Contents

CONTENTS

CONTENTS

PART FOUR

List of Illustrations

Section Two

Introduction

WHEREVER ONE LOOKS in the nineteenth century, there is a Victor Hugo – each one accompanied by its contradiction: the angelic child prodigy of the early Romantics and the satanic 'Attila of the French language';[1] the militant monarchist and the revolutionary socialist; the symbol of a corrupt aristocracy and defender of the *misérables*; a represser of revolts and instigator of riots.

By the time he fled the country in 1851, Hugo was the most famous living writer in the world, the founder of two distinct phases of Romanticism. His influence on French literature was second only to that of the Bible. In the long night of exile, faced with a new audience – the ocean – he discovered a new set of identities: the visionary poet who invented a religion and received personal compliments on his work from Jesus Christ and Shakespeare; the hero of freedom-fighters from Serbia to South America.

Hugo returned to Paris at the end of the Empire in 1870 as a gigantic oxymoron who seemed single-handedly to represent the history of France since the Revolution. When he died in 1885, he was followed to his tomb by a crowd which outnumbered the usual population of Paris. The obituaries turned out to be premature: it emerged that only two-thirds of Hugo's work had been published in his lifetime. Seventeen years after his death, the corpus had swollen to include seven novels, eighteen volumes of poetry, twenty-one plays, a small museum of paintings and drawings, and approximately three million words of history, criticism, travel writing and philosophy. Now that the fragments of *Océan* and the coded diaries have been published, Hugo seems to have erred on the side of modesty when he hoped that his complete works would form 'a multiple book that sums up a whole century'.[2]

Our own century has added several Hugos of its own: the prophet of Surrealism, two World Wars and the European Community; the principal saint of a Vietnamese religion; the General de Gaulle of French letters and hero of the French Left; the popular classic whose works have spawned adaptations often profoundly opposed to the spirit of the originals; the cross-party monarch of a French Republic which commemorated the centenary of his death in 1985 with a nationwide spate of exhibitions, postcards and videos.

This proliferation of Victor Hugos has had an unexpected conse-quence: each separate Hugo has fallen into a kind of obscurity or been tidied away under the heading of Cocteau's distracting paradox: 'Victor Hugo was a madman who thought he was Victor Hugo.'[3] The disputatious rabble of his writing was not invited to the celebration of its own revolution. Twelve years on, the epic edition of the *Corres-pondance Familiale* has been arrested at 1839 by the commercial *coup d'état* of a publisher. France now has several miles of Boulevards Victor Hugo and a small population of busts, bas-reliefs and statues, but there is still no complete, scholarly edition of his works and letters. It was in exile in the Channel Islands that Hugo plumbed his own depths and found his widest audience. Definitions of 'Hugoesque' in *The Oxford English Dictionary* unfortunately suggest a similar eclipse of the work by the image in Britain. In 1893, 'Hugoesque' was a synonym of Romantic–Medieval. By 1960, it had acquired a different connotation: 'Almost Hugoesque in his unflag-ging pursuit of maids'.[4]

*

THIS BIOGRAPHY had one of its origins in the bowels of the ferry that mysteriously stops its engines in mid-Channel and sits in total darkness for several hours before sailing for Guernsey with the first light of dawn. Trapped on the ocean, I began to read the novel which George Saintsbury called 'the maddest book in recognized literature':[5] *L'Homme Qui Rit*. It had been written a short distance across the water on the top floor of a house which might be called the maddest building in the history of domestic architecture: Hauteville House.

A few months later, I started work with a sense of righteous excitement that the magnificent delusions of works like *L'Homme Qui Rit* were still being locked away during official visits, and with a nagging sense of personal ignorance. Hugo always ended up occupying a large part of anything I wrote on the French nineteenth century. His name came up in conversations and tutorials on apparently unrelated subjects. Several of his poems had recorded themselves in memory to be declaimed in moments of guaranteed privacy. Hugo himself remained a mystery. I knew the Romantic boot that marched into the Comédie Française in 1830, the fist that 'confiscated' French verse for the best part of a century, the eye of conscience that stared at Napoleon III from the Channel Islands, and, inevitably, the token of another kind of virility that Hugo poetically called his 'lyre'; but I had never seen the giant as a whole.

This book is an attempt to explore Victor Hugo in his entirety by using the work on which he lavished the greatest amount of love and ingenuity: his life.

*

THE FIRST BIOGRAPHIES of Hugo were a small, inbred community spawned by two squabbling parents: the adulatory account of Hugo's life up to 1841 written by his wife and doctored by his disciples – possibly the most plagiarized book in French literature – and Edmond Biré's three vitriolic testaments to the disappointments of growing up (1883, 1891 and 1894). A devout Catholic and passionate admirer of Hugo in his youth, Biré followed the advice of his Bishop to treat *Les Misérables* as a thing of Satan and produced a relentlessly negative image of a self-inflated balloon who held the gaze of the myrmidons below for seventy years, showering them with lies and beautiful poems. For one side, Hugo was 'a hero of humanity'; for the other, a hypocrite and a traitor who cheated and scrimped his way to fame and fortune.

Each of these biographers wrote with only one eye open at a time, and while, from a scholarly point of view, one might prefer Biré's black eye-patch to the rose-tinted monocle of the Hugophiles, both sides laboured under self-imposed constraints which made it impossible for them to be honest. Hugo was so enmeshed in French cultural institutions and their historical controversies that studies written by his compatriots were often more closely related to polemic than to literary criticism. Significantly, the fairest early biographies were Frank Marzials' *Life of Victor Hugo* (London, 1888) and J. Pringle Nichol's *Sketch of His Life and Work* (London and New York, 1893).

Even when scholarly habits began to prevail, Hugo's biographers were hampered by the self-defeating discretion of the forty-five-volume 'Imprimerie Nationale' edition (1904–52), flaunting its omissions on unnecessarily large and expensive pages. It ended with four volumes of carefully weeded correspondence, edited by a woman who was rumoured to be one of Hugo's unacknowledged daughters. It presented the image of a model father and husband, the tireless grandfather of French letters who suffered five generations of little poets to worship at his feet. Similarly asphyxiated by incense, Hugo's mistress of fifty years, Juliette Drouet, had her 20,000 love letters boiled down by Paul Souchon to 1001 monotonous examples of self-macerating devotion, offering the unnuanced image of a clinging psychopath – an 'act of piety' which was in reality a monument to the editor's unconscious misogyny and a serious distortion of a complex relationship.

A new age of Hugo biography began in 1954 with André Maurois's reputable *Olympio*, continued in its benign spirit by Alain Decaux's *Victor Hugo* (1984). Both lean heavily to the early years, before Hugo sailed for England. Hubert Juin's three-volume *Victor Hugo* (1980–86) is a narrative chronology which turns the Jean Massin 'Édition Chronologique' into continuous prose. All three decline to investigate the parts of Hugo's genius that appeared to take the form of deliberate deception. Biographers may still be prone to what Macaulay termed the 'disease of admiration'. Hugo's biographers have suffered more particularly from the disease of discretion. The best biographies of Hugo, in fact, are not biographies at all but editions and studies in which analysis or simple fidelity to the texts makes it possible to peel away the layers of legend to see whether anything is left in the middle: Jean Gaudon's *Le Temps de la Contemplation* (1969), Victor Brombert's *Victor Hugo and the Visionary Novel* (1984), and the editorial explorations of Pierre Albouy, Jean-Bertrand Barrère, Evelyn Blewer, Jean and Sheila Gaudon, Pierre Georgel, Henri Guillemin,

A. R. W. James, René Journet, Bernard Leuilliot, Jean Massin, Guy Robert and Jacques Seebacher.

The last life of Victor Hugo in English (1976) deserves a special place as an example of political propaganda surviving the regime that produced it: in this case, the Second Empire (1852–70). As Hugo wrote of a similar historical anomaly: 'This rejuvenation of a corpse is surprising.'[6] Nourished by lies long since disproved, it briefly describes a self-serving, ignorant megalomaniac inexplicably adored by the French as their greatest poet. It is in parts an unacknowledged paraphrase of other biographies. The plot summaries, also unattributed, are lifted, with minute changes, from the old *Oxford Companion to French Literature* (1959). Each borrowed passage is followed by a judgement from the biographer's own pen: 'cumbersome plot', 'the plot and characters ... do not bear analysis', 'has long since become unreadable', etc. Works – even major works – not described by the *Companion* are not mentioned in the biography.

Hugo's fond belief that misdeeds come with their own punishment does not in this case seem overly optimistic. It is fair to assume that the magpie biographer never had the pleasure of reading some of the most exciting works of Romantic literature. According to the introduction, 'The task of writing a life so full, so complex, so exhaustively documented, has clearly daunted many biographers. No English writer, until now, has attempted to write a critical biography'. This remark has remained true.

The present biography was intended primarily to provide its author with an excuse to spend four years reading the works of Victor Hugo. It contains new letters, verses, anecdotes, facts and sources. Some mysteries have been solved, others created. Unknown editions and publications have come to light. Information on 'the most obnoxious'[7] of French exiles as he appeared in the prying eyes of Scotland Yard and the Home Office is new. Many of the quotations from Hugo's works and letters have never before appeared out of French – not necessarily a sign of progress in Hugo's view: 'How does one recognize intelligence in a nation? By its ability to speak French.'[8]

Translations from the poems are unavoidably utilitarian and give about as much idea of the original as a written description would of a piece of music. Elucidations which concern the history of Hugo's biographies rather than the story of his life or which open up divergent lines of enquiry have been removed to the archival attic, accessible by the hidden staircases marked with note numbers. The largest of these has been given a room to itself (Appendix III).

A handful of anachronistic allusions to computers and the like are intended to illuminate rather than trivialize, to suggest that Hugo's brain is not the exclusive property of the nineteenth century, and to serve as reminders that the past is not a theme park or a refuge from the present.

This is the first fully referenced biography of Hugo in any language. It is based on direct exposure to the works of a writer who was once described as 'an element of Nature'. I have accepted the umbrellas of other biographies only when they had some precise find to offer or when they exemplified a particular attitude. Since approximately 3000 words are published every day on Victor Hugo, it will be several lifetimes before I can claim to have read everything that has ever been written about him. The exhaustive, 'definitive' biography is in any case a myth: the only possible complete biography would be the life of a plant or a worm – unless, that is, one accepted Hugo's view that even stones have souls. The test of a biographer lies in the willingness to discard and select. I have tried to offer the reader a mine of information without including the slag heap.

Biographers of famous writers who believe in their own originality are of course happily deluded. It is usual to talk of one's 'debt' to editors and critics. In most cases, 'free gift' would be nearer the mark. The mainstays of this biography are the epic Jean Massin edition and the more recent *Oeuvres Complètes* in the 'Bouquins' series, which became more complete as it went along. Without the work of several generations of editors, it would be impossible to survive in the subterranean labyrinth of Hugo's works, to identify unknown objects and observe its processes before re-emerging in the expected place and in a more or less presentable condition.

For illumination, I am grateful to Jean-Paul Avice, Alain Brunet, Robert Ellwood, Jean and Sheila Gaudon, Charles Hambrick, Danielle Molinari, Geoffrey Neate, James Patty, Claude Pichois, Stephen Roberts and Adrian Tahourdin, and to the following institutions: Taylor Institution Library, Bodleian Library, Bibliothèque

Nationale de France, Bibliothèque Historique de la Ville de Paris, Public Record Office (Kew), Maison de Victor Hugo (Place des Vosges), Maison d'Exil de Victor Hugo (Hauteville House), Jersey Archives Service, Jersey Museum (Catherine Burke), St Saviour Parish Hall, Jersey (M. R. P. Mallet), National Army Museum, Royal Society of Literature, Madame Tussaud's (Undine Concannon), Archives Municipales de Strasbourg (J. -Y. Mariotte), Universitetsbiblioteket i Oslo (Steinar Nilsen), Family History Library of the Church of Jesus Christ of Latter-Day Saints.

For all sorts of help, I should like to thank Gill Coleridge and, for their editorial tact and kindness, Starling Lawrence and Tanya Stobbs. Thanks also to Helen Dore. May Peter Straus find his encouragement justified.

I am happy to say that every page of this biography owes an unreasonably large debt to Margaret.

GRAHAM ROBB

139 Hollow Way
Oxford OX4 2NE

Part One

CHAPTER ONE

A Sabre in the Night

(1802–1803)

Victor-Marie Hugo, according to his father, was conceived 'almost in mid-air', by which he meant 'one of the highest peaks of the Vosges mountains'.[1]

There is some doubt as to what else Major Hugo and his wife were doing in May 1801, 3000 feet above sea-level, overlooking the Rhineland which had just been incorporated into Bonaparte's France. The mountains were infested with bandits and smugglers – or rather, they had been until Major Hugo arrived a few weeks before with his special battalion. He may have returned so that his wife could enjoy the view and his account of the campaign. Or, when he made this claim in a letter written shortly after the mother's death in 1821, he may simply have been trying to take some credit for Victor's 'sublime muse' – a poor substitute, as he pointed out, for the army or the civil service.

Anyone who climbs the 3000-foot Donon mountain today will find the exact spot of Hugo's conception marked by a block of sandstone in section 99 of the Donon forest, just below the summit, near the ruins of a Celtic temple:

IN THIS PLACE
ON 5 FLORÉAL, YEAR 9
VICTOR HUGO
WAS CONCEIVED

This remarkable piece of detective work was the idea of a former Head of Strasbourg Museums, Hans Haug, who erected this memorial-to-end-all-memorials in the mid-1960s as a practical joke. Hugo himself preferred a different site. When he retold his father's story, he usually replaced the Celtic temple with a Roman 'Temple of Love', the Vosges with the Alps and the Donon with Mont Blanc, which has the advantage of being 3000 feet higher, internationally famous and at the intersection of France, Switzerland and Italy.[2] More importantly, it meant that the embryo of Victor Hugo came into existence at a major crossroads of world history: even before he had legs to walk on, he was following in the footsteps of Hannibal and Napoleon. With such unhumble origins, it would take an enormous quantity of successful ambition to ensure that the rest of his life was not an anti-climax.

*

VICTOR HUGO'S father had met his wife in similarly dramatic circumstances four years before.

Sophie Trébuchet was a Breton, born in Nantes in 1772, the third of seven children. Her mother died when Sophie was eight, and her father had spent most of his life sailing from Nantes to the West Indies, filling up with slaves at West African ports on the way out, and returning with sugar and molasses. In 1783, during a fruitless voyage to Mauritius, he caught a disease and died 5000 miles from home. The remains of Hugo's maternal grandfather now lie somewhere at the bottom of the Indian Ocean. For Hugo's mother, the past was something to be locked away or remodelled to suit present needs. All that Victor Hugo thought he knew on the subject was that his grandfather 'was one of those respectable bourgeois who never change their home or their views'.[3]

Having lost both parents, Sophie was taken in by her Aunt Françoise and was still living in Nantes when the Revolution broke out in 1789.

According to Hugo, whose writings have supplied the spectacles through which the following events have traditionally been viewed, his mother was a half-wild royalist Amazon, chased through the Breton undergrowth by republican soldiers, risking her life to rescue persecuted priests. Brittany itself, in Hugo's Parisian view of the country, was an antediluvian land inhabited by hairy, tattooed peasants, squatting in their cottages or holes in the ground, surviving on milk and chestnuts, fanatically loyal to King and Church, their world-view bounded by the horizons of the ancient forests in which they hid, bristling with Druidic superstition and mindless animosity – a contrast, in Hugo's personal mythology, to the mountain-born genius. Only the 'wash-basin' of the Atlantic Ocean was equal to the filth of Brittany, he wrote on a visit in 1836.[4]

When Sophie Trébuchet was a young woman and the republican soldiers came to stamp out the counter-revolutionary fires of the monarchist Bretons, the forests in which Hugo imagined his mother running wild were 'enormous, dark sponges from which, under the pressure of that gigantic foot, the Revolution, civil war spurted out'.[5] The metaphor was clearly inspired by wet socks and shoes, but also by the murkiness of his own past.

One of the heaviest boots belonged to Hugo's father, Joseph-Léopold-Sigisbert Hugo (usually known as Léopold). He was the third son of a wood merchant and a governess from Nancy in the east of France.[6] For a soldier, Léopold Hugo was unusually well educated, but had thrown away the chance to pursue his studies in order to join the Army. Camaraderie and adventure were preferable to life behind a desk. When he met Sophie Trébuchet, he was twenty-two years old, a short, broad-chested man with a ruddy face and a fat nose, swerving constantly from deep dejection to violent elation, full of flattering stories about himself, delighted to have been shot through the neck and to have had two horses blown to pieces while he was riding them in battle. He was unashamed of his plebeian roots but keen to provide himself with aristocratic forebears. He worshipped his commanding officer, Muscar, and, like him, wrote bawdy songs and dragged a mistress around with him on all his campaigns. 'I often press her to my breast,' he told Muscar in a letter, 'and, through two pretty spheres, I feel the forces which move the world . . . Draw the curtains!'[7]

The Revolution stimulated his ambition: he renamed himself 'Brutus' and proved to be an enthusiastic republican. Brutus Hugo played his part in the 'cleansing' of Brittany with no obvious relish but without shirking his duty. He presided over the massacre of entire villages, executed congregations, and, like many soldiers in similar circumstances, adopted an abandoned child. When his own children began to arrive, the orphan would be given away.

In 1793, shortly after the execution of Louis XVI, Hugo's regiment (the Eighth Lower Rhine) was ordered from the most distant part of France. The idea was to minimize those conflicts of loyalty which are the principal military inconvenience of civil war. It was this efficient management of resources which provided Victor Hugo with the convincing antithesis of a republican, atheist father and a royalist, Catholic mother: blasted into existence by the collision of modern history's most powerful opposites.[8]

In Hugo's version of his own prehistory – parts of which appear to have found their way back into local legend – his parents met in the winter of 1795 while this paragon of republican virtue was scouring the lanes and thickets in the vicinity of the small town of Châteaubriant, a few miles from Nantes. Châteaubriant was the country home of Sophie's Aunt Françoise and was supposed to be safer than the city. Charging along between the hedgerows, Brutus suddenly came upon a frail, dark-eyed girl. When she heard that he was hot on the trail of some renegade priests, she cleverly invited him home to tea.

Brutus, still smouldering from battle, showed off his shattered foot, his uniform with its seventeen bullet-holes and recited his verse. Sophie seems to have impressed him more than he impressed her: she was reserved, even secretive, proud of her self-control. 'A mother who made provision for the moment in life when one finds oneself alone,' Hugo wrote in 1822, 'and who accustomed me from childhood to keep everything to myself and let nothing out'.[9] She was also seventeen months older and better educated than Brutus, a different creature altogether from his battle-scarred mistress and far more intimidating than a band of Breton peasants brandishing their pitchforks and axes.

Six months later, when Brutus was summoned back to Paris, he promised to write. Sophie promised nothing but reflected on the fact that she would soon be twenty-five and too old to marry. Perhaps in order to impress her with his potential for stability, Brutus took a desk job at the Conseil de Guerre in Paris and tried to be patient. Finally, in November 1797, Sophie arrived from Brittany with her brother, only to discover that Brutus had been unfaithful – as he himself admitted in a jovial letter to his commanding officer. Rather than face a humiliating return to her home-town, she married him, without a priest, on 15 November 1797. There had been talk of a dowry, but, to the disappointment of Brutus, it turned out to consist mainly of bed-linen.

Victor Hugo knew his parents well enough to flesh out the details of their early relationship – a domestic image of the devastation he witnessed as a child in various parts of Napoleon's Empire. But the reality differs from his reconstruction of it in one crucial respect. Far from being royalists, Sophie's family, like many of their fellow-Nantais, had actively contributed to the establishment of the Republic.[10] They prided themselves on their modern views and were more likely to be found reading Voltaire than the Bible. Her grandfather had worked with the notorious Carrier, who distinguished himself under the Terror by loading excess prisoners on to boats and then sinking them in the Loire. Sophie's young Aunt Louise – one of her best friends – was Carrier's mistress, and when Sophie and her Aunt Françoise left Nantes for Châteaubriant in 1794, they were not fleeing from republican troops but from their fellow Bretons – those who were appalled by Carrier's brutality, or those whose festering bodies were spreading disease, piled up in the open graves to which Sophie's grandfather had contributed in his capacity as public prosecutor in Nantes.

Throughout Hugo's childhood, recent history was subjected to that blithe simplification which retrospectively divides entire populations very neatly into patriots and collaborators. In Hugo's case, the misrepresentation of his own family history owes something to his mother's silence and his father's love of stories in which he was the hero. More than that, it reflects the battle-lines drawn up by his parents as their marriage fell apart. From the very beginning, the idea of a royalist mother and a republican father was highly acceptable because it suggested that historical forces, and not Hugo himself, were responsible for his parents' incompatibility.

*

AT THE TURN OF the century, under the Directoire, the city which Victor Hugo was to call 'the native city of my mind'[11] was a wrecked museum of recent French history, its palaces infested with beggars and rubbish, more like post-revolution Zanzibar than modern Paris. The Tuileries Gardens had suffered the indignity of spades and potatoes; statues had been toppled, inscriptions erased. Employees of the Conseil de Guerre occupied the Hôtel de Ville (renamed 'Maison Commune'), where the only intact decorations were the busts of revolutionary leaders.

In Part Five of *Les Misérables*, Hugo paints his most memorable picture of the period, dating it, significantly, to the year of his birth, 1802.[12] It was then that 'the conscience of the city' – its enormous network of sewers – flooded it with its own filth. A characteristically Hugolian view of history – compromising, inscrutable and blatant: 'The mind seems to perceive, straying through the darkness amid the rot of what was once magnificence, that huge blind mole, the Past.' In Hugo's case, the past would be unusually difficult to contain and analyse, but it carried with it the strong smell of a suspicion that the individuals who embroiled his childhood in momentous historical events were subject to even greater forces.

The popular promenade of Directoire Paris was the Jardin d'Idalie near the Champs-Élysées. In the months leading up to Bonaparte's *coup d'état*, free enterprise was sprouting among the ruins. The Jardin d'Idalie was an excuse for open-air pornography: *tableaux vivants* and women dressed as sylphs, disporting themselves in mid-air, attached to balloons. Major Hugo took his wife there and ran into an old acquaintance, Colonel Victor de Lahorie, Chief of Staff of General Moreau, who was at that time Bonaparte's main rival.

Apart from his later involvement in Moreau's conspiracy against Bonaparte and his role in Victor Hugo's childhood, very little is known about Lahorie. Even his name changes from one page of his biography to the next.[13] He was six years older than Sophie and came from the same part of France. A fervent republican, but with the manners of a royalist, he was a pleasant contrast to 'Brutus': he wore a blue suit and breeches, white gloves and a black cocked hat with a tiny cockade – the first sprouting of a more elegant age. A 'Wanted' notice posted by the Minister of Police in 1804 asked citizens to be on the look-out for a man of 5 feet 2 inches, with black hair, dark, deep-set eyes, a pock-marked face and a sardonic smile. He was also said to be slightly bow-legged, like a man who spent a lot of time on horseback.[14]

With the support of Lahorie, Hugo resumed active service. In 1799, he and his wife moved to the more rural setting of the École Militaire in the west of Paris. In a room overlooking the Champ-de-Mars (now dominated from the other end by the Eiffel Tower), a first son, Abel, was born exactly one year after the marriage. He was nursed by Mme Hugo to the sound of drums and marching soldiers.

In June, they left for Hugo's home-town of Nancy. As Stendhal describes it in *Lucien Leuwen*, Nancy had been turned into a barracks, its streets continually muddied by regiments leaving for the Eastern front. The Major stormed off to conquer Bavaria, earning the patronage of Bonaparte's older brother Joseph with his 'courage, activity and intelligence'[15] – the first sign of that stream of coincidences which intermittently connects the history of the Hugos to that of the Bonaparte family. Sophie was stuck in Nancy with a finicky mother-in-law and a jealous sister. The only relief was the gentlemanly Lahorie. It has been suggested that they became lovers, but the circumstances were hardly propitious. In Nancy, a second son, Eugène, was born on 16 September 1800.

Almost immediately, Hugo was put in charge of the nearby garrison at Lunéville, where a treaty was signed in February 1801 consolidating Bonaparte's France. Great days were dawning. In the words of a song which Major Hugo hummed at home often enough for his youngest son to remember it perfectly half a century later, the future Emperor issued a stern ultimatum to all the sovereigns of Europe: 'Kiss my ass, and you'll have peace . . . And peace there was!'[16] Mme Hugo did not consider her husband a suitable companion for the children.[17]

One other important event coincided with the stay in Lunéville: the excursion into the Vosges during which Major Hugo exercised his conjugal rights on the mountain-top.

In August 1801, he descended with the Twentieth half-brigade to the town of Besançon. The Hugos took a first-floor apartment in an old house on the Place Saint-Quentin. There, one evening towards the end of winter, a third son was born at what turned out to be precisely the worst moment. It was a Septidi in the month of Ventôse,

Year X of the Republic (in the old calendar, 26 February 1802). A significantly insignificant event:

> This century was two years old. Rome was replacing Sparta;
> Already Napoleon was emerging from under Bonaparte,
> And already the First Consul's tight mask
> Had been split in several places by the Emperor's brow.
> It was then that in Besançon, that old Spanish town,
> Cast like a seed into the flying wind,
> A child was born of mixed blood – Breton and Lorraine –
> Pallid, blind and mute, . . .
> That child, whom Life was scratching from its book,
> And who had not another day to live,
> Was me.[18]

Major Hugo had been hoping for a girl. The plan was to name her Victorine-Marie – 'Marie' after a family friend and 'Victorine' after Victor Lahorie, who agreed to be the child's godfather. Since 'Marie' was also a boy's name, the baby was named 'Victor-Marie Hugo'. There was no baptism[19] – another sign that Hugo's mother was not the fervent Catholic he thought she was.

It had been a difficult birth and the child was clearly a runt. To judge by his mother's description – 'no longer than a knife'[20] – he may have been premature. The midwife predicted imminent death and a week passed before the Major reported the birth to Lahorie.

According to the opening poem of *Les Feuilles d'Automne* – one of the great verse autobiographies of the Romantic period – a double order was placed with the carpenter for a cradle and a coffin. Victor's sturdy seventeen-month-old brother, Eugène, already enjoying his father's rude health, saw the puny creature and offered the first subjective judgement of the future poet: '*bébête*' ('silly').[21]

Six weeks later, the family was to break up.

*

FROM A ROMANTIC point of view, it was a disappointing, untidy origin. In Hugo's lifetime, a critic tried to prove that he must have sucked in at birth the stubborn spirit of the Franche-Comté and was a recognizable product of the region; a typical Easterner.[22] His place of birth, however, is significant only in its almost total irrelevance. Hugo was an Army child, swept along in the storm created by Bonaparte.[23] He never saw Besançon again, and his next direct contact with his native city was in 1880 when the local council unveiled a plaque commemorating his birth. On that occasion, Hugo sent a letter of thanks describing himself as 'a pebble of the road on which humanity marches onward'.[24] For all his grasping after symbolic coincidences, Hugo, unlike some of his even more neurotic biographers, accepted the arbitrariness of his birth and saw his eccentric personal geography as a sign of innate internationalism. He had a mother from Brittany, a father from Lorraine (which was alternately German and French), and a native city which had once belonged to Spain. A natural candidate for the presidency of that embodiment of cultural unity he was one of the first to call 'The United States of Europe'.[25]

Hugo saved his biggest distortions for the family. Here, the quest for autobiographical appropriateness veers off into pure fantasy, gradually consolidated and confirmed over the years by layers of imagined memories. But to accept Hugo's version for the sake of narrative convenience and then denounce it as comical arrogance is to ignore the unpleasant reality he spent much of his life trying to comprehend or conjure away.

He later considered himself to have been baptized symbolically by the substitute father, Lahorie, 'who witnessed my birth'. Lahorie may indeed, as Hugo claims, have suggested that the Germanic 'Hugo' be softened by the Latin 'Victor'.[26] But when the baby was born, Lahorie was in Paris.

The puniness of the infant Hugo also belongs to both legend and reality. When Hugo dictated the details of his early life to Alexandre Dumas in 1852, he revealed that, even at the age of fifteen months, he still had difficulty holding his head erect: it kept lolling on to his shoulders.[27] The peculiar precision of the detail betrays the mythologizing instinct. He may have been a runt but he had an enormous, compensatory head – his proudest physical possession, not entirely unconnected with his boasts of unusually powerful sexual desires and accomplishments. He even boasted of having been diagnosed by an alienist as a cured hydrocephalic.[28] The insistence on his puniness, in texts which in other respects are far from modest, casts an ambiguous light on his inferiority to his two older brothers. In one sense, he was practically a Quasimodo. On the other hand, the feeble corporation struggling to support the vast brow of genius meant that Hugo was born with the perfect Romantic body.

Seen in relation to his intense rivalry with his two brothers, Hugo's weakness has another unexpected advantage. The opening poem of *Les Feuilles d'Automne* explains, apparently in contradiction of itself, that mother's milk, by divine dispensation, is shared equally, but that each son receives it all: the ideal, miraculous solution to sibling rivalry. Yet at the same time, the extra care lavished on the sickly baby 'Made me twice the child of my obstinate mother'.

In the autobiographical texts, the cruel calamity of Hugo's early days is plastered over: 'Abandoned by all, except by his mother', the child was loved back to life. Then the whole family left for Corsica together and 'the infant quickly reached the age of one'.[29]

The interest of this imaginative re-creation of his origins lies in its exact untruth. For all the concern about Victor's poor chances of survival, the family set off for Marseilles when he was only six weeks old. Major Hugo was in deep trouble: he had reported his commanding officer for embezzlement and slanderous accusations were being made about him. Only one thing could save his career: an appeal to his protectors in Paris, Lahorie and Joseph Bonaparte.

So, on 28 November 1802, while the Major remained on active duty, trusting in his wife's persuasive powers, Sophie Hugo left her baby in the arms of a certain Claudine, the wife of Hugo's orderly, and travelled back to Paris, where she stayed in the Rue Neuve-des-Petits-Champs, close to the Place Vendôme, and even closer to the Rue Gaillon, home of the recently retired Lahorie.

*

THE SINGLE MOST IMPORTANT fact of Victor Hugo's formative years is that his advent coincided with the collapse of his parents' marriage.

Because of Hugo's silence about his broken home, emphasis tends to have been placed on the eventual, apparent reconciliation with his father, after his mother's death. This cheerful view may have something to do with the personal lives of his biographers, or it may simply be an effect of traditional biography, crossing off events as they occur. Hugo, on the other hand, with his huge capacity for never recovering from grief, lived in circles rather than on a straight line, and the disasters of his life should be imagined as continually recurring events, differing only in the degree of intensity.

> When the dreaming soul descends into the body
> And numbers in the heart, which cold at last has touched,
> As if counting dead bodies on a field of battle,
> Each departed grief and extinguished dream, . . .
>
> There, in that night where no light shines,
> The soul, in a dark fold where all things seem to end,
> Feels something still fluttering under a veil . . .
> You who lie sleeping in the shadows – sacred memory![30]

Since the sight of a bickering couple always induces someone to offer a helpful diagnosis, Sophie has been accused of being too dry, frigid and even mulish: a quality her husband attributed to the fact that she came from Brittany.[31] It should be remembered that her coldness and apparent lack of sense of humour had the contrasting background of the Major's perpetually active volcano: 'I wish I could break down the narrow bounds of language,' he wrote in 1800, 'and give full expression to my feelings, to deify the woman I adore, to hold her in my arms and press against my breast the mother of my little children.'[32]

Whether or not this rampaging style is the sound of sincerity, as is often supposed, the Major's letters also demonstrate his familiarity with the popular literature of the time: exaggerated, simple emotion. It served him well when he came to write his first adventure novel.

The little children, who were suffering the same 'deprivation' as their father, were stuffed with sweets. Victor kept asking for '*mamaman*'[33] and had to be fobbed off with macaroon – which is conceivably what he was asking for anyway ('*macaron*').

In January 1803, the Major struck camp and sailed with his three sons to Corsica, where the French Army was preparing to defend itself against plague and the British. Sophie seemed to be in no hurry to resolve the Major's dispute or even to answer his letters. For the first time in her life she was free and enjoying the company of Lahorie.

Meanwhile, living conditions for the rest of the family deteriorated rapidly. From Corsica, they sailed to Portoferraio on the tiny island of Elba in June 1803, eleven years before the deposed Napoleon tried to drag it into the nineteenth century by building proper roads. They lived in a house in the present Via Guerrazi.[34] A nurse took the boys to play by the sea. There would be no postal service in the winter. The Major felt abandoned. He freely admitted that he did not make a good mother. Victor was teething, suffering from the heat, and appeared to have worms. He hardly ever cried but looked around him as though he had lost something. In Corsica, a local woman had been found to take him out in a pram but the child seemed uncomfortable with a non-French-speaker. Hugo later claimed that one of the first words he learnt was the Italian '*cattiva*'[35] – the feminine form of 'wicked', which might reflect a later suspicion that all was not well in his father's house.

For all the Major's semi-religious outpourings, the bottom line of all his letters is that he was desperate for sex. In his view, Sophie had been given fair warning. Now he was hanging on to fidelity by his fingertips: 'Do you think that at my age and with my character it's a good idea to leave me to my own devices?' He pretended to set her mind at rest by pointing out that women in that part of the world were in the habit of stabbing their lovers to death, not to mention the additional 'guarantee' of possible 'maladies'.

It was clear that the marriage was over. By insisting on his impressive desires, the expert in self-justification was writing out his absolution in advance. But he was also genuinely bemused. His wife had managed the unusual feat of not appreciating his merits: 'Born with a character which has made me no enemies and brought me many friends,' he wrote the following year, 'I have seen you grow unhappy with me, contriving to live apart from me for specious reasons, abandoning me to the ardent passions of my age.'[36]

At last, having secured the Major's future in the Army with the help of Lahorie, Sophie made the long journey from Paris and reached Elba in July 1803. Four months later, she left with the children for Paris.

The only window into the Hugo household in those disastrous four months is the petition drawn up by Sophie in 1815 when she was suing for divorce.[37] According to Mme Hugo, her husband had taken a 'concubine' called Catherine Thomas, the daughter of a hospital employee at Portoferraio. This is the woman who called herself Comtesse de Salcano, Major Hugo's future second wife. She was probably the model for the transvestite soldier in his conventionally melodramatic novel written in retirement, *L'Aventurière Tyrolienne* – intrepid, childless, and eleven years younger than Sophie. Suspecting nothing, Sophie was persuaded to sail for France with the three boys before the British came and took them all prisoner. Hugo was left to indulge what his wife described in her petition as his 'unbridled desires'.

Subsequent letters from the Major suggest that he had tried, one last time, to stir up some passion in his wife. He missed his sons and it was probably only later that he attached himself to Catherine Thomas. Sophie's petition dates from a time when she was busy constructing the legend of a royalist Amazon manacled to a republican vandal which her sons inevitably accepted as the truth.

The only certainty is that when Victor Hugo arrived in Paris at the age of one and three-quarters, his parents had begun the long and painful separation which continued throughout his childhood and dragged him on a tour of Napoleon's Empire.

*

HUGO NEVER PRETENDED to remember anything from this period. In the splendid vision attributed to the mothers of children born at the turn of the century, and then, much later, to his alter ego, Marius in *Les Misérables*, 'the Revolution was a guillotine in the twilight, the Empire a sabre in the night'.[38] Like most writers of his generation, Hugo had the impression of having entered the world in a mythical age – the child of a giant, wrapped in a banner, laid on a drum and baptized with water from a helmet.[39]

If, as he claims, his early years were lived through a fog of cultural prejudice and twenty years of political and domestic unrest, his parents' mistake made it an unusually thick and representative fog. Little by little, a curiously similar situation materializes in Hugo's future, as if the adults around his cradle – or his coffin – had created roles that other actors would fill.

The 'sacred memory' which survives and predates all other memories is also the unconscious recollection of childhood, and a suspicion of the truth. The rediscovery of that truth is one of the stories of Hugo's life. It was a far more dramatic tale than the ingenuous narrative according to which Victor Hugo became the dominant figure of French Romanticism because he was a megalomaniac with an unshakeable belief in the reality of his own image. That would have been comparatively simple. Extracting a means of expression for unacceptable truths from a literature bound by convention was something far more worthwhile, something almost worthy of a giant's son conceived on a mountain-top.

CHAPTER TWO

Secrets

(1804–1810)

HUGO'S EARLIEST MEMORIES are of his first Paris home: 24 Rue de Clichy, across the road from the Tivoli Gardens. There was a courtyard with a well, and a willow which dipped its branches in a water-trough. While Abel went to school, Victor and Eugène were sent to a nursery in the Rue du Mont-Blanc (now Rue de la Chaussée-d'Antin).

If *Victor Hugo Raconté Par un Témoin de sa Vie* is to be believed,* Hugo's adventures at his first institution were amazingly prophetic. Every morning, Victor was deposited by the maid in the bedroom of the schoolmaster's daughter. If she lived long enough to read the book, Mlle Rose would have discovered that as she clambered out of bed and pulled on her stockings, the infant Hugo was registering the image of her naked legs.

The schoolmaster's daughter also became the victim of a more dramatic display of infant sexuality. Like the narrator of Proust's *À la*

---

* *Victor Hugo Raconté* ... is the 'official' biography by Mme Hugo, based on conversations with her husband and her own memories, ending with Hugo's induction into the Académie Française in 1841. It was published in 1863 and has supplied the basis – sometimes even the text – of the early chapters of almost every biography of Victor Hugo. However, the published version differs dramatically from the original drafts: Hugo's son, Charles, and his disciple, Vacquerie, rewrote it in a 'literary' style, expunged what they felt were embarrassing details and digressions, smudged the traces of Hugo's sense of humour, and generally brought it into line with the Hugo legend. Both versions are revealing in their own way. Preference is given below to the original drafts, the last of which has a note in Hugo's hand, suggesting that he was more interested in preserving the truth than his hagiographers gave him credit for: 'Manuscripts of my wife which were going to be burnt and which I pulled from the fire. 8 March 1867.'

Recherche du Temps Perdu, Hugo's deepest well of memories contains the story of Saint Geneviève de Brabant, the Countess who was falsely accused of adultery and took refuge in the woods with her baby son – a potent transposition of Hugo's fantasies about his mother: the fugitive, the martyr, the abandoned woman transferring all her affection to her child. Proust's character learns the story from his magic lantern. Hugo's involvement, as befits an age of heroes, was more physical. It was the school play. Mlle Rose was Geneviève and Victor her baby son, dressed in a sheepskin. While she tried to read her lines, he stabbed at her legs with the iron claw that was part of his costume.

Plausible as they are, these memories of a precocious hankering after female flesh are also commonplaces of Romantic autobiography.[1] They belong to the same Herculean tradition that has Victor and Eugène devouring the roasted thigh of an eagle – the imperial bird – on their forthcoming journey to Italy,[2] and might serve as a reminder that even memories are subject to changing fashions. It should be said, in defence of the use of such early impressions, that Hugo enjoyed a spectacular, long-term photographic memory: he once correctly counted, in his mind, the number of buttons on his father's uniform,[3] and – even more remarkable – lived into old age and never told the same story to the same person twice.[4] But even if these memories were selected and contrived, they should not be dismissed as lies: the original choice may not have been conscious.

The child in sheep's clothing stabbing at his mother's fictional counterpart with his fifth member is an unusually crisp expression of unconscious desire, perhaps too an unconscious allusion to the expression *mouton à cinq pattes* ('a five-footed sheep'), meaning a phenomenon or a prodigy.[5] The megalomania which is supposed to be the distinguishing feature of Hugo's autohagiographies is certainly present in these memories; yet they also show that his attempt to give his life the quality of a myth entailed the rejection of a myth: the innocence and purity of the child.

The only objective glimpse of Victor Hugo in his third year is a disappointing contrast. It comes from his father's former colleague at the Conseil de Guerre, a compatriot of Mme Hugo called Pierre Foucher – Victor Hugo's future father-in-law. When he visited the house in the Rue de Clichy, Foucher always found the youngest child sitting in a corner, whining and drooling on his bib.[6]

The other place in the nursery where little Victor was deposited was a window-sill, from where he watched the construction of a town-house belonging to Cardinal Fesch.[7] A sign that both the economy and the Church were recovering from the Revolution. One day, as he watched the masons at work, a huge block of stone plummeted to the ground, crushing a worker beneath it. On another occasion, a rainstorm turned the streets around the nursery into rivers and the two brothers were stranded until nine in the evening.

The fact that Cardinal Fesch was the uncle of Napoleon and had celebrated his nephew's marriage with Josephine in 1804 may be purely coincidental, although it does reveal another segment of that labyrinth which, in nineteenth-century Paris, connects everything to everything else. Both stories, in any case, form a kind of allegorical vignette of Hugo's childhood – a childhood which is littered with more real dead bodies than the imaginations of his Romantic contemporaries.

The violence and danger in Hugo's earliest memories are also an accurate reflection of the adult world. Strange men were often seen dawdling in the streets around the nursery and the family home. A plot to assassinate Napoleon had been uncovered (the Moreau conspiracy) and Lahorie, as one of the ringleaders, was being hunted by the police. In the autumn of 1804, in the month of Fructidor (September), a dawn raid took place at 19 Rue de Clichy. It was the home of a close friend of Lahorie. Meanwhile, across the road, a man answering only to the name 'M. de Courlandais' was spending four nights with his friend, Sophie Hugo, before continuing his oddly erratic tour of the provinces.[8]

Hugo's determination to 'construct a faith for himself',[9] to evolve an infallible eye for Evil and to plant his feet on solid ideological rock is the paradoxical result of the enormous, fragile confusion which presents itself in history as the growth and consolidation of Napoleon's Empire. A bureaucracy had turned a large percentage of the population into spies. Sophie's relations with republican conspirators and their royalist allies were certainly not a secret. Lahorie might have been arrested at any minute; but he appears to have enjoyed the clandestine support of the Minister of Police, Fouché, whose information network was a subterranean empire within an empire which survived his dismissal in 1810 and, for that matter, the fall of the Empire.

The only person still in the dark was Major Hugo – still wondering why he was only a major after nineteen years' distinguished service and no lack of ambition. Nameless men who sat in offices knew that Major Hugo's wife was carrying on with a conspirator. Any request for promotion would have reached Napoleon with a cross-reference to the file on Lahorie. Hugo could only bang his head against the trap-door at the top of the ladder while a bureaucrat kept it shut.

A few weeks after the Battle of Trafalgar concentrated the war effort on the Continent, Major Hugo was given another chance to prove his worth. He took part in the conquest of the Kingdom of Naples. The Austrians were expelled and the Kingdom was given to Joseph Bonaparte. Now able to act on his own initiative, Joseph made the intrepid Hugo one of his aides-de-camp and sent him into the mountains of Calabria to exterminate the followers of the bandit leader known as Fra Diavolo ('Brother Devil').

The Fra Diavolo campaign, which ended with the arrest of the bandit and the decimation of his guerrilla army,[10] became one of the Major's principal claims to fame and the attention of his dinner guests. 'He would wrinkle up his nose like a rabbit – a characteristic expression of the Hugos – wink as though he had a new joke up his sleeve, and then tell us what we had already heard twenty times before.'[11]

What they heard was the version of the occupying army. The more Romantic and, as it happens, accurate version was well known to Victor Hugo and his contemporaries. The 'bandit' was a leader of popular resistance, an Italian Robin Hood who had been ennobled by the exiled King of Naples and refused to recognize Major Hugo's authority when he came to interrogate him in his cell.

When the six-year-old Victor saw his father again for the first time in five years, the story would have provided rich soil for his doubts and suspicions. Who was the hero: his father or his bandit victim? The fact that Hugo's childhood universe contained a genuine outlaw in open revolt against his father helps to explain the huge aesthetic and symbolic triumph of the Romantic drama, *Hernani*. The righteous bandit-prince was already a cliché in 1830; but when that legendary figure was fuelled by the real disappointments and anxieties of the child, it stimulated the fantasies of a generation which had grown up under the shadow of the Empire. Two decades on, the bandit struck back:

> Vengeance limps and hobbles along,
> But eventually arrives . . .
> Remember that I hold you yet! . . .
> Small and puny in my hand,
> And should I clench this too-loyal fist,
> I'd crush your Imperial eagle in its egg![12]

In December 1807, without telling her husband, Mme Hugo suddenly decided to transport the family to Italy. Hugo had been promoted to the rank of colonel and installed in the palace at Avellino, east of Naples, as governor of the province.

Mme Hugo hated travelling, but it was an excellent opportunity to force a decision on the children's future, fix the monthly allowance and find out about the Thomas woman. According to the Colonel, Mme Hugo had been 'building castles in Spain'[13] (a prophetic image), implanting in the minds of her three sons the fantasy of an immense fortune which their father was frittering away on prostitutes and easy living. This intangible treasure-trove became part of the family myth. Its non-existence, combined with a financially incompetent father and a mother who scrimped and splurged in equal measure, made the adult Victor Hugo an enthusiastic saver – a highly unRomantic trait which earned him a reputation as a miser.

For two months, the family lived in a coach, crossing the Alps in January by the Mont Cenis – Abel and Eugène on mules, Victor and his mother in a sleigh; or, as the ode 'Mon Enfance' (1823) puts it: 'High Cenis, whose eagle loves the distant rocks, / From its caverns, where the avalanche grumbles, / Heard its ancient ice cry out beneath my childish feet.'

Victor saw Parma under floodwater, glimpsed the white waves of the Adriatic sparkling in the distance, stared at the severed highway-men's heads which had been nailed to trees at the roadside, waved straw crosses at peasants just to see them cross themselves[14] – which casts more doubt on his mother's devoutness – and worried that the coach might tip over at any moment. In Rome, he marvelled at the toe of St Peter, eroded by fifteen centuries of pilgrims' kisses.[15] From there, Mme Hugo announced that the family was about to turn up on the Colonel's palatial doorstep.

Colonel Hugo quickly arranged accommodation in Naples, claiming that the palace at Avellino was unsuitable – which was undoubtedly true. The thirty-four-year-old stranger in a dazzling uniform had the boys signed up as members of his regiment, the Royal-Corse.[16] It was a gesture which enabled Victor Hugo to describe himself, years later, as a soldier since childhood – the career he abandoned in favour of poetry or which he successfully combined with it. The Colonel was too busy to spend much time with his boys. They waited in Naples while their parents fired angry letters at each other.

Naples, for Mme Hugo, was like Hell, swarming with aggressive beggars who cooked their fish and macaroni in the street outside the house.[17] This was the city which, three years later, made Stendhal wish he was back in Paris:[18] rotten company, bad music, noisy plebs and carriages driven far too fast on appalling roads. Vesuvius was in full spate – 'one of Nature's finest horrors', enthused the Colonel in a letter.[19] His son described it in a heroic, classical vision which dates from his early twenties – the story of a whole year in miniature, and in code:

> Naples, on whose scented shores Springtime washes up,
> And which fiery Vesuvius covers with a burning canopy,
> Like a jealous warrior who, witnessing a feast,
> Casts among the flowers his bloodied plumes.[20]

For Hugo, this is a powerful, personal image. In the gardens of his childhood, his mother's flowerbeds were sacred. She seems to have lavished on plants the attention she denied her husband. In the poem, the warrior's helmet has the same destructive effect as the boys' football.[21]

From Naples until the return to Paris the youngest child's memories are skewed and inaccurate, which is just as revealing as an exact recollection: four months in the palace at Avellino; a bedroom with a long crack in the wall (earthquake damage), through which he peered at the countryside.[22] He also remembered, in a curious image, 'sitting astride' his father's sword 'in the barracks at Rome'[23] – presumably because *Rome* rhymes with *homme*, whereas *Naples*, in French, can only be rhymed with *Étaples*, which is a small town in northern France. A clear indication that the autobiographical content of these poems is not to be looked for in geographical and chronological details.

In reality, the visit to Avellino, which Hugo remembered as a long stay, was a mere excursion, in the absence of Hugo's mistress. The family remained in Naples for a whole year, perhaps because Mme Hugo fell ill. In July, Colonel Hugo was asked to join Joseph Bonaparte in Spain and, though he was under no compunction to do so, left like a shot. The only reliable report on what happened during the year in Italy comes from an unjustifiably optimistic letter written by the Colonel in Vitoria on 10 October 1808. He had just sent 6000 francs to his wife in Naples and promised to invest money for the boys:

> The children will thus receive an education which will enable me to promote their careers. In this way they will suffer no ill-effects from our decision to live apart. We must ensure that they remain ignorant of our decision and take care not to implicate them by heaping insults on each other.
>
> We have proved that we cannot live together, and now that our children's interests have prevailed against a public, judicial separation, you must raise them to respect both of us equally.[24]

To judge by letters written by Victor Hugo on and shortly after his mother's death, his father's hope was not quite as vain as he obviously thought it was: 'She never spoke of you in anger and it was she who engraved in our hearts the deep feelings of respect and affection we have always had for you' (28 June 1821).

The second letter is closer to the ambiguous truth: 'We have always been proud of the brilliant reputation you earned, and our beloved mother, even in the midst of her worst sufferings, was always the first to inspire us with respect for it and to make us aware of the worth we should attach to our name' (28 November 1821).

Here, the father is an abstraction – 'it' instead of 'you'[25] – the embodiment of status rather than personal virtue.

For Mme Hugo, in 1808, the remark about promoting the boys' careers would have sounded an ominous note. France had been at war since the birth of the eldest son, and every peace treaty was the signal for battles on a new front. Her boys were being raised to be cannon-fodder for the Emperor.

*

SHORTLY AFTER RETURNING to Paris in February 1809, Mme Hugo found the perfect hiding-place. Close to the southern edge of the city, a quiet cul-de-sac led off the Rue Saint-Jacques. At the far end of the Impasse des Feuillantines, an iron gate opened on to a courtyard and a house which had once been part of a convent. Under Louis XIV, the Feuillantines convent had served as a remand hostel for adulterous wives – a custom which survived elsewhere in Paris for most of the nineteenth century. Later, it doubled as a rest-home, because of the silence and clean air. During the Revolution it had been closed down and was falling into disrepair.[26]

At the back of the house, two rooms with tall, south-facing windows gave on to a vast, overgrown garden and an ancient avenue of chestnuts – 5 acres of wilderness enclosed by high stone walls.[27] Looming over the secret garden and creating a special light and climatic zone (according to Balzac, who in *Les Petits Bourgeois* chooses the area as the natural habitat of a retired civil servant[28]), were the 'gigantic spectre' of the Panthéon and 'the leaden head' of the Val-de-Grâce. Through the knee-high grass, behind the drooping vines and espaliers, Victor and his brothers discovered the wall of a ruined chapel. Two decades before, a hand had stencilled on to it the words '*Propriété Nationale*'.

That June, a makeshift bed appeared behind the altar and a man was sometimes seen walking in the garden, reading a book. The other families in the house were told that it was an eccentric relative of Mme Hugo who had odd sleeping habits. To the boys, he was 'M. de Courlandais' – the gentleman who helped them with their homework, joined in their games and put their mother in a good mood.

Every path in Hugo's brain leads back eventually to the Feuillantines garden[29] with its chattering birds, its 'flowers opening like eyelids',[30] the smoke from neighbouring chimneys and the moon moving behind the branches. Confirmation that a safe, secret place existed in the world, a stone's throw from the turbulent city. This is what gives the commonplace of Mother Nature such resonance in Hugo's poetry. It was under his mother's eye that he acquired that intimate knowledge of Nature which he always refers to as an education and an antidote to the academic. When, a few years later (in the poem, 'Ce Qui se Passait aux Feuillantines Vers 1813'), a headmaster, 'bald, black' and 'ugly', came to urge Mme Hugo to send her boys to his boarding school, it was the garden that persuaded her to keep them:

> Even the most vulgar man has grand, impressive phrases
> – 'It is essential! It is fitting! It is important!' –
> Which sometimes unsettle the strongest of women.
> Poor Mother! Which path to choose? . . .
> It was then, as I mentioned before,
> That the beautiful garden, that shining Eden,
> Those old crumbling walls and young roses,
> Those objects which think and gentle things,
> Spoke to my Mother by water and air,
> And whispered softly, 'Leave that child to us!'

In the Feuillantines, for the first time, Victor Hugo comes to life in his own right. He now had a group of playmates: the children of the Delons and the Fouchers, whose fathers were civil servants at the Conseil de Guerre. The Delon boy was eight years older than Victor, notorious for never using pavements: he got about the *quartier* by crawling along gutters, jumping from one rooftop to the next. Victor Foucher was the same age as Victor Hugo; the daughter, Adèle, was almost two years younger. The eldest Foucher, Prosper, had caught fire while playing by the stove and burned to death as his parents tried to break down the door which, for some reason, he had locked.[31] An important consequence for Victor Hugo was that Adèle's mother became extremely protective of her children. She cursed herself for having forced Prosper to go to school and especially for having thus followed Mme Hugo's advice. According to Adèle, Mme Hugo's recommendation that Prosper be educated somewhere else was motivated by the fact that she 'could never stand the sound of other people's children'.

Her own sons were not noted for their contemplative natures. When the family was in Naples, Colonel Hugo had described his youngest child as a studious boy with a sweet face who always thought before he spoke and got on well with his brothers.[32] In the Feuillantines a few months later, he proved to be quite normal. He played with lead soldiers, tortured frogs and insects, had a knack of dislocating his playmates' wrists, and pushed Adèle on the swing until she disappeared into the branches: a fitting start to their relationship.

The only vestige of the horrors Victor had seen on the roads of the Empire lay at the bottom of a dried-up well. It was the home of a black, scaly, pustular creature of hair and slime which 'observed but was never seen'. Its name was '*le sourd*', possibly by confusion with the Deaf School which still stands nearby on the Rue d'Enfer.[33]

When he wasn't playing, and when his mother released him from flower-watering duty, Victor was sent with brother Eugène to collect books at the local *cabinet de lecture* on the Rue Saint-Jacques.[34] There, a man in a powdered wig allowed them up to the entresol where the interesting books were kept: degenerate descendants of the French classical novel which 'were inflaming the amorous souls of Paris concierges' – books in which Mme Thénardier, in *Les Misérables*, 'drowned what little brain she had'.[35] Mme Hugo marked off clear bounds, within which she allowed her boys complete freedom. Ignorance of life, she thought, was a natural shield against the immorality of novels. Thanks to this enlightened régime, Victor had learned to read before he went to school. Applied to home life, his mother's theory was to have a disastrous effect.

The most unusual and disturbing detail in the garden paradise is also the detail which is subject to the greatest distortion – Lahorie – and it is fascinating to see the child's confusion reflected in his later depictions of the period. Several times he places his father in the garden – though Colonel Hugo never visited the Feuillantines. (Hugo may have been half-remembering visits from the Colonel's younger brothers, Louis and Francis, who were both Army officers.[36]) In two separate poems, he records a sighting of Napoleon in a military parade and gives the impression that his father was marching along among the other uniforms, though he was 600 miles away at the time:[37] Napoleon's enemy, Lahorie, is replaced by his loyal subject, Hugo. The objective truth of these poems lies in the association of his father with the Emperor. Now and then, the mouth that mutters away in Hugo's verse like a voice from the audience is clearly heard and his ambivalent feelings towards his father and Napoleon break through: 'Children of six, we lined your route; / Seeking a father's proud face in the procession, / *Nous te battions des mains.*' A strangely gauche expression which is supposed to mean, 'We applauded you', but which first strikes the mind as 'We hit you with our hands'.

In a later text, Hugo even makes his father responsible for Lahorie's presence in the chapel: 'My Father opened his house to him.' Yet, at the same time, he comes close to acknowledging the fugitive's true role in his upbringing: Lahorie 'fastened his eyes on me and said, "Child, remember this: above all, Freedom." Then he placed his hand on my little shoulder, and the tremor I felt is still with me.'[38]

This symbolic scene in the garden brings to mind – as it was certainly supposed to – another, more famous scene of revolutionary history: Benjamin Franklin taking his grandson to see Voltaire so that he could receive the great man's 'blessing', '*Dieu et la Liberté*'. But it also shows how a political ideology could be used to make sense of a confusing childhood. 'This word', says Hugo in his capacity as champion of democracy-in-exile, 'was the counterweight to a whole education.'

*

EDUCATION AT THE FEUILLANTINES eventually consisted of a six-hour day in a dingy little school in the Rue Saint-Jacques – actually more a repository for neighbourhood children, with private tuition for the intelligent. It was run by a former *abbé* called Antoine-Claude de La Rivière.[39] During the Revolution, La Rivière had taken the triple precaution of leaving the Church, dropping his '*de*' and marrying his servant. Regulation of primary schools was not introduced until the Restoration in 1815.[40] Before then, the official recommendation was to teach reading, writing, the rudiments of grammar, arithmetic and draughtsmanship, and the new decimal system. Instead, with Mme Hugo's approval, La Rivière poured Latin texts into the open mouths so that, by the age of nine, Victor could recite swathes of Horace and translate Tacitus – a remarkable feat, even with such an uncluttered syllabus.

At four o'clock, Victor and Eugène walked home past the cotton factory where street urchins 'threw stones at us because our trousers were not torn'.[41] In the evening, they competed to see who could translate more Latin: an early sign of a rivalry which La Rivière unwisely encouraged.

Later in life, Hugo painted a black picture of his education at the hands of 'a priest',[42] and described senility, in teachers, as a contagious disease.[43] But this was at a time when he was conscripting his own past as a political ally, when he saw, in every village in France, 'a lighted torch' (the schoolmaster) and 'a mouth trying to blow it out' (the priest).[44] Even then, La Rivière himself was exempted: he was the victim of cultural prejudice. As Hugo told his father in 1825, when La Rivière, in extreme poverty, had asked for a ten-year-old bill to be paid: 'What little we are worth we owe in large part to that venerable man.'[45] A pointed remark which underlines the fact that, in contrast to his sabre-rattling father, all his positive images of men were associated with reading: La Rivière, Lahorie and the open-minded owner of the *cabinet de lecture*.

*

ON THE MORNING OF 30 December 1810, the local police superintendent entered the Impasse des Feuillantines, followed by a squad of soldiers. A few minutes later, they left with the mysterious 'M. de Courlandais'.[46]

Lahorie's former friend, Savary, had just been appointed Minister of Police and was determined to prove his efficiency. Lahorie was taken straight to prison. His godson never saw him again.

As an accomplice, Victor's mother should have been arrested at the same time and deported. According to her, she 'owed her salvation to her knowledge of certain facts which Savary did not wish to be revealed'.[47] Mme Hugo would certainly not have made this astonishing claim – in a letter to the Minister of War in 1815 – if she had no story to tell. Her secret intelligence may even have something to do with the fact that Savary was sentenced to death in 1816, the year after she wrote her letter.

An ability to blackmail the Minister of Police does not suggest a purely passive involvement in the conspiracy against Napoleon. Since the conspiracy actually gained momentum after Lahorie's imprisonment, someone on the outside must have been taking messages, coordinating efforts and, as Colonel Hugo complained, spending inexplicably large sums of money.[48] The real situation beyond the garden walls is far more remarkable than the pleasant myth of the brave little Breton risking her life for the conspirator she loved. While Colonel Hugo was helping to spread the branches of the Empire, his wife was sawing at the base of the trunk.

This is where Hugo's florid legend of a 'bandit' mother engaged in counter-revolutionary espionage begins to come true, with some slight chronological adjustment. It was in the childhood paradise of the Feuillantines that he first heard 'History addressed in the "*tu*" form'.[49] This familiarity with the minutely human origins of cataclysmic events revealed the possibility, on a deeper level, of acting out his own private dramas through history – which can be seen either as astounding arrogance or as a splendid opportunity and a psychological necessity. In Hugo's words: 'The company of great men made it easy for me, later on, to keep up a long *tête-à-tête* with the Ocean.'[50]

*

TWO MONTHS AFTER the abrupt disappearance of Lahorie, Mme Hugo presented her sons with a Spanish dictionary and grammar, announced that their father was now a general and that they would shortly be leaving for Spain.

By now, General Hugo had been in charge of three different Spanish provinces. The King of Spain, Joseph Bonaparte, had made him a count (this was before brother Napoleon pointed out that Spanish grandees were technically equal to kings). Hugo was offered a choice of titles and opted for Siguenza where, by demolishing a church wall, he had uncovered a large treasure previously thought to have been carried off by guerrillas. King Joseph sent a message, behind the new Count of Siguenza's back, urging Mme Hugo and her family to join him. A large army was holding Spain against

Wellington, whose troops were massing in Portugal. In Spain itself, the occupying French were effectively besieged inside the towns and cities. Joseph was trying to create an impression of permanence and stability.

Mme Hugo's story was that she hoped to 'bring him to his senses'.[51] Hugo and his concubine 'were squandering the considerable income he received as a General, while his virtuous spouse and unhappy children were forgotten in Paris, where they lived on whatever M. Hugo felt he did not need for his life of luxury'.[52] Which was to say, a lot of money: in 1810 alone, General Hugo sent his wife 51,000 francs (about £153,000 today).*[53] When the family left for Spain in 1811, Mme Hugo hired a whole coach and drew 12,000 francs from the bank. Even with inflation, it was a fortune: the price of a single ticket from Paris to the south of France was enough to live on for a month.[54]

They took with them a manservant and a maid, leaving behind a cat and a canary. The schoolmaster's wife, Mme Larivière, was to look after the plants. On 10 March 1811, they set off for the war-zone, with the boys still poring over lists of Spanish vocabulary. At the age of nine, Victor was heading once again for a country he had never seen; but this time it was a country where he would begin to discover the puzzle of his own identity. Even without the adult Hugo's embellishments, the journey to Spain and back can be counted as one of the great Romantic expeditions – not only in the extraordinary incidents of the journey, but above all in its consequences.

* For approximate US dollar equivalent, multiply by 1.6

CHAPTER THREE

The Disasters of War

(1811–1815)

MME HUGO, Abel and the two servants sat inside the coach. Victor and Eugène grabbed the two seats in front, protected only by a leather hood. From there, they could watch the driver and his whip, enjoy the scenery and prove their physical endurance. Heroes had a new enemy: modern comforts. The departure from Paris is the first sight of Victor Hugo deliberately exposing himself to the breeze of real experience – a lifelong habit which, even in the cushy age of railways, 'made him a terrible travelling companion for anyone who was afraid of draughts'.[1]

Progress was slow, every able-bodied horse in France having been pressed into service by Napoleon. They stopped at Blois, Angoulême and Bordeaux, crossing the Dordogne by ferry, and arrived nine days later at Bayonne in the far south-west. Mme Hugo rented rooms, and there they waited for a convoy which was due to leave a month later with bullion for King Joseph.

Somewhere beyond the Pyrenees, General Hugo was doing battle with another bandit, the hero of Spanish resistance known as El Empecinado ('The Stubborn'), perpetrating some of the horrors depicted in Goya's engravings, *Los Desastres de la Guerra*. A local specialty adopted by the General consisted of creating a display of severed heads to set an example. His personal innovation was to arrange the heads over church doors. The French Revolution was still exporting its anticlericalism, annihilating the spirit of the Inquisition with its own fire and torture. Surveying the historical drama from the vantage-point of the future, Victor Hugo comes close to exonerating his father on the grounds that he was serving a greater morality: 'That

Army carried the Encyclopedia in its knapsack.' 'It threw open the monasteries, snatched away the veils, aired out the sacristies and slew the Holy Office.'[2]

Interestingly, this notion of a Voltairean Salvation Army was current in the paranoid milieux which Hugo encountered as a child in Spain: it was the view of the progressive *afrancesados* (pro-French). But his remarks were more than just an ambitious historical analysis or a return to the prejudices of childhood. Hugo was remodelling his father's footprints before planting his own feet in them. Half a century later, he boasts of 740 attacks on *Les Misérables* in Catholic newspapers and merrily records the revelation of '*La España* – a priest-paper from Madrid – that Victor Hugo does not exist and that the true author of *Les Misérables* is a creature called Satan'.[3] Hugo's father had been acting on the side of Good, and, as if by divine ordinance, the agents of progress were also quite nice people: 'Let the Army of today take note: those men would have disobeyed if ordered to fire on women and children.'

The last remark is blatantly untrue. It was this savage campaign which had earned General Hugo the title of Count of Siguenza, and he was not being rewarded for his scruples.

While they waited in Bayonne, Victor and his brothers gorged themselves on the theatre, which had been a yearly treat in Paris. They saw *Les Ruines de Babylone* – a popular melodrama with a genie, a caliph, a eunuch and a trap-door. The following night, they saw *Les Ruines de Babylone* again. After the fifth performance, they stayed at home in disgust: evidently, dwindling audiences did not guarantee a change of programme. Instead, Victor collected birds which he bought from local boys, coloured in the pictures in his copy of *The Arabian Nights* (a present from Lahorie), and listened to the landlady's daughter reading him stories.

One of these readings was the occasion of a momentous event which Hugo later wished to see recorded in the biography by his wife. The sight of the girl's heaving breast gave him his first adult erection – or, as an unpublished draft of *Victor Hugo Raconté* puts it, 'his virility declared itself'. Hugo also described the great moment in a text which he intended to publish: 'I blushed and trembled [when the girl noticed his wandering eye] and pretended to play with the big door-bolt. . . .

It was there that I saw that first inexpressible light beginning to shine in the darkest corner of my soul.'[4]

This typically heavy-handed yet subtle periphrasis is a splendid demonstration of the fact that the literary proprieties, even prudishness, have certain aesthetic advantages. It also serves as a reminder that the babbling brook of Romantic fiction carries darker currents. Without the discipline of what are now seen as constraints and euphemisms, these otherwise trivial details would have lost their visionary depth. Hugo's text represents the vital moment, not just as the revelation of sexual desire at the age of nine, but as the first inkling of a means of expressing the 'inexpressible', of preserving the mysterious imprint of sounds and objects on the mind. 'As she read, I paid no attention to the meaning of the words; I was listening to the sound of her voice.'

At last, the great day arrived: the theatre announced a new play, and a grenadier covered in white dust came to escort Mme Hugo and her boys over the border to Irún, where the convoy was to assemble. For the first time as a fully conscious being, Hugo saw the curtain go up on a new world. Thirty-two years later, he rediscovered Irún and tried to scrape away the veneer of urban 'improvement' which threatened to erase his own past:

> It was there that Spain first appeared to me and astonished me so with its black houses, its narrow streets, its wooden balconies and fortress doors – I, a child of France, raised among the mahogany of the Empire. My eyes were accustomed to star-patterned beds, swan-neck armchairs, fire-dogs shaped like sphinxes, gilded bronze and turquoise marble. Now, with something approaching terror, I saw those great sculptured sideboards, the tables with their twisted feet, the canopied beds, the massive, convoluted silverware, the leaded windows – that old New World which spread itself out before me. – Alas! ... Irún now looks like the Batignolles.*[5]

The family left Irún with the convoy in a tubby museum-piece of a coach, lined with cast-iron to stop the bullets. It was pulled by six mules, with four oxen for the hills. Alongside and far behind, 2000 soldiers and cavalry marched along, with a hundred other coaches

---

* In the 1840s, a modern garden-suburb of Paris.

painted green and gold – the colours of the Empire. In the mountain passes, high on the ridges, figures stood silhouetted against the sky, and everyone remembered that the last convoy had been massacred at Salinas. The women were raped, the children dismembered (someone had told Victor that guerrillas were especially fond of children), while the men were roasted on spits. Since Mme Hugo's convoy was one-third the size of the last one, it was considered to be safer. They were shot at only once.

At each stop, they were billeted in houses whose owners left food and disappeared, muttering, behind locked doors. In the face of fleas and rancid oil, Mme Hugo's courage almost failed her. The closer they came to Madrid, the less fresh food there was, and the more signs of French activity. At Torquemada and Saladas, there was nowhere to sleep: both towns had been razed to the ground. Victor and his brothers played among the ruins. One day, a 'cripples regiment' passed by in the opposite direction – the mutilated remnants of French battalions who were strung together and left to make their own way back to France. Few saw home again.

Why Mme Hugo decided to endanger the lives of her children becomes clearer in the light of an incident which occurred just beyond the town of Mondragon. On a downhill slope, a mule collapsed and the coach hurtled towards a precipice. One of the wheels caught on a boulder. While some grenadiers tried to force it back on to the road, Mme Hugo ordered her boys to stay in the coach and not to behave like silly girls. The manuscript version of *Victor Hugo Raconté* observes that Mme Hugo 'was very firm in her educational system'. For her, this baptism of fire was simply parental duty. Once, when he was five or six years old, Victor had been found crying and, as a corrective, was taken out for a walk dressed as a girl.[6] Both parents believed that undesirable aspects of a personality could be removed as if by surgical operation. The trip to Spain would be an invaluable part of Victor's upbringing, if he survived.

Mme Hugo's educational system did not take account of the fact that its beneficiary was likely to try to re-create similar opportunities on his own initiative. Hugo's life is punctuated, at almost regular intervals, by situations which called for conspicuous acts of bravery and an assumption that his family and loved ones would happily follow him over the precipice. The other drawback was that, for Mme Hugo, 'courage' was part of keeping up appearances – a heroic conceit which was just as likely to produce a person who felt the need to inflate his own achievements and had the nerve to betray his friends.

But the journey was also supposed to be a cultural excursion, and in this it was a huge success. In Burgos, half-way through the journey, Victor Hugo discovered his passion for architecture. He was fascinated by the cathedral, with its firework-display of pinnacles and the mechanical man who shot out of a window high up on a wall, clapped his hands three times and disappeared. The revelation of Gothic whimsy at Burgos might explain why some readers found the cathedral of Hugo's novel about a hunchback a poor likeness of Notre-Dame de Paris.

Two years later, during the French retreat from Spain, General Hugo demolished three of the pinnacles and shattered the famous stained-glass windows while blowing up the fort and part of the town. In 1811, the French had already left their mark on Burgos. Mme Hugo took her sons to see the tomb of the warrior hero, El Cid. French soldiers, stupidly oblivious to the effect on Spanish resolve, had used the tomb for target practice.[7] Meanwhile, as Governor of the garrison at Madrid, General Hugo was busy destroying and exporting significant portions of the national heritage. He oversaw the removal of masterpieces by Velázquez, Murillo and Goya to the Louvre and the Luxembourg Palace – a fact which only the author of the entry on General Hugo in the Spanish *Enciclopedia Universal* has seen fit to record.

It is worth remembering that Victor Hugo, who did so much for the conservation of medieval works of art and buildings, was the son of a man who stole them and blew them up. Much of Hugo's work can be seen – as he saw it himself – as a kind of reparative pilgrimage: the epic of El Cid in *La Légende des Siècles*, or the two plays which take their names from places on the journey in 1811 – *Torquemada* and *Hernani*. For all his proprietorial treatment of history as a supply depot for writers, there is always a certain unease when he talks about his father's activities in Spain. He tends, significantly, to exaggerate his own gifts to the country, not to mention his knowledge of the language.[8] Along with everyone who has written about it, Hugo was under the impression that he had endowed the little town of Ernani with the totemic 'H' of his own name. In fact, it always was Hernani.[9]

The final irony is that the picturesque Spain appropriated by the son of General Hugo for his poems and plays was re-imported by his Spanish admirers and contributed to the creation of a spurious cultural identity.

*

AFTER MORE THAN three months on the road, the convoy reached the outskirts of Madrid. It was important to put on a good display. The soldiers were ordered to wash, comb their hair and change into clean uniforms. The guns were polished and Mme Hugo had her carriage swept out. Then they trotted into a dust-storm and arrived in Madrid, filthy, exhausted, but safe.

It was then that the battle began. A cavernous apartment in the palace of the former ambassador to France, Prince Masserano, had been sealed off and assigned to Mme Hugo. General Count Hugo was in Guadalajara at the time, exterminating bandits, and welcomed his wife to Spain by suing for divorce. In support of his petition – addressed to 'His Majesty José Napoléon, King of Spain and the Indies' – he noted that his 'ambitious', 'imperious' wife had managed to spend 12,000 francs simply travelling, uninvited, from Paris. Proof that his authority was being flouted.

When Joseph Bonaparte returned from the baptism of Napoleon's son in Paris, he appears to have engineered a specious reconciliation since General Hugo sent a giant crate of candles and oranges in August, along with a selection of his uniforms, as if to say that part of him at least would now be residing with the family.

While they waited for the legendary General to materialize, Victor and his brothers explored the palace.[10] The main attraction was a gallery lined with portraits of Masserano's ancestors, magnified by giant mirrors, glittering with chandeliers. Mme Hugo designated it as the play area. The three boys chased each other along the gallery, wondered what other treasures lay behind the sealed doors and found two enormous Japanese vases which were just the right size for hide-and-seek. At night, Victor washed in a marble bathroom and fell asleep under a Virgin Mary pierced by seven arrows.

Sometimes, he was joined in one of the vases by a local girl called Pepita.[11] 'She was sixteen, tall and beautiful', with a silk hairnet sewn with doubloons and 'a toreador's jacket'; blue velvet and black lace. Pepita was being courted by at least one soldier and seems to have allowed the French boy to kiss her in order to provoke her suitors.

Pepita was an impressive contrast to Adèle Foucher, the little *bourgeoise* back in Paris. She was the daughter of the pro-French Marqués de Montehermosa. Her mother took her francophilia to the point of becoming Joseph Bonaparte's mistress. It seems almost too good to be true that Victor Hugo should have been frolicking with the daughter while the elder Bonaparte was enjoying the company of the mother (strangely, Hugo never mentions this), and especially that Hugo's sweetheart should have sat for none other than Goya. It thus becomes possible to compare Hugo's description of her in *L'Art d'Être Grand-Père* (in the section entitled 'What Grandfather Got Up To When He Was A Child') with the portrait by Goya, and to examine the face which Hugo tried to hold in his memory for the rest of his life. This was the Spanish face he looked for later in his fiancée, Adèle, which haunts the last hours of the prisoner in *Le Dernier Jour d'un Condamné* and which may have inspired the gypsy girl, Esmeralda, in *Notre-Dame de Paris*. There is a certain similarity between Adèle and Pepita: dark hair and eyes, a strong, slightly chubby face, the seriousness and ostentatious self-control. Besides that curious, corpse-like flatness of Goya's portraits, Pepita's face also has a certain playfulness and daring, both qualities lacking in Adèle, who would never have allowed herself to climb into a vase with an excited boy.

Victor's parents were playing their own game of hide-and-seek. In September 1811, the General stumbled on the awful secret: his wife had been living with another man. Legally, this was far more serious than his own alternative household. General Hugo's cruel genius (Sophie's expression) led him to deny the help he had once received from Lahorie and to denounce his own wife to King Joseph as 'a traitor to the State'. Whether or not he took the risk of revealing his wife's political rather than personal infidelity, the effect was to place the boys at the General's disposal.

Abel was signed up as a page of King Joseph, which meant that he suddenly became a grown-up in the eyes of his younger brothers:

pages at the Franco-Spanish court wore a blue uniform with gold trimmings, silk stockings, a white-plumed hat and – every boy's dream – a sword.[12] Before entering the service of the King, Abel was to join Victor and Eugène in a school for sons of the nobility in the nearby monastery of San Antonio Abad, known to the French as the Collège des Nobles.

Mme Hugo left her children in the sunless, echoing corridors with two monks – one thin, the other fat, both smelling of the crypt. True to her Enlightenment upbringing, she informed the monks that her sons would be unable to attend Mass because they were Protestants. As children of a French general, they would have to be treated with respect. They were also several years ahead of the other boys in Latin and leapfrogged into the top class. This instant promotion might have consoled them for the loss of their mother, but it only served to increase the confusion. Power and impotence combined. The General sometimes took them out in his carriage with his mistress, the self-styled 'Comtesse de Salcano', but the boys saw their father more often through the words and actions of others than in the flesh. It was a deeply impressive image. The seemingly boastful exaggerations of the ode 'Mon Enfance' are probably an accurate description of the child's impression:

> Through the lands of ten vanquished races,
> I passed defenceless, amazed at their fearful respect.
> At an age when one is pitied, I seemed to be a protector,
> And when I uttered the cherished name of France,
> The foreigner turned pale.[13]

Hugo's memories of the Collège des Nobles in Madrid are happy or unhappy depending on the ideological context in which he chooses to place them. On the whole, any unpleasantness seems to be a trans-position of turmoil in the family. There was famine in the city and rationing in the school, but his memory retained only the delicious watermelons and *olla podrida*, an improvised stew which he later re-created at his own dinner-table. The dormitories were almost deserted and freezing cold in winter, but they were tended by an unhappy little hunchback whom the Hugo boys treated as their personal servant.

Dressing his earlier self in one of its more unlikely costumes, Hugo claims to have fought for the Emperor, inside the school, attacking anyone who dared to call him 'Napoladron'.*[14] Yet only twenty-four of the original 500 pupils remained in Madrid and practically all were from afrancesado families.[15] The monks themselves were careful to compromise only their principles. The nastiest Spaniard was objectionable mainly for aesthetic reasons – a lazy pig of a boy with enormous, claw-like hands called Elespuru, who reappears, with the same name, in the third act of Hugo's Cromwell (1827) as a court jester.[16]

One of the most enduring effects of school life in Madrid lies at the point where the personal meets the political. Instead of calling each other by their Christian names, pupils at the Collège des Nobles used titles – Marqués, Conde, etc. A far cry from Larivière's grimy little schoolroom in the Rue Saint-Jacques. Hugo's first sight of himself in the eyes of a larger society was unlikely to inspire him with modesty. Victor and Eugenio Hugo were better at Latin than anyone else, the monks were afraid to punish them, they had a brother who carried a sword, their father was a friend of the King, their mother lived in a palace, and now everyone called them 'Viscount'.

The eight months of domestic misery and social grandeur in occupied Spain can be seen as the start of Hugo's peculiar relationship with his own name. 'A name is an identity,' he claims in Les Misérables;[17] but for the ten-year-old Visconde Hugo, which name was the real one? He shared in the glory of his father's title, just as he was used to hearing his mother addressed as 'Mme la Générale'. But now, when she travelled, she called herself Mme Trébuchet, sometimes aristocratically appending her aunt's little property in Brittany to her maiden name: Mme Trébuchet de la Renaudière – a complete rejection of the General, marital, social and geographical. Victor's Christian name, on the other hand, was a souvenir of the man in the Feuillantines garden. With such a choice of signposts at the beginning, it is hardly surprising that the map of Hugoland should become increasingly complex.

*

* 'Ladron' = 'thief'.

IF NAPOLEON'S EMPIRE had lasted, the writer known as Victor Hugo would probably have been a Spanish poet called the Count of Siguenza. 'My works would have been written in a language which is not widely spoken and would thus have had little effect.'[18] The survivor's privilege is to write history with a sense of humour. In this view, the fall of Napoleon I – and, later, of Napoleon III – paved the way for Victor Hugo, the punch-line of the Second Empire.

In the spring of 1812, the French were streaming out of Spain by the thousand. Wellington was advancing on Madrid. A travel warrant was hastily issued to Mme 'Hugau' and she was reunited with Victor and Eugène. Abel stayed behind with his father, a soldier at the age of thirteen – which says more about French desperation than his abilities as a soldier. Hundreds of families had already left on foot and died of thirst on the plains of Old Castile, where the wells had been poisoned with manure and dead animals.

Hugo's memories of the return journey are fragmented and horrific.[19] They cast a shadow over the rest of his life which is easily missed: odd, unreal incidents in what would soon appear to have been an almost imaginary interlude in their life in Paris.

At the gates of Vitoria, the bleeding limbs and severed head of a bandit leader's nephew had been gathered up and nailed to a crucifix. At Burgos, Hugo saw a procession of lantern-bearing penitents, escorting a man seated back-to-front on an ass: he was about to be garrotted on the public square. With its scaffold and cathedral, Burgos is the birthplace of Hugo's obsessions: the preservation of the past and the abolition of the death penalty – both strongly associated with his father.

Finally, after the huge relief of crossing the border at Saint-Jean-de-Luz, in the courtyard of an inn, 'an enormous wagoner's cart, unhitched, with its chains hanging down. – Why, in such a long and eventful journey, which certainly had its share of curious and remarkable things, should something so insignificant be remembered? Is that not a mystery?' A mystery which Hugo's mythologizing mind tried to rescue from its unfathomable banality in *Les Misérables*: 'a fat chain worthy of the convict Goliath, with the air of a gaol about it, turning rusty and getting in the way like outmoded institutions'.[20]

*

THE FATHERLESS FAMILY arrived back at the Impasse des Feuillantines in April 1812. Nothing had changed. 'M. de Courlandais' had
not returned. For the next two years, Victor Hugo effectively
disappears in the apparent uniformity of a safe and almost normal life:
the lessons of Larivière, the richer, improvised curriculum of the
cabinet de lecture, and games in the garden with Adèle Foucher, who
reminded him of Pepita. Their mother often went out alone on
unexplained visits. The only echo of the disintegrating régime in
Spain was the increasing lack of money: Joseph Bonaparte had
delegated one of General Hugo's salaries to Sophie, but payments
were irregular. Most of the French Army now consisted of unpaid
conscripts.

Only once in that quiet period, as the *Grande Armée* was leaving
the smouldering rubble of Moscow for 1000 miles of Russian winter,
did Hugo's childhood world feel the tremor of historical events. It
was a drizzly evening in October 1812. He was playing with Eugène
outside the church of Saint-Jacques-du-Haut-Pas, opposite Larivière's
school, when they spotted a poster on one of the columns. Some
generals who had tried to depose the Emperor in his absence were to
be executed. They were struck by the name of one of the condemned
men: Soulier ('Shoe'). The other names – Malet, Guidal, Lahorie –
meant nothing.

As they found out later, the execution marked the end of their
mother's career as a conspirator. On 23 October, General Malet had
proved that the Empire was an upside-down pyramid poised precari-
ously on one man. A forged document convinced Malet's jailers that
Napoleon had perished in Russia. Lahorie was freed and then helped
to arrest two government ministers and the Prefect of Police. For half
a day, Mme Hugo's lover was Minister of Police. When the deception
was discovered, reprisals were swift and extreme – probably to prevent
a proper investigation by Napoleon when he returned. Lahorie was
shot by firing-squad among the vegetable plots on the edge of Paris,
while undercover agents were sent to every second-hand clothes shop
in the city with orders to buy up all the General's uniforms in case it
happened again.

Hugo later decided, at the age of seventy-three, that he had lived
this moment of history at his mother's side. It was evening; the

Retreat from Moscow had begun and a 'terrible shadow' was falling over the Empire. She held his hand and pointed to the large white poster: '"Lahorie," said my mother. "Remember that name." Then she added, "That is your godfather." Such is the ghost I perceive in the depths of my childhood.'[21]

These fantasies of old age, with their patina of retold stories, are an eloquent reversal of the truth: a sense of exclusion from his parents' world, and an attempt to determine the precise nature of childhood influences by appealing to the comparatively straightforward narratives of history.

At the time, the only perceptible influence of history on Hugo's life was the enlargement of Paris, which was about to swallow up part of the Feuillantines garden and raise the rent. At the end of 1813, the family moved to the ground floor of a modest *hôtel*, next door to the Fouchers, at 2 Rue des Vieilles-Tuileries (now 42 Rue du Cherche-Midi). A tiny courtyard left room for only a few flowers; Sophie was disappointed and claustrophobic. As if sensing imminent anarchy – or by contrast with the more confined setting – the boys' games became more violent. Their mother was determined more than ever to maintain her hold over them. A letter written to Abel in September 1813 gives some idea of that steely affection which created such a strong bond between Victor Hugo and his mother and imbued his closest relationships with a sort of monumental stiltedness, as if friendship were a form of personal discipline and love itself indistinguishable from the abstract notion of it.

> I shall not scold you, my dear Abel, for not having written earlier, since I attribute it to thoughtlessness and a failure to consider my inevitable anxiety rather than to any lack of affection on your part. Whatever the case, my dear, do not let it happen again.
>
> I doubt your father could forbid you to write, but if that were so . . . your duty would be to disobey, just as your brothers should disobey were I to be so forgetful of the sacred laws of Nature as to forbid them to write to their father. . . . Let us hope, my dear Abel, for better times and above all that our common misfortunes might serve as a lesson to you. See where a lack of principles and extravagant passions can lead us. What a fine destiny your father has ruined! . . . How horrible to see a father despoiling himself and his family for such a woman![22]

Abel came home in time for the death-throes of the Empire. Cheerful bulletins had been arriving in the capital giving the latest position of the troops. For the first time, Napoleon's soldiers were fighting on French soil. Some of the 'victorious' regiments named in the bulletins consisted only of officers with no troops to command. Some had ceased to exist altogether.

On 29 March 1814, the Hugo family woke to the sound of fighting at the gates of Paris. The armies of the European coalition had over-run the country like a disease invading an exhausted body. Next day, the dreaded Cossacks arrived. Some were billeted in the Hugos' house. Overawed by the great city, they turned out to be as docile as sheep.

Napoleon went down immediately in the boys' estimation, which effectively makes the point that, in contrast to the supposed two-stage evolution of the poet – ardent monarchism followed by ardent republicanism – the political background of his early years was a sea of constantly changing and conflicting loyalties.

Mme Hugo decided to press what she thought was her advantage: her husband would now be recognized officially as a villain, a henchman of the defeated tyrant Napoleon. She rushed out to buy a white dress, a straw hat and some tuberoses (real *fleurs de lys* were too big to wear). Her objective now was to exact a financial commitment from the villain and to ensure a stable future for the children. In May, she set off, with Abel as a human shield, for Thionville, 12 miles from the border with Germany and Luxembourg. General Hugo had been holding the town since January and had managed to hang on, even after Napoleon's abdication in April.

Having sustained the siege for several months, General Hugo had honed his strategic abilities and his blood was up. He refused to send his 'concubine' away and forced his wife and son to sleep next door to his adulterous bedroom. One night, he threatened Sophie with a whip, locked her out in the street, and generally acted as though the siege had transferred itself to his own house. While this was going on, in a cunning rearguard action, he had the seals affixed to 'the Demon''s house in the Rue des Vieilles-Tuileries, using his sister in Paris as his agent. Sophie returned to find herself evicted and her two younger sons legally kidnapped by the General's sister, Mme Martin, who found the boys impertinent and profligate.

Sophie managed to reconquer her home and her children for a time, but the General descended on the city in September and emptied the house of all its linen – '10 shirts, 24 pairs of stockings, 19 cambric handkerchiefs for the use of the plaintiff, all the silver, a vermeil opera-glass, and placed the lot (as the plaintiff believes) in the hands of his concubine'.[23] Messy, but effective. He then succeeded in regaining custody of the boys and wrote on 9 January 1815 from his temporary lodgings in Paris, thanking them for wishing him a Happy New Year:

> I accept your wishes, my dears. My own wishes, and all my actions, will always have your happiness as their principal object.
>
> Soon you will be restored to me and you shall see me unceasingly concerned with the completion of your education.[24]

Their worst fear ... A month later, the boys were 'imprisoned' in a boarding school nearby in the Rue Sainte-Marguerite, where Victor Hugo landed, at the end of the Empire, after so many heroic adventures, feeling like a plucked eagle, his feathers swept away with the classroom rubbish.[25]

*

ON 6 MARCH 1815, a month after Victor and Eugène were placed in the Pension Cordier, the *Journal des Débats* reported that that 'coward', Bonaparte, dripping with the blood of generations, had escaped from his island-empire of Elba and, with a motley band of foreigners, had dared to set foot in France. 'All France will have but one cry: "Death to the tyrant; long live the King!"'[26]

Two weeks later, the same newspaper reported the 'miraculous return' of Napoleon and the restoration of freedom, honour and virtue. Peasants, 'drunk with joy', flocked to see him pass and hardened soldiers wept openly in the streets. Only a few 'miserable pamphlets' opposed the hero's triumph. 'As we write, the streets, squares, boulevards and *quais* are covered with an immense throng, and cries of "Long live the Emperor" ring out everywhere, from Fontainebleau to Paris.'

One hundred days after the landing at Fréjus, the telegraph brought news of a tremendous disaster in the north. It was the battle Hugo calls 'the hinge of the nineteenth century', when the 'thinkers' took over from the 'swordsmen'.[27] The name of the spot where Napoleon lost his final battle, 'the first knot to resist his axe', is given in *Les Misérables*, with more than a hint of its etymological significance: a little walled farmyard near the paltry village of Waterloo called Hougomont ... 'For a long time after, all over the gateposts, the prints of bleeding hands could be seen. ... The breaches cry out, the holes are wounds, the trees, shivering and bending over, appear to be trying to flee.'[28]

It is customary to chortle smugly, from the safety of our own century, at those who preferred to keep their jobs and lives by signing an oath of allegiance to the King, then, during the Hundred Days, to Napoleon, and then, once again, after Waterloo, to the King.

As a professional soldier, General Hugo acknowledged Louis XVIII in April 1814. But his letter could hardly be called a volte-face: he proclaimed his fidelity to 'the fatherland' and – with an interesting choice of verb – to 'the oath which chains us to King Louis XVIII'.

Hugo's father had behaved like a hero. He had been the last general to leave Madrid. During the disastrous retreat from Spain, he hatched a plan to kidnap Wellington (over-cautious comrades refused to help). In the musical chairs at the end of the Empire, he saved Thionville for France and stuck to his guns even after the war had ended and the royalist reprisals known as the White Terror had begun. In the spring of 1815, he enjoyed a triumph which mirrored Napoleon's return to Paris. He was sent back to defend Thionville against the Prussians and received a standing ovation at the town theatre. When Victor Hugo visited Thionville in 1871, he found that his father was practically worshipped as the town saint.[29] General Hugo flooded the moat, executed deserters, ignored all messages from the outside world and held the town until 13 November 1815, by which time civilization had moved on a stage and several of Napoleon's generals had been shot as traitors.

This extraordinary resistance gives Hugo's father the great distinction of being the small but final full-stop to the history of Napoleon's Empire. It has an exact parallel in his son's resistance to the Empire of Napoleon III. The famous words he applies to political exiles of the Second Empire could easily be applied to General Hugo in 1815: 'And if only one remains, I shall be that one!'

Hugo's first recorded reaction to the defeat of Napoleon and his father dates from later that year. Inspired by monarchist propaganda, he wrote a political song of his own. Entitled 'Vive le Roi! Vive la France!', it lunges straight to the point in the first line: 'Corsica has bitten the dust!' But even in such a conventional piece, assembled almost entirely from clichés, echoes of his own experience and of a more confessional form of literature can already be heard:

> A dark and dreary sadness
> Reigned o'er our dejected hearts . . .
> Return, black demon of war,
> To the hell which spat you out . . .
> At last, that treacherous Marshal –
> Ney – will go to meet his death.
> Tremble, regicidal cohort,
> Jacobins, such is your fate.

When Hugo wrote this song, the fate of the treacherous Marshal Ney might well have been awaiting General Hugo, which means that the General's youngest son was virtually signing his father's death warrant: 'Tyrant, you can no longer vent / Your stupid rage on us.'

He then goes on to consider the sins of his childhood from the height of his thirteen years:

> Oh you whom a shameful glory
> Has dazzled for too long,
> Give up your hateful error
> And learn to cherish the King!

The need to adopt a clear position is obvious, but also the attempt to convince himself that his monarchist mother had been right all along and that the confusion was over. His behaviour inside the school was proof of the opposite. The 1815 equivalent of Cowboys and Indians was Napoleon against the Rest of the World, and the boy who most often got to be leader of the civilized world was the precociously authoritative and authoritarian Victor Hugo.

His father had been on the winning side and the losing side, a figure of power and a fugitive who continued to act as a tyrant towards his own children. It was impossible to reject or identify with him entirely, and this impossibility should serve as a warning against interpretations which impose a grid of simplistic antitheses on Hugo and all his work. His childhood had not been the plot of a melodrama, but a series of contradictory certainties. After Spain, every simplification was both implausible and necessary. How was it possible to detect any trace of divine justice in the victories and defeats of Napoleon, that 'parody of God's omnipotence'?[30] Besides which, disputatious parents were always an excellent source of alternative interpretations. Inspected with the attention they deserve, the violent contrasts of Hugo's works have that same cold sense of a necessary discipline as Goya's *Desastres de la Guerra*; the same stark divisions of reality which make it possible to contemplate the dismembering of Truth.

After all his adventures in Paris and the Empire, the thirteen-year-old *Visconde* had acquired a vast frame of reference for his own identity, but so far the only guiding principles had come in the form of political and domestic propaganda. The monster in the Feuillantines garden was still there – not only in the secret places of childhood, but imprisoned in his own brain. Any insights into his own condition would have to be founded on an original blindness, an intense curiosity about events which part of his mind had blotted out. The seemingly accidental wisdom of his mature work owes much to that endless patience with insoluble riddles which Hugo describes as the principal advantage of a miserable childhood.[31]

With all the distortions and untruths piled up in his past, it seems quite natural that Hugo should come to an understanding of the universe long before he comprehended the circumstances of his own birth and upbringing; also, paradoxically, that his work should help to provide the psychological foundations of later, empirical discoveries. The universe as it reproduces itself in Hugo's brain has at its centre that revolting phenomenon now called a Black Hole: 'A dreadful black sun radiating darkness'.[32]

CHAPTER FOUR

Metromania

(1815–1818)

A RESTORATION, according to Hugo, is like the restoration of a painting.[1] The recent past is scraped off to reveal the old order underneath. Louis XVIII returned from exile in England, brushed aside the last twenty years and dated his reign from the death of Louis XVII in 1795. But the damage had been done. France now had a Charter which recognized the principles of liberty and equality. A dangerous precedent, according to the royalist extremists known as the Ultras, who would soon be able to call on the formidable voice of the nation's youngest great poet: Victor-Marie Hugo.

Almost as soon as Napoleon set sail for St Helena, business picked up – especially for sign-writers: Paris was redrafting its own history. The Place de la Concorde, formerly Place de la Révolution, was now the Place Louis XV. The square which had been the Place de l'Indivisibilité and then the Place des Vosges was once again the Place Royale. Capital 'N's were chiselled off the face of monuments, and the four horses on the triumphal arch in front of the Louvre were unbolted and returned to Venice, where Bonaparte had stolen them.

In Mme Hugo's milieu, General Hugo and his fellow 'Republicans' were known as 'Brigands of the Loire' (from the final position of the defeated French Army). The name of their murderous ringleader was pronounced '*Buonaparté*' to make it sound as foreign as possible. In 1815, a young Englishman, Viscount Palmerston, crossed the Channel and recorded the unsurprising fact that the worst thing you could say to a Frenchman was 'Filthy rabble of a vanquished nation'.[2] But for many Frenchmen, only 'the Ogre of Corsica' had been vanquished. The Prussians who camped in the Champs-Élysées and the

Cossacks whose horses munched the grass in the Tuileries Gardens were 'the Allies'. In conservative circles it was fashionable to affect an English accent. For a time, the return of the *émigrés* and their powdered wigs concealed the fact that irreversible changes had occurred. The Empire had provided an administrative and social foundation for the ideals of 1789, and produced a generation of old men and orphans to put them into practice.

Three decades later, Hugo learned from an English newspaper that shiploads of skeletons picked up on Napoleonic battlefields had arrived in Hull to be crushed into fertilizer: 'the final by-product of Napoleon's victories: fattening up English cows'.[3] Almost a million Frenchmen had died since the Revolution, half of them under the age of twenty-eight.

In 1815, Hugo's hero was Chateaubriand. Already at the age of forty-seven a grand old man of French letters, Chateaubriand had launched his political career as a constitutional royalist. This was the moderate line which Mme Hugo followed – an affiliation which made her and, therefore, her sons more accepting than they might have been of those strangely sensual, melancholy fragments of Chateaubriand's *Le Génie du Christianisme*, 'Atala' and 'René' – soon to be associated with something called '*Romanticisme*' and disowned by their author. Chateaubriand proved his genius for poignant, diplomatic symbols when he went with an official deputation to exhume what remained of Marie-Antoinette from the common grave. In the piles of skeletons, he claimed to recognize her by her 'smile'.

Meanwhile, the youngest child of one of the 'Brigands of the Loire' was looking for plausible explanations of what had happened to France and to his own family. Victor Hugo was filling up notebooks with hundreds of lines of verse, scribbling 'graffiti in the latrines of history'.[4]

*

VICTOR AND EUGÈNE spent the first three-and-a-half years of the Restoration in the Pension Cordier, wedged in a narrow street under Saint-Germain-des-Prés.[5] It was a dark and noisy *quartier* of scrap-metal merchants, the most densely populated part of Paris. At one end of the street was a prison, at the other, across the Rue de l'Égout

('Drain Street', where, exceptionally, the drain was covered), a stone dragon carved over a gateway gave its name to the Passage du Dragon.

When Hugo revisited the school in all his glory at the age of forty-four, pupils and teachers recited tributes to the poet who, according to school legend, had sat, Buddha-like, under the school tree (an Indian walnut), writing his first poems. It was the only vegetation on the premises, though an optimist had painted the walls of the inner courtyard to look like a park, with leafy bowers and silvery fountains. Here, the boys were incarcerated by their father from 13 February 1815 until 8 September 1818, forbidden to see their mother and placed in the care of an old teacher called Cordier, remarkable for his snuff-filled nostrils and his taste in clothes: M. Cordier wore a Polish cap with ear-flaps and a fur-lined coat because he thought they made him look like Jean-Jacques Rousseau – a predilection which seems to have had little effect on his pedagogical practice, since he used his metal snuff-box to hammer important points into his pupils' heads.

The timetable was easy to remember. This one is taken from their second year, when most of the classes were held three-quarters of a mile away at the Collège Louis-le-Grand. The emphasis on Mathematics reflects the General's desire to see his boys obtain a place at the École Polytechnique and thus, eventually, in the Army.

> 8.00: Mathematics and Algebra.
> 12.30: Lunch at the Pension, followed by Drawing.
> 2.00–5.00: Philosophy.
> 6.00–10.00: Mathematics and homework.

Any spare time was taken up with obligatory walks. Holidays consisted of 'work in moderation' and longer and more frequent walks. 'Viscount Hugo' had fallen prey to the French education system.

After several washings in Hugo's memory the colours of the Pension Cordier are still authentic and the details of his accounts amazingly accurate, even the suspiciously symbolic antithesis according to which one of his classmates became a Prefect of Police, while another – a boy called Joly – became a convict: the former a threat to Hugo's freedom, the latter to his purse. One detail, however, reflects the personal Restoration in Hugo's mind, when his father retrospectively became a hero. The General supposedly requested that his sons be accommodated in a private room instead of being lumped together with the other boys in the common dormitory. As a result, Victor and Eugène shared a room with the future Prefect of Police. But official statistics suggest that the special treatment was a fantasy: in August 1817 the Pension Cordier had only four boarders and twelve day-boys. If the common dormitory existed, it was even more exclusive than the private room.

General Hugo was in no mood or position to pay for luxuries. He had retired, temporarily he hoped, to Blois, where he lived with his mistress in a little white house by the banks of the Loire. Painfully ignorant of the needs of growing boys, he developed a nasty suspicion that Sophie was encouraging them to destroy their clothes. The General's sister in Paris was instructed to 'have the holes plugged with scraps and then they will only have themselves to blame if they are not decently dressed'.[6]

Eugène and Victor responded with enormous dignity, at first in letters written by Eugène and signed by both of them. From their mother, they had learned the power of consistent moral principles in the face of a sporadically apoplectic General. The woman they refused to call 'Aunt' was driven to distraction – though the fact that she later left most of her money to Abel and Victor suggests an improvement in relations and some blackening of the picture. They complained that she withheld the money they needed for knife-sharpening, mathematical instruments, book-binding (since books were sold in paper covers) and pew-rent[7] (probably a stab at the old atheist rather than a sign of piety: the thought of General Hugo giving money to a church . . .). Experts in domestic warfare, they tried to drive a wedge between the General and his sister:

> You told us that she was to see to our needs. No doubt you issued her with instructions, but we cannot believe that you ordered her to treat your sons as she would like to treat us. We can ask her for nothing, *not even shoes*, without her immediately exclaiming . . . If we try to prove that we are right, we are forced to endure a torrent of crude insults and, if we try to escape, we have to hear ourselves being called stupid and impertinent. . . . We have reason to believe that she is being less than honest with you.[8]

The General himself received an even lower moral rating. In an 'open letter' (presumably a note passed on by M. Cordier), he had referred to their 'unhappy mother'. 'What would you have done', they asked him, 'in the days when you were pleased to find happiness with her? What would you have done to the person who had the temerity to use such language? She is and always has been the same, and we still think of her now as you thought of her then.'[9] Both the sentiments and the style of writing evoked the more courtly age of the Ancien Régime.

There is no doubt that the boys were shabbily treated, that their father pretended not to have received some of their letters, lied about reductions in his pay and failed to calculate the expense of prolonging an education as far as the École Polytechnique. It is equally certain that he became a testing-ground for one of literature's great emotional manipulators and that Victor and Eugène successfully turned the situation to their moral advantage. For the time being, circumstances agreed with Hugo's conscience.

*

WHEN HUGO COMPLAINED that the fantasy superhuman known as 'God' had made a mess of human existence by putting old age after childhood,[10] he might have cited himself as an exception. The *enfant terrible* of the French Romantics was practically an adult at the age of fifteen. Whenever any serious discipline problem arose in the Pension Cordier, the teachers appealed to his authority. Shortly after their arrival, he and Eugène had divided the territory into two 'nations', Victor's being the larger. He sat in the courtyard on a makeshift throne, punishing offenders and rewarding the faithful with medals made of gold and silver paper and a lilac-coloured ribbon. (According to Victor's research, the colour was not in official use.) Sometimes, to supplement school meals, a day-boy called Léon Gatayes was sent by King Victor to buy a slice of Italian cheese, half rind, half fat. When Gatayes returned, the cheese-slice was inspected. If it failed to match the instructions, Gatayes was kicked in the shins.[11]

Later in life, Gatayes became a noted horseman, swimmer, marksman and duellist. He also rebuilt the Hugos' fireplace for them in the Place Royale. Noticing that he was a foot shorter than Gatayes, Hugo asked him why he had never retaliated. The answer was obvious: because Hugo would not have entrusted him with any more errands.[12]

This sounds like a happy tale of survival and suggests a successful assimilation of at least one aspect of his father. But it also reveals a delicate dilemma, which Hugo spent most of his early life trying to resolve. He was in the tricky position of having to rebel against an iconoclast. He had to be as gentlemanly and as self-disciplined as the General was not, to look down on him, as it were, from below, whilst asserting his independence. The most awkward corollary of this was that the ideal of uprightness which the age and Mme Hugo had implanted in his mind included unquestioning respect for fathers. But how was it possible to revere a patricidal generation which had decapitated its King and, in the Romantic imagination, murdered God?

At school, the anger which could not be expended on his father found a target in Mathematics – 'the hideous rack of Xs and Ys' on which the General had decided he should be stretched.[13] The records of Louis-le-Grand show that Hugo obtained merits in Philosophy, Geometry and Physics, but none in Mathematics,[14] and he seems to have done his best not to enjoy it. Well into old age, he boasted of a rare aptitude for Mathematics which allowed him to reach the correct answers by paths unknown to his teachers, extrapolating solutions 'of singularly rare construction and complicated symmetry'.[15] On one occasion, he calculated, 'to the nearest hundred', how many horses it would take to pull the Earth out of orbit.[16] At the Pension Cordier, it was precisely this capacity to generate clear and unavoidable evidence which met with strong mental resistance. Mathematical formulae were 'hydras, each with their fateful secret, squatting on the inert pedestal of obscurity'. Theorems – according to one of the most revealing images Hugo ever gave of his mind's relationship to objective truth – 'attached their leaden weights to the feet of the lugubrious diver'.[17]

These ambiguous metaphors indicate a kind of intellectual allergy to the world of fact, where 'proof reigns in the pitiless air'. His natural preference was for long journeys through forests of images which perpetually defer the final evidence. An enormous curiosity coupled with an enormous desire not to know. His only happy memory of the subject is of the teacher at Louis-le-Grand who, after an hour of calculation, arrived at the sign of the Infinite and stopped: ∞. Hugo calls this symbol the pair of spectacles which sits on the thinker's nose.[18] Excellent for long-range vision, but as good as a blindfold for the immediate.

*

HAPPILY, HUGO DISCOVERED the perfect medium for rebellion early in his school career. It was his greatest educational achievement and something which he claimed he never had to learn: French versification. It simply sprouted in his brain, complete with all its rules.[19]

To dismiss this as a boast (like the critic Gustave Planche who said that Hugo would claim to have discovered the propositions of Euclid 'by intuition'[20]), is to miss a splendid opportunity for understanding Hugo's real strangeness, to see him as a kind of literary functionary who chopped his thoughts into twelve-syllable segments simply because every poet before him had done the same.

The evidence provided by Hugo's work is that the seemingly arbitrary regimentation of language known as French verse is not an artificial construction designed by malicious pedants to obstruct the free expression of ideas, but a spontaneous creation of the collective unconscious. The structures of French verse correspond to structures in the mind and even, according to a more ambitious view, to structures in the material universe: an idea more familiar nowadays in its application to twelve-bar blues and reggae. To attribute the twelve-syllable alexandrine, for instance, to the author of a rule-book would be like trying to identify the copyright holder of a Greek myth.[21]

If Hugo had formulated his instincts in the theoretical manner of a Coleridge or a Mallarmé, he would have ensured himself a place among the intellectual seers of Modernism. Instead, the didactic trees of Hugo's odes – and his own enormous ego – have hidden the magical forest. It rarely occurred to him to dwell on the 'obvious': that each vowel has its own colour, that words are living beings with complex physiognomies of which their dictionary definition is only a trait. His life, on the other hand, is full of beautifully concrete proofs of the mysterious logic of verse. Some explanation of the sheer size of

Hugo's output can be found in the fact that, as early as 1816, in the Pension Cordier, complete alexandrines and even whole poems were forming themselves in his mind while he slept and survived the passage from dream to paper. His daily correspondence is littered with fragments of verse like driftwood from imaginary vessels abandoned in other parts of the brain. Hugo actually complained about this involuntary activity as a nuisance, as if it had been a speech impediment or a tic.[22] In the nineteenth century, it was practically a recognized mental illness: 'metromania'. At least one person is known to have been imprisoned for it.[23]

This untranslatable idiom was Hugo's mother tongue, and to ignore the phenomenon would mean writing part of his biography in reverse. He already had a form of expression; the task now was to find a reality to fit it.

It may well be that 'metromania' saved him from a more serious form of insanity. The conventionality and rules of French verse were an official guarantee that the feelings he expressed were authentic and that society, like French prosody, had a place for them. The added advantage was that, by imposing constraints, it greatly increased the possibilities for that disciplined revolt which seemed to be the only answer to his father.

It seems strange today to call this activity rebellious. In the early days of public education there was no such thing as a swot. The 'creep', who devotes every waking hour to academic work, is the invention of a more democratic age. By writing poems – no matter how conformist the subject – Hugo would inevitably be rebelling. The University, which dictated school policy, pursued a line of active discouragement: 'For pupils of sixteen or seventeen, the study of French versification ... can only be a dangerous distraction or a sterile torment.'[24] One enlightened pedagogue actually published his treatise on versification as a kind of prophylactic for juvenile rhymesters. One might as well admit, he wrote, that the vice exists and at least make sure that the boys are doing it according to the rules.[25]

The quality of the poems, therefore, was a secondary consideration. Hugo in any case had few illusions on the subject, though there is no sign that he ever despaired of becoming a great poet. It was simply a matter of time and determination. The main problem in the days of the Pension Cordier was that his progress was so fast that by the time he had completed the third act of *Athélie* (a classical-style tragedy set in Romantic Scandinavia), he found the first act so intolerably puerile that he had to start from scratch. In one of the three notebooks which contain his earliest poems, he informed his hypothetical reader that anything which had not been crossed out could safely be read, and then crossed out almost the entire notebook. Later, he drew an egg with an embryo inside and entitled the contents 'The rubbish I wrote before I was born' – surely an example of his famous false modesty: the free-range poet produced a vast anthology of contemporary trends in French poetry which is so up-to-date that he was obviously being fed from the outside by brother Abel, who now had a job in the civil service and several literary friends.

Sometimes averaging thirty faultless lines a night, Hugo wrote *romances* (the equivalent of pop song lyrics), imitations of Ossian – raging torrents, birds of prey and a wild-eyed bard with bristling hair, steering his 'frail barque' under Gothic battlements. He lampooned the common variety of epic poem which applied the Homeric style to topics such as horticulture: 'I should sing the endive, swelling with the sap of clear streams ... The tortuous contours of the enormous cucumber.' Still at an age when famous inventions are a source of patriotic pride, he enthused about that 'vast breast swollen with subtle air' (the balloon), and those 'tutelary orbs attached to the flanks of huge furnaces' (the steamship). The poet who was to boast of giving a home to that '*misérable*' of the dictionary, the word *merde*, seems to have sensed that the classical refusal to call a spade a spade, however ludicrous, had certain poetic virtues – an imaginative skirting of the truth which was somehow more illuminating, potentially, than mathematical exactitude.

He also tried his hand at the *fable* – a genre which was still widely practised 150 years after La Fontaine. The fable entitled 'L'Avarice et l'Envie' is one of Hugo's least-known poems but it sticks in the mind along with his finest allegories. Avarice and Envy meet Desire, who promises that the first to speak will have whatever she wishes, and the second will have it twice over. Envy thinks for a moment, then says, 'Put out one of my eyes.'[26]

This little fable opens a door into the cruelly ingenious mind which ruled the roost at the Pension Cordier. With different protagonists, the same story might have been an allegory of heroic self-sacrifice. As it is, it constitutes a sharp comment on the ideal of military glory on which General Hugo based his self-esteem.

Other poems were more in keeping with schoolboy concerns. The lines 'on a broken cornice' are the earliest description in French poetry of a game of football.[27] Equally noteworthy are some examples of a tiny sub-genre: riddles to which the answer is a fart – of which the French language distinguishes two varieties. In one, Hugo cleverly conceals the word for the silent variety (*vesse*) in a rhyme on *esse*. This is the sort of Byzantine virtuosity on which Mallarmé was to base an entire poetics. In Restoration France, it was just silliness. Perhaps Hugo was thinking of himself when he wrote, in a *chanson* dated February 1818:

> Many a great poet is often
> Nothing but a literary giraffe:
> How great he seems in front,
> How small he is behind![28]

There is a surprising professionalism in Hugo's juvenilia which has led some critics to suspect him of copying out the work of other poets – not that any theft has come to light. His alexandrines already have that gorgeous orotundity which makes it almost impossible to read them silently or sitting down. This is poetry in search of a context – ideally, a large crowd cheering at the end of each stanza. Hugo himself compared his style to the flowing lava of a volcano which has since solidified.[29] At the age of fifteen, the volcano was just as capable of coughing up a little poem on chamber-pots as a touching fantasy in the Racinian style entitled, 'A Father Mourns the Death of His Son'.

On the surface, everything had been sorted out: his father, according to another 'Élégie', was the agent of 'implacable Destiny' which kept him apart from his sainted mother. The only problem seemed to be that 'sincerity' depended on a judicious use of rhetorical devices: 'This Elegy represents two hours' work ... Why does the mind say so poorly what the heart feels so well?' It was the dilemma of the confessional poet:

> If, in order to be a good poet,
> One must be full of one's subject,
> Then how, when the subject is myself,
> Could I be fuller than I am?[30]

That wooden formality which seemed to drain the poems of the emotional reality that inspired them in the first place was an essential part of the project. Poetry was also a means of repression. Words inscribed on paper could be erased from the brain; doubts turned into certainties. Painful memories could be altered and then re-remembered from the written version. The following lines, from 'Mes Adieux à l'Enfance', were intended for his mother, but they might just as well have been addressed to the art she encouraged him to practise:

> You who supported the wavering steps of my happy childhood,
> Come and repress the ardent unruliness of my mettlesome youth.

This peculiar injunction to his mother should be read with its historical context in mind: an age in which schoolboys could swear passionate, undying love to their mothers without fear of ridicule. But the obvious reference to puberty indicates a potentially disastrous regimentation of the mind: 'Duty and discipline, those lamp-shades of the heart and soul'.[31] Amazingly, the evocation of Hugo's childhood world says nothing at all of Italy or Spain. Everything appears to have passed off harmlessly within the walls of the Feuillantines garden, where the only hint of the horrors of war, according to the poem, was the occasional experiment with gunpowder.

*

HUGO'S CONTENTION that disobedient schoolboys are a product of their teachers' intolerance was confirmed in May 1817 when a professional sadist called Decotte took over from Cordier. A slyly sarcastic report from a school inspector noted that Emmanuel Decotte was 'full of pride, ambition and energy' and obviously, therefore, the right man for the job.[32]

The new teacher identified Victor Hugo as the chief threat to his authority, and earned his place in literary history by forcing Hugo's drawer and confiscating his private journal. The journal contained a declaration of political and literary ambition dated 10 July 1816 – 'I want to be Chateaubriand or nothing' (as common a desire in the 1810s as a desire to be Victor Hugo was in the 1830s and 1840s). There was also some poetry, which Decotte might have compared to his own rhymed discourse on education policy, and a detailed character sketch which concluded that Decotte was a 'scoundrel'. Hugo was accused of 'ingratitude' – an especially grievous sin since he had been enjoying 'care and attention the like of which no pupil has ever seen'. *Victor Hugo Raconté* records the exchange:

VICTOR: It is I, Monsieur, who should be reproaching you. You have
    sought out my secrets, violated my mind and laid bare my soul. . . .
DECOTTE: Take care, Monsieur, you shall be sent back to your family.
VICTOR: Send me back to my family. That is my greatest wish.

In its nineteenth-century form, the tale of the hero's origin almost always includes a confiscation episode. It establishes the hero as a threat to the old order, demonstrates the latter's criminal nature whilst supplying the former with a motive (revenge), and, since the work is invariably lost or destroyed, allows its precocious brilliance to swell in the reader's imagination.

The value of the episode in Hugo's case lies in his reaction. His 'insolence' prefigures his response to later accusations and confiscations by other tyrants such as the French press or Napoleon III. But even here, the attempt to manufacture sturdy moral positions for himself has a dark side: the inevitable impression of his own guilt. After years of wrangling, his parents would soon be legally separated, and, like most children in similar circumstances, Hugo was unable to imagine himself as an innocent victim. When he tells the story of Adam and Eve in *La Fin de Satan*, original sin is not associated with a hunger for knowledge. Evil enters the world with the next generation; specifically, with Abel's jealous brother.

Fortunately, the tyrannical Decotte was complemented by a fairy godmother: a young man with a pock-marked face and a happy smile called Félix Biscarrat[33] – the school dogsbody who supervised the pupils and led the same sort of dismal boarding-school life as today's *surveillants*, but with even worse career prospects.[34]

Biscarrat was the first person after Hugo's mother to recognize his poetic genius. He was even relaxed and modern-spirited enough to admire such lines as 'Making their bones cry out 'neath his devouring teeth' or 'Intoxicated with gore and brimming with blood', from Hugo's verse translation of *The Aeneid*.[35] This enlightened reader was the guiding spirit in the two events which marked Hugo's transition to the adult world.

One of Biscarrat's duties was to take the pupils out on walks. Once, he had deviated from the prescribed route to lead them up inside the dome of the Sorbonne. His girlfriend – the daughter of the school laundress – knew someone who worked there. They climbed a series of ladders and, from the top, heard the Allied armies approaching Paris. Hugo was struck by the sunny landscape beyond the city gates and its apparent indifference to the beings who called it France – a recurrent theme in his poetry: Nature obliviously pursuing its eternal circle. It was also his first experience of vertigo in the true sense: a fear that his own mind was going to make him jump off the parapet.

The scene from the top of the Sorbonne should be imagined with Hugo's phenomenal vision: an extraordinary far-sightedness, with curious distortions of colour and perspective. This useful defect lends an unexpectedly literal nuance to his definition of the genius as a creature with a microscope in one eye and a telescope in the other, 'rummaging about in the infinitely large and the infinitely small'.[36]

Hugo's eyesight also served him well on the ascent, when he was able to inspect the equally vertiginous view under the girlfriend's skirt ... If his separate memories of childhood are assembled in chronological order, they show his rise in the world coinciding with the gradual, piecemeal discovery of the female body: the legs of Mlle Rose, the breasts of the girl at Bayonne, the lips of Pepita, and now the more impressive panorama inside the dome of the Sorbonne.

There is no attempt in *Victor Hugo Raconté* to draw a moral from the story as a whole. Yet, as on so many other occasions, Hugo's day-to-day life appears to have ordered itself as though his mind were a magical sieve through which reality fell like dust to arrange itself in meaningful patterns. He climbs to a position of prominence in the city and, almost at the same time, discovers the historical moment which signals the defeat of his father, the source of earthly satisfaction, the indifference of Mother Nature and a desire to jump into the void. All this takes place inside the main seat of French learning. Normally, this spontaneously metaphorical vision, the instantaneous translation of every event into an allegory of something else, would be described as psychosis, and there is a disturbing similarity between some of Hugo's later poems and the almost tediously astonishing images produced by garrulous psychotics.

If Hugo continued to inhabit the reality recognized by the rest of society, it was perhaps because his point of departure was always a concrete object and because his relationship with the visible world had a strong sexual foundation. Even his explicitly sexual activities should be seen, on one level, as applications of an intellectual method. In old age, he was simply more prolific in flesh than on paper. In his youth, this mode of perception often appears in a trivial or ridiculous light. The schoolboy Hugo was also in the habit of gazing at naked statues in the Luxembourg Gardens. Once, he hid in the wardrobe of an attic-room in his mother's house in order to observe the maid as she got out of bed.[37] The fact that in each case the female figure was unaware of the probing eye marks him out as a voyeur. But it was the same eye which wrote *Les Contemplations* and which 'lifted up the skirts of Nature'. The voyeur was also a *voyant*, a seer in both senses.

Biscarrat's second contribution to Hugo's career brought him his first taste of fame. For their annual poetry competition in 1817, the forty ageing 'Immortals' of the Académie Française had set one of their deeply uncontroversial titles: 'The Happiness to be Derived from Study in All the Circumstances of Life'.[38] When he saw the announcement, Hugo wrote a 334-line ode to the joys and uses of reading books, with the faintest of hints that school (represented by 'noise, disturbance and imposition') was inimical to study and the predictably royalist sentiment that literature teaches us to hate 'cruel conquerors and wild warriors'.

When the poem was finished, Biscarrat directed the crocodile of pupils towards the dome of the Institut* on the Left Bank of the Seine, ordered them to study the stone lions outside, ran up the steps with Hugo and deposited the poem in the Academy's office.

A few months later, brother Abel came to tell Victor the news: he

---

* The Institut de France is the corporate body formed by the five Académies (four until 1832).

was a blithering idiot. If he hadn't let it be known in his poem that he had 'scarce seen three lustres* complete their course', he probably would have won first prize. No one believed he was only fifteen. Hugo, whose triumph seems to have earned him the right to wander more freely, rushed to show the Perpetual Secretary of the Académie Française his birth certificate and was told, with an off-handedness which shocked him, 'Our incredulity will be of service to you.' The Secretary was right: Hugo's poem made him instantly famous. There were official attempts to revive public interest in the arts. These competitions and the exchange of epigrams and odes that followed them were major literary events. The Academy was delighted to have discovered an infant prodigy, especially a prodigy who held the correct political views.

Hugo's first academic success was also a turning-point in the history of relations with his family – not only because it demonstrated his embarrassing superiority to Eugène, who was also writing poems and competing for their mother's admiration. On 26 August 1817, Abel sent one of his 'impertinent' letters to the General in Blois. At the age of fifteen-and-a-half, he announced, Victor had been awarded a *mention honorable* by the Académie Française. (Literally, this was true: the poem was 'mentioned' in the Academy's public meeting and this was certainly an 'honour'; but a *mention honorable* was a particular rating, which Victor had not received.) 'And yet,' wrote Abel, 'these are the children whom you persecute with such fury.' For an objective opinion, the General could refer to the latest issue of the *Journal de Commerce*. There, he would learn that 'a military career is not the only career that brings glory'.

If General Hugo looked at that day's *Journal de Commerce*, he would have seen an accusatory finger rising off the page: 'What grave censor would not be moved by a child of fifteen who ingenuously sends his poem to the Academy and who, perhaps without knowing it himself, writes verse which anyone would consider a good literary fortune?' The anonymous journalist, sounding suspiciously like Abel Hugo, reported the surprise and delight of the Academy's mainly female audience. Victor's description of what he felt when reading

---

* Lustre: a period of five years.

about the tragic passion of Dido in *The Aeneid* was a perfect, unthreatening vignette of a sentimental young man aware of vague stirrings. A heart-throb was in the making:

> There, my heart is more tender, better able to share
> The sorrows which perhaps one day it must feel.

Hugo's success was a moral victory over his father, and it was entirely appropriate that the first review of his work should take the form it did – literary criticism combined with practical advice on child-rearing:

> Parents to whom this disciple of Virgil belongs ... see with what care and tenderness this sweet and innocent creature should be raised. Preserve it from those travails which eat away at time and the heart, the rigours which wither talent before it has fully bloomed, and perhaps we shall owe to you a successor of Malfilâtre.*

The General's reaction is unknown, but from now on, he was more inclined to comply with his sons' requests. They were to be allowed to study law – in other words, to be free agents who signed up for classes and occasionally transported their bodies to an amphitheatre in the Sorbonne.

*

THE OFFICIALLY RECOGNIZED child prodigy launched his literary career without waiting to be released from 'prison'. The short period between the Academy's competition and his last day at school (8 September 1818) brought the most revealing incidents of his 'apprenticeship' period: the 'sweet and innocent creature' venturing out into the world he hoped to conquer, with a great deal of sweetness but, tragically, saving all his innocence for his private life.

His first ploy was to send obsequious little odes to several Academicians, thanking them for 'snatching [his] feeble essay from oblivion's abyss'. Hugo's 'inept muse' begged the Perpetual Secretary's pardon for 'interrupting such noble works', but it was to the Secretary's 'flattering organ' that he owed his undeserved success. *Victor*

---

* Malfilâtre (1732–67), poet and author of a work on Virgil, who died young and unrecognized.

Hugo Raconté calls this unseemly grovelling a lack of discernment. In fact, Hugo's bowing and scraping was far from naive. He was marketing himself as a budding genius in the fawning idiom of the age and proving that he was willing to suffer a little self-inflicted humiliation for the sake of a glorious future.

One ode went to the translator of Ossian, Baour-Lormian, known to the later Romantics as Balourd-Dormant ('Slumbering Fathead'). Yet this was the man whose epistle to Louis XVIII, recommending mild constitutional reform, had brought a fierce, monarchist response from Victor Hugo – a poem which marks him out clearly as one of the Ultras. Fortunately for Hugo, the poem had not been sent to the newspapers 'because', he wrote in his exercise-book, 'Eugène was too slow'. (Mme Hugo was to have decided which was the better poem.) 'It would have been like mustard after dinner, as common people say.'[39]

By far the most successful ode was the poetic begging-bowl held out to 'M. le Comte François de Neufchâteau, de l'Académie Française'. It earned Hugo a powerful patron and embroiled him in his first literary adventure. The sordid mystery at its centre is worth exploring since the episode opened his eyes to the literary establishment before he had time to form many illusions on the subject: a significant advantage over other writers of his generation.

On 30 August 1817, he measured out the correct quantities of arrogance and servility and reminded Neufchâteau (who needed no reminding) that Voltaire had 'brightened your dawn with the fires of his sunset' – meaning that Voltaire had hailed the thirteen-year-old Neufchâteau as his poetic heir. Now, Neufchâteau was asked to do the same for Victor Hugo. The Academician's reply took the form of an ode, inviting the 'tender friend of the nine muses' to come and receive the benefit of his advice.

Neufchâteau had twice been Minister of the Interior and helped to establish the Louvre Museum. In old age, he was busy carving out a new role for himself as the patron saint of that vastly underrated vegetable, the potato, which he thought should be renamed the *parmentière* after its discoverer. '*Pomme de terre*' was an insult. Everything on his table – stew, pasta and something resembling cutlets – turned out to be made from potato. His modern-style home

– an imitation Greek temple – stood in the north of the city next to a field of potatoes. Neufchâteau was also an authority on the carrot, but occasionally remembered his roots and returned to literature.

When Hugo went to see him, he was working on an edition of Lesage's picaresque novel, *Gil Blas*. He wanted to test Voltaire's claim that Lesage had plagiarized a Spanish work, and now here was a young man who knew Spanish. Hugo sat for several days in the Bibliothèque Royale, compared the texts and produced a long and detailed refutation – a model of scholarship which Neufchâteau inserted in his edition, signing it 'François de Neufchâteau' and earning himself a reputation, which survived well into the twentieth century, as 'one of the most profound and ingenious critics' of Lesage.

Long after Neufchâteau's death, in *Les Misérables*, a love-sick Marius tells himself that the exquisitely beautiful Cosette 'could hardly help but have some esteem for me if she knew I was the true author of the dissertation ... which Monsieur François de Neufchâteau included in the preface to his edition of *Gil Blas*, passing it off as his own work!'[40] Despite this broad hint and explicit accounts by Hugo's wife and daughter, the learned 'dissertation' is usually said to have been the result of a friendly agreement. It has even been claimed, presumably so as not to spoil the heart-warming spectacle of the old nurturing the young, that Neufchâteau was not a thief. But the evidence is overwhelming. A few pages into the preface, Neufchâteau's doughy, self-congratulatory prose suddenly gives way to a rapid, aphoristic style full of gleefully sarcastic comments on 'thieves and plagiarists', 'the lies and flattery with which dedications are ordinarily swollen' and an unacademic reference to a scene in *Robinson Crusoe* – one of young Victor's favourite books.

The dirtiest fingerprint is the assertion – by Neufchâteau himself – that Lesage was born on the Rhuys peninsula in Brittany. Had Neufchâteau bothered to check the gift-horse before he sent it to the printers, he would have noticed that, twenty-four pages earlier, the pseudo-Neufchâteau tells us that Lesage was not born, as is often believed, at Ruys (spelt thus), but at Vannes. A sign of the faith that Neufchâteau placed in Hugo's scholarly integrity and a possible explanation of why the François de Neufchâteau section of the Bibliothèque Nationale catalogue is so large.

It would have been necessary to mention this incident if only for the sake of bibliographical accuracy and simple justice: the first, unrecognized prose text published by Victor Hugo. But it also offers a rare glimpse of the schoolboy in private. When he writes in front of an audience, a certain stiffness comes into his hand and makes him sound like a young fogey – 'a walking book', as he describes himself in 1820. In the dissertation on *Gil Blas*, unaware that his notes would be published, he projects the image of a confident, witty young writer, with the maturity to extract the lessons from the shortcomings of previous scholars without wallowing in their stupidity.

Even more illuminating is Hugo's reaction to the theft. The journal he published with his brothers from 1819 to 1821 – *Le Conservateur Littéraire* – contains several pleasant comments on the 'Neufchâteau' edition of *Gil Blas*. These comments have been interpreted as a sign that he was a willing provider. Intentions are hard to prove, but a simple experiment should make it possible to form a strong opinion: reading the following remarks by Victor Hugo with the eye of François de Neufchâteau.

> Almost all [Neufchâteau's] works are written with the interests of young people at heart. One can easily see that his greatest desire is to render his old age of service to youth.

> M. Bignan [a Homer translator who had 'borrowed' lines from other translators] has not had the audacity to steal entire passages from his predecessors. But then M. Bignan is not a member of the Institut.

> M. François de Neufchâteau, in thus defending our national glory, has made a worthy contribution to his own glory.

> True scholars are as rare as borrowed erudition is common.

Finally, one of Neufchâteau's notes to *Gil Blas* is 'recommended to writers of melodramas: these four lines contain the substance of a splendid piece of plagiary'.

To talk about the politeness of Hugo's remarks is to miss the point. If Neufchâteau was capable of feeling remorse, he would have been as red as a beetroot when he read *Le Conservateur Littéraire*. Hugo's sophisticated blend of insolence and respectability shows a remarkable understanding of that type of self-deceiving personality. Neufchâteau

[66]

was soon to obtain a royal pension for the young poet and on that occasion announced, with (one assumes) a breathtaking lack of self-awareness, 'I enjoy your own successes more than you do yourself.'

Hugo's rare ability to satisfy, at the same time, personal ambition and a sense of justice shows how well his first sixteen years had prepared him for life as a famous writer. He had seen a whole society destroy itself and his family fall apart; but already he was replacing the ruins with a world of his own.

CHAPTER FIVE

Passion

(1818–1820)

THE DRAIN WHICH ran past the Pension Cordier emptied itself into the Seine at the far end of the Rue des Petits-Augustins (the present Rue Bonaparte). Nearby, at number 18, Mme Hugo was living in a third-floor apartment – a sign of straitened circumstances in a city which divided its inhabitants vertically according to social position and, increasingly, income: nobles on the first floor, servants in the attic. The separation settlement had provided her with 3000 francs a year: a mere token of the treasure General Hugo was believed to have amassed in Spain.[1] She was only forty-six but nearly always ill. She sat reading books, taking snuff and talking to visitors – ghosts of another age to whom her sons were not to speak unless spoken to. They included a distant relative, Count Volney, the author of *Les Ruines, ou Méditations sur les Révolutions des Empires* (1791).[2] Volney had camped among the buried temples in the deserts of Syria and Egypt. His precise, elegiac accounts had been used by Napoleon's invading army and inspired the first French Romantics. They, too, had seen a civilization crumble away.

Delighted to have regained their freedom and their mother, Victor and Eugène slept in a corner of the dining-room and worked in a room at the back of the house. Mme Hugo had made her home inside another history lesson. Like the Feuillantines, it had a monarchist moral. The room she slept in was the chapel of the defunct Petits Augustins convent. When he sat at his desk, Hugo looked out over a Parisian Valley of the Kings: the convent cloisters[3] were a repository for tombs which had been removed from the royal burial ground at Saint-Denis. Considering their circumstances, the Hugos had excellent neighbours: quiet and hugely respectable. For Mme Hugo, the yard of tombstones was evidence of the Revolution's brutality. Abel was writing a book about it from the royalist point of view.⁴ But for an English visitor who followed the tourist trail to the 'Ancien Couvent des Petits Augustins' in 1814, the improvised graveyard showed that the period had some saving graces:

> a collection of ancient French monuments which were saved from destruction at the moment when the fury of the revolution was directed against all the symbols of superstition and tyranny. They are arranged according to their dates, in halls so constructed as to be illustrative of the style of architecture which prevailed in the thirteenth, fourteenth, fifteenth, and sixteenth centuries.⁵

The poems Hugo wrote at his window can usefully be read with the view in mind – a concrete illustration of a new sensibility: entire societies disappearing into time but recoverable by the imagination. Hugo's vision of a wasteland Paris in the year 5000 is also a mental image of the city in post-revolutionary Europe: 'When the banks where the water breaks on sonorous bridges / Are covered once again with the murmuring reeds ... When the Seine flows on over obstacles of stone, / Eroding some old dome which has tumbled into its stream ...'⁶

Next door to the museum–mausoleum, Hugo lived his lost childhood, often staying up all night to nurse his mother. His life seemed to be gradually unsticking itself from events and heading backwards in time. His most remarkable achievement had nothing to do with literature but reflects his desire to consolidate the family. He learned how to plaster walls and to dye the silk that was used as wallpaper. He went shopping for food, swept the house and polished the furniture.⁷ His future fiancée, Adèle Foucher, was amused to see him following his mother to market like an overgrown child, very serious and handsome, with – according to Hugo's self-description – 'wide, passionate nostrils'⁸ (like a Delacroix horse), 'a frank, composed air, his whole face exuding high-mindedness, thoughtfulness and innocence'; 'timid to the point of grimness'.⁹

In *Les Misérables*, Hugo manages the unusual feat of describing himself seven times over in the various members of 'The ABC Society', a band of young idealists who enjoy the easy camaraderie that was missing from Hugo's youth and who each share several moral and physical traits with the author. All these descriptions might have been deduced from letters and pictures, but they have the advantage of shading in an extra perspective – the later Hugo's almost paternal affection for his younger self:

> His manner was reserved, coldly courteous and unforthcoming; but as his mouth was charming, his lips exceptionally red and his teeth abnormally white, this air of severity was quite altered when he smiled. . . . His eyes were small but far-seeing.[10]

> In common with certain young men of the beginning of this century and the end of the last who became famous early in life, he had the extreme youth and fresh complexion of a girl but with moments of pallor. Already grown to manhood, he still appeared a child. . . . He was solemn and seemed not to be aware that there existed on earth a creature called Woman.[11]

Hugo's portraits of himself as a young man are false in only one physical detail: thick, dark hair. In fact, it was fair, slowly turning brown, but he did possess the principal qualification for masculine beauty, 'a high, intelligent forehead': 'A lot of forehead in a face is like a lot of sky on a horizon.'[12] But as Hugo likes to point out, long before the age of space travel, the 'sky' is simply a trick of the light, a projection on darkness.[13]

The story of the first part of Hugo's adult life consists largely in the shoring up and disintegration of this carefully constructed personality. At school, he had developed an infallible technique which enabled him to memorize thirty lines of Latin before falling asleep.[14] On waking, he translated them all into rhyming couplets. Reading the Classics, he thought, would supply all his mental needs for the journey into adulthood.

> I manufactured experience for myself with the advice which the great minds of the past continually offer to the little minds of the present. . . . I was ready for anything . . . For every eventuality I had a Greek proverb, a classical allusion or a line from Virgil.[15]

Already, this is the self-sufficient Hugo appraised by the ironic eye of the young Baudelaire in 1841: 'He seemed to me a very gentle, very powerful man, always master of himself, sustained by an abbreviated wisdom made up of a small number of irrefutable maxims.'[16] A prefabricated genius, with a vast store of literary data at his disposal. As a result, beyond the age of thirty, Hugo read very little of other writers' work, which might explain why a century's worth of influence studies show such heavy traffic – themes, images, phrases – pouring from Victor Hugo into the works of other poets, with just a trickle of possible borrowings and reminiscences in the opposite direction.

The other main source of information on Hugo's mind in this period is, of course, his poetry. For most of his poems, he was using the paradoxical verse form called the dithyramb: a combination of regular lines of different lengths. Because of its slightly ragged appearance on the page, it was supposed to evoke the 'fever of inspiration', in the same way that gestures in a melodrama indicated certain moods: a hand across the forehead for grief or a leg in the air for joy. To the modern eye, the regularity of the form is more striking than its eccentricity, and it seems more likely to be a vehicle of repression than revelation. An understanding of Hugo's early work depends to a large extent on a realization that the two go hand in hand.

Hugo used this form for the odes which he entered in the annual competition of the oldest Academy in France: the Jeux Floraux, founded by troubadours in Toulouse in 1323.[17] The Académie des Jeux Floraux owed its renewed prestige to a growing interest in the indigenous treasures of French culture, even those of the 'barbaric' Middle Ages. A rare and short-lived example of provincial influence on the capital. Mme Hugo identified the competition as another gateway to success and ordered her sons to compete. Like other families in the street, the Hugos were practically a cottage industry. Eugène won a prize in 1818. In 1819, Victor sped past him, winning a Golden Amaranth for an ode on 'Les Vierges de Verdun'* and, for another ode on the re-erection of a statue of Henri IV, the Academy's highest honour: a Golden Lily. Winners could either accept the prize in cash or go to a jeweller's shop in Paris and collect the flower itself. Hugo nobly chose the latter. The following year, he won again and

---

* The 'Virgins of Verdun' were imprisoned during the Revolution for greeting invading Prussians with flowers. The Restoration turned them into royalist martyrs.

was named *Maître ès Jeux Floraux*, which meant that, as a judge, he could no longer compete.

The winning poems were published in a special anthology and had first to be purged of anything incorrect or controversial. French verse was still operating as an elaborate penal system. The would-be helpful comments Hugo received from the Guardians of the Rule-Book in Toulouse are a valuable set of clues to the secrets of his art. In many cases, conservative strictures seem to have led him to an understanding of his talent which he might never have reached by other means.

His ode on Moses, for example, was criticized for presenting only one character's view of a great event, instead of maintaining the classical pretence of omniscience. He was asked to expunge the word 'carnage' and to amend the expression 'chaste pleasures' (applied to the frolicking of Pharaoh's daughter) because it was too suggestive. Like most original poets, he was accused of 'obscurity'. Hugo's timid rejoinder lights the way to the poetic revelations of a later age. Perhaps some areas of experience were inherently obscure?

> While writing the poem, I had noticed that disjointedness which the Academy observed in the ideas, but finding no remedy for it, I successfully persuaded myself that lyric poets enjoy the privilege of leaving unfinished the thought which first struck them in order to develop the thought which occurred to them next.[18]

Despite this daringly modern defence of deliberate obscurity, Hugo was displaying a perfectly classical temperament. The implication is that when he wrote an ode, he was not himself a lyric poet; he was an educated writer pretending to be a lyric poet, producing the sort of verse that that imaginary figure was conventionally supposed to produce. The idea of a writer who also 'lived' his poetry was highly suspect. Some would claim that when Hugo became the head of the French Romantic movement, he was still a classical poet, but one who was better than anyone else at pretending to be a Romantic.

*

SUCCESS AT THE JEUX FLORAUX gave Hugo instant respectability, but it also brought to the surface the less innocent aspects of his personality.

Eugène's prizes were the pinnacle of his brief career.[19] The looming catastrophe was masked in the family correspondence with references to his poor health. Symptoms of insanity had appeared from time to time, but, like a tidal wave far out at sea, were ignored. Psychiatry was still applied only to the spectacularly insane; quirky behaviour was the domain of discipline and morals. When Eugène threw his food at the wall or stayed at home and sulked while his brothers went out, his actions were taken to be a sign of his naturally obstreperous temperament. Any other interpretation carried a stigma: madness in the young was usually thought to be a side-effect of masturbation.

At the Pension Cordier, Biscarrat more perceptively christened Eugène 'the Energumen' ('one possessed by a devil'). This 'possession' manifested itself in a curious absence of affection and a jealous conviction, which his paranoia probably justified, that his mother preferred Victor. The youngest brother pressed his advantage. In a birthday ode to Biscarrat, he compared his own effortless tribute to that of 'the Energumen': 'You know the gentleman I mean / All a-sweat, he painfully forges / A long-winded epistle.'

Years later, when it was known that Hugo had a brother in the lunatic asylum, a myth grew up that he had risen to greatness by sucking out the life-blood of a genius even greater than himself, consigning the corpse to oblivion.[20] As late as 1924, Pierre Dufay's neurotic study of Eugène alleged a conspiracy of silence; but as far as literary criticism is concerned, the silence was simply a lack of interest. As he must have realized himself, Eugène's poems were patently inferior to Victor's. The eerily appropriate title of Eugène's most celebrated work, 'Le Duel du Précipice', conceals a quite conventional prose poem, at least linguistically: two Celtic warriors hurtle down a mountainside, slashing and stabbing at each other, and, as they lie in a writhing heap at the bottom of the cliff, are eaten by a bear.

The irony is that Hugo himself was partly responsible for the myth – first by helping to popularize the pre-Freudian notion that the burblings of the insane sometimes yield nuggets of oracular truth. Second, by leaving what can best be described as clues, as if inviting punishment for the crime which, in his mind, he had indeed committed. In 1839, he wrote three acts of a play, *Les Jumeaux*, based on the Man in the Iron Mask story (the legend of Louis XIV's twin brother, made famous by Voltaire and then by Dumas): 'a thinking corpse, still alive in its coffin' remembers an idyllic childhood garden while his brother usurps the throne.[21]

A more cryptic clue is buried in the pages of *Notre-Dame de Paris*. On a door in one of the towers leading to the cell of the evil Frollo, a hand has scratched the name 'UGENE':[22] 'EUGENE' had lost his head and, in one world, it was his brother who cut it off. The fantasy of a 'mad genius' brother was the ghost which condensed from Hugo's feelings of remorse – feelings which were all the more potent for having no concrete basis in reality, or rather, objective reality.

With Abel, rivalry rarely came to the surface. Yet the notion that Victor was somehow responsible for Eugène's mental collapse has disguised the fact that he had real reasons to feel guilty about his treatment of his older brother. After his own marriage, he flirted with Abel's fiancée and published a strangely indelicate poem in which he imagined her last night as a virgin in some detail: her 'anxious sighs', 'a husband's caresses' and 'the trembling crown' which was about to fall from her 'blushing brow'.[23] In 1825, he attributed Abel's important rediscovery of the Spanish Ballads to himself and a friend.[24] Later, he went on holiday with the three volumes of Abel's descriptive atlas, *La France Pittoresque*, and made free, unattributed use of them for his own book on the Rhineland.[25] Abel either didn't notice or didn't mind.

The most telling document dates from 1817: an anonymous treatise by Abel and two of his friends on how to write melodramas, attributed to 'Messrs A! A! and A!'. Reading the treatise with hindsight is a peculiar experience. It precisely catalogues some of the principal elements of Hugo's Romantic revolution of the stage twelve years before it happened:[26] the abolition of the classical unities; the exploitation of plebeian forms of literature which the hated Revolution had brought to the attention of educated, bourgeois audiences; the grandiloquent manifestos; maxims in which the image drowns out the thought (intended to be sarcastic echoes of General Hugo's florid prose):[27]

> Sentiment is the escape-valve of the soul.
> The soap of repentance alone can erase the blackness of crime.
> Reputations are refined in the crucible of the tomb.

Were it not for the date on the title-page, the treatise by A!, A! and A! would sound like a set of instructions on how to write like Victor Hugo, and the possibility that it was a friendly tease should not be discounted: the addressee is a young reader 'who aspires to become one day the leading light of the French stage'. Abel's joke was Victor's artistic credo.

Abel did however make a deliberate contribution to Victor's career. On the first day of every month, he proudly took his genius brother to a restaurant in the Rue de l'Ancienne-Comédie. With his two co-authors, he had organized a monthly 'literary banquet' – mostly an excuse for a slap-up meal, but also a showcase for Victor's poems. Abel then provided him with a wider audience by founding a literary review called *Le Conservateur Littéraire* (by allusion to Chateaubriand's *Le Conservateur*).[28] It appeared from December 1819 to March 1821, often twice a month, but always irregularly, since regular periodicals were subject to censorship and tax.

Victor's 112 articles and twenty-two poems are one of the great marathons of French journalism. He managed to summon out of his own confusion a tone of authority which established the journal as the organ of a new generation – but it was a generation which, as some subscribers suspected, consisted primarily of one person with eleven pseudonyms.

It says much about the reactionary nature of early French Romanticism that its future leader was the most conservative of the *conservateurs*. As books came in for review, he scoured them for grammatical mistakes, puns, peculiar images, neologisms, vulgarisms, barbarisms and any trace of literary and linguistic revolution. This, incredibly, is the writer who claimed, in a famous poem published in 1856, to have 'placed the red cap of the Revolution on the old dictionary'.[29] *Le Conservateur Littéraire* projects a kind of optical illusion: the young Victor Hugo castigating his future self. He decreed that women should not be banned from writing because then they would all be at it. He struggled to reconcile his admiration for Voltaire with his reputation as a father of the Revolution and decided that 'Voltaire was essentially a Monarchist.' And when someone launched an appeal for donations to build a town where only Latin would be spoken, he pointed to the greater urgency of founding a town for francophones, 'for the Revolution has created a new French language which will eventually render the old one unintelligible'.

Irony, in Hugo's later work, is the rhetorical symptom of a dissatisfaction with the state of things, a figure of speech which implicitly calls for correction; in *Le Conservateur Littéraire*, it is a sign of violent disagreement with himself. He warned his readers that 'erotic' poems would not be accepted and then printed an example from a certain Gaspard Descombes, who described an unspecified sexual activity being interrupted by his mother. One of the alter Hugos was an old, arthritic pedant. But another was a young man obsessed by a father who dismisses him as a 'nincompoop' and a 'chatterbox'.

When Hugo republished his articles in 1834 in *Littérature et Philosophie Mêlées*, he surreptitiously made hundreds of changes to the original text. To his stuffy criticism of Chénier's verse, for example, he added a prophetic suspicion that Chénier's 'faults' were perhaps the seeds of poetic progress. Because of this tampering with his own record, Hugo has been accused of deceiving both his readers and himself. Yet insights do not always come with their conclusions already in place like price-labels. Hugo was implicitly acknowledging the fact that no writer is ever fully aware of the meaning of his work, that 'all great writers create two oeuvres, one deliberate, the other involuntary'.[30] Even in 1820, he was obviously surprised by his own admiration of Lamartine's *Méditations Poétiques*: a new form of poetry which acknowledged the effects of passing time and, therefore, questioned the unchanging precepts of classicism. The great happiness of Romantic poetry was that it suggested the possibility of freedom from pedants – even from the pedant within. Its vagueness and local colour, he wrote, thoughtfully, 'cast, over the very imperfections, a sort of magical spell'.

Hugo's falsification of the articles from *Le Conservateur Littéraire* was an attempt to renovate the past: he could then appear as a young prophet whose billowing cloak had flapped over the faces of other writers (especially the writers whose names were deleted in the 1834 edition). This, however, may have been the accidental effect of a desire to pick out patterns in a sustained explosion, to prove that 'the apparently divergent notions of his earliest youth had been leading to the single, central idea which gradually emerged' (the idea of social reform).[31] In other words, he was treating his life as any traditional biographer would treat it. In 1819–21, no such coherence existed: this extraordinary literary energy was generated, not by a passionate commitment to social reform, but by the friction between Victor Hugo and his family. Some of the early issues contain what amounts to a crushing condemnation of General Hugo: 'I know from my father that it is never too late to say what our conscience directs us to say, when we stand to gain by it.' *'Eat little, but often* ... My father [changed in 1834 to 'my great-uncle'] applied only the first part of this precept in the running of his household.'

Hugo seemed none the less to be in tacit agreement with his father when, as the result of a wager at one of the literary banquets, he wrote a long short story in fourteen days: *Bug-Jargal*, serialized in *Le Conservateur Littéraire* in May and June 1820. The unconventional hero is the black leader of a slave revolt in San Domingo. The story is remarkable for its portrayal of a Negro, not just as a victim, but as an embodiment of Christian virtue; remarkable, too, because Hugo appears to have written it from his father's liberal point of view. In 1818, General Hugo had published a pamphlet on 'the means of replacing the trade in Negroes with free individuals'.[32] When Hugo expanded his story into a short novel in 1825, he predated the first version, significantly, to 1818 – 'a memory of that period of serenity, audaciousness and confidence when the author squared up to that enormous subject'.

This period – which was anything but 'serene' – is our last sight of the professional Victor Hugo before his originality fully asserted itself, and it offers the faintly disturbing spectacle, not of a young genius forging new paths, but of a greedy emulation, the baby of a family of writers snatching food from every plate on the table.

*

THE SIXTEENTH ISSUE OF *Le Conservateur Littéraire* was more than usually pregnant with personal messages. It contained a poem entitled 'Le Jeune Banni': 'At dawn, I wandered, filled with sweet expectation, / And I saw the long folds of your dazzling dress.' 'In the evening, supporting your father's heavy step, / I entered your home, / Seeing and admiring everything, / ... Your timorous dove was resting in my hand.'

For one reader, this moving specimen of the new style was an urgent plea, probably not meant to be taken literally but alarming all the same: 'Be warned: when dawn breaks, / Flee, and tie your long, ebon hair in another place ... Lest, oh my Emma, 'neath yon shady trees, / That pure water in which your eyes seek your image, / Show you a frozen corpse.'

Adèle Foucher was only fifteen when Hugo declared his love (on 26 April 1819) and exacted a similar confession from her. The little girl he used to push on the swing in the Feuillantines garden was now an angel – as he told her in a letter: 'more beautiful yet by her modesty than by her charms', 'as virginal in her thoughts as in her actions', 'dutiful and submissive'.[33] Just the sort of unspoiled, unerotic creature which modern poets worshipped in their elegies.

In contrast to some of Hugo's other affairs, his first passion was perfectly timed. Mme Hugo seems to have contracted pneumonia, and her failing health may have kindled a feeling that it was time to start a family of his own. Perhaps he realized, too, that Eugène was secretly in love with Adèle. The youngest brother was about to win again: he now had a focus for all his thoughts and a subject for all his poems.

> In the tumult of my feelings I can distinguish only one thing: an insurmountable passion. . . .
>
> It would be impossible now for me to live without being loved by you, and to stop seeing you would condemn me to a slow but inevitable death. . . . From now on, we must maintain the greatest reserve with one another in public.[34]

'Public' often meant the open-air ball which was held every Sunday in the nearby country town of Sceaux.[35] It was a weekly debutantes' party for the bourgeoisie where respectable girls could show themselves off to suitors. One day, Victor Hugo stood watching with one of his first literary friends, a stiff young lieutenant called Alfred de Vigny: 'Seeing some young ladies décolletées as one is for dancing, he said to me, "Would you not say those are whited sepulchres?"'[36] Hugo's biblical tone may also have had something to do with his shyness, his unimpressive wardrobe, and the fact that neither parent had ever paid for dancing lessons.

But 'public' also referred to home life. The heavy-footed father of the poem in *Le Conservateur Littéraire* was Mme Hugo's old friend, the civil servant, Pierre Foucher. Foucher had often bravely acted as a buffer between Mme Hugo and the General. Now, when the Hugos visited in the evening, he sat with his wife by the fire, bent into the shape of his chair at the Conseil de Guerre, chatting about his rheumatism or his manual on recruitment procedures (incongruously reviewed in *Le Conservateur Littéraire*), while the children sat quietly round a table. After years of seeing superiors come and go, Foucher had the slightly smug impartiality of an underling and the patience to put up with Mme Hugo's haughtiness. He prided himself on his sense of humour, which expressed itself in flowery euphemisms: Foucher was a man who knew how to talk to writers. He was secretly excited at Victor's literary success, but he also knew that Mme Hugo would consider their daughter a poor catch for her brilliant son. Adèle was to be inoculated against infatuation with warnings that young Victor was vainglorious, volatile and lazy (still no sign that he was looking for a proper job). Foucher's counter-propaganda made Hugo's letters an intricate experiment in reconciling his professional image with the 'true' Victor Hugo: 'the Victor Hugo who is thought by all the salons where – very rarely – he shows his sad and frosty face to be preoccupied with some serious conception when in fact all his thoughts are on a sweet, charming and virtuous girl who, happily for her, is a stranger to all the salons'.[37]

Parental resistance created the ideal tragic situation for two lovers. They slipped letters into each other's hands and began the long and perilous process of emotional negotiations which, in Hugo's mind, would inevitably lead to marriage: his very first letter was signed, 'Your husband'. The combination of delicious anguish and the powerful conviction of a foregone conclusion proved to be practically, if not emotionally, irresistible.

'Despite the obstacles, marriage will still be possible, if only for a day. I would have been happy and no one could blame me. You would be my widow. . . . A day of bliss is worth a life of unhappiness.' This was the romantic Hugo, the optimistic elegist; but there was also the disinherited Viscount, the defender of King and Family whose parents had separated: 'One more thing. You are now the daughter of General Hugo. Do nothing that is unworthy of you. Allow no one to treat you with disrespect: Mama is very firm about such things.'

The dilemma was identified by Adèle from the very beginning: if her suitor was such a stickler for propriety, how could he respect a girl who, by scribbling passionate letters while pretending to sew, was deceiving her own parents? Worse still (she thought), she had no feeling for poetry, had been brought up to be an ornament and could never replace the redoubtable Mme Hugo. The 'angelic creature' tried to climb off her pedestal: 'I must tell you that you are wrong to think me superior to other women.' 'You shall have a wife, dear Victor, who will be good for nothing except for loving you. It truly upsets me but it is not my fault – which is even more unfortunate.'[38] More unfortunate still that this is exactly what Victor wanted.

Adèle's assessment of herself as a poor little girl with very bourgeois ideas is often judged to be accurate. She wondered whether girls were allowed to kiss boys before they were married, never understood why Victor stayed up all night writing, and had heard that 'passion' was the demon which destroyed domestic harmony. Victor defined it for her etymologically as 'suffering': 'And do you truly believe that there is any *suffering* in the affections of the common herd? ... No, immaterial love is eternal ... It is our souls which love each other, not our bodics. – Note, however,' he went on, with an eye to the future, 'that nothing should be taken to extremes. I am not saying that bodies are of no account in the most important of affections, for then what purpose would be served by the difference between the sexes, and who could prevent two men from loving one another?'[39]

Adèle's self-denigration was also a timid criticism of Victor's view of marriage. It gives the correspondence – which ran to almost 200 letters – a certain lopsidedness, as if a Jane Austen character were being wooed by the hero of a Gothic novel. The leitmotif was Victor's jealousy: it was a frame of mind which, like a well-defined genre, found a place for every detail of daily life, concentrated the mind on one object, removed all doubt and suffering to certain parts of the body and, as his skill as a literary lover increased, supplied a more interesting, intellectual focus for lust:

You do not know, my Adèle, how much I love you. Whenever I see anyone even approach you, I shudder with envy and exasperation. My muscles contract, my chest swells up and it takes all my force and circumspection to contain myself. You can well imagine what I suffer when I see you waltzing.[40]

Even such an uneventful life as Adèle's provided food for jealousy. The frenzied suitor was retrospectively jealous of her ten-year-old brother Paul because she had sometimes been forced to share her bed with him; jealous of her Uncle Jean-Baptiste whom he judged to be 'a libertine'; jealous of her whole family when they left for a holiday at Gentilly because 'your house might catch fire and I would not be there before anyone else to carry you off in my arms'.[41]

The greatest threat was perceived to be her friendship with a painter, Julie Duvidal de Montferrier, a pupil of Gérard and Abel's future wife. At first, it was because 'the venomous ingredients which constantly rise in a subtle vapour from the colours ... attack the internal and external organs of the body'. Adèle took to pencil drawing. Then it was the profession itself that troubled him:

A woman has only to belong to the public in one respect for the public to believe that it possesses her in all respects. Moreover, how can one suppose that a young woman will have conserved a chaste mind and, consequently, pure morals after undertaking the studies demanded by painting? ... Does it befit a woman to descend into the class of artists – a class which encompasses actresses and dancers?[42]

Hugo's all-seeing eye made the Latin Quarter a very small place. One day, he caught sight of Adèle crossing the Rue des Saints-Pères and, the following evening, broached a delicate subject:

I wish, Adèle, that you were less fearful of muddying your dress when you walk in the street. ... I know that you are simply obeying your mother's stubborn advice – somewhat singular advice, since it seems to me that modesty is more precious than a dress, though many women think differently. I cannot tell you, my darling, what torture it was for me to think that the woman I revere as much as God himself was, unwittingly and under my very eyes, the object of impudent glances.[43]

This old-fashioned young Hugo was to become an inexhaustible source of interest for the later Hugo, whose travel accounts record several astute sightings of peasant women stepping over puddles or climbing fences. In *Les Misérables*, a gust of wind lifts Cosette's dress and Marius catches sight of an exquisitely shaped leg: 'He was furious and exasperated ... determined to disapprove and jealous of his own shadow.'[44]

Hugo's analysis of jealousy – as of all other emotions – seems doggedly superficial when snatched from its context, but with all the juxtapositions supplied by character and plot, surprisingly subtle. Conjunctions like 'because' are omitted, and it is partly this deletion of explicit causal links which explains his enormous readership and his seemingly accidental sense of humour: two levels of reading are always possible.

The context of Marius's jealousy is that, while courting Cosette, he is torn between hate and admiration of his father, a 'Brigand of the Loire' like General Hugo. His jealousy then appears in a wider setting as a symptom of the masochism which has been described as characteristic of the Romantic generations, an internalization of the father's tyranny. In Eugène, it took the catastrophic form of mental suicide. Hugo was more successful. From now on, he would be responsible for his own 'suffering'. But for this, an accomplice was required: Adèle, explicitly posed by Hugo as a substitute for his mother. The recurrent tragedy of his life is already sketched out in his instructions to the bride-to-be: a dependence on finding fresh victims for the reconstructed ego. Though she could only express it in the clichés of the age, Adèle saw this quite clearly. His jealousy was not a sign, as he claimed, of the potency and purity of his passion, but a mark of its fragility.

*

SOME OF HUGO'S STUFFINESS – and the self-confidence which allowed him to pursue Adèle in defiance of his mother – can be attributed to fame. Even if he was unsure of his own identity, other people now could tell him who he was.

His latest notoriety was the result of a murder. On 13 February 1820, the Duc de Berry, son of the future King, Charles X, was stabbed by a Bonapartist fanatic on the steps of the Opéra. The ensuing panic ousted the moderates and shifted power to the Ultras who, naturally, fanned the flames of outrage. An isolated terrorist act was used to lever in repressive measures: tighter censorship, arrest on suspicion and double votes for certain members of the electorate.

Hugo threw the full weight of his rhetoric behind the Ultras. His ode on 'La Mort du Duc de Berry' was published as a pamphlet in March 1820. It was to be followed by equally ecstatic odes on the birth and baptism of the Duke's posthumous son – the so-called '*enfant du miracle*', hailed by Hugo as a second baby Jesus and swathed in all the mystical symbols which had once been applied to Napoleon: 'A thousand cries, striking the flaming cloud, rise in the air from the distant, shimmering city.' The tone of the ode is almost gleeful. There is a strong identification with the fatherless prince and a sense that he too was well on his way to becoming a young Messiah: 'Deprived of the paternal eye, / In suffering born, / May you comfort the long grief / Of your Mother and of France.'

Louis XVIII was said to have cried when he read Hugo's exhortation in the assassination ode: 'White-haired monarch, hasten your step, / A Bourbon is returning to his ancestors' home.' Royal tears fell in the form of a 500-franc tip – surely a mark of genuine appreciation, since the Ultras were the King's political enemies.

The great Chateaubriand himself issued an invitation.[45] After days of nervous anticipation, Hugo turned up at the Rue Saint-Dominique and was dismayed to find 'a genius, not a man'. He was sickened by his hero's aloofness and the chilly reception of Mme de Chateaubriand, who finally turned unctuous on the third visit and asked him to buy some chocolate in aid of her 'poor old priests'. (Hugo bought 3lb of it for 15 francs – enough to pay for twenty days' food.) The only time the great man himself brightened up and chattered politely was when he had all his clothes taken off in front of Hugo to be rubbed down by the servant.

Hugo declined the opportunity to work for Chateaubriand at the embassy in Berlin: he wanted to stay near Adèle and pursue his literary career.[46] Future relations would be distant and symbolic: Hugo continued to admire Chateaubriand the writer and the royalist, but the two poems addressed to him are rich in ambiguities. 'À M. de Chateaubriand' compares him to a self-consuming volcanic asteroid and then invites him to 'fulfil [his] destiny'. The 1820 ode, 'Le Génie', depicts him as an albatross – a bird, Hugo informs us in a note, which is able to pursue its 'noble flight' while fast asleep.[47] As far as Hugo was concerned, there was now a vacancy for the job of greatest living French writer.

Fame had also produced a standing invitation to the inner circle of poets who represented the literary élite of Paris. Most of these poets were ten years older than Hugo: Émile Deschamps, whose translations helped to open up a treasure-house of German and English literature, and three men from the Académie in Toulouse – the tragedian, Alexandre Soumet, whose wind-swept toupee gave him the requisite 'inspired' look; Jules de Rességuier, a former cavalry officer; and Alexandre Guiraud, an aristocrat with some experience in business, who, in Hugo's memory, stammered, bit his nails and 'looked like a cross between a wild boar and a rabbit'.[48] (This was an age when the sciences of physiognomy and phrenology gave a certain respectability to cruel physical descriptions.) Guiraud is remembered, but only just, for his plaintive elegy, 'Le Petit Savoyard'. Now too glutinous to be read with comfort, it was considered rather daring for its reference to humble realities like money; its most famous line was the revolutionary, 'A little penny saves my life'.

Like much of the group's poetry, which harked back to the chivalrous age of patronage and inherited wealth, 'Le Petit Savoyard' was sold for charity: a device which allowed the poet to remain 'pure' whilst canvassing readers. In line with this principle, Hugo would refuse to curry favour with the newspapers or, like many of his contemporaries, write reviews of his own work.

The members of this nostalgic avant-garde sat in the salon of Sophie Gay in the noble Faubourg Saint-Germain, sipping tea, reciting their sentimental poems, discussing the position of the caesura and the question of whether or not the word '*mouchoir*' ('handkerchief') might be used instead of '*tissu*'.[49] Like latter-day *précieuses*, they practised the art of extravagant praise. Hugo was 'the Angel Victor', 'the hope of the muses of the Fatherland'; Chateaubriand dubbed him '*l'enfant sublime*' and the name stuck to Hugo well into middle age.[50]

This first ripple of French Romantic poets was easily absorbed by the Académie Française: their gauzy visions still had a visibly classical anatomy. They manipulated a tiny repertoire of phrases and images as if rearranging the ornaments in a room. Meeting in a quiet area of a city which was still a conglomeration of villages, this cosy club lends support to the view that European Romanticism was closely tied to industrialization, both revolutions coming almost half a century later in France than in Britain and Germany.

Even in this dainty mileu, there are signs of a remarkable coincidence of Hugo's personality and cultural trends. Although his rumbustious odes must have rattled the tea-cups, the self-observant rigidity of his verse suggests the artificial friendships of the lonely child, the etiquette and rituals which take the place of shared experience and a private language. When the Abbé de Lamennais, then living in the Feuillantines, tried to coax Hugo into joining his Catholic revival, he found a perfect example of the 'angelic' type of young Romantic:

> M. Victor Hugo has the purest and serenest soul I have ever encountered in the sewer of Paris. He is trusting and unaffected. He met me for the first time in the house where he once lived with an adored mother.... He will give wings to Catholic thought, which our pious writers often drag through the streets and even through the gutter.[51]

For the same reason, the former capital of the Empire, in Hugo's early verse, is a city of domes and monuments – broad stepping-stones over the mire in which the *misérables* of royalist mythology fermented their revolutions and worshipped Bonaparte – the medieval Paris which Hugo had been forced to inhabit by his father.

The tone of this coterie can also be heard in Hugo's letters to Adèle. His insistence on virginity ('not that opportunities have been lacking, but the thought of you protected me'); love as the union of two souls exiled from heaven; poetry as 'the expression of virtue' ('a beautiful soul and a fine poetic talent are almost always inseparable'); and his true 'vocation': 'a life of peace, tranquillity and obscurity, if possible'.[52]

A very different Victor Hugo was about to emerge. The decisive incident occurred on 26 April 1820. Adèle was tying her shoelaces in front of her mother when a letter fell from her corsage. The secret was out. Mme Hugo was informed and broke off relations with the whole Foucher family. For several months, there were no more letters. But the *enfant sublime* had found a new outlet for his passion: Mme Hugo had inadvertently helped to revolutionize French Romanticism.

CHAPTER SIX

The Demon Dwarf

(1821–1824)

FORBIDDEN FROM SEEING VICTOR, Adèle took comfort in her daily routine. But now, when she set off for her drawing lesson, a figure lurked in doorways, trying to catch her eye. When she went to bed, it stood on the street-corner beneath her window; once, it woke up the cat;[1] and when she went to confession at Saint-Sulpice with her mother, it hid behind the pillars. Sometimes, she whispered a quick message, 'like an angel conversing with a devil'.[2] Hugo was happy to learn a few months later that when she prayed to God his own face occluded the divine presence: 'There are occasions when I dare to imagine that I am all things to you.'[3] This was the 'Voltairean Royalist' teasing the daughter of devout parents – perhaps, too, a reader of the latest European bestseller, a masterpiece of 'Phrensied Literature', Lewis's *The Monk*.

When the angel had left the church, the devil scribbled notes on long rectangles of paper. Since Mme Hugo had banished the Fouchers to social oblivion and since Eugène was in the habit of going through his drawers, they were written in code:

Dimanche 4 – à 12^h ½ (récip^t) ⸭ sa m. d.l.b.[4]

This means that Adèle was sighted on Sunday, 4 (February 1821) at half-past midday, arm-in-arm with her mother at Saint-Sulpice and exchanged glances with Victor. For someone 'whose mind conceives twenty pages before his pen has written a single line',[5] it was a painfully concise form of expression. Sometimes, the notes were interrupted by fragments of verse or mysterious aphorisms which would have surprised the admirers of 'the Angel Victor': 'I wish there were a God so that I could blaspheme'; 'Robbing a rag-picker'; 'Rendezvous at the scaffold'.[6]

A month later, the dam burst. Hugo had hit upon the perfect medium for secret messages – a novel, set in seventeenth-century Norway, entitled *Han d'Islande*. It was designed to be fully understood by only one person – not, for example, by a disgusted Stendhal, who was to review the first edition (February 1823) in the English press: 'The most extraordinary and *ultra* horrible production of a disordered imagination', he punned, 'that has ever frozen the blood and blanched the cheeks of romance readers'.[7] For Hugo, it was an escape-valve, the result of a pressing 'need to give vent to certain thoughts which oppressed me and which French verse cannot contain'. *Han d'Islande*, he told Adèle, was a *roman àclé*,[8] the verbal equivalent of a clandestine visit to her bedroom. The heroine, Ethel Schumacher, was Adèle Foucher, and the hero, Ordener Guldenlew, Baron de Thorvick ('Victor' inverted), 'not myself as I am, but as I should like to be'.

The love story was predictably frenetic. Ethel's father has been imprisoned as a traitor by the Viceroy of Norway. The Viceroy's son, Ordener, has fallen in love with Ethel and sets out to prove her father's innocence. The idealized Hugo has a graceful body and the complexion of a young girl; solemn and self-assured, he sneers at superstition but is not insensitive to the supernatural aura of wild landscapes. In spite of the model's protestations of ordinariness, Ethel is a sublime Romantic specimen in black crêpe and white gauze, melancholy, sensible and appetizing:

> Her eyes and her long hair were black (a very rare form of beauty in the North). Her face, raised to heaven, seemed to be kindled with rapture rather than dimmed by meditation. She seemed a virgin from the shores of Cyprus or the fields of Tibur, clad in the fanciful veils of one of Ossian's characters and prostrate before the wooden cross and stone altar of Christ Jesus.[9]

A living anthology, indelibly dated to the French 1820s: Classical, Celtic and Christian; a Scandinavian Mediterranean. In the fantasy Paris of dungeons and fjords, Thorvick Hugo finally had his way: '"My adored Ethel ... tell me, do you love me?" He fastened his flaming eyes on her tear-stained face. The maiden's answer was not heard, for Ordener, in an ecstasy of passion, snatched it from her lips.'

The dance of the frantic hero around the ripe virgin was quite conventional and the characters were cloned from the trashy novels Hugo had devoured in the *cabinet de lecture*; and yet, when it was published in 1823, *Han d'Islande* dealt a hammer-blow to the wall which separated French literature from European Romanticism. The reason was that Hugo's unconscious had added several hundred pages.

The novel opens promisingly in the morgue at Trondheim. Bodies have been found torn to shreds as if by a long-nailed beast. Meanwhile, among the icy crags to the north lurks a weird, red-haired dwarf, the son of a witch and the last descendant of Ingulphus the Exterminator. Abandoned in Iceland, the hideous infant Han was taken in by a saintly bishop (a forerunner of Bishop Myriel in *Les Misérables*). Immune to Christian charity, he torches the bishop's palace and sets sail by the light of the flames on a tree-trunk, bound for Norway. There, he incinerates Trondheim cathedral, whose flying buttresses now resemble the rib-cage of a mammoth's carcass. He slaughters regiments, hurls mountains down onto villages, extinguishes beacons with a single breath, carries a stone axe and rides a polar bear called Friend. He also provides a tenuous link with the rest of the novel by stealing the casket which contains proof of the father's innocence.

Han of Iceland is the first of Hugo's evil red-haired dwarves, the prototype of Quasimodo. Hugo himself was shorter than his older brothers, and this may conceivably have something to do with his dwarf obsession.* But the fact that one of the terms of endearment used later on by his mistress was '*Le Petit Poucet*' ('Tom Thumb') does not suggest any unusual sensitivity. No doubt there was some anxiety about his changing body: no one goes through puberty without considering the possibility that they might end up a monster, and the child of warring parents was more likely than most to consider himself deformed. When Hugo learned that Heinrich Heine had called him a hunchback, he flew into a rage, climbed to a cliff-top on Guernsey,

* Hugo was about 5 feet 7 inches or 8 inches tall. The average height of a young male Parisian in 1843 was 5 feet 6 inches.[10]

removed all his clothes and asked his publisher, 'Am I a hunchback?' His publisher generously concluded that 'if Heaven had bestowed no other gift on him, he could have earned his living as an artist's model'.[11]

To look for graphic representations of Hugo's own physique is to belittle his creation. The real power of the literary dwarf lies in its ability to draw evil from others. This is not the pathetically nice monster of *Beauty and the Beast* but a perverted Christ-figure, incarnating the sins of other people – and the fact that the deformity has a soul calls the supposed metaphysical coincidence of reality and morality into question. Han himself has a certain Nietzschean, apolitical purity which sets him far beyond the other characters – pure, misanthropic instinct, unmarred by petty human motives. Royalist soldiers and seditious miners are crushed and maimed with equal relish. The spattered brains and palpitating flesh which he wraps around his body like a cloak conceal a surprisingly subtle view of Evil. Han is not defeated by the hero of the novel. He destroys himself, and the final battle never takes place. Hugo's *roman à clé* opened doors only on to other doors. His whole complicated self could not after all be crammed into the elegant frame of Ordener, and almost half the motley cast of characters is tattooed with the totemic letters of Hugo's name: Gormon, Guldenlew, Guldon, Guth, Oglypiglap, Orugix, Spiagudry.[12]

Apart from a hesitant reference to some notebooks full of 'originality and imagination'[13] (*originalité* had connotations of eccentricity), Adèle's opinion has not survived but was presumably similar to her later reaction to another ambiguous gift. At the Fouchers' holiday home in the village of Gentilly, on the southern edge of Paris,[14] Victor handed her a thick envelope which proved to contain a live bat and a terrifying poem about that 'dark and hairy' 'sister of the funereal owl', 'vainly seeking the night'. An obscure but vital moment in the history of French literature: the maiden flight of a new breed of poem which refused to sit dutifully on the page.

In a preface to the second edition of *Han d'Islande*, Hugo assured his readers that he was not in fact a frizzy-bearded monster who feasted on infants and never cut his nails. He even agreed with Adèle, after shocking her parents with a disquisition on the social necessity of executioners, that a man should never 'sully his mouth with the hideous and ignoble names of torture instruments'.[15] Yet a change of some sort was obviously taking place. When the correspondence resumed, Adèle's virginal suitor had become a ravening beast who 'embraced his bed with convulsions of love', plotted elopements, complained that his darling submitted to his kisses 'like a victim'[16] and, later, boasted of having made love to his bride nine times on her wedding night.[17]

The secret message of *Han d'Islande* remained indecipherable. The Gothic background which was originally intended to pad out the novel was a development of the cryptic notes in his diary. These notes offer a first glimpse of the nocturnal Hugo, a man who had taken to prowling about the 'amphibious' zone of barracks and cemeteries on the edge of Paris, 'where the pavement begins and the furrows end', where Lahorie had been executed.[18] Piecing together the various memories of torture and executions in Hugo's autobiographical writing, a curious fact comes to light: most of them fall within this period of courtship, and although they are presented as accidental sightings, a clear picture emerges of a ghoulish connoisseur, an intellectual jackal, watching the Duc de Berry's assassin being led to the scaffold;[19] a servant publicly branded with an iron;[20] the executioner slicing off the right hand and head of a parricide.[21] Searching for realities to compare with the images which had been burned into his eyes in Spain, Hugo was still determined to believe in official, royalist justice, as if it was possible to come to a final, irrefutable judgement on a human life. *Han d'Islande* made it easier to contemplate these horrific extremes – even to look for the answers to unformulated questions by feasting the mind's eye on seemingly gratuitous images, objective correlatives of a state of mind, or by resorting to the morbid sententiousness of the genre: 'All of us are condemned to death with indefinitely suspended sentences. A strange and painful curiosity impels us to observe the wretch who knows at what precise moment the sentence will be enacted.'[22]

*

HAN D'ISLANDE and the letters to Adèle spanned two years of unrequited lust and formed a ramshackle bridge over the abyss opened up by his mother's death.

Early in 1821, the family had moved a few streets away to 10 Rue Mézières, close to Saint-Sulpice. Mme Hugo had a small garden again but was too weak to tend it. On 27 June 1821, she died, after a long and expensive illness. A watch and some silver were pawned to pay for the funeral. Returning from the cemetery, Victor wrote to his father, calling a truce, asking him to continue the allowance and promising not to be a burden to him much longer.

General Hugo blethered on about lost fortunes, property tax and repair bills and negotiated a delicate compromise: he would be allowed to marry his mistress in peace; in exchange, Victor could marry his little sweetheart – but on one extra condition: that he earn enough money to support a family. This, he assumed, would force him to go and study Law.

Hugo accepted the challenge as a palliative. Even before his father's ultimatum, his mourning had taken a dramatic, physical form. Fearing passionate advances from a grief-stricken Victor, M. and Mme Foucher had whisked Adèle away to visit a relative in Dreux on the borders of Normandy. The 25-franc coach ride would put her beyond Victor's reach while he regained his composure. A week later, on 20 July 1821, Adèle was amazed to catch sight of her 'husband' in Dreux. He had walked 50 miles 'under a burning sun, on roads without a shadow of shade', staring 'insolently' at passing carriages and 'proving that it is possible to use one's feet for walking'.[23] After bathing in the river, he made his way to the Hôtel du Paradis and wrote a careful letter to M. Foucher, remarking on the extraordinary coincidence. He just happened to be in Dreux 'in search of Druidic monuments'. However,

> It would be dishonest of me if I did not confess that the unhoped-for sight of Mademoiselle, your daughter, caused me great pleasure. I am not afraid to say it openly: I love her with all my soul, and in my complete abandonment and profound grief only the thought of her still affords me some happiness.
>
> As for yourself, Monsieur, you know with what sincerity and whole-hearted devotion I have the honour to be
>
> Your very humble servant,
>   Victor-M. Hugo.[24]

Foucher, to his credit, was hugely impressed: to a man who had spent most of his life in a chair, 50 miles on foot was an astronomical distance. In future, Victor was to be allowed to stay with the Fouchers in their rented holiday house in Gentilly. He was lodged, appropriately, in the most picturesque part of the building – a fifteenth-century tower with views of the countryside in all directions. The Fouchers' landlady employed inmates from the local asylum, Bicêtre. And so, while a gloomy lunatic turned the sods in the garden below, Hugo sat at the top of his tower writing Gothic odes. 'A tower inhabited by Vertigo, / That cruel and curious dwarf, which hovers o'er the peaks ... And tosses pale travellers to the vultures of the abyss.'[25]

The correspondence with Adèle entered a new phase: they were busy carving out the informal, unalterable marriage contract which precedes the written agreement. She worried about his lack of experience and, implicitly, future infidelity. Mme Hugo's body became a battleground: Adèle was still smarting from her undisguised contempt, and Victor admitted that his mother had tried to wean him off his sweetheart and 'intoxicate' him with 'the pleasures of vanity' and 'worldly dissipations', forgetting, ' – poor mother! – that she herself had implanted in my heart disdain for the world and scorn for false pride'.[26] When one argument was exhausted, they set to work on another. Victor accused her of having only 'a sòrt of compassion', 'a habit, perhaps even friendship, but not love'.[27] She then pointed to his own unpredictable frostiness. Expectations had imperceptibly been lowered, but Hugo was already savouring the intimacy of married life and the sharing of her 'little secrets'. He would nurse her through her monthly 'indisposition': 'I shall warm you in my arms with my kisses and caresses and my love will be a shield to protect you from your pain.'[28]

Although one of his odes described Nightmare 'sitting on [his] panting breast',[29] the 'orphan' seemed to have escaped the clutches of grief. His mother's death had cleared the way to married bliss, and his father was a greatly deflated tyrant – too selfish to be invincible, although his faintly ribald references to Victor's young damsel were infuriating. Anguish came in unexpectedly subtle forms. His feelings refused to obey his brain. When he ran into the General's 'concubine' in Paris, strangely, his head did not explode: 'The evil genius of my noble mother's life and of our childhood', he told Foucher, 'dared to speak to me, and the amazing thing is that I heard her voice without all my blood spurting from my veins.'[30]

Practical obstacles were a welcome distraction. Later in life, Hugo might even be said to have created them for precisely that purpose. First, Mme Foucher rather suspiciously became pregnant again at the age of forty-three and insisted that Adèle would have to stay at home and nurse her: 'Mama told me ... that children ought to be capable of suffering boredom for their parents' sake.'[31] Foucher himself was easily won over. He was happy to be supplied with the latest works from 'England' – Walter Scott and Southey – and concerned only that Victor would become the tool of a political party. Or even a martyr. Hugo had boasted of receiving a poem from an anti-royalist threatening him with the guillotine[32] – the first of several death-threats; almost as gratifying as a good review.

There remained the problem of money. Hugo's heroic description of himself as 'a cloud fettered by an iron chain'[33] nicely conveys the ambiguous nature of the dilemma. This was one of the happiest periods of his life – a period, he noted in the 1833 preface to *Han d'Islande*, 'when the commonplace and ordinary obstacles of life are converted into imposing and poetic impediments'. It was also a period when, for the first time, writers who were willing to accept the new disciplines and constraints of public demand could expect to live by their pen.

Leaving Eugène with Abel, he moved to a sunless two-room garret close to the Pension Cordier at 30 Rue du Dragon. In one room, the Golden Lily from the Jeux Floraux sat proudly on the mantelpiece. The other room was an 'inextricable chaos' of furniture and papers which he shared with his cousin from Nantes.[34] Adolphe Trébuchet had come to Paris to study Law and was now referred to as 'our fourth brother'. This strengthening of ties with the maternal side of the family was an act of devotion to Mme Hugo, the sequel to her own revised version of family history. (She had once told Alfred de Vigny that Victor was a native of Brittany.)

For the first time in his life he was free. His 800-franc allowance was roughly equivalent to a student grant today, but poverty was an enjoyable mental exercise and proof of a virtuous existence. A cutlet, he discovered, could be made to last three days: meat on Monday, fat on Tuesday, bone on Wednesday.[35] If he dined out, he went to a restaurant in the Rue Saint-Jacques run by a man called Rousseau 'the Aquatic', because all his customers drank water. Dinner cost 80 centimes – the cheapest recorded meal anywhere in Paris, *pace* Balzac.[36] The price of breakfast varied with the price of eggs but averaged 20 centimes. Housekeeping was performed by the concierge for 5 francs a month and probably included hot water in the mornings. After rent (400 francs per annum), laundry, lighting and fuel, he still had money left over. In contrast to Cousin Adolphe, who seems to have received part of his inheritance in shirts (he sent them back to Nantes twice a year to be laundered), Hugo had only three, which he wore, hot from the iron, before the bleach had turned them yellow. He also bought a cornflower-blue suit with gold-coloured buttons. A letter to his prospective mother-in-law talks of a perilous shopping expedition among the 'pirates' and 'sirens' who 'took advantage of my ignorance and stupidity: I had only the vaguest notion of current fashions'[37] – especially disastrous at a time when tailors expected their customers to haggle.[38] The result is apparent from one of the earliest physical descriptions of Hugo. The socialist philosopher and reformer, Pierre Leroux, was typesetting one of Hugo's odes and saw the young genius when he came to correct the proofs: 'Your blue suit was too short for you, and your arms, which had grown, stuck a long way out from your cuffs.'[39]

The cornflower-blue suit was also seen in the waiting-rooms of Government offices, doing something which would later be thrown in the face of the socialist Hugo: trying to obtain a pension from the King's purse. A signature from Louis XVIII and he would be financially stable enough to marry Adèle. Despite his royalist odes and the support of François de Neufchâteau and Chateaubriand, the file on 'Victor Hugot' grew for over two years before it produced any money.

One possible reason for the delay is a letter Hugo had sent to the mother of Delon – the boy from the Feuillantines who used to go walking about on the rooftops.[40] Delon had been accused of taking part in an attempted coup by the international Republican underground known as the Carbonari.[41] A warrant had been issued for his arrest and he was about to be condemned to death *in absentia*. Forgetting the possible repercussions for Mme Delon, Hugo grandly offered to hide the fugitive: 'My profound attachment to the Bourbons is known; but this very circumstance is a reason for you to feel secure, for it removes all suspicion from me.' The letter was intercepted and read by the *cabinet noir* – a secret Government agency which Hugo had always thought was an invention of republican propagandists.

His memory later seized on this story – or rather, on contradictory versions of it – in order to explain how an annual pension of 1000 francs landed in his lap on 25 September 1822, followed by another pension from the Ministry of the Interior on 23 June 1823. The King was impressed by his reckless courage and decided to reward him for his virtue rather than have him imprisoned for abetting a conspirator. According to a more plausible version, the bibliophilic King sent his reader to buy a copy of Hugo's first book of odes and rewarded him for his poetic virtues.

The fact is that Hugo forced himself to beg in order to earn the right to marry Adèle, and it might have been better for his reputation if he had simply told the truth. But there was no strong tradition of truth-telling in the Hugo family. Impeccable moral credentials would justify the deception. Once the principle was accepted, the possibilities were endless, and a hundred years of deliberately credulous biographies testify to the excellence of his arrangements.

In negotiating the final hurdle to marriage, he proved that religion, too, could be manipulated. His anti-clerical parents had never had him baptized and Hugo did not believe in a church-going God. He assured his father, knowing it to be untrue, that he had been baptized in Italy – which shows how much General Hugo was expected to know about the past. He then persuaded the Abbé de Lamennais to certify the baptism and supply him with the *billet de confession* without which a church marriage was impossible.[42]

The pensioned poet who stood at the altar in Saint-Sulpice on 12 October 1822 could congratulate himself on a splendid achievement. The 'orphan' had turned himself into a decent proposition almost single-handed. Unlike Eugène, he had pushed his boat out just in time to escape the legacy of his parents. Confusion, frustrated rage and even debts had all been consigned to oblivion by his pen. Neither parent was at the wedding. Sixteen months before, Mme Hugo's coffin had stood in the same chapel. The General, who married his mistress in September 1821, did not attend: something had happened to his vineyard in Blois which required his urgent attention.[43]

The wedding feast was held in a hall at the Conseil de Guerre. A hinged partition separated it from the courtroom where Lahorie had been sentenced to death. In his last letter to Adèle, Hugo had talked of the impotence of his pen – his happiness could only be expressed in clichés – and he drew the moral of their heroic story: *'vouloir fermement c'est pouvoir'*[44] – where there's a strong will, there's a way. But will-power alone offered no control or even knowledge of the wishes that would be miraculously granted.

*

WHILE HUGO, 'like an inebriated grape-picker', harvested his wife's virginity[45] in the rooms they had been assigned in the Fouchers' house, Eugène marked the occasion with a violent fit of madness and had to be restrained and sedated. On the day that Victor lost his virginity, Eugène lost his mind.

With this chronological conceit, *Victor Hugo Raconté* smothers the screaming lunatic in the gauze of tragic love. The truth is that Eugène's madness had come into full bloom long before the marriage. The latest incidents included an unspecified 'profanation' of one of Victor's mementoes of Adèle – so disgusting that Victor spent a thousand words telling her that he could not bring himself to describe it.[46] There were also suggestions that Eugène was stealing money to pay for prostitutes.[47] He was treating his brothers like 'enemies'.

As Eugène's thoughts became increasingly obscure, the motive force of his behaviour came into focus. In April 1822, he had run away from Paris 'in his worst suit', according to Victor, and was arrested without a passport somewhere between Chartres and Orléans.[48] Apparently, he was on his way to verify the unbelievable fact that his father had married another woman. Eugène's schizophrenia was finally recognized as something other than a nasty personality:

the word '*pantophobie*' was used.* But the General was convinced that paternal authority would prevail. Eugène was sent to stay with him and his new wife at Blois: the human barrel of gunpowder was to be showered with sparks. Electrical shock treatment, already in its eternal infancy, proved ineffective. One day at the dinner table, his mind confused by fever and the smell of coriander (someone was obviously trying to poison him – coriander was used to mask the taste of medicine), Eugène lunged at his stepmother with a knife but succeeded only in ripping her shawl. General Hugo pushed him up against the wall, as he told Foucher in a letter which says far more about the General's mental condition than his son's.

> Unable to snatch the knife from his hands, I decided to bend the blade under his eyes, and this intimidated him sufficiently to make him drop it. Then he allowed me tie him up unaided and I kept him in that state for just a moment: it distressed my heart to see him laid low, unable to keep up a struggle with me.[49]

This is the father for whom Victor was about to discover an unexpectedly strong affection.

Eugène was locked up in a reputable Paris asylum, his father still convinced that his brain had been befuddled by the full moon and, before that, by the late Mme Hugo. In the letter to Foucher, he went on to deny, at length, the rumours of his Spanish fortune which had apparently been one of Eugène's themes. He was also concerned that three 'strangers' had witnessed the incident. Tongues would wag and it would all be 'very disagreeable for the family'.

Victor visited his brother in the asylum, and wondered whether 'solitude and idleness' were really the best treatment. Eugène thought he was in prison. 'He told me in a whisper that they were murdering women in the dungeons and that he had heard their screaming.'[50] Soon, the doctors forbade all visits from the family and Eugène descended with ever larger steps into his real-life Gothic fantasy. His body survived in a padded cell until 1837.

'Who has not witnessed this horrible drama in the high grass of Springtime?' Hugo asks in *Promontorium Somnii*: a mayfly captured

* 'Manifest fear of all things, observed especially in Melancholia' (Littré). 'Paranoia' was first used in French in 1838.

by a beetle. 'It lays open the belly, pushes in its head, then its brassy corselet, rummaging and scooping, disappearing up to its middle in the wretched creature, it eats it alive on the spot.' 'This is a man possessed by madness.' This horrific evacuation is explicitly compared by Hugo to the poet's descent into that 'vertiginous spiral, the self'.[51] In one sense, as the youngest brother settled safely into family life, Eugène was still ahead of him. A pioneer in another world.

For those sympathetic vampires known as biographers, Eugène's insanity is an extraordinary stroke of good luck. While Victor reconstructed his social identity, predating his love for Adèle to 'earliest childhood' and cultivating what had been at first a purely formal reconciliation with the General, Eugène enacted his own version of happy families. His letters from the asylum to General Hugo offer a crazed image of Victor's own tender messages to his 'kind and dear Papa'.[52] With their odd insistence on 'political events which occurred before we were born into this world in which all the friends of our parents and our parents themselves had preceded us', they imply a view of madness which did not gain currency until well into the twentieth century: the view from inside the sick brain which expands the environment of the illness from the family circle to include social and historical influences. Eugène, the failed Romantic poet, had become a very modern sort of lunatic. This is one of his more coherent lucubrations:

> Whatever political events might have occurred since that period [childhood], they cannot have made you forget all the happiness I gave you and the memory that I should have liked it to engrave in your mind. . . . It is worth pointing out to you that the various political events by which the State and France have not been unaffected have been unable to force us to deviate from the principles to which we were compelled to adhere as the sons of an officer and as subjects of a Government formed principally to attend to the salvation of all and the particular tranquillity of each individual.[53]

These 'principles', the public and domestic wisdom of two generations which straddled the Ancien Régime, the Revolution, the Terror, the Empire and an increasingly turbulent Restoration, were all contradictory, riddled with double negatives in which all attempted compromises cancelled each other out. Eugène's rambling letters, like vastly extended Freudian slips, are a foretaste of Victor's increasingly brilliant and implausible attempts to force all these contradictions into the same syncretic mould.

*

THE WIDENING GAP between the messy reality and the uniformed image was already noticeable in Hugo's first two books – a diptych of his mind at the end of bachelorhood.

Four months before the wedding, he had been agonizing over the question of his literary virginity. Abel helped out once again: he stole the manuscript of Victor's poems and took them to a printer. A few days later, the concierge delivered a bundle of proofs. Hugo made corrections, added a short preface and, on 8 June 1822, fifty copies of a small, sloppily printed volume on dirty grey paper were taken by Abel to the book-buying centre of Paris, the Palais-Royal, and foisted on a bookseller who grudgingly gave them a place next to his novels.

The *Odes et Poésies Diverses* – a bland, descriptive title, typical of the period – contained all of Hugo's prize-winning and occasional odes, along with fresh evidence of his 'monarchical ideas and religious beliefs': another blasting of the Satanic 'Buonaparte' and a 'Vision' in which God sends the entire eighteenth century tumbling into the eternal abyss like a hurricane pursuing a snowflake. After some favourable reviews, 1500 copies were sold in four months, bringing the author the huge sum of 750 francs (almost two years' rent). A second, revised edition appeared in January 1823 with two extra odes: passionately slavish tributes to Louis XVII and Jehovah.

A critic on the royalist *Gazette de France* perceptively pointed to a new hybrid: the lyrical ode in which historical events are described as if they were personal experiences. But no one seemed to notice the peculiar assertion, in the preface, that the poet's 'political intention' was the result of 'the literary intention'.[54] This is an exact contradiction of Hugo's famous boast, in 1831, that he was 'cast into the literary world at the age of sixteen by political passions'.[55] Could it be that this intensely earnest poet was an extremist 'Ultra' principally because the Catholic and royalist point of view made it possible to present the chaos of History in a crisp, axiomatic form? In a literary sense, Hugo had founded his own dynasty. It is significant that his first five volumes of poetry (1822–8) were all cultivars of the original book of odes. The imperceptible originality of the dingy little volume was that, instead of being a mere anthology, it was a living plant in its own right, with its roots in the heart of an individual.

By contrast, the four pocket-sized volumes of *Han d'Islande* (the one-volume novel was a rarity) appeared anonymously in February 1823, when Adèle was already four months pregnant. When the publisher declared bankruptcy, a second edition, attributed to a certain 'Oguh',[56] appeared in July, almost at the same time as a sickly child, christened, in honour of the General, Léopold-Victor. The baby was handed to a nurse and put on the coach to Blois where country air, goat's milk and the General's wife were supposed to toughen him up. Adèle stayed in Paris: she was ill and had never been away from her parents. Even so, her anxious letters suggest that the child was sacrificed to improving relations with the General.

Han d'Islande fared slightly better. It was not an immediate success, but it rode the wave of dwarfmania, then at its height,[57] and *Hans of Iceland* was eventually translated twenty-three times into English in the nineteenth century, twice subtitled *The Demon Dwarf*.*[58] A Norwegian translation in 1831 testified to Hugo's hastily acquired erudition.[59] The first English translation appeared in 1825, with four etchings by George Cruikshank, greatly abridged but by no means edulcorated, and aimed, impressively, at 'juvenile readers'.[60]

Reviewing the French edition in London, the *Literary Gazette* noted the 'contemptible pretension' of *Flan d'Islande* (*sic*) 'to imitate the productions of Sir Walter Scott'.[61] For Vigny and the respected eccentric, Charles Nodier – who must have noticed that these 'barbarous fantasies of a sick mind' owed something to his own fantastic novels – this was a point in its favour.[62] Under the umbrella of Walter Scott, *Han d'Islande* met the seemingly unrelated *Odes*: the dramatic, non-linear organization of character and description

---

* Since the monster is named after his grunt ('*han!*' is the standard French interjection for the noise made when lifting a heavy object), the correct name is 'Han', not 'Hans'. Directly translated, the title would be *Oof of Iceland*. However, given Hugo's habit of toying with the letters of his own name, *Ugh of Iceland* would be preferable.

attached symbolic weight to every detail, however trivial or gory, and made the novel an organic whole. The painfully old-fashioned Victor Hugo had an innate modernity which protruded like his arms and legs from the cornflower-blue suit.

A more subtle originality lay in its seriousness. *Han d'Islande* is often said to be typical of the Gothic novel and therefore, like the blood-curdling melodramas which Balzac was churning out at the same time, tongue-in-cheek. The final epigraph seems to confirm this and is usually interpreted as a warning to over-earnest readers: 'You took seriously what I said in jest.'[63] Yet the epigraphs themselves are patently not meant to be taken seriously. Hugo was nodding to the Romantic connoisseur – to the melancholy few who had discovered that real experience could be conveyed by the most extreme and unrealistic forms of literature.

*

ON 10 OCTOBER 1823, Léopold died at the age of three months. Sad but not surprising. Hugo wrote to his father: 'We should not think that God had no purpose in sending us that little angel, so soon recalled. He wanted Léopold to be another tie between you, tender parents, and us, your devoted children.'[64] General Hugo was associated now with a rational, benevolent God.

There was further consolation in the belief that Adèle's second pregnancy announced the imminent return of the spirit which had briefly inhabited little Léopold.[65] On 28 August 1824, the second edition emerged in the form of a fat and noisy baby. It was a girl, Léopoldine, obviously destined to survive – destined too, by her father's intense, determined happiness, to be the subject of some of the saddest and most skilfully written love poems in the language.

The first poem Hugo wrote after the birth of his daughter shows a curious choice of subject, curiously treated: 'Les Funérailles de Louis XVIII' – the finest of all political odes, according to Sainte-Beuve.[66] On the day of the child's baptism, the King died, and for the first time since childhood, Hugo allowed Bonaparte (so spelt) a certain glory: the exile on his 'black rock, beaten by the waves' and deceived by the heavens.

The King, of course, is the ultimate victor. But the short, panting lines of the final stanza, 'Plumbing with uncertain eyes / Death's great mysteries', suggest that these heroic figures may simply be passers-by in a vast, inscrutable cosmos. From now on, it would take all his poetic ability to maintain the facile loyalties of family and fatherland. The baby completed a family circle, but her birth was also the funeral of an earlier Victor Hugo and the messenger of his real subject:

> Who art thou, proud God?
> What arm throws towers beneath the grass
> And changes purple to vile rags? . . .
> What unseen hand
> Holds the keys to the tomb?

Léopoldine brought with her the first suspicion of a God who existed independently of convention and human wishes. An adversary worthy of the vision.

Part Two

CHAPTER SEVEN

Traitors

(1824–1827)

THE POET WHO had recently been 'descending the great precipice of life in a barrel full of nails'[1] was now negotiating a gentle river, half oblivious to the rumbling cataract downstream. He had a loving wife, a healthy daughter, a respected father, an annual income of 3000 francs and his own armchair in the drawing-room of French literature. When Byron died in 1824, Hugo described his death, significantly, as a 'domestic calamity':

> A man who has devoted his life to the cult of letters feels the circle of his physical existence close around him, while the sphere of his intellectual existence grows ever wider. A small number of cherished beings occupy the tenderness of his heart, while all poets – dead and contemporary, foreign and compatriotic – take hold of the affections of his soul. Nature having provided him with one family, poetry supplies him with another.[2]

There was obviously something comforting about the death of a fellow writer. With its dated vocabulary, its short phrases flung down like handfuls of soil on the coffin-lid, the axioms which allude to unchanging realities and the beliefs of a stable community, the Byron article showed an odd resistance to the changes which Hugo himself was promoting in the same piece of writing and which had already divided cultural life into two opposing camps – Classics and Romantics: 'Let there be no mistake: it is in vain that a small number of little minds attempt to drag the general trend of ideas back towards the dreary literary system of the last century. . . . One cannot return to the madrigals of Dorat* after the guillotines of Robespierre.'[3]

---

* Claude-Joseph Dorat (1734–80), frivolous poet and musketeer.

The author of this optimistic obituary is the beautifully supercilious cherub of the 1825 portrait by Jean Alaux: Hugo's golden head blossoms from the black suit with the serenity of a Renaissance Christ, supremely confident of something. Half the face is taken up with forehead – the unruffled reservoir of genius; but the crude particulars of Hugo's passports reveal a far more turbulent physiognomy. Having oneself described by a tetchy bureaucrat could be just as dispiriting as seeing one's face parodied by a photograph booth today. In April 1825, he has 'an average forehead', a 'large nose' and 'brown eyes'. Three months later, 'a small brow', 'grey eyes' and an 'ordinary nose'. By 1834, without the help of a receding hairline, he had acquired a 'high forehead' and an extra inch-and-a-quarter in height.[4]

Hugo was under the impression that he and French literature had undergone a change. The evidence of his own writing is that both had entered a world where change would be the norm.

*

Hugo's obituary of Byron appeared in the timidly Romantic successor to *Le Conservateur Littéraire: La Muse Française*. Hugo and Vigny were the youngest contributors: the others belonged to the older generation and were already knocking on the doors of the Académie Française. A frontispiece showed the rancorous Medusa of Revolution blasted out of the sky by a zigzag of royal lightning, while a Gallic cock looked on approvingly, one leg in the air. On the cover, a debonair Apollo sported the paraphernalia of a medieval knight, warning readers to expect a bizarre mixture of periods and cultures.[5]

For want of anything more blatantly rebellious, *La Muse Française* is usually cited by literary historians as one of the principal organs of early French Romanticism. At the time of its creation, it was the mouthpiece of a reactionary club called the Société des Bonnes Lettres. The explicit aim of the club was to exterminate revolutionary ideas by propagating 'good and healthy doctrines'.[6] Propagation took place at public meetings where members of the Society basked in mutual admiration and concocted press-releases for newspapers sympathetic to the cause. *Le Réveil* reported 'veritable transports' when the 'energetic, sensitive and graceful' Victor Hugo recited his ode on

Louis XVII: 'each line [there are eighty-six] was greeted with a salvo of applause'.[7]

Soon, the salvoes would turn into a barrage of insults. The poets of *La Muse Française* might be political reactionaries, but they were fomenting a revolution in literature, writing in a style which appealed to a large and poorly educated audience, opening the gates to another foreign invasion. Hugo's first attempt to resolve the contradiction, in the preface to the *Nouvelles Odes* of March 1824, is notably feeble and betrays a sense of contaminated origins: 'Modern literature', he decreed, 'may be the *result* of the Revolution, without being its *expression*'.

Lamartine predicted that *La Muse Française* would be sustained for a time 'by the stupidity of its opponents', and this now seems to have been its principal function: to attract hostile criticism and thereby enable the Romantics to reach an understanding of their own position. The word *Romanticism* had already become an epistemological bucket-with-a-hole into which any number of definitions could be poured. The most accurate were also the vaguest. For Hugo, a Romantic was a writer who refused to imitate: 'anyone who imitates a *Romantic* poet necessarily becomes a *Classical* poet'; or, as he put it thirty years later, 'A lion who copies a lion is an ape.'[8] The Romantic was also a creator who, quite literally, did not know what he was doing: 'As a person, one is sometimes a stranger to what one writes as a poet.' Hugo prophetically observed that this had worrying implications for critics: if the final judgement of a work of art lay with each reader's sensibility, the professional critic would be out of a job.

The confusion of critics may have been 'stupidity', but it presented a more dynamic perception of the movement than the dogmatic manifestos of the Romantics. Some of the most rewarding literary criticism of the Romantic period is also the most abusive: critics, like poets, did not necessarily have access to the true meaning of their work. From now on, attacks on Hugo's writing would be an essential element of his art: the final, irritating incantation which turned his words into a screen on which he saw himself projected. A good reason to be as famous as possible. As each book appeared, he would see his recent self exposed to a hundred professional analysts. In such conditions, naivety would have to fight for survival.

The first blow to Hugo's literary illusions came from within the establishment. The Director of the Académie Française, Louis-Simon Auger, had sounded the alarm on 24 April 1824. The forty 'Immortals' had reached the word *romantique* in their dictionary and were trying to come up with a suitably pejorative definition.[9] Auger took it upon himself to explain what it meant. Beyond the Rhine, a sinister confederation of vandals had been systematically copying those barbaric geniuses, Shakespeare and Lope de Vega, grubbing about in 'the chaos of ancient chronicles or the jumbled mass of old legends'. Cultural explorers like Mme de Staël had imported the first seeds of a new 'sect', which called itself 'Romanticism' and which threatened now to split into countless 'little secondary schisms', thus creating an uncontrollable plague of grammatical errors, incomprehensible phrases and 'febrile excitation'. France, renowned for her clarity and precision (at least in France), would soon be swimming in 'the foggy atmosphere of Great Britain or Germany'.[10]

Like most cultural reactionaries, Auger revelled in self-inflicted ignorance and refused to believe that anything new could be invented, especially by the young. But he made a brave attempt to overcome the contradictions which still bedevil any attempt to define the movement. Romantics were unconscious hypocrites – patriotic traitors, aristocratic demagogues, creating their melancholy characters with cheerful arrogance. Sometimes they were repulsively literal; sometimes they pursued their lurid images until they lost sight of the thing they were supposed to be describing. For 200 years, a small élite had been bringing the language and a handful of literary genres to the point of unalterable perfection, and now the children of the Revolution were giving it all away to foreigners and plebs.

Auger's speech had two immediate effects. First, Romanticism was officially recognized as the Enemy. Second, *La Muse Française* was forced by its older contributors to turn its lightning-bolt on itself: it folded after the twelfth issue (15 June 1824). Hugo's friend, Alexandre Soumet, thought he deserved a seat in the Academy and knew that the admission price would be the death of the subversive organ he had helped to found. Moral pressure was brought to bear on Hugo and produced a characteristically two-sided reaction. He promised not to keep the *Muse* alive for a thirteenth issue, then he wrote a letter to a newspaper dissociating himself from the turncoats.

This desertion of Hugo's fair-weather Romantic friends had the effect of locking him into his principles like a knight in his armour. Responsibility for progress had passed to Victor Hugo and his generation. That month – July 1824 – he wrote one of his first *ballades* (a 'foreign' form which harked back to pre-classical times): 'La Fée et la Péri', in which the fairy of the West and the elf of the East compete for the soul of a dead child. The poem seems to have nothing whatsoever to do with current events, but, in context, it has the force of an avant-garde manifesto. All the qualities Auger castigated as 'Germanic' were trumpeted in the rhymes – 'vaporous', 'nebulous', 'misty', 'smoky' and 'mystical'. Pedants would have noticed that the poem contained a provocatively odd number of lines (199) but would have failed to spot the logical connection between the Gothic churches, the pink-roofed pagoda, Fingal's cave and the twelve elephants of Delhi.

Hugo seemed to have deliberately set out to illustrate Auger's sarcastic question: 'What would one say of a painter who omitted the foreground, in which everything must be distinct, and reduced his landscapes to those distant backgrounds in which everything is vaporous, confused and indeterminable?' The *enfant sublime* was turning into an *enfant terrible*.

The lesson in literary mores supplied by the cowardly Soumet was closely followed by another lesson in the *Journal des Débats*. A critic called Hoffman who signed his articles 'Z' (because he always had the last word?) reviewed the *Nouvelles Odes* and accused Hugo of being a Romantic. There was an exchange of letters in the press, during which Hugo discovered that critics sometimes lied, used other writers' work as an excuse for showing off, hinted at non-existent faults too heinous to be mentioned, and prevented letters of rectification from being printed.

Hugo's exquisitely insolent replies showed that he was absorbing the lessons. The basis of his extraordinary success in the years to come was the realization that, instead of using literature to fight political battles, literature itself could be politicized. The quarrel of Classics and Romantics, however nugatory its intellectual content, would provide a polemical framework for his writing, in the same way that abstract notions of friendship provided the basis of his relationships with other writers. Large-scale manipulation made life much simpler. It brought everything together under the same umbrella and made it possible to interpret every emotional incident as a professional event. Thinking of the attacks by 'Z', he told Vigny in December 1824,

> As soon as I see passions and self-interest enter the fray, all my ideas fly away and I am vanquished. Little injuries kill me. I am – I hope you will forgive the arrogance of the comparison – like Achilles: vulnerable by the heel.

But presumably invulnerable everywhere else. This is typical of Hugo's early letter-writing style – stilted and unconvincing, but perfectly readable if one assumes that the 'I's and 'me's refer to a third person. Hugo was constructing an ego for himself and trying it out on his friends. The good thing about friends was that they could easily be construed as having 'betrayed' the friendship, like the founders of *La Muse Française*; and betrayals, as Hugo knew from his parents, were a powerful justification for single-minded action.

As Hugo picked his way over the rubble of his illusions to the highest point on the battlefield, a mist descended over the personality which earlier events had laid bare. It was a colourful mist in the Romantic style which might happily be taken as the complete picture for the next few decades. In letters, he began to refer to his odes as '*rêveries*' or '*rapsodies*', hinting, implausibly, that they were the fruit of idle musing.[11] He showed off his modern sensibility by praising the 'charming bizarreness' of things.[12] On a letter to Adèle's fifteen-year-old brother Paul, he traced the shadow of some ivy as it fell across the page and sketched a verbal vignette of himself as a model Romantic:

> Please do not laugh at the bizarre lines which I have drawn, as if haphazardly, on the back of this sheet of paper. Use your imagination. Tell yourself that the drawing was traced by the sun and the shade and you will see something charming. This is how those lunatics called poets proceed.[13]

This passage – even the single phrase 'as if haphazardly' ('*comme au hasard*') – could form the basis of a whole chapter in a history of

French literature: the analytical, self-observing nature of a supposedly spontaneous movement which had long since established firm traditions in Britain and Germany. Hugo's studiedly indiscriminate sketch is a highly representative gesture: a gratuitous act with an ulterior motive.

A similar sort of performance was offered to visitors to the Hugos' new home. In the spring of 1824, they moved from the Fouchers' house to a second-floor apartment at 90 Rue de Vaugirard: six small rooms, a maid's room, a cellar, a wood-shed, and 'exclusive use of the WC on the landing'.[14] The annual rent, excluding door and window tax, was 625 francs – easily covered by Hugo's income from writing. Visitors included the painters, Achille Devéria and Louis Boulanger, who illustrated Hugo's works and family life as if they belonged to the same Romantic universe. The poet, Adolphe de Saint-Valry (another refugee from *La Muse Française*), saw an adorable domestic scene, like something from Thomas Moore's *The Loves of the Angels*, but 'a lot more poetic'. The literary allusion is a slight but significant irony: like most young couples, Victor and Adèle acted out their ménage in public and invited visitors to be the mirrors of their bliss. The editor of a new, liberal newspaper, *Le Globe*, knew exactly what he was being asked to admire:

> In the entresol of a joiner's workshop in the Rue de Vaugirard, I saw a young poet and a young mother in a tiny little drawing-room. The mother was cradling in her arms a child of a few months, teaching her to join her little hands in prayer in front of some engravings of Madonnas and Infant Jesuses by Raphaël. Though it was always slightly contrived, the scene, naive and sincere, moved me and delighted me.[15]

The dramatist was already at work, keeping up appearances, offering beautiful scenes to an audience which was happy to be deceived.

*

IT WAS ONLY OUTSIDE the home that the frame sometimes failed to keep up with the face, and without the three journeys of 1825, there would be little to add to our knowledge of Hugo besides a list of poems and payments.

General Hugo had invited Victor and his family to visit his little estate near Blois: 'If you enjoy hunting, you will be able to kill some rabbits, partridges and other creatures which I allow to live there in peace.'[16] Hugo boarded the mail coach on the evening of 24 April 1825 with Adèle and Léopoldine. The rhythm of the carriage had its usual effect. Overnight, he wrote a long ballad, 'Les Deux Archers', averaging one line every two kilometres: 'It was the deathly hour when the night is so dark ... When the traveller goes scurrying through the clearing ...'

He was in the jolly frame of mind that makes it easy to write a gloomy poem. First, he had just been chosen as the official poet of the coronation of Charles X, which was due to take place at Rheims in a few weeks' time. Second, as the coach was being loaded in Paris, a liveried messenger came running up with a large sealed letter. Victor-Marie Hugo had been made a *chevalier* of the Légion d'Honneur – a civil and military award instituted by Napoleon and adopted by the Restoration. Both honours showed that the court was well aware of the propaganda potential of Romanticism: it, too, was trying to establish its cultural legitimacy by harking back to medieval roots.

In his later account, Hugo probably telescoped the three events – the departure for Blois, the Légion d'Honneur and the ballad – for the convenience of future biographers.[17] The false coincidence forms a symbolic self-portrait and establishes Hugo's equality with his father. He could not have known, of course, that a later generation would interpret the ballad, in which two blaspheming bowmen camp next to an isolated tower and are murdered overnight by a mysterious supernatural force, as a tale of two Victor Hugos racked by Oedipal guilt.[18]

For three weeks, General Hugo and his youngest son behaved like old friends. Since the General's wife was there, and with a new baby to monopolize the conversation, sensitive topics like politics, Eugène and the first Mme Hugo could easily be avoided. The General had taken up treasure-hunting and conducted Victor on a tour of Roman and Gallic excavations – a craze which Hugo was soon to turn into a national campaign. They visited the magnificent, decaying shell of the Château de Chambord, where Hugo exemplified the older approach to ancient monuments: 'All sorts of magic, poetry and even *madness* are represented in the admirable *bizarrerie* of that palace of knights and fairies,' he told Saint-Valry, using all his favourite words. 'I carved my name at the top of the highest tower, and from the summit I took away with me a little stone and moss as well as a piece of the window frame on which François I inscribed the lines: "*Souvent femme varie / Bien fol est qui s'y fie!*" '*[19] A good example of Hugo's contention that the printed word spelt the end of that older form of writing, architecture.

The most revealing moment of the visit to Blois has slipped between the cracks of the larger events of 1825. One evening, as he sat on the terrace of the General's country retreat, looking out over the sand-flats and poplars, the poet who was about to celebrate the Monarchy's great moment wrote a strangely unspecific little poem about a captured city in the East: 'Hymne Oriental'.[20] It was the first of the future *Orientales* and one of the very few poems he had written which did not appear to commemorate any public or private event, though it was written on the day that he was officially inducted into the Légion d'Honneur.

'Hymne Oriental' might easily have been a scene of modern warfare and a defence of French imperialism; yet the dying inhabitants of the unnamed city are little more than pretexts for a pretty evocation of the flames skipping merrily over the disaster area. Just when the imagined reality is most horrific, the butchered priests are drowned out with an amazing fusillade of plosive alliteration which would have had the red pens of the Academy furiously twitching:

> *Les prêtres qui priaient ont péri par l'épée.*†

And the 'tiny little children, squashed under paving-stones' (an interesting image for a doting father) die a luscious, lingering death in a daringly Romantic line with an enjambment and a displaced caesura.

Hugo's gory vision is all the more surprising since, at this stage in his life, he could hardly be called an inspirational poet. From 1824 to 1827, he averaged only two lines a day. The sheer size of his complete

* 'Women are often fickle, / 'Tis folly to trust them!' Used in *Le Roi S'Amuse* (1832) and in Verdi's adaptation, *Rigoletta* ('*La donna e mobile . . .*').
† 'The praying priests have perished by the sword.'

works and the length of his life suggest constant, regular motions producing an ever larger pile of manuscripts. Close up, large gaps appear in which his brain seems to have resorbed almost everything it imagined. Only one poem was written in 1826, and the frequency of his verse is visibly tied to the dates of publishers' contracts. 'Hymne Oriental' belongs to that other, unprofessional oeuvre which, as he learned to exploit the unexpected deviations of his mind, gradually became indistinguishable from the marketed commodity.

Seized at the moment of its creation, the oriental fantasy from the Loire Valley is a clue to the direction his mind was taking. The poem in which he devolved power to the words themselves was also the first poem in which an uncaring sovereign is seen through the eyes of the masses. Something that would soon amaze Hugo's royalist friends had already happened in his verse, on a level where political allegiances hardly seem to exist and where different life-forms are in control: 'Words know the secret of that sphinx, the human mind.' 'A sullen horde, they come and go within us.' 'At their breath . . . obscure enormity slowly drops its leaves.'[21]

The impression that another mind was already whispering in Hugo's verse, in contradiction of the poet, can be tested by a statistical experiment. Calculating the number of matching sounds in each rhyme-pair gives the following averages, at three-yearly intervals:*

$$1816 - 2.14$$
$$1819 - 2.23$$
$$1822 - 2.58$$
$$1825 - 2.67$$

The size of his rhymes had been steadily growing. Since 1822, they had reached a size that is almost never found in French verse, and then only before the classical period. These figures indicate an increasing tendency to allow the words to dictate the meaning of the poem, to fit the sense to the sound. They also reveal a vital connection between Hugo's verse and his perception of reality.

When the French army stamped its way through the Spanish Civil

---

* Rhymes in French are based on the number of matching phonemes. A rhyme is said to be 'poor' if only one phoneme matches (*vin – libertin*), 'sufficient' if two phonemes match (*vérité – beauté*) and 'rich' if three or more match (*Adèle – fidèle*).

War in 1823 to restore the Bourbon king, Hugo had used the expedition as a pretext for an ode to his father, rather artificially associating the destroyer of Burgos with the royalist mission:

> Sometimes I dream that I take up your sword,
> O my Father, and, borne by my ardour,
> I follow our glorious soldiers to the land of El Cid.

Why, then, had this model of militarism invoked his prizes at the Jeux Floraux to negotiate a legal precedent which granted him special dispensation from military service?[22] Why had he not followed Alfred de Vigny to Spain? The whole idea was deeply unconvincing, personally and politically.

In this least plausible of poems, the average size of the rhymes is enormous: 2.81 – and though the fact is invisible to the mind's naked eye, this is one of the most richly rhymed poems in French literature. Just when he was trying to bring the two opposing armies of his mind together – the King and his father, Napoleonic Spain and Bourbon Spain – these apparently arbitrary coincidences of sound were setting out from the decorative edge of the poem, pushing back into the body of the verse, as if to reinforce the structure. Academic critics were right: incomprehensibility – or a different kind of sense altogether – was eating away at the rhetoric.

Ironically, the General's role in the poetic revolution signalled by 'Hymne Oriental' may have been more decisive than any political influence. Before the visit, he had been encouraging Victor to try out his 'little remedy' for chest colds: a decoction of opium poppies mixed with milk and honey.[23] If the remedy was administered at Blois, it might have had the appropriate effect: the flippant omnipotence, the disappearance of the narrator's personality, the sense of uninterpreted symbols, even the oriental setting, are all characteristic of opium-inspired literature.[24] Some of Hugo's fantasies may in any case be transpositions of actual hallucinations. He appears to have enjoyed unusually detailed phosphene images – the patterns that swim about under the eyelid[25] – or an unusually strong desire to cultivate them, for example by the Promethean habit of staring at the sun.[26] This might explain the dark patches which had begun to affect his vision and which led a medical student in 1828 to predict imminent blindness. On that occasion, Hugo thought of Homer and Milton and 'started hoping that perhaps one day I would go blind'.[27]

*

WHETHER OR NOT his father's remedy helped to change the course of French Romanticism, Hugo had recently come under the influence of a man who had a stronger effect than any drug: Charles Nodier.[28] After three weeks in Blois, Hugo left Adèle with her parents-in-law to join Nodier in Paris. From there, they set off on the specially sanded roads for the coronation at Rheims.

Nodier was twenty-two years older than Hugo and had done everything except produce his definitive masterpiece. He had been a botanist, an entomologist specializing in antennae, an opium-addict, a gambler, a Romantic theoretician before French Romanticism existed, and a bibliographer with a passion for accuracy and for perpetrating hoaxes (a surprisingly common combination). When Hugo was born in Besançon in 1802, Nodier, the son of a local judge, had just returned there from Paris with gonorrhoea and a well-deserved reputation as an anarchist. He wrote his autobiography, *Moi-Même*, at the age of twenty, with a chapter consisting entirely of punctuation marks; apocryphal memoirs which are still sometimes used as genuine historical documents; and an anonymous *Histoire des Sociétés Secrètes de l'Armée* which might now be celebrated as one of the first French historical novels had it not purported to be a faithful summary of conspiracies against Napoleon, including an abortive ambush which Nodier helped to organize. He was the author of a selection of maxims, some of which were his own and which he published under the title *Pensées de Shakespeare*, and of a dictionary of onomatopoeic words – one of the most readable dictionaries ever written – designed as an antidote to the miserably proscriptive *Dictionnaire de l'Académie Française*.[29] After working for Johnson's collaborator, Sir Herbert Croft, he took his wife and daughter to Illyria, where he ran a tetraglot newspaper in Ljubljana and collected local vampire legends. He even, apparently, met a vampire in the flesh, which gives his Gothic tales an unusual claim to accuracy.

When Hugo met him, Nodier had just been made librarian of the second library in France, the Bibliothèque de l'Arsenal. Its *salon*, which now smelled of Mme Nodier's home cooking and was soon to be adorned with a bust of Victor Hugo, had become a refuge for writers from *La Muse Française*.[30] It was the only non-sectarian salon in Paris. The regulars came to be known as the Cénacle. With a capital 'C', the word normally designated the room where the Last Supper took place. Nowadays it is usually taken to refer to Hugo and his disciples.

The reason Hugo found himself sitting next to Nodier in a carriage bound for Rheims in the late spring of 1825 was that Nodier had had another good idea. He had suggested to the Arts Minister that he, Nodier, be named official historiographer of the coronation, which, of course, he would describe in his official account – which he never wrote – as 'the positive end to the disastrous age of revolution' (because the royal succession was now assured).[31]

Nodier was duly appointed and suggested that Hugo apply for the non-existent job of official poet. Hugo was reluctant to be seen cadging favours. He wrote to Vigny with the acceptable version:

> Before you hear from anyone else, I must tell you, dear Alfred, of the unexpected favours which have sought me out in my father's retreat. The King has given me the Cross [of the Légion d'Honneur] and is inviting me to his Coronation.

And to another friend, Jean-Baptiste Soulié, sandwiched between an 'I' and a 'my': 'I assure you that the pleasure this news will bring you greatly increases my own satisfaction.'[32]

The fact is that Hugo had specifically requested the award,[33] and a letter from his father-in-law proves that he had also asked to join Nodier at Rheims.[34] It was an excellent career move, guaranteeing mass publicity for whatever he chose to write.

The coronation itself was a disappointment and a revelation.[35] The cardboard scenery erected in front of Rheims Cathedral seemed to symbolize the flimsiness of the regime, but at least it was Gothic: 'Such as it is,' he told Adèle, 'the decorations are another sign of the progress of Romantic ideas. Six months ago, they would have turned the old Frankish church into a Greek temple.'[36] Medieval sculptures which protruded from the façade had been lopped off by masons in case they fell on the King. Hugo picked up a head of Christ and later remembered this as one of the crucial incidents which turned him in the direction of socialism.[37] His own interpretation of the event refers to only one aspect: the dereliction of the cathedral. The other elements – Jesus Christ chiselled off the face of his own church and his recuperation by Victor Hugo – are left to haunt the mind.

At the time, Hugo's main worries were the cost of his uniform – culottes, stockings, buckled shoes, feathered hat and sword – and the price of food: his account book shows two dinners costing 15 francs each.[38] He fretted at having to occupy a room in a house rented by an actress (a notoriously promiscuous profession)[39] and stood in the rain under Rheims cathedral reading tear-stained letters from Adèle. The General's wife had turned cold and unsympathetic. Adèle was spending hours alone in her room, feeling sorry for herself. She clung to her baby and the thought that she would soon be reunited with 'the greatest poet of the age, the most adorable and most adored of men!'[40] With Victor away, the decorous front had collapsed, and from now on, relations with the General would be shored up with polite formulae and a very public display of devotion.

In other words, nothing had changed: a disintegrating family and an increasingly successful attempt to integrate himself into French history. Professionally, the coronation was one of the highlights of Hugo's career. His stunningly old-fashioned ode – one of the last of its kind to be written by a major poet, excluding poet laureates – was published in several newspapers. The King, who 'shone like a beacon o'er the undulating crowd', bought 300 copies, ordered a special luxury edition from the Imprimerie Royale and rewarded Hugo with a Sèvres dinner service.[41]

The lasting benefit of the trip to Rheims was far more valuable than royalties, prestige and a dinner service that was too good to use. Hugo had spent a week in the company of the man who came to be known as 'the Schoolmaster of Romanticism', and learned his lessons so well that he effectively banished Nodier to the suburbs of literary history.

The word 'influence' normally conjures up a pleasant image of collaboration or natural affinity. Hugo engaged in a literary equivalent of asset-stripping. Virtually every new aspect of his work from 1824 until the Romantic putsch of 1830 can be traced back to Nodier: the attack on the classical unities, the deification of Shakespeare (whose works Hugo did not discover for himself until the 1850s),[42] parodies of the classical style in the *Nouvelles Odes*,[43] an erudite interest in folklore and the supernatural, a subversive sense of humour, and the detection of vanished civilizations in the ruins that were being cleared away in the name of progress or for profit.[44]

Nodier also taught Hugo how to exploit the commercial potential of Romanticism: 'Classical writers are approved of, but Romantics are read,' he observed in his review of *Han d'Islande*, going on to reveal that 'M. Victor Hugo thinks in four or five languages' and that *Han d'Islande* had sold '*12,000 copies*' (not bad for a book with a print-run of 1200).[45] Hugo took the hint. In a preface to the second edition of *Han d'Islande*, he alluded serenely to 'the immense and popular success of this work'.

By appropriating Nodier's work, Hugo was taking advantage of his suicidal instinct – the instinct that led him to vandalize the guillotine in Besançon town square, to shatter his life's work into fragments, to attribute some of his best work to pseudonyms, and to become the evangelist of remarkable individuals whom he tried to re-create in an image worthy of his enthusiasm. For Hugo, a talent for self-effacement was an irresistible attraction.

Socially, the trip to Rheims had been a great success. Nodier had enjoyed the spectacle of the straitlaced Victor Hugo being forced to have a good time. He now planned another free trip. He, Hugo, the two wives, Léopoldine and a painter called Gué would go on holiday to the Swiss Alps, calling in at Lamartine's estate near Mâcon. The holiday would be funded by a publisher, Urbain Canel. In exchange, Canel would receive a collection of drawings, prose and verse to be entitled *Voyage Poétique et Pittoresque au Mont Blanc et à la Vallée de Chamouny*. '2250 francs for four paltry odes', Hugo told his father. 'It's a good price. . . . Nodier is coming with us.'[46]

They set off in two coaches on 2 August 1825. It was an adventure, but not as heroic as Hugo had hoped. The route to Switzerland was already well trodden by tourists, and even as long ago as 1825 a conscious effort was needed to produce the unexpected. There were some good snapshots for the album, though: a slim, fair-haired Victor Hugo arrested by a gendarme for wearing the ribbon of the Légion d'Honneur (how many twenty-three-year-olds had the Légion d'Honneur?); Victor Hugo scaling the Montenvers and nearly led to his death by a careless guide; Adèle vowing never to go gypsying again. In her life, it was a tremendous experience, which she recorded forty years later in the biography of her husband with a passionate recollection of the discomfort.

Hugo himself produced a short account which sounds like an edited recording of Nodier's voice and which could almost have been written without leaving Paris. The formative incident of the journey was the exact opposite of what his Romantic readers would hope to find in the book, and so he never mentioned it. But Adèle remembered the deep impression it made on him. In keeping with his chivalric image, Lamartine had invited Hugo in a recent volume of Épîtres to visit the unkempt ruins of his ancient pile – two turrets 'veiled by Time's dye', clad in tufted ivy and haunted by the crow: ''Tis there that friendship calls thee.' Hugo arrived to find a flat-roofed, modern villa with yellow walls. In answer to his query, Lamartine explained that grey stone was depressing and ivy caused rising damp. So much for the Voyage Poétique et Pittoresque. Hugo was horrified at Lamartine's 'improvements'. He had been deceived.

This at least is a real insight into Hugo, far more revealing than the snapshots: his descriptions of places are not the fantasies of Lamartine and his contemporaries, but reproductions of what he actually saw. Hugo was harbouring a serious misconception about the Romantic movement hc proposed to lead. He failed to see that the Romantic journey was Romantic precisely because it failed to meet the ideal expectations of the traveller. Nodier supplied him with a point of view to be going on with, and, rather eerily, the role of 'Victor Hugo' in 1825 seems to have been taken by Charles Nodier. He behaved exactly as Hugo would behave on his later travels – eating local food, concocting an anecdotal soup of popular legends and his own tall stories, leaving witty reminders of his passing. Next to 'Purpose of Visit' in the hotel register at Geneva, he wrote, 'Come to overturn your Republic': the result of too many 'Keep off the grass' signs. Hugo reproduced this 'Bohemian' behaviour on his later journeys with a studious attention to detail.

*

THE *VOYAGE POÉTIQUE ET PITTORESQUE* was never published because Canel – one of the unsung subsidizers of the Romantic movement – went bankrupt.[47] Hugo set to work instead on a less recent version of himself. He took the story of the slaves' revolt in San Domingo which had appeared in *Le Conservateur Littéraire* and inflated it into a short novel, notably by adding a volatile, voodoo-practising dwarf called Habibrah.

Bug-Jargal II was published anonymously in January 1826 and criticized for its blatant lack of realism. Strangely, the bone of contention for most critics was not the dwarf but the enslaved African prince. Even sixty years on, Bug-Jargal was felt to be 'too violent a call upon the imagination'.[48] At the time, Lady Morgan found the hero 'too virtuous' because, 'according to physiologists, the African organization does not lend itself to such qualities'. *Le Globe* observed that few White men – let alone Negroes – were such models of courage, generosity and good taste . . .[49]

In short, *Bug-Jargal* is a splendid example of the creative imagination escaping the prejudices of its age. Though the fantasy of extreme sexual potency survives, and though the Black characters are sinister or comical because they try to ape their White superiors, when Bug-Jargal hurls himself between the White heroine and a ravening crocodile, Western literature acquires one of its first wholly admirable Black heroes.

Even more remarkable, Hugo was also escaping his own prejudices. The White hero had a new name, Léopold (his father's Christian name) d'Auverney (a place-name from Mme Hugo's region and one of Hugo's early pseudonyms): an ideal composite of both parents, which might explain why the character is so psychologically unconvincing. But it is the Black hero who owns the emblematic 'ug', like the Negro mentioned fleetingly in *Les Misérables*: Homère Hogu.[50] He also has the face of a Black Hugo: 'a large forehead – especially surprising in a Negro; the disdainful swelling of lip and nostril which gave him such a proud and powerful air'.[51]

Is this why the conservative Hugo had espoused one of the great liberal causes and was displaying what *Le Globe*'s reviewer saw as 'revolutionary' tendencies? Written by the eighteen-year-old, re-modelled by the twenty-three-year-old, *Bug-Jargal* showed that sympathizing with social, political and racial outcasts made it possible to feel compassion for the outcast in himself.

So far as can be judged from the measurements of the head, his brain was by no means above the average in size; his face was unduly large and broad as compared to the head, and gave an impression of animality; there were many signs of lack of facial symmetry, and the lips and the nose were thick, the eyes small.[52]

This is not a description of Bug-Jargal but of Hugo himself. An anthropologist with a measuring stick was given access to a cast of his head and produced this 'scientific' confirmation of the idea that Victor Hugo was not entirely Caucasian, a 'savage' who saw the world in images not in concepts. This was also Hugo's worry. His sensitivity about the shape of his body – specifically, a slightly protuberant hip[53] – was part of a deeper anxiety that he did not after all belong to the noble race whose glory he had just celebrated at Rheims. The post-revolutionary ego was outgrowing society's institutions – but only in the novel; and even then, Hugo rather oddly decided after all that the slaves were not ready for emancipation.

Apart from the publication of *Bug-Jargal* and the *Odes et Ballades*, the writing of one poem and the elaboration of a huge, unwieldy play called *Cromwell*, 1826 is practically a blank in Hugo's life. A period of gestation. A son, Charles, was born in November. The few letters which survive show Hugo rushing about Paris, talking to publishers, building up the family business: 'The mother feeds the children, the father feeds the mother. More happiness means more work.'[54]

The absence of finished products can be explained in several ways: Léopoldine was a new outlet for the urge to instruct and entertain, and in some ways a model for Hugo's relationship with his readers. His working day was shortened even more by the need to rest his eyes – usually a sign in Hugo of some internal struggle. And then there are the reasons which hover in the margins of any biography: periods of passivity and fogginess which Hugo came to associate with the magnetic influence of the Ocean.[55]

It was on 9 February 1827 that a brand-new Victor Hugo shot into view and showed what his mind had been mulling over, the thoughts he had been sharpening into a conviction. An explosive ode 'À la

Colonne de la Place Vendôme' appeared in the *Journal des Débats*. It was a response to an incident which had occurred at the Austrian Embassy in Paris. Four French dukes had been announced at a reception without their titles – understandably, since these titles were the names of battles in which Napoleon had massacred the Austrians. Hugo interpreted the incident as an insult to his father. The visit to Blois had ended as a diplomatic disaster, but the ode, written in defence of his father's memory, was a public triumph. It was a nationalistic hymn to the great phallic monument, the 'indelible trophy' forged from enemy cannon which still stood on the Place Vendôme, although the Napoleon on top had since been melted down to make the statue of Henri IV whose re-erection Hugo had celebrated in 1819.[56]

Hugo had read *Le Mémorial de Sainte-Hélène* – the record of Napoleon's life in exile, published after his death in 1821 – and had already inducted the Emperor into his personal mythology.[57] Since, in the imagination of the masses, Napoleon was now a mythical, revolutionary messiah, a focus for every kind of social disgruntlement, Hugo's defence of his father's role in Napoleon's victories was an implicit criticism of the current, monarchist regime.

The ode to the Vendôme column meant that Hugo had re-organized his political prejudices and rationalized his contradictions: he was drawing a line between himself and the legitimists, publicly declaring himself to be the son of a Napoleonic general, and thereby allowing himself to exploit the full potential of his colourful past: 'I who not long ago was stirred / By the sound of my Saxon name, mingled with battle cries!'; 'I whose first toy was the gold rosette of a sword!'

For the generation born around 1810 which had glimpsed the Empire through the nursery window, Hugo's splendid ode was a poetic validation of their experience and, by implication, a giant leap sideways to the left. The liberal press was won over at a stroke: Victor Hugo was a good thing.

Hugo's 'desertion' of the legitimist cause has been hugely exaggerated, not least by Hugo himself. It should be noted that his royalist odes had never offered the slightest argument in favour of a monarchist system of government. Neither did he present a reasoned case for favouring liberalism until several months after his defection. In any case, the extremist, Ultra point of view was already a form of opposition, as Hugo had shown by protesting in *La Muse Française* against censorship of the press.

The disturbing aspect of the new Hugo is not that he changed his mind about politics. At this stage in his life, the destiny of France is a red herring. Hugo mentions his own desertion of legitimism so often precisely because it was so easy to defend. But another, related desertion deserves more attention. When *Cromwell* appeared in December 1827 with its manifesto-preface, the man who had done so much to fertilize French Romanticism in general and Victor Hugo in particular was barely acknowledged: only two bland references to Charles Nodier but dozens of phrases and ideas lifted directly from his work.[58]

The erasure of Nodier testifies to Hugo's anxiety about the extent of his influence: a few acknowledgements would hardly have diluted Hugo's glory. But Nodier also belonged to the same liberal generation as General Hugo and he may unwittingly have been paying the price for Hugo's reconciliation with his father.

The friendship survived in a fossilized, ceremonial form until 1829, when Nodier appeared to suggest in an article that Hugo's *Orientales* owed more to the East India Company than to oriental scholarship.[59] Hugo decided to believe he had been betrayed like Julius Caesar or Jesus Christ: 'You, too, Nodier . . . I care not about the daggers of my enemies but I do feel the pinprick of a friend.'[60] Nodier's reply was an example of that velvety sarcasm which so impressed and exasperated Hugo, combined with the abject devotion from which he had decided to unstick himself: 'All my literary life is in you,' wrote Nodier. 'If I am to be remembered, it will be because you willed it and because I was, not even the obscure precursor *who is unworthy to unloose your shoe's latchet*, but simply an old friend who cherished your young glory and celebrated your birth.'[61]

The real volte-face took place in the world of literary politics and the new hero was Hugo himself.

A month before the ode on the Vendôme column, a dazzling, two-part review of the *Odes et Ballades* had appeared in *Le Globe*.[62] It explained in great detail precisely why Victor Hugo was not as famous as he might have been: the solemn, mystical, royalist side of his work

– the declamatory Hugo of *La Muse Française* and the namby-pamby Société des Bonnes Lettres – was out of tune with the age. The new generation was liberal.

By the time the next edition of the *Odes et Ballades* appeared in 1828, Hugo had learnt the lesson and firmly believed in what was best for his career, though he inadvertently gave away his true thought. The new generation was the army that would fight his battles: 'A strong school is rising, and a strong generation is growing in the shadows for it.' As if the audience existed for the poet . . . A *coup d'état* was in the air.

*

ON 15 APRIL 1827, the Hugos moved to a new home at 11 Rue Notre-Dame-des-Champs: a first-floor apartment separated from the street by an avenue of trees.[63] From his window, Hugo looked down on an overgrown garden with a pond and a rustic bridge – long since sacrificed to the Métro and the Boulevard Raspail.[64] One gate led to an alley and the Jardin du Luxembourg; another led to the open country and the road to Vaugirard, with its taverns and windmills, and its gorgeous sunsets. An ideal setting for the poet who, in the preface to the *Odes et Ballades*, contrasted the ordered classical gardens of Versailles with the New World virgin forest of modern poetry. Here, Hugo was to start a Cénacle of his own. It already had its intellectual guru – masquerading as the master's devoted servant – a distractingly ugly and timid young man with ginger hair, huge ears, a 'proboscis', and a tendency to dribble; he rubbed his hands and mumbled, never looked anyone in the eye and said brilliant, memorable things: Charles-Augustin Sainte-Beuve, author of the review of the *Odes et Ballades* which had explained to Hugo how much he had to gain by becoming a liberal.

The first characteristic act of the new Hugo was to send out a scout to reconnoitre the land he hoped to conquer. He took from his drawer a play which he had begun with Alexandre Soumet in 1822 and finished on his own: a prose adaptation of Walter Scott's *Kenilworth*. *Amy Robsart* was a risky mixture of historical melodrama and fairground farce. It had a red-haired dwarf called Flibbertigibbet and several tendentious comments about arrogant aristocrats.

No general risks his finest troops on an exploratory mission. Hugo handed the manuscript to his eighteen-year-old brother-in-law, Paul Foucher, and told him to offer it to the Odéon as his own work. The play was accepted, Delacroix designed the costumes, and it opened and closed on 13 February 1828. *Amy Robsart* was laughed off the stage and torn to pieces in the newspapers, mostly because of its 'trivial expressions': it was a tragedy with jokes, and had a heroine who, when she was about to be rescued, worried about the state of her hair.[65] Since the theatre director had leaked the information that the true author was Victor Hugo, the cat-calls were probably aimed at him and the Romantic movement in general.

When the play reached its inaudible conclusion, the director, according to tradition, came to the front of the stage and, as the auditorium fell silent, named the author: M. Paul Foucher.

The morning after, a letter appeared in the *Journal des Débats*: Victor Hugo confessed that he was 'not entirely unconnected with the work. The play contains a few words and a few fragments of scene which are by me, and I should say that these are perhaps the passages which were booed the most.'

This, of course, was several acts short of the truth and has been interpreted as a disgraceful betrayal of young Foucher. The most revealing aspect of the account in *Victor Hugo Raconté* is that, even after being doctored by Hugo's loyal disciples, it still contains the incriminating contradiction: Hugo's authorship of the play and the letter in which he simultaneously accepted and absolved himself of responsibility. The only possible conclusion is that Hugo genuinely believed that he was acting – or would be seen to have been acting – in Foucher's interests.

It may well be that a partial confession was less embarrassing for the bogus author. Foucher did in fact survive to become a successful playwright and journalist, with the help of Hugo. It should also be said that there was something about Foucher that attracted practical jokers: probably his extreme short-sightedness, the fact that he never bore a grudge, and an indestructible gullibility which sent him hurrying off to non-existent fancy-dress parties and made him publish any piece of news that landed on his desk, even if it contradicted what he had said the day before.[66] Hugo was simply making a more efficient use than most of his brother-in-law's personality.

Nevertheless, the *Amy Robsart* incident, and later episodes like it, leave a residue of unanswered questions and niggling doubts. The temptation is to head for the nearest moral certainty and to say either that Hugo was shamelessly exploiting his brother-in-law or that he was bravely carrying the can. The idea behind this approach is that one particular moral trait presides over each episode in a life and continues to prevail until the episode has come to an end.

But if the ambiguities are allowed to survive, they begin to point to something far more disquieting than personal courage or brazen egotism: Hugo's self-incrimination by betrayal and the creation of circumstances in which he himself was likely to be betrayed. Some of his letters show a tendency to revel in the 'disease of hate, calumny and persecution' which he seemed to bring on all his supporters.[67] Real guilt was preferable to an irrational malaise. All this time, brother Eugène had been mouldering in the asylum, incontinent, dropsical and catatonic.[68] Further back in time, there was another source of vague guilt: his parents' separation – especially troubling now that the reconciliation with his father had made it harder to preserve the image of a perfect mother.

Hugo's continual polishing of his halo should not be allowed to disguise the fact that he was also directly responsible for the damaging attacks on his moral integrity which continue to this day. The persistent ambiguity of his actions is, after all, extraordinary. Whether it was intentional or not, the effect of his self-glorification and manipulation was to focus on himself the critical eye of biographers. 'And so,' he wrote in the *Préface de Cromwell*, 'the author delivers himself up once again to the anger of journalists', while his play 'exposes itself to the eyes of the public, like the cripple of the Gospel – alone, poor, and naked: *solus, pauper, nudus*'.[69]

When Hugo talks about his audience, he normally means, potentially, the rest of the world and – as the *Préface de Cromwell* implies – God. Consequently, the more notorious he became, the easier it would be to carry on the argument with his conscience and, eventually, win it over to his side.

General Hugo died of a heart attack on 29 January 1828. A month later, Hugo described him as 'the man who loved me more than any other, a kind and noble being ... a father whose eye never left me'.[70]

Biographically, the last phrase is blatantly untrue, but in the context of Hugo's work, it has a peculiar resonance – a reminder that, for a lonely person, remorse is the most faithful and communicative companion.

> Then he descended alone beneath the gloomy vault;
> And when he had sat on his chair in the darkness,
> And the cavern had been closed on his brow,
> The eye was in the tomb and was staring at Cain.[71]

CHAPTER EIGHT

H

(1828–1830)

GENERAL HUGO WAS BURIED on the hill to the east of Paris, in the Père Lachaise cemetery, on 31 January 1828. Almost alone among Romantics, Hugo despised the cemetery for its 'hideous, frilly little buildings with their boxes and compartments where good Parisians tidy their fathers away into drawers ... Family vaults: the ultimate bourgeois chest-of-drawers!'[1]

The General was filed away and labelled with all his honours by a remarkably unbourgeois group of people: 'Madame la Comtesse Hugo [the General's widow]; Monsieur le Comte & Madame la Comtesse Abel Hugo; Monsieur le Vicomte Eugène Hugo, Monsieur le Baron & Madame la Baronne Victor Hugo'. Needless to say, 'Monsieur le Vicomte' was unable to attend, being detained in a padded cell.

This announcement of General Hugo's death – and not the invitation to an audience with Charles X in 1829 – was the first public appearance of 'Baron Victor Hugo',[2] an adopted title which has generated hundreds of pages of pious sneering, perhaps confirming Baudelaire's sarcastic aphorism: 'The immense appetite we have for biography comes from a deep-seated sense of equality.'[3]

The commonest sneer is that Hugo dubbed himself a baron just when he had supposedly woken up to the injustice of the monarchist regime. But the paradox is illusory. The General's hereditary title,[4] which had never been recognized by the Restoration, represented what Hugo's funeral oration pointedly called 'the glorious wars of the Revolution' and 'that marvellous history of the Empire'.[5] Like the ode on the Vendôme column, the fanfare of names in the death announcement was a political protest. The connotation is made plain in *Les Misérables*, where Marius marks his father's death and his own abandonment of royalism by having a set of visiting cards printed for 'Baron Marius Pontmercy'.[6]

The other source of ill-informed gloating is Hugo's letter to the Minister of the Interior in August 1829. He then extended his noble ancestry back another 300 years: 'My family, noble since the year 1531, is an old servant of the State.'[7] No such connection has ever been established. The Hugo family tree rises rapidly into the unmapped obscurity which usually denotes peasant origins.* But this, too, was part of the paternal inheritance. 'My relationship with the Bishop of Ptolémaïs [Louis Hugo] is a family tradition,' he told a genealogist in 1867. 'All I know is what my father told me.'[8] When the Hugophobe biographer, Edmond Biré, triumphantly produced a document proving that Hugo's grandfather was a labourer, Hugo was still able to point out that, like 'everyone else', his forebears included cobblers as well as lords. (A private note on the subject replaces 'cobblers' with 'carpenters', and 'everyone else' with 'Jesus Christ'.)[9]

In view of the fact that Hugo was about to turn the Romantic movement into an independent society with its own sacred texts and anniversaries; considering, too, that he became the focus of adulation unknown since Napoleon, his self-ennoblement might just as well be criticized as too modest. Genealogical niceties are in any case a distraction from the real eccentricity of his ancestral fantasies. A whole fairyland of Hugos inhabits his work: sometimes they were people he supposed to be real ancestors, like Hugo of Besançon, who 'practised the black arts' in a secret cell in Notre-Dame; sometimes, half-fabulous creatures who just happened to share his name, like 'Hugo Eagle-Head', skulking in his Rhineland cavern. By the dictionary, he was connected with a German word meaning 'intelligence' or 'spirit' and with the English 'high' and 'huge'. The H of 'Hugo' is also the mighty rock formation at the centre of *Les*

---

* This did not prevent the anonymous reviewer (Mary Duclaux) of Gustave Simon's *L'Enfance de Victor Hugo* in *The Times Literary Supplement* of 23 September 1904 from asserting, inexplicably, that Hugo's 'most remote known ancestor . . . was an English knacker settled in Lorraine – a point that has escaped M. Simon'. The point also escaped Mary Duclaux's own biography of Hugo, published in 1921. On Hugo's most famous, unknown relative, see p. 482.

Travailleurs de la Mer with a shipwrecked steamer as its bar; and in the capital city which, if some had had their way, would now be called Hugopolis, stood a giant medieval hieroglyphic, 'an enormous two-headed sphinx squatting in the middle of the city' – the building which came to be known as Victor Hugo's cathedral: Notre-Dame.

These harmless distortions – typical of the Romantic age – are negligible compared to the blatant rewriting of modern history in Hugo's funeral oration. In Brittany, apparently, his father had been a model of 'humanity' and 'courage'. Later, unpublished remarks make it clear that Hugo had a more accurate impression of his father's qualities:

> My father was very kind. But one day a traitor is brought to him.
> He says, 'Shoot the blighter,' and turns his horse away.[10]

The ability to take a long-term view of things was also part of the inheritance – far more valuable than the mess of debts and legal fees which the General left behind. In 1829, Alfred de Vigny noticed a new tone creeping into Victor's conversation. 'Brutus' Hugo lived on:

> The Victor I loved is no more. He used to be a touch fanatical in his royalism and religion, chaste as a young girl and rather timid, too. It suited him quite well ... But now he likes to make saucy remarks and is turning into a liberal, which does not suit him – but it's only to be expected! He started out mature and is entering on his youth, living after writing, whereas one really ought to write only after having lived.[11]

In Vigny's view, the pure could only be corrupted from without. Hugo's personal Satan was the young man who had reviewed the *Odes et Ballades* in 1827. The review was one of Sainte-Beuve's first attempts to establish himself as a critic after abandoning his medical studies – or after deciding to put his medical studies to a new use. When the Hugos settled in the Rue Notre-Dame-des-Champs, Sainte-Beuve moved with his mother to a flat in the same street. It was the start of the most productive and mutually destructive friendship in French literature. The two men organized themselves into a machine which consolidated Hugo's reputation and eventually crushed the friendship: Sainte-Beuve converted Hugo's poetic genius into intellectual insights which then became an influence on Hugo's poetry.

The following character sketch was written by Vigny after a bad review by Sainte-Beuve of his novel, *Cinq-Mars*, but the irritation probably only sharpened his critical faculties:

> Sainte-Beuve is a rather ugly little man with a common face and very round shoulders. When he talks, he looks like a servile, reverential old woman.... Without being an instinctive poet, he has written some excellent verse by dint of sheer intelligence. He behaves very humbly and has made himself a henchman of Victor Hugo, who encouraged him to turn his hand to poetry. But Victor Hugo, having spent his entire life going from one man to another, helping himself to whatever they had to offer, manages to extract from Sainte-Beuve a vast amount of knowledge which he did not possess before. Though he addresses him like a master, Hugo is Sainte-Beuve's pupil. He is well aware that Sainte-Beuve is providing him with a literary education but he does not see to what extent that clever young man dominates him politically.[12]

Neither did he notice that Sainte-Beuve was also drawn to the family home by the dark eyes of Mme Hugo, like a critic drawn to a mysterious text: 'one of those strange and rare beauties to which our eyes must first grow accustomed'.[13]

*

THE VICTOR HUGO who descended from the necropolis of Père Lachaise in January 1828 had already provided the Romantic movement with the magisterial text which, according to Théophile Gautier, 'shone in our eyes like the Tablets of the Law on Mount Sinai'.[14]

The *Préface de Cromwell*, published on 5 December 1827, was the codification of the precepts, the hoisting of the Romantic flag, the hors-d'oeuvre of an unperformable play which turned into the main course. Hugo's 25,000-word manifesto may have contained a lot a twaddle, as one of Musset's characters complains, 'but at least it was something'.[15]

Though he had it up his sleeve all along, Hugo pretended to extrapolate his main point from a brief disquisition on the history of human civilization. Art was now in its third phase – old age, verging on second childhood. Since the advent of Christianity, it had been impossible to believe that perfect beauty could exist on Earth. Hence the coexistence in modern art of the grotesque and the sublime, the ugly and the beautiful. The idea was translated by journalists into the famous phrase, which Hugo never wrote: 'Ugliness is Beauty.'

The so-called 'theory' of the Grotesque is a splendid example of Hugo's ability to reconcile productivity with ideology: 'Ugliness is one detail of a great whole which escapes us and which harmonizes, not with man alone, but with all creation.' This meant, first, that art would in future perform a quasi-religious function and the artist himself would be a prophet (the verb '*harmoniser*' is a significant borrowing from the language of mystical socialism); second, that absolutely any aspect of existence could be used as raw material. Flattering, unforgettable and convenient, it was the most influential aesthetic treatise of the century.

The *Préface de Cromwell* is designed to be read once and enjoyed for its invigorating effect. Anyone who reads it twice is condemned to read it a hundred times. Walking back down the tracks along which Hugo's ghost-train has just propelled us shows it to be a muddle of hastily erected placards, and there is something of a cruel joke in the fact that generations of students have been asked to study the *Préface de Cromwell* and come up with a coherent description of the Romantic movement. Ideas which are still sometimes considered revolutionary, such as the natural fluidity of language, or art as a deliberate distortion of reality, go hand in hand with a defence of monologues and the classical unity of action; verse as a dam against 'vulgarity'.

In practice, the content mattered less than the tone and the inspiring sense of new possibilities. Very few of Hugo's imitators were stupid enough to think that he was being objective. But instead of being irritated by his arrogance, they were grateful to him for having shown that it was possible to apply such belligerent enthusiasm to literature. The *Préface de Cromwell* created writers as Kitchener's poster created soldiers in 1914: 'Let us take a hammer to theories and systems! Let us tear down that old plasterwork that hides the façade of art. There are no rules, no models; rather, there are no rules other than the general laws of Nature.'

Reading Hugo's works in chronological order, it is here that

Cocteau's paradox first comes to mind: 'Victor Hugo was a madman who thought he was Victor Hugo.'[16] The *Préface* certainly contains some gorgeous self-compliments: 'modern genius – so complex, so varied in its forms, so inexhaustible in its creations'; 'one of those men who, like Napoleon, are always the oldest in their family, whatever the order of birth'. But Hugo was also a madman who had come out on the other side of madness with a kind of super-rationality. He now believed that he could also convince other people that he was Victor Hugo.

*

AS IF TO PROVE his point about the versatility of modern genius, Hugo published two entirely different works in the space of two weeks: *Les Orientales* and *Le Dernier Jour d'un Condamné* (19 January and 3 February 1829).

The latter, described by an English reviewer as 'a book too terrible to be perused more than once – too remarkable not to be perused at all',[17] is written from inside the mind of a man condemned to death for an unspecified crime. The man recalls his childhood and observes his surroundings with a preternatural clarity, uncluttered by the embellishments of Romantic prose. It had a lasting effect on Charles Dickens. Dostoevsky remembered it as he waited to face the firing squad.[18]

Le Dernier Jour d'un Condamné is a masterpiece of the interior monologue and still seems Hugo's most modern work. The concentratedness of the narrative was felt to be an odd use of prose (supposed to be more diffuse than verse), and it may well be that the book was the result of a happy accident in the mental laboratory. Hugo had set out to write a short story without first making the appropriate adjustment to his brain: it was still in ode-writing mode. During the period covered by the writing of *Le Dernier Jour* (14 October to 26 December 1828), he wrote sixteen poems – his most prolific spell of verse-writing so far. This crossing of wires was perceived instinctively by an Italian writer who translated the book into *terza rima*, the measure used by Dante for *The Divine Comedy*.[19]

Further evidence of the book's modernity can be found in the fact that it was a direct influence on Albert Camus's *L'Étranger*. Here, an even more peculiar literary phenomenon might be mentioned: the contention that writers are as it were 'influenced' by their future imitators.[20] The unnamed prisoner himself is an Existentialist *avant la lettre*, haunted by a phrase which might have come from a play by Jean-Paul Sartre rather than from Chapter 48 of *Han d'Islande*:

> Condemned to death!
> Well, why not? 'All men,' I remember reading in some book or other – it was the only good thing in it – 'are condemned to death with indefinitely suspended sentences.' So has my situation really changed?[21]

The most influential critic of *Le Dernier Jour d'un Condamné* has also been the least trustworthy: Hugo himself. For the 1832 edition, he added a long preface which is practically a student's guide to his own text. He revealed his work to be 'nothing less than a plea, direct or indirect, as one wishes, for the abolition of the death penalty'. Why had he not made this clear before? Because 'the author preferred to wait and see whether or not his work would be understood'. Cynics might have added that he had also waited until there was a popular and parliamentary majority in favour of abolition.

The urge to stamp the book with a philanthropic message is a sign that something else, something less sociable, was lurking in its pages. Suspicions are raised by the fact that the condemned man's childhood memories are the same as Hugo's: the secret garden near the Val-de-Grâce, a playful Spanish girl called Pepita. The monologue ends, of course, before the execution – though Hugo later hoped to persuade the ghost of Louis XVII to write a sequel. The preface, on the other hand, with its real-life stories from the *Gazette des Tribunaux*, wallows in the horror of decapitation: victims of insufficiently sharpened guillotines; a man left supporting his half-severed head while it was cut off with a carving knife; a woman whose head had to be tugged, screaming, from her body. Coincidentally, Hugo also mentions an arsonist called Camus whose execution was celebrated as a public holiday.

In the *Préface de Cromwell*, Hugo had observed that 'all men of genius, however great, are inhabited by a beast which parodies their intelligence'. Here, bristling with synonyms, he vaunted the close-cropped style of his book: the author had 'comprehensively pruned his work of the contingent, the accidental, the particular, the specific, the relative, the modifiable, the episodic, the anecdotal, the incidental and the proper nouns' – Hugo could talk for hours about concision. With the addition of a stodgily sarcastic playlet, 'A Comedy about a Tragedy', in which a group of snobs and fuddy-duddies complain about the poet whose name sounds like '*Visigoth*' and who tries to make his readers experience actual physical pain, the prefatory material takes up over one-third of the book.

The snobs sound very much like the voice of Hugo's conscience in disguise. Like the ghoulish sightseers mentioned in the book,[22] he, too, had gone to watch the convicts being put in irons for the journey to the hulks at Toulon. He had seen them stripped naked in the rain to have their genitals inspected in front of a crowd. His campaign against the death penalty was also a cloak of respectability which allowed him to feast his eyes on punishment and cruelty, and to imagine his own execution. According to Sainte-Beuve, Hugo often saw ghosts, had terrifying dreams of talking corpses and, after attending the death-bed of one of his young Romantic supporters in 1832, was unable to sleep alone for several weeks.[23] Without Hugo's critical dilution, *Le Dernier Jour d'un Condamné* was not just a piece of polemic. It was a plea for the abolition of death.

In contrast to *Le Dernier Jour*, *Les Orientales* seemed to be set in a Never-Never Land which resembled Spain, Algeria, Turkey, Greece and China, and called itself 'The East'. In the critics' view,[24] Hugo had taken French poetry back to the play-pen. 'What is the point of these *Orientales*?' asks Hugo's preface. 'The author has no idea.' 'He has never seen any road maps of Art, with the frontiers of the possible and the impossible drawn in red and blue. He did it because he did it.'

Opening the book, instead of the thick battle-lines of alexandrines, readers discovered acres of blank space and a motley collection of poems which sat on the page like abstract designs. It was a showcase of exotic verse forms, some revealed by Sainte-Beuve in his study of the neglected poets of the French Renaissance, others, like the Malayan *pantoum*, imported by the orientalist, Ernest Fouinet.[25] Some were made up by Hugo. The passover of the demons called 'Les Djinns' (later set to music by Fauré, Franck and Saint-Saëns) begins with two-syllable lines, reaches a screaming climax with lines of ten syllables, and fades away, syllable by syllable, to almost nothing:

> *On doute*
> *La nuit . . .*
> *J'écoute: –*
> *Tout fuit,*
> *Tout passe;*
> *L'espace*
> *Efface*
> *Le bruit.*

The source of countless disastrous imitations for the next half-century.

The karaoke of classical forms, with their set structures and subjects, had given way to a more pervasive inventiveness. *Les Orientales* opened the eyes of several generations of poets, not only in France. Anyone, it seemed, could achieve originality by allowing the rhyme dictionary to write the poem.

To readers brought up on the kind of poetry Hugo had been practising until now, the effect on the meaning of the poems was catastrophic. Everything seemed to be profoundly insignificant and deeply symbolic at the same time. A writer called Edmond Géraud spent a reading evening with some friends rolling about on the floor, helpless with laughter.[26] The sea was a flock of sheep or a barking dog; tigers had 'the feet of gazelles', horses fled like locusts; a star was 'odourless'. Waves 'kissed the flanks of a rock', which was quite conventional, except that, three lines later, the foot of the rock was lacerating the entrails of the sea. A sixty-four-line poem contained the names for twenty-eight different kinds of ship (actually twenty-seven, since a *'barcarolle'* is a song, not a boat), and, for nineteen stanzas, a girl wearing no clothes, blushing like a pomegranate, swung in a hammock for no apparent reason other than laziness.

Critics experienced a rush of blood to the head – probably also to other parts. Twisting clichés was far more provocative than devising something completely new: the result was a kind of verbal disorientation akin to culture shock. Breasts were 'ebony' instead of the usual 'alabaster',[27] and hair which would normally have been ebony was red: 'One must not forget', says Hugo's erudite note, 'that red hair is considered beautiful by certain Oriental peoples.'

> Between two rocks of ebon black
> Do you see that sombre thicket
> Bristling in the plain
> Like the tuft of wool
> Betwixt the horns of a ram?
>
> . . . . .
>
> There, monsters of every form
> Creep about: the dreaming basilisk,
> The enormous-bellied hippopotamus,
> The vast and shapeless boa
> Which seems a living tree-trunk.
>
> . . . . .
>
> Alone and naked on the moss,
> In that wood I'd be more at ease
> Than in front of Nourmahal-the-Red
> Who talks with a soft voice
> And looks with soft eyes!

To call *Les Orientales* 'unconvincing' or 'artificial' is to miss the point – or rather, to hit it without realizing. Their superficiality is not the sign of a less sophisticated age. In 1829, all these pashas and sultanas had already worn paper-thin after half a century in fashion. By attaching them to a new form of poetry based on words rather than concepts, Hugo reactivated the fears which underlay the Oriental vogue. Political unrest resulting from the collapse of the Ottoman Empire (to which some of Hugo's poems allude) was only part of the story. This is what the best contemporary comment on *Les Orientales* suggests. An admirer of Hugo, Joseph Méry, reported in *Le Sémaphore de Marseille* that a band of pirates had sailed up the Rhône as far as Beaucaire and made off with all the virgins of a nearby village.[28] Since Beaucaire was the site of an international fair and since Hugo's *Orientales* had everyone thinking once again about swarthy corsairs and sultry harems, the story had an air of plausibility. The Minister of the Interior asked the local Prefect for a report. Eventually, it was discovered that neither the village nor the virgins existed.

The real fear was the introduction of an irrational mode of thought, vaguely associated with Islam and the smoking of hashish. Hugo himself believed in a progressive softening of the Western brain and saw a new centre of energy forming, not in Europe but in the United States.[29] These are the sorts of grandiose statement which have encouraged his compatriots to think of Hugo as primarily a political creature. But if Hugo's analysis is applied to his own poetry, and his poetry disengaged from literary history, he can be more accurately described as a dangerous individual. An anarchist with a genius for organization.

*

HAVING OCCUPIED the high ground in poetry, prose and literary theory, Hugo set his sights again on the stage – or rather, on the national institution known as the Comédie Française.[30]

A Trojan horse called Baron Taylor – the new director of the theatre and a friend of Nodier – was already in position, sympathetic to the Romantic cause and eager to accept anything Victor Hugo cared to write. For the first time, Romantic literature would gain a foothold in the establishment. With an increasingly old and nervous government, this had a strong political connotation: Romanticism, defined by Hugo as 'liberalism in art', was the voice of the younger, republican generation. It stood for freedom, imagination and a furious fear of being bored, a determination never to grow old and conservative.

The explosion caused by the introduction of Hugo into the Comédie Française is known as the 'Battle of *Hernani*'. The expression refers primarily to the mayhem at the first performances of Hugo's play; but it also refers to the symbolic showdown of an older, rule-bound form of literature with a literature based on individual sensibility – in other words, what we now think of as literature. Probably the most famous and most obscure moment in the history of European Romanticism, it is normally depicted through a heavily romanticized account written by Gautier forty-two years after the event. It established Hugo's public image, pulled most young writers and many artists into his orbit, and created so many myths that the precise manner in which he pulled off the biggest cultural coup of the century has practically been forgotten.

The key to Hugo's *coup d'état* was centralization. 'French literature' in most contexts actually means 'Parisian literature', and Parisian literature had as its focal point the Comédie Française: the great bell at the heart of French culture. In most theatres, the centre of attention was the fashion parade on stage and the social drama in the auditorium. Of thirty-one phrases in the 'Theatre' section of Blagdon's *French Interpreter* for English businessmen (1816), fifteen are for describing the 'beautiful lady' in the box, 'whose teeth are as white as ivory'.[31] But the Comédie Française was supposed to be different. William Hazlitt had attended a performance of Racine in 1825 and was amazed at the order and decorum, 'such as would shame any London audience':

> There was a professional air, an unvarying gravity in the looks and demeanour of the whole assembled multitude, as if every one had an immediate interest in the character of the national poetry ... Not only was the strictest silence observed, as soon as the curtain drew up, but no one moved or attempted to move.[32]

It was this living museum which Hugo's *Hernani* was about to turn into a boxing-ring and a public urinal, five months before the revolution in the streets.

Once the battleground had been chosen, the next step was to push any rivals and precursors into the background. The Comédie Française, in fact, had already begun to emit some strange vibrations. Dumas and Vigny had presented Romantic dramas there in 1829 which were in some ways as inflammatory and innovative as *Hernani*.[33] Since then, the unthinkable had happened. Racine's *Athalie*, one of the crown jewels of French literature, had been hissed.[34] Educated audiences had begun to drift off to the smaller boulevard theatres, already simmering with popular forms of Romanticism. A favourite on the boulevards that year was *L'Enragé*, in which the heroine was bitten by her lover and died of rabies.[35]

Most of these early rumblings have now been forgotten except by specialists. Hugo tends to be seen as the lone trailblazer, in the same way that modern youth movements are reduced to a few well-publicized individuals. His procedures are an object lesson in hijacking a revolution.

First, he pointed out, over and over again, that a vacancy existed for a revolutionary hero and then removed himself from the list of candidates with a flourish of self-effacement: 'Other nations say, "Homer, Dante, Shakespeare". We say, "Boileau".'* The fact that the person who indicates the vacancy more memorably than anyone else is most likely to be asked to fill it seemed to be purely incidental. Hugo's points of reference ensured that any other interpretation would have implied unbelievable arrogance (although, in this, he may have miscalculated): 'Why should we not now expect a poet', he asked in 1831, 'who would be to Shakespeare what Napoleon was to Charlemagne?' Whether or not anyone saw Victor Hugo as the Jesus Christ of his own John the Baptist, the association was made and from then on he would have to be attacked on his own terms.

The next step was to bathe his enemies' attacks in a kind of epic grandeur as if the Empire had never ended. In 1829, the critic Hyacinthe de Latouche published an article on 'Literary Camaraderie'.[36] He crept behind the puppet-master's box to reveal Hugo's 'Cénacle' as a kind of life insurance company for works of art: members' products were praised in newspapers and other works of art; 'French literature' would eventually turn into a giant chain-letter and critics not yet born would have to explain why so many mediocrities had been so important. 'Ever since we all became geniuses,' wrote Latouche, 'talent has become singularly uncommon'.

Hugo immediately cast the article, with its harmful trivialization, into the stormy sky lowering over the heads of the embattled Romantics:

> Those wretches, Janin and Latouche, have taken up position in all the newspapers and are pouring out their envy, hate and rage. They have fatally deserted our ranks at the decisive moment. A terrible storm is gathering above me ... A dual intrigue is being organized against me and is merely sharpening its swords on *Othello* in preparation for *Hernani*.[37]

This subtle relegation of Vigny's *Othello* to the role of precursor, the freshening breeze that announced Hugo's hurricane, is typical of his apparently blameless opportunism.

---

* Nicolas Boileau-Despréaux (1636–1711), so-called 'legislator of Parnassus'. His *L'Art Poétique* was treated as the definitive classical rule-book.

The overt campaign was quite straightforward by comparison. Originally, Hugo had been intending to present a different play. On 1 June 1829, he took a theme from Vigny's historical novel, *Cinq-Mars*, and wrote a five-act play in verse: *Un Duel sous Richelieu*, later retitled *Marion de Lorme*.[38] It was accepted by the theatre reading committee, then submitted to the censor, who threw it out. The problem was not the controversial 'rehabilitation' of a prostitute, Marion de Lorme, nor even the scandalous line, 'Love has given me a new virginity'. The problem was Act IV. It portrayed a dithering, pusillanimous Louis XIII presiding over his country's slide into absolutism and pining for the hunt. Just like the present King of France.

Hugo went to see the Minister of the Interior, Martignac[39] – a man whose sensitivity to political allusions was heightened by the fact that he was about to lose his job. Hugo protested his scorn for works of art which contain snide contemporary allusions, and Martignac told him what he already knew: these days, a Paris theatre audience was a giant ear which resonated at the faintest subversive innuendo.

Hugo left the Ministry, sensing victory. He requested an audience with the King. The audience was granted and, on 7 August 1829, Baron Victor Hugo turned up at the Palace of Saint-Cloud with the proper court dress, supplied by brother Abel, a copy of Act IV on expensive vellum, and a bad case of nerves. The King graciously claimed to be an admirer of Hugo's work and promised to read the offending Act IV.

A week later, the verdict was made known: the play could not be performed. As a consolation, Hugo was offered an extra 4000 francs on his royal pension and a post on the Council of State: part of a patronizing attempt to win over the younger generation. If the regime lasted, it meant comfort for life. While the messenger waited, Hugo wrote an ostentatiously dignified letter. He mentioned his noble ancestors (a contrast to the upstart aristocrats recently ennobled by Charles X), his royalist odes, his father's lost fortune, his numerous dependants, and the fact that he lived by his pen. 'I had asked for my play to be performed, and I ask for nothing else.'

In a few hours, the text of Hugo's letter was known to every newspaper in the city. This first symbolic encounter of the young

Romantics with the generation in power made a hero of Victor Hugo: 'The youth of France', wrote *Le Constitutionnel*, 'is not as corruptible as Ministers would hope.' Next time, banning a play by Victor Hugo might have serious consequences.

Now, instead of rewriting the fourth act, Hugo chose a new subject: *Hernani, ou l'Honneur Castillan*. A Spanish bandit and disinherited noble, Hernani, loves and is loved by Doña Sol, who is also being courted by her aged guardian and by the future Holy Roman Emperor, Don Carlos – hence the subtitle of the original edition, *Tres Para Una*, 'Three For One'.

Subjectively, it was the story of a beautiful young girl who loves a handsome, persecuted hero but is forced to suffer the senile advances of disgusting old men. This brazenly unrealistic drama, in which the two lovers needlessly poison each other at the end (such is 'Castilian Honour'), was the perfect vehicle for Hugo's unorthodox verse. Ironically, his wit was less stagey than in his everyday conversation, and when they heard the play read aloud by the twenty-seven-year-old author, the actors of the Comédie Française hated it. How was it possible to be comic *and* tragic in the same scene?[40] Why was the language so disgracefully intimate and idiomatic? It has often been said that *Hernani* was a very timid revolt because it was written in verse. In fact, verse acted as an amplifier. It was far more shocking to hear the French language expressing Romantic sentiments when it was wearing its Sunday best. The old war-horse of classical drama, Mlle Mars, playing the barely nubile Doña Sol at the age of fifty-one, would have to be wooed and bullied by Hugo into agreeing to call 'that respectable M. Joanny' (the actor playing Hernani) her 'proud and generous lion' – a phrase which seemed to her to suggest a rather suspect relationship.[41] Yet it was precisely this combination of irony and passion that appealed to Hugo's young audience: it seemed to prove that one could live in the prosaic, modern world without emotional compromise.

This time, the pickings for politically minded spectators were even richer than in *Marion de Lorme*. In the first scene, a lusting sovereign called Charles hides in a wardrobe, asking Doña Sol's nurse as he squeezes in, 'Is this perchance the stable where you hide / The broomstick-horse on which you ride?' The censors – four playwrights, three of whom were on the verge of retirement or death – rubbed their hands with glee. *Hernani* was rubbish: 'The bandit treats the King like a brigand, the daughter of a Spanish grandee is a shameless hussy, etc.' It should be performed exactly as Hugo wrote it, and 'the public will learn how far the human mind can go when it is freed from every rule and every form of decency'.[42]

As soon as rehearsals began in the autumn of 1829, war was declared. A consortium of classical playwrights, headed by Casimir Bonjour, had sent an unsuccessful petition to the King asking him to ban all Romantic plays from the Comédie Française. *Le Figaro* called this 'demanding a monopoly on sending the audience to sleep'.[43] One by one, members of the Academy were stirred into action, oblivious to the fact that their parodies and epigrams simply proved the ability of the new literature to activate the mind. Baour-Lormian's *Le Canon d'Alarme* contained the sinister phrase, 'Hugos are writing poems with impunity.'[44] Others, like the Academician in Stendhal's *Le Rouge et le Noir*, recommended corporal punishment where literary criticism had failed.[45] Viennet, author of a stupendously dull 30,000-line epic poem (someone said it would take 15,000 people to read it), suspected a foreign plot to discredit the French stage.[46] The academic arsenal was hopelessly outdated. It was hard to be offensive about offensive language. Their insults came out as incomprehensible circumlocutions: 'It seems, when I hear them grunting in my path, / That Circe's wand in my hand they have seen.' If Baour-Lormian had been a Romantic, he could simply have called them swine.

On the other side of the battlefield, an army of artists and poets trooped up and down the stairs day and night, to the dismay of the Hugos' landlady. Hugo had made contact with the younger generation. These '*Hugolâtres*'* were the 'soldiers' who would prevent *Hernani* from being booed off the stage as *Amy Robsart* had been at the Odéon two years before. A valuable resource, 'the generous youth of today – devoured from within by misunderstood genius, stifled from without by a badly organized society'. Hugo's meticulous housekeeping accounts, in which every haircut, broomstick, bar of

---

* From *idolâtre* ('idolatrous'): 'One who blindly supports the works and literary theories of Victor Hugo' (Littré).

H

soap and umbrella repair is recorded, show a strong aversion to waste, human or otherwise. 'What great things one might achieve', he mused, 'with that legion of minds, if the will were there!'[47]

This untapped resource was to be smuggled into the Comédie Française as a reinforcement for the paid claqueurs, who were known to be susceptible to bribes.*[48] Passes on red paper stamped with the word '*Hierro*' ('Iron')[49] were distributed to 'battalion leaders' who were then to recruit their own cohorts in the cafés and studios of the Latin Quarter.

In this way, as the first night drew near, *Hernani* became the banner which united a generation, many of them still in their teens:[50] Gautier, who claimed to have given up painting for poetry when he read *Les Orientales*; Petrus Borel, the 'Lycanthrope', who dressed like a Spanish grandee and recited sections of the *Préface de Cromwell* without the text; an artist and melodramatist, Joseph Bouchardy, who memorized all five acts of *Hernani*; a sculptor known as Jehan du Seigneur (a medievalized form of Jean Duseigneur), who dressed in black and parted his hair on both sides to form a pointed crest above his forehead symbolizing 'the flame of genius'. The best known *Hernaniste* was Gérard de Nerval, who had just adapted *Han d'Islande* for the stage and was seen at a restaurant called the Petit Moulin Rouge, sitting with a skull to which a brass drawer-handle had been screwed, ordering 'sea-water' because that was Han of Iceland's favourite drink.[51]

The group which came to be known as the 'Petit Cénacle' was living proof that Hugo's medieval and oriental fantasies had been realism in advance of reality. Merovingian curls, cloaks, daggers, skulls and hookahs were coveted possessions. For the first time in 400 years, long pointed shoes were seen in provincial towns. Spanish tobacco was smoked in a form which the cognoscenti called the 'cigarette'.[52] A petition was drawn up asking the Government to institute bull-fights in Paris.[53] Hammocks swung from the ceilings of studios. Young men from respectable families turned themselves into

---

* Legend has it that Hugo dispensed with the claque, but his accounts show payments to the head claqueur totalling 280 francs between February and June 1830. The significant break with tradition consisted of bringing in claqueurs from one of the more popular, down-market boulevard theatres.

living masterpieces and their names into works of art: Augustus Mac-Keat (Auguste Maquet), Napol Tom (Napoléon Thomas) and the author of some remarkably Baudelairean poems, Théophile Dondey, who rearranged the letters of his name and went down in literary history – and disappeared – as Philothée O'Neddy. For most of the Petit Cénacle, the Battle of *Hernani* was their first and last hour of glory.[54]

*

BY ONE O'CLOCK on the afternoon of Thursday, 25 February 1830, a long queue had formed outside the Comédie Française and was clogging up the Rue Richelieu. Much of the queue looked as though it was about to go and sit for Velázquez – long hair, beards, clothes several centuries old. One frightening specimen wore a broad-rimmed hat, pale green trousers with black velvet stripes, vast lapels and – after several sessions with a baffled tailor – a doublet, padded like a breastplate, in purplish-red satin. An important nuance. Bright red would have had a political connotation, whereas the doublet stood for pure, militant aestheticism. This was Théophile Gautier and his famous 'red waistcoat', which was neither red nor a waistcoat (waist-coats were bourgeois).

It now became evident that Hugo's tactics had been, if anything, too mild. The police had ordered the entrance to the auditorium to be closed at three o'clock, forcing the Romantic rabble to arrive four hours early. It was hoped that something that might be called a riot would ensue, which, naturally, would be heroically repressed by the forces of order. Responding to an ancient siege instinct, theatre employees on the roof pelted the queue with waste from the Comédie Française kitchens.

The queue refused to be provoked and ran the gauntlet of sabre-wielding guardsmen into the dark cathedral of the Comédie Française. They had come equipped with bread, sausages, cheese, chocolate sticks and oranges. They sang subversive songs, discussed the lines that would have to be cheered to victory and, according to the fantasies of people who were not there, fornicated with their working-class girlfriends. The usherettes, who held the keys to the toilets, did not arrive for work until shortly before the performance. Undaunted,

Hugo's army dined at five, spread out over the seats like banqueting Romans, then wandered off into dark corners. They were still eating when the rest of the audience began to trickle in, filling up the boxes, their slippers and evening dresses trailing through something moist and pungent.[55]

While the Comédie Française was being rebaptized, Hugo spent the afternoon drumming up support, visiting newspaper offices, asking critics to join the revolution.[56] An obstreperous old ticket-lady had been undermining his plans by selling tickets to his enemies, and it was vital to ensure that reviewers would not be influenced by organized booing. With an hour to go, he dined with Sainte-Beuve in a restaurant in the Palais-Royal. Then he walked to the theatre, where Baron Taylor was in a flap about the improvised toilets. Hugo was taken to the dressing-room of Mlle Mars, where he found her half-naked and fuming – a fearsome sight. 'Fine friends you have, M. Hugo,' she is reported to have said. 'Madame,' answered Hugo, 'you may be very glad to have my friends this evening. For this evening, my enemies are yours.'[57]

At seven o'clock, Hugo was standing alone in the wings. He heard the stage manager give the order for the curtain to be raised and experienced a sensation which he described in 1852 with a variation on the theme of literary virginity: 'I felt the skirt of my soul lifted up.'[58]

Sixteen hundred over-excited spectators found themselves staring into Doña Sol's darkened bedroom in Saragossa. Someone was knocking at her secret door . . .

> *Serait-ce déjà lui?*
>> (Un nouveau coup)
>>> . . . *C'est bien à l'escalier*
> *Dérobé.*

*

CONTRARY TO POPULAR LEGEND, the first line, with its daring enjambment on 'hidden staircase' (a serious breach of the classical rules), passed without comment – as did the first scene and part of the second. Then came Hernani's speech about Doña Sol's lecherous old guardian – 'Go get yourself measured for a coffin, old man.' This struck a chord. The Romantics cheered and stamped their feet. There was some concern for the building. It had not been designed to cope with audience participation.

Five acts later, it was obvious that the first night was a victory for the Romantics. Michelot (Don Carlos) smirked and overacted in case anyone thought he was taking it seriously. *Le Corsaire* reported that the actors had performed 'like epileptics'.[59] But Mlle Mars rose to the challenge (though she did insert the innocuous word '*Seigneur*' in place of '*lion*'). Cheers drowned out the booing and part of the performance. A few grumblers were punched in the face and there was a nasty argument at the end of Act III when someone jeered at the words, '*Vieillard stupide!*', which he heard as '*Vieil as de pique!*'[60] Hugo's bold image of an 'Old Ace of Spades' was hotly defended – proving, first, that the pleasure of the text now lay less in recognition than in the creation of a state of mind which could transform even chance elements into poetic beauties; second, that it was difficult to hear what was going on on the stage.

News of the battle spread quickly. Someone had shouted 'Guillotine the knee-heads' – baldness being synonymous with decrepit classicism. 'One was surrounded by terrifying men whose inquisitorial glances spied out one's true opinion,' wrote an Academician whose nephew, the painter Amaury-Duval, was cheering with the Romantics, 'and if one's face had the misfortune to betray boredom or disgust, one was attacked with the epithet, *épicier*' ('grocer'): Romantic slang, he explained, for 'outrageously stupid'.[61] Young barbarians danced round the bust of Racine in the foyer, shouting, 'One in the eye for you!'[62] On the way home, Théophile Gautier and his friends scrawled '*Vive Victor Hugo!*' on the walls of houses.[63]

Similar battles had been fought before *Hernani*. In 1809, at the Odéon, Népomucène Lemercier had cunningly subverted the unity of place by setting his *Christophe Colomb* on a ship: several thousand miles later, the characters were technically still in the same place. The student audience – in those days opposed to innovation – was unconvinced. The actors performed behind a line of soldiers. On the second night, after a stage invasion, part of the audience was bayonetted and the survivors packed off to the Eastern front by

Napoleon for a final lesson in the artificiality of the unity of place rule.[64]

The main difference in 1830 was that revolutionary fever affected only the young. With its shocking mixture of plebeian and courtly language, *Hernani* was simultaneously translated in the mind of every 'knee-head' into subversive rhetoric.[65] Even in England, the political connotations were more obvious than they had been to Hugo himself when he wrote the play. Lord Gower's 1831 translation included a prologue in which he begged indulgence for the author's 'liberal muse' – a sensible precaution since the audience on one occasion was the British Royal Family:

> Against the unities our Muse has made
> Full in their front a perfect barricade;
> Whence with a dagger, and a poison bottle
> She sticks Voltaire, and pelts at Aristotle![66]

Almost every account of the first night of *Hernani* is actually a digest of all thirty-nine performances – an unusually long run in the days before railways enlarged the theatres' catchment area.[67] The real Battle of *Hernani* lasted several weeks, degenerating into a three-way struggle for supremacy between the actors and a bipartisan audience. In a theatre the size of the Comédie Française, the Romantics were always in the minority. One night in March, Hugo followed the proceedings in his newly printed copy of the first edition, noting every reaction in the margin: 'laughter' (109 times), 'hissing' (30), 'sniggering' (9), 'noise' (5), 'stirring in the audience' (2), one 'laugh in anticipation' and one 'noise – nothing can be heard' next to the Emperor's speech on the populace, that 'mirror which seldom shows a King in a flattering light'.[68]

The actor playing Doña Sol's guardian had lost two fingers fighting under General Hugo; under the General's son he fared little better. As Hernani and Doña Sol expired in each other's arms at the end of Act V, something far more tragic was taking place beyond the footlights: simultaneous booing and cheering; fisticuffs and arrests. Acting had never seemed so pointless. 'There appears to be some contradiction here,' the actor wrote in his diary on 5 March. 'If the play is bad, why do they come and see it? And if they are so keen to come, why do they hiss?'[69] He sensed danger. There was a fine line between noble adversity and everlasting ridicule. Even the stage-hands were avoiding him. At midnight, on returning home, he wrote to a friend, Paul Lacroix:

> The takings from the first two nights have already reached 9000 francs, *which is quite without precedent in the theatre* [i.e. at the Comédie Française]. Yet we must not sleep; the enemy wakes. . . . Therefore, in the name of our cherished literary freedom, send out a call to every last one of our strong and faithful friends for Monday. I am counting on you to help me extract this last tooth from the old classic Pegasus. . . . The great cause is at stake – not myself.[70]

Half-way through March, unexpected reinforcements arrived. The pupils of the Collège Bourbon and the Collège Charlemagne (Nerval and Gautier's old school) had requested a special performance. The twelfth *Hernani* was played to an orchestra-pit of cheering schoolboys. When the curtain fell, they tried to bring Mlle Mars back on to the stage. But curtain-calls had been outlawed. The police moved in and evicted the entire contingent, which then hurried round the side of the theatre to the stage-door and cheered 'Doña Sol' into her carriage.[71]

Within a few days of the first night, a whole industry of *Hernani* parodies sprang up, showing that the play itself, like many innovatory works of art, contains elements of self-parody. Four were premièred in March alone: *N, I, Ni* ('N, O Spells No'), 'Romantic Claptrap in 5 Acts and Sublime Verse Interspersed with Ridiculous Prose'; *Hernani*, 'Romantic Stupidity in 5 *Tableaux*'; *Oh! Qu'Nenni!* ('Oh! No!'); and the beautifully rhymed *Harnali*, in which the hero is a ticket-tout in love with the daughter of a theatre shareholder. There was even a Battle of *Harnali*: on its second night, Hugo's supporters turned up to throw firecrackers on to the stage. When *Hernani* reached the end of its run, the parodies were still going strong. In June, the Gaîté Theatre was already on its second: *Les Massacres*, 'Cerebral Fever in 3 Attacks'.

Many journalists had waited to see which way the wind would blow before expressing an opinion. As the booing increased, so did the insults. The conservative press talked of lunatics and devil-worshippers. A few weeks before the July Revolution, violence was in the air. One night, Hugo returned home to find a bullet-hole in his window. He also received a letter which told him, 'If you don't withdraw your filthy play, we'll do you in.'[72] The *Universel* condemned the death threats by suggesting a slight attenuation of the punishment.[73] In some minds, *Hernani* was now firmly associated with all that was rotten in the fatherland.

By the time *Hernani* reached the end of its run, it was clear that Hugo had been a prophet. *Hernani* was a literary virus which modified the world around it. On the stage, it was sixteenth-century Spain; in the auditorium, it was an enactment – even, in some minds, a direct cause – of what was about to happen on the streets.

*

IF *HERNANI* WAS Hugo's Battle of Austerlitz (Sainte-Beuve's expression[74]), his landlady was the peasant whose hut happens to be on the battlefield. For several months, the entire Romantic movement had been stamping on her ceiling. The Hugos were a nice couple, 'very fond of their children', but M. Hugo had chosen 'such an arduous profession'. Poor Mme Hugo. They would have to move.

In Hugo's lifetime, the population of Paris had risen by 45 per cent and was now washing up on the fields on either side of the Champs-Élysées. Hugo chose a second-floor apartment in the Rue Jean-Goujon. Described as number 9, it was still the only house in the street. They moved in in May 1830: 'Trees, air, a lawn beneath our window, grown-up children in the house to play with our little ones . . . much solitude and no more *Hernanistes*.'[75]

There were now three little Hugos: Léopoldine, Charles and Victor, whose birth had briefly interrupted the writing of *Le Dernier Jour d'un Condamné*. Adèle was pregnant again, this time with a girl conveniently referred to as Adèle II.

Because Hugo allowed his visitors to wait in his study and because some of them rummaged in his papers, the room in which he wrote one of the great Romantic novels can be described in some detail:[76] five red leather chairs, two couches and several tables supporting very neat piles of books; two folios on the history and antiquities of Paris bristling with bookmarks. An odd assortment of objects: two boot-hooks, a dagger, a bronze head, a stuffed white bird, and some strange little earthenware pots (probably relics unearthed by General Hugo). There were pictures of children and 'scenes of blood and death – the St Bartholomew's Day Massacre or one horseman slaying another in a lonely spot'. Elsewhere, lithographs by Hugo's friend, Louis Boulanger, and a painting, 'The Witches of *Macbeth*'. A journalist on the *Mercure* interpreted the painting as an allegory of the young Romantics: 'All hail, Hugo! that shalt be king hereafter!'[77]

The books were the raw material for Hugo's tale of fifteenth-century Paris, *Notre-Dame de Paris*. It was supposed to have been delivered to the publisher, Gosselin, on 15 April 1829.

On 28 May 1830, when the worst of the Battle was over, Hugo sat at his window, listening to his favourite sounds – birdsong and twittering children – writing one of his first visionary poems, 'La Pente de la Rêverie', in which the mind abandons itself to dream and hurtles down the spiralling slope of an inverted Tower of Babel to the invisible world – a poem which belongs to the history of the 'stream of consciousness'; it showed that it was possible to make the deliberate meandering of a mind the organizing principle of a poem. Meanwhile, in the upper world, a compromise was being negotiated for him by the editor of the *Revue de Paris*, Amédée Pichot. A new deadline was set: 1 December 1830. This time, for every week the novel was late, Hugo would forfeit 1000 francs.

He bought a grey woollen body-stocking, a new bottle of ink, locked his clothes in the wardrobe and 'entered his novel like a prison'.

These sporadic bouts of extreme self-discipline suggest that Hugo's frequent references to his 'idleness' were not simply an attempt to project an image of Romantic indolence. An observer of literary life called Antoine Fontaney saw Hugo one morning in August 1831, shaving:

> A most curious spectacle: he draws the razor over his face with incredible slowness, then he places it in his fob for a quarter of an hour to warm it up; then he starts on his ablutions and finally pours a whole jug of rose-water over his head.[78]

During the day, Hugo made cardboard coaches, boats, castles and puppet theatres for the children.[79] Sometimes he sat under the trees in the Champs-Élysées or ambled along a terrace in the Tuileries Gardens, watching the Seine, composing in his mind. Nerval told a friend he ought to be delighted to receive a note from Victor Hugo, since 'he is not a natural scribbler'.[80] Instead of answering letters, he left his door open. Considering the number of visitors, this can hardly be interpreted as a time-saving device.

But as the novel would show, attempts to overcome laziness and the prospect of more idleness at the end of it could inspire huge quantities of writing and efficient research, while laziness itself prevented him from fussing over the finished product. Hugo's obsessive reconstruction of his own past might easily have ruined his best works. Instead, as he told Fontaney, he had 'a religious respect for inspiration. Even for a comma, I would always consult my first draft!'[81] 'It is the author's method', he had revealed in the *Préface de Cromwell*, 'to correct one work only in another.' This meant that he could calculate precisely the time it would take to produce each book. Fontaney was shocked to learn that Hugo tackled his work like a farmer measuring a field. His financial future was secure. 'After twenty dramas, he will conclude his literary career with two great works – one in prose, the other a gigantic epic on Napoleon, in every form and metre.'[82] In reality, Hugo practised a form of mental crop rotation, alternating poetry, prose and drama. Otherwise, the long-term plan was quite prophetic, with its hint of a second life after the 'literary career' and the epic on Napoleon – not, however, the Napoleon he was thinking of in 1830.

With *Notre-Dame de Paris*, there was a slight miscalculation. On 5 August 1830, he already knew that it would not be finished on time; but he had an excellent excuse. Because of fighting in the Champs-Élysées, he had evacuated his manuscripts to his brother-in-law's house on the quieter Left Bank. A notebook containing two months' research had gone missing. 'No doubt this is one of those *cas de force majeure* provided for in our contract', he prompted Gosselin, who agreed to a two-month extension.[83]

If Gosselin read the 1823 edition of *Han d'Islande* before he published the third edition in 1829, he might have thought twice before agreeing: a note explained that the author had been forced to write a serious novel, 'having had the misfortune to lose the notebook

– in the vicinity of the Fontaine des Innocents – in which he habitually inscribes his future quips and witticisms'.

In 1830, Hugo's excuse was the July Revolution which sent Charles X into exile and the Hugos running for cover, while bullets smashed the tiles on their roof, to a country inn at Montfort-l'Amaury. In what was effectively a *coup d'état*, Charles X dissolved Parliament and abolished freedom of the press on 25 July 1830. Next day, there was a general strike. The King – like Louis XIII in *Marion de Lorme* – went off to spend the day hunting. Newspapers appeared as usual. When the troops tried to close down a printing works, barricades went up all over central Paris. Notre-Dame fell to the insurgents, who included a large number of students and intellectuals.

For the time being, the bloody three-day revolution ('Les Trois Glorieuses': 27–29 July 1830) was a victory for the generation which had cheered at the first night of *Hernani*. Louis-Philippe was crowned 'King of the French', and it was not immediately apparent that the July Monarchy represented the triumph of money, bureaucrats and the bourgeoisie.

A statement was expected from Hugo. It came in the form of an ode, 'À la Jeune France'. He saluted the noble students who had helped to restore freedom, but he also herded them all together, under the paternal umbrella of his rhetoric, with the other heroes of recent French history: the students were the fledglings of the great Eagle, Napoleon, himself a child of the Revolution. Nothing of the past should be erased; 'the scars of combat' should remain on the face of the city. The iconoclast of *Hernani*, the liberal with the manners of a royalist, was intent on preserving idols. Even old Charles X, 'plodding into exile', should not have his 'crown of thorns' rammed down on his 'hoary head'.

In other words, history was a force which ignored political loyalties. From a sufficiently lofty point of view, the Victor Hugo who celebrated the coronation of Charles X, the Hugo who glorified Napoleon and the Hugo who hailed the July Revolution – the son of Sophie and the son of Brutus – had all been right.

When it appeared in *Le Globe* of 19 August 1830, Hugo's ambiguous ode was preceded by a short, anonymous note written by Sainte-Beuve. Like a publicity manager at a press conference, he presented the ode as a mark of Hugo's support for a free and liberal France. The expression Sainte-Beuve later applied to his note is significantly brutal: 'I deroyalized him'. 'My intention was to pilot the ode through the still narrow straits of triumphant liberalism'.[84] Since every young Romantic wanted to believe that Hugo was a republican at heart, it worked amazingly well.

With the help of Sainte-Beuve, Hugo sailed serenely into the new dawn, flying the appropriate colours,[85] unaware that the pilot had also been busy in the hold, levering up the planks.

CHAPTER NINE

What the Concierge Saw

(1831–1833)

'THE MOST ABOMINABLE BOOK ever written'[1] appeared in the bookshops on 16 March 1831. *Notre-Dame de Paris. 1482* was the emotionally exhausting tale of the penniless poet, Gringoire, the demonic, lecherous priest, Frollo, the handsome, empty-headed guardsman, Captain Phoebus, the deaf bell-ringer, Quasimodo, with his hump and his wart-obscured eye, and the beautiful gypsy-girl they all fall in love with: Esmeralda, whose only friend in the world is her performing goat, Djali (the name Emma Bovary gives to her lap-dog twenty-six years later).[2]

The eye of the novel is the Gothic cathedral. In the minds of progressive Parisians, it was a shabby relic of the barbarian past. Hugo himself valued it at first mainly for the view. He climbed the bell-towers, emerged from the spiral staircase on to the narrow platform and stood, hallucinating with vertigo, next to the stone Quasimodos, peering down over 'that surprising thicket of pinnacles and towers and belfries', 'the inextricable web of bizarrely twisted streets' which, like the plot, converge on the cathedral and the 'great ship' of the Île de la Cité, 'moored' to the two banks of the Seine by its five bridges.[3]

It was during one of these exploratory visits, he claimed in a prefatory note to the novel, that he discovered the mysterious graffito from which the story was extrapolated:

A few years ago, when he was visiting Notre-Dame or rather, sniffing about in it, the author of this book discovered in a dark corner of one of the towers this word which a hand had etched on the wall:

ΑΝΑΓΚΗ

'Fate'. A pagan idea carved on the stone of a Christian church. Some critics were disturbed by what they saw as the godlessness of *Notre-Dame de Paris*. It was a forerunner of the urban detective novel: an obsessive individual scours the nooks and crannies of the city for clues to an unknown crime and reasons to believe in final justice. The story ends with the discovery in the catacombs of the two main protagonists, Esmeralda and Quasimodo, their decayed skeletons entwined in a hideous embrace. A parody of a happy ending.

The oddest character of all is the narrator himself: the pedantic Hugo, shattered into a thousand images and reconstituted as a linguistic rubbish-heap – dog Latin, medieval French and shaky Spanish, culled from a handful of old books and an astonishing verbal memory, fed through the collective brain of a historian, a town-crier and a population of demented gossips, brilliantly evoking a chaotic melting-pot of a Middle Ages. In this idiom, the wisdom of the centuries is reduced to eerie, erudite slogans: '*Tempus edax, homo edacior*, which I would happily render thus: Time is blind, Man is stupid.'

Hugo's first full-length novel shows a sense of revolutionary intoxication far removed from the tidy world of politics, a sense of the gradual suicide of civilizations which curiously recalls the other great novel to emerge from the July Revolution: Balzac's *La Peau de Chagrin*. In the 'eighth edition' (actually the second), Hugo handed his readers a theoretical key, as if he was talking about someone else's novel. The chapter entitled 'This Will Kill That' explained that the story was sited at the historical crossroads when the modern world was struggling to be born and when the printed word began to dominate and annihilate that older form of writing – architecture. This contaminates the whole book with an interesting paradox. Hugo was contributing his own 'basketful of rubble' to 'the second Tower of Babel of the human race' – the Babel of books – helping to destroy the civilization embodied in Notre-Dame of Paris.

From our own point of view, the effects of Hugo's destruction are apparent: the disintegration of the structure under a bombardment of exotic words which invites comparison with Rabelais and James Joyce; the tendency to hand the narrative over to elements which, until then, had only been picturesque embellishments of the plot.[4] Hugo was calling for the architectural treasures of the past to be preserved in a novel which subverted the very traditions it exploited. Here, at the dawn of 'heritage' movements, was the now familiar irony: a determination that the past should be preserved, but 'only on condition that it consent to be dead'.[5]

The cathedral itself was a model of the author's mind, the ruined temple of his royalism and catholicism, 'which I sometimes contemplate with respect but where I no longer go to pray'.[6] The book is littered with secret references to his private adventures – the headless 'UGENE' scratched on a wall, the tower at Gentilly, and a whole street-map of allusions to his Paris homes. But since few readers could be expected to understand the allusions, this ransacking of his own life serves as a warning that autobiographical elements are not necessarily confessional. They may be part of an act of concealment or an attempt to see beyond the trivia. Hugo was sweeping out his memory to find what lay underneath. The last word of the novel is '*poussière*': 'dust'.

The immediate effect on readers of the time was horror verging on intense pleasure.[7] Victor Hugo had written a very smelly book: there was a pile of rags with a pair of feet, teeth chipped 'like the battlements of a fortress', a heroine who trembled 'like a galvanized frog', a boy who used his tongue as a handkerchief, and a man so tortured by his thoughts 'that he took his head in both hands and tried to pull it off his shoulders in order to smash it on to the paving-stones.'

It was partly this portrayal of extreme states that made *Notre-Dame de Paris* a standard popular classic for the next century-and-a-half.* *The Hunchback of Notre-Dame* (Hugo loathed the English title),[8] 'with a sketch of the life and writings of the author', *Esmeralda, or The Deformed of Notre Dame*, by Edward Fitz-Ball, and dozens of other translations and adaptations[9] made Hugo the most famous living writer in Europe and sent thousands of tourists to Paris and the Île de la Cité where they were disappointed to find an 'old church thrust away into a corner'.[10] But they could also find a guide (as Hugo did)

---

* Anyone who has ever twisted their body into an imitation of Lon Chaney or Charles Laughton and screeched, 'The bells! The bells!' is in for a surprise if they read the original bell-ringing scene. For Quasimodo, the bells are a 'harem' of mothers and girlfriends – huge, resonant cavities with little clappers on which the monster jerks and swings in an orgy of mutual gratification.

who would show them the little room close to the bell-tower on the side nearest the Seine where M. Hugo had supposedly written his novel, and the famous mystery inscription. By the 1840s, 'Victor Hugo's Cathedral' was firmly on the tourist map of Paris, but there were soon so many ΑΝΑΓΚΗs on the wall that no one was sure which was the original.[11]

*

ONE RECURRING MOTIF in *Notre-Dame de Paris* could be fully understood only by Hugo's closest friend: 'Let us not affix our gaze too firmly on our neighbour's wife,' says Gringoire, 'however much her beauty might tickle our eyes. Fornication is a most licentious thought. Adultery is an expression of curiosity about someone else's sensual pleasure.'[12]

A traditional character sketch of Charles-Augustin Sainte-Beuve would be a long list of adjectives cancelling each other out until the negatives prevailed, and ending with the observation that he was the greatest French critic of the nineteenth century. Two details stick in the mind more than any abstract quality: his secret disability – a type of congenital arrested development, known as hypospadias, which causes the urethra to open before the end of the penis and usually produces impotence; and his most characteristic act. On a rainy morning in the eastern suburbs of Paris, Sainte-Beuve turned up to fight a duel with the editor of *Le Globe*. He was holding a pistol in one hand and an umbrella in the other. When the seconds objected – umbrellas were against the rules – Sainte-Beuve retorted that he was quite prepared to go to the grave 'shot dead but not soaking wet'. Four shots were fired without injury and then they all went off to have breakfast.

This mixture of ironic modernity and Romantic ennui is the twisted thread that runs through Sainte-Beuve's verse: a photographing of subtle shades of mind with a cruel, acidic eye overseeing the operation. A translation of one of his early poems made in 1830 by Lady Morgan preserves the crippling self-awareness, but it should be imagined with the perverse counterpoint of Sainte-Beuve's suave verbal harmonies. This is poetry which simultaneously aspires to Hugo's grandeur and revels in its failure:

Should you wish in the waters a cold bed to find,
The place where we stand is just made to your mind.
Choose your day and set off. Ere you sink in the billow,
Pack your clothes in a bundle snug under yon willow.
Souse not head over ears, as if conquered by wrath,
But go, step by step, as you'd enter a bath: . . .
And when you're in order, prime up to the mark,
(That is half killed with cold), take 'the leap in the dark'.
Don't keep yourself waiting, but down with your head,
And be sure you don't lift it again till you're dead.[13]

In this dismal landscape, Hugo shone like a warm red sun. In July 1830, Sainte-Beuve was asked whether Victor Hugo believed in God. His reply shows a surprising blindness, but also the delicious pain of envy:

Oh! Victor Hugo is not tormented by things like that. His talent constantly provides him with such grand, pure and delicate pleasures! His work is so beautiful and so perfect! He is so abundant! He is a full and happy man. He lives contentedly in his family. He is jolly. Perhaps too jolly.

Writing to the happy man, Sainte-Beuve spread himself at his feet and bent his style into the shape of Hugo's: 'I now live only through you,' he wrote in October 1829. 'The small amount of talent I possess has come to me by your example and from your advice disguised as praise.' Years later, Sainte-Beuve carefully corrected all his earlier comments on Hugo's character:

No, his is not a noble heart: deceitful and immodest, deep down he is vain. All those who have had close dealings with him have discovered this sooner or later. But I was fooled for a long time. I was in the cave of the Cyclops and thought I was in the grotto of a demi-god.[14]

In fact, the change was not so much in Sainte-Beuve's feelings towards Hugo as in his analysis of those feelings. His own false imitations fed his mistrust of Hugo's grand simplicity, and it was this, along with the catastrophe he engineered, that makes his affair with Adèle a thorough dissection of Hugo's personality.

Throughout 1830, Sainte-Beuve had been seeing less and less of

Hugo. He even refused to write a review of *Hernani* on the grounds that he knew the play too well. Anyway, he claimed, it was a waste of time trying to feed Art to the masses (an interesting conviction for a socialist): Hugo would only be 'compromising his chastity'. Hugo was puzzled. On 5 July 1830, a miserable Sainte-Beuve wrote to explain his absence: 'I sometimes have atrocious bad thoughts – hate, jealousy, misanthropy. . . . But you must believe – you will believe, won't you? – that I am still the same person, changed as I am. Believe that by some miracle of friendship I am present in all that is dear to you.'

'Present in all that is dear to you' . . . Sainte-Beuve had been secretly meeting Adèle in churches and rented rooms. Hugo's Aunt Martine, soon to be comfortably installed in an adjoining apartment in the Place Royale, acted as a messenger and was paid for her trouble by Adèle. What else could she do? Her nephew was so 'stingy'.

The tone of their liaison is a stale, almost passionless intensity, coloured only by Sainte-Beuve's sense of pantomime. The concierge often noticed a nun climbing the stairs to the Hugos' apartment when the master was out. Sometimes, it was an old woman with a handbag, a veil and a wig half-concealing some patches of carrot-coloured hair.[15] Deceiving Hugo seemed to be an essential part of the business. In a poem which remained in his drawers until 1843, the master of disguise complained to Adèle that ever since Victor Hugo had popularized the Middle Ages, the churches had been full of 'young prowlers who might know who we are'.[16] But they overcame the obstacles and achieved a kind of satisfaction which Sainte-Beuve recorded in some of the most innuendo-ridden love poems in the language:

> Was it me you meant when yesterday you grasped
> Convulsively, as it lay there in your lap,
> My head, whose blooms are now so sparse,
> And murmured: ''Tis he – the precious darling!'[17]

Loved by the two best poets of the age, it seems a shame that Adèle was not very fond of poetry, though she did enjoy her husband's plays, or at least the stage-sets and costumes. She saved her imagination for practical arrangements. Sometimes, they met in cabs which trundled aimlessly along city streets with the blinds pulled down. Sometimes, Adèle would signal from her window like a lover in a Victor Hugo play. Hugo himself was easily dealt with:

> There is no question of his regaining his marital rights and if I pretend to be ill like this he will not be able to ask for anything ... He sometimes mentions bed, but only because he wants to sleep in a room which isn't quite so cold ... I tell him that I go to bed at a different time and that the slightest noise wakes me up and that once I'm awake I can't doze off again ... To make sure he doesn't suspect anything, I am kind and attentive. His eyes are poorly. I read to him and write for him. I look after him like a son taking care of his father. He seems to be grateful and is kind to me. I think this is the most sensible way to proceed, don't you?[18]

The life Hugo had built for himself since the death of his mother is dismantled here bit by bit: his working partnership with his childhood sweetheart, the pride of supporting several dependants, the friendship chiselled out of his own monumentality. Even the baby in the cradle was soiled with suspicion.

After some copies of Sainte-Beuve's privately printed poems leaked out in 1843, it was generally believed that Sainte-Beuve was the father of Adèle II.[19] Hugo tried not to speculate. His only attempt to deal with the subject in writing is a fragment which contrasts sadly with the love poems to his beloved Léopoldine: '(before the cradle) ... I know not, sleeping angel, if I am your father ... but I adopt you with my blessing.'[20]

Sainte-Beuve's expert opinion can be deduced from a poem 'À la Petite Ad ...', which is so slyly ambiguous that it has often been interpreted as a confession. He portrays Léopoldine, with her disdainful mouth, as the unmistakable image of her imperious father. Adèle II, by contrast, was conceived at a time when Sainte-Beuve 'was swimming every night into [Mme Hugo's] warm thoughts'. The answer lies in the following lines: 'Oh you who came then, child, you whom I see / Pure, yet in some ways resembling myself!'

The implications are clear: Adèle II was indeed the fruit of her father's loins (the loins of a 'furious lion'), but all along the silent Sainte-Beuve had been there with them in bed, penetrating Mme

Hugo more profoundly by another organ. Adèle II was sentimentally illegitimate.

The keys to Sainte-Beuve's relationship with Adèle are, first, that it waned with his admiration for Hugo; second, that he allowed so much of it to seep out – even in full view of Hugo himself. The poems of *Les Consolations*, published in 1830 and admired by Hugo, are fine examples of using honesty to deceive: descriptions of surreptitious visits to Adèle when her husband had 'gone out to dream'. He even sent messages to Adèle via the pages of the *Revue des Deux Mondes*, inserting meaningful quotations from Diderot's love letters – knowing, surely, that Hugo was far more likely to read the articles than Adèle.

The first crisis came towards the end of 1830. Sleeping with Adèle Hugo was a rare form of literary analysis, one of the early practical experiments of a critic who became famous for his ability to talk from inside his subject. With Hugo, such intimacy was impossible, especially now that his drawing-room was always full of hangers-on. The next step, therefore, was to confess. If Sainte-Beuve could never feel what it was like to be Victor Hugo, then Victor Hugo would know what it was like to be Sainte-Beuve. He told him that he had fallen in love with Adèle – 'How guilty and foolish I am!' – but said nothing of Adèle's feelings for him.

Honour now demanded an end to the friendship, but Hugo refused to let go:

> Let us not bury our friendship: let us keep it chaste and whole, as it always has been. Let us be indulgent with one another, my friend. I have my wound, you have yours. This painful shock will pass. Time will heal everything.... My wife has read your letter. Come and see me often. Write to me always.
> Remember that *after all* you have no better friend than me.[21]

Hugo's later references to Sainte-Beuve as a creature of indeterminate sex, a man who 'lifts his loathsome skirt and says, "Admire me!"', show an insight he lacked in 1830. Sainte-Beuve's confession was a perverse advance, almost a declaration of love for Hugo.

Meanwhile, the affair was flourishing. Most of Adèle's love letters were incinerated after Sainte-Beuve's death as an act of piety; but before they were thrown into the fire, their owner scribbled some notes which were published in 1957. The passages which survive have the horrible effect of shining a light straight through Adèle's personality.

One of her most passionate concerns was the expense: 'Victor would be very unhappy to see money being spent, when he is so parsimonious with himself, so eager to put money into savings.' It seems that after all those lake-like eyes concealed an expanse of very still water. Adèle's own father talks of her 'stultification',[22] and for every description of her 'Spanish majesty', there is another which calls her 'stupid'. She sat in the salon, interrupting conversations with dazzlingly trivial questions, suddenly silenced by her glowering husband. In June 1830, the champion of liberal Catholicism, Montalembert, spent an evening in Hugo's salon and was astounded by his 'muse':

> Hugo was very entertaining, very animated and very friendly. But his wife! Ye Gods! What a disappointment! Is that the woman who inspired her husband and his friend Sainte-Beuve with such delectable poems? . . . I who was already half in love with her simply from having heard her celebrated in the works of my favourite poets, I was thrown into consternation by her coarse appearance, her rough voice, her common tone.[23]

It should be said that Montalembert slightly modified his opinion of her manners (though not of her mind) when Adèle complimented him a few months later on his newspaper, *L'Avenir*, and her 'coarseness' may have been an attempt to shrug off the angel's wings Hugo had been trying to make her wear since 1820. But even Sainte-Beuve admitted, in 1838, that she had to be loved to be admired: 'an astounding and truly stupid gullibility gave me the measure of an intellect which is no longer enlightened by love'.[24]

By the spring of 1831, the friendship was riding up and down on Sainte-Beuve's conflicting desires to 'kill' Hugo (as he told him) and to continue worshipping at his feet. He was beginning to suspect that Hugo's naivety was a front. Hugo, still unaware that Adèle had deceived him, snatched at every sign of friendship, expressing himself in that Olympian style which was so stirring in fiction and so unconvincing in life.

Three months later, he knew the full extent of the damage. It has often been said that he never realized that Adèle was unfaithful. The reasoning behind this is that he would have been 'dishonoured' if he knew and didn't try to run Sainte-Beuve through with a sword. But this was real despair. He wrote to Sainte-Beuve on 6 July 1831, hoping to salvage either his friendship or his marriage:

> I have lost you and you have lost me. There is something between us. It is terrible to feel this, when we are together in the same room, seated on the same sofa and can touch each other's hands.... Even the obligation, imposed on me by *a person whom I must not mention here*, of being always present when you are there, reminds me constantly and very painfully that we are not the friends of old.

Realizing that Adèle had come under suspicion, Sainte-Beuve warned Hugo not to 'make reality overflow with your fancies'. Hugo wrote back the same day with a mixture of gratitude and desperation:

> You are right in all things; your actions have been impeccable and loyal ... I love you more than ever and I hate myself, without the least exaggeration, I hate myself for being so sick and stupid. Whenever you want me to lay down my life for you, you shall have it, and the sacrifice will be small. For you see – I say this to *you alone* – I am no longer happy. I have acquired the conviction that it was possible for the object of all my love to cease to love me, and that you perhaps had very little to do with it.

Sainte-Beuve responded at once with some intimate advice, which Hugo accepted as a mark of friendship:

> Try, my friend, to allow this limpid water [Adèle] to start running at your feet again without disturbing it and soon you will see in it your image restored.... I have always thought that a woman married to a genius was like Semele: the clemency of the god consists in divesting himself of his rays and blunting his lightning-bolts. Where he thinks he is simply playing and shining, he often wounds and consumes.

From then on, the friendship slowly rotted away behind a polite façade. The only echoes in the family correspondence are Adèle's allusions to vague illnesses and tactical complaints that Hugo didn't love her enough. A pathetic letter from Hugo, written from a house in the country on 17 July 1831, shows that he was still trying to resuscitate the past:

> I am nothing without you, my Adèle.... This bed where you might have been (though you don't want to any more, you naughty girl!), this room where I might have seen your dresses, your stockings, your clothes draped over the armchairs next to mine, the very table on which I am writing and where you would come and interrupt me with a kiss: it is all so painful and agonizing. I didn't sleep last night. I was thinking about you as if I was eighteen years old again. I dreamt about you as if I hadn't slept with you. Dear angel!

The most passionate part of Adèle's reply was the last line: 'I shall probably see you tomorrow, dear friend.'

*

ON THE EVENINGS when there were no visitors, the Hugos' drawing-room was like the opening scene of a play which never began. Adèle sat with her embroidery or made hats for herself out of Victor's old coats. It was the atmosphere of repressed scandal he had known as a child. But how could he have known, when he asked Adèle to take the place of his mother, that pieces of the past could not be detached and brought back to life in isolation?

Hugo now seemed to have been working out one of his own circuitous plots – a long path, doubling back on itself and eventually describing an ironic itinerary: futile premonition, catastrophe, delayed insight. The part of his mind that was an extension of his pen knew, long before the rest of him, that something sinister was going on. Every time he wrote about Sainte-Beuve, an odd clumsiness had contaminated his sentences with insulting ambiguities.[25] Even his first ode (December 1827) appeared on a first reading to compare Sainte-Beuve to a viper in a nest of eaglets – an image he used more than once and which Sainte-Beuve himself may have unconsciously picked up when he gave his god-daughter Adèle a 'boa' (a type of scarf).[26]

Hugo's contention that the mind is not just a passive observer of the universe but a spider poised on an infinite web seems peculiarly appropriate. Many years later, he wrote a poem entitled 'L'Affront'. It remained unpublished until 1910 and its human subject – described as a 'ghastly serpent' – has never been identified. But the biographical allusions all point quite clearly to Sainte-Beuve.[27] Written on 14 October 1869, the poem is obviously supposed to be about a man who is still alive. Unbeknownst to Hugo, Sainte-Beuve had died in Paris a few hours before.

The insights spawned by Sainte-Beuve's deception came in years late, in the darkness of exile, like light from distant galaxies: 'An ardent enemy is always more passionate than an ardent friend.' 'The smaller the heart, the more hate it contains.' 'An elephant who is hated by an ant is in danger.' 'The pedestal hates the statue because it can smell its feet but cannot see its beauty.' And, the most valuable insight of all – the realization that the Poet also had to be the Fool, punished by the crowd he entertained: 'All great men are cuckolds.'[28]

Hugo's personal tragedy has also proved to be a disaster for the truth. Less than a month after Hugo discovered the affair, Sainte-Beuve published an epic summary of Hugo's career in the *Revue des Deux Mondes*. It provided the raw material of virtually every biographical account for the next three decades. But like so many of Hugo's enemies and admirers, Sainte-Beuve was using Hugo's story to tell his own, talking to Adèle through her husband's lips:

> *Han d'Islande* – who would have believed it? – was originally a tender love message designed to deceive the watching eyes and to be intimately understood by one particular young girl. . . . I am entitled here only to hint at the ruses, stratagems and secret schemes of that marvellous love affair which was a novel in itself.

In 1833, Hugo made a final attempt to push aside the mirror and explain to his biographer that skilful writing need not be a sign of slyness – which is not to say that he didn't use some literary cunning to make his point:

> You know little of my true nature, Sainte-Beuve. You have always believed that I live by my mind, whereas I live only by my heart. To love, and to need *love* and *friendship* . . . that is the basis of my life . . . You have never sufficiently recognized that in me. Hence more than

one capital error in your otherwise benevolent judgement. Even at this, you may shake your head, yet it is certainly true.

As a biographer, Sainte-Beuve had every reason to want to believe in a calculating Hugo. It was safer and more interesting to assume deliberate deceit, and Hugo's style seemed to prove him right. The idiom in which Hugo had made his home was a model of the world of opposites he had grown up in, characterized, notoriously, by its heavy use of antithesis. The practical advantage was that the vehicle had a high centre of gravity: any number of words and images could be piled on top of one another without collapsing the syntax. But the obviousness of the device made him sound inherently insincere.

Contrary to the usual supposition, Hugo was sensitive to his rhetorical habits and their effect on the reader. His best defence was to point out that antithesis was 'God's favourite stylistic device'[29] – light and dark, male and female, good and evil. A more enlightening comment is hidden in an apparently frivolous letter dated 15 June 1833. It shows that, in Hugo's mind, literature was not just a vehicle for ideas but a machine for transforming the world:

> Poor old Paris continues to be very boring. . . . Dead calm and sunny. It's very tiresome. No crowds in the street, no clouds in the sky. – Excuse me, I'm wrong: yesterday it poured with rain. That's what happens when you have a mania for writing symmetrical sentences.[30]

*

THE DISCOVERY OF Adèle's infidelity had the effect of visiting the parents' antagonism on the children. Hugo made his first daughter the foundation of his happiness, his only tie with a coherent, just universe:

> It is the hour when children converse with angels.
> While we go rushing off to our strange amusements,
> All the little children, their eyes raised to heaven, . . .
> Beg the universal father to forgive us!
> And then they fall asleep.

Adèle now decided to sever this tie: she wanted to have Léopoldine sent away to boarding-school. Hugo eventually prevailed and had her enrolled in a nearby day-school. But his letter to Louise Bertin – the daughter of Bertin the Elder and the children's favourite playmate – shows what subtle violence Sainte-Beuve had stirred up: 'Saint-Denis is one of my poor wife's desires. For the last ten years she has been terribly taken up with motherhood. She wishes to rest a little. I am weak and shall probably give in.' This was the public image. But the letter ended with a curious echo of the period of courtship, when Hugo urged his fiancée not to lift up her skirts when she crossed the street:

> Please forgive this dirty letter – late, crumpled, and frayed at the bottom like an old winter dress which has had the mud scraped off it once too often.[31]

The poem on the praying children took its place in a collection of forty poems with the melancholy title, *Les Feuilles d'Automne* (November 1831). Most were happy evocations of family life, ironically showing the influence of Sainte-Beuve's domestic poetry, but, like the Hugos' drawing-room, opening on to a metaphysical landscape: in the evening, he stood on the balcony with Léopoldine, pointing out stars in the clear night air. (Most Parisians cooked and heated their homes with charcoal, which produced very little smoke. Hugo's references to nebulae and the colours of different planets are not necessarily poetic embellishments.)

In his glowing review of *Les Feuilles d'Automne*, Sainte-Beuve detected a new tone: 'scepticism invading the poet's heart'; 'a memorable example of the corrosive energy of our age and its gradual triumph over the sturdiest of personal convictions'. The implication was that, by cuckolding Hugo, Sainte-Beuve was acting as an agent of the Zeitgeist.

Yet this was also Hugo's perception. In the preface, he projected his fireside meditations into a wider sphere. The whole continent was an objective correlative of his own predicament: 'entire races wiped out, deported en masse or put in chains; Ireland turned into a graveyard, Italy a prison, Siberia populated with Poland . . . something worm-eaten which is crumbling away and, for attentive ears, the rumbling sound of revolutions . . . driving their subterranean galleries under all the kingdoms of Europe, ramifications of the great central revolution whose crater is Paris'.

With *Les Feuilles d'Automne*, Hugo began in earnest a systematic attempt to present his life as a working model of human history. The idea was to replace the crude narratives imposed by clocks and calendars with the more illuminating coincidences of heart and history. In this, he succeeded so well that it is impossible to tell the story of his life accurately without feeling a constant tug of regret that events arranged themselves with such callous disregard for genius.

Hugo's own versions of life in the early 1830s produce a sequence of what a traditional historian would have to describe as 'lies' – although these helpful fake coincidences have been used by most of Hugo's biographers, right up to the present, to make the life and times cohere:[32]

Notre-Dame de Paris did not appear in the bookshops on the very day that a mob – as if in imitation of the final chapters – ransacked the Archbishop's Palace and threw his library into the river.

Les Feuilles d'Automne was not published on the day an insurrection broke out in Lyons.

Performances of *Marion de Lorme* were not interrupted by fighting in the streets and the audience did not have to clamber over barricades in order to reach the theatre.

Le Roi S'Amuse was not performed for the first time on the day a shot was fired at King Louis-Philippe.[33]

The myth which is hardest of all to relinquish is the birth of Adèle II on the second day of the July Revolution. Her cries did not drown out the gunfire because she was born twenty-seven days later on 24 August 1830.[34]

On the other hand, in the privacy of his study, Hugo was able to wait until the first stroke of midnight on New Year's Eve 1830 before writing, in *Notre-Dame de Paris*, 'That will be the hour of the people striking.'[35]

These lies are probably closer to the truth that matters than accurate statements. By adjusting his chronology, Hugo was hinting that, though he himself may have been deaf to the evidence, his work had always known that it was on the side of the masses. Gradually, he was learning to listen to his own voice.

*

ON 5 JUNE 1832, impatience with the Government of Louis-Philippe and the effects of economic depression exploded in a revolt which might have established a full republic once and for all had it not been swiftly and brutally repressed.

Hugo had been writing a play in the Tuileries Gardens. Towards evening, the sound of gunfire drifted over from the direction of Les Halles. The Gardens were deserted and the park-keeper had to unlock the gates to let him out. Instead of hurrying home, he followed the sound through the empty streets, unaware that one-third of Paris had already fallen to the mob. The area around Les Halles was choked with barricades. Hugo headed north up the Rue Montmartre. Then he turned right into the Passage du Saumon, the last turning before the Rue du Bout du Monde (World's End Street).

He was half-way down the alley when the grilles at either end slammed shut. A band of rioters appeared at one end; at the other, Government troops took up position. The shops had long since closed their doors and shutters. Hugo flattened himself against the wall, between the half-columns which divided the shop-fronts, trapped between the forces of order and anarchy. For a quarter of an hour, bullets flew both ways down the alley.[36]

Next day, news came in of a horrendous massacre at the church of Saint-Merry near Les Halles. In all, about 800 rioters – legitimists as well as socialists, workers as well as bourgeois – had been killed or wounded. The compromise Government which had been entrusted with the ideals of the 1830 Revolution had shown its true face.

Hugo had begun to keep a diary – the thoughts of a tax-paying, property-owning father of four with timorous leanings to the left. 'Follies drowned in blood,' he wrote. 'One day we shall have a republic and when it comes of its own free will, it will be good. But let us not harvest in May the fruit which will not ripen until July.' 'We should not allow barbarians to bespatter our flag with red.'[37] This is a perfect example of the over-cautious policies which Hugo derides in Les Misérables, where the 1832 uprising is seen as one of the great hinges of modern history: 'to wrap that giant called the People in flannel and put it quickly to bed'; 'to treat Hercules as a convalescent'; 'to fit the revolution with a lampshade'.[38] At the time, his only other comment on the 'follies drowned in blood' was that they would make an excellent subject for a poem.

No such poem appeared – though a later, less cowardly piece on the subject was redated to make it look as though it was written immediately after the rebellion.[39] And even then, the main objection to the Government's clumsy concessions and repressions made him sound like an irritable bourgeois sitting up in bed to write to his *député*: the result of all this civil strife was that 'At the hour when sleep demands its moment of peace / One hears the heavy cannon trundling over the cobbles of the city streets!'

The biggest outward change in Hugo's life that year indicated a need to retreat from the evidence and even from the nineteenth century.

The Place Royale, now known again by its older name, the Place des Vosges, is a magnificent square of tall, early seventeenth-century town houses in red brick and white stone. Its cosy monumentality appealed to Hugo, who was willing to pay a high rent for bigger rooms and historical connections. The house in the south-east corner – number 6 – was said to have been the home of Marion de Lorme. A secret rear exit had been used by lovers of the famous courtesan to reach the safety of the crowded Rue Saint-Antoine. It had the extra advantage of sharing the corner with the house where Théophile Gautier lived with his parents. Hugo would lean out of his second-floor window, leave bread for the birds (like Esmeralda), and chat with Gautier over the void about art and literature.

This island fortress of Renaissance architecture stood on the edge of the once aristocratic Marais, turning its back on one of the poorest areas of Paris: its blue-slate roofs rose over the Faubourg Saint-Antoine, the notorious breeding ground of sedition which spread like an open sewer from the Hôtel de Ville to the Place de la Bastille.

In October 1832, Hugo signed a lease for two apartments with an annual rent of 1830 francs (about £5500 today).[40] The smaller apartment was for the conniving Aunt Martine. The move had been delayed by a cholera epidemic which claimed the life of the Hugos' concierge and almost carried off little Charles. When the epidemic was over, they moved 'with the aid of those supposedly convenient machines which helped so many poor devils to move to their final resting-place during the epidemic. For a week, I have been living in chaos, nailing and hammering, dressed like a burglar.'[41] By the time Hugo laid down his hammer and nails, Marion de Lorme would have felt quite at home.

When Charles Dickens visited in 1847, he saw 'a most extraordinary place, looking like an old curiosity shop, or the Property Room of some gloomy vast old Theatre'.[42] Entering from the main staircase, guests found themselves being out-stared by David's larger-than-life marble bust of the master.[43] The hall or antechamber was lit by a long, narrow window in the corner. Wooden coffers lined the walls, which were hung in red damask: Hugo had learned from set designers how to create an appearance of regal luxury at low cost. In the twilight of the dining-room and drawing-room, odd, massive objects sat like remnants of *Les Orientales* stranded in three-dimensional reality: an antique musket, a Turkish yataghan of silver and steel, Auguste de Châtillon's life-size painting of 'The Red Monk' reading his Bible on the haunch of a naked woman. An antique compass was said to have helped Columbus discover America, and there was a crossbow that might have belonged to William Tell.[44] There were tapestries and pieces of armour, and even a canopy of state, believed to be Hugo's armchair, but actually the first sign of his habit of providing seats for invisible guests. Watching for the sliver of Sainte-Beuve as it passed between the columns in the square below, Mme Hugo might have felt like Rapunzel. Hugo had carried off a counter-*coup d'état*: it was obvious that this was his home.

The *genius loci* sat in the red gloom with green eyeshades completing what he called a 'bilogy' (cf. 'trilogy'). *Marion de Lorme*, banned by the last Government, had been performed in August 1831 and, surprisingly, was only moderately successful, perhaps because it was two years late. It found its audience through re-editions and revivals. By the end of the decade, the poor and principled orphan, Didier, who falls in love with the courtesan, Marion de Lorme, had become an anti-establishment role model; his disillusionment and dress sense (all black) were enormously attractive to the next two generations of young Frenchmen. It cast their affairs with working girls in a poetic light.

The next play, by contrast, was instantly influential. A fiasco on the stage, it was so successful as a book that customers of *cabinets de lecture* were allowed to keep it for only an hour at a time.

Read in the light of Hugo's life, the plot of *Le Roi S'Amuse* sounds like a condensed reaction to Sainte-Beuve's treachery.[45] The words scratched by François I on the window-frame at Chambord had been singing in Hugo's mind: 'Women are often fickle . . .'. He constructed his tragedy around the philandering King who tries to seduce the daughter of his fool, Triboulet, mistaking her for the hunchback's secret mistress. It was the mental equation involving Sainte-Beuve, Adèle and Léopoldine, but with the two women merged. If any further proof were needed that Hugo knew what was going on, the guilty pair should be imagined sitting in the Comédie Française on the first night, witnessing the opening scene: King François, lusting after a married *bourgeoise*, meets her secretly in a church, disguised in 'a grey dress' (a monk's robe). The fool supplies the misogynistic moral: 'A woman is a very sophisticated form of devil.'

The final scene offered an eerily convincing solution to the equation, though, at the time, it seemed to belong to the realm of pure fantasy. Triboulet is about to drop a sack into the river Seine, believing it to contain the dead body of the King. But then he hears a voice from the back of the stage singing, '*Souvent femme varie . . .*'. The horrible truth dawns on him: 'I have murdered my child!'

The play had only one performance (22 November 1832). The painters Achille and Eugène Devéria turned up for the first night with some relatives, one of whom was a hunchback. They were hoping that Victor Hugo had exhausted his obsession with cripples. (Another human gargoyle had lolloped across the stage in *Marion de Lorme*.) When Triboulet appeared with his hump, they left in disgust. The respectable members of the audience decided to be angry with Hugo for taking liberties with the great names of French history. François I, played by an actor described by Hugo's brother-in-law as 'a butterfly in boots',[46] expunged the jokes as he went along and made large parts of the play incomprehensible. The title itself suggested a French Nero and was felt to be an incitement to revolt. Worst of all, the fool's subversive outburst – 'Your mothers prostituted themselves to lackeys! / You are bastards, one and all!' – was taken to refer to the well-known fact that King Louis-Philippe's mother and grandmother had been unusually fond of servants. The body in the sack was the last straw. Since the noise in the auditorium made it hard to follow the plot,[47] these scenes tended to materialize in the storm like little islands of pure absurdity or fragments of popular farce: a clown holding a long and miserable conversation with a sack ... If Hugo's plays could be re-created with the original audiences, he might appear much closer to Ionesco and Beckett than to the costume dramatists of the nineteenth century.

The main problem, however, was Hugo's army of supporters: the idealistic sons of the bourgeoisie were outnumbered now by a wine-sodden rabble who sang revolutionary songs and came from a different part of Paris. Word was out that Hugo's plays were a humorous variety of pornography. *Le Roi S'Amuse* and *Marion Delorme* were just as likely to be seen by his concierge as by his neighbours in the Place Royale. With each play, his audience was expanding, with an alarming downward trend.

Next morning, before he had time to organize reinforcements, he heard that the Comédie Française had been ordered to suspend performances immediately, which was strange because censorship had been abolished after the 1830 Revolution.

It was now that he realized what he had seen in the Passage du Saumon. A criminal government, conducting a series of tiny *coups d'état* in the name of 'public order'. It may even be that, despite Hugo's denials, *Le Roi S'Amuse* had after all been a conscious attack on the Government. His contract with the publisher contains a clause declaring it null and void if the play is censored, which does rather suggest precognition. His diary records his reaction in an obscene image – a verbal equivalent of the caricatures which served as propaganda for the illiterate: the Government of Louis-Philippe was a monster whose excremental organs were several times the size of the rest of its body.[48]

In this frame of mind, Hugo composed a speech. Knowing that it was useless to sue the Government, and worried that student demonstrations in support of the play might be treated as a riot,[49] he had decided to take the Comédie Française to court: since censorship no longer existed in law, the theatre had no right to ban his play.

On 19 December 1832, the Tribunal du Commerce had the atmosphere of a first night. A large crowd had gathered to witness Hugo's maiden speech.

He turned out to be a natural orator. For half an hour, a regime whose petty hypocrisy was compared to Napoleon's epic despotism was peppered with grotesque images. At least under Napoleon loss of liberty had been the entrance ticket to a 'sublime spectacle'. Today's Government was a highwayman crouching in its forest of laws, picking off one freedom after another.

The frustrated anger of the last two years had found a target in the comparatively simple deceptions of the Government. Hugo's elegantly insulting speech showed the stylistic effect of Adèle's infidelity. She had proved that middle-class decorum was a thin disguise and even that the bourgeoisie itself was not a separate class but simply 'the satisfied portion of the populace'. 'The bourgeois is someone who has the time to sit down. An armchair is not a caste.'[50]

Hugo was catching up with the insights of his own work. A few days later, when he asked for his Government pension to be discontinued, he was marking the transferral of the artist's allegiance from the traditional patron, the King, to a more volatile but potentially more lucrative sponsor, the people. Essentially, this was the speech he was to give for the rest of his public life, and it seems fitting that he ended it with a glimpse of his own future:

> Today, my freedom as a poet is taken by a censor; tomorrow, my freedom as a citizen will be taken by a policeman. Today, I am banished from the theatre; tomorrow, I shall be banished from the land. Today, I am gagged; tomorrow, I shall be deported. Today, a state of siege exists in literature; tomorrow, it will exist in the city.

The judges wisely declared themselves incompetent and ordered Hugo to pay costs. But by that time, a new play was already in rehearsal at the Porte-Saint-Martin Theatre. Hugo was going 'to prove to the Government that art and freedom can sprout again overnight under the bumbling foot that squashed them flat'. 'The literary work and the political struggle', he wrote in the preface to the new play, 'will henceforth be undertaken simultaneously. It is possible to do one's job and one's duty at the same time. Man has two hands.'

Lucrèce Borgia was the second half of the 'bilogy', conceived at the same time as *Le Roi S'Amuse* and 'at the same point in his heart'. According to Hugo's interpretation, the first play showed 'paternity sanctifying physical deformity', the second, 'maternity purifying moral deformity'.

This crisp bisection of a complex body of work is what students call 'a good quote' and is so typical of Hugo that copies of his texts in university libraries tend to be more than usually stiff with annotations and asterisks, as if reverting to their original manuscript state; sometimes, only a few lines of his prefaces, often the most revealing, escape the pencil. Hugo's handy formula hardly did justice to the savagery of his imagination. Lucrezia Borgia falls in love with the young and parentless Gennaro, whom she accidentally poisons along with the other anti-Borgia conspirators. To avenge the murder of his best friend, Gennaro stabs Lucrezia to death. As she dies, she reveals the awful truth – 'I am your mother!' – with a note of happiness in her voice which was psychologically acute enough to be condemned as unrealistic.

Depicting a young man who ignores the desperate pleas of a woman who is both his mother and his would-be lover is an odd way to demonstrate the 'purifying' power of motherhood. From Gennaro's point of view, the real tragedy, which casts a pall over the entire moral universe, is the worthlessness of instinct:

> Oh no! My mother is not a woman like yourself, Madame Lucrèce! I feel her in my heart and dream of her in my soul as she really is.... In his heart, a son is never wrong about his mother.... Something in me cries aloud that my mother cannot be a demon of incest, lust and poison like the beautiful women of today.

As rehearsals progressed, it began to look as though, in writing his bilogy, Hugo had unconsciously been plotting a kind of revenge.

At the preliminary reading of the play, a young actress called Mlle Juliette caught his eye. He remembered seeing her a few months before, perhaps at a reception following one of Dumas's plays – 'Pale, dark-eyed, young, tall and radiant'.[51] Why had he not spoken to her then? Because 'the barrel of gunpowder is afraid of the spark' – an image which suggests that his attraction to a woman who belonged to a 'dangerous', disreputable profession and very likely had working-class origins, was closely related to the curiosity that had driven him to go and watch the insurrection at close quarters.

Now, as the play took shape in the first days of 1833, contact was unavoidable. Mlle Juliette had asked the theatre director, Harel, to obtain for her the tiny role of the Princesse Negroni, who supplies the poison, declaring, diplomatically, 'There is no such thing as a small role in one of M. Victor Hugo's plays'; and Hugo had agreed, despite the fact that she was known to be jittery on stage and relied heavily on the prompter.

He seems to have fallen instantly in love: it was the first shot of an addictive drug, the traces of which fill his works with memorable depictions of the vital moment: 'The day when a woman who passes in front of you gives off light as she walks, you are lost: you are in love. There is only one thing to do: think of her so intently that she is forced to think of you.'[52]

The outside world saw only the humorous side-effects. Actors and journalists who sat in on rehearsals of *Lucrèce Borgia* were entertained by the sight of Baron Hugo – furrowed brow, green eyeshades, trousers held up by braces (a detail noticed by Juliette) – treating a minor actress like a great lady. (Actresses were normally addressed in the familiar '*tu*' form.) He stood with stop-watch in hand, timing the scene changes,[53] instructing experienced actors in the minute nuances of diction; but with Juliette he was untypically soft. The leading man, Frédérick Lemaître – an authority on the sexual politics of actresses – had seen it all before: 'She will capture him by saying, "You are great!" and keep him by saying, "You are handsome!"'[54]

Meanwhile, Hugo was making enquiries of Harel. What he learned about Juliette might easily have frightened him off. On the other hand, it was a chance to test the thesis of *Marion de Lorme*: fallen women could be 'redeemed' by love.

Julienne-Joséphine Gauvain was born in Fougères in Brittany on 10 April 1806. Before she was two years old, both parents – a tailor and a housemaid – were dead. Her uncle, a coastguard called Drouet, rescued her from the poor house. While he looked out for smugglers,

Juliette ran wild in the Breton countryside – an image which, for Hugo, would have conjured up his mother's childhood. At the age of ten, the little savage was sent to Paris to be educated in a convent on the Montagne Sainte-Geneviève. She grew up in the heart of the Latin Quarter inside the silent, antiquated institution which is one of the models for the Petit-Picpus convent in *Les Misérables*.

By 1825, the world beyond the convent walls had no more secrets. Mlle Drouet was modelling for the sculptor, James Pradier, thanks to whom she can now be seen as 'The City of Strasbourg' in the Place de la Concorde.[55] Erotic sculptures of her body were sold to private collectors.[56] Pradier, then in his mid-thirties, liked to think of himself as her guardian, and his letters to Juliette, signed 'your friend, lover and father', form a very Balzacian set of precepts for young actresses. It was Pradier who advised her to use the name 'Mlle Juliette': 'It is, I believe, a waste of time to pass yourself off as a married woman. I feel it lessens the interest, for, as you know ... whenever a man offers help, he always hopes. In certain cases, therefore, you should not remove that hope.'[57] Along with the advice, he gave her a child, Claire, who now lived with her father.

Since 1826, Juliette had had at least four lovers, including the millionaire Prince Anatole Demidov, the estranged husband of Napoleon's niece, Mathilde – a smutty little man who set her up in an apartment in the Rue de l'Échiquier – and the journalist Alphonse Karr, who borrowed all her money and never paid it back: 'Pawn your jewels if necessary and lend me 500 francs,' he wrote. 'I shall have no hesitation or qualms about taking half your little fortune. ... And anyway, my pretty girl, I can't really see how I'd manage to live apart from you.'[58] (Karr is now remembered for the saying, '*Plus ça change, plus c'est la même chose.*')

To insure herself against poverty, Juliette made her lovers overlap. It was probably she who taught Hugo the actress's proverb, 'A woman who has one lover is an angel, a woman who has two lovers is a monster, and a woman who has three lovers is a woman.'[59] To Paris society, she was a typical courtesan: a mediocre actress, a brilliant dresser, a fluent spender, equally familiar with pawn-shops and casinos, physically confident, with a boisterous sense of humour, unashamed to show her plebeian origins and, of course, amazingly beautiful. In a *roman à clé* published in 1833, Alphonse Karr painted a more realistic picture. The following passage is almost certainly a direct transcription of one of Juliette's letters:

> I feel that my soul has desires just like my body – and a thousand times more ardent. . . . You give me pleasures which are followed by exhaustion and shame. Yet I dream of calm and constant happiness. Listen, I am too proud to lie: I shall leave you and abandon you all – the earth itself and even life – if I can find a man whose soul caresses my soul as you love and caress my body.[60]

When she asked for a role in *Lucrèce Borgia*, Juliette may have had something very different in mind, as the recently published correspondence of James Pradier reveals. On 8 January 1833, in mid-rehearsal, she received a note from Pradier. He asked if she could help him to obtain a commission for a statue from an influential *député*, M. Debelleyme.[61] Louis-Maurice Debelleyme was a close acquaintance of Victor Hugo, and a later, undated note from Pradier to Juliette shows that Hugo was the ideal intercessor: 'Your influence on our excellent Victor H. has already served me well with that kind M. de Beleme' . . . Was Juliette performing a role for Pradier within the role written by Hugo? If so, she soon found that the mask had stuck.

Hugo was equally guilty of professional misconduct. From one rehearsal to the next, he padded out the tiny role of the Princesse Negroni and inserted a little dialogue which is strictly unnecessary and which even distracts from the climax: 'One can scarcely describe the Princesse Negroni as a role,' he admits in a note to the published play. 'It is a sort of apparition, a beautiful, young and fateful figure.' Night after night – and soon with the rest of Paris – he watched the beautiful apparition listening to the words which had been hammering in his head. It was one of the most public declarations of love ever made. (This is Juliette's role in its entirety.)

PRINCESS NEGRONI, *to Maffio, pointing at Gennaro*: M. le Comte
  Orsini, you have a friend who appears to be very sad.
MAFFIO: He is ever thus, Madame. You must forgive me for having
  brought him without your kind invitation. . . . We never part. We
  live together. A gypsy once told us we would die on the same day.

NEGRONI, *laughing*: Did he tell you whether it would be night or day?
MAFFIO: He told us it would be day.
NEGRONI, *laughing even louder*: Your gypsy didn't know what he was
    talking about. – And are you very fond of that young man?
MAFFIO: As much as one man may love another.
NEGRONI: Well then! You have each other. You are happy.
MAFFIO: Friendship does not fill the heart, Madame.
NEGRONI: God! What can fill the heart?
MAFFIO: Love.
NEGRONI: You always have love on your lips.
MAFFIO: And you in your eyes.
NEGRONI: How odd you are!
MAFFIO: How beautiful you are!
          [He puts his arm around her waist.]
NEGRONI: M. le Comte Orsini, let me go.
MAFFIO: A kiss on your hand?
NEGRONI: No!
          [She slips away.]

When Henry Bulwer translated some scenes from the play in 1834,
he seems to have suspected some theatrical hanky-panky and, interestingly – allowing for cultural differences – came very close to the truth:
'The reader will observe that it is not my fault if the Count Orsini
and the Princess Negroni behave a little too much like a young
Oxonian and a Dover chambermaid.'[62]

The first night of *Lucrèce Borgia* (2 February 1833) was a triumph
which expunged the failure of *Le Roi S'Amuse*. The poisoning, the
incest and the adultery were shocking, but the whole performance
was stamped with the bullying authority of Frédérick Lemaître – the
only actor in Paris who could stare an audience into silence. An
embarrassing moment was averted when Hugo noticed that a hand
had painted a 'secret door' to look like a ceremonial archway –
possibly not unconnected with the fact that the set designer was
Charles Séchan, one of Juliette's former lovers. Between Acts I and
II, Hugo grabbed the buckets and brushes and repainted it as a
continuation of the tapestried wall. Some veterans of *Hernani*, meeting in Delacroix's studio, had been horrified to learn that Hugo was
going to have his characters talk in prose 'like vulgar bourgeois'. A

deputation was sent to the Place Royale to demand an explanation. Hugo quelled the revolt by convincing them that 'it was the duty of Romanticism to renovate prose just as it had smashed the old alexandrine mould'.[63]

It was partly this subtle compromise that ensured the play's success – not that every newspaper was prepared to change its mind so soon after *Le Roi S'Amuse*. Hugo still showed a fine disregard for the rules of drama and the entertainment needs of the average family. A term was coined – '*quasi-héros*' – to describe all those quasi-Quasimodos who seemed to imply that everyone in authority was corrupt and that nobility of heart increased as one descended the social ladder. The *Revue Théâtrale* – soon to change its name to *L'Anti-Romantique* – claimed to be sick to death of Hugo's morbid imagination: 'The production of M. Hugo's next dramatic work will be entrusted to the association of funeral directors.'

> We have learned that M. Hugo is threatening us with a twelve-act drama covering a period of 300 years. We shall thus have the pleasure of seeing four or five different generations pass before our eyes. Much praise has been lavished on a delectable scene in which two women give birth on stage to two pretty infants who are later seen dying of old age.[64]

The majority opinion was that of Adèle's father. He wrote to his son-in-law after the first night: 'Everyone in the theatre had goose pimples. Where were all the enemies? As for myself, you almost gave me a heart attack. I am now surrounded by foot-baths and all that.'[65]

When the curtain fell, Hugo refused to join the actors on stage. He ran out into the rain and escaped in a carriage. According to one version, the carriage was unhitched by Hugomaniacs and towed back to the Place Royale, where a party went on until four in the morning.

For fourteen nights, Hugo watched the Princesse Negroni flirting with the guests she is about to poison. She wore a pink and silver dress, pearls and feathers in her dark hair; 'supple and serpentine', according to Gautier, 'like a snake standing on its tail'.[66] One evening, Hugo declared his love in person. On 16 February, a note was handed to him at the theatre, addressed to 'M. Victor':

Come and fetch me tonight at Mme K.'s.*

I shall try to make the hours pass quickly by loving you. Until tonight. Oh! tonight will be everything!

I shall give myself to you entirely.

J.[67]

That night, Hugo did not return to the Place Royale. It was the Saturday before Mardi Gras. The streets were full of revellers in costumes and masks. Adèle must have assumed her husband had been taken off to a party. But Hugo was celebrating his 'second birth':

On 26 February 1802, I awoke to life; on 16 February 1833, I awoke to love. My mother made me, and you created me. . . . I was suckled by my mother, who was my nurse; I drank your soul from your lips, and you were also my nurse, for you filled me with perfection.[68]

*

IN THE SMALL HOURS OF 17 February 1833, a man in his early thirties left the apartment owned by Prince Anatole Demidov in the Rue de l'Échiquier. He stepped out into the street and opened his umbrella.

Day was dawning, it was pouring with rain; the masks, all ragged and spattered with mud, were descending noisily from La Courtille,† inundating the Boulevard du Temple. They were drunk and so was I: they on wine, I on love. Through their cries I heard a song which my heart was singing. I saw none of the spectres that surrounded me – ghosts of dead happiness, phantoms of the faded orgy. I saw you – a soft, shining shadow in the night – your eyes, your brow, your beauty, your smile which intoxicates as much as your kisses. Oh, that morning, so cold and rainy in the sky, so gloriously warm in my soul! Memory![69]

* A village of open-air cafés and dance-halls to the east of Paris.
† Juliette's friend, Laure Krafft.

CHAPTER TEN

Olympio

(1833–1839)

T HE ENTIRE CITY OF PARIS could now enjoy the sort of view that was normally reserved for concierges. Writing to his future wife in March 1833, Balzac sensed a novel in the making: 'Victor Hugo, who married for love and has pretty children, is in the arms of an infamous courtesan.' Details followed in June:

> He has fallen in love with an actress called Juliette who, along with other tokens of affection, has sent him a bill from her laundress to the tune of 7000 francs. Hugo was forced to sign promissory notes in order to pay for his love letter. Imagine a great poet – for he is a poet – working to pay off Mlle Juliette's laundress.[1]

For Balzac – as for Hugo – courtesans were a dangerous drug in human form, spreaders of disease and destitution. Others, like the young dandy, Barbey d'Aurevilly, welcomed the news that Victor Hugo had gone 'stark staring mad': 'The reason? An utterly untalented actress from the Porte-Saint-Martin called Juliette.' After spending the last four years amassing a fortune, Hugo had succumbed to Nature's revenge – an Aphrodite 'raised among the seaweed on the shores of Brest': 'By the God who made woman, she is worth a blade or a bullet in the heart of any man who has one.'[2]

Sainte-Beuve guessed correctly that Hugo's 'beautiful poems' to his mistress would 'cover up and glorify' his 'sin'.[3] There was a feeling in any case that someone of Hugo's stature was entitled to a small harem.[4] The actress was the missing piece in his image and was expected to fill a gap in his work. The poems of *Les Feuilles d'Automne* were full of dove-like children with rosy eyelids and sunny haloes; the 'love' poems were all about mothers and virgins; and the poet himself, as 'thought' ploughed its daily 'furrow' across his brow, saved up all his passion for 'fatherland' and 'freedom'. It sounded like a curriculum vitae in rhyming couplets: the Academy and Parliament could not be far away. There was just an occasional trace of 'rising sap', 'suddenly spraying verses at thy feet', and some flimsy erotic fantasies like naughty lithographs: 'To contemplate, veil-less in her bath, / An innocent-eyed girl'.

The new source of inspiration proved difficult to master, but the audience was waiting. A woman who had captured the heart of the great Victor Hugo had a right to expect something more than a verbal assurance. Hugo lifted up the barbells of his epic-intimate style and, on 7 March 1833, sent her the first love letter he had written for over a decade.

> I love you, my poor angel, as you well know, and yet you want to have it in writing. You are right. We must love each other, and then tell each other, and then write it down, and then kiss each other on the mouth, on the eyes, and elsewhere. You are my beloved Juliette.
>
> When I am sad, I think of you as one thinks of the sun in winter; and when I am happy, I think of you as one thinks of shade on a sunny day. As you can see, Juliette, I love you with all my soul.
>
> You look as young as a child and as meek as a mother, and so I enfold you in all those different forms of love at once.
>
> Kiss me, beautiful Juju!
>
> V.[5]

There is no better proof that Sainte-Beuve was wrong to confuse rhetoric with insincerity. Hugo's letter was a serene depiction of a violent relationship. It reads like the prose draft of an ode. Each paragraph contains the substance of a well-balanced stanza: words and action, sun and shade, childhood and motherhood.

Forgetting Pradier's advice always to write in a small, elegant hand,[6] Juliette practised a more inspirational form of Romanticism. Her letters have a wider emotional repertoire than Hugo's, which is fortunate since she wrote almost 25,000 of them in fifty years.

> Poor poet! You wrote *Les Feuilles d'Automne* with love, childish laughter ... and lots of happiness, and you never noticed how a dismal,

rainy day like today makes the greenest and most firmly attached leaves turn yellow and fall off the trees. You have no idea – for you are astonished when I cry and almost angry with my grief.[7]

She complained of her own clumsiness, using an image later made famous by Baudelaire: 'I stumble over words and ideas like a drunkard on uneven paving-stones.'[8] But she had a superbly modern style, a combination of melodrama and the language of her convent education, which gave Hugo the interesting illusion of corresponding with one of his own characters:

The corpse which lies cold between our kisses must at all costs be buried; and then, like martyrs, we shall begin a new life, a heavenly life of oblivion and bliss – happiness as pure as my soul, for my soul has remained pure while my body was defiled.[9]

The first months passed with no sign that Hugo was willing to leave his wife. Once, he smuggled Juliette in to the Place Royale to show off his treasures, but it only served to emphasize what she called her 'crouching, humiliating posture'.[10] She was still living in Prince Demidov's apartment, harried by usurers and bogus creditors, fulfilling her contract with the Porte-Saint-Martin, sometimes appearing two or three times the same night in different plays. Her last role, at the end of 1833, was as a dancing apothecary in *Le Malade Imaginaire*.[11] Anonymous letters threatened Hugo with blackmail or kindly informed him that his mistress was paying debts with her body. Worse, there was the ineradicable stain of her past and the certain knowledge that reproductions of her body, sculpted by Pradier, were on sale all over Europe. Hugo used his jealousy to sever her ties with the world in which she made her living. His anguish produced some very rare and revealing letters, in which all his masks are jumbled up – the heroic lover, the orator, the angry child, even the comedian:

How can you fail to see that all I do – even when I hurt you – is love? It may be insane, absurd, extravagant, malicious, jealous, nervous – whatever you will – but it is love. – And are you so good yourself? I long to be lying at your feet, kissing them. If you love me, when you have read this letter, you will smile.[12]

The battering-ram of adjectives should be imagined with Hugo's parade-ground voice, which, according to two poets who attended the same play-reading at his home, was either 'vast and sonorous, admirably suited to his verse', or 'a disagreeable organ', 'composed of two extreme tones – high and low – continually oscillating between one and the other'.[13]

This was not a gentle idyll. Hugo was terrified by his own behaviour. What if she decided to use his letters against him? Actresses were notoriously fickle. In response, Juliette threw the first six months of correspondence into the fire.[14] Hugo admired the sacrifice but was upset that a priceless treasure had been lost: 'those letters were the truest, most deeply felt things I have ever written'.[15]

Humming in the background of these early letters is the twenty-four-hour gossip network which made Paris such an efficient cultural factory and such an inconvenient place for lovers. Hugo had access to the network and 'friends' like Alphonse Karr to keep him well informed. Juliette parried his suspicions with just enough ambiguity not to be guilty of lying: 'As God is my witness, I have not deceived you in our love a single time in the last four months.' 'The most significant love letters', says Hugo, 'are those which have to be deciphered. A woman's modesty takes refuge in illegibility.'

In a poem written in the late 1830s, he describes a Parisian standing alone in a cellar 30 feet underground, whispering something nasty about an enemy: the word leaves the cellar, finds the enemy's home, opens the door and says, 'Here I am, I come from the mouth of so-and-so.'[16] Whether it was this miraculous diffusion of embarrassing information or something simpler (Juliette's maid may also have worked for Frédérick Lemaître's mistress, Atala Beauchêne), the actor had a ringside seat for the great affair of 1833. The sordid details were recorded by Sainte-Beuve:

> She even tells him how great he is in the housekeeping accounts which she submits to him (because he's also a skinflint). She makes notes like this: 'Received from my *too* precious darling ... received from my *King*, my *angel*', etc.[17]

Hugo actually spent large sums of money paying off Juliette's debts, which explains why the family accounts show a sudden increase in charitable donations: 'alms', 'aid', 'good work', etc. – not necessarily false descriptions in Hugo's mind. Nevertheless, the sheer quality of the gossip is astounding. Frédérick Lemaître's titbit, though reported second-hand, matches Juliette's monthly account book very closely indeed:[18]

	francs	sous	liards*
Cash remaining	4		3
1st: money earned by my Toto	51	4	
4th: money from the purse of my beloved	5	10	
Carried over	60	14	3
6th: money earned by my darling	44		
9th: money from my Toto's purse	10		

Hugo was drilling her in the art of home economics in preparation for their secret life. For Juliette, it was a drastic change, to judge by the list of clothing she pawned to pay creditors (January 1834): 60 cambric blouses, 48 towels, 35 dressing-gowns, 33 petticoats, 32 handkerchiefs, 25 dresses, 12 bodices.[19] In July 1834, when the bailiffs moved in to the Rue de l'Échiquier, Hugo installed her in two tiny rooms and a kitchen in the auspiciously named Rue de Paradis, slightly closer to the Place Royale. She would then be able to offer proof of her love in her 'coarse slippers, dirty curtains, iron spoons, and the absence of any prettiness or pleasure unconnected with our love'.[20]

*

ALTHOUGH HUGO WAS BLESSED with an inability to blush,[21] Adèle found out about Juliette almost immediately and was quick to tell her father. From Rennes, Foucher wrote to his sister-in-law in his man-of-the-world style:

> That fine lady from the Porte-Saint-Martin – the one who, as part of her reform programme, has left her grand apartment for a more modest one – the Princess Negroni – is that still causing Adèle anxiety?

* 4 liards = 1 sou; 20 sous = 1 franc.

How is the conversion of the Princess coming along? I wish that liaison, which was still continuing when I left, would come to an end – to the satisfaction of my daughter.[22]

Adèle's main 'anxiety' was Victor's unimaginative savings policy and the discrepancies which were creeping into the accounts. She used her father to persuade Victor to invest in a life insurance policy.[23] 'A good husband after all', was Foucher's verdict when Victor finally bought into a pension scheme. With the occasional reminder that she was the senior of the two wives, Adèle appears to have settled into her new role as she defined it in 1840: 'I consider myself, vis-à-vis yourself, as a stewardess with the job of supervising and keeping house for you as efficiently as possible, and as the governess of our children.'[24] There may even be some truth in Alexandre Dumas's claim that Adèle had asked him to find her husband a lover.[25]

The most revealing aspect of Hugo's affair in the early days is the almost total absence of efficient deccit, a revelling in imperfect disguises and the constant possibility of discovery which seems to contradict his fear of what people might think. The official line would always be that Victor Hugo was a faithful husband with a close friend called 'Mme Drouet'. Even in the 1947–52 edition of Hugo's *Correspondance*, the story is that Juliette Drouet was that nice lady who copied out half a century's worth of Victor Hugo manuscripts, helped him to escape to Belgium in 1851 and metaphorically kept his bed warm after the death of Adèle. Hugo himself was never so discreet. When the poet was writing, the whole world was his confidant. His next collection, *Les Chants du Crépuscule* (1835), was a detailed report on the state of his heart: it contained several poems which were obviously not about Adèle – notably the famous 'Oh! Never Insult a Falling Woman!', in which prostitution is blamed on capitalism and greed.

Behind the mask of the hero was an anxious face which wanted to please as many people as possible, if need be, by stirring up violent disputes – a man who claimed to be afraid of meeting his enemies 'in case they become my friends'.[26] Hugo listened to his public as he listened to the advice of his tailor. Even when he went into exile, he did so with the conviction that he was filling a vacancy.[27] This is the humble sense of what appears to be a swaggering hymn to his own glory, 'Ce siècle avait deux ans . . .' – though hundreds of identical claims can be found in the uncut pages of books by Hugo's obscure contemporaries: 'Many an old man without passion or hair . . . Would blanch if he saw . . . My soul, which my thoughts inhabit like a world.'

> If it please me to hide away my love and grief
> In some corner of a sardonic romance;
> If I set the stage atrembling with my fancies . . .
> It is because love, death, glory and life . . .
> Make my crystal soul vibrate and shine –
> My thousand-voiced soul which the God I adore
> Placed at the centre of all like a sonorous echo!

The development of Hugo's art in the 1830s can be seen as a progressively finer tuning of the bell. His courageous stand in *Le Dernier Jour d'un Condamné* had coincided with a swing in public opinion against the death penalty. In 1834, when he published a documentary short story on a real murderer called Claude Gueux, demanding universal education as an antidote to crime, he was espousing the increasingly respectable views of the philanthropic bourgeoisie, satisfying the Romantic taste for prison tales and gore (in *Claude Gueux*, it was the hacking to death of a prison warder), and placing a Christ-like arm around that faceless 'crowd, multitude and *majority*', its orphans, convicts and prostitutes, who would one day be able to read his books:

> The head of the common man, that is the question. A head which is full of useful seeds. . . . The man who has murdered on the highway might, with better guidance, have been the most excellent public servant. Take that head and cultivate it, weed it, water it, fertilize it, enlighten it, moralize it and put it to good use. There will then be no need to cut it off.

When Hugo undertook to 'fertilize' Juliette, he was proving himself equal to his precepts. She was Marion de Lorme and he was the redeeming lover, Didier – although his letters reveal a slight gap between personal and public morality: 'Unlike other men, I make allowances for fate', he told her. 'Nobody has the right to cast the first stone at you – except me.' Juliette provided him with a running critical commentary on his work. She had a sharp eye for the Hugolian phrase, its tendency to climb up its own ladders and then kick them away. She even made fun of *Claude Gueux*:

> I too have some bad educational habits which disturb my natural dignity more frequently than is desirable. I too have reason to complain about fate and society – fate, because it forced me into a position which is beneath my intelligence, and society, because it robs me of some of the portion of love and happiness which you so generously share with me, my beloved Albin.*

Juliette's tragedy was that the 'fallen woman' had to be saved over and over again in order to maintain the relationship. Eventually, the metaphorical 'collar, chain and other ornaments of slavery'[28] would be incorporated into every aspect of their life.

*

HOW FAR HUGO might have been carried by his ego without the ballast of Juliette's honesty can be deduced from the two-volume work which appeared in March 1834.

Littérature et Philosophie Mêlées is a deliberately scrappy-looking collage of miscellaneous texts, some of which date back to 1819. The idea was to show the 'mysterious and intimate' unity of his intellectual life dominating the 'superficial' contradictions – and, in the process, to fund his new life as a lover. The book was sold to Renduel for a sum that would pay the rent at the Place Royale for the next four years.

In order to demonstrate this 'unity', Hugo snipped and pasted his way through the thirty yellowing issues of *Le Conservateur Littéraire*, erasing names, adding witty remarks, modifying conclusions, changing dates and interpolating passages from encyclopedias and biographies. When he rediscovered his review of a play by J.-C. Royou, who had since died, he removed the bibliographical data and replaced it with the title, 'Outline of a Tragedy Written at School': his strictures now looked like precocious self-awareness. An essay 'On Genius' – conclusion: 'Genius is virtue' – was reprinted without the name of its

---

* Albin is the young man who shares his prison bread with Claude Gueux.

original author, Eugène Hugo, who was in no position to object or even notice. He concocted a spurious diary, the 'Journal des Idées et des Opinions d'un Révolutionnaire de 1830' – meaning himself.

1830 Hugo was given a quiet lesson by 1833 Hugo. He took a jittery letter written to Lamartine in the aftershock of the Revolution. The first part was excised – 'In this dizzying whirlwind which envelops us, I have been unable to collect my thoughts . . .' – and a new section tacked on in its place: 'Men of art in particular are utterly stupefied and haring about in all directions in pursuit of their scattered thoughts. Let them set their minds at rest.' 'We are in 1830,' he reminded himself.

'No artificial arrangement', says the preface of *Littérature et Philosophie Mêlées*, 'has interfered with the composition of this volume.' Everything had been reproduced 'exactly as it was found'. 'The author offers this compilation to the public in all candour and good faith . . . believing that some lessons may perhaps be drawn from the development of a serious, upright mind which has yet to be directly involved in any political cause.' 'It is above all a work of probity.'

The great stumbling-block in Hugo's past – as his critics always pointed out – was his abandonment of royalism. This was now presented as a natural progression and blamed on his parents: liberalism had come upon him like puberty. He took a sheet of paper, dated it 'December 1820' and recorded a 'recent' conversation in the Feuillantines garden. An imaginary General Hugo listens to young Victor defending his royalist views; 'then he turned to General L[ahorie], who was there, and said, "Time will have its way. The child agrees with his mother. The man will agree with his father."' Memorable, convincing, and even, on one level, true.

This collage technique is still found sufficiently shocking for some editors to be almost ludicrously discreet in cataloguing Hugo's untruths and distortions. This is a shame, since *Littérature et Philosophie Mêlées* is a brilliant experiment in autobiography. It may be that Hugo was so insistent that nothing had been changed because he had promised his next new work to a different publisher. But the alterations were also a means of thickening the lines he believed to be essential to the true portrait. The result is a surprisingly postmodern view of the ego: not a chip off the block of tradition but an organic substance continually pummelled and moulded by events. Putty with its own pair of hands.

Hugo's first major work as a sexually satisfied adult exudes a huge, invincible happiness. He had made a great discovery. There was no need to remain faithful to a particular personality. The artist was free to forge his documents, to leave the prison of the past. The work of his first thirty-two years was now presented as the culmination of two opposing forces in Western civilization: art for art's sake (an expression he always denied having used, though he did eventually claim to have invented it)[29] and art with a message. The new, super-art would be governed only by its own aesthetic needs, but this technical purity would allow it to transcend the pettiness of political debate and achieve universality. Then, he claimed, alarmingly, 'the crowd will be drawn to the drama as the bird is drawn to a mirror'.[30]

Any Romantic philosopher might have made similarly extravagant claims for Art; but Hugo went a little further. Like many entertainers in his position – seeing an unhappy childhood wiped away by love, wealth and popularity – he had begun to think of himself as a Messiah. The conviction that he was to help usher in a new age for the human race was firmly rooted, but the path had yet to reveal itself, and there was the immediate problem of conveying the information. For the time being, he favoured two devices. One was the use of the conditional and the third person, which he had been practising since the *Préface de Cromwell*: 'If the name which has signed these words were an illustrious name, and if the voice which now speaks were a powerful voice...' Or: 'the biographical value which only a more important name on the title page could have given this book'.

The other device was to dispense with the rhetorical trimmings altogether and project himself into a substitute figure. In *Littérature et Philosophie Mêlées*, it was Mirabeau. Hugo's mini-biography of the great orator of the French Revolution offers a clear view of the mind that inhabited his brain for the next ten years – the vision in the shaving-mirror on happy mornings: 'When he came into the world, the superhuman size of his head put his mother's life in danger.' As an orator, he 'scattered the crumbs of his great intelligence' over the hungry masses, converting 'the vague instincts of the crowd' into thought. His face was 'washed in mud but continued to shine', and he survived the insults of his contemporaries to be buried (as Hugo would be) in the Panthéon, 'a Pope, in the sense that he directed minds, and God, in the sense that he led events'.

Juliette was the plinth on which Hugo erected his new self-image. She teased him, criticized him, threatened to chop him into tiny pieces if he betrayed her or to set about him with 'the club of the savage and those rifles which fire eighty rounds a minute',[31] but she also, literally, worshipped at his feet. Throughout the 1830s, Hugo increasingly refers to the poet as a 'prophet', a 'pastor of souls', a light-emitting 'head touched by God'; and, increasingly, Juliette accepted her role as Mary Magdalene: 'Without you and without your love, I would have been lost to this world and the next. You are my saviour and my *Christ*.'[32] 'I cannot bear it if you won't let me serve you on my knees. I consider it an insult that you won't allow me to choose you the biggest asparagus and the *crème de la crème*.'

Psychologically, she gave him a kind of diplomatic immunity which Hugo called 'indulgence'. Forgiveness of society's 'sinners', like Claude Gueux, was also forgiveness of himself; and, in Hugo's mind, 'God will be lenient with the indulgent man'.[33] Victor Pavie – a writer from Angers who had reviewed the *Odes and Ballades* and since become a friend of the family – heard about Hugo's adulterous liaison and expressed concern. Hugo explained everything on 25 July 1833:

> The theatre is a type of church, humanity is a type of religion. Think on this, Pavie. Either it is very impious or very pious. I believe I am accomplishing a mission . . .
>
> This year, I have committed more faults than ever before and I have never been a better person. I am much better now than in my days of *innocence* whose passing you regret. Once, I was innocent; now I am indulgent. It is a great step forward, God knows. . . .
>
> I see my future clearly, for I walk with faith, my eyes fastened on the goal. It may be that I shall fall by the wayside, but if I do I shall fall in the right direction.

The determination to present his smallest utterance as part of an all-enveloping oeuvre, as if each work were a phoneme in a gigantic, definitive sentence, is a reaction to commercial success which Hugo shares with some of his contemporaries: a marketing device, but also an attempt to sidestep the continual assessment of his work and set the date of his own Day of Judgement. Balzac erected the giant hoarding of *La Comédie Humaine* as a kind of protective screen behind which he could happily contradict himself. Hugo devised a persona called 'Olympio', a rhetorical mirror which enabled him to address himself – or one of his selves – in poems which might otherwise have seemed too personal or even mentally implausible: 'There comes a time in life when, with an ever-widening horizon, a man feels himself too small to speak in his own name. He then creates ... a figure in which he personifies himself.'[34]

In the *Revue des Deux Mondes*, Gustave Planche, who had had his persona imposed on him by other people and was known as 'the Danube Peasant', suggested that Olympio-Hugo was the figurehead of a new religion called 'Autotheism', because the priest and his god were the same person.[35] In fact, Olympio was just the first of several alter-Hugos:

> My self is made up of:
> Olympio: the lyre
> Herman: love
> Maglia: laughter
> Hierro: combat[36]

This filing system for the psyche was a highly practical arrangement. Not only did it give Hugo a set of sub-personalities to which thoughts and deeds of a compromising nature could be ascribed, it also supplied him with an alternative to the seemingly inevitable 'I': 'the *moi*, that weed which always sprouts afresh under the pen of the writer given to familiar outpourings'.[37] Hugo's dissatisfaction with the confessional mode was a recognition that the writer is never entirely identical with himself, an early version of another egotist's insight: Rimbaud's '*I* is another person'.[38] He was simply moving the productive part of himself to larger premises. Each separate Hugo would now be able to carry on its business without getting in the way of the others.

*

SEEING HER INDEPENDENCE slip away, Juliette was desperate to consolidate her acting career. Hugo had been inspired by a picture on his bedroom wall to write a prose drama on the abuse of power and the dilemma of being a woman and a queen at the same time: *Marie Tudor*, originally announced as *Bloody Mary*. Queen Mary has been betrayed by her lover, Fabiani, who seduced the adopted daughter and fiancée of an honest engraver, Gilbert – a dramatic association of monarch and worker which was boldly underlined by the title of the 1842 American adaptation: *Mary Tudor, or Gilbert the Mechanic*.[39] The play was set in that misty realm called 'Angleterre', famous for the University of Exford, but the theme was dangerously close to home. 'Resuscitating the past for the benefit of the present', it implied that in 1830 the masses had been manipulated by a small clique which abdicated simply in order to absolve itself and then regain power. The conversation between Queen Mary and the hangman was taken to be an insulting allegory of the French State: the legislature in cahoots with the executive. Juliette was to play the Queen's rival, Jane.

Hugo must have known that he was putting her in an impossible position. His enemies would be her enemies, and the other actors would hate her for being the author's pet, though perhaps this made her the perfect choice for Jane, the cowering 'gazelle' to Bloody Mary's 'panther', played by the formidable Mlle George. Hugo himself was being confirmed in his heroic isolation by what amounted to a boycott of his works. The Comédie Française refused to revive his earlier plays as agreed, while the director of the Porte-Saint-Martin inexplicably printed Hugo's name in very small letters on play-bills and replaced his *Lucrèce Borgia* with far less lucrative offerings. Hugo retaliated by suing the Comédie Française for breach of contract in 1837 – 'I need a trial to vent my fury' – and by challenging Harel to a duel. But the literary establishment had decided that Victor Hugo had had his fair share of success.[40]

He was known to be intimate with the editor of the *Journal des Débats*, Bertin – the Lord Beaverbrook of his day – his plays were attracting '*titis*'* to respectable theatres, and he thought he could

---

* 'Artful Dodgers'; young working men from the suburbs.

dominate French literature without the help of reviewers (which he obviously could). Before, when the satirical *Figaro* attacked him, Hugo had simply visited the hole in the Boulevard Poissonnière where it conducted its business and won over the entire editorial team. Now there were too many enemies for hand-to-hand combat. He resorted to explosive generalizations about critics who thrive like fungus at the foot of oaks[41] or who look at the sun through the darkened glass of their jaded minds and see only its spots.[42] The effect was to turn his black-and-white vision of literary Paris into objective reality. For the rest of the century, virtually all French writers can be divided into those who were for or against Victor Hugo.

On the first night of *Marie Tudor* (6 November 1833), Juliette was crushed by the anti-Hugo publicity machine.[43] 'She was not bad,' wrote Gustave Planche, 'she was hopeless.' To convey humility, she bowed her head, and the result, apparently, was that whenever she turned her back she looked like a headless corpse. 'You nobly kept your head lowered,' Hugo told her. 'It was beautiful, simple and intelligent. You played before 2000 people and only one of them understood you – me.'[44] Next evening, the role of Jane was taken by another actress.

Marie Tudor was the end of Juliette's acting career. Hugo failed to have her chosen for a role in his *Angelo, Tyran de Padoue* (1835), a pale, prose melodrama in which an actress and a tyrant's wife stand at opposite points of a love parallelogram. It seems likely that he always had in mind a 'contest' in the two leading roles between the old warhorse of classical theatre, Mlle Mars, and the untutored darling of the boulevards, Marie Dorval. A final attempt was made in 1837. Juliette was promised the role of Queen of Spain in *Ruy Blas*, but when he returned from a short holiday, Hugo was presented with a new cast and, unusually for him, gave in. The director of the Théâtre de la Renaissance had gratefully succumbed to the influence of the legitimate Mme Hugo. While Hugo and Juliette were on holiday, Adèle had written to the director:

> The role of the Queen has been assigned to a person who was partly to blame for the rumpus at *Marie Tudor*. . . . I hope you will find a way to give the role to someone else. I do not need to tell you that my only

concern in this matter is to see the interests of the work prevail ... I am quite certain that this will all remain ENTIRELY between the two of us.

Hugo was spared the agony of seeing his mistress exposed to 4000 eyes, while Juliette was left to suffer more than one kind of jealousy:

I, too, am jealous – but not of the purchase of a box of tooth powder, or the presence of a new apron made from an old shawl, or a missing curlpaper.

I am jealous of a woman of flesh and blood [Marie Dorval], who has the most concupiscent character imaginable, who is there with you every day, looking at you, talking to you, touching you. . . .

And I am also jealous of those thousand women who send you letters, who admire you, and who think they have the right to tell you so.[45]

For Juliette, acting was the most intimate form of intercourse, 'a marriage of the actress's mind with the author'.[46] Now, she had to resign herself to performing in front of the faceless audience which Hugo called posterity. She began hoping instead for a baby but, perhaps as a result of one of her many illnesses, or, as one letter reveals, a kick in the stomach from Hugo, Claire Pradier was to be her only child.[47]

As a consolation, Hugo wrote plays for her to perform in real life. For two summers, he rented a room in a gatekeeper's cottage, 2½ miles by muddy, toad-infested forest paths from the Bertins' home at Bièvres, 8 miles south-west of Paris.[48] Depending on whether or not one looks at the cottage through Hugo's poetry, it was either a sylvan paradise or a cheap hovel in the back of beyond. They met half-way in the woods, made love while sheltering from the rain or trudged back to the house and played at being peasants. Sometimes, Hugo set off from Bièvres early in the morning and left poems for her in a hollow chestnut tree. One rather formal poem, previously written in praise of another actress, was padded out and given to Juliette, but others were clearly inspired by her and the pantheistic fever which took hold of him in the forest:

While you wait, tired from walking,
Under the tree beside the lake, far from meddling eyes,

With the scented valley at your feet . . .
Grass and leaf, wave and furrow, shadow, light and flame,
Let everything acquire a voice, become a soul,
    And say my name to thee!

Most of the time, Juliette was alone in the cottage with the old couple who lived there, rehearsing for the comeback that would never take place, waiting 'like the poor old beaten dog that I am', making a new career out of her love: 'I talk to your portrait, I kiss your chair, I use your handkerchief when you have left it behind. I immerse myself as much as possible in your memory and rub up against the things that have touched you.'[49]

It was after a visit to the far side of the forest in 1837 – but without Juliette – that Hugo wrote one of the great Romantic poems, 'Tristesse d'Olympio', the elegy of rented accommodation. The lover returns to the scene of his passion to find that all the objects that were imbued with his memories have changed. The house fails to recognize him. Nature has forgotten. 'The fields were not black, the sky was not grey, / The sun was shining in a limitless blue.'

The magic of the poem is that it seems to evoke a remote past, though Hugo returned to the cottage only two years after his last visit. Juliette was disappointed not to be taken along, but Olympio had to prepare his canvas, and a happy, passionate woman would have ruined his train of feeling. By projecting the lyrical 'I' into a persona and by siting the act of remembering in the past, he places the reader at two removes from the author and at two removes from the past. The illusion of memory is created and the poem installs itself at such a level in the mind that, even on a first re-reading, it seems to be dredged up from the reader's own distant experience.

Juliette's other consolation was the annual summer expedition, which allowed Olympio to pit himself against the trivial irritations of modern life.

In 1835, he was appointed to the Comité des Monuments Inédits de la Littérature, de la Philosophie, des Sciences et des Arts – recognition of his campaign against 'the Demolishers' and a good excuse to go on holiday. The Committee was supposed to produce a list of the national treasures which the Government should try to preserve. Partly to keep up the pretence, Hugo sent long letters to Adèle, full of dates and obscure architectural terms which she found extremely boring. They were written with an eye to publication. The family was catered for in short personal sections at the end which could easily be deleted later on.

In 1835 and 1836, Hugo and Juliette journeyed north to Brittany and Normandy. The following year, they went as far as Belgium, and then the exploration of the Rhineland began. In 1836, on a 600-mile circuit of Normandy, they took with them the illustrator, Célestin Nanteuil, a veteran of *Hernani* who was said to resemble one of his own wispy, stained-glass-window figures. In the event of unexpected callers in hotels, Nanteuil was to pose as Juliette's husband and even climb into bed with her, having first been sewn into a bag.[50]

Just in case Adèle ever felt like joining him, Hugo took every opportunity to remind her of their 'sweet, enchanting journey' with the Nodiers in 1825, which Adèle had found excruciatingly inconvenient.[51] He sailed down the Loire on a 'filthy, stinking, incommodious steamship', was crushed between blubbery peasants in coaches which were always full, burned by the sun, pestered by guides who lay in wait in every monument and church, and kept awake by carousing salesmen. His luggage was trampled and his shoes split open after covering vast distances, though in each case the 'walk' had been completed in a hired coach.

He became a connoisseur of low-class inns. Every festering chicken and rotten fish was recorded. Before packing his bags, he scratched insulting poems into the dirt on the bedroom wall: 'Your inn, like your face, / Is as graceful as a boar's head / And as clean as a pig's snout'[52] – an insult which, if preserved by the proprietor of The Boar's Head at Laon, would have paid the bill many times over. These experiences are the origin of an important leitmotif in *Les Misérables* – the parody of hospitality known as innkeeping: 'The duty of the innkeeper ... is to know how much wear and tear a shadow causes the mirror and to fix a rate for it', 'to make the traveller pay for everything, even the flies consumed by his dog!'[53]

Olympio on the road was a jovial misanthrope, a handsome prince in the land of the ugly and deformed. On the coach to Meaux, he sat between a hunchback and a policeman, like an allegorical painting on wheels.[54] In 1834, he left Orléans in a rickety coach with 'the Fetid Fairy and the Stinking Gnome'. In Normandy, in 1836, he was stuck with a snooty Englishwoman, 'a blue-stocking dressed in white with red hair – a sort of English tricolour'. Hugo imagined the tricolour to be Mrs Trollope (Anthony's mother), whose popular *Paris and the Parisians in 1835*, published in English and in French, is a good example of how travelling abroad narrows the mind of the narrow-minded. Mrs Trollope thought that Victor Hugo should be 'chastised' with 'a stouter and a keener weapon than any a woman can wield': 'Sin is the muse he evokes', 'horror is his handmaid'; 'it is the occupation of his life to disgust the world.'[55]

A few days after meeting 'Mrs Trollope', Hugo, Juliette and Nanteuil came into view through someone else's eyes. They arrived at the fishing-port of Barfleur on the northern coast of the Cherbourg peninsula and fell foul of the local mayor.

Hugo had begun to write poems on the entity which was to provide him with his clearest line of communication to God: the Ocean, which he hadn't seen since 1807. He was drawn to it by a kind of homesickness: the sight of the sea invariably brought Léopoldine to mind, and the marine poems of this period are also poems about his daughter. Strangely morbid poems. He prayed for her in the seaside chapel where women prayed for their sailor husbands, 'but without kneeling or putting my hands together, with the foolish pride of our time'.[56] He thought of her when giving money to a hideous cripple who habitually wandered down to the sea to drown herself.[57] At Étaples, he traced her name in the sand: 'The high tide will erase it tonight, but nothing will erase your father's love for you.'[58]

By the time they reached Barfleur, Hugo had discovered that he was immune to seasickness and was determined to spend a night at sea.[59] The first boat they hired returned to the harbour at dusk and a conversation began, in which a large part of the population of Barfleur took part, on the wisdom of putting to sea in total darkness. Word reached the mayor, who asked to see the travellers' passport. Hugo had failed to have it stamped and in any case it was valid only as far as Soissons. The mayor refused to authorize the excursion.

Next day (5 July 1836), on arriving at Valognes, Hugo lodged a complaint with the *sous-préfet* of the *département*, who apologized profusely, offered champagne, and forced them to take a tour of the library and the school. He promised Baron Hugo that the Mayor of Barfleur would write and apologize for being so officious. But when the mayor's report came in a few days later, a different picture emerged:

> When he arrived, the famous Romantic author was accompanied by a young man with a thick red beard, a Phrygian cap, no tie, no waistcoat, and an unbuttoned shirt. There was also a shabbily dressed woman whose attire was so grotesque that the women thought she was a man in disguise.

Knowing that playwrights were prone to 'generous impulses', the mayor suspected a plot to help a political prisoner escape to England. For all he knew, the strange woman might be the Duchesse de Berry.[60] A man was sent to keep an eye on them.

> I myself went out towards nine o'clock to see what was going on. As I drew near to the harbour, a large group had assembled and I was not a little surprised and dismayed to hear M. Hugo talking to the sailors' representative, saying things like, 'In twelve hours you will be dismissed. You are not Frenchmen. As for the mayor, if we had mayors like that in Paris, we'd soon kick them out. He will be the ruin of your borough.' 'Here is the Mayor,' someone said to him. He came up to me without lowering his voice or changing his manner. I begged him to observe that we were in the street. He paid no attention, and all the way to his inn he talked only of the twenty newspapers in which the arbitrary and despotic act of the Mayor of Barfleur would be recorded. . . .
>
> You say this was an unfortunate incident. He was going to celebrate Barfleur and encourage foreigners to prefer our sea to the lakes of Switzerland. I know the lakes of Switzerland better than M. Hugo and I am not such a simpleton as to think that he will persuade Romantic travellers to turn on their heels at the sound of his voice and come and admire the Saint-Marcouf Islands and eat oysters at Saint-Vaast or lobsters at Barfleur.

Between the two of them, the Mayor of Barfleur and the *sous-préfet* of Valognes had a nicer understanding of the Romantic temperament than many professional critics. M. Hugo inhabited a special universe in which a poet's whim could send entire continents rushing to an obscure Norman fishing-port. A mere provincial had deprived him of a symbolic experience.

Hugo's arrogance was an intellectual form of his father's imperialist zeal. In the duplicitous accounts of his journeys, he was inventing a new kind of travel literature in which the journey is a pretext for testing the mind's ability to poeticize reality, a drug which dislocates the landscape and brings the contemplative self to life. Chartres Cathedral was a behemoth filled with stalactites.[61] Hedgerows had knobbly fingers like a print by Dürer.[62] The cliffs at Étretat, which Hugo sketched long before Courbet and the Impressionists, were a Piranese.[63] The sea was 'rococo'.[64] Some of these images found their way into his poetry, where they would have to wait many years before finding readers willing to enjoy them: reviewers of *Les Rayons et les Ombres* in 1840 were outraged to see trees on a misty horizon described as 'a large, red-haired herd of gigantic hedgehogs'.[65]

The severest test of Hugo's ability to interpret the evidence of his eyes as mysterious clues to a vast unity came the following year during the trip to Belgium. A chance discovery produced one of the first great battles between art and technology, and a violent enactment of the competing tendencies in his writing.

Hugo first saw the railway at Mons, where some coal-trucks were being pulled by horses.[66] Then, at Malines, instead of the horses, 'a smoking, groaning machine'. A crowd had gathered to watch the locomotive setting off for Brussels. Hugo stood next to a coachman who was staring pitifully at the train.

'"It goes faster than your horses," I said to him. "What's so amazing about that?" he retorted. "It's driven by a thunderbolt."'

The Brussels line had opened two years before, but passenger trains were still a novelty: in 1837, France had only 110 miles of track, much of it in industrial use. The French railways were still the baby of a small group of socialist engineers, who saw them as the key to free trade and world peace – a view Hugo was soon to adopt and which is represented in Flaubert's *L'Éducation Sentimentale* by an allegorical painting showing Jesus Christ driving a steam engine through a virgin forest. In the words of a contemporary poem, 'Only God's work goes faster than the locomotive!'

At first, Hugo was rather sniffy about the railway. It was 'very ugly' and only slightly more impressive than another form of transport popular with the Belgians: 'a wheelbarrow with a dog in front and a woman behind'.

Three days later, at Antwerp, he realized that he was seeing something quite new. He bought a return ticket to Brussels and spent the next four hours in a different universe. As the train hurtled through the Belgian countryside at over 30 miles an hour, a whole new art and literature exploded into view through the carriage window:

> The motion is magnificent. You have to have felt it to know what it's like. The speed is unbelievable. The flowers at the track-side aren't flowers any more; they turn into blotches or red and white stripes. There are no points, only stripes. The corn is a huge mass of yellow hair; lucerne, long green tresses. Towns, steeples and trees dance about in a crazy jumble on the horizon. Now and then, a shadow, a shape, the upright figure of a ghost appears and disappears in a flash beside the door ... Inside the carriage, people say, 'It's three leagues from here; we'll be there in ten minutes.'

> We passed the train heading for Brussels. Nothing could be more terrifying than two velocities juxtaposed. From the passengers' point of view, one speed is multiplied by the other. . . . Carriages, men, women, nothing could be seen distinctly, only light or dark shapes passing in a whirlwind emitting cries and hoots and laughter.

This was the first trial run on the rails of modern reality of Hugo's contention that art should be able to contain all experience, not just the parts which had already been earmarked as useful or beautiful. Instead of treating the kettle-on-wheels as a joke or discussing its socio-economic implications, he managed the extremely unusual feat of describing exactly what he saw: forms disengaging themselves from concepts; familiar objects turning into abstract shapes.

But Hugo's description comes in two parts. As he wrote, his mind applied the brakes and set off backwards in time. The first part was a Turner, the second a Leonardo:

> You have to try very hard not to imagine that the iron horse is a real creature. You hear it breathing when it rests, groaning when it has to

leave, and yapping when it's under way. . . . Along the track it jettisons its dung of burning coals and its urine of boiling water; . . . its breath passes over your head in beautiful clouds of white smoke which are torn to shreds on the track-side trees. . . .

Of course, if you actually see the iron horse, the poetry is lost. When you hear it, it's a monster. When you see it, it's just a machine. Such is the sad infirmity of our age. Bare utility without beauty. Four hundred years ago . . . the boiler would have been fashioned into a monstrous scaly belly, a huge carapace. The funnel would have been a smoking horn or a long neck supporting a mouth full of burning embers. The wheels would have been concealed under enormous fins or pendent wings. . . . It would have been a magnificent sight.[67]

A whole history of modern art could be written around these two passages. In the first, Hugo tries to twist up the spaghetti of the landscape on the prongs of metaphor. The main prong is the word 'raie', which was mistakenly used in the 1830s in place of the English 'rail'.[68] The word is then split into two: its normal meaning ('stripe') is applied to the whizzing flowers, while its secondary meaning ('parting') supplies the hair image. This rapid use of metaphor, which readers of the time found needlessly confusing and esoteric, implies that, on one level, all perceptions are equivalent, that there is no final, base reality to which everything can be referred. Through the carriage window, the world did not simply look different; it was different. A theory of relativity was just around the corner.

In the second passage, Hugo loses his metaphorical nerve and pulls the locomotive back into a mythological age, with its built-in meanings and morals. A coherent description now becomes possible, but at what cost? For it also becomes apparent that the 'poetry' of the vision – the quality that allows it to be described coherently – is dependent on the deliberate blindness of the poet. Hugo blames the engineers: 'They gave me Watt entirely naked, when I'd rather have him clothed by Benvenuto Cellini.'

In other words, in the age of railways, the Romantic writer is faced with a new choice: an accurate account and a fragmented text, or a cogent metaphor and a knowingly false representation.

*

ON RETURNING FROM BELGIUM, Hugo inevitably chose the latter. Adèle and the children had been spending the summer at Fourqueux in the Forest of Marly, west of Paris. The poet Ulric Guttinguer, a friend of Adèle and Sainte-Beuve and, ostensibly, of Hugo, was there when Hugo arrived: 'I found him thinner and rather cool,' he told Sainte-Beuve. 'He had run all the way from the coach. Was it eagerness or suspicion? . . . I don't know.'[69]

Certainly eagerness to see Léopoldine, who sent dainty letters to her wandering father and was so much his child that she even seems to have inherited his symmetrical phrase:

> Your letter is very nice, and even if the paper is horrible, the letter entirely makes up for it. I do not have the same advantage. My paper is very nice but my letter is very horrible, my dear papa.[70]

Other letters showed the competing influence of mother and education. Léopoldine had succeeded in having a piano installed in the Place Royale, a brash, modern instrument to which Hugo was aurally allergic, though he did learn to pick out a few tunes.[71] From Fourqueux, she wrote to her mother, who was spending a few days in Paris: 'Ask papa if he'd like to make me a present of a song called "The Convent Washerwomen", it's very pretty. If he doesn't want to, buy it anyway and he'll just have to pay for it.'[72]

In 1836, the favourite child took her first communion, wearing a gown made from one of Juliette Drouet's old dresses. The scene was painted by Auguste de Châtillon, who also commemorated her first catechism in a luscious portrait.[73] It shows her sitting prettily on a Chinese-patterned chair, holding a Book of Hours: both possessions of her father. Considering Hugo's perfect Latin, it is surprising to discover that the words on the page can be traced to Psalm 116, which is used in the service for the dead.

The less time Hugo spent with his family, the more time he spent on its image. On 20 February 1837, Baron Hugo became Viscount Hugo when brother Eugène died in the asylum of 'chronic enteritis'.[74] That day, Hugo had been writing a poem about an 'antique garden' 'where every flower that opens seems a censer'. Five days after Eugène's death, he wrote another poem on a young girl who admires her own reflection in the waters of love and drowns in the river.

Finally, after two more unrelated poems, he wrote the official threnody, two weeks late: 'À Eugène Vte H.', published in *Les Voix Intérieures* (1837). It was a moving farewell to their shared childhood – 'You must remember the green Feuillantines', 'When Napoleon was blazing like a beacon' – though Hugo's confidence in the inscrutable designs of providence imparted a curious curl of the lip to the sad smile:

> Since it pleased the Lord to crush you, O poet;
> Since it pleased the Lord to compact your head
>   With his sovereign hand
> And turn it into a holy urn to contain the ecstasy,
> To place the genie in the vase and seal it
>   With a seal of bronze . . .

The cost of the funeral (182.60 francs) was shared by Victor and Abel, who was recovering from the various business disasters which had sent him fleeing to London: he was publishing the encyclopedias which would supply his brother Victor with some erudite passages for his travel accounts.

Eugène's death enabled Hugo to tidy up the graveyard. The plot which General Hugo had acquired for himself and his second wife – who was still alive – had never been paid for in full. Hugo completed the payment and had his mother and brother disinterred and reburied with the General under a small pyramid. He thus achieved his greatest unfulfilled ambition: to evict the evil stepmother from the nest – this time for all eternity.

Having taken his father's wife away from him, Hugo handed him a laurel wreath. The Arc de Triomphe had been inaugurated in 1836, with the names of Napoleonic heroes inscribed on its walls – but not General Hugo's. *Les Voix Intérieures* was dedicated by 'his respectful son' 'To Joseph-Léopold-Sigisbert, Count Hugo . . . Not Inscribed On the Arc de l'Étoile': 'He offers his father this poor sheet of paper, which is all he has, with the regret that he has no granite. . . . A nation is great, a family is small. That which means nothing to one means everything to the other.'

Except, of course, in certain cases, like the Hugos. As a famous cartoon implies, Hugo seems to have drawn up a list of all the major monuments and institutions with which he hoped to be historically associated: the Vendôme Column, the Comédie Française, Notre-Dame, the Arc de Triomphe. Soon, he would add the Académie Française, the Assemblée Nationale and, eventually, the Paris sewer-system and the Statue of Liberty before it sailed for America. Another famous landmark was only an idea at the time of his death, though he was described in 1893 by an English biographer as 'the Eiffel Tower of literature'.[75]

Yet the prefaces of *Les Chants du Crépuscule* (1835) and *Les Voix Intérieures* (1837) – eagerly read by young writers as definitive bulletins on the state of literature and society – suggested a Hugo who had run out of ambitions: 'this strange crepuscular state of society and the modern soul – mist on the outside, uncertainty within'. The poet 'must hold himself above the tumult, unshakeable, austere and benevolent'. But what then? Attentive readers might have noticed the gradual formation of a new religion which came into view like a new planet rising above the cloud-layer of Christianity in *Les Rayons et les Ombres* (1840).

There would also be hints of a less wholesome Hugo. Juliette was in a position to spot the more subtle signs of change. He flirted with her seamstress, neglected his appearance – despite a habit of practising speeches in the mirror[76] – and, suspiciously, subjected her to long periods of 'chastity'. A letter from Juliette dated Saturday afternoon, 29 September 1838 proves however that Olympio was still capable of Herculean feats – specifically, a feat he later claimed to have performed on his wedding night: 'Yes, you must be very tired, my love. You *kissed* me nine times – *that's enormous*. You are my ravishing little prankster and I love and adore you, yes, yes, yes. What more do you want, eh?'[77] Interesting, though, that she had the presence of mind to keep count.

Significantly, Juliette saved her best plebeian language for what seemed to be his most respectable ambition – as if there was something dangerous about applying to the venerable institution she liked to call the '*Cacadémie*':*

So there you are applying for a nasty, insignificant little chair which has all those old idiots' snot on the arms and their droppings on the

---

* From '*caca*': a child's word for faeces.

seat. Personally, I'd rather have a wardrobe so I could lock your mind up, because it looks to me as though you must have lost it or at least mislaid it on the day you let them wrap your head up in the candidate's hat, which doesn't suit you at all.[78]

CHAPTER ELEVEN

'Dark Doors Stand Open in the Invisible'[1]

(1839–1843)

THE VICTOR HUGO who had been ingratiating himself with the 'Immortals' of the Académie Française – making the obligatory visits* while Juliette waited outside in a carriage – was expanding his field of operations.

Every three or four years, he reported on the state of his ambitions in books of poems which he presented as episodes in a private drama of universal significance: *Les Feuilles d'Automne*, *Les Chants du Crépuscule* and *Les Voix Intérieures*. Instead of forming the usual sheaf of sporadic postcards from the poetic regions of the mind, these collections were arranged so as to suggest an underlying progression. Each title alluded to a line in the previous collection, and there were some vast, vague hints in the prefaces. In *Les Rayons et les Ombres* in 1840, it was the emergence of the open-air poet who collects his thoughts like flowers in the field and returns to the city to scatter them over the vegetating masses:

> The poet, in impious times,
> Comes to prepare better days.
> He is the man of utopias:
> His feet are here, his eyes elsewhere.

Reviewers usually drew a sharp distinction between Hugo's thought and what they saw as the true source of his prestige and popularity:

* On the death of an Academician, candidates visit the thirty-nine survivors, who then vote in a secret ballot.

his technical mastery, the astonishing variety of poetic forms, a vocabulary larger than that of any writer since Rabelais, an ability to write songs that seemed always to have been a part of French folklore. Philosophically, he was beginning to sound like the dummy of his own ventriloquism: a vaguely Christian idealism which seemed to owe more to the clichés of French verse than to personal beliefs.

Yet this philosophy proves surprisingly difficult to define, and if a crisp, clear view of Hugo's personality emerges from this period, then the biographer is guilty of over-tidying. *Les Rayons et les Ombres* is filled with misty atmospheres and muddy swirls. After reading Hugo's amazing fantasy of 'Indian wells', dungeons and other intestinal monuments, 'a roiling mass of steps and rails', dripping walls and hands that clutch like tree roots, George Sand suffered a kind of mental indigestion. Even stranger poems lurked in the darkness of his unpublished papers. A peculiar piece on Saturn, 'jail-house of the heavens', was saved for a later collection, perhaps because it suggested an eccentric belief in the transmigration of souls (though it was astronomically accurate and up-to-date).[2]

One face of planet Hugo was liberal-monarchist, but the other had begun to swarm with the dark currents of mystical socialism. This was interpreted as simple professional expediency: just as the medieval pageants of the restored monarchy had inspired the Romantics two decades before, socialism now offered the most rewarding package of poetic procedures, images and ideas.[3] After all, these first products of the visionary Hugo went hand in gnarled hand with some truly Victorian verse which betrayed a huge philosophical smugness. God was working his purpose out and anyone who was full of 'love' could find out what it was: 'The mind alone is a feeble light, / And a woman's heart is often / The explanation of God!'

To the outside world, Hugo was becoming more respectable by the year, as if the mind which plummeted into the bowels of a bizarre imagination sent its presentable counterweight hurtling into the light of day. Victor Hugo was a revered national figure: the man who had forced Romanticism into the mainstream and whose greatest poems were inseparable in the public mind from the events they commemorated. When *Hernani* and *Marion de Lorme* were revived in 1838 at the Comédie Française, they seemed so unobjectionably entertaining that some 'knee-heads' from the Battle of *Hernani* swore that all the 'bad' lines had been taken out.

Hugo's campaign to confirm his status as a pillar of the State had begun in 1836. Since then, Academicians had died with sufficient regularity to allow him five candidacies. But so far the Academy had remained loyal to its miserly tradition. The first four elections gave seats to a historian, a politician, a doctor and a prolific writer of vaudevilles called Dupaty, who took to carrying a pair of pistols in case a Hugo supporter decided to re-create the vacancy.

Eventually, the barrel-scraping would have to stop. Support on the inside was growing – Lamartine and Nodier were already members – and all the Academicians he visited were surprised by Hugo's modesty and good manners. Only one question remained: why did he want to be a member? The 83 francs a month he would receive for contributing to the *Dictionnaire de l'Académie Française* hardly seemed a sufficient incentive, especially since Hugo had calculated that by the time the Dictionary was completed, the French language would no longer exist.[4] The answer, as everyone soon realized, lay in the fact that Hugo was not a landowner and did not pay enough taxes to stand for Parliament. Academicians however could, if the King saw fit, be elevated to the peerage and take their place in the upper chamber.

Hugo had seen the first door to this golden future swing open in 1837. He was invited to a party at Versailles to celebrate the marriage of the Duc d'Orléans, heir to the throne.[5] The invitation itself was not hugely significant, but the effects of it were. The young Duchess, Helena von Mecklenburg-Schwerin, turned out to be one of Hugo's greatest fans. In Germany, she told him, she had discussed his works with Goethe and knew his poems by heart, which was more than could be said for Hugo, who once complimented his daughter on a poem he had written himself. The Duchess's favourite was 'Dans l'Église de ***'. It contained a daringly modern image which had been ridiculed by reviewers: a hand squeezing music from organ-pipes like water from a sponge. The Duchess obviously understood the Romantic temperament.

The poet who had publicly denounced the covert censorship practised by Louis-Philippe's government was now well on his way to becoming an unofficial court poet for the second time in his life. He was promoted in the Légion d'Honneur and given a large oil-painting by the Duke and Duchess. The following year, the Duc d'Orléans asked Prime Minister Guizot to grant Hugo and Dumas the right to have their plays performed at a new theatre, the Théâtre de la Renaissance: no modern writer had ever been offered such a privilege.

None of this was likely to speed him on the road to revolutionary socialism. For the inauguration, Hugo wrote his finest play, *Ruy Blas*, in which the Romantic alexandrine is wielded with a swashbuckling elegance not found again in French drama until Rostand's *Cyrano de Bergerac*.

Considering the circumstances in which it was performed, Hugo's choice of subject has an air of extraordinary personal indiscretion. *Ruy Blas* is set in seventeenth-century Madrid. A grandee, Don Salluste, has been banished by the Queen (or so he thinks) for having seduced her favourite lady-in-waiting. Just before leaving for exile, he discovers that his valet, Ruy Blas, is in love with the Queen – 'an earthworm enamoured with a star'. Plotting revenge, he introduces him to the court as a long-lost relative. Ruy Blas becomes a powerful spokesman for the poor and wins the heart of the Queen. But the triple dream of social justice, royal patronage and requited love is shattered at the end of the play when Don Salluste returns to reveal the deception. Ruy Blas runs his master through with a sword and poisons himself in front of a horrified Queen.

The knives were still out for Hugo and critics tried hard not to enjoy themselves: the play was historically inept, it showed egalitarian tendencies, and in Act IV, a character entered through the chimney. To make matters worse, the theatre had only just been finished: the doors were not properly hung and the central heating was useless.[6] Most irritating of all, *Ruy Blas* was a financial success, though the management acted as if it was bound to fail without a barrage of irrelevant publicity: free albums were handed out to the ladies during the intervals, a waxwork dummy modelled expensive dresses in the foyer, and at the end of the play there was a ball with a 200-piece orchestra and a tombola at midnight.[7] Hugo's product was sacrificed to the packaging. Relations with men of his own profession and generation were now at their lowest ebb. There was a feeling among critics and theatre directors that Hugo had upset a balance: one man was hogging all the prestige that should have been shared out among his fellow writers.

The gutter press of the day practised the art of literary criticism with an admirable attention to detail. *Ruy Blas* was construed as a coded message from the 'worm' Hugo to the 'star' Duchess.[8] The theory that Hugo was courting a woman who might one day be Queen is still vigorously denied, perhaps rightly so. It may, for instance, be pure coincidence that the Queen in *Ruy Blas* is a composite of an earlier Duchesse d'Orléans and a German princess; that Ruy Blas is an ideal image of Victor Hugo, the voice of the downtrodden in the court of a privileged élite; and that Hugo drew the Duchess's attention to the rumours: 'I must confess to Your Royal Highness that I hesitated for a moment before sending Her this work. It has been interpreted in such a strange manner.' Only the draft has survived and so the letter may never have been sent, though the Duchess did receive a copy of *Ruy Blas*, and since she signed her thank-you note, 'Yours affectionately, Helen', it would be surprising if the thought of carnal royal patronage never occurred to him.

It certainly occurred to Juliette in 1842 when Hugo went to offer his condolences to the widowed Duchess – 'that woman bathed in the glamour of great misfortune – which is to say, after physical beauty, the thing most likely to seduce you';[9] and again in February 1848, when Hugo risked his life in an attempt to have the Duchess proclaimed Regent. As one of the most ambitious fantasizers in the nineteenth century, Hugo was perfectly capable of having designs on a future Queen of France. King Victor I? . . . Similarly implausible things had happened to him before. The preface of *Les Rayons et les Ombres* suddenly appears in a different light: 'Where is the poor shepherd who has not cried out, at least once in his life, as he dangles his feet in the stream from which his lambs are drinking, "I wish I were an emperor!"'

*

FROM NOW ON, it is impossible to account for Hugo's extraordinary status if he is seen simply as a successful careerist who contributed to a pension scheme called 'Victor Hugo's reputation' and engaged in unprofessional activities in his spare time. The first serious attempt to simplify him in this way was made by Juliette Drouet. Her twice-daily letters to her darling 'Toto' seem at first to provide a short-cut to the 'real' Hugo. Who else could have revealed the filthy state of his underwear or his habit of borrowing her toothbrush and leaving it in the wash-basin?[10] How else would we know that Hugo gave her fleas?[11] But her depiction of a shabby, middle-aged bourgeois dressed in 'an old dead dog' (his overcoat) was an affectionate distortion, intended to isolate the Victor she loved from all the others.

By now, Hugo was not just a real person with several masks but a limited liability company of egos, each one feeding off the other and maintained by an army of commentators. The space he had created around his name was only partially filled by the 'enormous gaseous emissions'[12] of his verse. The rest was taken up with a stream of hostile or obsequious discourse to which Hugo adapted himself so skilfully that it appears to have been a self-generated source of energy.

Face to face, the company of egos turned out to be very pleasant company. Emboldened by reports of his affability, large crowds attended the Sunday soirées at the Place Royale, despite the fact that only water was on offer (though not always easy to obtain) and smokers were banished to the square outside. Refreshments aside, everyone was received with the courtesy Hugo had been disgusted not to find in the heroes of his youth. 'I am nothing but a door that is always open and a heart that is never closed,' he told a worker-poet who had been 'prowling for the last three years under the arcades of the Place Royale hoping to catch a glimpse of you'.[13] Hugo maintained one of the busiest and most eclectic literary salons in French history for well over a decade – an achievement which places him on a par with the great hostesses of the age, though it was remarked upon by very few writers. Liszt's lover, Marie d'Agoult, came closer than anyone to defining Hugo's charm, perhaps because she observed his behaviour with other people:

> Believe it or not, I find him the exact opposite of his works ... I find him unpretentious, kind, above all charming, neither arrogant nor timid, with a good hearty laugh like that of a child and a caressing voice. Very polite with the men, very flattering and almost respectful with M. Ingres, delicately assiduous with me, jocular with Balzac ...[14]

Marie d'Agoult's comments are borne out by Balzac's sketch of Hugo in 1840. He too had a sharp sense of Hugo's compatible contradictions, but was able to offer a theory, based on a more informed impression of his private life. Fitting his conversation to Balzac's bawdy joviality, Hugo had obviously been boasting about his manly exploits:

> You asked me for some details on Victor Hugo. Victor Hugo is an excessively witty man; as witty as he is poetic. His conversation is absolutely delightful, a little like Humboldt's, but superior and leaving a little more room for dialogue. He is full of bourgeois ideas. He execrates Racine and calls him a second-rate writer. He is quite fanatical on that score. He left his wife for Juliette and his excuses are uncommonly hypocritical: he was giving his wife too many children – note, however, that he isn't giving any to Juliette. All told, there is more good than bad in him. Even though the good things are a continuation of pride, and though everything he does is very carefully calculated, he is on the whole a likeable man, quite apart from his being a great poet. He has lost a lot of his talent, his power and his qualities because of the life he has led. He has loved a great deal.[15]

These descriptions of Hugo as he appeared to people who treated him as a human being are rare islands of sanity in a sea of fantasy which inevitably had its effect on Hugo himself. The phenomenon of Hugomania had long since spread to the provinces, carried by touring theatre companies and the new mass-circulation newspapers. In Toulouse, a student had died defending *Hernani* in a duel.[16] A corporal in the dragoons asked for his tombstone to be inscribed with the words, 'Here Lies One who Believed in Victor Hugo'.[17] Two stories were written about an undertaker who was so obsessed with Hugo's novel about the slave revolt that he was rechristened Bug-Jargal.[18]

Whatever the truth of these anecdotes, the important fact is that the people who reported them expected to be believed. They were a dramatized version of the letters Hugo actually received in which young writers talked of laying down their lives for him, just as their fathers had died for Napoleon. The image of the folk-hero, Napoleon, was disseminated in the same way as the works of Victor Hugo, and the association of the two was sealed in 1840 by the publication of a small book, 'within the reach of every purse': *Le Retour de l'Empereur, par Victor Hugo*. It was a collection of all his poems on Napoleon, including his celebration of the recent return of Napoleon's ashes from St Helena. 'Tributes from the great poet to the great emperor', said the Hugo-inspired 'Note from the Publishers'. The key words were 'popular' and 'popularity'. The modern sense was still just a nuance: '*popularité*' referred to the disenfranchized majority. A popular writer was one 'who endears himself to the people with sweet and insinuating manners or by excessive promises'; popularity was 'conduct likely to win the favour of the people'.

A practical disadvantage of fame was that, just as the domestic market was flooded with foreign pirated editions of Hugo's books, counterfeit copies of Hugo himself were running about Europe. There was a spurious sighting in Brittany, where he was said to have gone to recover from the death of his wife. In Paris, a wedding was called off at the last minute when it was discovered that the bridegroom was not, as he claimed, Victor Hugo. (The bogus Hugo later married the daughter of François de Neufchâteau – the potato-growing Academician who stole Hugo's work on *Gil Blas*.) An actress at the Hugos' local theatre changed her name from Victorine Hugot to Victorine Hugo and spread rumours that she was a relative.[19] On a visit to La Roche-Guyon, Hugo had his own name pointed out to him in the visitors book: 'A servant told me, "Victor Hugo was here" ... and showed me half a line of verse which a tourist had inscribed with my name underneath.... Why disabuse them? My name is uttered here every day.'[20]

Hugo's linguistic *coup d'état* was confirmed by a new set of words which entered the language, making 'Hugo' one of the most prolific eponyms in history: '*Hugoïen*', '*Hugolien*', '*Hugonien*', '*Hugotien*', '*Hugolique*', '*Hugoniste*', '*Hugotiste*', '*Hugocrate*', '*Hugolin*', '*Hugolisme*', '*Hugoïste*' (said by Heine to be the superlative form of '*égoïste*'),[21] '*Hugotique*' (from '*Gothique*') and '*Hugolâtre*' (from '*idolâtre*'), with its corresponding verb, still in use today: '*hugolâtrer*'. Later contributions from English included 'Hugoesque', 'Hugolesque', 'Hugoish', 'Hugolian', 'Hugonian' and 'Hugonic' (the bastardized language spoken by Hugo and his followers). Most of these words – like the earlier

'*Hernanisé*' (from '*hypnotisé*') – started out as pejorative allusions to Hugo's neologisms (or '*hugotismes*'). Sometimes they were a sarcastic acknowledgement of Hugo's influence, or, in some cases, quite serious: in the 1860s, a newspaper devoted to the doctrines of 'the Calvin of Literature' called itself, adoringly, *Le Victor Huguenot*.[22]

In schools, Hugo was still considered a 'Decadent': a word which referred to the gaudy, ungrammatical period of Latin literature but was acquiring connotations of picturesque depravity.[23] Hugolatrous pupils were placed in detention and their Hugo books confiscated.[24] At the Collège Royal in Rouen, Gustave Flaubert had been excited by Hugo since the age of thirteen – 'a genius of the stature of those who have been admired for centuries'.[25] Two years above him in the same school, a boy called Auguste Vacquerie was showering his hero (and his future father-in-law) with letters and poems so long that they seemed to contradict his main fear:

> Sometimes I thought you might die before your work was finished, and tears came to my eyes, and I wished I might perish if I could be certain that you would live for a long time.[26]

Hugo always dreamed of undermining the education system by writing alternative text-books which pupils would buy with their own money and read in secret,[27] but this is how his books were used in any case, and it should count as one of his greatest achievements that he managed to remain a forbidden pleasure even as he became the national poet.

His personal influence on fashion was comparatively slight. Balzac and Gautier both reported a spate of head-shaving:[28] one or two inches off the forehead expanded the brow to Hugolian dimensions, though some claimed that Hugo achieved the effect by bending his head forward when sitting for portraits. He was famous for his ability to keep the same pose for several hours, apparently out of politeness to the painter – literally an excellent poseur. Those who visited him at home or found him scouring the book-boxes on the Seine – but never sitting in cafés – discovered that he wore the most bourgeois item of clothing in existence: a starched white shirt collar. Hugo's clothes reflected the tastes of his tailor and were always four or five years behind the times, thus creating the spectacle of a private Hugo belatedly catching up on the fashions that the public Hugo had helped to create.[29]

The lunatic hero-worshipping fringe was undeterred. 'Le Père Hugo', so called when he was barely thirty, was their ideal parent. This was still an age when the fashionable rebel was an orphan in search of a family. Hugo's domestic bliss was celebrated in newspaper articles and poems like 'The Toys of Victor Hugo's Children'.[30] Cheap imitations of 6 Place Royale sprang up: leaded-glass windows, frescoes painted on wood, second-hand church furniture. For students, essential possessions included a skull, a rapier, anything Eastern, and a well-thumbed copy of Marion de Lorme.

Familiarity with Hugo did nothing to dispel the rumours that he was not entirely human.[31] He could eat half an ox at a single sitting, fast for three days, and work non-stop for a week. He went out in the worst weather and walked through unlit streets after dark, armed only with his house-key. In the countryside, his mighty ear picked up the sound of ants and moles moving underground. One day, from the top of Notre-Dame, he spotted Nodier's daughter walking about in the drawing-room of the Arsenal. At a distance of one kilometre and with the guiding frame of a window this is just possible and when his eyes were working properly, they do seem to have acted as binoculars. According to the authoritative testimony of Hugo's barber, his bristles blunted the razor three times as quickly as a normal beard.

There was an immense hunger for heroes, which Hugo satisfied to the limits of immodesty. Auguste Vacquerie likened him to the sun; his voice resembled 'the sigh of the ocean'; his portrait by Louis Boulanger showed his 'magnanimous face' to be the living bibliography of his 'glorious hymns'. When Vacquerie invited the Hugos to visit his family mansion on the banks of the Seine at Villequier, he compared himself, unironically, to the centurion of the Gospels: 'Lord, I am not worthy that thou shouldest come under my roof.'[32] Vacquerie went to live in Paris – 'in fact, it was Hugo I was going to inhabit'[33] – and one day when he was sick, he wrote to Hugo instead of calling out the doctor, 'for I feel that a word from you would heal me'. Perhaps Hugo had told him that he once cured his son Victor by 'magnetizing' him with his hands.[34]

Vacquerie was comparatively restrained in his adulation and never lost sight of his own ego. He was building a career as a disciple of Victor Hugo, just as he might have joined the Army or the civil service. Others tried to sacrifice their personalities. A young poet called Philoxène Boyer vowed to devote 'every breath of [his] soul' to Hugo and hailed him, in a 250-page *Lettre à Victor Hugo*, as a Joshua who would lead humanity out of the desert. Entering Hugo's salon for the first time, Boyer fell to his knees and waddled across the room to the master's feet. In his farewell letter, desolate at having to return home to Grenoble, he cheered himself up with the thought that he would 'fight and die in the service of the man-god, obscurely, without glory and without his even knowing about it'.

Replying to this sort of fan mail was certainly a major influence on Hugo's style: 'I arrive home, Monsieur,' he told Vacquerie in August 1836, 'to find your poem, your charming poem. . . . You are a thinker and you are a writer. March onward. . . . I congratulate you on your talent.'[35] The vagueness of Hugo's exhortations meant that they could be used in almost any letter, while the short, self-contained sentences could easily be shuffled to avoid repetition. It thus became important to have a set of axioms ready to be dispensed. Anyone who finds Hugo's replies overblown should consider that when the writer has been hailed as the successor to Moses, polite disagreement is practically an insult.

Maxime Du Camp, later described by the monarchist Barbey d'Aurevilly as 'a fly born on Victor Hugo's excrement',[36] sent his hero a poem in 1840. A week later, he received a superb example of the Hugo thank-you letter:

> My claim to fame, Monsieur (if I have any claim at all), lies not so much in what I say as in the replies I receive, not so much in my voice as in my echoes. You alone would be sufficient proof of this. I know not whether I am a poet but I do know that you are. Take heart, Monsieur: study, meditate, learn and grow in every way. You are already a poet; now become a man.[37]

After the first flush of excitement, Du Camp re-read his poem, found it painfully inept and came to the conclusion that Hugo was making fun of him. This was a common reaction. A law student called Farcinet was persuaded by Hugo's 'encouragement' to give up writing poetry altogether.³⁸ Arsène Houssaye showed Gautier what he thought was a sarcastic letter thanking him for a puny sonnet in which 'the vine and the trees' recite the poems of Victor Hugo to each other. 'Your sonnet', wrote Hugo, 'is worth a book and your book is worth a library. You are a direct descendant of Virgil and Theocritus.'³⁹

It was one thing to heap praise upwards at the idol; it was quite another to see the same undiluted blandishments coming back down again. Gautier explained that Hugo could 'get passionate about anything'. He might have added that Hugo saw the modern world as the most recent layer of an ancient, archetypal onion: Houssaye's poems were stale and sticky but, in Hugo's view, not intrinsically worthless, since he was also an incarnation of the ur-Poet and the great pastoral tradition.

Hugo's unbelievable modesty created a vacuum which sucked hysterical praise from his fans. Things they might have whispered to themselves in private moments of optimism were said out loud to Hugo. If Hugo was a god, then the whole scale of literary values had been shifted up a key. Even someone as greedy of fame as Franz Liszt noticed the effect: 'Whenever I have spent a few hours with V.H., I feel a host of silent ambitions stirring in the depths of my heart.'⁴⁰ Some of Hugo's admirers eventually rebelled against their own idolatry. Others, at first suspicious, underwent a kind of conversion, almost embarrassing to witness:

> What a man is Hugo! . . . He is divine, he is infernal, he is wise, he is foolish, he is People, he is King, he is man, woman, painter, poet, sculptor. He is everything. He has seen everything, done everything, felt everything. He astonishes me, repels me and enchants me.⁴¹

When Hugo described the Poet as a new spiritual force in society, he was simply agreeing with his guests and correspondents.

*

As Balzac suspected, Hugo now enjoyed a more direct relationship with his public than his ceremonial style suggests. Men offered him odes, women offered their bodies.

As early as 1837 there were clear signs that he was no longer content with purely intellectual dissemination. The sculptor, David d'Angers, spotted the first symptoms of the disease that destroys Dorian Grey:

> It is time I started work on the bust, for the sensual part of our friend's face is beginning to put up a vigorous struggle with the intelligent part. In other words, the lower part of the face is now almost as wide as the brow.[42]

The causes of this mysterious face-widening might have been found in Hugo's unpublished verse. Unknown figures had begun to appear in fragments: in 1837, an 'angel dressed in homespun'[43] – a coarse material which neither Juliette nor Adèle nor either of his daughters would have worn; a 'blonde with blue eyes',[44] perhaps the same woman whose trail was picked up by Juliette in 1840: 'It was very nice of me just now, and very trusting, to concede that a *blond* hair could and did come from your brown mop.'[45]

Hugo was certainly offered physical bribes by actresses who were keen to be given a role in one of his plays. A later note to Gautier, who earned his living by reviewing, suggests some cooperative arrangement for sharing the spoils.[46] The strongest evidence is a letter from Juliette in 1843. She told him he ought to find her devotion more flattering than the flirtatious letters he received: 'Mine is not the infatuation of a bluestocking nor the wantonness of a woman who marries M. Ourliac in order to go to bed with M. Hugo.'[47]

Édouard Ourliac was a short-story writer and journalist who was often seen in Hugo's company in the early 1840s. His marriage was a famous disaster, and his wife, being the daughter of a senior official at the Ministry of War, would have known Adèle's side of the family. No definite trace of an affair has been found, though there are signs that Hugo was on equally intimate terms with the wife of his solicitor.[48] The arrangement referred to by Juliette is also reminiscent of a note attributed by Hugo to his playboy persona, 'Maglia'. It sounds like a potted history of his sex life from Sainte-Beuve to the present:

> I had a wife and a friend. I worshipped my wife and I loved my friend. My friend was caressing my wife. I found out. I wanted to kill

myself but I didn't. I thought I would die. I suffered greatly, then less, then not at all. Now it's my turn. I have a friend who has a charming wife. I shake his hand and I sleep with his wife. I have the impression that this sort of thing is quite widespread.[49]

To see this as evidence that Hugo was a rabid fornicator making up for a slow start in life implies a somewhat patronizing view of the women involved. The phenomenon of 'groupies' is well attested long before the age of rock bands, and there was clearly a passionate, resourceful curiosity in Hugo's female admirers which his critics might have done well to imitate.

It was this accommodating poet, with his compartmentalized lives and consciences, who was finally elected to the Académie Française on 7 January 1841. He made his acceptance speech on 3 June. Unusually, the audience was full of women, many of them under eighteen and most of them known to Hugo in one capacity or another. Some had been queuing for hours. They were pushed aside by soldiers while the Duc and Duchesse d'Orléans processed to their seats: a rare royal visit to the Institut. Hugo smiled at Juliette in the front row (one of her proudest moments, she told him)[50] and then recited the speech in which he was expected to excoriate the institution which had once denounced him as 'the Attila of the French language'.[51]

An hour later, Hugo had sung the praises of almost every regime in modern French history, including the Revolution and the Terror, which for many people were still a painful memory. Sainte-Beuve was shocked:

> His speech would have been just the thing to bellow out in a Colosseum in front of Romans, Thracians and savage beasts, but it was completely out of place under the cupola of the Institut in front of that elegant audience.[52]

Special praise was reserved for Napoleon, 'the man who, as he later said at St Helena, "would have made Pascal a senator and Corneille a minister".'[53] Could this possibly be a gigantic hint intended for the Duc d'Orléans? The seat Hugo was about to occupy had once been Corneille's. Yet surely a ministerial portfolio would be a piffling reward for a man who claimed to see the Académie he was entering as 'one of the principal foci of that spiritual power which, since Luther, has been displaced and which, 300 years ago, ceased to belong exclusively to the Church'.[54]

The official reply, by the statesman, Salvandy, was described by journalists as the ritual bucket of water poured over the new boy's head. Salvandy snidely congratulated Hugo on having 'courageously defended your poetic vocation against all the seductions of political ambition' and complimented him on the impetus he had given to '*l'art scénique*' – a synonym for 'theatre' which caused a lot of sniggering because it sounded like '*l'arsenic*':[55] Mme Lafarge had just been sentenced to death for poisoning her husband. The suggestion was that the anti-establishment heroes of Hugo's plays had somehow been accessories to the crime.

In this strangely petty and monumental fashion, Victor Hugo and the Académie Française 'effected their laborious and memorable conjunction'.[56] Since no new collection of poems had been announced and since Hugo had not produced a play since 1838, it was assumed by many people that this was also a funeral service for the Romantic poet. In one sense, they were right.

*

THE NEW ACADEMICIAN returned home that evening with his green uniform and ceremonial sword to several hundred pages of a highly idiosyncratic political manifesto disguised as a travel account. Seven months later, it was published under the deceptive title, *Le Rhin, Lettres à un Ami*.

The male 'friend' who was supposed to have received the letters was actually, in most cases, Adèle, and the singular journey was an amalgam of three separate trips: ten days in the Champagne in 1838, part of a journey to Strasbourg and Nice in 1839, and an expedition to the Rhineland itself from August to November 1840 – all in the company of Juliette Drouet, who is removed from the account as completely as a stencil from a finished picture.

Le Rhin was twice translated into English in 1843 and remained in common use as a guide-book for many years. In *Excursions Along the Banks of Rhine, by Victor Hugo, author of the 'Hunchback of Notre Dame'*, readers were reassured that, 'while apparently vacillating between the embroidered uniform [of the Académie] and the ambition of reigning as the demigod of the *cabinet de lecture*, [the author] is, in private life, a man of high integrity and domestic worth'. The clean-living Victor Hugo had 'repoeticized, by force of genius, a tour which was becoming, by force of steam, prosaic and vulgar as a trip to Margate or Gravesend'. At the same time, he had managed to supply the traveller with 'much valuable information'.

This is something of an understatement. According to Hugo's preface, the letters were scribbled down in taverns, fresh from the brain, unaided by any book. 'Letter XXV' alone contains approximately 360 names, seventy dates, the dimensions of buildings, population figures, timetables, and so on. Hugo's memory was not quite as good as he seemed to remember it being. It was supplemented by a battery of guide-books, including his brother Abel's *La France Pittoresque*; but acknowledging these sources would have ruined what he thought of as the book's authenticity. This was Victor Hugo *en déshabillé*, even if he did spend a long time arranging his state of undress.

The result is one of the first *romans-fleuves*: Hugo himself points out that the title, *Le Rhin*, also refers to the book itself. The long rhythms of his prose massage the reader's brain into the meditative state which Hugo associates with travelling: 'the rising tide of thoughts which invades and almost submerges the mind'[57] – an effect which he enhances by describing things he had seen in daylight as if they had swum into view through the twilight gloom.

Most of the images which stick in the mind have to do with the traveller himself: a man who uses picturesque aliases like 'M. Go', who prefers talking to statues and gargoyles instead of people; a 'hard-working idler' who sets distressed beetles back on their feet, rescues drowning flies, and helps to extinguish a fire which completely destroys his hotel at Lorch.

Only two things appear to worry him: boredom, which descends with the rain in Zurich and which he defines, in a phrase which is worth several pages on the intimate origins of his world-view, as a state in which 'life seems entirely logical';[58] and the present, which occasionally interrupts the Rhineland legends (one of which Hugo invented himself) and visions of the future Europe – omnibuses trundling over ancient bridges; the volcanic landscape of furnaces and factories near Liège.

On one revealing occasion, while poking about in a ruin, he meets three young girls and tries out his English on them. Taking him for an idiot, the girls run off to ask their father for a translation of a Latin epitaph. 'It had not even occurred to them to ask me. I was somewhat mortified to think that my English had given them such a poor opinion of my Latin.' Before the girls return, he scribbles a perfect verse translation of the epitaph and slips away, unseen. 'Did they ever find the translation I left for them? I have no idea. I plunged into the meandering paths of the ruin and never saw them again.'[59]

This pedantic will-o'-the-wisp, performing his little miracles and disappearing, is a creature of Hugo's favourite form of mental distraction, a game which was becoming the basis of all his work and which makes even his most enigmatic descriptions instantly comprehensible: taking a God's-eye-view of the world.[60]

At Lausanne, Hugo's Black Forest of fact and legend opens on to a vast 'Conclusion' which occupies one-sixth of the book. The pieces of the mosaic are now assembled, or swept away and replaced with one he had made up earlier. The left bank of the Rhine should be given back to France. The Prussians would be placated with the gift of Hanover. A united Germany and France would then form a bloc strong enough to withstand those two incarnations of 'egotism': Russia and Great Britain. 'Providence' would pursue its course uninterrupted towards universal suffrage and peace.

The keystone of the European federation would be France, and the new lingua franca would be French, because, in Hugo's view, it has enough consonants for the North and enough vowel sounds for the South. Its popular monarchy was the latest step on the road to full democracy, while its capital was the intellectual powerhouse of the continent: 'Vienna, Berlin, Saint Petersburg and London are only cities; Paris is a brain'. 'The whole universe' agrees that 'at the moment, the greatest political, literary, scientific and artistic minds are all French'. French literature is 'not simply the best, but the only literature there is'.[61]

Political speeches for domestic consumption do not travel well, especially when written by a man for whom patriotic sentimentality was a way of purifying his memories of childhood. (The two English translators of *Le Rhin* discreetly amputated the conclusion.) Hugo was setting up his ideological stall much further to the right than even political ambition required. His motto seemed to be 'Democracy, but not yet'. Revolutionaries were 'a bunch of drunken good-for-nothings'.[62] Algeria was ripe for civilization: 'Strange but true,' wrote the poet who opposed the death penalty and who was to become the world's most famous anti-imperialist, 'what France lacks in Algiers is a little barbarism. The Turks acted more quickly, more surely and made more progress: they were better at cutting off heads.'

Six years later, without any real change having occurred in his political philosophy, Hugo wrote a speech on the same subject: 'But, people will say, when in Africa, do as the Africans do. One must show a little barbarism with those savages ... Messieurs, that of all arguments would be the most deplorable, and I do not accept it.'[63]

Hugo's constant shuttling from one apparent conviction to another ends up looking like hypocrisy, not only because he was constructing a marketable foreign affairs policy, but also because of his habit of appending philosophical conclusions to every fact that came his way, especially if it entered through his eyes: 'I am a great one for looking at things. I try to extract the thought from the thing.' A reluctance to express himself hypothetically meant that, unlike his more naturally ironic contemporaries, Hugo needed several square feet of textual space in which to develop his thought. This is why some of the jokes in *Les Misérables* have punch-lines which go on for several pages.

The other Hugo – the Hugo who was responsible for the half-tamed chaos of the main part of *Le Rhin* – emerges with full force in the notes which he was now amassing more assiduously than ever and which eventually appeared, after his death, as *Choses Vues*.[64] This vast collection of personal and historical anecdotes is usually pillaged, as it is in this biography, for its illustrative gems. But it is also worth considering as a composition in its own right – a fragmented view of what his work might have become without the all-consuming desire to be a financial success and the owner of a coherent philosophy. Without the need to make all the data point in the same direction, Hugo could have gone on collecting information ad infinitum, spontaneously generating whole libraries of text like one of those super-efficient organisms he found so engrossing: 'In four years, a poppy would cover the Earth and a herring would fill the seas.'[65]

A long meditation on the death of the Duc d'Orléans, for instance, reads like part of *Les Misérables* filleted of its plot.[66] The Duke had fallen from his runaway carriage 'between the twenty-sixth and the twenty-seventh tree on the left ... on the third and fourth paving-stones'. 'The house where the prince expired is number 4b and stands between a soap factory and a wine merchant's.' What did it all mean? What lurked beneath the compost heap of apparently useless information? The notes of *Choses Vues*, like the mad minutiae of *Le Rhin*, occasionally resolve themselves into a question which Hugo only seemed to have answered in his published work: was a benign hand doctoring events, or was Providence powerless in the face of Chance? The entry for 9 March 1842 showed that this dabbling in the metaphysical and the hunt for the missing link between mind and matter might produce some surprising results:

> It was dark. A Winter's night. A great wind was blowing, shaking the building from top to bottom. The rooms had some strange life of their own. Doors opened and closed; cupboards rattled. The furniture cried out as if someone had sat down on it. It was like listening to invisible inhabitants coming and going in the house.
>
> This nocturnal wind frightened us. The children, half awake, trembled in their cots. The adults, half asleep, shivered in their beds.[67]

The nocturnal wind appears to have blown away, at least for the time being. But somewhere in psychic space a door had been opened that would never close again.

*

THE OTHER PUBLISHED WORK to emerge from Hugo's Rhineland excursion had a more tangible effect on his daily life. It was a gloomy three-part play about the burgraves – the thirteenth-century robber-barons who skulked on cliff-tops overlooking the Rhine in their labyrinthine, bat-infested dungeons:

> There, father and grandfather, lost in thought, heavy with years,
> Of all they have done seeking the dark trace,
> Meditating on their life as on their race,

Contemplate, alone, and far from exultant laughter,
Their evil deeds – less hideous yet than their sons and daughters.

Hugo's pre-Wagnerian drama[68] of the progressive degeneration of a family of giants, haunted by its crimes until the Holy Roman Emperor, representing 'Providence', absolves it, was performed thirty-three times at the Comédie Française in March and April 1843. By Hugo's standards it was a flop. The audience not surprisingly failed to see it as a moral manifesto for the future United States of Europe. It hooted at Job instructing his sixty-year-old great-grandson, 'Young man, be silent!'[69] It noticed that Hugo's giants were played by unusually short actors.[70] And it giggled at Daumier's cartoon of Victor Hugo asking why comets have '*queues*' ('tails' and 'lines') when *Les Burgraves* have none: Hugo had blamed poor attendances at the theatre on the Great Comet of 1843. The 'brain' of Europe voted with its feet and wandered off to watch the usual crop of parodies: *Les Hures-Graves*, *Les Barbus-Graves*, *Les Buses-Graves* and *Les Bûches-Graves*, (The Serious Boar's-Heads, Bearded Ones, Dunderheads and Dolts).

The relative failure of *Les Burgraves* is generally thought to account for Hugo's abandonment of the theatre, but the play itself showed that his metaphysical preoccupations needed more room than a stage could offer: it was after all supposed to be performed by giants. With the appropriate technology, it might have been written as a screenplay and should count as one of the first signs of that impatience with bourgeois realism which led to Baudelaire's interest in the Japanese Noh and the experiments of Antonin Artaud. Hugo was trying to be Aeschylus in the age of gas-lamps and railways. When he left the theatre for politics, he was not simply exchanging one career for another, he was providing himself with a broader canvas, manipulating events instead of characters, dispensing with actors and directors, manoeuvring himself into a better position from which to 'interview' God.[71]

Hugo's habit of bombarding the ticket-buying public with vast, unanswerable questions couched in unquestionably beautiful verse was unlikely to make him popular anyway, as Baudelaire explained:

The public was so tired of Victor Hugo, tired of his indefatigable abilities, his indestructible beauties, sick to death of hearing him constantly referred to as 'The Just', that it had already decided some time before in its collective mind to accept as its idol the first block of wood to fall on its head.[72]

The block of wood, which became the literary event of 1843, was a pleasantly mind-numbing, pseudo-classical play by an unknown provincial called François Ponsard. Ponsard's neatly turned-out *Lucrèce*, starring the classical actress Rachel, sealed the fate of *Les Burgraves* by attracting capacity crowds to the Odéon. Thousands hung on its dull, predictable lines and persuaded themselves that a new Racine had arrived. Hugo agreed and recast the affair as Victor Hugo against Racine: 'Listening to Racine tragedies and fishing with a rod – same sort of pleasure'.[73]

Because of this coincidence, *Les Burgraves* – one of the most frequently mentioned and least read works of the nineteenth century – is traditionally said to mark the end of the Golden Age of French Romanticism. But the direct cause of the fiasco is so astoundingly trivial that Baudelaire was surely right to remove the debate from the committee rooms of literary history to the great outdoors of the collective unconscious. The event called *Lucrèce* was engineered by a talent scout who advertised Ponsard as a genius before anyone had heard his work. The joke caught on. Joseph Méry pretended to have seen the manuscript and improvised two acts of the play in a literary café next door to the Odéon. They were printed in *Le Globe* as the work of Ponsard and when the real *Lucrèce* was performed, *Globe* readers wondered why all the best lines had been left out.

The real significance of Hugo's failure goes far beyond the village square of literary Paris. The new generation – the real, impoverished Bohemia of *La Vie de Bohème* – enjoyed *Lucrèce* more than it was later willing to admit. It was beginning to realize that it would have to fight for jobs in an overcrowded establishment and accepted Ponsard's conformism as a convenient substitute for rebellion. Ponsard had dared to be timid. He cheered up his audience with the news that there was glory in blandness. The hero, Brutus, pretends to be a dimwit in order to bore his way to power and restore the grandeur of imperial Rome (i.e. Paris), while the heroine, Lucretia, is practically a negative image of Hugo's female monsters. She sits at home, sewing tunics for her husband, urging 'housewives' to do the same – for, as Ponsard's memorable axiom would have it: 'Busy fingers strengthen the mind.'

As Baudelaire hinted by talking of a 'conspiracy', the bourgeois despotism of Napoleon III was already on the horizon, and Victor Hugo, still determined to inject the obscene products of a weird imagination into the mainstream of capitalist culture, was already being ushered into exile.

*

THE UNCOMMERCIAL CLOUD of depression and congenital decay which hangs over *Les Burgraves* was partly the result of what was supposed to be a happy event.

Léopoldine had fallen in love with – or chosen as her husband – the brother of Hugo's head disciple, Auguste Vacquerie. Charles Vacquerie was a limp and self-effacing man who might have made a suitably compliant partner for the eldest child of Victor Hugo.

The courtship had been conducted with truly Hugolian artfulness. Auguste was used as a secret messenger and the powerful eye of Hugo swept over the comings and goings that were undermining his happiness like the beam of a lighthouse. 'Don't say anything in your letter about you know what,' Léopoldine instructed her ten-year-old Aunt Julie Foucher in May 1842. 'Papa reads them all. . . . Don't use any names. You might give the whole game away.'[74]

When Hugo was asked for his consent, he prevaricated for months, pretending to consider the matter carefully and hoping it would all go away. The anguish of losing his 'angel' was complicated by half-formed feelings which he had already treated unconsciously in one of his most imitated poems, 'Regard Jeté dans une Mansarde'.[75]

Peering down from a steeple, the poet spots a virgin sitting in her attic-room with its twin icons of proletarian rectitude: a Virgin Mary and a picture of Napoleon. The telescopic eye picks out every detail of her little nest but then recoils in horror at the sight of a book by Satan's emissary (and one of Hugo's closest cultural relatives) – Voltaire: 'Take care, child! . . . Voltaire is in a corner of your blessèd chamber! / With his burning eye, he spies on you and laughs.'

'Regard Jeté dans une Mansarde' is probably the worst poem Hugo ever wrote. It simply does not appear to have occurred to him that the moralistic eye is engaged in the same erotic activity as the nefarious Voltaire, and it is precisely this painful lack of self-awareness that makes the poem so aesthetically poor and psychologically rich. A corresponding scene in *Les Misérables* is, perhaps, a more conscious exploration of the theme:

> The reader may at a pinch be introduced into a nuptial bedchamber, but never into the bedroom of a virgin. Such a thing would hardly be dared in verse; in prose it must not be attempted.
>
> It is the inside of a flower which has yet to open.... A budding woman is sacred.... That bosom which veils itself before a mirror as if the mirror were an eye, that chemise hastily pulled up to hide a shoulder when the furniture creaks or a carriage passes in the street ... the successive phases of clothing, none of that must be described.... A man's eye must show even more reverence at the rising of a young girl than at the rising of a star. The possibility of touching must convert itself into increased respect. The down on a peach, the dust on a plum ... the feathery powder of the butterfly's wing are coarse matters compared to that chastity which does not know that it is chaste.... The indiscreet touch of the eye is a ravishment of that vague penumbra.[76]

The sexual torment of watching Léopoldine grow up and fall in love was exacerbated by the fact that she was now almost the same age as the actresses whose names and addresses had begun to appear in her father's secret diary. The wife of André Maurois once suggested that a much later note on the ten-year-old Aunt Julie in the most private of his private journals – 'For the first time at Fourqueux' – means that the Ogre Hugo deflowered his daughter's little friend at the time of her first communion.[77] Hugo and Julie Chenay, as she then was, probably knew each other sexually in the 1870s, but Hugo's coded notes often refer to what are technically remote relations. He received the same erotic charge from sight that most people receive from touch, and was just as likely to record a sighting as a capture. The phrase, 'For the first time at Fourqueux' commemorates the worrying and, for Hugo, shameful revelation that young girls are not just hermaphroditic 'angels'. Tragically, these feelings were about to be frozen in time.

Hugo finally gave in to the inevitable. On 15 February 1843, Léopoldine married Charles Vacquerie at the church of Saint-Paul in the Marais, where the 'Christ' by Delacroix had reportedly been modelled on Hugo. She went to live with her husband's family in Le Havre. While the burgraves expiated their ancient crimes in front of a yawning audience, Hugo sent passionate letters to the new Mme Vacquerie:

> If you received all the letters I send you, dear child, the postman would be rousing you from your sweet pleasures at every hour of the day and night. For the last month, in the middle of this maelstrom, with my enemies stirring again on every side . . . my eyes in a bad way and my mind tugged in all directions, I can truly say, my darling child, that not a moment has passed without my thinking of you. . . . Your beautiful blue sky consoles me for my cloud. My heart is heavy, but my heart is also full: I know your husband to be kind, gentle and charming . . . Happiness resides in unity. Guard that unity well, my children.[78]

Léopoldine's replies paint a powerfully symbolic picture of what might have been future relations with her father:

> I had a wonderful surprise the other day: your bust arrived. It is wonderfully lifelike. The smallness of our room forced us to leave it with my sister-in-law and so I asked Mama to get me your portrait – true to life – or a reduced copy of one of David's busts. I shall place you in front of my prie-dieu, above the stoup and the rosary of pearls which you gave me so long ago.[79]

Evicted from his daughter's bedroom but promised a place on her altar. This was a girl who knew her father well.

Missing Léopoldine and embarrassed by *Les Burgraves*, Hugo was desperate for a holiday. For the first time, he decided to return to Spain and the opening scenes of his childhood – a decision perhaps related to the fact that Gautier's colourful *Voyage en Espagne* had been serialized, very successfully, in a newspaper. With one eye on a future political career, he would also be reinforcing his credentials as an expert on Iberian affairs. On 13 June 1843, he wrote to Léopoldine explaining why he had to leave, apparently with every impression of being honest. Spain was not mentioned. He was going to take the waters at a Pyrenean spa:

A journey for my health ... but also a working journey, as you know, like all my journeys. When I have my booty and my sheaf is tied, I shall come back and embrace you all, my beloved. God owes me that at least.

Victor and Juliette set off from Paris on 18 July 1843 with a deliberately erratic, improvised itinerary. Newspapers liked to plot the progress of travelling writers as a kind of supplement to the court circular, and Hugo had always enjoyed a game of hide-and-seek. They passed through the Loire Valley, which Hugo deemed to be overpopulated with poplars, the vegetable correlative of the alexandrine, 'one of the classical forms of boredom'[80] (the spectre of Ponsard still looming). But when they crossed the border, the past exploded in his mind with the power of affective memory. Hugo's equivalent of Proust's madeleine in a tea-cup was the excruciating screech of the unoiled axles of a Spanish ox-cart:

The mere sound of it suddenly rejuvenated me. I felt as though my whole childhood were alive in me once more. Some strange, inexpressible, supernatural effect made my memory as fresh as an April dawn. I was a child, I was little, I was loved. I had no experience and I had my mother. My fellow travellers plugged their ears. I was in ecstasy.[81]

Parts of a more recent Hugo had also merged with the landscape. His own poetry was in the air. A setting of a pseudo Spanish folk song from *Les Rayons et les Ombres* was the latest hit from Paris.*[82] Hugo heard it first at Biarritz, which was then a quiet fishing-port. A peasant girl was swimming in the rock-pools by the sea. Hugo stood on a rock and listened:

> Gastibelza, the man with the carbine
> Was singing this song:
> Has anybody seen my Doña Sabine –
> Anybody here?
> Villagers, dance and sing; night is falling
> Over the Mont Falù.
> The wind which blows over the mountain
> Will drive me mad!

* In the setting by Hippolyte Monpou. See Appendix III.

1. General Léopold Hugo, father of VH, with his brothers, Louis-Joseph and François-Juste (Francis). On the left: VH's brother Abel.

2. Sophie Hugo, mother of VH.

3. Eugène Hugo, VH's brother.

4. Marquesa de Montehermoso ('Pepita'), by Goya, c. 1808–10.

5. Adèle Foucher, VH's fiancée, in 1825, by herself.

6. VH at the Coronation of Charles X (Rheims, 1825).

LES

ORIENTALES,

PAR VICTOR HUGO.

SEPTIÈME ÉDITION.

PARIS

CHARLES GOSSELIN, LIBRAIRE
DE S. A. R. MONSEIGNEUR LE DUC DE BORDEAUX,
RUE S.-GERMAIN DES PRÉS, N° 9.
HECTOR BOSSANGE, LIBRAIRE,
QUAI VOLTAIRE, N° 11.
1829.

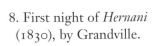

CLAIR DE LUNE

7. *Les Orientales* (1829), title page and frontispiece.

8. First night of *Hernani* (1830), by Grandville.

9. Sainte-Beuve, 1844.

10. Juliette Drouet in 1832.

11. Léopoldine, daughter of VH.

12. VH with his son François-Victor in 1836.

13. VH in 1837.

14. Adèle, wife of VH, in 1838.

15. 6, Place Royale (Place des Vosges).

16. VH in Benjamin Roubaud's 'Panthéon Charivarique' (1841).

17. 'Barricades before the attack', Rue Saint-Maur, 25 June 1848.

18. Marine Terrace (Jersey), by VH.

Noticing that she had an audience, the girl emerged from the water and asked in a mixture of French and Spanish, '"*Señor estrangero, conoce usted cette chanson?*"[83] "I think so, yes," I said, "A little".' – 'Is this not rather reminiscent of Ulysses listening to the siren?' Hugo asks the reader. 'Nature is forever throwing back at us, rejuvenating them as she does so, the countless themes and motifs on which the human imagination constructed all the old mythologies and epics.'[84]

Across the border at Pasajes he heard the song again. Two boats were anchored under his balcony and a sailor was singing *Gastibelza* as he worked:

> She would have made the Queen look plain
> When, as night drew on,
> She passed on the bridge at Toledo
> In her black bodice.
> A rosary from the time of Charlemagne
> Hung around her neck.
> The wind which blows over the mountain
> Will drive me mad!

Perhaps it was this constant mirroring of his own past that gave the journey an increasingly morbid tone. In places, Hugo's account becomes so eerily prophetic that one is constantly led to rehearse the evidence that it was indeed written on the road and not tailored afterwards to fit events. At the icy Lac de Gaube, a bilingual epitaph recorded the death by drowning, in September 1842, of an English barrister and his young bride.[85] At Gavarnie, two children playing on the edge of the abyss had disappeared.[86]

On 4 September 1843, 400 miles away, Léopoldine, Charles, his Uncle Pierre and Cousin Arthus had arrived at Villequier and were preparing for a boat-trip. The Seine at Villequier was notorious for accidents,[87] but the weather was fine, Uncle Pierre was a retired sea-captain, and the yacht, though slightly top-heavy with sail, had won first prize in the Honfleur regatta. At exactly the same moment, Victor and Juliette were exploring the cathedral at Auch, admiring the stained-glass windows on which pagan figures mingled with Old Testament characters. In one, a woman was holding a skull and a mirror. 'She appeared to be comparing Beauty to Death.'[88]

Four days later, on 8 September 1843, they arrived at the Island of Oléron, half-way up the west coast of France. The salt marshes, the gangs of convicts and the 'sinister' appearance of the island depressed them. It was the first time Hugo had been truly miserable by the sea. The locals were blaming the heatwave for a mysterious plague which had claimed the lives of several children. On the boat across, sailors were discussing a recent spate of drownings.

> *Diary of Juliette Drouet*: Since I arrived in this region a vague anxiety has taken hold of me. I shudder at the delays which prevent us getting news from Paris. When I left my daughter in Paris she was poorly and now I can't stop thinking about her. I fear some terrible misfortune.[89]

> *Diary of Victor Hugo*: I walked along the shore, stepping in the seaweed in order to avoid the mud. I followed the castle moat. The convicts had just returned and were being counted in. I could hear their voices, one after the other, answering the voice of the inspecting officer.... To my right, the marshes stretched away as far as the eye could see ... Low in the western sky a huge round Moon appeared.... Death was in my soul.... The island seemed to me a large coffin laid in the sea, with the Moon as a torch.[90]

They spent the night in a hotel on the island, but fearing the fevers that drifted off the marshes, they retreated to the mainland and arrived at Rochefort, tired and thirsty, on 9 September. The coach for La Rochelle was not due to leave until six in the evening.

On the town square a large sign said 'Café de l'Europe'. It was almost deserted. They ordered some beer and sat down in a corner. In front of them, some Paris newspapers were spread out on a table. Juliette took *Le Charivari* and Victor took *Le Siècle*. 'Suddenly my poor darling leant over me and, pointing to the paper, said in a choking voice, "*Something horrible!*" ... His poor lips were white, his eyes stared blindly, his face and hair were wet with perspiration, his poor hand clutched his breast as if to prevent his heart from bursting out.'

It was an article which had appeared in the *Journal du Havre*, written in the flowery style which Mérimée blamed on the influence of Victor Hugo ... In all the superfluous verbiage, terrible phrases stood out:

The sinister report of an appalling incident which will cast a shroud over a family held dear by the world of French letters has this morning afflicted the inhabitants of our town . . .

M. P. Vacquerie . . . took with him in his yacht . . . his nephew M. Ch. Vacquerie and the young wife of the latter, who is, as everyone knows, the daughter of M. Victor Hugo. . . .

News reached the steamboat *La Petite Emma* that a yacht had capsized . . . The corpse of M. Pierre Vacquerie was recovered. It was first assumed that M. Ch. Vacquerie, who is an experienced swimmer, had been washed further downstream in the attempt to save his wife and relatives. . . .

The net dredged up the lifeless body of the unfortunate young woman . . .

Mme Victor Hugo had been residing for some time in Le Havre with her two other children . . . She left immediately for Paris. M. Victor Hugo is presently engaged on a journey. He is believed to be in La Rochelle . . .

Léopoldine, Charles, his uncle and cousin had all drowned. By the time Hugo saw the article, his daughter was lying in the cemetery at Villequier.

He stood up and moved to the other side of the table, facing Juliette. 'He told me we must not attract the attention of the people around us.'

Then they left the café and walked for hours under the blazing sun, along the town walls, through the suburbs, back to the square. People were staring. Most of the country had heard the news a day or two before. 'At one point', Juliette remembered, 'we sat down on a stone bench, then on some grass. Some women and young girls looking after children were sewing. As they worked, they sang. One of them was singing *Gastibelza*.'

Hugo sent a note to Adèle. It ended with the ambiguous phrase, 'My God, what have I done to you?'

Shortly before six o'clock, a small crowd of people gathered round the coach, trying to catch a glimpse of Victor Hugo. Out of sympathy, the driver left early. At ten o'clock that evening they arrived under a heavy sky at La Rochelle. It was still unbearably hot; a thunderstorm was trying to break. A room would have to be found and seats reserved for the next stage of the journey. They passed in front of a crowded café where a singer was belting out the inevitable *Gastibelza*. For the fourth time that journey, Hugo heard his own words returning; but as he knew from the girl at Biarritz, this was no longer the voice of Victor Hugo. It was the 'siren' voice of Nature with her uninterpretable omens.

> Villagers, dance and sing, night is falling!
> Sabine, one day,
> Sold all she had, her dove-like charms
> And her love,
> For the sake of Count Saldagna's golden ring,
> For a jewel . . .
> The wind which blows over the mountain
> Has driven me mad!

CHAPTER TWELVE

Criminal Conversation

(1843–1848)

A T SAUMUR, Hugo asked to see a newspaper. A garbled report in *Le Siècle* implied that his son, François-Victor, had also drowned. Juliette tried to tell him it wasn't true. 'He looked as though he was going to die.... Then he wanted to read all the horrific, moving details of that atrocious catastrophe.'

Three days passed before they reached Paris. Hugo rushed to the Place Royale to find François-Victor still alive. The funeral had already taken place at Villequier. Mme Hugo sat in the salon, clutching a clump of hair which had been shorn from the head of the corpse. Hugo answered letters and received visitors. Pictures of the young couple were set out on the tables. The dress in which Léopoldine drowned had been folded into an embroidered satchel. Hugo labelled it, 'What my daughter was wearing when she died. Sacred relic'.

A few streets away, Juliette waited for news, praying to Léopoldine to watch over the rest of the family. Days later, Hugo brought her some 'relics' and gave her the job of recording the last stages of their journey. On the way back, he had numbered the pages of a notebook, but they were never filled.

These blank pages have proved to be an irresistible temptation. In the face of death, even scholarly integrity falters, and the story which has emerged from 150 years of misguided commiseration is that Hugo interpreted the drowning as a divine reprimand: adultery, neglect of his children, expensive foreign holidays with his mistress, resulting in the eternal confiscation of his daughter. What should make one deeply suspicious is the fact that the main contemporary authority for this is a letter from Balzac to his future wife. In December, he went to ask for Hugo's vote in the forthcoming Academy elections:

> Victor Hugo has aged ten years! It may be that he has taken the death of his daughter as a punishment for the four children he has from Juliette [*sic*]. He is all in favour of me and has promised me his vote. He execrates Sainte-Beuve and de Vigny.[1]

Business as usual. The only definite sign that Hugo felt he was being 'punished' comes much later – a fragment of a poem asking Léopoldine not to make him feel guilty about 'kissing' other women.[2] Yet the compacted, flabby face of Victor Hugo in the portraits of exile clearly shows the dent of a great disaster, or, by then, several disasters.

Mourning, for Hugo, did not dawn for years. A thought had taken up residence like a parasite. The single obvious fact was that God had deprived him of his daughter for no discernible purpose. A career publicly devoted to the moral improvement of humanity had been impeded by the ultimate authority. While his face grew old, his mind was plunged into childhood and the moral vertigo of having a father like General Hugo: 'It cannot be . . . that I am better than the Father / Or that man is greater than God!'[3] This disillusionment with the divine Father is a valuable key to Hugo's seemingly squalid behaviour in the years to come: sin and depravity were infinitely preferable to the thought of a malevolent Creator.

Meanwhile, Hugo had to compose a public face. Sympathetic poets were tackling the subject of the Villequier disaster as if the Académie Française had set it in a competition, and Hugo was forced to thank them for their 'simultaneously heart-rending and ravishing lines'.[4] The sculptor David, reviving an idea he had hoped to use on a monument to Nelson, wanted to cast the ill-fated yacht in bronze, set it over the four coffins and show 'two frantic hands protruding from under the rim, which is what actually happened', he explained, 'for it was only with the greatest of difficulty that the poor drowned woman's hands were prised open: they were practically incrusted in the wood'.[5]

Responding to these images of his own despair, Hugo was able to construct a coherent, optimistic interpretation for his audience. On

23 September, he wrote to the critic, Édouard Thierry, who had just lost his father:

> Let us bend our heads under the hand which destroys. . . . Death brings revelations. The mighty blows that open the heart also open the mind. Light penetrates us at the same time as pain. I am a believer. I anticipate another life. How could I not? My daughter was a soul. A soul which I have seen and, as it were, touched. . . . Even in this world, she was visibly living a higher life. . . . I suffer as you do. Hope as I do.[6]

Ludicrously, Hugo's balanced prose – and some perfect alexandrines written on the journey back to Paris – have been cited as proof that his grief was insincere. Those who expect to see tears bursting punctually from the eyes of the bereaved as if activated by a mechanism in the coffin-lid have expressed surprise that the first poems Hugo wrote, less than two months after the drowning, were calm, soft-hearted celebrations of life:[7] a child unravelling a spindle while her grandmother nods off at the spinning-wheel; the poet in Nature, 'listening to the lyre within himself', while the flirtatious little flowers shimmer and shake like pretty girls: '"Look!", they say, "Our lover is passing!"'

The fact that Hugo redated these poems to fit the expected chronology shows that he was as disturbed as his critics by the mind's inability to perform on cue.

Eventually, the death of Léopoldine would turn out to be one of the great opportunities of his career. It prepared the way for a conviction far more powerful than any speculation on the personal attributes of God: the realization that the universe is not indifferent but formed from the same substance as the human mind. This realization was already latent in his verse. Throughout his life, the months in which he composed his poems consistently fall into a poetic year corresponding to the solar year. April, May, June, July, August and October are his richest months; September, November, December, January, February and March his poorest. The most prolific is always June and the least prolific February. The poem-writing Hugo, the 'lover' of little flowers, was more profoundly affected by the annual death of Nature than by the death of his own daughter.[8]

This permeability to a more deep-seated influence than the ups-and-downs of daily life is normally recognized only as a social shortcoming: a great respectful intimacy with the universe at large, and an apparent insensitivity to individuals in the immediate vicinity. But it explains why he set about exterminating the parasite of despair by incorporating the death of his daughter into a myth – the merging of male and female beyond the grave. The final 'official' version of the tragedy – Charles Vacquerie, realizing that Léopoldine was doomed, had held on to her as she drowned – echoes the consummation-in-death at the end of *Notre-Dame de Paris*, thirteen years before: 'Two skeletons were found, locked in a curious embrace. One of the two skeletons – the skeleton of a woman – still wore a few scraps of dress of a material which had once been white.'

*

THE EVERYDAY HUGO underwent more noticeable changes. As usual when his mind was over-occupied, his eyes began to hurt. He had a pain in his 'dear little knee', as Juliette's letters reveal – perhaps the result of praying, which he did now every day. He also became extremely rude and grumpy and began to snore.[9]

Superstitions sprouted in his mind. When Adèle and the children went to stay with brother Abel at Versailles, Hugo insisted on seeing them again either on Thursday or on Saturday: 'You know how weak and fearful I have become since the blow which has just struck us, and I should not like us to meet again on a Friday.' A conviction that all things are interconnected meant that Hugo had always been prone to superstition. Now that the possibility of a malevolent God had presented itself, some personal intervention seemed advisable.

The letter sent to Versailles was one of the longest he wrote in the days following the accident, and its longest section has been taken by some as confirmation that he was a heartless father, preoccupied with his own little needs:

> You and Charles took my umbrella with you when you left on Saturday. Watch out for it. It is easy to recognize. The wood of the handle is plain, yellow and knotted. Take care of it and make sure it does not get lost.[10]

A more charitable, Freudian reading might associate his anxiety about the lost umbrella with the new theme of exposure to the elements – the drowning of Léopoldine, a recent allusion to Brunel's tunnel under the Thames (a tiny crack, and the waters of destiny come crashing in),[11] and the great elegy, 'À Villequier': 'The tomb which closes on the dead / Opens up the firmament'; 'I who was weak as a mother, / Kneel at Your feet under Your open skies.'

In an ominous development, Hugo's three remaining children were ordered now to follow the impeccable example of their sainted sister. Little 'Dédé' was repeatedly told to stop stammering: 'A little girl may stammer; a young girl must not.'[12] In the eternal absence of her older sister, Adèle II began to blossom. Balzac described her in 1843 as 'the greatest beauty I shall ever see'.[13] But she was a dark flower, well adapted to the funereal habitat, and there was already something odd and intense about her, the aura of a well-populated fantasy world which her father's almost vindictive protectiveness would allow to fester.

The whole tragic tribe was almost too much for Charles Dickens when he saw it in 1847. Compared to the fluttering heroines of his own novels, the Hugo women were black ravens which he quickly labelled and cast into his museum:

> I was much struck by Hugo himself, who looks a Genius, as he certainly is, and is very interesting from head to foot. His wife is a handsome woman with flashing black eyes, who looks as if she might poison his breakfast any morning when the humour seized her. There is also a ditto daughter of fifteen or sixteen, with ditto eyes, and hardly any drapery above the waist, whom I should suspect of carrying a sharp poignard in her stays, but for her not appearing to wear any. Sitting among old armour, and old tapestry, and old coffers, and grim old chairs and tables, and old Canopies of state from old palaces, and old golden lions going to play at skittles with ponderous old golden balls, they made a most romantic show, and looked like a chapter out of one of his own books.[14]

Dickens's flair lay not so much in his gift for raising ghosts and laying them humorously to rest as in his detection of the dangerous smell of sex – the only incense that wards off death. That year, Adèle II was allowing herself to be courted by the sculptor, Clésinger,[15] famous for his mouldings of Mme Sabatier's body, which found their way into the poetry of Charles Baudelaire and even on to wallpaper, and for a 'Bacchante Sprawling on Vine Branches' which may also have been inspired by the partly imagined body of Mlle Hugo.

Mme Hugo responded to death by developing flirtatious friendships with Auguste Vacquerie and their neighbour, Théophile Gautier. Warm, bossy letters invited that naughty man Gautier to the local swimming baths or scolded him for letting his chocolate grow cold every evening. Persistent rumours allege an affair between Mme Hugo and her daughter's brother-in-law. One of Vacquerie's poems does seem to be a coded description of morning visits to his bedroom from Mme Hugo and it is quite possible, as the rumours also suggest, that Hugo encouraged him.[16] He too was craving a fresh injection of life and a moral victory over death. For this, there would be a heavy price to pay.

*

THE WOMAN COMMONLY referred to as 'Mme Biard' was introduced to Hugo by a mutual friend, probably in 1843.[17] She was famous for being the first Frenchwoman to visit Spitsbergen, 700 miles inside the Arctic Circle. The expedition had been a pre-marital honeymoon with the painter, Auguste Biard, 'the man of frigid follies', according to Baudelaire's *Salon de 1846*.[18] Auguste was twenty years older than Léonie, violently jealous and, apparently, easy to deceive.

The details of Léonie Biard's personality are almost entirely swamped, in Hugo's descriptions, by the tide of sexual desire. Other writers show her as a witty, courageous, well-educated woman who designed her own clothes and those of her pet monkey, Mouniss.[19] The only exception is Flaubert – 'There is something of the *grisette* about her – probably not a gourmet dish'[20] – but Flaubert was only twenty-three at the time. According to the usual microscopic, pathological accounts of male connoisseurs, she had fair hair, which she wore loose, cheeks as appetizing as 'a ripening peach', 'supple nostrils' and pouting lips. Hugo compared her eyes to diamonds. 'Mme Biard' suggests an older woman. In fact, Léonie was just four years older than Léopoldine. When she and Hugo began meeting secretly some time in 1844, she was pregnant with her second daughter and was hoping to obtain a separation from Biard.

Léonie was a pleasantly distracting challenge. Her later account of one of Hugo's seduction attempts suggests a long and arduous campaign. Hugo's feverish unbuttoning is constantly interrupted: first she thinks of her husband, then of her children, and then she remembers God. Finally, a spent force, Hugo sighs, 'You can safely come and lie with me now.'

Several of Hugo's letters to Léonie Biard have survived because he copied out his own purple passages before going to the post, first adding the precautionary phrase, 'He said to her . . .', in case they fell into the wrong hands. In order to conjure up the air of authenticity essential to a love letter, he retrained himself by consulting the 6000 or so he had received from Juliette. But even in a new context, phrases retain the watermark of a personality, and borrowed traits of Juliette show up quite clearly in the letters to Léonie:

> *Victor Hugo to Léonie Biard*: I shall lock myself up with the memory of you ... I see around me all the adorable traces of your visit, the unmade bed, the disordered room, the stool on which you rested your foot, the pillow which bears the imprint of your ravishing head ... I shall religiously respect that charming little turmoil you left behind you.[21]

These days, Juliette's affectionate fetishism had a more earthy, domestic quality which underlines the difference between the two ménages:

> *Juliette Drouet to Victor Hugo*: I drank everything you left in your glass, and I shall nibble your little piece of chicken wing. I shall eat with your knife and sup from your spoon. I kissed the spot where you rested your head. I placed your walking-stick in my bedroom. I surround myself and steep myself in all that was close to you.[22]

It is ironic that Juliette had often complained about her poor writing: 'Only in bed do I feel I can compete with the abundance and richness of your language, which I utterly lack when I am wearing shoes and corseted.'[23] Even more sadly ironic that Hugo involved Léonie in the deception: 'This is a letter from that poor girl I told you about. I am sending it to you along with my reply . . . Please have it posted . . . The stamp will convince her that I have gone to the country.'[24]

In Hugo's mental universe, there was sometimes little difference between an act of cowardice and an act of courage: both meant ignoring the usual code of conduct. The subterfuges that make up a work of art could also be used to satisfy a need, while prevailing attitudes to the other half of the human race allowed an impression of moral freedom to survive. And yet the magnificent portrayals of injustice in *Les Misérables* show that he was storing up shame deep inside like a treasure. 'Noble spirits!' he writes in one of the rare first-person interventions in *Les Misérables*. 'Often, you present us with your hearts and we take your bodies'.[25]

Even then, the last part of the phrase should probably be read as an echo of back-slapping conversations with male friends. The potency of the national poet has been a favourite theme with French critics for the last hundred years, and whether the theme is treated with awe or outrage, the assumption is that Hugo was different in this respect from the normal run of humanity. Juliette's sexuality is not usually submitted to the same jovial scrutiny, except by misogynists. Yet it was Hugo who came up with all the excuses – her periods and his ailments. He claimed that his doctors had warned him against the potentially damaging effects of orgasm. Juliette complained that her cat, Fouyou, spent more time in her bed than Hugo.[26] She was starved of food, fuel, money and sex. She threatened to cut off his 'appendix'.[27] She broadened her repertoire, promised to drink his 'nectar', and tried to encourage the 'little man' to behave like a lover.[28] But as a careful reading of the texts inspired by Léonie reveals, the man with three households had embarked on something far more adventurous and nutritious.

Eleven poems, most of them written in 1844 and all published posthumously, form a mini 'Mme Biard' corpus, dissolved in the great flood of Hugo's verse and traceable now only because they were arranged consecutively in the same dossier by one of his executors.[29] The Mme Biard poems are all intensely sexual, all good examples, superficially, of what Verlaine described as the typical Hugo love poem: '"I like you. You yield to me. I love you. – You resist me. Clear off." ... The joy of the cock and then its full-throated cry.'[30]

The first poem (29 December 1843) helpfully announces a break with literary tradition: 'Love is no longer that ancient, lying Cupid, / The puny, naked child with a blindfold on his eyes.'[31] In contrast to his other love poems, the woman in the Mme Biard poems is either naked or about to be naked. Except for a sunny Sunday afternoon in bed, the setting is almost always the starry sky (force of circumstance). The 'darkness' surrounding the light of their happiness does not refer to Léopoldine but to the fact that neither of them is free to go and live on 'a wonderful desert island'.[32] Léonie's large eyes appear in all but two of the poems, but their colour is never mentioned by Hugo: another trace of the peculiar vision which makes his drawings such subtle studies of light and the mind's interference with reality.[33] Colour is confined to her face, which on one occasion is said to be 'alternately pale and pink', though this is clearly a rare allusion to orgasm, 'that sweet abandon known only to the angels'.

The great contribution these poems make to our knowledge of Hugo is the information that sex, for him, was a form of *contemplation*. Léonie's body was the Sibyl's tripod. 'Reason', he once wrote, 'is intelligence taking exercise. Imagination is intelligence with an erection'.[34] When Hugo entered her body, he was plunging into the 'firmament' which the death of Léopoldine had opened up. It was in the tomb of Léonie's bed that the mythological interpretation of the drowning took on a real existence:

> When I have you, when I hold you naked in my arms, I am no longer a man, you are no longer a woman, we are two sovereign beings, emperors of paradise!
>
> The pleasure of the senses flows in amongst the pleasure of the soul ... My eyes are filled with stars, my mouth is filled with perfumes. I feel myself dying – dying a death which is life.
>
> I penetrate you. ... O ravishing contemplation! For me, you are transparent. Through your clothes I see your body and through your body I see your soul.
>
> Thus you hold my heart in your talons, O beautiful victor, as an eagle holds its prey.

Words fail me. This is an inexpressible, divine form of life. Did I say divine?! This is to be happier than God, for God has no wife!

The noteworthy absence of drugs in Hugo's life is misleading. Léonie's bed was the propagator of a new kind of hallucinatory composition. Hugo's letters are filled with what looks like Surrealist imagery and are even several years ahead of his own poetry. The nearest equivalent in his published work is the mystical verse of the 1850s: '[The Poet's] transparent skull is full of souls, bodies / And dreams whose light can be seen from the outside.'[35]

The versatile Léonie was a secret gate back to the sense of wholeness he found in Nature and in crowded city streets,[36] so that, without a title, it would often be hard to tell whether some of his poems were descriptions of sex or religious meditations.

It seems especially cruel that this seventh heaven was about to be penetrated by the long arm of the Paris gendarmerie.

*

WHILE HUGO was perfecting himself with Léonie Biard, his public career had been reaching new heights, and revealing greater expanses of emptiness than he had supposed to exist in the upper spheres.

Under the cupola of the Institut, he sat with his fellow academicians, marvelling at their ignorance of the French language, wittily recording their pearls of unwisdom. It was like school without the teachers. Mérimée described the scene on an average day in the Academy: 'Everybody talks at once. Only V. Hugo maintains his gravity.'[37] In Sainte-Beuve's view, 'Hugo thinks that people are more stupid than they really are.'[38] But his portrayal of his colleagues as overgrown children shows a keen awareness of the mental stagnation endemic in institutions, and a desire to dig out the underlying personalities. Hugo's most successful relationships were always with people under the age of ten or with the ten-year-old parts of their personality.

In 1845, Hugo was assigned the job of welcoming into the Academy the moralizing, anti-Romantic Professor of French poetry at the Sorbonne, Saint-Marc Girardin,[39] and his old ex-friend, Sainte-Beuve.[40] The speeches were delivered by a truly noble Victor Hugo who could conjure up an act of unquestionable virtue like a perfect poem. He used the opportunity to remind the Academy that 'writers must take themselves seriously'; 'always respect the fundamental laws of language, which is the expression of truth'; and, while the other Hugo listened quietly, he courageously defended the cause of women – a huge incongruity which brought the air of a socialist club meeting into the conservative Academy, even if it did perhaps reflect the unusually high number of women who attended whenever Hugo was to speak:

> For her, social laws are rough and stingy. Poor, she is condemned to labour; rich, to constraint. Prejudices ... weigh more heavily on her than on man. ... The more adept she is at loving, the more she suffers ... And yet, what a contribution she makes to the total sum of providential acts which result in the continual improvement of the human race!

Not for the last time, Hugo was proving that hypocrisy was one of the essential ingredients of an effective desire for justice, because then, the inspired reformer was driven by the evidence of his own shortcomings. Charity begins at home, but not necessarily in the form of charity.

This was the distinguished, honourable Hugo who was now being regularly invited to soirées by King Louis-Philippe, later described in Louis-Philippe's favourite part of *Les Misérables* as a man who loved his family before his country, had his bedroom shown to visitors to prove that he slept with his wife, carried an umbrella and wore a toupee; a professional monarch, immune to depression and fatigue, but somehow emotionally neutral and lacking a sense of the 'inner aspirations, the dark, concealed upheavals' that seethed in the masses.[41]

Hugo was a good listener, a therapist rather than a counsellor. The King chatted at him for hours about the mental incompetence of Europe's rulers and the lazy schoolboys in his Cabinet. Once, Hugo was kept so late that His Majesty had to light him down the stairs. Both men had lost their favourite child, both considered themselves fundamentally decent and misunderstood, and both were interested in the problems of ordinary men in extraordinary positions.

Hugo had two reactions to royal favour. He was slightly crestfallen to see how bourgeois palace life had become (nothing like Madrid under Joseph Bonaparte); yet he was perfectly bourgeois himself in his excitement. Hobnobbing with the great names of European politics enabled him to admire his miraculous career and the little ironies of fame. One minute, he was listening to the Prince of Bavaria calling him 'the European poet'; the next, he was waiting for the bus.[42]

The son of a soldier, married to a civil servant's daughter, Hugo was a spectacular example of what the Revolution had done to French society. On 13 April 1845, the rise of the Hugos was complete – from labourer to lord in two generations. At the age of forty-three, Viscount Hugo was made a *pair de France*. Politically, it was a sensible appointment: he was internationally famous, intimate with the royal family, worshipped by the young, historically connected to several regimes, and a conservative with an interest in philanthropic causes. A thoroughly good example.

On 28 April, he took the sacred oath and went to sit among the lords who helped to forge the destiny of the nation. Fans of the old, Romantic Hugo considered it a betrayal, the second nail in the coffin after the Académie Française. As Alphonse Karr put it, 'What was the point of going to all the trouble of becoming Victor Hugo?'[43]

A few weeks later, before he had the chance to make his maiden speech in the Upper Chamber, the brand new Victor Hugo fell flat on his face with his trousers round his ankles.

*

HUGO HAD BEEN looking for a 'lair' where he and Léonie could enjoy each other's company without fear of interruption or blackmail. He found it in a quiet side-street, conveniently close to the Academy and Parliament: the Passage Saint-Roch.

If Hugo had had the criminal experience and supersensitive ear of Jean Valjean in *Les Misérables*, he might have held his house-key more tightly in his hand on certain evenings when he made his way to the Passage Saint-Roch. A man had been watching while he passed along the shop-fronts and disappeared through an iron gate on the left. When the street was empty, the man came and stood at the gate and stared up at a gloomy-looking tenement. There was no concierge to ask him his business, just a sign advertising 'Furnished Rooms'. He might have waited for days without ever seeing his prey emerge. A second key allowed the occupants of the house to slip away by another street into the crowded Rue Saint-Honoré.

On the night of 4 July 1845, Hugo and Mme Biard were communing with each other in their rented lair when a cab drew up in the alley outside. A few seconds later, the door was opened and two men appeared at the foot of the bed. One was holding a pen and some paper; the other was the local *commissaire de police*. While the culprits dressed, the significant facts were recorded. They had been found 'in criminal conversation' and 'in uncrumpled attire', which meant that they were committing adultery and were wearing no clothes.

Back at the police station, it was ascertained that Madame was the wife of M. Auguste Biard. Monsieur was known to the investigating officer only as 'M. Apollo' – the name under which the room had been rented. At first, the man insisted that Apollo was his real name, hoping that the husband would relent. Léonie had been suing for divorce on the grounds of mistreatment and Biard had launched a pre-emptive strike by hiring a private detective. He refused to drop the charges. Léonie was taken to Saint-Lazare, the prison for prostitutes and adulterous women. Hugo was forced to reveal his identity. His medal proved that he was a *pair de France* and thus immune to prosecution. While his lover went to jail, Hugo left the station a free man and returned to the Place Royale, where he woke Adèle up at four in the morning and poured out the whole story.

At times like this, the Paris gendarmerie acted as a clearing-house for salacious information. Mysterious channels led directly from the file cabinets of the Préfecture to the editorial rooms of avant-garde newspapers like *La Silhouette* and *Le Corsaire-Satan*.[44] While editors assigned their wittiest reporters to the job, news of the incident reached the Tuileries Palace. The King was said to be furious. The inviolability of peers was a politically sensitive issue. Veiled threats were issued by the Palace and had the usual effect: a rumour went about that the Biard affair was an attempt to cover up a liaison between Victor Hugo and a member of the royal family. As a result, the man at the centre of the scandal was identified in the papers only as a famous poet of the modern school who was an Academician, a *pair de France*, and had reached the '*feuilles d'automne*' period of his life. 'As for *notre dame*, she comes from *Paris*.'[45]

Soon, every newspaper reader in Paris knew that Victor Hugo had been found in bed with the wife of Auguste Biard.[46] They also knew that a deputation of angry peers had visited Hugo at his home and been mollified by his promise to leave Paris for a long vacation in Spain. Hugo obtained a passport and set off for the Rue Saint-Anastase four streets away, where Juliette, who did not read the papers, was surprised to have him to herself for a few days.

After two months in cell 13 at Saint-Lazare, Léonie was transferred to the Convent of the Dames de Saint-Michel. Article 337 of the Penal Code allowed husbands to show their clemency in this way. Mme Hugo, pleased to see that the beloved Juliette had a rival, took up Léonie's cause and visited her in the convent. Léonie had been helping the nuns to choose a selection of Victor Hugo poems which might safely be shown to girls of fifteen.[47] She was still in love with Hugo and expecting support. Meanwhile, Biard, with more business sense than passion, was determined to see Hugo's guilt established in the Chambre des Pairs. The King was persuaded by the peers to placate him with a commission. Biard relented, and a few months later the Château de Versailles acquired some unusually mediocre frescoes.

In November 1845, while Léonie was still in custody, Hugo began work on a novel, his first since *Notre-Dame de Paris*.[48] The working title was *Jean Tréjean*, soon to be changed to *Les Misères*. It was the story of a convict and an abandoned woman, a plea for natural justice written by a man who was above the law. But the book which a Protestant minister would describe as 'the Magna Carta of the human race'[49] was not necessarily the work of a penitent. He simply had more time for writing – including more lusty poems to Léonie. His own life had just supplied him with a dramatic example of the injustices he condemns in the novel. The 'penitence' theory is somewhat weakened by the fact that when she left the convent, Léonie became a frequent visitor to the Place Royale and was accepted almost as a member of the family. Mme Hugo helped her with her new career as a writer in exchange for advice on clothes and interior decorating. Hugo continued to sleep with her. The recent death of his father-in-law, Pierre Foucher, may have created a more relaxed domestic regime.

The Mme Biard affair caused only a slight delay to Hugo's new career. In the eyes of his fellow peers, who were not noted for their continence, his crime was that he had allowed himself to be caught. The lasting damage was to his image, which is to say an important part of his personality. The recurrent figure of the Fool in Hugo's work betrays a fear that he was little more than a clown. How could he convincingly plead the cause of the poor when he himself was legally immune – something he considered 'just as stupid' as the laws on adultery?[50]

This discrepancy was not an insuperable intellectual obstacle to Hugo himself; but his 'aristocratic' behaviour was responsible for a new tone in the papers – not the bracing ridicule of envious reviewers, but the affectionate laughter of a younger generation. According to *La Silhouette*, 'Olympio I' was daily surrounded by fawning women, scattered handshakes and autographs wherever he went, and called the editor of the *Quilleboeuf Courier* 'the leading critic of our time'. One day, said the anonymous article, a playwright called Camille Bernay had been strolling along the boulevard with Hugo. A strap on Bernay's trousers came loose. Hugo reattached it for him, saying as he did so, 'One day you will tell your children, "It was on this very spot that HE repaired my trouser-strap."'[51]

La Silhouette also revealed that, as a very young man, Olympio had drawn up 'the complete programme of his life and never deviates from it: in a file he keeps poems, written in advance, in which he talks of his white beard and bowed head. They will be published at the appropriate time and place.' Hugo had turned into an ageing dandy, unquestionably the greatest living writer, but also an eccentric artefact, the national treasure of a state which was rapidly losing control of its destiny. In his poetry, he was still a visionary who had conversations with God, but in the outside world, the sphinx appeared to have forgotten the answer to its own riddle.

*

THE BEST ARTICLES written on Hugo in the late 1840s were published in the satirical press: only a combination of praise and ridicule could bring together the two paths he was following and which were diverging rapidly, as the immovable obstacle of the 1848 revolution drew near.

The public Hugo became increasingly proficient at commemorating his daughter's death (rather than celebrating her life). Plotting his annual output of verse produces a line of almost regular peaks and troughs. Before the drowning, it reaches a peak shortly before the publication of each new volume. A punctual, businesslike pulse of poetic activity. After 1843, the line becomes a cardiograph of Hugo's inner life. A sudden surge of poems in 1846 can be explained by the death of Juliette's daughter, Claire Pradier. Hugo had supported her financially, and when she died at the age of twenty on 21 June 1846, despite the damage already done to his image, he publicly attended the funeral. Mourning Claire seems to have allowed him to mourn his own daughter and made 1846 by far his most prolific year until the great unblocking of exile. Unless, of course, this was simply the usual pre-publication increase in output.[52]

Hugo was well aware that if the poems he wrote were sufficiently beautiful, such petty speculations would be set aside. According to him, the more beautiful the work, the nobler the sentiments that inspired it in the first place. His refusal to allow himself to be bogged down in the endless internal debate of 'sincerity' made his visits to the little riverside cemetery at Villequier one of the lasting images of the nineteenth century and produced some of the most deeply pleasing poems on tragic death in French literature. Poems like 'À Villequier', which shocked the schoolboy Verlaine with its gentle reminder to God, who had never had a daughter, that losing one's child was very painful. Or 'Demain, dès l'aube . . .', in which the first-person narrator summons up an audience to which he remains ostentatiously oblivious.[53] Whatever the motives of the actor himself, the performance, with its grand gestures and simple phrases, would be validated and purified by the emotions it drew from the spectators:

> Tomorrow, at dawn, when light falls over the land,
> I shall leave. I know you are waiting for me.
> Through the forest, over the hills,
> I can no longer stay apart from you.

I shall walk with my eyes on my thoughts,
Seeing nothing beyond me, hearing no noise,
Alone, unknown, hunched, my hands clasped
In sadness; and day for me will be as night.

I shall not look as the gold of evening falls,
Nor see the distant sails bound for Harfleur,
And when I arrive I shall place on your grave
A bunch of flowering heather and green holly.

While Hugo's image climbed its Calvary, the rest of him was busy elsewhere – but doing what? Arranging every known fact about Hugo's life in chronological order is an alarming experiment, the biographer's equivalent of the missing mass problem. Hugo usually made appointments to the nearest quarter of an hour,[54] suggesting a full timetable; yet the evidence seems to show that he was a man of leisure.

His total verse output from 1843 to 1848 comes to only 143 poems and fragments of poem – an average of fewer than two lines a day or less than one poem a fortnight for six years.[55] He worked on his novel, *Les Misères*, like 'a convict', but sporadically, often setting it aside and filing it away for years when revolution broke out in February 1848. Most days, he added scraps of miscellaneous information to his diary – 'The breath of whales is fetid'; 'Soot is the best fertilizer for carnations'. But even after his fifteen speeches and political texts (six in 1848), meetings at the Academy, Parliament and the Société des Gens de Lettres, letters of recommendation and trips to Villequier, he should have been relatively idle. 'Like all old men and most thinkers', he slept soundly, but only for a few hours on a hard bed with a pillow like 'a Greek pediment' ('sinking into a feather-bed frightens me').[56] The time-consuming process of reading had been streamlined as if it was a form of housework. Hugo had a method:

I take a book – let's say *La Petite Fadette* by Mme Sand . . . I open it at any page and if nothing grabs my attention, I open it a second time at random; if it still says nothing to me, I open it a third time, again at random; if the page contains no trace of any thought or idea, I close the book and deem it bad.[57]

The only drawback to this method was that, after he went into exile, books on which he had expressed an opinion were found in his library with their pages uncut.

A huge amount of time is still unaccounted for. Very little of it was spent with Juliette, as she often complained. He attended plays and dinners, deposited frivolous poems in albums and became a master in the art of *bouts-rimés*.* One such quatrain, never included in Hugo's complete works, is signed 'Victor Hugum', to rhyme with 'album'.[58] Another, also unpublished, tells the Irish actress Mme Doche that since she has *'oignons'* on her feet (meaning 'onions', 'bulbs' and 'bunions'), she should have been a tulip.[59] One of his best impromptu poems wandered about Paris on a piece of cardboard belonging to a blind beggar:

> Like Belisarius and like Homer, blind,
> With but a child to guide his feeble steps,
> The hand which feeds this pauper bread
> He will not see. God sees it in his stead.[60]

Hugo's social activity was subordinate to his passion for saving money: in 1845 he valued his investments at 300,000 francs – just under a million pounds today.[61] 'I have worked too hard to live into old age, and I do not want my wife and children to receive pensions when I am dead.' He walked to the Chambre des Pairs, worked without fire, wore his clothes until they were rotting off his body, and was never seen in cafés or casinos; but 'I have always had the two possessions without which I could not live: a clear conscience and complete independence.'

Only an engrossing hobby or an addiction could account for all the missing time. This was also Juliette's conclusion. Two of her letters, written in February and March 1847 and prudently omitted by Paul Souchon from his adulatory edition, are practically a menu of the sexual sports available to a man with spare time and influence in mid-nineteenth-century Paris. Timidly threatening revenge, she mentioned his *'tableaux vivants'*, his 'lithographs in action or delivered to the home', his 'aristocratic amusements', his *'bonnes fortunes'* on the

---

* Poems improvised on a given set of rhymes.

omnibus, his telltale demeanour – that of a 'conquering, *spontinian* Academician' – and a series of what were obviously excuses and alibis: 'frequent visits to the town hall' and 'your unherculean labours'.[62]

Juliette's litany of misdemeanours can be deciphered with a little help from Hugo's secret records. The word 'spontinian' has been interpreted, inexplicably, as an allusion to the composer, Spontini; Hugo's later notes show that it was his code-word for ejaculation. The '*tableaux vivants*' refer to the English 'actresses' who re-created famous works of art wearing transparent body-stockings. Full porno-graphic details are given in Hugo's diary: he had once observed in a mood of frustration that society women showed far more naked flesh than their available counterparts in the lower orders, and was excited on this occasion to see nipples on public display. He hired prostitutes who specialized in stripping, which was cheaper and safer than physical contact and in any case a favourite activity with Hugo. He also picked up women while travelling on the omnibus – which might explain his generous donation in 1878 to the bus-drivers of Paris.

When Hugo kept turning up at the Rue Saint-Anastase shortly after midnight, supposedly having just laid down his pen, Juliette began to suspect the impressive social range of his operations. 'I cannot understand how your brain manages to function with such clockwork regularity.' Midnight, she observed, 'is the hour at which one leaves a society woman with whom one cannot spend the night'.[63] But she was aware of only a tiny fraction of Hugo's other life. Unlike most of Paris, she still knew nothing, for example, of Léonie Biard. Hugo's notes (some in his 'diary of what I learn every day', others in a special address book) reveal liaisons with actresses and courtesans of every shade: Héléna Gaussin, 'beautiful but very thin', who was imprisoned for theft;[64] an Englishwoman called Amanda Fitz-Allan Clarke;[65] the actress, Mlle Plessy, 'pretty but with a poor figure, not much bust and long legs'; Mme Richy, the wife of Hugo's hair-dresser;[66] Esther Guimont, who became the mistress of Hugo's friend, the newspaper editor, Émile de Girardin, and, later, of Hugo's son Charles.[67] Some women are represented only by furtive notes, abbreviations of brief liaisons, oddly reminiscent of the notes he took while pursuing his fiancée in 1821: '133. f Temps. 4ᵉ a dr. la der. p. à ga Bigot' – presumably a fourth-floor address in the Rue du

Faubourg-du-Temple, which was a street of tailors and small factories.[68] Several notes refer to addresses in the proletarian district surrounding the Place Royale. Prostitution was now one of Hugo's major sources of information on the class of *misérables*. Even without a complete record of his doings, a statistical analysis shows that from 1847 to 1851, he had sex with more women than he wrote poems.

Hugo had always tried to exploit each of his talents to the full and always accepted any source of 'inspiration', any chance to try out his talent. Charles Hugo, who turned twenty-one in 1847, discovered this to his cost. He had fallen in love with the actress and model, Alice Ozy, and was devastated to find she had been 'unfaithful'.[69] The watered-down version which appears in Juliette's letters suggests a tearful Charles pouring his heart out to the family in the hope that Dad would go and fix everything. In a sense, he did. When Charles began to sacrifice punctuality at mealtimes to his mistress, Hugo cancelled his daily cutlet. Then, having met Alice at a dinner, he unleashed a salvo of erotic odes – valuable autographs which he used in the same way that other men used money: Venus emerging from the Ocean ('I should rather see Mlle Alice climbing into bed'), Jupiter visiting Danaë in a shower of rain.[70] Alice joined the list of Hugo's 'conquests' and used her influence to have Charles's daily cutlet reinstituted. By then, Charles had seen enough. He wrote to Alice:

> Why did you write that letter to my father? On the one hand, you have the son with a pure heart, profound love and limitless devotion. On the other, the father and glory. *You choose the father and glory.* I cannot blame you. Any woman would have done the same. But you will understand that I am not strong enough to withstand the pain that your love, *shared in this fashion*, would cause me.[71]

Hugo's victory over his own son gives some measure of the rivalry that existed between him and Eugène thirty years before when they were both in love with Adèle. The situation is possibly not as uncommon as it sounds. Certainly in Hugo's case, the Oedipal complex has been emphasized to the exclusion of its opposite. With Alice Ozy, Hugo was the potent patriarch, and Charles an unwitting Isaac. Hugo drew the moral for him in another little poem: he was too young to meddle with actresses – 'You see only their eyes; I see their wings.'

'Fallen women' and courtesans were a pleasant antidote to the hypocrisy of high society: 'they have as much heart, soul and spirit as society women, but are frank where society women are prudish.'[72] This would-be laudable sentiment does not specify the manner in which Hugo enjoyed their 'frankness'. His secret life was also a form of inverted aspiration. The great Victor Hugo, secure in the knowledge that the block of his everlasting statue was already half carved, occasionally – more than occasionally – felt the need to wash the gilt off with some dirt, the healing dirt of 'the *plebs*, the *vulgus*, the *turba*'. Significantly, something very similar was happening to his prose in *Les Misères*, his sturdy, well-marshalled periods slimed with the vocabulary of the street, the tavern and the jail.

The confusing coincidence of a fornicating, 'aristocratic' Hugo and the magnificent, well-informed sense of justice in *Les Misères* has been explained by supposing that the novel was a guilt offering. This seems to be borne out by the fact that Hugo's donations to beggars and charities usually came hot on the heels of his sexual splurges, especially those at which no other person was present. But Hugo had no real desire to free himself from a sense of shame. The point of the mental transaction was to confirm the powerful reality of his conscience. An addiction to live pornography and the campaign to create a humane society were mutually dependent, like God and Satan.

Not surprisingly, Hugo never left an image of himself creeping out of a brothel, but he did describe a man who, one day in September 1846, emerged from the Conciergerie prison in the centre of Paris and was mistaken by two passers-by for a released convict.[73] The man with long, lank hair, a grubby black overcoat and a frown on his face had just been inspecting the dungeons where Society continued to punish the monsters it created itself. One of these monsters was a little boy of twelve, accused of stealing some peaches from a tree. Hugo summed up the encounter in one of those symmetrical phrases which seem to contain a hundred years of social history: 'True, we might ask them, "What have you done with our peaches?"; but they might answer us, "What have you done with our intelligence?"'

The original reason for Hugo's visit to the Conciergerie is not mentioned in his notes, but it completes the picture nicely: he was playing truant from the Académie Française, where the winner of the annual Prix Montyon for virtuous fiction was being chosen. A journalist had pointed out the incongruity of an adulterous Victor Hugo awarding prizes for virtue.

*

THREE YEARS AFTER the death of Léopoldine, Hugo had ostensibly reached a kind of equilibrium: the repudiation of his own past in debauchery and the espousal of the probable future in a social philosophy which was beginning to look like socialism. The virginal monarchist and the *enfant sublime* belonged to history. As a *pair de France*, he now had a vast stage on which to act out the adult drama of his conscience – the Upper Chamber – and it seems entirely appropriate that he compared political oratory to sex: 'I find that delivering one speech is as exhausting as ejaculating three times – even four!'[74]

For once, however, Hugo seriously underestimated his own importance. He failed to notice how closely his own mental progress matched recent developments in France – abuse of privilege and desire for reform. And now there was the additional distraction of his latest creation – Victor Hugo, the political orator.

The nightmare version of his parliamentary début in the novel, *L'Homme Qui Rit* (1869), is a fairly accurate summary of what actually happened, several times, in Hugo's political career. The hideous Gwynplaine, his face wrecked and reset in childhood into a silent laugh which spreads from ear to ear – the fixed laugh of the professional entertainer – enters the House of Lords at Westminster, filled with the great revolutionary message, 'My Lords, I have come to inform you that the human race exists', and is greeted with gales of hysterical laughter.[75]

Hugo was a nervous speaker, reading his theatrical speeches from a carefully prepared text, too earnest to be taken seriously, buffeted by interruptions and sarcastic allusions to his literary works. 'To be comical on the outside and tragic within: nothing is more painfully humiliating or deeply infuriating.'[76]

This appealing image has convinced even his most suspicious

critics. It gives the reader of Hugo's speeches the stirring sense of belonging to the persecuted, enlightened minority and somehow erases the significant facts: that Hugo had lived in front of an audience almost since childhood, that he was entirely familiar with the irrational aggression which topics like vagrancy and the death penalty never fail to arouse, and that, over a hundred times in the last sixteen years, he had seen huge, disgruntled audiences hurling abuse at his most private creations.

Convincing the most fervent Hugophobes (and even himself) that he was a naive evangelist, wounded by the misbehaviour of his fellow politicians, is one of Hugo's greatest victories as a writer. Behind his image, the self-confessed clown was innovating in the art of oratory as he had revolutionized the French stage. His first major speech, for example, was a wonderfully bizarre intervention in a debate on the budget of the Ministry of Public Works (27 June and 1 July 1846).[77] It was typical of his courageous style – faintly ridiculous and deeply impressive:

> Messieurs, if someone came and told you, 'One of your frontiers is under threat. You have an enemy who ... is constantly encroaching and stealing territory day and night' ... this Chamber would immediately rise up and find no power too great to defend the land against such a peril. Well, my Lords ... this enemy exists. It is the Ocean.

His two finest speeches were devoted to prison conditions and the law on child labour, the latter containing a typically inflammatory, irrefutable phrase: 'The Law must be *a Mother*.'[78]

Unfortunately, neither speech was delivered because the Chambre des Pairs suddenly ceased to exist.

*

AT THREE O'CLOCK on the afternoon of 22 February 1848, Hugo went out in heavy rain to find the Chambre des Pairs about to close. He hailed a cab, forced the driver to negotiate the Rue de Lille, where a crowd of workers was facing a line of soldiers, and arrived at the Chambre des Députés. In the Salle des Pas Perdus, he joined a group of jittery politicians.[79]

A revolt was under way. Hugo predicted the imminent collapse of government. If only they had listened to him: for years, he had been insisting that 'politics' should give way to 'social questions'. Anarchy now seemed inevitable. 'As far as I can see,' said Hugo, 'the Cabinet has been sending bailiffs and summonses to a lion.' Bad harvests, a severe winter during which the Seine had frozen over, bankruptcies, unemployment and the scarcity of credit had created misery not seen in France since the Revolution. After eighteen years of Bourgeois Monarchy, the middle classes were sandwiched between a new aristocracy – a tiny clique of fabulously rich individuals – and, something quite new, a politically educated working class.

Outside, cavalrymen were swirling across the Place de la Concorde, swinging their sabres at rioters. During the night, crosses had been painted on the doors of some of the richest *hôtels* as a guide to looters. Barricades were going up. All day long, Hugo wandered through central Paris, witnessing skirmishes between workers and soldiers. Ammunition trucks thundered over the cobbles. At sunset, he returned to the Faubourg Saint-Antoine. The street lamps had been smashed and the Place Royale was full of soldiers armed with bayonets. He heard a man shouting, 'It's 1830!' 'No,' Hugo said to himself, 'in 1830, the Duc d'Orléans was waiting behind Charles X. In 1848, behind Louis-Philippe there is a hole.'[80]

On 23 February, the National Guard took the side of the people. The King dismissed Prime Minister Guizot, too late. That evening, on the Boulevard des Capucines, army cannon tore into the mob and baptized the revolution in its own blood. News of the massacre spread like a landslide. Parisians woke on the 24th to find the city bristling with barricades: a total of 1574, according to Hugo's note, comprising 4013 trees and 15,121,277,000 paving-stones ... [81] A civil service gone mad. Louis-Philippe changed his name to 'Mr Smith' and fled to Surrey, abandoning the Tuileries to the mob. A provisional government was proclaimed.

As the most prominent personage in his *quartier* – a *quartier* which was always the hub of any revolt – Hugo found himself in a position of huge potential influence. Battles had always excited him and brought out that suicidal sense of an overriding mission which he attributed to his army childhood. He and the local mayor went to see the new Prime Minister, Odilon Barrot. After a panicky discussion, they returned to Hugo's home to announce, from the balcony, the formation of a provisional government and – Hugo's idea – a Regency, with the Duchesse d'Orléans as acting head of state. Loud cheers greeted the first announcement; the second caused a rumble of dissent. Undaunted, Hugo had himself escorted by two soldiers of the National Guard down the road to the Place de la Bastille, mounted the steps of the Colonne de Juillet and, at two o'clock that afternoon, proclaimed the Regency to an angry sea of insurgents. A man pointed a gun at Hugo's head and shouted, 'Down with the *pair de France!*' A Regency, it seemed, was out of the question.[82] Meanwhile, at the Hôtel de Ville, another poet, Lamartine, had declared his support for the Republic and was sworn in as one of the eleven members of the provisional government.

The man who wanted to kill Victor Hugo was, for the time being, in a small minority. The Hugo who shot to political fame in the February Revolution was one of the fantasy figures thrown up by the cauldron of mysticism and political philosophy broadly labelled socialism. A typical example of 1848 idealism – a tract explaining how the world should be governed by 'sages', 'sacerdotal souls' and 'poets' – paints a portrait of the perfect ruler which corresponds almost exactly to Hugo's popular image: 'natural genius, popularity, compassionate kindness'; a hermit of the metropolis; a Christ of the barricades.[83] This was the Victor Hugo of the *cabinets de lecture*, the well-loved author of *Notre-Dame de Paris*, *Claude Gueux*, patriotic anthems and parlour songs, the nemesis of the death penalty, the Napoleon of the Romantic movement.

Hugo himself had allowed this Messianic image to swell in the popular imagination. It was the basis of his imminent political success, but it had the inconvenience of implying more radical views than he actually held. The revolution which Marx saw as one of the founding events of modern history was about to call his bluff. In the months to come, Hugo's extreme ideological discomfort was partly a result of his own conception of the Poet-as-Priest. He would now be asked to follow in the footsteps of his own image by a working class which was likely to remember at any moment that he was also a *pair de France* who slept with other men's wives and had metaphorically been to bed with every royal regime since the fall of Napoleon.

On Friday, 25 February at the Hôtel de Ville, Citizen Hugo made his way through an excited crowd to present his respects to the acting head of the provisional government, Lamartine, who offered him the Ministry of Education. The hasty reasoning behind this was that the new government included some full-blooded anti-capitalists – Louis Blanc and a man known only as 'Albert the worker'. A popular moderate like Hugo was more likely to win the support of 'the provinces' (i.e. the rest of France). Hugo refused the Ministry. In his mind, the provisional government was a solidified riot; a people's republic was not a practical solution – this was 1848, not the distant utopian future. Lamartine persuaded him instead to serve as acting mayor of his *arrondissement*, while his younger son, François-Victor, was hired as Lamartine's secretary, one of his duties being to sleep in front of Lamartine's door with a pair of loaded pistols.

Some people in Hugo's *arrondissement* had different ideas. An anonymous letter accused him of being 'haughty' and 'aristocratic', and a newspaper claimed that his so-called republicanism went all the way back to last Thursday. There were ominous signs that the alliance of bourgeois and worker which brought the July Monarchy to power in 1830 had given way to class war. Demonstrators carried placards saying '*Kill the Rich!*' – sometimes misspelt – and the walls of the Place Royale were daubed with its old revolutionary name, the Place des Vosges.

Hugo 'reigned' over the eighth *arrondissement* for eight days, during which he addressed his subjects several times from his balcony, urging moderation. As mayor, he organized policing, had the barricades removed, the streets repaved and the lamps repaired. Hugo was tidying up the revolution. He was relieved to see his popularity surviving: 'Workers blew kisses at me as I passed in the street.' Nevertheless, his only recorded speech as mayor, delivered on 2 March 1848 during the planting of a 'Tree of Liberty' in the Place des Vosges, shows him tiptoeing with feigned insouciance through a red minefield: 'The first Tree of Liberty was planted eighteen hundred years ago by God Himself on Golgotha. (*Cheers.*)' 'Let us not forget: . . . the revolution of our fathers was great in war; yours [*sic*] must be great in peace. . . . This is the task of the future – and in the times in which we live, the future comes quickly. (*Applause.*)'

While Hugo dragged his feet, almost 60,000 people were planning to vote for him in the forthcoming Paris elections. Hugo's 'Lettre aux Électeurs' declared his willingness to be elected but hinted strongly that he would be eternally beholden to the good people of Paris if they left him alone. His private notes show a fearful conviction that the revolution had started too soon, but also real affection for the people, exactly analogous to his preference for working-class prostitutes. On the one hand, he was the peace-loving bourgeois whose mistress had reacted to the troubles by making him a money-belt. On the other hand, he was the sympathetic anarchist, the cynical parliamentarian who picked up his pearls of popular wisdom on the street:

> A three-year-old was singing *'Mourir pour la Patrie'*. His mother asked him,
> 'Do you know what that means, "To die for the fatherland"?'
> 'Yes,' said the child, 'it means walking in the street with a flag.'[84]

Hugo was not elected, but the 59,446 votes he received on 23 April 1848 – without being a candidate[85] – persuaded him to launch a proper campaign for the next elections in June. Backed by a committee of right-wing moderates, he devised a conciliatory manifesto: free education, penal reform, an ambitious railway-building programme, with the long-term goal of world peace and a population of property-owners. Property should be democratized but not abolished. The immediate goal was freedom from civil unrest. If the shops and factories remained shut much longer, France would be facing an economic Waterloo. 'England' was already rubbing its hands.

Despite continuing unease about Hugo's class loyalties, he was elected as a Paris representative on 4 June 1848 with 86,695 votes. An amazing achievement, which he might justifiably have bragged about had he been less concerned with appearing consistent: in 1845, he had been elected by the King; in 1848, he was elected by the people who had deposed the King. Six days later, he entered the new Assemblée Nationale for the first time and sat far up on the right-hand side, politically enfeebled since he belonged to no particular party, and depressed by the ugliness of the place: 'Wooden beams instead of columns, partitions instead of walls, tempera instead of marble. . . . The tribune, which bears the dates of the February Days, looks like the musicians' stage at the Café des Aveugles.'[86]

The first speech Hugo launched into the hullabaloo of the new Assembly was a mild success which turned into a huge personal disaster. On 20 June, he tackled the crucial question of the National Workshops. The Ateliers Nationaux had been set up by the provisional government to solve the problem of unemployment. There was still no work, but now 100,000 Parisians were receiving a wage for doing nothing. Hugo's notes on the subject differ in tone from his public pronouncements but the general idea is the same.

Men in overalls have been playing *bouchon** under the arcades of the Place Royale, which is now called the Place des Vosges. Playing *bouchon* is one of the functions of the Ateliers Nationaux.[87]

In the Rue Bellechasse a passer-by has added an 'R' to a National Workshop poster. It now says, 'R ATELIERS NATIONAUX' ['National Troughs'].[88]

For Hugo, the Ateliers were a humiliating trick played on 'the noble, worthy people of Paris'. The sentimental patriot was embarrassed and insulted. He urged the Assembly to pursue a more rational course.

Too late, Hugo realized that he was adding his weight to a reactionary battering-ram.[89] Two days after his speech, the Ateliers were closed. Workers under the age of twenty-five were to be conscripted; all others were ordered to go and work in the provinces. It was a political purge disguised as a new employment policy. As expected, the poorer areas of Paris immediately reached boiling-point. General Cavaignac prepared to assume emergency powers. Barricades the size of buildings marked out the battleground. On 23 June, at the Porte Saint-Denis, a prostitute taunted the National Guard, lifting up her skirts. She was shot to ribbons. Whole *quartiers* fell silent, every street was watched by snipers. February had been a revolution of hope. June was the revolt of misery and despair. A splendid excuse for the moderate majority to make everything return to 'normal'.

---

* A game in which a small disc is thrown at coins piled up on a cork.

The Assemblée Nationale sat all night (23–24 June 1848) – the people's assembly discussing the means of repressing the people's revolt. At six in the morning, Hugo left for the Faubourg Saint-Antoine hoping to see his family. He walked along the river as far as the Hôtel de Ville,[90] spoke to General Duvivier, who was later shot by insurgents, dodged whistling bullets and reached the edge of the Faubourg. It was completely closed off by a low barricade. Behind it, the Rue Saint-Antoine, its rooftops shining in the June sun, snaked away into the heart of proletarian Paris, silent and deserted. Soldiers were lying flat along the top of the barricade. Some officers advised Hugo not to proceed. He might be killed or, worse, taken hostage.

By eight o'clock, Hugo was back at the Assemblée Nationale in a state of intense anxiety. General Négrier informed him that the Place Royale was in flames but that his family was safe.[91] He scribbled a note to Adèle: 'What a terrible business! How sad to think that the blood which is flowing on both sides is brave and generous blood!' A state of siege was declared and full executive powers were conferred on General Cavaignac. Victor Hugo, the people's friend, had voted for a temporary dictatorship. Later, he adjusted the chronology – departure from the Assembly at 6 a.m., return at 11 a.m. – suggesting that he played no part in what was effectively a *coup d'état*: 'Civilization defending itself with barbarism'.[92] But even then he suspected, with Lamartine, that Cavaignac was allowing the insurrection to spread, virtually unchecked.[93] When the Army launched its full attack, the rabble would be decimated once and for all.

What happened next was a turning-point in French history equal in importance to Waterloo; it was also the central event in the life of Victor Hugo. Yet the next forty-eight hours have been tossed into the confusion and allowed to drift away with the smoke.

Hugo and fifty-nine other representatives were chosen to go and inform the insurgents that a state of siege existed and that Cavaignac was in control. Their mission was 'to stop the spilling of blood'. Nine of the representatives would be shot dead before they had a chance to complete their mission.

At two o'clock that afternoon Hugo left with the mandate in his pocket and headed for the Porte Saint-Denis. For the first time, his conscience was unsighted. He was acting in accordance with his principles, 'saving civilization', as he told himself shortly after the event – indeed, 'saving the life of the human race'.[94] But behind the barricade was the power that would eventually prevail, the starving heroes who, for Hugo, at that moment, represented the voice of God; 'the rabble who followed Jesus Christ'. The incomplete accounts and contradictory hints in his work relating to the June Days are centred on an unmentionable abyss: the possibility that one can obey one's conscience and not be on the side of Good. 'Four months ago, the situation was unspoiled. Who will ever recover that virginity? No one. Everything has been ruined and compromised. The mind wanders from the difficult to the impossible.'[95]

Slight confusion translates itself as hesitancy. The utter disorientation Hugo had been concealing from himself since the death of Léopoldine and even since the wreck of his parents' marriage translated itself in the only possible way: an appearance of absolute conviction. When the author of *Les Misérables* came face to face with the people in June 1848, he went far beyond his remit from the Assemblée Nationale. The representatives had not been asked to lead a full-scale assault on the barricades, backed by cavalry and heavy artillery ... The Assembly had just bestowed its full legal powers on a man who was going to spend the next forty-eight hours hanging on to his sanity for all he was worth.

Part Three

CHAPTER THIRTEEN

Mount Sinai and a Pile of Rubbish

(1848–1851)

DURING THE ALL-NIGHT SITTING of the Assembly, the old Hugo had still been functioning as normal. A man called Onézime Seure had sent him a long, deeply unfunny poem on the subject of Divorce. Why, he asked, had Victor Hugo not opposed the legalization of 'debauchery'?[1]

Taking a sheet of parliamentary notepaper, Hugo allowed the debate that was deciding the future of France to fade into the background and constructed one of his firm but supple pronouncements. The rising tide of disorder was funnelled into the beautifully coordinated irrigation system of his prose:

> From the Assembly, Friday, 23 June [1848]
>
> This morning, Monsieur, I read your fine verse and my mind was filled with it when the riot came and snatched me away from poetry. Now, in this hour of trouble, amidst the tumult and the impending storm, I think of you, Monsieur, and of the noble inspirations which moved me, and my thoughts rest for a moment on yours.
>
> Your opinion on a very grave and very delicate question appears to me a trifle absolute; yet you express it with such nobility of heart and decency of soul that all my objections vanish before your talent. The thinker murmurs a little, but the poet applauds.

This letter – cited here for the first time – was Hugo's last message to the outside world before the June massacre. The furnace burning in the Faubourgs was about to give birth to a new society, good or bad, and it was there that Hugo might find the answer to all his questions.

A few hours later, the protesting 'thinker' and the applauding 'poet' stood in front of a mind-boggling piece of architecture which seemed to have dropped through a hole in time and landed on a street in nineteenth-century Paris:

> It was a collaboration of the paving-stone, the rubble-stone, the beam, the iron bar, the rag, the shattered window, the broken chair, the cabbage-stalk ... It was great and it was small.... Sisyphus had cast his rock upon it and Job his potsherd. In a word: terrible. The ragamuffins' Acropolis.... In the chaos of despair, rafters and pieces of garret with their coloured paper could be made out ... fireplaces ripped from the wall, wardrobes, tables and benches. The Faubourg Saint-Antoine seemed to have swept it all out into the street with a colossal broom, turning its misery into a barricade ... It was enormous and living, spitting thunder and lightning as if from the back of an electric beast. The spirit of revolution covered that peak with its cloud in which the voice of the People rumbled like the voice of God ... It was a pile of rubbish and it was Mount Sinai.[2]

The ragamuffins' Acropolis had been erected across the main road leading into the Faubourg Saint-Antoine. Half a mile to the north stood another barricade in the Faubourg du Temple. Hugo appears to have gone first to the Faubourg du Temple. It was two o'clock on the afternoon of 24 February. The cobbles were already strewn with corpses and the whole area was covered by invisible snipers. Hugo remembered seeing a white butterfly fluttering down the street: 'Summer never abdicates.'

A well-built barricade could not be breached without artillery, and several decades' experience had gone into the making of the 1848 models. It either had to be blown apart from the front or attacked from above by soldiers who smashed their way through the dividing walls of the tenements. According to a witness in the summary commission of enquiry held in July, Hugo favoured the frontal approach:

> Victor Hugo and I obtained from General Lamoricière seventy-five men of the Republican Guard [professional soldiers]. We went to fetch

a cannon and led it at a gallop on to the Place Boucherat. The first volley momentarily stopped the firing which was coming from the Rue Saint-Louis, and my colleagues Hugo, Saint-Victor and Breymand went and took possession of it at the head of the National Guard.[3]

Another witness saw an unarmed man in a grey overcoat, 'with no insignia of any kind', standing alone in the middle of the street, calling to the soldiers who were darting from doorway to doorway: 'Let's get it over with, my children.'

> Twice, I tugged at his sleeve, saying, 'You'll get yourself killed!' He answered, 'That is why I am here,' and continued to shout, 'Forward! Forward!' With such a man to lead us, we reached the barricades and took them one after the other.[4]

Even General Hugo would have been impressed.

For the next three days, pausing only to sit for a few moments on a pavement, Hugo harangued insurgents, stormed barricades, took prisoners, directed troops and cannon, and unexpectedly remained alive. This means that he was directly responsible for the deaths of untold numbers of workers, whom he himself considered innocent and heroic; misguided, but justified by their misery. While a band of rioters broke into the apartment at the Place Royale, which had been vacated shortly before by Adèle and the servants, Hugo was preparing to launch an attack on another barricade. This one flew the white flag of the Carlists – a monarchist faction which had joined forces with the workers. Politically and sentimentally, the white flag symbolized a large part of Hugo's life. It was the flag of his monarchist mother.

Seven years later, in a conversation recorded by his daughter, he described what happened next:

> I broke through the barricade and took two prisoners, the Comte de Fouchécourt, a former guardsman aged sixty, and his son, a young man of twenty. Mlle de Fouchécourt, a beautiful young woman of thirty, came to see me and begged me to release her father and brother. Since a representative of the people, a *pair de France* and a Royalist could not possibly be seen to be granting special favours to a former fellow legitimist . . . I refused point-blank.[5]

The Comte de Fouchécourt was sentenced to twenty years' hard labour. His son was deported to the prison camps of Cayenne, which was effectively a death sentence.

On Sunday, 26 June, an exhausted Hugo was back in the Assembly, 'heart-broken', desperate for news of his family, sitting with what he called his 'mandate of order, peace and reconciliation' – bitter words, considering the horrendous, half-erased visions in his eye:

> Leaving a barricade, one no longer knows what one has seen. One has been ferocious, yet one has no recollection of it. Swept up in a battle of ideas endowed with human faces, one's head has been in the light of the future. There were corpses lying down and phantoms standing up. The hours were colossal – hours of eternity. One has been living in Death. Shadows have passed. What were they? Hands with blood on them. A horrific deafening din. An atrocious silence. Open mouths shouting; other mouths, also open, but soundless. . . . One seems to have touched the sinister perspiration of unknown depths. There is something red under one's fingernails. One remembers nothing.[6]

By 26 June, order had prevailed and reprisals began. Hundreds were deported or executed. Insurgents were herded into cells, bayoneted through the grilles when they came up for air, left to die in their own blood and excrement, tortured by shopkeepers and civil servants in National Guard uniform, and made to pay for five months of social and economic instability. The new Republic had defended itself like a tyranny.

Later that day, according to Hugo's passing reference in *Histoire d'un Crime*, 'I went to the Rue Saint-Anastase and I saved four men'.[7] While soldiers made a house-to-house search, the four men had been hidden by Juliette Drouet in the attic of her apartment at number 12 – an offence punishable by deportation. One of the men was a wine merchant called Auguste. When Mme Drouet's friend came to announce the surrender of the Faubourgs, Auguste was amazed to see the familiar face of Victor Hugo: 'To think that an hour ago, knowing you were in front of us, I was wishing that the barrel of my rifle had eyes so it could see you and shoot you dead!'

If, as he claims, Hugo released the men who were hiding in the

Rue Saint-Anastase, this is the only moment at which he failed to do his parliamentary duty during the June Days. But was his memory telling the truth? The account of the trial of the Comte de Fouché-court – the man supposedly captured by Hugo on the monarchist barricade – contains a disturbing little detail.[8] The Count's address is given as the Rue Saint-Anastase: an amazing coincidence, especially considering how short the street is ... On the other hand, it might explain why four insurgents happened to throw themselves on the mercy of their neighbour, Juliette Drouet, who was not particularly sympathetic to revolutionaries. The unanswerable question is this: did Hugo capture the Count and his son on the barricade, or did he find them hiding in Juliette's attic and hand them over to the authorities? Hugo re-remembered his actions in the June Days so many times and in so many different contexts that even he might not have been able to provide the correct answer.

Adèle had taken refuge with a neighbour[9] and the apartment had not after all gone up in flames. The invading workers had been cowed by the unearthly atmosphere, Hugo supposed. His antique sabre and musket were untouched, as was the manuscript of what became *Les Misérables*. Only one thing was missing: a sheaf of paper which had lain on top of the manuscript. It was a petition from the sailors of Le Havre asking for leniency to be shown to mutineers because of their atrocious working conditions. Naturally, Hugo had signed the petition. It was taken by the insurgents to prove to their comrades in the square outside that Victor Hugo was 'a true friend of the people'.[10]

After thirty years in the public eye, Hugo tended to see the nation as an audience composed of loyal fans and a handful of hecklers. And yet, if the performance had ended in June 1848 with a well-aimed bullet, the final image of a carefully planned career would have been Victor Hugo leading a murderous assault on the people. The ultimate public relations disaster. Worse still, he had become convinced that the people were a direct manifestation of God. 'Not to believe in the people', he told Guizot the following January, 'is to be a political atheist.'[11] Like Moses on Mount Sinai, Hugo on the barricades had seen the 'back parts' of God,[12] the rude underside of History; unlike Moses, he had no tablets to show for it.

On the Mount Sinai rubbish heap, the laws of morality had ceased to function. It was impossible to be a hero simply by rushing out into the streets. But it was equally impossible to be a villain. One of the interestingly dubious aspects of Hugo's lacunary accounts of the June Days is the search for sequences of events that suggest the possibility of assuming guilt. Citizen Hugo had done his best: 'I offered myself,' he wrote on 1 July, 'but God didn't want me ... What a mournful victory!' Once again he had failed to fit together the pieces of his own puzzle, and, as usual, his own distortions and silences conceal a true picture which is perhaps more flattering than the invented image: a man who had the courage of his lack of conviction, who found the only logical solution to a moral dilemma in a three-day-long suicide attempt.

Anyone with a taste for extreme symbolic events might relish the thought that Baudelaire also took part in the June Days, but on the other side of the barricades. He fired at the troops with his brand-new rifle. The possibility thus arises that the last great poet of Romanticism might have been murdered by the first great poet of Modernism ... The age of heroes had ended, and while Baudelaire chose the relatively simple expedient of aesthetic terrorism, Hugo decided to create a new heroic age.

*

Since the apartment in the Place Royale had been defiled by terrorists, Mme Hugo insisted on moving.[13] For two months that summer, they suffered the noise and dust of the Madeleine district at 5 Rue d'Isly. Léonie Biard recommended her own *quartier*: the grassy streets which climbed up among the vineyards and windmills of Montmartre were quiet, almost provincial; the air was clean, and the Faubourg Saint-Antoine was just a dark smudge on the horizon.

In September 1848, the Hugos transported themselves and their museum to a bright, roomy apartment at 37 Rue de la Tour-d'Auvergne. From the balcony on the first floor the eye soared over the city: one of Hugo's drawings makes the view look like a giant slipway with a harbour wall and the stormy sea beyond.[14] In November, Juliette moved into 'a sad and black little dwelling' in a nearby cul-de-sac, the Cité Rodier (now Rue de l'Agent-Bailly). Hugo's three wives now lived within 200 yards of each other. Good timekeeping was more important than ever.

Moving to Montmartre meant that Hugo had now occupied the two poles of the capital – the Christian and the Pagan. From the Martyrs' Mount in the north he looked over to the slopes of Mount Parnassus (Montparnasse) in the south, where he had written his royalist odes over thirty years before. Part of his mind had already gone into exile. When he returned each day from Parliament, he entered a luxurious cell, padded with the visions of its occupant – a home within a home, which was more like the Musée Victor Hugo now installed in the former Place Royale than the Place Royale had been when Hugo lived there:

> A naked Venus laughs above my bed,
> Canopied with scarlet damask and gold tassels.
> Monkeys on my wall . . . do a thousand things . . .
> Crockery, bas-reliefs, stoneware, Bohemian glass,
> Enamels compose a poem on my sideboard.
> A whole world stirs on my chest-of-drawers,
> And in my mirrors pass the eye-bedecked peacocks.
> Dragons, magots and Chinese demons.
>
> In this strange world my mind thinks more freely,
> Like a bird that yearns for distant seas,
> Dreaming, it slowly spreads its wings.[15]

Even in this period of poetic hibernation,[16] Hugo was managing to keep one foot in the avant-garde. The description of his Montmartre interior is typical of the *l'art pour l'art* poetry of the 1850s and 1860s: the ivory tower with its miniatures and mass-produced objects – an early form of kitsch;[17] the allergic reaction to Nature, the cultivation of illusion and political indifference, with just a smear in the background like smoke from a factory chimney – the dispiriting defeat of the February Revolution. An implicit celebration of the bourgeois lifestyle which saved its subversion for forms and techniques. This was Victor Hugo pretending to be a dandy, the clean-handed curator of his own exquisite thoughts.

At the foot of Hugo's mountain, Cavaignac and the Army held the reins for several months. Savage reprisals had failed to settle bourgeois nerves. With much of the working class still heavily armed, the Red Menace was suspected everywhere. In Parliament, 'a cormorant in the storm',[18] Hugo flapped his wings at the military dictatorship – theatres had been closed, newspapers banned and their editors imprisoned. Cavaignac, he declared, was confusing the necessary state of siege with the suppression of law.

The cormorant was not exactly fishing for compliments. He later claimed to have been saved from an official reprimand only by his reputation for being a buffoon. Critical of both sides, he stood for the seemingly incompatible causes of 'people, order and freedom', 'red, white and blue' – a 'tricolour' Victor Hugo.[19] This meant resisting the temptation to indulge in a very common, even respected intellectual habit: 'giving secret caresses to our opinions so that they will turn into convictions'.[20] The image was obviously connected in Hugo's mind with his attempts to give up masturbation[21] – which was after all another form of grasping after certainties where none existed. The result was something which looked like intellectual honesty – keeping an open mind as he kept an open house, where people and ideas were allowed to come and go, except in certain rooms.

The hidden thread of Hugo's thinking, well into 1849, was the need to ignore the evidence of June. For the first time, he sounded almost pathetic, a prey to psychosomatic complaints. He kept losing his voice. A persistent 'affection of the respiratory organs' now replaced poor eyesight as his favourite excuse.[22]

On 4 November 1848, martial law ended when the Assembly came up with its constitution: a single chamber and a single head of state with full executive powers, both to be elected by the entire male population. Fears that the Republic was advertising for a new Napoleon were ignored by three-quarters of the Assembly and justified on 10 December when a strikingly unimpressive individual who shuffled his feet, stammered and spoke in what sounded like a German accent was elected President with a majority of four million. His name – and only apparent asset – was Louis-Napoléon Bonaparte: he was the son of Napoleon's brother Louis, though some claimed that he was the illegitimate son of a Dutch admiral, which, for Hugo, explained why he looked nothing like the Emperor. The conservatives were happy to have 'a sleeping parrot'[23] at their beck and call, a man who perched on the presidential chair dozing off behind his drooping eyelids. During debates, he folded paper shapes and doodled on his files.[24] Outside Parliament, according to someone who approved of him, he was 'frigidly affable and repulsively polite'.[25] 'This man of weary gestures and a glazed expression', Hugo wrote with hindsight in 1852, 'walks with an absent-minded air amidst the horrible things he does, like a sinister sleepwalker.'[26]

Louis-Napoléon had been swept to power on a tide of voluntary amnesia and wishful thinking, characteristic of the movement called 'Bonapartism'. There was a great yearning for the innocuous, for a passionless, peace-loving Napoleon who would restore order without trying to conquer the world. His curriculum vitae was the comedy version of Napoleon's epic. Its high points so far were two idiotic coup attempts, at Strasbourg and Boulogne, where he landed in 1840, supported by a small platoon and an eagle in a cage. He was arrested and imprisoned at Ham. This *coup d'état* habit was forgotten, as were tales of his merry life in exile: unpaid debts and misdemeanours in the brothels of London and New York.[27] Prison was said to have matured him. The 'prisoner of Ham' wrote a book on 'the extinction of pauperism' which made him sound like a socialist, although, in retrospect, he may have been referring to his own poverty. When he escaped from Ham wearing a labourer's smock and carrying a plank of wood, Louis-Napoléon went to London where he signed up at Marlborough Street police station as a special constable: the new President had wielded a truncheon against the Chartists. Another point in his favour. A careful reading of *Des Idées Napoléoniennes* – Louis-Napoléon's *Mein Kampf* – might have caused some disquiet. He wanted all sections of society to enjoy the benefits of democracy and was prepared to suspend civil liberties to see that they did.

Hugo allowed himself to share these false hopes. After all, he was partly responsible for opening the gates to the Trojan parrot. In 1847, he had asked Parliament to end the Bonapartes' exile: in his view, this would prevent them from becoming the martyred heroes of seditious movements. Before the election, apparently out of gratitude for Hugo's role in his return, Louis-Napoléon visited his new home and impressed him with his virtuous intentions. 'I am not a great man,' he assured him, 'I shall not copy Napoleon. But I am a decent man. I shall imitate Washington.'[28] With a nephew of the great Napoleon sitting on a packing-crate in his front room, Hugo was easily convinced.

Some have doubted that the historic meeting took place – partly because Hugo's account of it in *Histoire d'un Crime* has Louis-Napoléon speaking pure Hugonic, but also because Hugo drastically down-played his own role in the presidential campaign: ironically, one of his most significant contributions to French political history had to be written off as a mistake, just as his death-defying assault on the barricades had to be swept under the carpet.

In fact, Hugo was an obvious target for the public relations genius. For one thing, the son of General Hugo was on better terms with Louis-Napoléon's uncle and cousin, Jérôme and Napoléon ('Plon-Plon') Bonaparte, than Louis-Napoléon was himself. They also had several friends in common: Alice Ozy, Esther Guimont, and a former mistress of Napoléon I, Fortunée Hamelin. This sexual–political network was as lively and effective as Balzac's novels claim it was: anyone who knew as many prominent courtesans as Hugo and Louis-Napoléon automatically had a power base and a source of up-to-date gossip.

Second, Victor Hugo was that rarest of parliamentary birds, a man of the middle who could sloganize moderate policies with the unignorable voice of an extremist.

Finally, as if by accident, Hugo had acquired a propaganda weapon to match those of his enemies.

The weapon was a newspaper launched in August 1848 by Auguste Vacquerie, Hugo's two sons, and Vacquerie's old school friend and fellow Hugophile, Paul Meurice. It called itself *L'Événement* and immediately achieved notoriety as the secret organ of a man who claimed in Parliament to have 'absolutely nothing to do with any newspaper'.[29] *L'Événement* did however print letters and speeches by Victor Hugo; its epigraph – '*Haine vigoureuse de l'anarchie, tendre et profond amour du peuple*' – was a quotation from Hugo's pre-election address in May 1848;[30] and Hugo regularly fed it with tendentious scraps of information which he called 'forage'.[31] Its contributors included Mme Hugo, Mlle Hugo and Léonie Biard. 'The editors of this paper', wrote the author of a descriptive list of the 480 new periodicals which appeared in 1848, 'seem to spend all their time listening at M. Victor Hugo's door, watching him think and never thinking themselves. *L'Événement* ought to call itself *L'Écho*.'[32]

This 'moderate, even reactionary' paper also owed its success to an invisible supply of money which made it the latest word in publishing technology:[33] it had a shop-front on the boulevards; the day's news was printed on an illuminated transparency fitted with an ingenious handle for the convenience of passers-by; and at eight o'clock every evening, paid workers dressed as bourgeois descended on the shop to grab the paper and disappeared, reading it with a look of urgent fascination.

Louis-Napoléon left Hugo with a signed copy of his book on artillery[34] (one of History's little jokes), and, a few hours later, *L'Événement* came out in support of his candidacy. On the eve of voting, it published a one-page supplement consisting of three words printed 100 times: 'Louis-Napoléon Bonaparte'.[35]

*

A FEW WEEKS into the new Presidency, Hugo found himself straddling an abyss.

The mood of the House was dramatically demonstrated in February 1849. The socialist Pierre Leroux moved that anyone convicted of adultery should lose the right to vote. It was supposed to be a sarcastic protest against the conservative attack on universal suffrage.[36] The so-called Leroux amendment was adopted ... When the new Assembly was elected in May 1849, the centre all but vanished into the abyss. The election was a triumph for the party of Order but also, surprisingly, for the radical Left. Even more remarkable in this climate of extremes, Hugo received 117,069 votes – the tenth largest vote in the Seine *département* (which returned twenty-eight members), almost ten times the size of Lamartine's vote in the national presidential elections.

It is far from certain that Hugo immediately knew what these votes represented. Intellectually, his position was far too subtle to appeal to a severely polarized electorate: defusing the time-bomb of socialism by adopting moderate socialist measures.[37] Morally, it was quite clear. He opposed the death penalty, defended universal suffrage, condemned cuts in arts funding ('Why not abolish one or two censors instead?'), called on his fellow representatives to 'have the courage of the opinions they express in corridors and committees', and championed the utopian belief that poverty could be eradicated for ever.[38] The former *pair de France* committed the ultimate parliamentary sin – making the other club members feel uncomfortable – although, of course, political debate is not quite as straightforward as Hugo would have us and himself believe. Hugo turned to the left because he suddenly spotted the solution to his moral discomfort. The ominous continuation of repressive measures gave him a firm platform for his own impractical views, and for the first time since the June Days, he was speaking with one voice:

> Here are the facts: ... There are in Paris ... whole families who have no other clothes or bed-linen than putrid piles of festering rags, picked up in the mud of the city streets; a sort of urban compost-heap in which human creatures bury themselves alive in order to escape the cold of winter.[39]

Hugo's attempt to adapt his conscience to events had enabled him to appeal to a group which normally lies buried under the rubble of great events: the peaceful proletariat – the same group which had imagined Louis-Napoléon to be a socialist hero and which cherished the image of a socialist Victor Hugo.[40]

It only remained for him to provide some concrete confirmation of the image.

Few people who undergo the kind of moral test Hugo had taken on the barricades in June are given a second chance to pass it. Fortunately, so to speak, France had also failed to resolve its dilemma. The same battles were brewing and the same choices would have to be made all over again.

The point of no return came in June 1849. A left-wing demonstration against the French military intervention in Italy was treated as an insurrection. Some socialist printing presses were vandalized by the police, but the culprits were never brought to justice. Hugo's suspicions were reinforced in July when newspapers were forbidden to say anything insulting about the President or to ask their readers for money when they were fined. Rumours of a Presidential *coup d'état* began to circulate, and as the sun began to set on the Second Republic, Hugo looked increasingly red.

This was all the more unexpected since he had recently been voting with the reactionaries. It is a little-known fact that Hugo – the future champion of anticlericalism – supported the education law proposed by the clerical party in June 1849 (the Loi Falloux). The reason this is not well known is that all the published versions of Hugo's speech change his final phrase, 'I support it' to 'I reserve the right to re-examine it.'[41]

Four months later, calling himself 'an obscure but devoted soldier of order and civilization', he denounced the bare-faced brutality of the unrepublican Republic on 19 October 1849. Six days later, *L'Événement* turned against Louis-Napoléon, and six days after that, Louis-Napoléon dismissed the entire Barrot cabinet, replacing it with one of his own – allegedly to ward off 'anarchy'.

Hugo can hardly be said to have been pleased by this battery of nails in the republican coffin; yet his speeches now began to exude a grim, determined joy. He had discovered the mouth of the tunnel at the end of which there might be light. The conservative majority had 'thrown off its mask',[42] and when Hugo stood up on 19 October 1849 amidst applause from the Left and cries of demagoguery from the Right, he used the image he had applied to his own side in June 1848. Victor Hugo had rematerialized on the other side of the barricades: 'those savages . . . who insult civilization by defending it with barbaric means!'[43]

It should now seem ridiculous that Hugo has been accused of turning his back on Louis-Napoléon because the President refused to give him a ministry, or even, according to one tenacious story, because they were both lusting after the future Empress[44] – the most unHugolian woman imaginable: thin-lipped, pious and – crucially – red-haired. The miserable truth is that these simple-minded fairy-tales come from the galvanized corpse of Second Empire propaganda – the lies of Government newspapers and the slanders of writers who stayed behind in France after the *coup d'état*, feeling guilty. For an equivalent, one would have to imagine a biography of Solzhenitsyn written from the point of view of the Politburo and documented with the memoirs of unrepentant KGB informers.

Hugo appears to have been offered embassies in Italy and Spain, and there are signs that Louis-Napoléon did have him in mind for a ministry.[45] But Hugo's thunderous speeches in 1849 show that a ministry was already out of the question when the Barrot cabinet was dismissed. This is not to say that his ambitions were more humble than previously thought; they were considerably *less* humble. Lamartine had shown how futile and humiliating partial political success could be. When Hugo joined the vanquished in 1849, he may still have been anticipating a left-wing coup which could easily have chosen him as a symbolic, compromise President; but the events of June 1848 had confirmed him in the role which had always come naturally to him: the pointing finger, the one-man opposition and conscience of the nation – a sort of super-ego President. 'Poetry goes to your head,' he writes in *William Shakespeare*. 'When you have been walking on the stars, you are quite capable of turning down . . . a seat on [the] Senate.'[46] Anyone who can imagine Victor Hugo sulking on a tiny island for eighteen years, consumed by impotent envy, has failed to grasp the great feat of mental management which makes his life an inspiring lesson in the art of surviving one's own personality: 'The good thing about pride is that it saves you from envy.'[47]

At its worst, the regurgitation of Second Empire propaganda is an excuse for reducing the central act of Hugo's life to one stingy motive. In its merely patronizing form, it shows a miscalculation of the price Hugo was willing to pay for his moral health. His early English biographers may perhaps be forgiven for considering the Channel Islands an acceptable substitute for Paris, even for failing to recognize the constant pain of exile; but they might have been expected to admire the rare form of courage Hugo was forcing himself to practise.

By defecting to the losing side, he was agreeing to rub shoulders with men of a very different background – men who, as Mme Hugo discovered, talked in loud voices, smoked pipes, were strangers to the handkerchief and never wiped their boots. Aspects of Hugo's life from 1849 to the *coup d'état* might have been scenes from a comedy on the then popular theme of the *déclassé*. The gulf – easy to bridge in principle but not in practice – first appears in his parliamentary jottings. Hugo's keen sense of what constitutes historical data led him to transcribe the hubbub which came from the Montagne – the far left of the House. The following is five minutes' worth from May 1849, before the dismissal of Prime Minister Barrot:

> 'Ah! 'ere comes Barrot! The big bass drum! Boom! boom! boom!'
> 'What's 'e saying?' . . .
> ''E's about as subtle as a bull dancing the gavotte.'
> 'Down with Louis-Philippe's last Minister!'
> 'If I 'ad my way, 'e'd get the Order of the Lantern!'*
> 'Curse you and your Louis-Philippe!'
> 'We never 'ad nothing to do with that twister!'
> *Someone, under his breath.* 'They'll think we weren't brought up proper. *Twister!* Nice word, that is!'
> *The other one, catching himself.* 'All right, then! Malefactor!'[48]

Most of the applause for Hugo's speeches now came from this side of the House. His parliamentary fortunes exactly mirror the evolution of his public: the social and economic status of the average Victor Hugo supporter was still heading sharply downhill.

At home, socialism entered Hugo's life in its most colourful forms. A man calling himself 'the Mapah' (a syncretic Mother–Father figure) had called on the Pope to abdicate and notified Hugo of a vacancy for 'Holy Spirit of the Christ People' (France).[49] The lunatic apostle of apocalyptic communism, Jean Journet, had offered Hugo a fifteen-day crash course in saving the human race and was a frequent visitor – loud, hilarious and impressive, almost a caricature of Hugo himself:

> Jean Journet told me this evening: . . . 'I have been weak. I agreed to feed and maintain my wife and children. I have failed in my duty. What I should have said was, "I am an apostle! Get out! Henceforth you are strangers to me!" . . . *But nobody's perfect!*'[50]

The salon in the Rue de la Tour-d'Auvergne was the scene of several entertaining experiments in the paranormal[51] – then a sign of socialist sympathies: the unity of creation as demonstrated by psychic phenomena proved that social inequality was artificial, not divinely ordained. Words had been read through envelopes, needles pushed painlessly through hands, Arsène Houssaye had recited the Book of Job from a closed Bible which Hugo was said to use as a footstool,

---

* An allusion to the practice of hanging aristocrats from street-lamps.

and Mme Hugo took to consulting a 'somnambulist' for news of her relatives in Normandy. Even the ghosts of Hugo's verse began to take on a more ectoplasmic consistency, long before the orgy of communication with the spirit world which is usually associated with the years of exile.

Hugo also found himself connected to the expanding network of international socialism. Since February 1848, there had been popular uprisings in Austria, Italy, Germany, Czechoslovakia and Hungary, and a new, alternative world of diplomacy existed. A deputation of Hungarians turned up one day on his doorstep to hail him, in Latin, as 'Gaul's greatest son', the Gallic equivalent of their revolutionary hero, Kossuth.[52] The editor of the *Liberty Bell* in Boston asked him for a letter urging the American Government to abolish slavery ('The Negro's chain riveted to the pedestal of Washington's statue,' wrote Hugo. 'Astounding. Nay, impossible').[53] Hugo later remembered making himself 'ridiculous' at an International Peace Conference held in Paris in August 1849, though Richard Cobden congratulated him on his excellent chairmanship. Things unimaginable a few months before fell from his lips – notably the phrase, 'our English friends'.[54] In his closing speech at the Peace Conference, he whipped an audience of 800 into a frenzy of hat-waving. The speech was practically a parody of his political philosophy: a hymn to railways, steamships, electricity and love – the pseudo-religion of material and moral progress which Baudelaire termed 'the salvation of the human race by the balloon'.[55]

These circumstantial texts have too often been quoted as definitive expositions of Hugo's beliefs. They should really be filed under the heading of etiquette. This was the paradoxical Hugo who had first been carried to the shores of socialism by a bourgeois sense of decency and who considered it bad manners to disagree with his guests. His famous comment at the grave of Balzac in August 1850 – 'Unbeknownst to himself, [Balzac] belongs to the powerful race of revolutionary writers' – was a polite echo of what most of Balzac's literary disciples were saying.[56] One observer recognized Hugo's funeral orations as a form of acting when he described a pale, portly, long-haired Hugo being led by the fingertips of his gloved hand to the grave-side 'like a soprano being led to the piano'.[57] Hugo's private account of Balzac's funeral shows a little more wit and a more poetic acknowledgement of the weight of Balzac's work. At the steepest point of the Père Lachaise cemetery, the horses faltered and he was nearly crushed between a tombstone and the runaway hearse: 'Without a man who clambered on to the tomb and hoisted me up by the shoulders, I should have presented the curious spectacle of Victor Hugo killed by Honoré de Balzac.'

*

THE STORY OF the next two years (1850–51) is that of an unavoidable event interminably postponed. Louis-Napoléon's ministers carried out a series of mini-*coups d'état*: a law which gave the Church the right to open its own schools; another which disenfranchised anyone who had changed his address in the last three years or been convicted by a court; this effectively wiped out the socialist vote. In June 1850, the Government gave itself the right to ban all 'dangerous' meetings. At the same time, the Faubourg Saint-Antoine was being covered in tarmac: as Hugo observed, this would make it difficult to build barricades and easy to move artillery.[58] In July, newspapers were taxed and thus brought under the control of a censor; all articles now had to be signed. As early as May 1850, a man was arrested with 150 copies of a Hugo speech, printed by *L'Événement*.[59] Two years after the revolution, the Red Menace barely constituted an excuse for repression. The farcical air of the final coup had much to do with the fact that there was almost nothing left to conduct a *coup d'état* against.

The same repressive spirit now reigned over the entire continent. The lamps which would be going out all over Europe in 1914 were already guttering. For decades, it would generally be accepted that socialism had seen its finest hour. In the lengthening shadows, only two idealists remained cheerful. One was Karl Marx, who, in his theoretical–hysterical mode, declared that the June massacre was a good thing because the workers would now be united in defeat.[60] The other – who embodied this position with too much anachronistic heroism for Marx's liking – was Victor Hugo.

Hugo's rhetorical fireworks showed up beautifully in the darkness. Speaking 'in the name of an anxious, expectant France', he castigated the parasitic priests in the Assembly who were plotting to 'confiscate' education. He talked, provocatively, about 'children's rights'.[61] He painted a spine-chilling picture of 'entombment 4000 leagues from the fatherland under a suffocating sun' – the notorious prison camps which he himself had helped to populate in 1848. Accused of fickleness, he defied the Assembly to find any moral contradiction in anything he had written since 1827: 'Indeed I am a strange man: I have taken only one oath in my life [to the Republic], and I have kept it.'

The last remark was aimed at the President. In July 1851, Louis-Napoléon tried to have his mandate extended beyond 1852 and just failed to obtain the necessary 75 per cent majority. Hugo's contribution to the debate was a one-hour speech which was extended to almost four hours by interruptions.[62] The ultra-conservative Count Horace de Viel-Castel – still one of the most frequently quoted 'authorities' on the period – called it 'the most cowardly and abominable speech it is possible to hear. It met with extremely vociferous cries of protest. That man is the most miserable scoundrel; he has the pride of Satan and the soul of a rag-picker.'[63]

Hugo's abominable 'cowardice' consisted in describing the Government as 'an enormous intrigue – History may call it a plot . . . to turn 500,000 civil servants into a sort of Bonapartist freemasonry within the nation': a fine pre-emptive analysis of the budding regime. This was Hugo's finest hour as an orator.[64] Some representatives suggested that he offer his speech to the Porte-Saint-Martin Theatre; others thought he had gone mad. In fact, Hugo had reached the final stage of a kind of religious conversion, shedding what he saw as the final layer of maternal, royalist prejudice.[65] The Revolution, which he had always baulked at as a historical obscenity, was now 'the first foundation of that vast future edifice, the United States of Europe'.[66] The Republic was no longer simply 'a form of government' but an 'essential, absolute truth'. Half-way through the speech, order broke down completely when Hugo hurled a custard-pie which has stuck to Louis-Napoléon's face ever since: 'What! Does Augustus have to be followed by Augustulus? Just because we had Napoléon le Grand, do we have to have Napoléon le Petit?! (*Applause on the Left, shouting on the Right. The session is interrupted for several minutes. Inexpressible uproar.*)'[67]

Hovering over Hugo as he stood on the podium was the republican, priest-hating ghost of his redeemed father, 'that sweetly smiling hero', he called him in a poem written in June 1850.[68] Hugo now occupied the same lonely promontory as General Hugo at the end of Napoleon's Empire; but there were two important differences. Whereas the General had been defending a small town near the Luxembourg border, his son stood at the very centre of 'the brain of civilization', marshalling its neurons for the final battle. The other difference was less inspiriting. Hugo's enemy was not the rest of Europe but a petty crook, an enigma too shallow to be fathomed, a man whose cousin, Princess Mathilde, wanted 'to smash his head open and find out what was in it' and whose image is still that of the nicest man who ever slaughtered innocent citizens and stamped on a democracy. Hugo's theatrical rage can be interpreted partly as an attempt to turn the cardboard Napoleon into a firm target, just as the anxiety of Louis-Napoléon's biographers has much to do with the fact that 'the first modern dictator' simply fails to lend himself to the sort of history which hangs its threads on prominent individuals.

Louis-Napoléon was unhappy to be dubbed 'the Little'. His insulter was legally immune, but the influential newspaper with which he had 'absolutely nothing to do' was a sitting duck. Charles Hugo was accused of 'contempt' for publishing an article in *L'Événement* on the horrific, bungled execution of a poacher. He was tried on 11 June 1851, defended by a lawyer as exuberant as he was inexperienced: Victor Hugo. 'Continuing his father's tradition! Some crime!' said Hugo, pointing to the crucified Christ on the wall at the back of the court:

> In the presence of that victim of the death penalty ... I swear that I shall continue to fight capital punishment with all my might! ... My son, today a great honour is bestowed on you: you have been deemed worthy to fight, perhaps to suffer, for the great cause of Truth. As of now, you enter the true virile life of our time.[69]

Hugo sat down to hear his son sentenced to six months in the Conciergerie. The critic Jules Janin wrote to his wife:

> M. Victor Hugo, by dint of eloquence and genius, has had his son Toto [*sic*] sentenced to six months in jail. With a tenth-rate lawyer,

poor old Toto would have got off with two weeks. . . . I saw M. Hugo yesterday. He is radiant! – perfectly oblivious to the futility of his gesture. He thinks he has won a great victory. So much for common sense!

It is just as likely that Hugo's widely reported speech stayed the judge's hand. On 15 September, without Hugo's help, his other son, François-Victor, and Paul Meurice were sentenced to nine months and fined 5000 francs for having invited the Government to extend political asylum to foreigners. *L'Événement* itself was suspended on 18 September and instantly replaced by a new paper called *L'Avénement du Peuple*. The first issue contained a letter in which Victor Hugo vowed to go and eat 'prison bread' every day at the Conciergerie. Six days later, *L'Avénement du Peuple* was suspended, its editor, Vacquerie, was sentenced to six months, and a cell in the medieval Conciergerie became the Hugos' daily dining-room.

By now, the Conciergerie was an informal socialist University. It offers two fascinating glimpses of Hugo as a revolutionary. Proudhon (author of *What is Property?*) was half-way through his sentence and had a long conversation with Hugo, but found his conciliatory policies too mealy-mouthed: 'He thinks that *fraternity* alone can resolve the social question.'[70] The father of French socialism and forerunner of Karl Marx was dreaming of explosions and purges. He wanted to replace the death penalty with legalized personal revenge and author-ize the murder of sexual deviants. The idea came to him immediately after meeting the Hugos:

> That family is a hive of impudicity. Every day there are visits from actresses and prostitutes: one minute they are in the arms of the father, the next in the arms of the son. . . . It's obscenity in action. Noise, shouting, loud laughter. A scandal.[71]

In Proudhon's view, Hugo lacked the brooding miserableness of the true revolutionary. It should be said, however, that while Hugo maintained a sceptical view of politics, enjoyed persecution to the full and stuck to his principles, Proudhon was about to convince himself that the dictator Napoléon III was the providential agent of social reform. The fundamental difference between them is that Hugo sited the ideological battle inside his own conscience, which is why he was able to embody socialist aspirations with the complexity, compassion and, irrelevant as it may seem, style that were missing in Proudhon.

Proudhon's cell-mate was a young journalist, Auguste Nefftzer, recently convicted of publishing apocryphal 'quotations' from the works of Louis-Napoléon which sounded so democratic that share prices had fallen. Unlike Proudhon, Nefftzer had a sympathetic eye for the social and political dichotomy in which Hugo was beginning to thrive:

> Our leftovers had been thrown into a corner – a horrible *arlequin*,* a mishmash of things like calf's liver and skate in brown sauce. Well, Hugo pounced on it! It was an amazing sight. We watched him, open-mouthed. You know, he simply gobbles things up like Polyphemus. . . .
> . . . He looked like a swindler or a student in his thirtieth year. And he was absolutely filthy . . .
> When I saw him again in Belgium [in 1852], he was a different man. He looked like an old cavalry officer. But I'll say this for him: his welcome was always seductive – elegant, courteous and charming.[72]

A General Hugo with the manners of an aristocrat. Hugo was ready to plunge into the cleansing 'ocean' of popular revolt, delighted to be eating 'prison bread', hungry for the struggle. God, his father and the people were all on the same side. On the other side, the parody of Napoleon Bonaparte, the evil father of the nation.

*

'TOWARDS THE CLOSE OF 1851,' wrote an English observer, Bayle St John, 'the atmosphere of Paris began once more to be charged with the electric fluid of Revolution'.[73] But something new was in the air. Before, 'even lads and women opened wide their nostrils to snuff the smell of gunpowder'; 'now, perhaps, for the first time, the sentiment of fear mingled with the anticipation of a struggle.'

Like most people, Hugo was expecting a coup. But he chose to ignore the plot which had been hatched against him in the bosom of his over-extended family. On 28 June 1851, the postman delivered a bulky package to the home of Juliette Drouet. She opened it to find a bundle of passionate lust letters sealed with Hugo's crest – '*Ego*

---

* Leftover pieces of meat and vegetable sold as pet food.

Hugo.[74] The letters were addressed to a woman called Léonie d'Aunet (Mme Biard's maiden name). In the accompanying note, Léonie informed Juliette that the affair was still going strong and that Victor had resisted all other attempts to force him to choose between his two mistresses.

Juliette left her cul-de-sac and spent the whole day walking through Paris, wondering whether to kill herself or go and live with her sister in Brittany. Her last seven years had suddenly changed in retrospect: she had been sharing her lover with a woman who dined with the Hugo family, while she was confined to her apartment with its caged bird and the tiny enclosed garden she called her 'exercise yard'.[75]

That evening, confronted with the evidence, Hugo swore to 'sacrifice' Léonie to Juliette. But with nineteen years' experience of Hugo, she had a good idea of the likely outcome: 'I should rather mourn your dead love for me than see you commit the hideous sacrilege of giving its corpse the appearance of life.' 'If I agreed to such a monstrous thing, in six months' time you would hate me and think me the cruellest and most cowardly of egotists.'

The plan, always attributed to Hugo, but actually Juliette's, was to have a trial period: Victor would continue to see both women and then make up his mind. Traditionally said to be four months, the period in fact runs from the discovery date, 28 June, to 5 October, when Juliette was 'granted permission to be happy': exactly 100 days – a symbolic length which was probably set by Hugo himself.

Napoleon's Hundred Days ended with defeat at Waterloo. Hugo's ended with a decision that would save his life. His sanguine adaptability to the unexpected gives even this fiasco an air of deliberation: it was time to sweep out the cupboards and prepare for a new life. Léonie had after all issued several explicit ultimatums: 'I cannot remain in the abyss of humiliation where you keep me, nor continue to play the odious role of a courtesan.'

Léonie's coup enabled Hugo to simplify his life. He reaffirmed his love for Juliette, confessed his guilt, obtained forgiveness and consigned his 'betrayal' to the past. The final cleansing of his conscience, muddied in the rubbish heap of June 1848, could now take place.

*

ON 1 DECEMBER 1851, a friend of the Englishman Bayle St John brought him a copy of an evening paper 'edited by the family of Hugos and a small society of young men'. Miraculously, *L'Avénement du Peuple* had survived its suspension and the imprisonment of its editor. The paper reported fresh rumours of a *coup d'état*, but 'then it went on to show, perhaps ironically, how utterly impossible it was that Louis-Napoléon could thus flagrantly betray the faith which he had pledged'.[76]

That evening, at 37 Rue de la Tour-d'Auvergne, Victor Hugo had just completed a dainty little poem about a figure on one of his Chinese vases: 'A virgin from the land of tea', 'in our dark Paris seeking your gold and azure gardens'; 'A happy dwarf paints the blue flower of innocence on your porcelain eyes'. Before going to bed, he made sure that his copy of the Constitution was on the bedside table. It had been there for several months now as a precaution – the pacifist's weapon of defence – open at Article 36. If anyone came to arrest him, he would recite it: 'The People's representatives are inviolable.'

Then he went to sleep under the scarlet canopy and the laughing Venus.

From Montmartre, lights could be seen going out all over Paris. Men with brushes and pots of glue were setting off for work, and a whole regiment of soldiers was spotted by an astonished passer-by in the Rue de l'Université, tiptoeing towards the Assemblée Nationale.[77]

CHAPTER FOURTEEN

Poetic Injustice

(1851–1852)

AT EIGHT O'CLOCK the next morning (2 December 1851), Hugo was sitting up in bed working when his servant burst in and announced the member for the Haute-Saône.[1] M. Versigny had dreadful news. Sixteen representatives had been arrested in their beds and sent to prison, the National Assembly was occupied by troops, bell-towers were guarded, municipal drums had been punctured, and the walls of Paris were covered in posters declaring a state of siege. Men had been hired to stand in front of the posters, making approving noises. In his 'Appel au Peuple', the President serenely accused the Assembly of plotting a *coup d'état*, vowed to protect all citizens against 'subversive passions', and promised to restore universal suffrage. In effect, a protection racket. France could keep its democracy on condition that it choose Louis-Napoléon to lead it.

Hugo threw on some clothes, grabbed his representative's sash, gobbled down a cutlet, took 500 francs from his drawer and left the remaining 900 with Adèle.

> Turning pale, she said to me, 'What are you going to do?'
> 'My duty.'
> Then she kissed me and said these two words: 'Do it.'

Outside in the street, everyone was going to work as usual. A group of men said good morning.

> I cried out to them, 'Do you know what is happening?'
> 'Yes,' they said.
> 'It's treason! Louis Bonaparte is butchering the Republic. . . . The people must defend themselves.'

'They will defend themselves.'
'Is that a promise?'
'Yes,' they cried. One of them added, 'We swear it.'

Sure enough, Hugo's *quartier* was one of the few to erect barricades; but another conversation he had later that day was more typical of the general mood and of Hugo's disappointment with the people:

HUGO: Follow my sash to the barricades.
A WORKER: That's not going to put another forty sous in my pocket, is it?
HUGO: You are a cur.

Two hours later, left-wing members of what used to be Parliament met secretly at 70 Rue Blanche. They found themselves completely naked: no newspapers, no telegraph, no soldiers. Hugo and some other representatives were sent out to sniff the air. Close to the Porte-Saint-Martin Theatre, Hugo was recognized and surrounded by a cheering crowd. What were they to do? 'Tear down the seditious *coup d'état* posters.' But what if they were fired on?

'Citizens! You have two hands. Take your legal rights in one and your rifle in the other and attack Bonaparte!'
'Bravo! Bravo!' cried the people.
A bourgeois who was shutting up his shop said to me, 'Keep your voice down. If they hear you talking like that, they'll shoot you.'
'In that case,' I replied, 'you would parade my body through the streets and my death would be a boon if God's justice came of it!'
'*Vive Victor Hugo!*' they all cried. I told them, 'Cry *Vive la Constitution!*'

Hugo's companion pointed out that he was about to cause a bloodbath. Artillery had just been spotted at the end of the street. They returned in a cab to the Rue Blanche, Hugo racked with doubt, contemplating visions of himself at the head of a popular army: 'Seizing such a moment might have brought victory or it might have caused a massacre. Was I right or was I wrong?'
With minor variations, this was the story of the next few days: isolated attempts to ignite the damp powder of popular revolt, followed by the awful sense of responsibility. Hugo's real contribution

to the Resistance was made with his pen: Louis-Napoléon's cynical proclamations – reassuring and righteous, beautifully printed by the Imprimerie Nationale – were pitted against Hugo's wordy counter-proclamations, crudely run off on secret presses, scrawled by illiterate typesetters on to a primitive form of carbon paper which had just been invented. His best decree was concocted that morning at the Rue Blanche. Thousands were pasted up and immediately torn down by soldiers.

TO THE PEOPLE

> Louis-Napoléon is a traitor!
> He has violated the Constitution!
> He has outlawed himself. . . .
> Let the people do their duty!
> The Republican representatives will lead them.
> To arms! *Vive la République*!

The Empire's official historian quoted this and other specimens of 'revolutionary typography' in his 1852 apologia of the *coup d'état*, gloating over the inadequate technology: 'The plaster still adheres to these scraps of stained paper on which the bandits' propaganda flaunts itself in misshapen characters and ink the colour of mud.' To think that 'the name at the bottom of this poster was once a synonym of genius'.[2]

By the afternoon of 2 December, secret agents were closing in on the underground Assembly. It agreed to reconvene that evening close to the Bastille. Meanwhile, Hugo and three of his colleagues set off to see their families. The cabstands were deserted but some buses were still running on the Boulevards. Stuck in a traffic jam, Hugo and his colleagues terrified their fellow passengers by leaning out of the windows and hurling abuse at a cavalry regiment: 'Those who serve traitors are traitors themselves!' 'You'll get us all killed,' said a woman in the street; but the soldiers ignored them. 'Was it too late? Was it too soon?' Hugo wondered. For that matter, was it even true? When Hugo's account appeared in 1877, one of the other representatives claimed that, far from insulting the troops, Hugo had tried to restrain his colleagues. He was in such a state of indecision that both accounts may be true.

Night was falling as Hugo made his way back up to the Rue de la Tour-d'Auvergne. A man under a street-lamp warned him that his house was surrounded. Munching a bar of chocolate, he headed back downhill towards the Faubourg Saint-Antoine where the meeting was about to begin. By now, he had at his side 'a generous, devoted soul' who had begged him to make use of her in an emergency – a person identified in Hugo's published accounts only as 'Mme D.*' (Juliette).[3] Shops were open on the Boulevard des Italiens; one of the theatres was showing *Hernani*. The glint of bayonets and the rumble of cannon were the only signs that Paris had fallen. Hugo must have realized that Louis-Napoléon had won, but the sense that a huge, historical disaster was occurring set him ringing like a great bell, his every word and action indicating the kind of energy normally associated with having the time of one's life.

7 p.m.
Hugo stands at the counter of a wine merchant's shop in the Rue Roquette. A mechanic tells him that the Faubourg Saint-Marceau will rise that night. Hugo agrees to lead the revolt: 'As soon as the first barricade goes up, I wish to be behind it.' But the Faubourg Saint-Marceau must have changed its mind or failed to get a message to Hugo. Perhaps the mechanic was only trying to be polite.

After 8 p.m.
Swollen by several journalists and, probably, spies, the Assembly meets in the home of a representative on the Quai Jemmapes. Proclamations are sent out but the couriers disappear without trace. Hugo is appointed to a seven-man 'Comité de Résistance'. A note asks him to meet Citizen Proudhon on the canal-bank near the Place de la Bastille. Proudhon insists that resistance is futile: 'What can you hope for?' he asks. 'Nothing.' 'And what will you do?' 'Everything.'

The Assembly reconvenes in two bare rooms in the Rue Popin-court. Hugo is asked to preside and improvises a speech which might have been written for a romanticized history of the *coup d'état*. It would be quite reasonable to assume that he made it all up later on. However, since every word was taken down by a stenographer and since the account was later published by someone other than Hugo, this is a reliable recording of his voice:[4]

Listen. Think about what you are doing. One side has 100,000 men, seventeen mobile batteries, 6000 cannon in the forts, and enough magazines, arsenals and munitions to fight the Russian campaign. The other side has 120 representatives, 1000 or 1200 patriots, 600 rifles, two cartridges a man, not a single drum for a call to arms ... nor a single printer to print a declaration ... Anyone who moves a cobble-stone will be sentenced to death; anyone found in a secret assembly will be sentenced to death; anyone who posts a call to arms will be sentenced to death. If you are captured in combat: death. If you are taken after the fight: deportation or exile. On one side, the Army and Crime. On the other, a handful of men and Justice. That is the struggle. Do you accept it?

... A unanimous cry went up: 'Yes, yes, we accept it!'

This transcript is extremely valuable, first because it shows that, even in the absence of exact information, Hugo was never short of a telling statistic; second, that his actual words came out in such a finished form, like the sketches of a great painter, that most accusations of *post facto* tampering are entirely plausible, though not necessarily justified.

Meanwhile, 300 right-wing representatives are arrested and sent to a prison outside Paris. A possible coup by the monarchist reaction – nicknamed 'the Burgraves' after the hoary-haired anachronisms of Hugo's play[5] – has been nipped in the bud. Its figurehead, the Duchesse d'Orléans, is still wondering why Viscount Hugo has deserted the cause. Displaying his talent for tactical humiliation, Louis-Napoléon has 'the Burgraves' taken back to Paris by bus and dropped off in the suburbs.

3 DECEMBER

1 a.m.

Friends and supporters vie for the honour of harbouring Victor Hugo. He chooses a friend of Abel Hugo's in-laws, M. de la Roëllerie. Arriving at the Rue Caumartin, he finds a beautiful young wife and a baby slumbering peacefully in a corner. A mud-spattered, grim-faced Hugo lies awake on a sofa in front of the fire under one of Mme de la Roëllerie's furs: 'I felt like an owl in the nightingales' nest.'

Dawn
Hugo kisses the sleeping infant and creeps out into a city which Bayle
St John compares to 'a South American town in the old buccaneering
times, when Captain Morgan was reported in the offing'.[6] Ripping
Presidential posters off the walls as he goes, Hugo returns home to
be told by a wild-eyed servant that thuggish agents in ankle-length
coats had come in the night to arrest him and were sent packing by
Mme Hugo.

8–9 a.m.
After persuading a trusty cab-driver to stop in the Place de la Bastille
so that he can harangue a general and his men (an apologia of the
coup d'état published in England calls this 'a reprehensible and insane
provocation'),[7] Hugo arrives too late to defend the barricade in the
Faubourg Saint-Antoine. The corpse of representative Baudin is being
carried away.[8] For Hugo, this murder of a fellow representative is
more disturbing than anything else. There is some suspicion, even
today, that his late arrival was deliberate, but it seems that other
representatives were also confused about the time of the meeting.
Hugo's feelings of guilt reflect his sense of poetic justice: surviving
the barricades of June, then perishing on the barricades of December
would have been a perfect martyrdom and the ideal end to his
biography . . .

3 p.m.
Discouragement sets in. Hugo suggests stirring the masses with some
great popular 'improvement' such as abolishing tax on alcohol. He
then drafts an enormous proclamation to the Army in an earthy idiom
evocative of the First Empire: 'Soldiers! The French Army is the
avant-garde of the human race!' Meanwhile, the loyalty of the troops
has been secured by a free distribution of brandy.

The emergency Assembly agrees to reconvene the next day on the
Right Bank at 19 Rue Richelieu. Hugo hides at number 15 in the
same street, between the Bibliothèque Nationale and the Comédie
Française, barricaded behind a sideboard. The apartment belongs to
an archeologist friend from earlier days, Henry d'Escamps – known
for his conformist views and therefore, Hugo supposes, unlikely to
come under suspicion.[9]

4 DECEMBER

Morning

A price of 25,000 francs has been put on Hugo's head and a gunman hired to dispose of him. The rumour – which has several different sources – is later dismissed by Louis-Napoléon's Ministers. (The Prefect of Police considered the price too high.)[10]

2.30 p.m.

While the Assembly collects reports of armed resistance, explosions echo down the Rue Richelieu from the north. An English officer whose account is published a week later in *The Times* and who is by no means a republican sympathizer, is amazed to see a broad phalanx of soldiers marching up the boulevards, firing indiscriminately at the windows.[11] People who try to run indoors or to help the wounded are stabbed to death. Children and even dogs are shot. Several witnesses see a drunken general joking outside the bullet-ridden Café Anglais with M. Sax (inventor of the instrument): 'We're having our own little concert!'[12]

Hugo arrives on the boulevards in time to hear rumours of his own death and to see the giant 'octopus' of Louis-Napoléon's crime 'stretching its tentacles through the streets'. So much plaster has been blasted from the houses along the Boulevard Montmartre that it seems to have been snowing. The true death figures are never known, but even the official figures run into several hundreds. Firing is heard throughout the night. Anyone caught whispering in the street is beaten up or killed. Many refuse to believe that the massacre has occurred and prefer to be shocked by false reports of 'Red' atrocities in the provinces.[13]

Hugo and Juliette find each other among the carnage. A writer called Plouvier recognizes Hugo and takes him to see a horrific scene in a nearby house. A seven-year-old boy has been shot twice in the head. His grandmother screams reproaches at Bonaparte, the Government and, since he is there, Victor Hugo. Hugo kisses the child. Juliette wipes the blood from his lips.

That night, Hugo has a dream: 'I saw again the dead child, and the two red holes in his forehead were two mouths: one said "Morny" and the other "Saint-Arnaud".'*[14]

* Duc de Morny, Minister of the Interior, and Maréchal Saint-Arnaud, Minister of War.

5 DECEMBER

The Assembly is dispersed. Representatives whose beards have grown sufficiently begin to leave Paris in disguise. A short man called Préveraud boards the train to Brussels as a woman and is molested by a gendarme. Another leaves as a priest, yet another as a railway inspector.[15] Hugo stays on in Paris, loath to abandon his sons in the Conciergerie, determined to be an eye-witness, half-believing rumours of an imminent uprising. In the Conciergerie, Charles and François-Victor hear of their father's 'death' and gauge the progress of the *coup d'état* from the increasing impudence of their jailers.

International outrage is tempered by relief that 'the Reds' have been quelled. Share prices begin to recover.

*

AT DAWN ON 6 DECEMBER, Hugo crumbled some bread on to the window-sill for the birds and left his hideaway in the Rue Richelieu for what turned out to be the last time. For the next six days, Juliette was kept busy hiding and feeding a certain 'M. Rivière'.

Information on the only week Hugo spent inside the France of Napoleon the Little is inevitably sketchy, but an important part of the background can be shaded in. According to one person, Hugo's flight was all hide and no seek. The Prefect of Police, Maupas, claimed years later in his *Mémoires* that 'we were perfectly acquainted with M. Victor Hugo's residence' and 'we might have arrested him ten times over', but 'had no motive for doing so'.[16]

Even if one accepts the word of a dictator's police chief (as many have done), the very fact that secret agents managed to keep their noses to every bend of Hugo's erratic route proves that his threat was taken seriously. Hugo was right to sense an eye at every window. A dictatorship is not just another form of government but a state of arrested anarchy which can change its face at any moment. In a private letter, Maupas himself admits that he countermanded an order from Louis-Napoléon's half-brother, Morny (the chief organizer of the coup) to have Hugo seized.[17] He also suggested searching the apartment of Hugo's brother-in-law, Victor Foucher, a career magistrate, 'where M. Hugo appears to be hiding'. None of this suggests the breezy indifference Maupas was keen to project.

Hugo probably owed his continued freedom to presidential policy: a regime which hoped to gain international respectability could not afford to give its most illustrious cultural representative the sounding-board of a cell.

A more serious accusation is that Hugo was careful to remove himself from 'the post of peril'. The remark is typical of a bully, who considers the mere threat of force quite innocent and its exercise perfectly 'natural' (Maupas's word for the 4 December massacre). It may also reflect a tendency in proponents of 'order' to overrate the deliberate endangering of one's life. Hugo was approaching his fiftieth birthday with a kind of morbid resignation and the sense of unfair invulnerability that comes to experienced mourners. Besides which, he was an old hand at lucky escapes: bandits and precipices in Spain; a bullet through his window in 1830; crossfire in 1832; an iron bar which smashed a seat he had just vacated during a rehearsal in 1838; a cannon which fell from its carriage and almost crushed him in 1844; then the barricades in June, Balzac's runaway hearse, and death threats from Right and Left.[18] The real root of his dithering during the *coup d'état* was the fear of other people's deaths – the responsibility and the further damage that might be done to his idea of divine providence.

The question also arises: how did Maupas's agents know where he was? Responding to a later report that his host in the Rue Richelieu was a Judas, Hugo refused to believe that he was anything but 'frivolous'. Yet in 1852 Henry d'Escamps published a resoundingly sycophantic book on the new Emperor.[19] Whether or not there was a price on Hugo's head, there were certainly rewards to be had for 'loyalty'.

When Hugo returned to his lair on 7 December, he was about to climb the stairs when a woman's hand grabbed his arm. According to Hugo's account, Juliette had come to warn him that men were waiting to arrest him. According to Juliette's account, she found him in bed and was cooking a meal for him when a shifty-looking boy knocked at the door and tried to look past her into the apartment.[20] Hugo incinerated the list of names and addresses he had used during the Resistance, and Juliette took him to the home of a friend, Sarrazin de Montferrier, who ran a Bonapartist newspaper – the perfect cover. An escape route had been organized. A former typesetter she had known as a servant in the home of James Pradier and then as her neighbour had obtained a passport for Brussels. Jacques Lanvin was described on the passport in vague enough terms, though his nose had been identified as 'large'.[21] 'This was not what we wanted,' wrote Juliette, perhaps reflecting a little-known aspect of Hugo's vanity: photographs of the early 1850s show a magnificent, bottom-heavy pear of a nose which might easily have passed as 'very large'.[22]

Three nights later, Hugo decided that it was time to make for the frontier. Juliette's apartment had been ransacked by policemen, and Montferrier had been told of a rumour that he was hiding Victor Hugo in his attic. On the evening of 11 December, Montferrier and 'Jacques Lanvin' arrived at the Gare du Nord half an hour before the night train to Brussels. Policemen were everywhere. Pictures of the revolutionary leaders, including Victor Hugo, were on display.

As they walked about in front of the station, people began to stare: Hugo was slightly over-disguised – a nine-day-old beard, a dark cloak with upturned collar, a cap with a leather peak pulled down over the famous expanse of brow, and a small parcel containing an orange and a ham sandwich. In an inside pocket he had a scrap of paper and a pencil. If he was carted off in a police wagon, he would throw a message through the little window at the back and hope that someone picked it up.

Having decided that the waiting-room would be less dangerous than a last-minute dash to the train, the two men found themselves sitting next to two policemen. A few minutes later, Montferrier was spotted by a journalist he knew and lured the man away from the biggest scoop in his life with the promise of an expensive meal – a cautionary tale for all investigative reporters.

Hugo was now alone.

At eight o'clock, the train pulled out into the darkness of the northern suburbs, Hugo's Montmartre home invisible on the right. In a freezing-cold second-class carriage, a toy-maker and two off-duty customs officers listened to two young men scaring each other with tales of firing-squads and blood on the streets. In one corner, a desperate-looking individual sat scrunched up in his cloak, trying to look like a typesetter with a large nose.

Three hours later, police boarded the train at Amiens. The carriage door opened. Seeing two customs officers, they moved on. At the next stop, the same thing happened. Finally, at three in the morning, Hugo looked out to see the word 'Quiévrain'. They had crossed the border. 'Jacques Lanvin' removed his cap in front of some French policemen and passed through Belgian customs. Another representative who had escaped on the same train caught sight of Victor Hugo waiting to reboard it, but, as he told him later in Brussels: 'I didn't dare talk to you – you looked so ferocious.' The caged animal was sensing freedom.

*

THERE ARE TWO quite different images of Victor Hugo settling into Brussels – both supplied by Victor Hugo. One is the battle-scarred prophet, trudging into the icy waste of exile:

> He leaves Paris on a winter's night. Rain, wind and snow – a good apprenticeship for a soul because of the similarity of Winter and Exile. The cold eye of the stranger is a useful adjunct to the dark sky: it hardens the heart in readiness for the trial.[23]

The other is the man of huge, happy ambitions who has just made the best career move in his life and who is already basking under 'the serene sky' of 'a clear conscience', planning an international publishing house 'which would be the intellectual factory of the entire world, with France working the bellows'. 'What an immense honour for me!' he wrote to Jules Janin. 'You should all envy me – I represent you!'

He spent his first six weeks in cheap hotel rooms, delighted to be forced to scrimp and save as in the early days of his writing career: no more income from plays, books, Parliament or, if they proved to be cowards, from the Académie Française. The Belgian Minister of the Interior came to warn him that he might be forced to expel him if he continued to agitate, and gave him some clean shirts. Hugo was a millionaire by today's standards, but a self-imposed ban on spending capital made him a pauper.[24] Complaints from disgruntled fellow exiles that he joined them at scurvy eating-houses only to gorge himself in private are a slur on Hugo's parsimony.

To his surprise, Hugo felt quite at home in Brussels. The Roman

Army had only recently gone home and the spirit of ancient Gaul was everywhere in evidence.[25] Belgian statesmen conducted their business in pubs and brothels, the city's favourite monuments were fountains of a vomiting man and a urinating child, and the Mayor of Brussels dropped in to see Hugo every day on his way to work. Apart from saving him from French kidnappers, was there anything he could do for M. Hugo? 'Yes,' said Hugo, 'don't whitewash the façade of your Town Hall.'

As 7000 French Republicans flowed into Belgium, bringing with them amazing, untrue tales of Hugo's heroic escape,[26] Hugo became the sun at which they warmed themselves. He chose his headquarters above a tobacco and umbrella shop in the splendid Grand-Place, the monumental square of baroque doll's-houses at the heart of the labyrinthine streets which have long since been swept away. Visitors passed between two grimacing gargoyles at number 27 and climbed the back stairs to a cavernous room: Hugo had also rented the apartment next door and had the wall knocked through. Without turning round, he would motion his visitors to wait and finish the sentence he was writing. There was a horsehair divan which turned into a bed, 'sheets the size of towels', a round table, a mirror, and a small, inadequate stove. A tall window opened on to the Town Hall opposite 'and illuminated the room with poetry, art and history'.[27]

As many as thirty people visited at once, turning Hugo's spartan bedsit into a combination of literary salon and courtroom. He was amassing testimonies for a devastating book that would enable him to 'lead Louis-Napoléon to posterity by the ear'. This garnering of fresh, eye-witness accounts makes *Histoire d'un Crime* a unique historical hybrid: a model of objective reportage, and one of the great examples of history as boy's adventure story. Some visitors came just to hear Hugo recite his latest page of invective. When they saw him rolling out his phrases, gesturing like a sower in a field, they would have noticed something which Hugo's convincing rendition of right-eous exasperation tends to conceal but which is clearly visible in his correspondence:

> Never has my heart been lighter or more contented. The events in Paris suit me well. They reach the heights of the ideal on both sides –

the atrocious and the grotesque. . . . Those wretches [Louis-Napoléon and his henchmen] are incomparable specimens. Epitomes of infamy. I find it quite beautiful.

Or, delving a little deeper into his mind in *La Fin de Satan*: 'Man is the prisoner of his own heart. Hating sets you free.'[28]

This sense of being released from his own prison and the resultant surge of creative energy help to explain the great mystery of Hugo's eight months in Brussels: why were the spectacular bazookas of *Histoire d'un Crime* packed away until 1877 and replaced by the one-volume hand-grenade, *Napoléon-le-Petit*? Opening *Histoire d'un Crime* at almost any page provides an answer. No one can write 600 pages in dramatic black-and-white and still appear entirely truthful. The literary merit of *Histoire d'un Crime* was its greatest handicap: 'People will think they are reading a novel when they are reading history!' Even the most incredible testimonies used by Hugo seem to be accurate, at least in a general sense. But he was incapable of freezing characters and events to set them all out like exhibits at a trial. Conversations he hadn't heard and rumours too perfectly symbolic to be omitted cast doubt on the rest of the story.

For instance, in the section on the secret executions which undoubtedly did take place, Hugo states that in the dim light of dawn on 13 December, 'a solitary passer-by in the Rue Saint-Honoré saw three heavily laden wagons trundling along between two lines of horse-soldiers. They left behind them a trail of blood. They came from the Champ-de-Mars and were going to the Montmartre Cemetery. They were full of corpses.' A splendid chapter-ending. But it asks the reader to believe that the blood was still flowing, uncongealed, after two miles, that the escort took a wrong turn after crossing the river, and that one of the main roads to the central markets was almost deserted on a Saturday morning.[29]

Overcoming his horror of wasted work, Hugo wrote *Napoléon-le-Petit* in one month (June 1852). This time, he confined himself to crisp invective, the evil character of Louis-Napoléon, the key moments of the coup, its social and political background. The author was relegated to fleeting, third-person appearances and hovered over the shameful episode like the finger at Belshazzar's Feast. 'This book is simply a hand that emerges from the darkness and snatches away the mask.' He showed the Skull-and-Crossbones flying from the Élysée, explained the Presidential con-trick of the plebiscite which, on 20 December, appeared to legalize the coup, and revealed the injustice of the notorious 'Commissions Mixtes': secret trials conducted by the Army and the civil service to judge 'all men hostile to the Government' and 'those with advanced ideas'. Although even such sympathetic readers as the Brownings felt that Hugo had simply 'lied' about events in Paris,[30] *Napoléon-le-Petit* is a brilliant, precise description of a modern police state, an unallegorical *Animal Farm*, with an Orwellian sense of sinister burlesque: 'M. Bonaparte's crime is not a crime; it is called necessity. M. Bonaparte's ambush is not an ambush; it is called defending order. M. Bonaparte's thefts are not thefts; they are called State measures.'

Hugo knew that as soon as *Napoléon-le-Petit* was published, his family in Paris would be caught in the explosion. Even Belgium was unsafe, anxious not to antagonize its unpredictable neighbour. On 23 July 1852, Leopold, King of the Belgians, wrote to his niece, Queen Victoria:

> We are very much plagued by our Treaty with France. Victor Hugo has written a book against Louis Napoleon, which will exasperate him much, and which he publishes *here*; we can hardly keep Victor Hugo here after that.[31]

With its dwindling liberal majority, the Belgian Government was under pressure not to give 'the rioters' the oxygen of publicity and had already responded by dropping heavy hints (tempered, perhaps, by the fact that Hugo had previously been awarded the Order of Leopold): he was marched off to a police station to explain his false passport. Conservative opposition members called for his expulsion. Coded dispatches left the French embassy in Brussels with amazingly detailed accounts of Hugo's attempts to find a publisher. Uncharacteristically, he had a lock fitted to his door. Until a proper study was made of State papers in 1961, it was widely believed that Hugo was suffering from paranoia.[32]

The first step was to gather his clan around him – an exercise which revealed the complicated feudal power structure which held it together. Juliette had arrived in Brussels a few days after Victor with a hefty trunk full of his manuscripts, and was already mending his shirts, making fair copies of his drafts and promising, bitterly, not to get in the way of his 'feminine visits' (no change there). Adèle II and François-Victor – now released from prison but chained to Paris by his infatuation with an actress – were advised to start learning English. Hugo's plan was to 'colonize a small corner of a free land'. He had been reading about the Channel Islands, where life was cheap, a form of French civilization survived in the Northern fog, and, more importantly from a poetic point of view, where Chateaubriand had spent four months in exile.

Mme Hugo's job was to arrange the auction of their furniture and to keep Victor Hugo's image clean. Strangers were greeting her in the street as the wife of a living symbol, and she proved herself an efficient public relations officer. When Hugo wrote in a panic to say that Léonie Biard was threatening to come to Brussels – 'My life here ... is profoundly austere and industrious'; 'All eyes are upon me' – Adèle moved into action: 'Don't worry,' she wrote, 'I *guarantee* that she will not leave Paris.' A quiet word with Gautier and Houssaye, and Léonie would have an outlet for her writing:

> I shall turn her in the direction of Art. It will be a noble and potent dis-
> traction, I hope. You may wish to write her some letters which would
> satisfy her pride, if not her heart. Make her your 'intellectual sister'....
> Dear great friend, I am watching. Work in peace and be calm.[33]

When Adèle tried to extend the tidying-up operation to Juliette, Hugo drew the line, but he was finally forced to do her justice – though it would still be many years before she was introduced to the family:

> Absolute and complete devotion which has never failed me in twenty
> years, not to mention profound self-sacrifice and complete resignation.
> Without that person ... I would now be dead or deported. She lives
> here in total isolation, *never going out*, and under an assumed name. I
> see her only at nightfall. The rest of my life is public.[34]

It is ironic that the need for secrecy opened so many drawers in the Hugo family – including a bulging drawer full of Hugo's sexual correspondence which Adèle was asked to destroy.

The caulking of the family Ark presented its biggest challenge when Charles arrived in Brussels at the end of January 1852. Father and son were to share the same apartment for several months. Charles was expected to help replenish the family coffers by writing something, and it now appears that Hugo's determination to be semi-destitute was partly an attempt to offer his sons the benefits of a tough apprenticeship:

> I told him to write a book about his six months in prison. . . . He promises and is as good as a girl, but then he doesn't start. I am not complaining, because I do not want you to scold him. I am working for us all. But I worry about the waste of time. The years go by and habits remain.[35]

Hugo is not the only father to worry about his children turning into slovenly parasites, or to suffer from a sense of frustrated generosity. But since his sons were willing to follow (or to disappear into) their father's footsteps, he suffered more than most. He was bursting with subjects and advice:

> Steep yourself for a few days . . . in the new world whose master you are to become. Lock yourself up with your characters and look them in the eye. Do not be afraid of the vague approximations that come to your mind . . . The outlines always swim about just before the work finds its feet and begins to walk.[36]

The similarity with meditation techniques is striking, and it shows what a triumph over the imagination Hugo's historical accuracies were. But it required a form of mental stamina and balance which Charles, unlike his studious brother, seems not to have inherited. He was pining for the cafés and brothels, as he told Nerval, who passed through Brussels on his way to the flesh-pots of Antwerp.[37] Hugo woke him up in the morning (usually more than once), bribed him with pocket money, watched him through the door sitting miserably at his desk in a cloud of cigar smoke, and tried to convince himself that this was 'the fertile idleness of gestation':[38] 'I need to see him at my side happy and contented, and if he doesn't want to work, what can anyone do? . . . I leave him entirely free and I do what I can to make him like living with me. It saddens me that he didn't mention it to you in his letter.'[39]

Charles was actually a talented writer, and was busy in his own way, planning plays and novels which sprouted only to wither under the shadow of *Hernani* and *Notre-Dame de Paris*: 'I have always been very timid with my father in literary matters. I had blackened reams of paper in sly seclusion without showing any of it to him.'[40]

Hugo may have adopted his father's belligerent optimism, but it is impossible not to be reminded here of his mother's character-forming zeal. She, too, had dragged her family into exile, forced them to learn a foreign language, extorted love, and cemented the clan by setting it up in opposition to an evil regime. Hugo was going to derive enormous pleasure from the spectacle of his sons' survival.

*

THE AUCTION took place in the Rue de la Tour-d'Auvergne on 8 and 9 June after an exhibition of Hugo's treasures on the 7th.[41] Jules Janin talks of three lonely figures – the two Adèles and François-Victor – standing at the windows of an empty house, gazing down onto a starlit garden; but for Mme Hugo the poignant pangs were dulled by the sight of all the bric-à-brac being swept away – the fruit of secret shopping trips with Juliette.

The sale was poorly managed. Prices were ridiculously low, reflecting the tatty condition of Hugo's antiques. Items filched by servants came to light in nearby shops, as did some unopened fan letters and unreturned library books. Some buyers came just to sit in Victor Hugo's armchair. An old woman was heard bemoaning the fact that poor M. Hugo had been reduced to beggary by his love of the people. In the papers, two courageous accounts of the auction appeared. Gautier and Janin both recognized it as a major event in French cultural history: it was the closing-sale of Romanticism, the public dismantling of the magical theatre – the Gothic trunks and coffers, the Renaissance bindings, the medieval arms and tapestries, the props of *Les Orientales*, dragged into the modern world and stamped with bargain-basement prices.

For Hugo, it confirmed the agony of exile and inspired the ferocious lament at the end of *Napoléon-le-Petit*:

Where are the songs one heard of an evening? ... Where is the street-lamp lit before one's door? ... And the auctioned furniture ... All flown away, those objects which bore the imprint of your life! Vanished, the visible form of memories!

Yet this was also the man, affectionately termed 'the Great Crocodile' by Flaubert, whose biggest contribution to 'liberalism in art' had been the commodification of Romanticism. Hugo had been the great auctioneer of Romantic imagery, the manipulator of words and writers, but also one of the first poets to make material objects the ironic vessels of spiritual longings. The sale of Hugo's possessions was certainly in Flaubert's mind when he symbolically placed the auction of Mme Arnoux's home and the offices of *L'Art Industriel* at the end of *L'Éducation Sentimentale* on 1 December 1851 – the eve of the *coup d'état*.

The Romantic sun was setting in the west, but it was going to sit on the horizon for the next eighteen years, observing its own apotheosis, reading its own obituaries: the 'father' whose absence exerted an unprecedented influence on the rest of the century's literature.

*

IN JULY, publication of *Napoléon-le-Petit* was imminent. The Ministry in Paris braced itself for a barrage of impressive insults. Two first editions were to be printed simultaneously – an 18mo and a tiny 32mo, the size of a pack of playing-cards: the smuggler's edition. To avoid embarrassing Hugo's liberal well-wishers in the Belgian Government, the title-page was to bear the name of a London publisher, though the book was printed in Brussels. In London, James Vizetelly was intending to publish a translation: *Napoleon the Little*. The French attaché paid him a visit and hinted that his next trip to France might end at the frontier. Vizetelly retorted that 'if M. Bonaparte wished to write a reply, I should be glad to publish his manuscript too, provided that he write with as much reason and no less power' than Victor Hugo.[42]

Leaving Belgium was now an urgent necessity. Hugo and Charles would travel together to the island of Jersey. Juliette would take the same train but a different carriage, still officially non-existent, though she was already copying out Charles's manuscripts for him. She was anticipating a new life much like the old one. The two Adèles would leave Paris as soon as they received Hugo's instructions: 'Go directly to Jersey, to *Saint-Hélier*, which is the main town. There ought to be some good hotels there. Settle in (*after fixing the price on arrival*, since, in hotels, one must always know in advance what one is going to spend) and wait for us.'[43] Enclosed was a letter for the love-sick François-Victor: 'You know me well enough to know that I sympathize deeply with that kind of grief; but you should also know that if I summon you at such a moment, it must be *absolutely necessary*.... Come at once, I beg you, dear child, or if need be, *I order you*.'

In the editions of his published speeches, Hugo boasts that he was driven into his 'second exile' by a law passed 'especially for him' by the Belgian Parliament: the Loi Faider, which made insulting foreign leaders illegal. In fact, the Loi Faider had not even been framed when Hugo left Brussels, though it certainly existed already in spirit – another poetic expression of the truth or a needless distortion of the facts. He told his fellow exiles that if he waited for the judicial hammer to fall, it might also fall on them. The future was looking rosy and a Hugocentric view of history more plausible than ever:

> They did not want to let me go. Three deputations came to discuss it with me.... I note with pleasure that they will miss me and that they all (more or less) love me and would be happy to have me as their leader. It may be a good thing for democracy one day if I become a banner.[44]

On 1 August 1852, a group of Belgian liberals and French exiles followed their departing banner to Antwerp. Speeches were made at a banquet. Hugo thanked them for their hospitality, compared them to early Christians in the Catacombs, urged them to set their ideological alarm-clocks for the dawn of the United States of Europe and, if 'the Bonaparte' invaded, to repel him with pitchforks.[45]

His other parting shot was a pamphlet which shows that he had already mastered the art of sending messages to the invisible ear.[46] Ostensibly addressed to his fellow Republicans, the pamphlet was clearly informed by detailed knowledge of French machinations: 'If M. Bonaparte took it upon himself to lodge a complaint against me in Belgium, I should appear with the deepest confidence before an honest Belgian jury, thanking Providence for the chance to speak out against that man before the conscience of every nation.'

Hugo obviously either knew or guessed that the French ambassador had orders to persuade the Belgians to suppress *Napoléon-le-Petit*, which was due to appear a week from then. After reading Hugo's pamphlet, the ambassador took the hint and reported back to the Minister of Foreign Affairs: 'I believe that M. Hugo's confidence would be justified.'

By the time Hugo set sail for England, Ambassador Bassano was beginning to develop a fine narrative style under the influence of Hugo's polemic. It made his dispatches unpleasant reading for the Minister in Paris:

> He embarked yesterday (1 August) at Antwerp for London with one of his sons, intending to take up residence on Jersey. Twenty or thirty refugees who reside in Antwerp or who made the journey from Brussels accompanied him to the quayside. Just as the steamer was starting its engines, M. Hugo cried out to them, 'Messieurs, we shall meet again!' The refugees waved their hats and answered, 'Yes – in France!'

CHAPTER FIFTEEN

Strange Horizon

(1852–1855)

H UGO'S FIRST ACT in English waters was to sign the 'List of
Aliens' which the master of every vessel from a foreign port had
to submit to the Chief Customs Officer.[1] The document shows, first,
the dutiful signature of 'Hugo (Charles)' – 'Quality / Profession:
Homme de lettres; Native country / Pays de naissance: *France*' – then
Victor Hugo, who ignores the line dividing the last two columns and
fills the space defiantly with the title that was no longer his, but that
was also his more than ever: *'représentant du peuple Français'*: one of
his finest enjambments.

The *Ravensbourne* steamed up the Thames into a polluted forest of
masts and rigging, dominated by a bloated Panthéon (Hugo's view of
St Paul's Cathedral). His encounter with the biggest city in the world
was to produce one of the great Impressionist urban tableaux of
French literature – an almost unknown passage which shows how
much of Hugo's electricity was passing through Rimbaud's optic
nerve when he wrote his English *Illuminations*. Even in the midst of
chaos, Hugo's drawing habit gave his eye a grid on which to organize
his impressions:

> 11 p.m. London Bridge. – Night. Mist. No sky. A ceiling of rain
> and darkness. Black vanishing planes lost in smoke; spiky silhouettes,
> misshapen domes. A big red circle glows on top of something which
> resembles a steeple or a giant: the eye of a Cyclops or possibly a clock-
> face. . . . In the darkness, four stars – two red, two blue – pierce the
> gloom and form a square. Suddenly, they start to move. The blue stars
> rise, the red descend. Then a fifth star, of burning embers, comes into
> view and rushes across the intervening space. A terrifying noise. It

seems to be passing over a terrible bridge. Large trucks go lumbering after it in the sky. Underneath, pallid clouds drop and disperse. A ghost, a woman, bare-breasted in an icy wind, passes close by me; she smiles and offers her cheek for a kiss.

Is it Hell?

No. It is London.[2]

Hugo's first words on English soil, to his son, in the taxi-cab – 'How do we get out of here?'[3] – are misleading, as is his famous definition of London as 'boredom in bricks and mortar'.[4] He was fascinated, as the following abandoned poem on 'the Black Babylon' shows – a negative image of Romantic communion with Nature:

> One blows one's nose and finds one's handkerchief all black . . .
> One blows one's nose again,
> And again one shudders to think
> That English soot lies deep inside one's brain.[5]

Hugo inhaled English soot for three days in the Hôtel de Normandie in Windmill Street. He visited publishers, met exiled revolutionaries – Louis Blanc and Mazzini – and found the French community split into acrimonious factions. On 4 August, he and Charles spluttered their way to Waterloo Station, with Juliette still travelling invisibly as self-transporting luggage. He marvelled at the sight of English interiors a few inches from his carriage window, and arrived at Southampton, where a pickpocket stole his handkerchief.[6] That evening, they boarded a steamer which Hugo identified as the *Royal Mail*. The Channel put on a magnificent storm:

> All the passengers were sick except Charles and myself. We spent the night alone together on deck, lashed and knocked over by enormous waves. At last, day dawned. We saw Guernsey and its delightful harbour in the form of an amphitheatre. Then, after a few hours' sailing, we saw a line of cliffs. It was Jersey.[7]

Several waves of exiles had already reached St Helier. Though some were deeply suspicious of 'the ex-peer', they all turned out to greet Victor Hugo, who, according to the report of the official French busybody, Vice-Consul Laurent, looked 'downcast'. The two Adèles, Auguste Vacquerie and a cat called Grise (a native of the Conciergerie prison), were already booked into the Hôtel de la Pomme d'Or, close to the harbour.[8] Hugo and Charles were taken to the hotel and then to the 'Société Fraternelle' of St Helier, where Hugo delivered a speech. Behind them, a grey-haired woman disembarked discreetly and was spotted by the Vice-Consul. Some onlookers identified her as George Sand.[9] When the report reached Paris, the Foreign Minister – by now an expert in Hugo's biography – added a note in the margin: 'Probably Victor Hugo's mistress, who was with him in Brussels'. The report went on cheerfully: 'It is unlikely that Victor Hugo will jeopardize the security of his new haven by imprudent manifestations.'

Five days later, the Vice-Consul heard about Hugo's speech:

> M. Victor Hugo has wasted no time in taking advantage of the licence that English law affords the spoken and written word, and of the false security offered him by the demagogic club of Saint-Hélier. He has fraternized with its members, delivering the most violent speeches against the French Government. He has even insulted Monseigneur the Prince-President in the most grievous fashion. I shall refrain from repeating his insults.[10]

Hugo's insults were not repeated because, apart from the phrase, 'the sinister premeditations of the Élysée', there weren't any. It was a plea for all the exiles to pull together, to present a united front to the enemy.[11] And between the lines it contained the surprising message that Hugo wanted to be left in peace. Now that the clouds of his conscience had cleared, he was discovering a new sky within himself. His life was regaining its pleasing symmetry: first, his political career had almost obliterated his imaginative work; now the events it had precipitated were about to give rise to the most astonishing artistic rebirth in nineteenth-century literature.

The rest of the family had been hoping to salvage some form of cosmopolitan life. St Helier had a theatre, a public library, seven booksellers and nine weekly papers, five of them in French. A grocer on the island owned the complete works of Victor Hugo. Not quite the desert they had feared. Unfortunately, Hugo was in a mood for symbolic acts. He spurned St Helier and settled on a white, rectangular house among the stubbly fields on the edge of town. It stood almost alone, staring out to sea. Hugo borrowed the name of the street and called his house Marine Terrace.[12] At the back, the dining-room and conservatory gave on to a broad terrace, then a stony, sloping garden full of marigolds (eaten locally with eel), and finally a windswept beach. Fort Elizabeth could be seen to the right; to the left, the Grève d'Azette and a bizarre, ancient breakwater, described by Hugo as 'an array of leg-bones and knee-caps afflicted with anchylosis'. At low tide and in fine weather, a pale cloud on the horizon was the French coast. The winking star in the east was the Saint Malo lighthouse. Hugo could see it from his bedroom window above the dining-room: 'The sun rises on that side. A good sign.'

No sooner had the Hugos arranged their books on mantelpieces and draped sheets over the packing crates than spies began to prowl about Marine Terrace. Like Inspector Javert in *Les Misérables*, Vice-Consul Laurent appears to have taken his quarry's existence as a personal insult. Rumours of a plot to smuggle a band of assassins into France were obviously true: M. Hugo had rented a house outside the town, close to the shore. When Charles bought a little boat, there was great excitement in the Ministry; battle cruisers were placed on red alert and when nothing happened, the Vice-Consul explained their cunning ploy: 'The refugees will probably take up fishing for a time in order to throw us off the scent.'[13]

Hugo's depiction of Marine Terrace in *William Shakespeare* as 'a heavy white cube ... shaped like a tomb' is painted with the dark palette he used for his portraits of exile. The scene was set in November, when François-Victor had been torn away from his actress lover, and when the winds were howling off the Channel. The road was deserted except for the occasional cartload of seaweed, and the dreaded sash-windows (*'fenêtres à guillotine'*) rattled endlessly in the storm. The house resounded 'like a reef'.

> Suddenly, the son raised his voice and asked the father:
> 'What think you of this exile?'
> 'That it will be long.'
> 'How do you intend to fill it?'
> The father answered:
> 'I shall gaze at the Ocean.'
> There was a silence. The father was the first to speak:

'And you?'

'I,' said the son, 'I shall translate Shakespeare.'

But in the summer of 1852, the view was very different: 'A little seaside nest which the island newspapers call "A superb residence on the Grève d'Azette". It's a hovel, but its feet are bathed by the Ocean.'[14]

*

HUGO'S LIFE AS A Jerseyman lasted three years, although it would be more appropriate to talk about his *lives*: the life of his work, the life of his mind, his life as an alien (mostly confined to occasional meetings with fellow exiles), and the life he had left behind in Paris and which was sadly represented among the 'compost heap' of books in a corner of his room at Marine Terrace by a cutting from a Jersey newspaper advertising *The Silent Friend*: a treatise on masturbation and how to give it up.*[15]

His first concern was to disseminate *Napoléon-le-Petit*: 'Let us make the wind blow.' The exiles' own newspaper, *L'Homme*, carried advertisements which show the enemies of Napoleon III market-gardening, clock-mending, hotel-keeping and teaching. Hugo contributed to the local economy by giving a new lease of life to one of the traditional industries of the Channel Islands – smuggling.[16]

Napoléon-le-Petit appeared in Brussels two days after his arrival on Jersey: 8500 copies vanished in less than two weeks. By the end of 1852, 38,500 were in circulation; they were read aloud at secret meetings all over France and passed around so that handwritten copies could be made. The rest of the Napoleon-hating world was served by three *Napoleon der Kleines* (Bremen, Gera and Murten), a *Napoleone il Piccolo* printed in London, a Spanish edition, and at least three pirated editions in French. Two translations were published in Mexico alone, as if in anticipation of the French invasion of 1862:

* The recommendations of Messrs R. and L. Perry's brochure, *The Silent Friend* (obtainable from a Jersey pharmacist) are an exact description of Hugo's daily routine on the Channel Islands: sleep on a hard bed, rise early, eat a lot of root vegetables, meat in moderation, drink pure water discoloured with a little wine, sponge the whole body with cold water every morning immediately after getting up, then rub down with a rough towel; go swimming, preferably in the sea.

Napoleon el Chiquito and *Napoleon el Pequeño*.[17] None of these brought Hugo any royalties, though the Mexican Government did award him a chased gold pen.[18] In London, 'Victor Hugo' and 'Napoleon the Little' were seen on sandwich boards, on the sides of railway carriages and 2000 walls in glorious tricolour, offering a choice between the 'Contemporary French Literature' series and the 'People's Shilling Edition'.[19] It was one of the autumn bestsellers. According to Hugo, extracts appeared in newspapers 'from London to Calcutta, from Lima to Quebec'. The total number of copies must have been 'more than one million'.[20]

Readers who wanted to know more about the hero himself could buy the two-volume edition of his *Oeuvres Oratoires* – a compendium of Hugo's public utterances since his maiden speech at the Académie Française in 1841. Edmond Biré's famous claim that Hugo manicured his own speeches, inserting politically correct remarks and jokes which he thought of years later, is hugely exaggerated.[21] One might just as well be impressed by the fact that, as the 'Publisher's Note' boasted, very few politicians would allow their last twelve years' worth of opinions to appear together in the same book.

While the pocket-, boot- or snuffbox-sized edition of *Napoléon-le-Petit* found its way into France via Belgium, Savoy, Nice, Switzerland and the Channel ports, dispatches went flying in and out of police headquarters, unintentionally assembling a detailed history of smuggling's finest hour until the French Resistance ninety years later, when many of the same channels would be used. Hugo's work reached its public like exotic produce, smelling of distant adventures. It came in bales of hay, packets of contraband tobacco, carriage clocks, lead-lined boxes which were lashed to fishing-boats below the waterline and unloaded at night on deserted beaches, hollowed-out blocks of wood which were thrown overboard just out of range of the coast-guard's telescope. Sandwiched between two sheets of metal, it slipped into France as a tin of sardines. French tourists arrived in St Helier wearing baggy trousers and left with bundles of pages strapped to their legs. Hugo's visitors proudly revealed their tricks: trunks with false bottoms, shoes with false heels, hollow walking-sticks and cigars rolled with sheets of *Napoléon-le-Petit*, specially printed on onion-paper. Hugo was delighted to learn that women were sewing his publications into their clothes and securing them under their garters: the ultimate compliment. A copy of *Napoléon-le-Petit* in the John Rylands Library gives evidence of another popular device: its plain binding is marked with the single word '*Paroissien*' ('Prayer-book').[22]

Even the most fantastic tales, once thought to have been dreamt up by Alexandre Dumas, are confirmed by French Foreign Office files:

> The latest mode of clandestine transmission [wrote the Vice-Consul in October 1852], consists of small balloons fashioned from sheets of printed paper which will be launched whenever the wind stands fair for France. Experiments have been conducted in the last few days and are said to have been entirely successful.[23]

According to Hugo's daughter, the first balloon-book was to be launched from the terrace at the back of their house. (There is only anecdotal evidence of a rumour that a balloon-borne Victor Hugo was going to scatter his books over Paris – presumably a few pages at a time.) A year later, plaster busts of Napoleon III began to arrive at the Gare du Nord in Paris, each containing a copy of *Napoléon-le-Petit*.

Hugo also sent out copies himself. Employing a smuggler was extremely expensive: 50 francs for a book which would be sold in France for 60 (forty-eight times the cover price).[24] Instead, he asked his correspondents to supply eight different addresses so that separate sheets could be dispatched in small envelopes and stitched back together in France. These 'letters' were sent via London and thus reached Paris without the telltale Jersey postmark, although Flaubert complained that Hugo's flamboyant false handwriting was far more suspicious than the real thing would have been.[25] Replies were sent to innocuous addresses – a hotel or an ironmonger's[26] – or stuffed into dead chickens: a scheme which may have been suggested by the other meaning of the word '*poulet*' (love letter).

The smugglers' ingenuity was almost matched by the vigilance of customs officers.[27] A carter wearing a very large hat was stopped on the road to Lyons. In the Channel ports, officials were instructed to be ruthless. A woman known to Charles Hugo was strip-searched in front of a male officer. The linings of her skirts and furs were unpicked and the notebook in which her little granddaughter had been doodling was confiscated and sent to Paris for decoding. The price of passports – on which 'Empire Français' was inserted above a crossed-out 'République Française' – went up from 25 centimes to 5 francs. The accounts of many British travellers to the Continent in the early 1850s mention hours of luggage searching and long interrogations by the passport officer: 'One would suppose', wrote a British journalist, 'that you had asked for the hand of his daughter in marriage.'[28] Boats were impounded if even a photograph of one of the exiles were found on board, and Jerseymen carrying seaweed to France were forced to spread their load out on the Normandy beaches so that the *douaniers* could go beachcombing for the works of Victor Hugo.

Suspicions that these extraordinary measures were designed to turn the locals against the refugees are still dismissed as a fantasy but are fully confirmed by police files – British as well as French. Strictly speaking, Jersey was a foreign possession of the United Kingdom with its own laws and currency, and although Hugo defined the English code of hospitality as 'Let them in and let them die', there was natural sympathy for the victims of a political bully. It was only in Whitehall that any attempt was made to distinguish between 'bona fide refugees' and 'mendicants' (today's 'economic exiles').[29] As long as Hugo and company were tolerated by the natives of Jersey there was little hope of persuading the British Government to extradite them.

The amazing, illicit success of *Napoléon-le-Petit* makes this an important moment in the history of modern democracy. It seemed to justify Hugo's belief that modern communications would bring about an international democratic republic. The balloon-books were an early demonstration of his prediction (proved spectacularly wrong sixty years later) that 'on the day the first airship takes to the skies, the last tyranny will return underground'.[30] It also endorsed Hugo's confident assessment of his new role: 'My function is somehow sacerdotal. I have taken the place of the magistracy and the clergy. Unlike the judges, I judge, and unlike the priests, I excommunicate.'

This may be the gentle raving of a satisfied megalomaniac, but, so far, his words had been completely justified by events.

*

WHILE HUGO'S WORK went about its Christ-like mission, the man himself kept a low profile. His initial view of the English seemed to date from the days of Claudius and Julius Caesar: 'a noble race of brutes'. The absence of mirrors in English homes was evidence of a stunted aesthetic sensibility. And there was the famous English '*cant*' (a word borrowed by the French to express what was supposed to be a peculiarly English form of piety). St Helier was thick with chapels: eight different denominations of 'superstition', not to mention a Temperance Coffee House. On Sunday, 'even the dogs stop barking'.[31] One day, Vacquerie was followed for miles by a strange man who finally crept up to him and told him that his shirt-tails were hanging out.[32] On visits to public urinals, Hugo noticed a curious inscription – '*Please adjust your dress before leaving*' – and inserted it in *Les Misérables* with the comment, 'History ignores almost all these little details and cannot do otherwise: it would be swamped by the Infinite.'[33]

For Hugo, the main drawback to the English-speaking world was that it spoke English: 'A cloud always floats in the English phrase. That cloud is a form of beauty. It is everywhere in Shakespeare,' he revealed in the preface to François-Victor's translation of Shakespeare's plays. Faced with this linguistic drizzle, he put up an umbrella of jocular remarks, some of which are not quite as silly as they sound:

> *Southwark* in those days was pronounced *Soudric*; today, it is pronounced *Sousouorc*, or something like that. Indeed, an excellent method for pronouncing English names is not to pronounce them at all. Thus, instead of *Southampton*, say *Stpntn*.[34]

An attempt to enunciate Hugo's non-word will in fact produce a reasonable approximation of the southern English glottal stop. It should be remembered that he was after all an able linguist, and there is something to be said for his ability *not* to become an English-speaker in nineteen years' habitation.

On one of his later trips through England, he shared a railway carriage with two English ladies. It must be inconvenient, they supposed, not to know any English. Hugo retorted, 'When England wishes to converse with me, it will learn to speak French.' ('They did not know who I was,' he explained when telling the story.)[35] This is really more a sign of his fondness for provocation than proof of his chauvinism. He could be far more insulting about the French provinces and, on the whole, managed to remain ambiguous. *Égalité* and *fraternité* may have been in short supply, but the spirit of liberty was so strong that dogs were allowed to go about unmuzzled.[36] For someone who belonged to one of the most Anglophobic generations in French history, any compliment was a noteworthy victory over prejudice.

This inoffensive man, who walked along the beach in a sweater and a floppy hat, confined his public appearances to the funerals of exiles, and planted beans in his garden which he suspected his neighbour's geese of digging up,[37] was busy writing one of the most savage collections of poetry in French literature: *Châtiments*, the verse equivalent of *Napoléon-le-Petit*. 'Louis Bonaparte has only been cooked on one side,' he told his publisher friend in Brussels, Pierre-Jules Hetzel. 'It is time to turn him over on the grill.'[38] When Hetzel hinted that this time Hugo had gone too far, like the ocean which flooded Marine Terrace in January 1853, Hugo explained his procedure:

> The fact is, I *am* violent. . . . Tacitus is violent, Juvenal is violent . . . Isaiah tells Jerusalem, 'Thou hast opened thy legs to the ass's member'*
> . . . Jesus was violent; he took a stick and cast out the moneychangers, and 'he struck with all his might', says St John Chrysostom.[39]

Hugo's reasoning was this: the violence of his poems would impress the masses and give him the authority later on to prevent violent reprisals. 'Keep my goal in mind: *implacable clemency*.' When a French tailor turned up on Jersey and asked Hugo's permission to assassinate Napoleon III, Hugo refused to give his blessing.[40] He was determined to put his view of the universe into practice. The just would be rewarded and the unjust punished. The meek would inherit the earth and there was nothing Napoleon III could do to prevent it. Some of the exiles accused him of pacifism, which reminded Hugo of the disciples urging Jesus to destroy the Roman Empire.

---

* Reminiscent though it is of Isaiah or Ezekiel, this appears to be one of Hugo's own additions to the Bible.

The two original editions of *Châtiments* were printed secretly in Brussels in November 1853.[41] The expurgated edition appeared with missing words and blank spaces to show the censor's dirty finger-prints. The complete, untreated edition used an old pornographer's trick on the title page: 'Genève et New York. 1853'. A foreign character set had been purchased to make the lie convincing.[42]

The full edition contained ninety-seven poems in almost every known genre – brilliantly vituperative lines, impossible to recite without spitting, and nicely defined by Hugo as 'God's vomit'. The poems are divided into seven books, each with a sarcastic heading inspired by Second Empire rhetoric: 'Society has been Saved', 'The Family is Restored', 'Stability is Assured', etc. In line with the corporal punishment connotation of the otherwise biblical title ('Chastise-ments'), he presented the Emperor as the silly nephew of popular comedy and contrasted his misdemeanours with the epic campaigns of Napoleon I (notably the Russian campaign, unforgettably evoked in the finest of all French historical poems, 'L'Expiation').

> We'll carve up History and take an equal share,
>   But he's not quite so canny;
> He'll get the glory and the trumpets' blare,
>   And I'll get all the money.

Since Hugo was now one of the major sources of alternative news in France, he made sure that his *Châtiments* were also a potted history of the last twenty-four months: the *coup d'état*, when Napoleon Jr 'stuffed all the laws into a sack and heaved it into the Seine'; his consecration in Notre-Dame, where 'Jesus had been nailed to a cross / In case he tried to leave'; and the proclamation of the Empire on 1 December 1852. No insult or news snippet was too small. 'Look, Messieurs,' the Emperor was reported to have said, 'here is *Napoléon le Petit* by Victor Hugo le Grand!' 'Ah!' comments Hugo, 'In the end you'll scream with pain, you wretch! . . . I hold the branding iron and see the smoke rise from your flesh!'

A fruitful comparison could be made with Hugo's earlier poems on children – for example, a chocolate-box poem from *Les Feuilles d'Automne* which still lives in the school memories of people on both sides of the Channel:

When the child appears, the family circle
Applauds and cheers; his sweet shining face
    Makes all eyes shine . . .

Twenty-three years on, the channel opened by these happy sounds was used to siphon in the horrible truth of 4 December 1851:

The child had got two bullets in the head.
The home was clean, humble, peaceful, decent;
. . . An old grandmother was there in tears.
We undressed the child in silence. Its pale mouth
Gaped wide. Death drowned its frightened eye.

Hugo was generally considered to have lied about the rivers of blood and the mutilated corpses buried with their heads above ground to facilitate identification. His depiction of a wretched city where 'gigantic pairs of scissors / Seem to reach up into the sky to snip the wings off birds' docs sound like an implausible contradiction of the glittering pageant of an economically rampant Second Empire. Yet it corresponds in spirit to independent accounts of Paris in the years following the coup: buses, once filled with chattering passengers, were silent; anyone who started a conversation was thought to be a spy; policemen had become aggressive, beggars were swept off the streets and flower-pots banned from window-sills: 'Whole quarters, refuges of poverty and democracy, have been cut down; broad streets, by which fresh air and artillery may penetrate in every direction, have been opened . . . Fine masonry is certainly an excellent substitute for liberty.'[43]

The effect of *Châtiments* in France is now almost impossible to imagine. Its innovative, pervasive use of proper nouns, the huge weight of meaning placed on the rhymes – so that language itself seems to confirm the poet's point of view[44] – made it a more modern work, technically, than it sounds today. With Baudelaire's *Les Fleurs du Mal*, it was the most popular forbidden poetry book in the generations of schoolboys which included Zola, Verlaine and Rimbaud. 'We felt that simply by reading his works, we were contributing to some silent victory over tyranny,' remembered Zola.[45] Every schoolboy knew that France's greatest living poet and patriot was Victor Hugo; but they also knew that he disapproved of the nation as it now existed. The fact that Hugo had continued to develop poetically proved that his insults were not simply the ramblings of a disappointed man. They were the outward signs of another literary revolution: the nuts and bolts of the modern world and the vast vocabulary Balzac had introduced into the novel entered French verse. Hugo had found another voice. Even his handwriting was growing larger.

The best description of the tutelary shadow Hugo had begun to cast over the Second Empire can be found in a letter sent to him by Flaubert in July 1853. Drawing his inspiration from Hugo's pungent, lavatorial images, Flaubert wrote a kind of admiring pastiche and offered confirmation that (as Hugo's poem put it) 'Times like ours are History's sewer.'

> Ah! if you only knew what filth we are sinking into! ... One can scarcely move without stepping in something foul. The air is thick with nauseating vapours. Air! I must have air! And so I fling wide my casement and turn to you. I hear the beating of your Muse's wings and inhale, like the scent of forests, the breath that rises from the depths of your style.
>
> Moreover, Monsieur, you have been an enchanting obsession in my life; an enduring passion which is as strong now as it ever was. I have read your works in sinister wakes and by the seaside, on soft beaches, under the Summer sun. I took you with me to Palestine, and it was you, again, who consoled me ten years ago when I was dying of boredom in the Latin Quarter. Your poetry entered my body like my nurse's milk.[46]

That same evening, before the stylistic effect had worn off, Flaubert sketched one of the great passages of modern prose fiction – the Comices Agricoles scene in *Madame Bovary*, where the pillars of rural French society pontificate among the animals and the dung. The resonances of Flaubert's realism – a conscious blend of *Notre-Dame de Paris* and *Napoléon-le-Petit* – go some way to explaining the political decision to prosecute *Madame Bovary* in 1857.

It is nice to see that the fifty-one-year-old *enfant terrible* has retained the power to irritate. His *Châtiments* are still treated as a hugely embarrassing faux pas, in line with the reaction of Empress Eugénie: 'What have we done to M. Hugo to deserve this?' (Hugo's answer: '*Le Deux Décembre*'). But Hugo was not performing for the ear of a nineteenth- or even a twentieth-century bourgeois. His audience was a cowed population, humiliated by its own surrender, which needed to be shown that its new master was not immune to rotten eggs. Hugo's music-hall Jeremiah is one of the first voices in modern French literature to ignore systematically the genteel rationalism of a critical tradition which turns even the most deliberately rebellious French poet into a self-conscious didact.[47]

The other main criticism is that Hugo simply did not know when to stop. It is true that even the willing victim of his verse sometimes has the impression of being washed by a giant wave on its way to somewhere else. But Hugo was looking far beyond the cheap seats towards the vast multitude of all his future readers with their potentially infinite attention-span. When Vacquerie claimed that he wanted to boil his oeuvre down to a few choice texts, Hugo told him (as if anticipating modern data retrieval systems): 'Every poet helps to write a Bible, and the library of the future will contain the Bible of Drama, the Bible of Epic, the Bible of History, the Bible of Lyric Poetry.'[48] For him, the only valid criticism was that he hadn't started sooner: 'What a shame I wasn't exiled earlier!' he would write in a note in 1864. 'I would have done many things for which I now feel I shall not have time.'

*

CHÂTIMENTS TURNED OUT to be a clearing of the throat before the great blast of visionary poetry in which Hugo adumbrated a new world religion. A religion to end all religions, which would complete 'the botched work of Jesus Christ' by putting the insignificant human ego in its place. This religion, which survives in the Cao Dai faith of Vietnam, was first confirmed in the drawing-room of Marine Terrace by an unusual group of visitors, constituting the greatest symposium ever held on the nature of human existence.

Far from being consumed by impotent rage, Hugo had been restraining his more gentle lyrical impulses. He had set aside the poems that would form the six books of *Les Contemplations* 'because it would look as though I was disarming'. After talking to the Ocean, skipping over rocks 'like a mountain goat', or sitting on 'The Rock of the Exiles' facing Chateaubriand's tomb off the coast of France, he left tender, flowery poems with Juliette, who was living in an apartment in Nelson Hall by the harbour, resenting the time he spent in his rare visits to town with those 'political bigots', his fellow exiles, 'bearded, hook-nosed, fungus-covered, hairy, hunchbacked and obtuse'.[49] Other poems were addressed to Léopoldine, who lay across the water in Normandy, out of reach but resting in the same Norman soil: in Hugo's mind, the Channel Islands were 'pieces of France which fell into the sea and were picked up by England'. Fishermen, he claimed in *L'Archipel de la Manche* (still one of the best general guides to the Islands),[50] navigated by the tree-stumps of the ancient forest which was submerged when a 'heavy swell' cut Jersey off from the mainland in 709[51] – a geological fantasy which appears as the literal truth in the latest edition of the *Robert* encyclopedia.

By the time *Châtiments* appeared, Hugo was in the ecstatic, windswept frame of mind previously induced by stormy first nights and falling in love: 'There have been two great affairs in my life: Paris and the Ocean.' 'At night,' he told his daughter, who wrote it in her diary, 'it is the Sea that wakes me up and says, "To work!"'[52] In a flattering letter to a young Belgian poet, Franz Stevens ('You are not a Belgian poet; you are a French poet'), Hugo described the curious effect of wind and tide on his brain:

> I am writing this a little haphazardly, just as it comes to me. Try to imagine the state of my mind in this splendid isolation: I live as if perched on the very tip of a rock, with the great foaming of the waves and all the great clouds of the sky beneath my window. I inhabit this immense dream of the ocean and slowly I become a sleepwalker of the sea. Faced with these prodigious sights and that enormous living thought in which I lose myself, there is soon nothing left of me but a sort of witness of God.
>
> It is from this unending contemplation that I rouse myself in order to write to you. Take my letter and my thoughts as they come, slightly disconnected and unravelled by that gigantic oscillation of the Infinite.[53]

This unpicking of the mind induced a state which sounds like the result of self-hypnosis: the sense of turning into an inanimate object while things and even concepts become sentient creatures. The English Channel should be counted as one of the main influences on Hugo's style: the characteristic phrase in which physical qualities are attributed to abstractions, and the grammatical oddity known as the '*métaphore maxima*' – the direct juxtaposition of two nouns ('the Hydra Universe', 'the Sphinx Human Mind', 'the monstrous Sperm Ocean'), which dissolves the distinction between image and reality. 'Each stanza or page that I write always has something in it of the shadow of the cloud or the saliva of the sea.'[54]

It was with his brain in this semi-soluble state that Hugo received the visit, in September 1853, of his old friend Delphine de Girardin, the wife of his comrade Émile. She brought with her a psychological germ which was to have a huge, catalytic effect on Hugo's work: the latest craze from America, known as Table-Turning or, to its more ambitious exponents, Spiritism.[55]

The practice of enlisting the dead in after-dinner entertainment was already in what scarcely deserves to be called its infancy: its ability to unbalance obsessive minds had not yet been recognized and it was generally believed to be a source of useful, authoritative footnotes to sacred texts. Neither had it occurred to a generation brought up on the mysteries of 'magnetism' to observe the less dubious, attendant phenomena of telepathy and telekinesis, nor even to refine the technology. The method in use at Marine Terrace required the spirits to rap the floor with a three-legged table, once for an A, twice for a B, and so on. This means that even the most concise revelations had the table hopping up and down from dusk to dawn. An alarming calculation based on Hugo's transcripts of the séances shows that the table must sometimes have kept up a rate of six taps a second for over three hours.[56] Clearly this is impossible, even for Hugo. Since he honestly believed that he was simply transcribing the words tapped out by the table, at least some of the texts must be considered an early form of automatic writing. He himself viewed the table as the modern equivalent of the Sibyl's tripod.

If all that happened at Marine Terrace was the usual sifting through the contents of mental rubbish-bins, Hugo's year-and-a-half of table-tapping would be worth mentioning only as an example of how long the evenings are in exile. But the texts themselves are one of the great masterpieces of the genre and give a unique insight into the workings of a poet's mind.

For several nights, the table behaved like a table. Patience was wearing thin and Delphine was about to leave for Paris. On the evening of 11 September 1853 (almost exactly ten years since Hugo heard the news from Villequier), the table twitched into life and spelt out the words *'fille'* and *'morte'*, then an amazing sequence of letters: l, e, o, p, o, l, d, i, n, e. Hugo addressed the silence:

> 'Are you happy?'
> 'Yes.'
> 'Where are you?'
> 'Light.'
> 'What must we do to be with you?'
> 'Love.'
> 'Can you see the suffering of those who love you?'
> 'Yes.'

Hugo understandably found it hard to be sceptical. Nobody would have used Léopoldine as a practical joke. Even more impressively, the table began to spell out ideas, images, whole lines of verse, even the final title of Les Misérables, which were known only to Hugo, often when he was not even in the room. His greatest anxiety, in fact, was that, having promised himself that he would never 'plagiarize the Unknown', the spirits of the dead might acquire an ethical copyright on some of his best work.

After Léopoldine, the table reverted for a time to its function as a parlour game. The Hugos and Vacquerie were joined by some fellow exiles: the Hungarian, Teleki, a former Republican representative, General Le Flô, and Hugo's hunchbacked side-kick, Hennett de Kesler, an excitable man whose company Hugo enjoyed because Kesler was an atheist who was easily defeated in argument. Hugo flirted with the female spirits, chatted to an incoherent fairy who claimed to be speaking Assyrian, and, from the corridor, roared with laughter at the following exchange with Vacquerie:

> 'Who is there?'
> 'Lope.'

'de Vega?'
'Yes.'
'For whom do you come?'
'For you.'
'Do you have a message for me?'
'Yes.'
'Speak.'
'Your.'
'Continue.'
'Seen.'
'Continue.'
'B p'
'Are you saying Bp?'
'No.'
'Did you say "Seen"?'
'No.'
'Did you say "Your"?'
'No.'
'You do not have a message for me, then?'
'No.'
'Are you Lope de Vega?'
'No.'

Like any form of meditation, table-turning improved with practice. When Hugo placed his hands on the table, almost nothing happened. After a few sessions, Charles was identified as the medium; yet the texts which emerged were pure Victor Hugo. It was as if Charles could be as fluent as he wished if only he let his mind be taken over by his father.[57]

This peculiar form of simultaneous creation soon produced some literary gems. On 12 September, in the darkened drawing-room, with the table tapping furiously, Hugo had a magnificent tête-à-tête which adumbrates the central pillar of his new religion.

The first letters of 'Bonaparte' were spelt out. 'Which one? Le Grand?' 'No.' 'Le Petit?' 'Yes.' It was then revealed that Napoleon III's spirit had left his body sleeping in the Élysée in Paris and had come to tell Victor Hugo that the Empire was due to collapse in two years. What followed was a dramatization of Hugo's mental state when he sat writing his *Châtiments*:

'Did you think I would forgive you?' 'Yes.' 'Why?' 'Out of genius. . . . I am afraid of the dark.' 'Do you see your victims in it?' 'I see light in it.' 'Speak.' 'Help me. I am afraid. The judge is there. The judge is there.' 'Who is the judge?' 'Death.' 'By death, do you mean God?' 'Yes.' 'Why didn't you say God?' 'I cannot see God.' 'Is that because you are evil?' 'Yes.'

The idea of divine and personal retribution was closely tied to the other main theme of the séances: Hugo's fame had spread further than anyone suspected. Dante announced himself with the words 'Caro mio' and congratulated Hugo on his recent poem, 'La Vision de Dante'. When Napoleon I called, he was asked if he had read Napoléon-le-Petit. He had, and deemed it 'an immense truth, a baptism for the traitor'. Chateaubriand also left his island tomb and expressed a more poetic view: 'My bones moved.'

Hospitable as ever, Hugo was entertaining the fictional audience which every writer carries in his mind,[58] although few writers operate in such a vast neighbourhood. The complete guest-list eventually included Cain, Jacob, Moses, Isaiah, Sappho, Socrates, Jesus, Judas, Mohammed, Joan of Arc, Luther, Galileo, Molière, the Marquis de Sade (whose comments have not survived), Mozart, Walter Scott, some angels, Androcles' Lion, Balaam's Ass, a comet, and an inhabitant of Jupiter called Tyatafia. There were also personifications – India, Prayer, Metempsychosis – and entities called the Iron Mask, the Finger of Death, the White Wing and the Shadow of the Tomb. The language was mid-nineteenth-century French, though Walter Scott tapped out a little poem in English (when an Englishman was present), Hannibal spoke in Latin, and Androcles' Lion imparted a few words of lion language. Hugo's dead audience could be used to construct a recipe for his style, a universal Esperanto based on grand, simple concepts that could be understood at any age and in any civilization, terrestrial or not; powerful, repetitive phrases with the volume and solidity of ships setting out on long journeys through time and space.

Hugo is usually assumed to have been almost insanely gullible, and it is true that flattery never activated his critical sense as much as disparagement. The spirits gave him the best reviews he had ever had. Civilization called him 'the great bird that sings of great dawns' and urged him to 'Finish Les Misérables, great man.' All his literary prejudices were confirmed. His *bête noire*, Racine, was made to pay for the sins of French Classicism and had to submit to the Romantic Inquisition:

> VACQUERIE: Do you acknowledge that Shakespeare is a tree and that you are a stone?
> RACINE: Yes.
> VACQUERIE: Do you acknowledge that you were wrong to write constricted plays?
> RACINE: I am embarrassed.
> VACQUERIE: Do you now feel remorse because your reputation is superior to your talent?
> RACINE: My wig is singed.

Having always insisted that his poems were simply an echo of Nature's voice, Hugo was quite ready to believe that the after-life expressed itself in a manner very similar to his own. However, he remained more open-minded about the phenomenon than mischievous biographers have suggested.[59] He weighed up all the usual hypotheses and tried, unsuccessfully, to test the spirits by asking them to supply a cure for rabies or the secret of steering balloons.[60] Even at the peak of his apparent credulity, he suspected some supernatural hanky-panky: 'It may be that a spirit is assuming these names in order to excite our interest.'[61] Hugo's questions, which are often as beautiful as the burblings from the putative Beyond, show a mind which had endless patience with the illogical and the miraculous, a mind which had perhaps acquired a certain imaginative fluidity in conversation during the days and nights it had spent alone with the unhinged brain of brother Eugène.

Hugo's 'faith' was partly a deliberate stratagem: the table evidently required a degree of gullibility to function properly, and there was no sense in wasting such a valuable source of free insights. Sometimes, the spirits came up with excellent ideas for plays and novels. Sometimes, they dictated amazing fragments of the sort that led the Surrealists to claim Hugo as one of their forebears:

> I am the night watchman of the innumerable tomb, emptying his eyes into empty skulls. I am the causer of bad dreams. I am one of the bristling hairs of horror.[62]

The spirits also had some handy tips. 'Death' produced an idea which Hugo later acted on almost to the letter:

> In your testament, space your posthumous works out at ten-yearly intervals, five-yearly intervals. . . . Jesus Christ rose from the dead only once. You can fill your tomb with resurrections. . . . As you died, you would be saying, 'Wake me up in 1920, 1940, 1960, 1980, in the year 2000.'

Compared to the soul-destroying banality of most séance texts, the Marine Terrace corpus (only a quarter of which has survived) is a literary masterpiece, the unconscious product of a naturally dramatic mind. Many of the spirits have such rich personalities that a very rare sub-phenomenon sometimes occurs: one spirit communicating directly with another. (This happens when the Shadow of the Tomb and the Wind of the Sea argue about their relative strength.)

The star of the show is without doubt a convincingly moody Ocean. The Ocean turned up in the spring of 1854 to dictate a piece of music but found itself talking to a group of musical incompetents. When offered a flute, it flew into a rage: 'Your flute with its little holes like the arse of a defecating infant disgusts me. Give me an orchestra and I will give you a song.'[63]

In Hugo's transcription, the Ocean goes on to list its musical needs:

> Give me the falling of rivers into seas, cataracts, waterspouts, the vomitings of the world's enormous breast, that which lions roar, that which elephants trumpet in their trunks . . . what mastodons snort in the entrails of the Earth, and then say to me, 'Here is your orchestra'.

Hugo politely offered a piano and asked the Ocean to dictate a new 'Marseillaise'. But, as the Ocean pointed out, a piano is incapable of expressing the synaesthetic dialogue of sounds, sights and scents. 'The piano I need would not fit into your house. It has but two keys, one white, one black – day and night; the day full of birds, the night full of souls.' Hugo then suggested using Mozart as a go-between: 'Mozart would be better,' agreed the Ocean, 'I myself am unintelligible.' Hugo: 'Could you ask Mozart to come this evening at nine o'clock?'

The Ocean: 'I shall have the message conveyed to him by the Twilight.'

As Jean Gaudon points out, Hugo's habit of appending reassuring conclusions to his most nightmarish poems suggests that he was frightened by his own imagination.[64] The table leg was a pen held by another hand – usually that of an exhausted Charles – which enabled Hugo to explore his visions in psychological safety. The disembodied responses were a hypnotic litany which smoothed the transition to pure, unconscious speech. It is therefore slightly unfair to diagnose a form of psychosis.[65] Everyone is a lunatic in the privacy of their own mind, and, considering the treasures in Hugo's unconscious, his apparent sanity is a far more remarkable phenomenon.

Hugo hoped that the photographs his sons were taking of him would reveal the actual process of discoursing with the Unknown, but the fidgeting furniture did this far more efficiently than glass and collodion. It separated the parts of his mind that normally acted in tandem and made it possible to observe the workings of his brain in extraordinary detail. Two main processes can be distinguished.

The spirits' favourite form of communication consisted of using the humans as secretaries. Brilliant poems were assembled by Androcles' Lion and André Chénier, with some prompting by Hugo. Shakespeare dictated a whole comedy, which a reviewer on the *Times Literary Supplement* once recommended to the BBC drama department,[66] though it sounds more like an early science-fiction film:

> ACT ONE. A starry sky. Serene night. The stars are twinkling. Their twinkling murmurs mysterious words. Suddenly, two of the stars begin to expand in a strange manner and become enormous, as if the audience's opera glasses had been changed into magic telescopes.

Night after night, Shakespeare returned to make minute changes, line by line – fortunately all in French because, as Shakespeare now knew, 'The English language is inferior to French.'

The explicitly religious texts came in a less formal manner. A typical pre-revelation exercise session (from 8 March 1855) went like this: first, a verbal limbering up, with the spirit dictating a sequence of opposites – '*Pur ou impur . . . Passe ou impasse*', etc. Then the same exercise, but with normal logic replaced by what seem to be purely aural connections: '*Immense ou anse. Oeil ou cercueil. . . . Dieu ou feu. Feu ou bleu. Bleu ou euh.*'* Next, with the mind loosened up, a torrent of favourite Bible quotations is fed into it like fuel: 'The last shall be the first', 'A prophet is not without honour, save in his own country', etc.

A passage has now been opened between the rational and the irrational mind, and the spirit begins a high-speed cosmological explanation of everything: 'The true religion is an immense taming of wild beasts'; 'The largest lip of the sky is placed not on the fold but on the jungle, the cave, the desert, the mane, the jawbone, the roar'; 'The kiss of Judas licks the starry darkness'.

The whole process is something like a verbal microcosm of Hugo's life – from sanity to insanity and back again, almost – and it confirms a suspicion that the starting-point of his poems was just as likely to be a word as an interesting idea.

If there is madness in the table-turning Hugo, it lies in his presumption that the publication of these texts would 'found a new religion which will swallow up Christianity just as Christianity swallowed up paganism'[67] – a view wholeheartedly espoused by the founder of Christianity himself on 11 February 1855.[68] The problem was that, according to Hugo's accurate prediction, the texts would be greeted with 'an immense guffaw'.[69] The Shadow of the Tomb shared his caution and advised posthumous publication. But the spirit world also egged him on and gave him the courage of his apparently insane convictions. As he told Delphine de Girardin in a letter which puts the Beyond in its proper place, the spirits had been spouting pure Victor Hugo all along, regurgitating his own eschatology:

> A whole quasi-cosmogonical system, which I have been incubating for the last twenty years and which is already half written down, was confirmed by the table with magnificent developments. We are living in a strange horizon which changes the perspective of exile.[70]

Cheered on by his dead predecessors, Hugo was soon able to produce large-scale revelations on his own. One day in October 1854, he walked to the prehistoric dolmen on the edge of the Rozel

---

* Literally: 'Immense or handle. Eye or coffin. . . . God or fire. Fire or blue. Blue or er.'

peninsula. There, 'the Mouth of Darkness' spoke to him. The resulting poem, 'Ce que Dit la Bouche d'Ombre', took its place with the other 'apocalypses' at the end of *Les Contemplations* in 1856, and though it was generally considered to be incomprehensible, it might almost serve as a key to the symbolism of all Hugo's work.

The central pillar of the system is the belief that the entire universe is sentient. 'Everything is full of souls.' 'Flowers suffer under the scissors and close like eyelids.' But only imponderable things were created by God. Anything possessing weight and substance is the product of original sin. The universe and all the mini-universes within it, from the merest atom to the mightiest nebula, are prison-cells on which crimes are horribly expiated. The worst evil inhabits stones, those 'dungeons of the soul'. Then come plants and animals, from maggots to monkeys, with archangels at the top. Man is an interme-diate, crepuscular creature, suspended between the light of heaven and the murk of the bottomless sewer.

Souls ascend or descend the universal ladder, migrating to other organisms or even planets, according to the weight of sin they have acquired. 'At death, every villain gives birth to the monster of his life.' 'The vile thistle we trample underfoot cries out to the heel, "I am the giant Attila".'

> Thus, a creature comes and goes, roars, shrieks and gnaws;
> A tree is there, its branches bristling in the air;
> A roof-tile falls into the middle of the street,
> Crushed by the cartwheel, destroyed by Winter,
> And under those thick layers of matter and darkness,
> Tree, beast, tile, weight that nothing can lift,
> In those dreadful depths a soul is dreaming!
> What is it doing? – It is thinking of God!

Fortunately, beyond the unknowable reality conveniently labelled 'God', nothing lasts for ever. The universe is slowly converging on its final transfiguration, impelled by the mysterious force of Love: 'Good deeds are the invisible hinges of Heaven's door.' This macrocosmic improvement is reflected in the attempts of individuals to clamber out of the slime of moral delinquency, as in the gradual progress of nations towards the Social-Democratic Republic – though there are exceptions, like Napoleon III: 'crayfish souls forever scuttling backwards into the shadows'.[71] One day, evil will expire, suffering will end, and 'there will be nothing left to say'.

From initial assumption to final punch-line, the system is an unmistakably Hugolian mish-mash of incongruous concepts and philosophical pantomime horses – politicized Buddhism, Christianized karma, fatalism fused with a belief in progress. The sort of religion that might have been constructed by a UNESCO committee. It reflects Hugo's serendipitous appetite for miscellanies, pot-boilers and encyclopedias, as well as his ability to remember everything except the context, to pluck a variety of fruits and arrange them on a tree of his own making. The metaphysical image of the house he would later build on Guernsey.

Apart from talking to the dead, the only religious practices associated with the new religion were a tendency to keep pets and a refusal to allow animals to be slaughtered on the premises.[72] The practical value of the system was its ability to account for the tiniest phenomena of everyday existence. Like most visionaries, Hugo was able to descend to an extraordinary degree of precision. When he went out walking after lunch, two dogs and a cat regularly came up to greet him. Hugo recognized these creatures as 'ex-Decembrists [plotters of the *coup d'état*] transformed into animals who come to beg our forgiveness for their sins'.[73]

It is impossible not to notice that this is a supremely convenient religion for a poet. It turns the universe into an infinite library of living symbols marshalled by a cataloguing system which is all the easier to use for being based on subjective impressions. It allows even the most eccentric images to exist as tiny islands of lunacy in a vast, coherent ocean. It does away with the moral nihilism which Hugo saw as the inevitable result of relativistic, evolutionist systems. It places 'God' far beyond the grasp of human beings, belittles religions as a parasitic growth – the 'lice' on God's scalp – and justifies Hugo's political anti-clericalism. It made it easier to be reconciled to doubt, ignorance and guilt. It confirmed the exiles' hope that the evil régime of Napoleon III was nothing but a primitive organism struggling vainly against the tide of cosmic progress.

The successful elaboration of the new religion may explain why the table-turning came to an abrupt end in the autumn of 1855. Hugo had acquired the art of sowing words in his mind and watching them grow into vast, complex visions. He no longer needed the support of a three-legged pedestal table. But there were other reasons. One of the devotees, a young man called Jules Allix, turned up one day with a loaded pistol, announced that he was God, and had to be sent to the asylum.[74] Unusually for her, Mme Hugo drew the line: she was tired of sharing her house with the Shadow of the Tomb and the Dove of the Ark. A headless ghost had been seen snooping about in Hugo's unpublished papers. The last straw appears to have been 'la Dame Blanche' – the ghost of a woman who had murdered her child in Druid times. The local barber saw her loitering in the vicinity of Marine Terrace.[75] She visited Hugo in his bedroom and became the subject of some unusual love poems – 'A Celle qui est Voilée' and 'Horror'. The depiction of a beautiful, prehistoric ghost playing hard-to-get shows that Hugo's sexual ambitions were as undaunted by the grave as by husbands: 'Emerge from the mist, O charming shade, / Show yourself, O ghost!'

The concrete result of these visitations was that Hugo began to suffer from insomnia. There was only one cure: to return to the battle and remind the civilized world that its moral destiny now revolved around a small rock in the Ocean.

CHAPTER SIXTEEN

'*Hu!* Go!'

(1855–1861)

THE CRIMEAN WAR worked wonders for Anglo-French relations. Napoleon III and Queen Victoria cemented their alliance against Russia with convivial visits to each other's countries. A waxwork Napoleon III stood in Madame Tussaud's, where Victor Hugo had been on display since 1833. The Home Secretary, Palmerston, had been forced out of office in 1851 when, without consulting anybody, he congratulated the French Emperor on his *coup d'état*. He became Prime Minister in February 1855. The little bastion of Jersey was in danger of being crushed by the rapprochement.

Hugo had only once tried to meddle in British affairs or, as he put it, 'to lay down the law in these parts'. A murderer had been condemned to death on the neighbouring island of Guernsey. Hugo published an open letter and sparked off a mass protest against the death penalty. Shortly afterwards, the man was handed over to an incompetent executioner who finished him off by jumping up and down on his shoulders. The next day, Hugo blasted off a letter 'To Lord Palmerston': 'I am but an exile and you are but a minister. I am ash and you are dust. One atom may talk to another.' He described the execution in a gory, forensic manner worthy of Edgar Allan Poe and insinuated that the French had asked Palmerston to proceed with the execution in order to teach the exiles a lesson. Palmerston had tightened his cravat with one hand, said Hugo, and the hangman's noose with the other – a heart-felt allusion to English mores:

To the English, I am *shoking, excentric* and *improper.** I fail to wear my tie in the correct fashion. I go to the local barber ... which makes me look like a *workman* ... I oppose the death penalty, which is not respectable ... I am neither Catholic, Anglican, Lutheran, Calvinist, Jewish, Methodist, Wesleyan nor Mormon and so I must be an atheist. In addition to which I am a Frenchman, which is odious, a republican, which is abominable, an exile, which is repellent, and on the losing side, which is infamous. To cap it all, I am a poet. Hence, not much popularity.[1]

The assumption has always been, first, that Palmerston ignored the Frenchman's puny letter and, second, that Hugo was suffering from paranoia. In fact, unpublished notes in Home Office files show that Palmerston had read and was disturbed by Hugo's account of the execution: 'a man ought not to be four minutes struggling with death'.[2] It led to a revision of the procedure. As for Hugo's paranoia, it is perfectly true that the French had been secretly pressing the British to extradite, muzzle or demoralize the exiles. It was also true – though not known until now – that the exiles had their own man in Paris with his finger in the diplomatic bag, which explains why Hugo seems so preternaturally well informed.[3] Since the epidemic of revolutions in 1848, espionage had become a cottage industry. A refugee called Hubert was found to be an agent of Maupas and only Hugo's plea saved him from the lynch mob. But another spy, a Hungarian exile, was never unmasked: his offer to supply Palmerston with information on his acquaintances 'the demagogues' is preserved in Home Office files.[4]

As the dead piled up in the Crimea, Hugo began to broadcast in earnest, referring to himself in letters and 'declarations' as 'the voice from beyond the grave': '*Exul sicut mortuus.*'[†][5] At the annual Polish banquet in November, he denounced the Anglo-French offensive as a direct result of Louis-Napoleon's *coup d'état*. This time, London responded. The son of Sir Robert Peel ('a small man with a big name') stood up in Parliament, glowing with righteous indignation. How dare these foreigners 'abuse the Sovereigns whom the people

---

* In approximate English in the original.
† 'An exile is like a dead man' (Ovid, *Tristia*).

and the Government of this country have accepted as their allies'! Peel first attacked the Hungarian Kossuth, who was saying similarly inflammatory things about the carnage in the East; then he turned to Hugo, who 'holds forth in the same strain at Jersey':

> This individual had a sort of personal quarrel with the distinguished personage whom the people of France have chosen for their Sovereign, and he told the people of Jersey that our alliance with the French Emperor was a moral degradation to England. What is all this to M. Victor Hugo? If miserable trash of this kind is to be addressed to the English people by foreigners who find a safe asylum in this country, I would appeal to the noble Lord the Home Secretary whether some possible step cannot be taken to put a stop to it.[6]

Charles translated the speech from *The Times* and Hugo reacted by hurling a piece of bread across the table and shouting, 'That's all I needed, the son of Robert Peel calling me an individual.'[7] The piece of bread turned into an 'Avertissement', which Hugo lobbed neatly over the head of Robert Peel at 'M. Bonaparte'. It appeared in several English newspapers, probably thanks to Hugo's connections with the former Chartist leaders, Ernest Jones and George Julian Harney:

> I hereby advise M. Bonaparte that I am fully aware of the strings he is pulling. . . . There is indeed a 'personal quarrel' between us: the old personal quarrel of the judge on the bench and the accused in the dock.

The next missile was more damaging. When Napoleon III visited England in April 1855, the walls of Dover and London were plastered with pamphlets in which Victor Hugo asked the English to imagine Regent Street riddled with machine-gun fire and Hyde Park turned into 'a grave for nocturnal firing-squads'. 'At night,' he told the Emperor, 'I ask God's darkness what it thinks of yours, and I pity you, Monsieur, as I stand before the formidable silence of the Infinite.' It was a beautiful combination of Hugo's rhetoric and the apocalyptic language of international socialism. French agents tore down the posters and a London bookseller advertising Hugo's pamphlet had his windows smashed.[8]

Hugo's text now sounds like the ranting of a street evangelist when set against the polite generalizations of history, but it was perfectly in tune with a certain current of popular opinion. It shared the walls of London with another home-produced placard:

ENGLAND'S DISGRACE.
THE REAL DAY OF HUMILIATION.
LOUIS NAPOLEON,

the murderer, the oath-breaker, the destroyer of the French and Italian Republics, who bribed the soldiers to massacre peaceful citizens on the Boulevards, exiled the best men of France, and paved his way to power with the dead bodies of honest, inoffensive men, women, and children, is coming to England.

Englishmen, do your duty!

If Hugo's actions seem slightly self-destructive, it should be remembered that he was expecting the Empire to crumble at any minute: the three-legged table had predicted it. Every 'chastisement' would be another qualification on his curriculum vitae when the Republic looked for a leader. Thanks to the exiles' secret intelligence, he also knew that, no matter what he did, he was almost certainly on the brink of his third expulsion. Mme Hugo was hoping he would accept an offer of asylum from the Junta in sunny Spain.

*

HUGO'S LAST ENGLISH biographer expresses the common view – or rather, the view that was common 140 years ago among those who stood to profit by the Second Empire: 'His egotism was so intense, his perspective so distorted, his introspection so unrelenting that he sometimes saw the politics of England and France as a personal campaign against him.' This view can usefully be compared to the facts.

In direct response to complaints from the French that the exiles were 'exciting to the assassination of the Emperor', a Sergeant J. Saunders of the Metropolitan Police was ordered to Jersey in March 1855. His expenses were to be paid, not by Scotland Yard but by the Foreign Office Secret Service. Sergeant Saunders wasted no time. He sent back copies of the exiles' newspaper, *L'Homme* – 'in which M. Victor Hugo takes a very prominent part' – underlining all the insults, snooped around for several weeks and did his best to confirm Palmerston's suspicions. He managed to obtain, for a few minutes, a letter in which the exiles named Victor Hugo as the 'centre of action' and listened in on meetings held at the homes of Ribeyrolles* and Hugo:

> They use in their speeches foul language, taking the most dreadful oaths, issuing threats against all the Kings and Queens, down with the Aristocracy and all persons in opposition to them.[9]

Anyone who had supported the Government of Napoleon III should be 'guillotined' and the Empress was 'worse than a prostitute'. Nuances were obviously unimportant – for example, the fact that Hugo was a pacifist and made it a point of honour never to insult a woman, even if she was the wife of Napoleon III.

The new official attitude to Victor Hugo either began to trickle down to the people of Jersey or, far more likely, undercover agents set to work. Two incidents related by Hugo have the strong smell of agents provocateurs:

> This morning, 11 June 1855, I found these words written in chalk on my door:

> *Hugo is a bad man*

> I ordered them not to be erased.[10]

> *Hugo, to Paul Meurice, 25 June 1855*: Yesterday, during a walk to the Rock of the Exiles, a large stone suddenly landed on my head; when I got up my face was all bloody; I plunged the wound into sea water, walked for two leagues and this morning I am fine. . . . I think it was just children larking about, but the exiles are determined to believe it was an ambush. I showed the stone to the urchins who play on the dyke and said, 'Next time, use smaller stones.' In the evening the exiles came en masse to find out how I was and St Helier was buzzing with the news.[11]

* Charles Ribeyrolles, member of Parliament, banished in 1851, chief editor of *L'Homme*, died in Brazil in 1860. Hugo was asked to supply his epitaph. A quotation from Hugo's accompanying letter 'To Brazil' was placed above the entrance of the National Historical Museum in Rio de Janeiro.[12]

Back in Whitehall, Sergeant Saunders's snippets were scoured by Palmerston for an excuse to get rid of the international embarrassment known as Victor Hugo. Palmerston had already hatched the idea of offering the refugees free tickets to New York. On 14 August 1855 – eight weeks *before* the incident which supposedly 'forced' the British Government to expel the refugees – the free passage idea still seemed the best option:

> I think these French either ought to be sent away from the Channel Islands where they are doing far more mischief to France and to England than they could accomplish in London. The best way would be to send them off gradually. The most violent first, the rest by instalments afterwards.[13]

On 22 September 1855, the perfect excuse presented itself. Some French exiles in London, led by the republican Félix Pyat, had published a *Lettre à la Reine d'Angleterre*, comparable in spirit to the Reagan–Thatcher '*Gone With the Wind*' poster of the 1980s. There were some feeble puns about the Orders of the Bath and the Garter (recently bestowed on Napoleon III) and crude hints that Queen Victoria was allowing grimy foreign potentates to paw her intimate parts.

In London, the letter passed almost unnoticed. Eighteen days later on Jersey, when it was reprinted in *L'Homme*, a mob threatened to burn down the newspaper offices and string up the editors. Hugo and some other exiles spent three days barricaded inside their homes. Ribeyrolles and two of his colleagues were given notice by Governor General Love to leave the island. Hugo thought the letter crass and clumsy, but he showed his solidarity by having a 'Déclaration' posted about the island on 17 October 1855, written by himself and signed by thirty-four other exiles: 'The *coup d'état* has just made its entrance into English freedom . . . Another step and England will be an annex of the French Empire.' He concluded, 'And now banish us!', which they promptly did, using an old edict originally directed against the Puritans.

Home Office correspondence relating to the Pyat incident fully justifies Hugo's egocentric view of events. He himself is repeatedly identified in dispatches as the arch troublemaker. He, his two sons and three other exiles are described as 'the most obnoxious'; the final 'List of Refugees Expelled from Jersey' begins with his name, and a tick beside his name marks him out as one of 'the most violent and mischievous'.[14] Writing to the new Home Secretary, Sir George Grey, Lord Palmerston summed up the situation with his usual firm bat: 'The question now is whether these Islands belong to us or to Victor Hugo and Co.' (23 October 1855).[15]

Hugo's *'expieulcheune'* (his transliteration of the English) was – as he himself always insisted – the culmination of an undercover operation directly inspired by French diplomacy.[16] One of the most revealing items in the Home Office files is a poster sent to London by Sergeant Saunders, 'just published and posted about Jersey': 'To the British Residents in Jersey and all not conversant with the French language, translation of the insulting letter addressed to the Queen of England'. The offending passages were conveniently italicized, capitalized and sprinkled with exclamation marks, corresponding closely to Saunders's underlinings in the copy of *L'Homme* which he had previously sent to London:

> *You have sacrificed ALL! – the Queen's dignity! – the woman's delicacy! – the aristocrat's pride! – the English woman's feelings! – the rank! – the kingly race! – the sex! – ALL – EVEN CHASTITY! – for the love of that ally!*[17]

The lynch mob can safely be said to have lacked spontaneity. The protest meeting itself had been called by a poster which was printed by a Jersey newspaper, *L'Impartial*. A few months after the expulsion, the editor of *L'Impartial* received a large sum of money from the Ministry of the Interior in Paris for 'upholding French interests on Jersey with notable vigour and proficiency'.[18]

*

ON 27 OCTOBER 1855, the local Constable* and two officials knocked on the door of 3 Marine Terrace and notified Hugo and his sons of their expulsion. They were given a week to pack their bags. Hugo assured the Constable that he had no desire to remain in 'a land which has lost its honour'.

---

* In the Channel Islands, roughly equivalent to a mayor.

Charles Hugo wrote an account of the interview, showing the snivelling officials embarrassed by their shameful mission, and a defiant, righteous Hugo. Governor Love (a name which delighted Hugo) sent a nervous note to Whitehall: Victor Hugo is 'threatening to hand the decree to posterity'.[19] The *Morning Advertiser* and the *Daily News* published translations of Charles's account, while *The Times*, which had changed its tune since 1851, pontificated about 'poets, philosophers and legislators' who soil the haven so generously offered by the British: 'they must expect that any claims which their previous career may have given them to the respect and forbearance of the world must be at once forgotten.'[20]

At dawn on 31 October, while most of the exiles were leaving for London, Hugo and François-Victor boarded the ship for Guernsey, two and a half hours to the north. (Like Jersey, Guernsey had retained a degree of independence.) It was pouring with rain and a strong wind was blowing. The ship would have to drop anchor off Guernsey and a trunk containing approximately one-fifth of Hugo's complete works would be lowered into a small rowing-boat and entrusted to the waves. Governor Love described the departure in a letter to the Home Office. He was anxious to project an image of patriotic unanimity. As the exiles boarded, 'they called out, "*Vive la République Universelle et Sociale*", which was answered by some of the bystanders with "Down with the Refugees", "Down with the bloody Reds"'.[21]

The idea that Hugo had been insufficiently grateful to his hosts has unfortunately proved irresistible and is now more widely accepted than it was in the mid-nineteenth century. It gives a false impression of prevailing attitudes in the United Kingdom and reflects a much more recent view of political asylum. Several pillars of Jersey society signed a petition and published pamphlets against the expulsion.[22] On the mainland, protest meetings were held in London, Newcastle, Paisley and Glasgow. The incident became known as 'the Jersey *coup d'état*'. The idea that Britain had bowed to French pressure was deeply shocking. Several newspapers predicted the fall of Palmerston's Government.

Hugo reacted in two ways. He was enraged and humiliated to be kicked off the island; but he was also thrilled to be banished by his third country. No one could possibly doubt the sincerity of his position.

A few years later, he noticed that his unofficial mandate from the oppressed peoples of the world was mystically inscribed in the two syllables of his name. Merely to say the name Hugo was to cheer him on his way: 'Wherever I go on Earth, I hear ... the *Hu!** of France and the *Go!* of England.'[23]

*

A SILENT CROWD removed its hats as Hugo disembarked at St Peter Port, capital of Guernsey. There was no trace of animosity. Anyone spurned by Jersey was likely to be welcomed by its smaller neighbour[24] – a tradition of mild antagonism which survives to this day.

Hugo booked into the Hôtel de l'Europe and spent a few days playing billiards with François-Victor. He was delighted to hear French again, the picturesque Old Norman French of the Channel Islands: 'Even in the rain and mist, the arrival at Guernsey is splendid. It is a real old Norman port, hardly anglicized at all. . . . The local authorities think of us as robbers,' he exaggerated, 'but buckets of water cannot extinguish craters.'[25]

When the rest of the family arrived with the luggage, Hugo rented a house in the elegant quarter of Hauteville at 20 Hauteville Street, which now belongs to the Quakers. He bought a letter scales and a telescope and wrote to Hetzel: 'I live in the upper town in a seagull's nest. From my window I can see the whole archipelago: France, whence I was banished, and Jersey, whence I was expelled.' In May 1856, he moved up the road to number 38 – a dull, dignified-looking, three-storey house with fourteen Georgian windows looking on to the street and a garden at the back commanding a view of the coast. Adopting the English custom of naming houses, Hugo called his 'Liberty House', later changing it to 'Hauteville House', perhaps after seeing the name on another building.[26] The *Gazette de Guernesey* announced the purchase as good news: 'Proof that the great poet is happy in our midst and intends to remain in Guernsey.'

Built in 1800 by 'an English pirate', Hauteville House had stood

* Gee up!

empty for the last nine years: its previous occupant, a vicar, had been chased out by a ghost.[27] Since then, several other ghosts had moved in. Hugo would soon be having silent conversations in bed with spirits who sang in sweet voices or tapped on the walls in what he assumed to be a kind of Morse code. But after Marine Terrace, this was quite normal. By 1862, when Hugo had transformed the house into the Aladdin's cave that can be seen today, the ghosts were probably more at home in it than the human beings.

The move to Guernsey marked what Hugo felt would be the final stage of his life. It seemed to fit a pattern, reminiscent of the life of a saint: precocious brilliance, worldly success and excess, political dominion followed by wilderness and exile, power in the spirit world, and then the dissemination of the message. This was the patriarchal Hugo who began to imprint himself on the French mind through the photographs which filtered into France. The heavy-jowled troglodyte of Jersey gave way to the white-bearded sea-captain, his sullen mouth concealed by a thicket of wiry hair; a moustache which remained black, and two small, dark eyes, each harbouring its own thoughts – interpreted variously as lust, avarice, envy and malice, or as the indomitable spirit of exiled democracy. The emergence of the beard would coincide with this description by Hugo of 'the monstrous sages of earlier times':

> They lived alone in horrid places;
> And while, deep in ecstasy, they said, 'God!
> God! God! God!', wild-feathered birds
> Made nests in the magi's hair.[28]

Hugo claimed that he grew a beard to protect his chest from the cold, but it allowed a powerful confusion to germinate in the collective unconscious. In 1866, someone wrote to tell him that a fifteen-year-old boy had asked on his death-bed to be buried with a photograph of Victor Hugo: 'for him you were almost a God'.[29]

At home, the god appeared as a clan chieftain, the head of a *ménage à plusieurs*. There were the maids who slept on either side of his bedroom – apparently because the master sometimes suffered 'fits of breathlessness' during the night (probably an effect rather than a cause of the sleeping arrangements). There was the elegantly dilapidated lady known to locals as Mme la Comtesse – Juliette, who moved into a house called La Fallue, further up the street. A dozen exiles had followed Hugo to Guernsey: some occasionally occupied the emergency bedroom which he had always set aside in all his houses and which he called 'The Raft of the Medusa'. Finally, there was the family, devastated to see him settling in so permanently.

Mme Hugo busied herself with the biography which would appear in 1863 and which is also an obituary to her own best years in Paris. The children, 'Charlot, Toto and Dédé', were described by their father in a phrase which soars far above any recognizable reality as 'great, proud souls. They accept their solitude and exile with gay, severe serenity.'[30]

Charles, still 'the indefatigable idler', was straining at the leash: his elegance wasted in the Channel Islands, he began to escape to the Continent for increasingly long holidays. François-Victor was the other half of the antithesis, doggedly translating Shakespeare and dealing with all the English correspondence in a style which chan- nelled the thoughts of Victor Hugo through a combination of Elizabethan and Victorian English.[31]

While the children watched the years evaporate, the rhythm of Hugo's life changed completely. He saw himself on the edge of a vast plain extending far beyond his own death and began to walk across it in huge strides. Apart from Balzac, no nineteenth-century writer produced so many masterpieces in such a short period. Yet there is also a tremendous passivity about the Guernsey Hugo: 'Exile has not only detached me from France, it has almost detached me from the Earth.' After writing all morning, he walked to Fermain Bay to find his favourite rock, 'a sort of natural armchair'[32] in which he sat like an acquiescent King Canute, watching the tide rise towards him.

The best self-portrait of Hugo can be found in the affectionate evocation of the Channel Islands which outgrew its original role as a preface to *Les Travailleurs de la Mer*. The Second Empire showed no sign of weakness, the dirty Paris of his youth was being swept away by Baron Haussmann, he now had 'fewer friends on earth than underneath',[33] and in February 1855 brother Abel had passed on to the realm of 'truth and light' where he would now realize that Victor had been right to devote himself to 'progress'.[34] On the other side of despair, Hugo discovered a kind of peace which, despite the daily twelve-hour traffic jam, can still be found on Guernsey:

> Rhododendrons among the potatoes, seaweed spread out on the grass all over the place ... The gloomy Celtic enigma strewn about in its various forms: standing stones, peulvens, long stones and fairy stones, cromlechs and dolmens ...
>
> Fertile, rich, heavy soil. No better grazing land anywhere. The wheat is famous, the cows renowned. . . .
>
> Gracious on one side, Guernsey is dreadful on the other. The west is ravaged, exposed to the wind of the open sea ...
>
> The rocks of the coast constantly try to fool you ... There are enormous stone frogs which stick out of the water, probably in order to breathe; giant nuns go scurrying across the horizon ... Move closer; nothing is there. Stones are known to perform such vanishing tricks ... Creation retains something of the anguish of chaos. Splendours bear scars.[35]

This was the island universe Hugo was to inhabit for the next fifteen years: 'the rock of hospitality and freedom, that corner of the old Norman land where live the noble little people of the sea, the isle of Guernsey, stern and gentle, my present refuge, my probable tomb.'

*

THE FIRST CONCERN of the happy castaway was to publish the poems which had been piling up in his trunks since *Les Rayons et les Ombres* in 1840. Bills were also piling up and, pending an injection of cash, 'sordid economy' was the order of the day. Touching the capital, which was salted away in the Belgian National Bank and British consols (Government securities), was unthinkable. Hugo took a long-term view of investments, as he did of his reputation and, for that matter, of everything else: fluctuations in the market, like the sins of benighted souls, concealed an overall upward trend.

The two volumes of *Les Contemplations* were set to appear in Brussels and Paris on the same day in a print-run of 5500 copies – a huge number for a book of poems, especially one which ran to over 11,000 lines. Hugo's loyal amanuensis in Paris, Paul Meurice (now a successful playwright), had obtained permission for the book to be published in France by promising the Directeur de la Sûreté Générale that it was a work of 'pure poetry'. This meant that nothing nasty was said in it about the Second Empire – a reminder that the aesthetic 'purity' of late Romantic French verse owes a large debt to political repression.

Held in the grip of Hugo's tyrannical courtesy, Paul Meurice and Hugo's other helper, Noël Parfait (once a ghostwriter for Dumas and Gautier) fought his battles with typesetters: '*lis*' (lily) should be spelt '*lys*' because the *y* represented the flower and its stem, just as '*trône*' should be spelt '*thrône*' because the *h* gave a side view of the object itself;[36] and the announcement of the long poem, *Dieu*, on the back cover of *Les Contemplations* should use founts of different size because 'GOD, BY VICTOR HUGO' might look 'strange'. Without telling Vacquerie, Hugo asked Meurice to delay the publication of Vacquerie's collected essays, in case they somehow detracted from *Les Contemplations*.[37] As Adèle II had recently noted in her diary: 'Victor Hugo says that for him the family does not exist when the fatherland is at stake.'[38]

On the morning of 23 April 1856, the Paris bookshops of Pagnerre and Michel Lévy were inundated with excited customers, many of whom would never normally have looked at a book of poems. Three days later, very little remained of the first edition. Michel Lévy rushed to the home of Paul Meurice and offered 3000 francs for the second edition. There was already talk of a third. It was Hugo's biggest commercial success as a poet, the last time that the publication of some poetry was a major public event, and, thus, a moral blow to Napoleon III more lasting and effective in its way than *Napoléon-le-Petit* and *Châtiments* combined.

Just when everyone was talking about the unsentimental excesses of '*réalisme*',[39] Victor Hugo had heaved into the stagnant pond of French verse a huge, Romantic compendium of 158 previously unpublished poems, many of which were instant classics. Almost two-thirds had been written since the *coup d'état*, but Hugo had altered most of the dates to suggest a steady flow of masterpieces from 1830 to 1856 and to fit the poems into a structure. The two volumes – *Autrefois* and *Aujourd'hui* – were 'separated by an abyss': a page near the beginning of the second volume was blank except for the date of Léopoldine's death. Morbid poems composed before the drowning were postdated, and jolly poems composed shortly afterwards were aged by several years. A poem on the supposed repudiation of his royalist roots, 'Écrit en 1846', had actually been written in 1854, just as a later poem, 'Écrit en 1827', was written in 1859.[40] A series recalling blissful days with Juliette gave the year only as '18..' – perhaps to prevent Adèle from reconstructing the true sequence of betrayals or, more likely, to symbolize the timelessness of the affair: 'The flame that cannot falter / And the flower that cannot die!'

The popular favourites were the cameos of Hugo's bird-like children frolicking in summer gardens and the heart-rending elegies to Léopoldine, especially 'À Villequier' and 'Demain, dès l'aube . . .'. Elizabeth Browning was so moved that she wrote a long letter to Napoleon III asking him to forgive the man 'who expiates rash phrases and unjustifiable statements in exile': 'What touches you is, that no historian of the age should have to write hereafter, "while Napoleon III reigned, Victor Hugo lived in exile".'[41]

The whole collection traced a slow march towards the grave, but the real chronology shows a continual process of rejuvenation. In exile, Hugo had become the rebellious schoolboy he never was in his youth. He recounted his career as the Romantic vandal in such gorgeously pugnacious poems ('Réponse à un Acte d'Accusation', 'À Propos d'Horace') that the history of French literature has never quite regained its footing in reality:

> I declared all words equal, free and of age . . .
> I removed from the neck of the stupefied dog
> Its collar of epithets . . .
> I violated the steaming corpse of verse.

Hugo's *post facto* appropriation of every significant change in French poetry and theatre since the 1820s still provides a cornerstone of many general guides to nineteenth-century French literature, so that evolutions appear as revolutions, and Hugo's contemporaries – Vigny, Dumas, Musset and the play-writing Balzac – have constantly to be rediscovered and given credit for their reforms.

Hugo was taking full advantage of longevity to set the first half of his life in order, but without the plangent mock-humility of most retrospectives. *Les Contemplations* marks the beginning of his influence on a fourth generation of poets, which explains why the book appears to have been written by someone who lived simultaneously in both halves of the century: the *états d'âme* ('soulscapes') of Mallarmé and Verlaine, symbols which seem to detach themselves from whatever they might have symbolized; the cultivation of what Baudelaire was alone in recognizing as deliberate obscurity and an unFrench avoidance of the *mot juste*;[42] the cosmic visions which impressed Rimbaud[43] and revitalized the creaking tradition of astronomical poetry which, before Hugo's colliding galaxies and planets torn asunder by rogue comets, had celebrated the spectacle of a Newtonian universe on its eternal best behaviour.

Professional critics were as tepid as it is possible to be when faced with a literary treasure. Lamartine and Sainte-Beuve said nothing. One of the commonest complaints was that Hugo used the same words over and over again. It was a criticism he had made no effort to avoid: '*Insondable* [unfathomable] is like *infini*, *absolu*, *éternel*, *inconnu*, *ineffable*,' he told Meurice, 'a word which has no equivalent and which inevitably, therefore, recurs frequently. Some words are like God in the depths of the language.'[44] An old enemy, Gustave Planche, boasted of having failed to understand a single word of Hugo's 'apocalypse'. Others claimed to be disgusted by the fact that Hugo had set poems about his daughter alongside frisky celebrations of his erotic exploits. Ulric Guttinguer found the idea so impossibly offensive that he read 'Elle était déchaussée, elle était décoiffée . . .'* as an allegory of the poet's 'union' with democracy.[45] Reviewers less concerned with their own moral rating might usefully have explored the religious aura of incest which is no more shocking in *Les Contemplations* than it is in some mythologies.

In the last thirty years, a more objective, archeological view has prevailed, as Hugo knew it would.[46] He called the book his 'Great Pyramid', referring to the tomb of Cheops and, probably, to the theory that the pyramid was astronomically aligned: 'At a certain sacred moment of the year, follow the line of Cheops towards the zenith and you will be stupefied to find yourself at the star of the

---

* 'She was wearing no shoes, her hair was untied . . .'

Dragon.'[47] Similarly, the poems of *Les Contemplations*, disposed around the sarcophagus of the girl-goddess, Léopoldine, open on to the final revelation, 'Ce que Dit la Bouche d'Ombre'. As James Patty has shown, the title itself alludes, by the root of '*contempler*', to the practice of watching the *templum*, the sacred space, for auguries.[48] The point of Hugo's careful redating was not to pull the wool over his readers' eyes (otherwise, why preserve the original dated manuscripts and make the deception so obvious?),[49] but to show his own life as a miniature model of human life. The point was hammered home in a peremptory preface: 'When I talk to you about myself, I am talking to you about you. How can you fail to see that? Fool, who think that I am not you!'

Hugo's fragmented epic was a partial realization of his plan to write a book entitled '*Nothing*, by Nobody',[50] an attempt to re-create the 'diary of a soul' which, as in any human being, was not ruled into a tyrannical grid of little boxes, each with its own name and number. Even with their fictitious dates, the poems are not set out in chronological order. Hugo's calendar was a snakes-and-ladders board of memories and premonitions, a deconstruction of historical time and a reconstruction of a mythical point of view, based on the central 'crucifixion' of the father and the daughter's descent into the underworld.

Esoteric as it may seem, this was certainly a cause of the popular success of *Les Contemplations*. Though he was increasingly out of touch with developments in Parisian literature, dismissed the yuppies of the Second Empire as 'senile adolescents',[51] read newspapers several months old and lived among the remnants of extinct religions, Hugo was now more than ever 'the voice of his century', the secular priest of a nation which had also been 'exiled' and was suffering in a world of science and industry, where 'progress gives a soul to the machine and takes it from man!'[52] Like the liturgy of private anniversaries which gave his affair with Juliette Drouet its surprising durability, *Les Contemplations* was a sign that the alienated individuals of modern society could reconstruct from the fragments of their lives the old religious calendar[53] – although, of course, they would need a poet like Victor Hugo to show them how to do it.

Hugo celebrated the unexpected success of *Les Contemplations* by buying Hauteville House with the proceeds. He added the word 'landlord' to his English vocabulary and felt safe for the first time since 1848. If they tried to expel him again, 'decent, prudish Albion' would be 'forced to trample an *at home* [*sic*] underfoot, the famous Englishman's castle'.

*

WHILE HUGO SAT AT the top of his castle, ringing for the invisible servants who came as soon as they were called (his description of the process of writing),[54] a plot had been hatched that threatened to deal a fatal blow to his contentment, and even to his interpretation of the past.

Les Contemplations showed that Hugo had remained on excellent terms with his dead daughter; but the living daughter was a closed book. The girl who had stunned Balzac with her dark beauty had grown long in the face; stale and two-dimensional, filling her time with little fads and habits. She listened to the sea and then wrote melancholy, wordless songs at the piano which were acclaimed at a public concert in St Peter Port; the composer Ambroise Thomas thought they should be published.[55] Hugo seems to have found Adèle's piano-playing more distracting than the sawing and hammering of the carpenters.

Having nothing else to do, Adèle had become obsessed with a young English lieutenant-colonel, Albert Pinson, who had been stationed briefly on Jersey. His regiment had since left for Ireland. The notes in Adèle's diary, most of which is a slavish record of Hugo's table-talk, betray a mild, intermittent form of dysgraphia (inconsistent errors and inverted syllables) which may indicate brain damage. More worryingly, they reveal her father's approach to relationships: 'You are an Englishman who loves a Frenchwoman' – she wrote to Pinson as if he were in the room – 'a royalist who loves a republican, a fair-haired man who loves a brunette, a man of the past who loves a woman of the future, a man of the material world who loves a woman of the ideal. . . . I love you as the sculptor loves the clay.'[56]

The spirit of Victor Hugo and the body of a twenty-six-year-old, nineteenth-century woman was a disastrous combination. Auguste Vacquerie had been Adèle's unofficial fiancé since the death of

Léopoldine. He was so frustrated by her glassy exterior that on one occasion he kicked her in the bottom and observed that he was unhappier than Pygmalion, who 'only had to animate a statue'.[57] All this was recorded in her diary in a strangely erotic, passionless style. Her feelings manifested themselves as fevers, delirium, constipation, gastro-enteritis and, probably, anorexia: Vacquerie complained that her arms looked like 'spindles'. The doctor advised her to take up billiards and to overcome her antipathy to the men's tobacco smoke, 'which is far from unhealthy'.[58]

Forty years before, Mme Hugo had seen Eugène stagnate under the shadow of her husband. Towards the end of 1856, she began to beg his permission to take Adèle to London or even back to Paris: 'A little garden and some needlework are not enough to satisfy a twenty-six-year-old girl.' To Hugo, this would have been a propaganda coup for Napoleon III, a sign that the Island Empire was crumbling from within. (Sightings of spurious Hugos in the capital were occasionally reported in pro-Empire newspapers.) Since he considered conversations to be public even if no guests were there, she conducted her campaign by internal mail:

> You said this morning at breakfast that your daughter *loves no one but herself*. I did not want to argue because our children were there and because it was not a good thing to say. Adèle has given you her youth without complaint and without asking for gratitude, and you find her selfish. . . . She may indeed have grown cold and somewhat starchy in appearance, but when she is deprived of emotional happiness, do we have the right to ask her to be like other young women?[59]

Hugo's authoritarian rule was not unusual for the time. He thought of himself as a good father. Despite his aversion to 'selected works',[60] he had recently agreed to allow Hetzel to publish *Les Enfants. Le Livre des Mères* – a 'safe' anthology of his poems on children which helped to establish the image of Victor Hugo the model father and had a certain influence on parental behaviour. Hugo himself was convinced by this image and there is nothing extraordinary in his ignorance of Adèle's predicament. The giant had to be protected from falls. The knowledge that the slightest insubordination would be a crushing blow to him had been enough to keep him in the dark. When

François-Victor called him 'a gentle tyrant', Hugo confided pitifully in his diary: '*Un tyran doux*. – Alas! How sad. My poor Toto whom I love so much, why that painful word?'⁶¹

His wife's observations amazed him. If the family were tired of living on Guernsey, it must be because they didn't love him. He had worked hard to protect his children from poverty; all he asked for in exchange was loyalty. And when he wrote in his account book – 'I want to help my wife settle her debts. She owes 1260. I shall cancel the 5 December bill and the monthly repayments of 50 francs' – there was no trace of bashfulness at the fact that these 'debts' were the result of his underestimating the housekeeping costs: 'I shall make her a gift of 200 francs. . . . She can pay me back at 20 francs a month.'⁶²

Mme Hugo persisted, sugaring her complaints with flattery, though she was unable to resist a tart allusion to the woman down the road:

> I quite understand that, with your fame, your mission and your personality, you should choose a rock which places you in such an admirable setting. I can also see that your family, which, without you, would be nothing, should sacrifice itself not only to your honour but also to your image. I am your wife and am simply doing my duty. Exile may have been a heavy burden for our sons, but it has turned out so well for them that I feel they have profited by it. But for Adèle, everything is detrimental. . . . A man might have a mistress who gave him the best years of her life and if that man were honourable he would compensate her for it. How could one refuse a daughter what one does not refuse a mistress?⁶³

Perhaps it was the threat to borrow money that finally convinced him. On 18 January 1858, Adèle and her mother were allowed to leave for a four-month holiday. Hugo recorded the event with the usual details. (Like all obsessive diary writers, he knew that tiny facts might eventually form interesting chains of coincidence.)

> My wife and daughter left for Paris at twenty past nine this morning on the mail steamer, the *Commander Babot*. They will go via Southampton and Le Havre.
> I am sad.

*

SAD, BUT NOT LONELY. From La Fallue, Juliette could see the '*torchon radieux*' ('shining rag') which Hugo tied to the railings every morning to show that he was up.[64] Passers-by in the street below sometimes spotted a robust body standing naked in a tub of water on the roof, rubbing itself down with massage gloves and showing itself to his neighbour like the morning sun.[65] When the Adèles' desertion turned into an annual holiday, Hugo began to take his sons to eat twice a week at Mme Drouet's house, where they were amazed to find a museum of Victor Hugo relics and a charming, elderly woman who adored them. It had taken Hugo twenty-seven years to acknowledge a situation which almost everyone else had long since accepted.

At Hauteville House, the missing family members were replaced by maids, workers, and a growing population of animals: two ducks, some goldfish and a bird-table; Vacquerie's cat, Mouche (daughter of the Conciergerie cat, Grise), a house dog, Chougna (Hungarian for 'ugly'), and Charles's dog, Lux, presumably named after the closing poem of *Châtiments*, which is a hymn to universal peace: Hugo's accounts show two sums of money paid to passers-by who lost pieces of clothing to Lux. His own dog, Ponto, had appeared in *Les Contemplations* as the thinker's silent conversation partner, but Ponto had since passed on to his next reincarnation and been replaced by a mongrel greyhound called Sénat ('Senate'). Hugo had a rhyme engraved on a medallion and attached it to the dog's collar:

> I wish that someone would take me home.
> Profession: dog. Master: Hugo. Name: Sénat.

The thought of an unpublished Victor Hugo couplet running about on a dog's neck was too much for some tourists and Sénat was regularly robbed in the street.[66]

It is tempting to see Hugo's Franciscan familiarity with the animal kingdom as a natural stage in his growing appeal to the uneducated. On a picnic one day, he was reading aloud from a book when a cow ambled over, leaned its head on the fence and began to listen. When the book was handed to Hugo's friend, Kesler, the cow lost interest and returned only when Hugo started reading again.[67]

Socializing with the human natives took two forms. Six days a week for the best part of seven years (1856–62), carpenters demolished partitions, turned door panels into windows, installed secret cupboards and, following Hugo's sketches, cobbled together the oak beams and coffers which he and Juliette had been rooting out in antique shops or salvaging from old barns and cowsheds. Hugo engraved them with mysterious Latin slogans using a red-hot poker.[68] He complained about the turmoil: 'Tortoises building the house of a bird'. But there was obviously something inspiring about the sights and sounds of manual labour and the mere fact of being able to refashion a whole building – the first he had owned – even if it did mean paying a feudal tithe of two capons a year to Queen Victoria.

His biggest contribution to the local economy however was the extra work he gave to a succession of cooks and chambermaids.

Henri Guillemin was the first to decipher the coded notes in Hugo's account books in 1954. They were written in a mixture of French, English, Latin and Spanish (or French constructions grafted on to half-remembered Spanish), abbreviated and encoded with puns and conundrums: 'Question délicate. Rhinocéros' refers to a servant called Catherine. The cry of the crucified Christ, 'Eli Sabactani', is a cipher for Elisa. References to 'vaults', 'ravines', 'hollows' and 'forests' are self-explanatory and should send even the most literal-minded critic back to Hugo's nature poetry with a fresh eye. Notes like 'Cloche, 1 fr.' are a reminder of the symbolic bell-ringing scene in Notre-Dame de Paris. Whereas other housekeeping items are missing from Hugo's accounts, there is an extraordinary proliferation of expensive 'toothbrushes', which, according to one unfortunately discreet editor, requires no comment.

These almost childishly mysterious notations are interspersed with trivial daily expenses, the commonest of which is 'sec[ours]' ('alms') – '9 October 1856. To the child who had fallen in the mud and was crying: 0.50' – or, more often, to distressed French exiles: a total of 730 francs in 1856, or £2200 today, which is far more than Hugo is generally supposed to have doled out. Prying eyes would not therefore have been surprised to notice several small sums given to 'pros.', though the occasional addition of a t shows that this was not always an abbreviation of 'proscrits' ('exiles').

Apart from brief encounters at Fermain Bay with market girls or prostitutes – sometimes more than one at a time – Hugo conducted his business high up on the third floor of Hauteville House which, before 1862, consisted mainly of his bedroom, the emergency 'Raft of the Medusa' room, a narrow, low-ceilinged library and the servants' attic. This cosy arrangement sometimes turned his eyrie into the set of a bedroom farce: '10 August 1860: S.-L. [= a maid called Coelina]. Situation. Leaving by one door while someone enters by another' – though this could conceivably be one of Hugo's oblique allusions to complicated sexual acts.

In the period in question, Hugo's records and the apparent absence of venereal disease suggest that he confined himself to touching and seeing. He liked to picture himself as Virgil or Horace, savouring the down-to-earth charms of a ruddy servant-girl, or, in a more religious mood, as Mohammed – described in the poem 'L'An Neuf de l'Hégire' (16 January 1858):

> He meditated at length before the holy pillar;
> From time to time, he had a woman undressed
> And looked at her; then he contemplated the cloud,
> And said, 'Beauty on Earth, daylight in Heaven'.

These surreptitious affairs were less sordid and superficial than is usually implied. In contrast to other sex-diaries of the time, most of the women are not anonymous. All were poor, and a surprising number are recorded as having died or gone mad – which offers an interesting alternative view of the 'island paradise' of Guernsey. Some were clearly devoted to Hugo. A seamstress called Mary Ann Green asked on her death-bed to have her grave chosen by M. Hugo and threatened to come back and haunt her brother if he failed to comply with her request.[69] The notes attached to the sums of money – for coal, clothes, food, medicine and the upkeep of babies – show these women as the happier sisters of the unmarried mothers in *Les Misérables*. Sometimes Hugo even named them after characters in the novel.

From a purely material point of view, the outstanding feature is Hugo's appetite. Early in 1859, he was able to draw up a list of fifteen 'servants we have had since August 1852' – probably with some ambiguity in the pronoun and verb since he added a short second column headed 'others'.

This hobby has certainly been emphasized to the detriment of other related activities like swimming, eating and writing, and is now one of the best known aspects of his life. But a self-styled Christ figure should perhaps expect to be made a representative figure and asked to carry the can for the commonest sins of his society. Even Sainte-Beuve was on intimate terms with his cook. Hugo's activities differ from those of his contemporaries more in quantity than in substance. What they reveal about Hugo himself is his constant hunger for visual stimulation, the passionate enjoyment of dangerous secrets, so redolent of his childhood, perhaps too his collector's instinct and his penchant for enumeration, also evident in his work. These women, none of whom appear to have attempted blackmail, were being asked to extend their spring-cleaning to the master's brain, to serve as reminders of the physical world. They were, in short, like theatre-goers, novel-readers, voters, ghosts, the Ocean, the cow in the field and the dog at the dinner-table, members of his audience; and Hugo was a writer who liked to test his influence at regular intervals.

*

FORNICATING AND INTERIOR DECORATING were just two aspects of a creative binge, most of which ended up on paper. The average size of Hugo's works had expanded with the horizon and, ironically, the period in which he produced his most popular and widely read books was also the period of epic, unfinished, and, often, unread poems – poems which represent his unsociable self, his need for solitude and the need to conquer his fear of it. But the two great monsters – *La Fin de Satan* and *Dieu* – came with the tide of poetry that also threw up *La Légende des Siècles*: Hugo's greatest victory over what his readers were beginning to see as a gigantic, incorrigible misunderstanding of his own genius.

La Fin de Satan (1854–62) began with the 10,000-year-long fall of Satan into the abyss and went on to tell the story of the universe from Satan's point of view: evil entering the world in the form of possessive love through Satan's daughter-lover, Isis-Lilith;* the discovery in

* In Rabbinical writings, Lilith is the first wife of Adam.

the mud of the future Paris of the three weapons used to murder Abel – a nail, a stick and a stone, which later become the instruments of social injustice – sword, gallows and prison; Jesus Christ recrucified by the established Church; finally, Satan's redemption by his other daughter, 'The Angel Liberty'.

Hugo abandoned *La Fin de Satan* at the point where four skeletons dug up in the Bastille are about to tell their horrid tale. As in so many epic fragments, the premature end is curiously appropriate: an evocation of the moment when all the plaster-board of the personality falls away and the body 'slowly fills up with disappearance'.

The other unfinished epic, *Dieu* (1854–6; 1869), also begins and ends with the Unknowable, represented by a row of dots – 'because God has neither beginning nor end'.[70] In between, in the version entitled *L'Océan d'en Haut* ('The Upper Ocean'), Hugo unfolds a pagan model of the universe, epistemologically comparable to the modern genre of computer adventure games, with which it also shares its colossal, picturesque personifications. There are nine levels, each beginning with the words, 'And I saw above my head a black dot'. Each black dot turns out to be a creature which initiates the poet into the next level: a bat, an owl, a crow, a vulture, an eagle, a gryphon, an archangel, a light with two wings and finally another black dot. Here, the poem ends, with the poet shaking 'as if from the blast of an enormous kiss'.

Dieu, which was not published until six years after Hugo's death, has twice been described as one of the finest things ever produced by human genius. Charles Baudouin, in his *Psychanalyse de Victor Hugo*, read it as a complete Jungian history of religion, from infantile Manicheism, Oedipal paganism, the Old Testament superego, the symbolic reconciliation of Christianity, and a post-religious super-rationalism which takes the poem well into the twentieth century.[71]

Usually, however, these famously interminable, oceanic poems are admired from a distance, though they can easily be explored if the normal reading rules are relaxed. This is not the concentrated verse of Baudelaire or Mallarmé, filtered through a mercilessly editing brain. Brute intelligence is not enough. They require a particular state of mind which, given a chance, they create: something like the detached concentration induced by walking along a pebbly shore.

The desire to comprehend may actually be an obstacle. To give a short quotation would be like using a cup of water to explain the sea. The single word which best characterizes them – a word much ridiculed at the time – is '*effaré*', conventionally applied to startled horses. In Hugo, it expresses the wild-eyed, ecstatic look of the poet who has stuck his head out of the carriage window as it hurtles through the infinite.

Hugo himself was alarmed by the size of the monsters he created and eventually separated smaller poems from the mass, like *L'Âne*, in which an ass explains to Immanuel Kant that words are simply a mask for human ignorance, or *La Pitié Suprême*, in which crime is shown to be its own punishment and pity a superior form of justice – the ultimate victory over tyrants.

Without the foothold in other people's reality supplied by commercial demands, Hugo might have lost a large part of his audience. His publisher, Hetzel, had been hoping for something more compact and accessible, and Hugo grandly conceded that 'on certain summits', 'the crowd does not have enough air to breathe'. *Dieu* and *La Fin de Satan* were filed away and replaced with a series of mini-epics strung together to form the first series of *La Légende des Siècles*. As far as Hetzel was concerned, this was a small concession to human frailty. Hugo donned his uniform and addressed the troops:

> You tell me anxiously that the book will be attacked. Who said it wouldn't be? . . . Which of my books has not been a battle? . . . I could write the reviews in advance: hideous! monstrous! absurd! criminal! abominable! barbarous!, not to forget hackneyed, banal, boring, deadly dull and lifeless. . . .
>
> See here, I attach very little importance to the immediate impact, as I think you know. A book always gets what it deserves in the end – glory or oblivion. The success of the moment is primarily the publisher's concern and to some extent depends on him. As for attacks, they are my lifeblood; diatribes are my daily bread![72]

La Légende des Siècles, Première Série appeared in Brussels and Paris on 28 September 1859. *Les Contemplations* had been the voice of the exile, travelling horizontally across the sea. *La Légende des Siècles* seemed to come from a vantage-point in space. According to the preface, Hugo had taken 'successive casts of the human face' in order to present humanity 'as a great collective individual'. In other words, he was redoing from the point of view of legend and for all centuries what Balzac, in *La Comédie Humaine*, had done from the point of view of history and for a mere half-century.

The work which Hugo called 'the first page of another book' contained almost 9000 lines divided into fifteen parts: 'From Eve to Jesus', 'Decadence of Rome', 'Islam', and so on, through the heroic Christian period and the Renaissance, to 'Now', 'Twentieth Century' and 'Outside Time'. The structure was said to reveal a providential message, but it was also a showcase for brilliant individual poems, and it might be said that the incongruously modern appeal of Hugo's work, as well as its power to irritate, comes from this grandiose showmanship: the gaudy *trompe-l'œil* of his painted hoardings and his fairground banter concealing a profound uncertainty, a contradictory religion of 'progress', a 'God' who is said to be unnameable, and a continuing unease that his opinions had changed since childhood. But it was Hugo's ability to convince himself that there was something real behind the hoardings ('fiction sometimes, falsification never') which produced such captivating poems: 'La Conscience', in which Cain tries in vain to escape from the staring eye; 'Le Crapaud', in which a toad, sitting contemplatively in the sunset, is stepped on by a priest, blinded by an umbrella, tortured by schoolboys but spared by an old ass. In 'Le Satyre', a lecherous Faun is arrested by Hercules and hauled before the pompous gods of Olympus: symbols of institutionalized pedantry. The Faun describes the universe in an encyclopedic performance which reduces the gods to stunned silence and turns him into Pan: 'Lost at the crossroads of his five fingers; / Nomadic races asked their way, / While eagles wheeled in his gaping mouth.'

The 'Twentieth Century' section consisted of two magnificent poems which impressed Jules Verne (though he may himself have been an influence on them):[73] 'Pleine Mer' and 'Plein Ciel'. The first described the gigantic, seven-masted steamship, 'Leviathan' – Brunel's expensive failure which was rusting away at Sheerness – as the symbol of the old world, weighed down by its war-mongering materialism. The second showed 'the giant leap of progress towards the sky' in the form of a gravity-conquering spaceship: a kind of flying Tower of Babel propelled by a combustion engine and a system of valves which suck the machine into a vacuum of its own making. (Almost an allegory of Hugo's own process of composition: 95 per cent of *La Légende des Siècles, Première Série* is in rhyming couplets, each line creating a void which the rhyme immediately fills.)[74] For the 1850s, this is a remarkably plausible contraption, possibly inspired by Pétin's 180-foot-long, four-balloon flying platform and in any case a technical improvement on the flying machine in *La Fin de Satan* where four eagles and a slab of lion's flesh operate according to the donkey-and-carrot principle.[75]

Hugo was right about the reviews,[76] though he lied about his indifference. *Macmillan's Magazine* and *The Saturday Review* both warned their readers, intriguingly, that these poems, 'contain many a passage which the husband will not read to his wife, nor the son to his mother'. Hugo had gone 'wading backwards and forwards up and down the centuries' to find the worst examples of human brutality. *La Légende des Siècles* was like a child's history of the world written by the Marquis de Sade. 'Cheerful scenes are few and far between in this book,' Hugo admitted in the preface. 'This is because they seldom occur in history.' But these horrors were also a result of his fondness for showing tiny feathers of virtue weighing heavier in the scales of justice than centuries of accumulated vice. This is why so many of his legends take the form of shaggy-dog stories. The problem was that the residual effect was the disturbingly pleasant impression of picturesque gore and invigorating violence.

In France, Flaubert was writing a novel, *Salammbô*, which shows a very similar wallowing in the sensual beauty of what are supposed to be essential, sacred facts, the same sense of a collective unconscious and the composting strata of dead civilizations and their gods.[77] Flaubert interrupted his writing to 'swallow' *La Légende des Siècles* in one sitting:

> I have just emerged from Hugo's two new volumes and I'm all dazed and dazzled. Suns are spinning before my eyes and there's a roaring in my ears. What a man!
>
> That book really boxed my ears![78]

The acknowledged *plat de résistance* in Hugo's bloody banquet was the beautifully peaceful 'Booz Endormi' ('Boaz Asleep'), based on the Book of Ruth. Unlike some members of the Hugo family, Ruth remains loyal to the exile and her moral prestige entitles her to sleep with the old patriarch, Boaz. In Hugo's poem, the venerable one looks suspiciously familiar:

> His silvery beard was like an April stream . . .
> A good master, a faithful parent;
> He was generous though thrifty;
> Women looked at Boaz more than at young men . . .
> For the eyes of young men have fire
> But the old man's eyes have light.

The poem ends with a tableau which stands with the seduction of Emma Bovary as one of the great implicit sex scenes, a model for cinematic euphemisms:

> All was at rest in Ur and in Jerimadeth;
> Stars studded the deep, dark sky;
> The fine, clear crescent among those flowers of night
> Was shining in the West, and Ruth was wondering,
>
> Motionless, half opening her eyes beneath her veils,
> What god, what harvester of the eternal Summer
> Had, as he went away, carelessly cast
> That golden sickle into the field of stars.

The disquiet of the modern reader at the respectable ancient practice of using lithe young bodies as poultices for the aged and infirm was not shared by Hugo, nor, according to him, by his doctor – though Dr Corbin apparently believed that boys were just as effective as girls.[79]

'Booz Endormi' is one of the most anthologized poems in the language, and one of the most frequently criticized. Hugo was fascinated by the pettiness of his critics[80] and would have been interested to see his poem exquisitely demolished by W. H. Hudson in 1918, referring here to lines which Proust considered among the most beautiful in French:[81] 'There are two errors of detail in this poem; asphodels are not found in Palestine (see l. 67) nor did the sheep of that country carry bells (see l. 78).'[82]

He would also have been delighted to learn that the place name 'Jérimadeth' (l. 81) has spawned half a bookshelf of commentary because it seems to have been invented by Hugo – no such place ever existed, though it is now effectively part of the French language. As he told a critic who objected that a word he had used was 'not French': 'It will be!'[83]

The solution to the mystery lies in the word itself. 'Jérimadeth' is one of those almost inaudible virtuoso touches which dare to threaten the integrity of the work at its moment of greatest gravitas. Typical of Hugo's determination to keep up appearances even while breaking the rules, '*Jérimadeth*' inserts in the poem a tiny vignette of the poet himself, writing the poem, looking for a rhyme on '*de*': '*j'ai rime à dé*' ('I have a rhyme on "dé"'). This sort of flippancy is more common in 'serious' French verse than is normally supposed, and Hugo was an enthusiastic exponent of it. 'A pun is the bird-dropping of the soaring spirit', says a character in *Les Misérables*. 'A white spot which splatters on the rock does not prevent the condor from flying.'[84]

*

MOST OF THESE POEMS were written standing up, ten lines to a page, and then left to dry on sofas which served no other purpose. The manuscripts were filed away in secret compartments in the panelling. Some were taken to be bound. When he was interviewed in 1903, the St Peter Port bookbinder remembered that, even though M. Hugo trusted him completely, 'before dark every night the manuscripts must be returned to the poet to be safely locked in a fire-proof safe'.[85] Downstairs, Adèle and her sister Julie – now thirty-six and unhappily married to an engraver, Paul Chenay – copied and collated the texts. Hugo was writing so much that Juliette could no longer cope on her own. The Chenays were pressed into service as secretaries, house-sitters and terrified couriers of Hugo's subversive tracts. Paul Chenay's only little rebellion was to refuse to join Hugo and his sons at Mme Drouet's house for dinner – apparently his 'upright character' would not permit it. He took revenge for his own obsequiousness by publishing a priggish volume of memoirs seventeen years after Hugo's death.

Apart from Hugo's epics, there were hundreds of pages of *Les Misérables* to copy – the great novel was finally nearing completion, sixteen years after conception – and, when he was called upon, messages to the international audience. Hugo lent his name to Republican movements in Italy[86] and Greece. He protested against the Anglo-French show of force in Beijing during which the Summer Palace was looted and destroyed: 'I hope the day will come when France, liberated and cleansed, returns its booty to the China it despoiled.'*

Two of these messages turned into great personal triumphs for Hugo and prepared the way for the global success of *Les Misérables*. First, on 2 December 1859, he wrote 'To the United States of America' on the Harper's Ferry incident: 'The murder [i.e. execution] of John Brown would be an irreparable mistake. It would create a latent fracture in the Union which would inevitably dislocate it.' This warning enabled Hugo to assert later on that if only America had listened to him, there would never have been a Civil War. In fact, America listened only too well. A nationwide spate of articles told him to mind his own business. What use was a 'high-strung intellect', asked *The Memphis Morning Inquirer*, without 'common sense'? Slaves had it better in America than anywhere else . . . [87]

It is true that Hugo's heroic image of John Brown as 'a soldier of Christ' is a poor match for the historical truth. It is also true that he was unwilling to investigate the facts once they had formed themselves into a coherent story. But his view of the symbolic truth is unquestionably accurate. In the Republic of Haiti he became a national hero. He corresponded with the President and with a newspaper editor who wrote to thank him 'in the name of the Black race'. Hugo called the editor 'a noble specimen of Black humanity' and used one of his favourite jokes: 'Before God, all souls are white.'

Since the other half of the island of Haiti had been the setting of

---

* This explains why the centenary of Hugo's death in 1985 was celebrated in China. The authorities were presumably unaware that, five years after the looting, Hugo purchased the embroidered silks which decorated the blue and red salons of Hauteville House 'from an English officer who was on the expedition'.[88]

Bug-Jargal in 1820, Hugo might be excused for considering his work a series of precise prophecies – not the final digest of influences, but the original nourishment. Throughout Central and South America, the author of *Hernani* and *Napoléon-le-Petit* was now the principal European catalyst of a literary and political *naissance* which fully justifies his equating of the Romantic revolution with a real one.

The other personal triumph began with a letter from his Chartist friend, George Julian Harney. In May 1860, five years after the '*expieulcheune*', Harney asked Hugo back to Jersey to help raise money for Garibaldi's 'Red Shirts'.[89] Italian unity had been one of Hugo's hobby-horses since the French restored the Pope in 1849. Garibaldi had become his hero: the lone republican fighting a French army backed by clerics. He even took to wearing a red shirt under his dressing-gown[90] and christened a room in Hauteville House 'La Chambre de Garibaldi'. However, Harney's invitation was not immediately acceptable:

> It would take at least twelve or fifteen hundred signatures to erase the famous *indignation-meeting*. I cannot return to Jersey by a back door. I must have the main entrance, with the doors flung wide. It is a question of dignity. A lofty soul like yours will understand. . . . If this invitation *by a very large number of people* is out of the question, hold your meeting without me. I shall applaud with all my might.

Hugo's request for what amounted to a local election victory has been described as 'breathtaking arrogance'. It could also be described as normal etiquette applied on an unusually large scale. (Hugo's target corresponds to roughly one-tenth of the population of St Helier.) And there was also the little matter of the expulsion order, which was still in force.

The lofty tone of Hugo's letter conceals a sophisticated manipulation of events. He was being cautious, preserving his dignity, taking revenge on the British Government and measuring his popularity all at the same time. 'It is because one has been prudent', he had told his sons after the *coup d'état*, 'that one is able to be courageous.'

The Garibaldi meeting was postponed while 427 signatures were collected. Hugo declared himself satisfied. On 14 June 1860 he docked at St Helier, risking imminent arrest. He was deposited by the boatman on the wrong side of the harbour, glowered at Juliette, who had landed there so as not to embarrass her heroic Toto in public, walked back across the quay and was greeted by a cheering crowd. Three days later, he wrote to Adèle, 'The walls are covered in enormous posters saying, "*VICTOR HUGO HAS ARRIVED!*"'[91]

He toured the town in an open carriage, attended a banquet and gave a long speech. It was published in England and recited in several towns by a travelling actor.[92] Hugo's old enemy, Vice-Consul Laurent, tried to have him arrested and sent a report to Paris in which, with an almost audible gnashing of the teeth, he announced that, despite the banquet attended by sixty people, nobody agreed with Victor Hugo anyway. In France, two newspaper editors who printed the Garibaldi speech were reprimanded for trying to stir up 'revolutionary passions'.[93]

Given this continuing official interest in his 'agitations', it should come as no surprise that Hugo declined the opportunity to return to France in August 1859. Napoleon III had granted an amnesty to all political exiles – or, as Hugo put it, 'the murderer forgave his victims'. While many refugees returned home to die, Hugo published a terse 'Déclaration':

Faithful to the undertaking I have given my conscience, I shall share the exile of freedom to the end. When freedom returns, so shall I.

Even today, Hugo is assumed to have been suffering from 'false pride', flailing at an enemy who no longer wished him any harm. This was also the view expressed by Napoleon III's pet journalists. But what exactly was on offer? An invitation to the exiles to come and place themselves under the control of a malevolent bureaucracy – a bureaucracy which had recently been forging pamphlets in order to implicate Hugo in Orsini's attempt to blow up Napoleon III.[94] The famous amnesty was not a change of policy. It was a trick.

Hugo's decision to remain on his rock was entirely practical; and, as he told François-Victor, it meant that his exile was now 'voluntary'. There was just the merest hint of embarrassment in his letter to François-Victor at the brevity and moderation of the 'Déclaration'. *Les Contemplations* and *La Légende des Siècles* owed most of their literary and financial success to the fact that they had been allowed to appear in France, and there was no sense in sacrificing *Les Misérables* to the pleasure of insulting 'M. Bonaparte'. As Hugo's poem on Cain makes clear, a conscience cannot exist without an audience.

*

ON 2 MARCH 1861, Mme Hugo left for Paris to have her eyes treated. Two days later, Hugo boarded the *Aquila* with Charles, Juliette, and the manuscript of *Les Misérables* in a waterproof bag. He was going to Belgium for a final piece of research, and his doctor had recommended a change. Since a severe case of anthrax, he had been anticipating an early death. It was the first serious illness he had ever had, and the resulting sense of urgency helps to account for the sheer size of *Les Misérables*: it might be his last chance to say everything. 'It has seven masts, five funnels, the paddles are a hundred feet across, and the lifeboats are battleships; it will not be able to enter any harbour [like Brunel's *Leviathan* on its voyage to Australia] and will have to weather every storm on the open sea. Not a nail must be missing.'[95]

Hugo landed on mainland Britain for the first time since 1852 at Weymouth,[96] which appears in the opening pages of *L'Homme Qui Rit*. They arrived in Brussels on 29 March. Juliette stayed in a furnished room at 91 Rue Notre-Dame-aux-Neiges while Hugo made himself at home in a *pension* at 64 Rue du Nord with the mistress of the establishment, her maid, and a selection of local prostitutes. The doctor was right. A rejuvenated Hugo zigzagged across Belgium and Holland, visiting towns and museums, ticking off sites in his tourist guide, filling up his diary in the usual manner: '*Garter. Shoes in my hand. Visto mucho. Cogido todo. No dorm. Osculum.*'[97] Almost no poetry was written in this period.

In early May, the original object of the trip took him 15 miles south of Brussels to Mont-Saint-Jean. He stayed at the Hôtel des Colonnes, where, nine years later, William Rossetti found a framed autograph note from Victor Hugo, 'testifying his great satisfaction at the treatment he experienced there in 1861'.[98] Hugo was gathering the evidence he needed to drive the final nail into *Les Misérables*: 'I shall say no more than a word on the subject in my book, but I want that word to be accurate.'[99] He had gone to the place where the founding event of the nineteenth century had occurred, where the 'door' of history had closed on the past and opened on Hugo's life. The visit is recounted in a section of *Les Misérables* which is probably the longest digression in the history of the French novel.

It was a sunny May morning, and 'the person who is telling this story' was on a long walk from Nivelles to La Hulpe. He had just turned off at a country inn to follow a rough path which disappeared into the bushes. After a while, he found himself skirting an old wall. In the wall, there was a doorway. Low down on one of the stone supports he noticed a large, circular depression and was bending down to examine it when a woman came through the door.

> 'That was a French cannon-ball did that,' she told him. 'And up there in the door, near a nail, that's a hole made by a big shell. The shell got stuck in the wood.'
> 'What is the name of this place?' asked the traveller.
> 'Hougomont,' said the woman.
> The traveller stood up and walked on a few steps to look over the hedge. Through the trees, on the skyline, he saw a little hill and on the hill something which, from a distance, resembled a lion.
> He was on the battlefield of Waterloo.[100]

Hugo returned to Waterloo in June to finish his novel on the battlefield itself. In 1815, the 'thinkers' had taken over from the 'swordsmen'. Now Victor Hugo was leading them to victory, but on a battlefield long since reclaimed by Nature. He celebrated the event with a servant girl known to us only from Hugo's diary as Hélène:

Helena nuda. Rubens. Anniversary of Waterloo. Battle won.

CHAPTER SEVENTEEN

'Merde!'

(1862)

N<small>O WORK OF ART</small> is finished only once. It was almost a year before Hugo completed his final revision of *Les Misérables*. Huge bundles of proofs arrived at Hauteville House, marked 'Works of Voltaire' or 'Translation of *The Iliad*'. For eight hours every day, he made corrections, adding far more than he deleted, spurred on by the Post Office timetable and the plume of smoke sent up by the mail boat in the harbour below.

In preparing his 'seven-masted' steam-ship for the open sea, Hugo had perpetrated what was said to be the worst in a long line of sins against the publishing profession.[1] Hetzel had been able to offer 'only' 150,000 francs for *Les Misérables* (equivalent to the annual salaries of sixty civil servants). Hugo stuck to his price – 300,000 francs for eight years, including translation rights – and signed a contract with Hetzel's Belgian rivals, Lacroix and Verboeckhoven.

Faced with a bitterly disappointed Hetzel, Hugo salvaged their friendship with one of those cordially domineering letters which suggest that he was after all a natural older brother:

> I have made a rule for myself: to be more than ever your friend in thought, word and deed ... Your letter is worthy, charming and kind, with a slightly bitter after-taste. If I am not wrong and if that aroma of bitterness is indeed there, it is an unjust aroma. Remove it from your heart. For me, you are a noble, staunch man, a deep and charming mind ... a *dependable friend*.[2]

Every detail of Hugo's negotiations was reported in the French press. '200,000 francs' (*sic*), drooled the Goncourts, 'for taking pity on the suffering masses'³ – thus setting a trend of innuendo which has dogged *Les Misérables* to this day. This deliberately naive view conceals a rather more complicated reality. Ignoring the superstition that intellectual entertainers should not be too rich, Hugo had always demanded huge sums for his work. This helped to establish not just his own fortune, but also the idea that serious writing could be a respectable, money-making profession. Hugo was one of the first writers to acquaint himself with the business which fed on his work, one of the first to realize that the bigger the advance, the more eager the publisher would be to disseminate the work.⁴ And since the price of intellectual property and Hugo's prestige continued to rise, it was important to test the limits whenever possible and even to wriggle out of contracts which had become retrospectively unfair. Lacroix was instructed to divide the first print-run of *Les Misérables* into several 'editions': a common ploy for making a book appear successful in the days before bestseller lists. Hugo had denounced the practice in the *Préface de Cromwell* and tolerated it in his own publishers. Modern editions of *Les Orientales* still show the original preface dated January 1829 and the preface to the 'Fourteenth Edition' dated February 1829 – which would mean that a new edition of *Les Orientales* came out every forty-eight hours for a month . . . ⁵ When the happiness of the human race was at stake, honourable obscurity was a crime.

On 3 April 1862, one of the biggest operations in publishing history went into action, directly inspired by Hugo himself.⁶ The first part of *Les Misérables* (*Fantine*) appeared in the wake of a mammoth advertising campaign in Paris, London, Brussels, Leipzig, Rotterdam, Madrid, Milan, Turin, Naples, Warsaw, Pest, St Petersburg and Rio de Janeiro. Hugo had been feeding Lacroix with press releases since September. Long before it came out, everyone knew that *Les Misér- ables* was not just a novel, it was 'the social and historical drama of the nineteenth century', 'a vast mirror reflecting the human race, captured on a given day of its enormous existence'; 'Dante made a hell with poetry; I have tried to make one with reality.' On Hugo's advice, the massive Waterloo episode was suspended over the heads of would-be censors: 'If you give quotations,' he told Lacroix, 'insist on *Waterloo*.'

Bring out the nationalist side of the book, play on patriotic sentiment, make Persigny [Minister of the Interior] feel ashamed in advance for suppressing a work in which [Marshal] Ney, his wife's grandfather, is finally vindicated. Make it impossible for them to impound it by saying that it's *the battle of Waterloo won by France*.[7]

Since some copies of *Fantine* leaked out in Brussels four days before the official launch, counterfeit copies swelled the tide: in June, there were already twenty-one illegal editions. Nine translators were hard at work. The London *Evening Star* of 8 April reported that '*The Miserables* of Victor Hugo [is] in the hands of all those who are able to purchase it and little circulating libraries have taken as many as fifty copies each.'[8] By the time Parts II and III appeared on 15 May, it was clear that Hugo had achieved the impossible: selling a work of serious fiction to the masses, or, for the time being, inspiring the masses with a desire to read it. It was one of the last universally accessible masterpieces of Western literature, and a disturbing sign that class barriers had been breached. The oxymoronic opinions of critics betray the unease created by Hugo – that the lower orders might also have their literature: 'a *cabinet de lecture* novel written by a man of genius,' wrote the Goncourts.[9] 'The most magnificent failure – the most "wild enormity" ever produced by a man of genius', according to Lytton Strachey half a century later, still fighting 'bad taste'.[10] In other words, *Les Misérables* was a jolly good book, but Victor Hugo never should have written it.

The view from the street was an inspiring contrast. At six o'clock on the morning of 15 May, inhabitants of the Rue de Seine on the Left Bank woke to find their narrow street jammed with what looked like a bread queue. People from all walks of life had come with wheelbarrows and hods and were squashed up against the door of Pagnerre's bookshop, which unfortunately opened outwards. Inside, thousands of copies of *Les Misérables* stood in columns that reached the ceiling. A few hours later, they had vanished. Mme Hugo, who was in Paris giving interviews, tried to persuade Hugo's spineless allies to support the book and invited them to dinner; but Gautier had flu, Janin had 'an attack of gout', and George Sand excused herself on the grounds that she always over-ate when she was invited out.[11] But the nameless readers remained loyal. Factory workers set up subscriptions to buy what would otherwise have cost them several weeks' wages.

Meanwhile, back on his island, Hugo had been correcting proofs with a furious attention to detail which belies his breezy comments about the immateriality of commas. The steam press in Brussels cracked under the strain, but the last two parts (volumes seven to ten) went on sale as planned on 30 June 1862. Gigantic posters were pasted up on walls which had once carried Hugo's call to the Army to oppose the *coup d'état*. Episodes from the novel were illustrated in bookshop windows. Hugo's characters were household names even before the last volumes were out: Jean Valjean, the ex-convict turned philanthropic factory owner; Javert, the maniacally dedicated police inspector; the saintly Bishop Myriel, who plants the seed of charity in Jean Valjean's benighted soul and antagonizes the Church (both in the novel and in reality) by following Christ's teaching to the letter; Fantine, the abandoned *grisette*, and her orphaned daughter, Cosette, rescued from the infernal inn-keepers, the Thénardiers, and raised as Jean Valjean's own child; Marius, the son of a Napoleonic general who joins a gang of young republicans and falls in love with Cosette; Gavroche, the snotty-nosed, street-wise, lantern-smashing gutter-snipe. Every character struck a chord and had such a profound effect on the French view of French society that even on a first reading one has a vague recollection of having read the novel before.

This is not the place for a full plot summary of *Les Misérables*: it would take up several pages and create the wrong impression. The main thread is quite simple, and strongly reminiscent of Sue's *Les Mystères de Paris* and Balzac's *Splendeurs et Misères des Courtisanes*, both dating from the years when Hugo began his novel: the pursuit of Jean Valjean by Inspector Javert, beginning with his release from the hulks at Toulon in 1815, and ending seventeen years later with the famous escape through the Paris sewers.

Les Misérables etches Hugo's view of the world so deeply in the mind that it is impossible to be the same person after reading it – not just because it takes a noticeable percentage of one's life to read it.[12] The key to its effect lies in Hugo's use of a sporadically omniscient narrator who reintroduces his characters at long intervals as if through the eyes of an ignorant observer – a narrator who can best be described as God masquerading as a law-abiding bourgeois. In this way, two points of view are constantly in play: Society's disgust and

God's pity. The title itself is a moral test. It invites a comparison of the human view with the godly-Hugolian view. Originally, a *misérable* was simply a pauper (*misère* means 'destitution' as well as 'misfortune'). Since the Revolution, and especially since the advent of Napoleon III, a *misérable* had become a 'dreg', a sore on the shining face of the Second Empire. The new sense would dictate a translation like *Scum of the Earth*. Hugo's sense would dictate *The Wretched*.[13]

This distinctive binocular vision accounts for the schizophrenic reception given to the novel. Several critics called it 'dangerous', as did Rimbaud's mother, who ticked off his teacher for lending him that pernicious book by 'V. Hugot'.[14] A man called Courtat published a list of eighty ridiculous phrases from the novel, itemized heinous errors (Jean Valjean is 'nailed' into a coffin whereas, as everyone was supposed to know, coffin lids are screwed shut), and gave the result of a manic calculation: 1053 of the 3510 pages were taken up with 'digressions'.[15] Others accused Hugo of soiling the great tragedy of French history by quoting the defiant cry of General Cambronne to the English at Waterloo: '*Merde!*', a word which had not appeared in decent literature since the eighteenth century. 'Perhaps the finest word ever spoken by a Frenchman,' wrote Hugo. To his disgust, it was omitted by the English translator.[16]

A certain Sergeant Deleau contradicted Hugo's account and was given a medal, which pleased Hugo enormously: 'To get a man the *croix d'honneur*, all I have to do is say *merde*.'[17] The critic on the *Journal des Débats*, Cuvillier-Fleury, observed that 'certain expressions are condemned never to be set down in writing by a self-respecting man', and Hugo addressed his reply to 'M. Villier-Fleury' (because '*cu(l)*' means 'arse').[18] Henri de Pène recorded a fake memory of Victor Hugo telling him that he wished prisoners were eligible so that he, Hugo, would be returned as 'the candidate of the convicts of France'. Perrot de Chezelles, in an 'Examination of *Les Misérables*', defended the excellence of a State which persecuted convicts even after their release, and derided the notion that poverty and ignorance had anything to do with crime. Criminals were evil.

One can see here the impact of *Les Misérables* on the Second Empire:[19] Henri de Pène worked for a newspaper which was edited by a personal friend of Napoleon III; Perrot de Chezelles was a public prosecutor; and M. Courtat was employed in the accounts department of the Ministry of Foreign Affairs. The State was trying to clear its name. The Emperor and Empress performed some public acts of charity and brought philanthropy back into fashion. There was a sudden surge of official interest in penal legislation, the industrial exploitation of women, the care of orphans, and the education of the poor. From his rock in the English Channel, Victor Hugo, who can more fairly be called 'the French Dickens' than Balzac, had set the parliamentary agenda for 1862.

One can also see the effect of that 'haunting and horrible sense of insecurity' identified by Robert Louis Stevenson as the root of the novel's power:

> The deadly weight of civilization to those who are below presses sensibly on our shoulders as we read. A sort of mocking indignation grows upon us as we find Society rejecting, again and again, the services of the most serviceable ... The terror we thus feel is a terror for the machinery of law, that we can hear tearing, in the dark, good and bad between its formidable wheels.[20]

This is the touchstone of all adaptations of *Les Misérables*, musical or cinematic: to turn Javert, the tenacious respecter of authority, 'that savage in the service of civilization', into the villain of the piece is to deprive the novel of its dynamite, to point the finger at a single policeman instead of at the system he serves.

For those who recognized Hugo's black-and-white vision as social reality seen from underneath – like the soldiers who read the 'Volunteers' or the 'Books for the Camp Fires' editions in the trenches of the American Civil War, or Dostoevsky, who was 'happy' to be imprisoned in 1874 because 'otherwise how would I have found the time to refresh my old, wonderful impressions of that great book?'[21] – *Les Misérables* was a moral panacea, the Bible of popular optimism. It stood for faith in progress and the end to misery of every kind – beautifully exemplified in the unexpurgated 'Sixpenny' English translation of 1887 with its cheering message on the inside cover: 'What higher aim can man attain than conquest over human pain? / Don't be without a bottle of Eno's Fruit Salt.'

The 'dangerous' aspect of *Les Misérables* is almost as evident today as it was in 1862. If a single idea can be extracted from the whole, it is that persistent criminals are a product of the criminal justice system, a human and therefore a monstrous creation; that the burden of guilt lies with society and that the rational reform of institutions should take precedence over the punishment of individuals.

Written for the masses, Hugo's novel placed itself at the side of the individual. It was history from the point of view of the scapegoat, which might account for the peculiar fact that so many who have practised on Hugo that glorification of the individual called biography have sided, perversely, with governments and a heavily censored press. With his seemingly unrepresentative life, his egocentrism, his isolation and his bizarre, patchwork religion, Hugo had produced the most lucid, humane and entertaining moral diagnosis of modern society ever written. For all the sniggering about his cranky predictions and self-serving idealism, it should now be said, 135 years after the novel appeared, that he was as close to being right as any writer can be, that a society based on the principles dredged by Hugo out of the sewers of Paris would be a just and a thriving society, and that, were biographers not far more prone to the petty professionalism commonly ascribed to Hugo, readers should be advised immediately to put down this book and go and read *Les Misérables*.

In the meantime, as a foretaste, something might be said of the novel's 'faults' since they are still identified as such and used as an excuse to doctor the text.*

The biggest supposed fault is Hugo's notorious tendency to go charging off on vast 'digressions', the longest of which are the mini-treatises on Waterloo, convents, the sewers, and slang. A key to the

---

* The best-known English translation (Penguin, 1982) is a Swiss cheese of unavowed omissions and bears out Hugo's comments on translation as a form of censorship.[22] The translator does admit to 'thinning out, but never completely eliminating, its lapses'. Hundreds of bizarre, arresting images are lost in the process. Typical remarks in the translator's introduction are: 'wholly unrestrained', 'no regard for the discipline of novel-writing', 'moralizing rhetoric', 'exasperating', 'self-indulgent', 'passages of mediocrity and banality'. This is strangely reminiscent of the passage on Aeschylus in Hugo's *William Shakespeare*: 'Barbaric, extravagant, emphatic, antithetical, bloated and absurd – such is the sentence passed on Shakespeare by the official rhetoric of today.'[23] 'One used to say: power and fertility. Today, one says: a cup of herbal tea.'[24]

installation of these vast plateaux in the labyrinth of plot-lines can be found in the second sentence of the first page: 'Although this detail has no bearing whatsoever on the substance of our tale . . .'.

Few novels begin with a digression (in this case, the engrossing fifty-page life story of Bishop Myriel); but few novels open their doors to such a wide arena. These interpolations were invitations to grasp the whole picture, to see that the Battle of Waterloo, for instance – described in a precise demonstration of Chaos Theory[25] – can be subsumed in the great strange attractor of destiny, the ineluctable equilibrium of everything. Napoleon had been defeated by God, not by the Duke of Wellington. (This was not well received in England.)

Even Cambronne's '*Merde!*' is a microcosm of the whole book, the ultimate act of linguistic democracy: 'the last of words' became 'the first' (cf. Mark 9: 35). 'Cambronne found the word for Waterloo as Rouget de l'Isle found the *Marseillaise* – in a visitation of the Holy Spirit.'

Pride of place in Hugo's digressions goes to the magnificent excursus on sewage, which is organically attached to the rest of the novel and can be read on its own as an allegory of the whole work: Jean Valjean pulling himself out of the slime of moral blindness into which society has plunged him. It also contained what some critics described as Hugo's only concrete suggestion for improving society.

When Hugo lamented the disappearance of the old Paris, his mind descended to the ancient medieval sewers, the intestinal city beneath the city. These had since been replaced by a super-efficient waste-management system which was shown off to tourists. With the Opéra and the Rue de Rivoli, it was one of the jewels of Haussmann's rectilinear Paris. For Hugo, the political connotations were clear: the old sewers had been 'the conscience of the city' where everything reverts to its true form and even the face of the Emperor 'turns frankly green'. 'The sewer never lies.'

This pungent metaphor was a manifesto. The revolutionary idea, previously floated by Eugène Sue and Pierre Leroux,[26] was that human beings produce exactly the right amount of manure to grow their daily bread. In *Les Misérables*, Hugo expanded the idea in several directions. For him, Haussmann's spanking-new sewage system was one of the great symbols and stupidities of the regime. The main intestine of the new Rome, the mighty '*Cloaca Maxima*', carried the guilty secrets of Parisians off to the sea – twenty-five million francs' worth of *merde*, 'the substance of the people' – while a cruel economy based on credit and social injustice held sway above ground. 'Parisian guano', he decreed, in an unusual example of patriotism, 'is the richest of all.'

Another, less flagrant 'fault' leads to the source of the novel's unmistakable smell. Hugo was extraordinarily careless about his dates. Twice, strands of plot overshoot their meeting point with other strands, so that Jean Valjean begins his second prison sentence six months before his arrest by Javert, and Marius has still not declared his love for Cosette in February 1833, which is the month of their wedding. At one point, Hugo writes, 'Some eight or nine years . . .', when it would have been easy to check and supply the correct date.[27] Yet the sense of passing time, the undertow of memory, the unwholesome interference of the past with the present are impeccably rendered.

The entire novel, by contrast, is predicated on two exact dates. The first is 5–6 June 1832: the insurrection which Hugo witnessed at first hand in the Passage du Saumon. This is the metaphorical and literal barricade at which all the strands and most of the characters converge like twigs floating up against a dam. (Almost one-fifth of the novel takes place on 5 and 6 June 1832.) The second date is 16 February 1833: the wedding of Marius and Cosette. It was also the night on which Hugo first slept with Juliette.

Like *Les Contemplations*, *Les Misérables* is a Great Pyramid with two routes to the centre: 'the historical drama of the nineteenth century', and the occult autobiography of Victor Hugo. Thus, 16 October 1823 is the date on which Jean Valjean jumps into the sea at Toulon and is presumed drowned. It is also the date on which Eugène Hugo wrote his last letter from the asylum.

On 7 September 1832, Jean Valjean is asked to give away his adopted daughter in marriage. On 7 September 1843, Hugo learned that Léopoldine was dead.

Finally, as the narrator himself points out, the writing of the novel straddles the great hole of December 1851. This would explain why the two crucial coincidences which tie the plot together both occur in the tenement of rented rooms at 50–52 Boulevard de l'Hôpital (a non-existent address) – the BC and AD of Hugo's life, and the crossroads of modern Europe.

Since the novel ends in 1833, it describes a society which was only just beginning to feel the influence of Victor Hugo. Its real theatre of operations is Hugo's memory of life before he was 'reborn' through Juliette: the Feuillantines garden, his mother's salon, the defeated General Hugo, along with fantasy memories of jolly student days and pretty mistresses. He was looking for a kind of redemption in literary excellence: if the story hung together, it would prove that the contradictions of the first half of his life were the necessary prelude to the second half. His warring parents reconciled in their youngest son, and the Battle of Waterloo won by France ... This sort of perfection is of course impossible, as the conjuring trick at the end of the novel suggests:

> No name can be read on the tombstone.
> But many, many years ago now, a hand wrote four lines of verse on
> it in pencil which gradually became illegible under the dust and rain
> and have probably now entirely vanished.

This final erasure is the only possible denouement, just as Hugo's insistence on the future was also a form of forgetting. The painful sense of homesickness in the Paris scenes is also the torment of a mind which could summon up all the moods and circumstances in which beliefs long since rejected were originally formed. The meandering, colonic structure of the novel is that of Hugo's mind and of the whole complex body he had always referred to in anticipation as his Complete Works – a vast, coherent work of art which historical change and his own changing views had always threatened to fragment.

Despite his huge achievement, Hugo had lost none of his capacity for being stung by reviews and reacted almost as if he had written the novel for the small group of writers who made up 'French literature'. 'The newspapers which support the old world say, "It's hideous, infamous, odious, execrable, abominable, grotesque, repulsive, shapeless, monstrous, horrendous, etc." Democratic and friendly papers answer, "No, it's not bad." '[28]

Reaction from the *misérables* themselves came in the form of begging letters: 'I am at Antwerp, about to set sail for the New World. I have no money. If you don't send me enough to pay my passage, dear master, I shall steal a candlestick and go to jail like Jean Valjean.'[29] Others helpfully enclosed the number of their bank account. In 1868, Hugo estimated that in order to satisfy all requests he would need an extra eight million francs a year.[30] Giving alms was one of his favourite pastimes, but reports of his stinginess appeared quite regularly in the press – even in Belgium – and while *Les Misérables* worked its effect on social legislation, its author was pilloried as a miser and a hypocrite.

That summer, Hugo escaped with Juliette to the Rhineland. He learned at Cologne that Charles's adaptation of *Les Misérables* had been banned in France, and returned to Brussels in September to attend a banquet organized by the publishers. Journalists came from all over Europe to hear Victor Hugo sing the praises of a free press.[31]

By the end of September 1862, he was back on his island fortress, talking to his old friend, the Ocean, 'which always agrees with me',[32] and which was full of cheering advice: 'Remember the advice that, in Aeschylus, the Ocean gives to Prometheus: "To appear mad is the secret of the sage."'[33]

*

THE HOUSE TO WHICH Hugo returned that summer suggests a serious attempt to follow the Ocean's advice. Six years after he bought it, its amazing transformation was practically complete.*[34]

When Hugo was away, visitors were taken on tours of the house by Mme Chenay and asked to sign a visitors' book in which Hugo noted a preponderance of 'English colonels and American pastors': 'almost a thousand' visitors in the summer of 1867.[35] They passed from the light of the street into a dim vestibule crammed with carvings, medallions and mementoes of Hugo's life and work, bathed in the coloured light that swam through the bottle glass. On the left was Vacquerie's bedroom, which now contains the cash register and

* Hauteville House can be visited from 1 April (unless a Sunday) to 30 September, 10–11.30 a.m. and 2–4.30 p.m.

postcards; on the right, the billiards room, doubling as a portrait gallery. The walls were covered in tapestries. Beyond the Gothic porch, inscribed 'VICTOR HUGO – NOSTRE-DAME-DE-PARIS', the 'Porcelain Corridor' ran like a gigantic Welsh dresser to the back of the house and the garden. It was painted brick-red to set off the plates. The prize exhibit was the Sèvres dinner service given to Hugo by Charles X in 1825. The corridor was lit by one of the fifty-six mirrors which, in Hugo's plan, would make the walls 'disappear'.

A staircase on the left led to the bedrooms of the two Adèles and to the Red Salon and the Blue Salon, modelled, miraculously, on Hugo's precise childhood memory of the Masserano Palace in Madrid.[36] A glass door in the Blue Salon opened into a conservatory where dinner was served in summer and where guests could reach up and pull grapes from the vines. The dining-room was dominated by the wooden bulk of the ancestors' armchair: in their eternal absence, it was used by the servants as a tray-rest and at other times by the dog, who may in any case have been an earlier Hugo reincarnated.

Bizarre maxims glowered in unexpected places: 'ABSENTES ABSUNT'* above the ancestors' armchair; 'EDE I ORA'† to the right of the dining-room door; on the back of a *bergère*, 'EGO**H**UGO'; in the oak gallery on the second floor, gilded studs on the back of three wooden thrones spelt out the words, 'FILIUS', 'PATER' and – a last-minute replacement for 'SPIRITUS' – 'MATER'. Above the fireplace and its four caryatids, a sculpted panel showed Abraham being blessed by Melchizedek – in Charles's Oedipal memory, it was Abraham sacrificing Isaac.[37] At the other end of the oak gallery stood 'Garibaldi's' four-poster bed. To the left of the bed, a small lavatory was adorned with peacock feathers and palm-leaf fans. A gilded engraving mysteriously warned those who entered, 'ERROR**T**ERROR', meaning either 'One is wrong to feel terror', or, more prosaically, 'Be in fear of error'.

These mottoes are virtually a parody of Victorian adages. Instead of 'Home Sweet Home' and 'Bless This House', 'TU QUI TRANSIS PER DOMOS PERITURAS SIS MEMOR DOMUS AETERNAE'.‡ Even today,

---

* 'The absent are present.'
† 'Eat. Go. Pray.' (Dictated by a spirit.)
‡ 'Thou who passest through perishable dwellings, be mindful of the eternal home.'

the carvings exude a sense of religious hospitality, the conviviality of a man who loved to share his mind and who never grew tired of his own company.

The last stop before the brain of the house on the top floor was a long library–antechamber,[38] strewn with books and papers like a robbed tomb. Hugo preferred to think of it, not as a library, but as a store of miscellaneous information, as interesting as someone else's attic. Like the rest of the house, it was a monument to serendipity. The secondhand bookshops of Jersey and Guernsey had supplied him with the seventeenth-century dictionary of 'curious facts', and the twelve-volume encyclopedia of religions which give *La Légende des Siècles* an appearance of bottomless erudition. The most dog-eared editions were pot-boilers and compendia – anything which, like hypertext, packed a lot of information into a small space and left its organization to the reader. There were about 3000 volumes, although there appears to have been some seepage after his death. Many of them came from admirers and show that Hugo was a magnet for cranks as well as for progressive thinkers: animal rights, extraterrestrial life, magnetism, universal languages, pneumatology, prostitution, public sanitation, aerial navigation, the sea, the *coup d'état*, capital punishment and slavery. Some were untouched, many were nibbled. Often, the pages had been cut, but rarely from start to finish.

The great advantage of allowing information to enter his mind in this way – piecemeal and by chance – was that each fact became a personal discovery, detached from the distracting hand of its originator. Fortunately, Hugo had the knack of thanking people for their books without having read them. Flaubert was plausibly congratulated on having 'Balzac's penetration, plus style'.[39] It was as if he had access to a constantly updated bluffer's guide to French literature.

At the far end of the antechamber, the direct light of day appeared for the first time since the entrance. An eighteen-by-ten-foot 'cristal palace'[40] had been built on to the roof, probably in imitation of other such structures on Guernsey. Hugo called it the 'look-out' (in English). The outside walls and the ceiling were glass and gave a panoramic view of St Peter Port, the gardens climbing up Hauteville, the beaches and inlets, the squat grey slab of Castle Cornet, the islands of Jersey, Alderney, Sark and Herm. Half the horizon was the thin grey line of the French coast. A side of the glass box could be opened on to a narrow wooden gallery.

Hugo worked in the blinding light reflected by two mirrors and the blue and white ceramic tiles. He wrote on a fold-down wooden shelf, opening his windows to the wind, sweating like an athlete. Heart-shaped pebbles served as paperweights. A cubby-hole contained some empty ink-bottles of a well-known English brand 'Used in the Government Offices':[41] these would later be marked with the name of the work that flowed out of them and given to friends. At his feet, an oval pane of reinforced glass lit the stairwell below and, by a series of slanting mirrors hung at either end of the landings, allowed him to spy on the comings and goings of the other occupants like a medieval God peering down through the layers of his universe.

No house ever said so much about its owner. The Gothic cathedral at number 38 is a very remote relative of that benign category of building known as the writer's house in which imaginations are reduced to their tools and trappings. Hauteville House gives one the distinct impression of having been swallowed alive by Victor Hugo; an oddly oppressive and inspiriting mixture of playfulness and solemnity, a giant act of aesthetic democracy in which every painted, carved or written product of the mind is slotted into a great scheme, as if to say that all things, however small or unsensible, are as real and significant as each other. The last stand of the nineteenth century against the age of mass-production.

For all its introspective gloom, Hauteville House is quite in keeping with its island setting, and the local workers employed by Hugo should certainly be given some credit. The cabinet-maker, who was interviewed in 1903 and again in 1927, deserves a place in French cultural history as the man who was Victor Hugo's closest collaborator for over a decade.

> Hugo was very quick in making designs for carving or engraving on wood. He would sketch either with chalk or pencil. Frequently, after a lapse of several days, he would ask me to return a panel, saying that he had omitted to put in a bird on a branch or a flower on a stem.

I was allowed to give him my opinion, but he wouldn't budge when it came to the varnish. Nothing could be coloured without his being present and without his express instruction.[42]

Today, no great effort should be made to imagine the house before it became a museum. As the following incident reveals, Hugo himself was the first curator of Hauteville House. On 22 January 1867, Mme Hugo met Juliette Drouet, for the first time, at Juliette's home. The meeting was more symbolic than social. Juliette was keen to appear grateful and considered Mme Hugo her social superior; but the conversation evidently attained a degree of intimacy ... Next morning, Juliette wrote to Hugo: 'You were right to give in to your dear wife by handing her the keys to all her beautiful salons yesterday.... I shall answer for Sénat's tail and everything else, and I am sure he won't let me down.' This combined assault on his domestic authority and the jealously guarded salons suggests that Hugo had reasons other than simple propriety for not bringing his two wives into contact before.

*

THE BIGGEST SURPRISE for many visitors to Hauteville House is the revelation that Victor Hugo was also an artist.

For almost fifty years now, he had been dotting his manuscripts with caricatures, drawing ruined castles on his travel accounts and developing an original style which reached its peak in the later years of exile. Almost 3000 drawings are known; hundreds of others are in private collections; many have disintegrated or been lost.

Some drawings appeared in reviews while Hugo was still in Paris.[43] In 1861, his brother-in-law, Paul Chenay, published his engraving of Hugo's powerfully pathetic 'Pendu'. Drawn in 1854 when John Tapner was hanged on Guernsey, it was retitled 'John Brown' and confiscated by the authorities in France because Chenay had stupidly added the date of Brown's execution: 2 December, which was also the date of the *coup d'état*. Finally, a few months after *Les Misérables*, a set of drawings etched by Chenay was published in Paris and marked the end of Hugo's public career as an artist until the posthumous exhibition at which Van Gogh and the Symbolists discovered an 'astonishing', unknown Hugo.

Hugo's objection to the album was not just that Chenay failed to follow his orders to the letter. The real problem was that the etchings were Victor Hugo at one remove: a Hugo who had been tidied up and rendered marketable. Since many of the drawings were inspired by etchers – Dürer, Callot, Rembrandt, Piranesi and Goya – Chenay was effectively undoing the work of transposition, colonizing Hugo's chiaroscuro with his lines and canals. Worst of all, the portrait of Hugo etched from a photograph was 'hunchbacked':[44] 'You have drawn a body where there was shade and given it two humps' ... In April 1864, Hugo wrote to the critic of the *Gazette des Beaux-Arts*:

> If I wished to restore my reputation I should produce an etching which would be myself and nothing but myself. But what's the point? ... In any case, etching would engross, captivate and seduce me. I should spend days and even nights on it. My time is not my own. I have not been put on this earth to amuse myself. I am a beast of burden yoked to duty.[45]

Unyoked from 'duty' and the need to satisfy a public, Hugo's talent quickly outgrew the medium. To the usual materials – charcoal, graphite, ink, gouache and gum – he added a whole pantry of other substances: blackberry juice, caramelized onion, burnt paper, soot from the lamp and toothpaste.[46] Coffee grounds imitated the texture of stonework; scraps of lace, steeped in ink and smeared with gouache, produced mottled, snake-skin skies; line drawings on white paper, cut out and pasted onto watercolours, gave a ghostly, 3-D effect. Brown-ink fingerprints became heads peering down a well. Damaged goose-quills spurted out blots which a broken match-stick teased into forests, castles, lakes and distant cities.

The volatile nature of the materials has ensured that only the more conventional pieces have survived,[47] and allowed purists to reject the evidence of several witnesses (including Hugo himself) and to deny that Victor Hugo ever worked in foodstains and smut. But these drawings were not born as expensive artefacts. They were as much a work of destruction as of creation and should be compared, not to published works, but to manuscripts, in which the text is seen emerging from the eradication of its earlier selves. Hugo's dabbling acted as a cultural sponge, absorbing trends that were in the air. If tradition must prevail, he can be placed on a line which runs from Leonardo to Jackson Pollock: 'Great artists', he wrote, 'have an element of chance in their talent, and there is also talent in their chance'.[48]

Under the expanding skies of the English Channel and in the optical illusion of Hauteville House, Hugo's face-haunted ruins grew into almost abstract scapes, sometimes resolving themselves into the letters of his name. Like Piero di Cosimo, who saw fantastic battles and landscapes on a wall on which invalids had spat, his starting-point was often a crinkle or a mottle in the vellum, a hole made by the scraper, a spilt drink or a raindrop, a crumple in his overcoat, the automatic scrawl of a spirit, or the folded splodges now familiar as Rorschach tests. An unfinished poem suggests that some of the painted panels in Hauteville House were drawn from the half-imagined shapes that swim about on the surface of polished wood.[49] As in his poetry, he was encouraging the medium to produce its own discoveries.

Even in the murkiest swirls a powerful sense of gesture survives – notably in a series of drawings called 'Le Poème de la Sorcière': a witch-trial in pictures which is a significant moment in the prehistory of the comic book. It is interesting to see that Van Gogh was sensitive to this gestural imagination, even when it manifested itself in writing: 'Take Bonnat's [1879 portrait of] Victor Hugo – fine, very fine – but I still prefer the Victor Hugo described in words by Victor Hugo himself, nothing but this: "And I remained silent, as one sees a cock keeping silence on the heath." Isn't that little figure on the heath splendid?'[50]

Anyone whose mind has wandered in Hugo's drawings or, like Van Gogh after reading *Les Misérables*, seen landscapes which look like 'a page from Hugo',[51] may find it odd that the Victor Hugo who regularly appears in histories of art is the sociable Romantic of the 1830s, the poet whose salons were an intellectual exchange for writers and painters and whose poems often sound like descriptions of paintings or were themselves transposed by painters. The point is not usually pursued beyond the anecdotal for several good reasons – comparative ignorance of his drawings, and his shortcomings as an art critic: he thought that Delacroix's women looked like 'frogs', and when he was shown a wall by Courbet (who asked to paint his portrait), he observed that a true '*réaliste*' would have painted in the inevitable lump of dogshit at the foot of the wall.[52]

This off-putting coexistence of the aesthete and the philistine goes straight to the heart of Hugo's mental apparatus. When he forced himself to think theoretically he was capable of saying spectacularly idiotic things, though not necessarily by accident: anti-academic poems like *L'Âne* show him using the rhetorical structures of philosophical argument as a kind of parody of logic, in much the same way (ridiculous as the comparison might at first seem) that Wittgenstein exploited a certain genre of philosophical discourse as a self-defeating art form. When he allowed his mind to continue thinking after it had reached its conclusions, when the words and arguments were mere cogs in the machine, he became a visionary. In his drawings, where the didactic component was reduced, the effect was all the greater.

The most perceptive art critic of the century turned the conventional view on its head. For Baudelaire, Victor Hugo had had a disastrous effect on French painting: his poetry had helped to spread the simple-minded notion that the subject was more important than the manner, inspiration more valuable than technique; Hugo was *not* the Delacroix of poetry – 'a prejudice which still encumbers many a feeble mind'.[53] By contrast, in 1859, Baudelaire used Hugo's drawings as a stick with which to beat the modern school of landscape painters: 'I have found in their work ... neither the supernatural beauty of Delacroix's landscapes, nor the magnificent imagination which flows through the drawings of Victor Hugo as mystery flows through the sky.'[54]

This is the true confluence of Hugo's work with modern art: a move away from the shackling of art to domains extraneous to itself and the exploitation of the means peculiar to that art; the use of chance coincidences – rhymes or slips of the pen; the development of devices which bring unconscious impulses to the surface. Hugo's stencils, collages, cartoons and blot-drawings should have a small but central place in histories of modern art: Romantic tableaux created using the techniques of post-Romantic art.

The fact that this is only a peripheral aspect of Hugo's work may be a testimony to his effortless genius; but one could also say that his art would not have had the significance it does if it was not peripheral, if it had been subjected to the traditions which were artificially preserved by salon juries and the market. Attempts to drag Hugo into the mainstream, to offer his work as it were the benefits of an institution, serve a useful purpose but entail a serious distortion. One simply cannot have one's hero being astoundingly original and well behaved at the same time. Anyone who investigates the origins of a new style should expect to find a mess. Hugo scribbled, smudged, scratched and toyed. He was a lover of substances and textures – inanimate and human – a *frotteur* and a voyeur, a hoarder and a thrower-out; a man who, in old age, stirred his food into an indescribable sludge which he called '*gribouillis*' ('scribble').[55]

The single aspect of his art that provides a key to all the others has been obscured by misplaced veneration. Georges Hugo claimed that one of the substances on his grandfather's palette was saliva; and there have been hints of even less respectable materials. When Hugo played with art, he was engaged in a religious exercise. It was a plastic demonstration of metempsychosis: the transmutation of base matter into spirit, the grime and excrement of the sewer-world purified and redeemed by the artist, though, of course, ultimately signifying turpitude.

In a passage of *L'Âne*, Man boasts about his glorious creations – his sculptures, his inventions, his pots and his books – and then the ass, losing patience with the egocentric fool, puts him firmly in his place:

> Very well then, spit on the wall, and now compare . . .
> The great starry sky is the spittle of God.[56]

CHAPTER EIGHTEEN

Salvage

(1863–1868)

IN THE AFTERMATH OF *Les Misérables*, Hugo's glass tower was the scene of an extraordinary act of mental salvage: a massive essay on Genius by which he hoped to prove to himself that petty literary squabbles were insignificant to an almost epic degree. But the self-aggrandizing maxims and sheer garrulity of the book called *William Shakespeare* (1864) are given a peculiar poignancy by the fact that the writing of it coincided with the first stages of a long disaster – a creeping shamefulness which poisoned the last years of Hugo's life and about which he said almost nothing in public.

Adèle II was thirty-two years old and apparently 'on the shelf'. Hugo noted in his diary that she had now turned down five suitors, including an unidentified 'marquis' and the Sicilian poet, Cannizzaro. That day (2 June 1863), Adèle left to join her mother in Paris.

She never arrived. A letter came from England informing François-Victor that his sister was on her way to marry Lieutenant Pinson. Hugo was 'overwhelmed by her *indifference*'. And there was the horrible suspicion that she had thrown herself on a man who did not want her. Hugo wrote to his wife: 'I fear the revelation of some latent impossibility. How else can we explain Adèle's preposterous behaviour, since we had given our consent and agreed to everything?' 'If, as I hope, the man is honourable, the dowry is ready.' So much for the theory that Adèle remained a spinster because Hugo was too mean to give her a dowry. The theory that he still believed her to be somehow contaminated by Sainte-Beuve is not so easily dismissed.

Worse news came in July. A letter arrived with a New York postmark. Adèle had crossed the Atlantic on the *Great Eastern* – the

Leviathan of her father's poem, since renamed and refitted for the laying of the Transatlantic Cable. By the time the letter reached Guernsey, she would be in Halifax, Nova Scotia, where Pinson's regiment was stationed. Hugo continued to send her monthly allowance. In September, she announced her marriage to Pinson, but then a few days later – writing to her confidant, François-Victor – she asked for more money. Her landlord was about to throw her into the street. The marriage to Pinson was a fantasy.

Hugo decided to seize the initiative. On 9 October 1863, he announced his daughter's engagement in two local newspapers and in the mainland press. Shame would force the scoundrel up the aisle before Adèle did any more damage to the family image: 'Her music must be muted,' he wrote, for once metaphorically. The announcement is easily the most surprising text Hugo published in exile. When family pride was at stake, the recent costume of the democrat and the pacifist fell away to reveal the Army child underneath, the man of 'honour' and tradition:

> Viscount and Viscountess Victor Hugo announce the engagement of their daughter to M. Albert Penson [*sic*], an English officer who distinguished himself in the Crimean War.

Next day, a furious Hugo told his wife about the latest begging letter from Adèle. Since François-Victor had urged him to think of Mme Hugo's health and moderate his rage, Hugo's summary should be considered a faint reflection of his feelings:

> My name is not mentioned. I appear in her letter only by implication, as a cashier. . . . People come up to me in the street, saying, 'Your daughter has married.' . . . It makes me look like a father who refused his consent and it forces me to deny the fact and to explain our family affairs to all and sundry. The newspapers hear about it before I do. . . .
>
> Let us now consider the husband. Adèle talks too much; he says nothing. He remains silent, plays dead, gives no sign of life; he doesn't even deign to send a note to the father and mother. A worthless little English trooper is granted the prodigious honour of entering the family of Victor Hugo, and that worthless little trooper doesn't even seem to notice.[1]

A week later, the fictitious marriage was announced in the papers, Pinson's family published a denial, and four weeks after that, Hugo wrote the words '*Non est*' in his diary: Adèle was unmarried and dishonoured.

By the end of 1863, the only reliable news of Adèle came from her landlords in Halifax.[2] They had noticed François-Victor's address on the back of an envelope and, supposing him to be a friend of 'Miss Lewly', wrote on her behalf. François-Victor summarized the letter. Adèle had almost stopped eating. 'Her fine clothes, they say, are much too flimsy for that harsh climate. . . . The officer who was to have married her has been to see her only two or three times since she took a room with them. He has not returned for several weeks.' The only messages from Adèle herself were worryingly bizarre. In June 1864, she was asking for 5000 francs, which would somehow enable her to hypnotize Pinson and marry him while he was asleep.

Hugo seems to have hit on what now seems the obvious truth in December 1863, when he used the word '*folie*'. But then he rejected the idea of insanity and, while still blaming Pinson, allowed himself at last to see what he had done to his second daughter. It is interesting to learn what he considered a suitable remedy:

> Six months from now, Adèle will return to Hauteville. She will call herself Mme Adèle. . . . The poor child has yet to know happiness. It is time that she did. I want her to. I shall hold parties for her at Hauteville-House. I shall invite all the great minds. I shall dedicate books to Adèle. I shall make her the crowning glory of my later years. I shall celebrate her exile. I shall make amends for everything. An imbecile may have had the power to dishonour her, but Victor Hugo will have the power to glorify. Later, when she is cured and happy, we shall marry her to a man of honour.[3]

The cure was simply a repetition of one of the causes: Adèle was to be turned into a second Léopoldine. Yet this is precisely what she had already done to herself. Her diary shows that she believed in her dead sister, more firmly even than Hugo himself, as the 'Virgin Mary' of the New Age, and now she, too, had effectively drowned and was sending messages back from another world, pursuing her sacred mission to marry the man of 'the past' (as she put it) to the woman of 'the future'.

The irony is that some of the most romantic adventures of the Hugos were censored as heavily as if they were a family of bourgeois functionaries dependent on the good opinion of neighbours and superiors. The true story of Victor's parents' marriage would have made a splendid historical novel, his dramatic courtship of Juliette Drouet had produced only a few lines of verse, and now Adèle's adventure – which supplied François Truffaut with the subject of one of his best films, *Adèle H.* – was to be entirely suppressed. Hugo had often talked of the constant need for secrecy in his childhood: 'Nobody keeps a secret like a child.'[4] He might have added that children of all ages are also adept at keeping secrets from themselves. It is worth considering the possibility that Hugo's astonishing sensitivity to what the people of Guernsey might think (not something that prevented him from performing his ablutions on the roof or going out in public with Juliette) was a projection of the censor in himself – not 'What will the neighbours think?' but 'What might I be forced to think?'

Adèle was acting out episodes from the family chronicles which Hugo had recently been retelling, in a purified form, for his wife's biography: Sophie Trébuchet throwing herself on the mercy of a brutish, philandering General Hugo with exactly the same mixture of helplessness and intrepidity; brother Eugène setting off for Blois to find out whether his father had remarried; Victor Hugo sailing into exile. Schizophrenia is now known to be genetically transmitted. It is also known to flourish in certain family environments. The theory that some families are pathological by nature might find some support in the Hugos, as might R. D. Laing's extreme contention that schizophrenia is not a disease at all, simply a logical response to an irrational world. Whatever the causes, Adèle's apathy, unsociability, apparent lack of emotion and quirky, obsessive behaviour are all classic symptoms.

The idea that mental illness was hereditary was sufficiently well established in the nineteenth century for Hugo to consider himself at risk,[5] and his allusions to the Romantic commonplace of creative lunacy should perhaps be taken more literally than they are. The lurking sense of a family destiny accounts for his fierce rejection of the new determinist systems, like Hippolyte Taine's. Blind fate – the ANAΓKH of *Notre-Dame de Paris* – was infinitely preferable to the notion of bestial impulses which left the human being with all the moral freedom of an ape. In *Les Misérables*, biological and kinship relations are curiously elided: Jean Valjean, Cosette and Marius are unrelated except by the marriage which brings the novel to an end; Cosette's mother dies and her father disappears; Marius is estranged from his grandfather and develops a relationship with his father only after his father's death. The only close family group is the hideous tribe of Thénardiers, a remarkably disparate group of personalities. In Hugo's novel about society, family relations are either non-existent, illegitimate, adoptive, bogus or posthumous. This, however, is one of the secrets of the novel's power: the resolution it seems to posit as a desirable end – a marriage and a new generation – is precisely what it unconsciously hopes to avoid.

*

IT WAS IN THIS ATMOSPHERE of half-uncovered secrets that Hugo wrote his next three major works. The sense of impending shame and 'the chill wind of hate blowing over the sea' (hostile reviews) helped him to construct a bloated image behind which he could grow old disgracefully, with every appearance of having survived.

The first of these three works was published in 1864 under the misleading title *William Shakespeare*. It began life as an introduction to François-Victor's translation of the plays. By the time it was finished, it was the size of a short novel and another, shorter introduction had to be written.

Starting with one of the most inaccurate lives of Shakespeare ever published, Hugo quickly moved on to his real subject – the greatest geniuses of all time, who belong to 'the region of Equals' and are therefore above comparison: Homer, Job, Aeschylus, Isaiah, Ezekiel, Lucretius, Juvenal, Tacitus, St John, St Paul, Dante, Rabelais, Cervantes and Shakespeare. 'Each new genius is an abyss. Yet there is such a thing as tradition. A tradition which passes from one chasm to the next.' Hugo himself is not explicitly excluded, since 'this is not a closed series'. 'These men climb the mountain, enter the cloud, disappear and reappear. They are watched and observed. They walk along precipices. A slip would not displease certain onlookers. . . . "How small they are!" says the crowd. They are giants.'

Hugo gave his prejudices free rein, relegating Goethe to the rubbish-bin of history because his 'indifference to good and evil went to his head'. He praised the 1830 revolution in literature which enabled his son thirty-four years later to translate Shakespearean phrases like 'the buttock of the night' into French. He attacked the mandarins of the French language: 'The dictionary had a mind of its own. Imagine Botany informing a vegetable that it does not exist!'

Very little of this was based on actual reading. It was literary criticism boiled down to pure enthusiasm: 'I admire everything, like a brute,' he wrote in the second section of the fourth book of Part Two. 'That is why I wrote this book. . . . It seemed to me that our age could do with this example of stupidity.' Vastly extended metaphors moved over the subject like weather systems; chapters were overrun by proper nouns or adjectives; showers of axioms filled entire pages, as if the whole book were a pretext.

Eventually, however, the moment comes when Hugo begins to take the collection. Beauty must serve Truth. 'The poet exists for the people. *Pro populo poeta.*' 'We should like to see a pulpit in every village explaining Homer to the peasants.' Geniuses and the people on one hand; on the other, the snivelling mass of envious reviewers: 'It seems there are some vagrant poets. The Prefect of Police, in his negligence, is allowing minds to wander. What can the authorities be thinking of?'

Underlying the sarcasm was a sense of injustice. 'Diatribes' may have been his daily bread, but it was a deeply unpleasant diet. *William Shakespeare* was a vast development of the 1824 obituary of Byron in which Hugo had imagined the great names of literature forming a new family around him. The blatant resemblance of 'the Equals' to Hugo himself, like the portraits of Scottish kings in Holyrood House, is not just a humorous foible but a poignant depiction of his tragedy: the real family replaced with a family of Victor Hugos.

William Shakespeare was laughed to pieces in France. Victor Hugo was a lunatic. Victor Hugo should have used a different title: *Myself.* Writing anonymously in the *Figaro*, Baudelaire was slightly more balanced: 'like all his books', *William Shakespeare* was 'full of beauties and stupidities'. Most stupid of all, in Baudelaire's view, was the politicization of Shakespeare: 'Shakespeare is a socialist. He never realized, but that's beside the point.'

'Old Will''s tricentenary was to be celebrated in the Grand Hôtel in Paris: a launch-pad for Hugo's book and his son's translation. The committee, which included Berlioz, Dumas, Gautier and Janin, decided to have Hugo represented by an empty chair draped in black. The Government heard about it and informed the management of the Grand Hôtel that the celebration was off. This negative victory might have consoled Hugo for the other attacks. But with the desertion of Adèle and the long absence of his wife and Charles, the critical failure of *William Shakespeare* had opened a deep wound. Hugo sounded old:

> I think I am beginning to get in the way. I shall keep silent for four or five years. . . . I do not have much time left. I shall spend it writing works rather than publishing books.[6]

It was the thirteenth year of exile.

*

IN EFFECT, the 1864 Shakespeare *was* a socialist. Organized opposition to Napoleon III was growing inside France, and even a book launch might become a focus for revolt. Pressure was once again exerted on Belgium to extradite the trouble-makers, and, this time, the Belgian Parliament responded by tightening controls on foreigners. Hugo was accused by the Belgian Foreign Minister of 'corrupting the young', which must set a record in modern literature: forty years of officially recognized youth corruption. He had been invited to chair the Students' Congress in Liège, and though he declined the invitation and sent a communiqué instead, urging the students to pass through the door marked '*Peace and Freedom!*', the damage had been done, apparently: simply by existing, Hugo had disrupted studies to such an extent, according to the Minister, that not a single one was ready to sit Finals that year.[7]

Meanwhile, Hugo's renewed status as socialist bugbear was confirmed in satellites of the French Empire. Copies of *Les Misérables* were burned publicly in Spain and, in June 1864, Pope Pius IX anticipated the choice of posterity by adding *Les Misérables*, *Madame Bovary* and all the novels of Stendhal and Balzac to the Index of Proscribed Books.[8]

The obvious anxiety of the Second Empire and its acolytes was, for once, a rational reaction to the shadow now being cast by Victor Hugo. No other nineteenth-century writer ever enjoyed such literary and political prestige. A world map showing the extent of Hugo's popular influence would be more monotonously red than a map of the British Empire is pink, and a full exposition of his part in several national histories would burst the banks of this biography (and strain the limits of the biographer's competence). There are, however, some valuable conclusions to be drawn about Hugo himself.

The three dozen or so declarations and open letters that represent Hugo's international presence in this decade stand under two banners: life and liberty. For many, his name was synonymous with the campaign to abolish the death penalty. In 1865, a new translation of *Claude Gueux* appeared in London under the title, *Capital Punishment*, and when six Fenians were convicted of terrorist acts in Ireland, their wives appealed to Hugo. Hugo wrote 'To England': how could the land of Wilberforce, Cobden and Rowland Hill (a passing tribute to the British postal service), the land which had shown the world how to colonize and civilize the savage, reinstate 'the political gibbet'? How could the widowed Queen Victoria bring herself to murder other women's husbands?

Florid, artificially emotional, riddled with illogicalities, Hugo's appeal had the desired effect, and his attempt to replace 'the Irish Question' in an ethical and constitutional context might usefully be compared to the disastrous British policy of indiscriminate outrage. He also played 'God's advocate'[9] in Jersey, Belgium and Italy, and was given most of the credit for removing the death penalty from the constitutions of Geneva, Portugal and the Republic of Columbia. He even asked for the Emperor of Mexico, Napoleon III's puppet, Maximilian, to be spared by Juarez: 'the noblest toppling of the scaffold is performed before the guilty'. He cheered on the freedom-fighters in Crete, urged Russian soldiers to stop massacring their Polish brothers, and published a long poem on Garibaldi's defeat by the French at Mentana near Rome: *La Voix de Guernesey*[10] was

translated almost immediately into English (by 'The Oxford Gradu-
ate', Sir Edwin Arnold), German, Hungarian, Spanish and four times
into Italian. Hugo's voice, wrote a Portuguese count, 'is heard with
respect from East to West and its echo reaches the remotest corners
of the universe'. Usually, it also reached the offices of the international
Courrier de l'Europe and was syndicated around the world. In Mexico,
French Army positions were bombarded with quotations from
Napoléon-le-Petit and leaflets bearing the famous message: 'What are
you? Soldiers of a tyrant. The best of France is on our side. You have
Napoléon. We have Victor Hugo.'

Even if Hugo's pronouncements now seem to verge on the
rhetorically inane, they were gobbled up by a large and hungry
audience. Their almost comical oscillation from the particular to the
universal, from the writer's blotting-pad to continental masses, is a
mark of Hugo's attempt to fit personal morality to industrial development, to manage the transition from the 'genius' of the Romantic
age to the intellectual of our own, to define a form of address that
might be used in speaking to the recently literate millions.

His rhetorical discrepancies are the cracks in a writing style which
straddled two distinct stages of civilization, and they can still be heard
today in the antiquated, mock-Victorian idioms peculiar to elected
Parliaments: 'Those poor stupid peoples', he wrote in a revealing
private letter, who 'allow themselves to be led by the nose.' 'How easy
it would be for them to be happy! . . . Let us enlighten them!'[11]

This was the voice of a President-in-waiting who believed in the
former excellence of the French Army (tragically misled by its
Government), in the inevitability of progress, and in the divine
mission of Paris, the 'pivot' of civilization. For once, the epithet
'imperialist' is entirely appropriate. The exile had become the true
spokesman of the Second Empire, which accounts for the seemingly
incredible fact that the main encyclopedic guide to the Paris Universal
Exhibition of 1867 – the last great public boast of the Second Empire
– contained a gigantic preface by Victor Hugo, rhetorically indistinguishable from the official propaganda:

> In the twentieth century, there will be an extraordinary nation. This
> nation will be great, yet it will be free. . . . It will be astonished at the

veneration with which conical projectiles [shells] are now regarded, and will experience some difficulty in distinguishing an army commander from a butcher. . . .

The capital of this nation will be Paris, and its name will not be France; it will be Europe.[12]

*

THE VERBAL PERFORMANCES which make up Hugo's political philosophy show how contradictory a personality can appear when it expresses itself in logical argument. In the flesh, his contradictions merged in a convincing whole.

The experience of meeting Victor Hugo was described by a young French master at the nearby Elizabeth College – Paul Stapfer, a colleague of George Saintsbury (who knew Hugo only through his books).[13] Expecting an unapproachable demi-god, Stapfer was surprised to see a young old man in a floppy hat, an overcoat slung over his shoulder, striding nimbly up the street, hands in pockets, his jacket half-unbuttoned, imparting an air of elegance to his scruffy clothes. He was 'very formal, *vieille France*, excessively polite', 'always saying that he was "honoured" to see me', but always keen to practise his bawdy sense of humour. The perfect gentleman who said ungentlemanly things advised M. Stapfer to cure his headaches with sexual intercourse and, when he left for a few weeks in Paris, urged him to 'yield entirely to the charms of Parisian women'.[14] Obviously a man who, unlike the author of *Dieu* or *La Fin de Satan*, was never troubled with the disappearance of his personality.

Hugo resolved his contradictions in routines. At dawn, Juliette's maid, Suzanne, would arrive from down the road with a pot of freshly brewed coffee and the daily letter from 'Juju' to her 'beloved Christ'. Having started the day with caffeine and compliments, he swallowed two raw eggs, then worked until eleven. Petals of torn-up manuscript fluttering down from the 'look-out' showed that he was hard at work. At eleven o'clock, he folded back his work shelf, opened the door to the roof-top gallery and stepped into a tub of water which had been left out overnight. Despite this, he was still prone to 'colds and cramps' (the 'despite' is Hugo's). Meanwhile, visitors had been gathering in the salons below: these were the days when prominent men were expected to have opening hours like museums. Hugo welcomed almost everyone, writers collecting snippets for their future memoirs, journalists who came to describe M. Hugo's famous dwelling for their female readers. As the clock struck twelve, he would appear in a grey felt hat and woollen gloves, looking like 'a well-dressed farmer', and conduct his guests to the dining-room. The senior guest was invited to occupy the 'ancestors' armchair' and could produce a rare display of impatience in Hugo by trying to refuse.

Meals were simple and copious. 'He seems to me to follow much the same dietary as that laid down for the prize-fighter described in *L'Homme Qui Rit*,' wrote Samuel Oliver, a guest of Hugo's neighbour, 'to wit, a slice of roast leg of mutton or a mutton chop (*sanglante*), washed down with cold coffee and *vin-ordinaire*. Abstemious himself, he always provides handsomely for his guests, to whom superior wines and liqueurs are handed.'[15]

Immediately after lunch, Hugo rushed out for exercise. This consisted either of a two-hour walk or a punishing routine on which Stapfer followed him only once because he almost died as a result: run until sweat breaks out, strip naked, jump off a rock into the waves, then lie down in the sun to dry. Most days, he went out with Juliette on a 'hygienic ride' in a carriage driven by a man called Peter who was ordered to stop whenever Hugo wished to digest a thought or look at something. Sometimes, he walked down the street in St Peter Port where no respectable gentleman was ever seen, looking for another form of inspiration. There was also the daily visit to Mr Blicq the barber. According to the surviving Blicqs, who were interviewed in 1903, the trimmings from Hugo's head and beard were never swept away: 'The poet insisted upon appropriating these cuttings himself, and bestowing them – no one says where.'[16] Perhaps they were offered to the birds as nesting material or given to Juliette for her Victor Hugo museum. Or perhaps, superstitiously, it was to prevent them from falling into the wrong hands: 'visitors would dog his footsteps along the seashore and pick up pebbles upon which he had trodden, to preserve as mementos of the great master'.[17]

Back at the house, Hugo continued to fill up his three manuscript trunks, allowing huge quantities of poetry and prose to accumulate like coral reefs from which he eventually hacked off his publishable works. Satchel-loads of letters arrived every day, even with bare addresses like 'Victor Hugo, the Ocean': in June 1862, he was writing 150 letters a week and was commonly accused of never answering his correspondents. Many of the replies were written by Juliette Drouet, who did an excellent imitation of his signature.[18]

As the sun set behind the look-out, Hugo descended into the bowels of Hauteville House to preside over the gloomy evening ritual. When the family were in attendance, he held forth after dinner on subjects of universal importance like the folly of atheism or the necessity of prayer, pausing only to make sure that his wife had not fallen asleep.[19] He always carried a little notebook in his pocket and, as Charles explained to the Goncourts in 1862,

> As soon as he has uttered the slightest idea – anything other than "I slept well" or "Give me something to drink" – he turns away, takes out his notebook and jots down what he has just said. Nothing is lost. Everything ends up in print. When his sons try to use something they heard their father say, they are always caught out. When one of his books appears, they find that all the notes they took have been published.[20]

Evenings at Juliette's house nine doors away were more boisterous. Hugo sprinkled himself with rose-vinegar, put on his blue tie, and turned up with the rest of the 'gang' for dinner.[21] They were seated at table in order of age, the youngest next to Juliette. The usual contingent was Hugo, his two sons, Paul Stapfer, his fellow exile Hennett de Kesler and the editor of the *Gazette de Guernesey*, Henri Marquand. They sat in the 'Chinese room' which Hugo had designed and which can now be seen in the Victor Hugo museum in Paris. They played cards until ten o'clock, while Hugo aired his views: 'There is only one classical writer in this century – only one, do you hear? Me. I know the French language better than anyone else alive.'[22] Of all the writers who resembled Racine, Lamartine was the best – 'not excluding Racine'. Musset was so vain that he thought he was as good as Victor Hugo.[23] Stendhal's *Le Rouge et le Noir* was a 'misformed thing' written in dialect: 'The only works which have a chance of traversing centuries are those that are properly written', which was why 'Balzac's hour to sink into oblivion will come much sooner than is thought.'[24] As the evening wore on, talk turned to women, in spite of Juliette: 'I do not wish to be made fun of,' she told him in a letter, 'nor have my heart treated like a twenty-five-sou accordion.'[25] (She later apologized to Hugo for having 'misunderstood' him.)

Every Tuesday afternoon, Hauteville House was the scene of a celebrated institution: the *Dîner des Enfants Pauvres*. Adèle and her sister Mme Chenay would go out looking for needy families, Catholic or Protestant, French or English, and invite the children to come and be fed and clothed at Hauteville House. In 1862, fifteen children attended; in 1868, there were forty-eight. Hugo gave a short speech, tasted the food, and – a concession to local 'superstition' – recited the Lord's Prayer. He even drank beer and ate roast beef. 'It is my attempt', he explained, 'to make this feudal country understand equality and fraternity.'[26]

Anyone with even recent experience of English rural traditions will recognize these dinners as a notable achievement. The idea was quite advanced for the time, even if the details seem outdated: 'They eat meat and drink wine – two great necessities of childhood.' The author of *Les Misérables* was offering the potential enemies of society a glimpse of society's benefits, showing them a model family which prayed and ate together. Victor and Adèle played the role of Mr and Mrs Hugo to perfection and the idea caught on in Italy, Spain, Sweden, Switzerland, Haiti, Cuba, the United States and London: in 1867, 6000 urchins were being fed in the Parish of Marylebone along the lines set out by Victor Hugo. Beyond the literary pages, most of the British press had decided that Victor Hugo was a good thing. Any suggestion of impropriety or excess could be excused on the grounds that he was French.

The Poor Children's Dinners also had a hearty effect on Hugo's local standing. There was gossip about his fancy woman, rumours of cruelty to his daughter, some attempts to be indignant about his failure to observe the Sabbath and to sing 'God Save the Queen' at a public function (not necessarily a political gesture on Hugo's part), but the dinners placed him almost on a level with Father Christmas and, ironically, had a powerful appeal for the feudal imagination. A photograph of Victor Hugo presiding over his symbolic flock of little paupers was a popular item at the local market.[27]

Edmond Biré's observation that these dinners cost Hugo next to nothing, brought him several thousand pounds' worth of excellent publicity and were originally devised by his wife is an interesting comment from a man who owed his fortune to a soap factory. The idea in any case was not to fling down pennies from the palace tower but to demonstrate the revolutionary possibility of treating the poor as equals. As for the myth of Hugo's stinginess, it says more about his accounting habits than his social conscience. He hated to tamper with investments and preferred instead to set aside certain sources of income for charity: royalties from musical adaptations and, often, performances of his plays, were donated to individuals and worthy causes. In a typical year, he doled out the equivalent of £20,000. Hugo liked people to ask him why he wore his coat inside out (instead of buying a new one, he gave the money to the poor), and the depiction of Bishop Myriel in *Les Misérables* – complete with household accounts – shows that he had a keen sense of the glamour of alms-giving. Hugo was too tight-fisted with his reputation *not* to give money to the poor.

It was this minutely organized existence, and the ability to enjoy his own company, that had enabled Hugo to survive the mass defection of his family to Brussels.

At the end of 1864, Charles left the island. He was tired of competing for a dwindling number of desirable women, convinced that his father was setting spies on his tail and infuriated at having his pocket-money withheld. (Charles was now thirty-eight.)

In October 1865, he married a 'sweet and gentle' eighteen-year-old orphan, Alice Lehaene, who reminded Hugo vaguely of Léopoldine. Alice brought the family something far more precious than a dowry: she had been raised by her godmother, the wife of Jules Simon, an important French *député* in the Republican opposition elected in the first genuine elections since the *coup d'état*.

Even the once dependable François-Victor abandoned ship. He had fallen in love with a local girl, Emily de Putron. She died of tuberculosis in January 1865. François-Victor heard his father's funeral oration, then left the Channel Islands for ever. Mme Hugo went with him to Brussels and did not return for two years. They rented a house, first in the Rue de l'Astronomie, then at 4 Place des

Barricades. Sacrificing 'happiness' to 'duty', Hugo stayed on Guernsey. 'Abandonment', he wrote in 1868, 'is the destiny of the old man. I can work well only here. My family is my happiness. I had to choose between my family and my work, between happiness and duty. I chose duty. That is the law of my life.'[28]

*

THE NEXT POEMS to issue from Hauteville House showed that duty and happiness were not completely incompatible. Seventy-eight relentlessly unmiserable poems called *Les Chansons des Rues et des Bois* were published on 25 October 1865. In contrast to the battalions of alexandrines, Hugo's *Chansons* went skipping down the page in lines of six, seven or eight syllables. This was supposed to be the poet on vacation or 'Pegasus put out to grass'. Like any stallion, Hugo's Pegasus was galvanized by the smells of spring and the scent of young fillies:

> Dawn at the door, a mattress in the nook;
> Eden can sometimes be a hovel;
> The creaking of a trestle bed
> Is one of the sounds of paradise.[29]

The old pacifist revolutionary was also present: discreet references to the military intervention in Italy added a little cloud to the sunny horizon. But the bullets had turned into buttercups:

> May, with mocking cries,
> Peppers the routed Winter
> With a grapeshot of flowers.[30]

The frisky nature of the poems delighted reviewers and almost made Hugo regret publishing them prehumously.[31] They were seen as the fruit of his dotage. The songs of 'M. Vertigo' were parodied, and almost lovingly ridiculed by Barbey d'Aurevilly (who had the grace to recognize them as a supreme example of French verse art): 'M. Hugo, broken by debauchery, with not a hair left on his head nor a tooth in his mouth, has just published an obscene book.'[32] Hugo hoped that Barbey would 'explode in his corset'.[33]

The idea of barely repressed paedophilia and a hoary Hugo

thanking heaven for little girls was reinforced in later years by a confusion of the fictitious 'Jeanne' of *Les Chansons des Rues et des Bois* with Hugo's granddaughter (born four years later in 1869). 'An outbreak of skittishness', wrote A. F. Davidson in 1912, 'which to some people seemed indecorous in an elderly gentleman of sixty-three'.[34] Davidson fortunately did not have access to the diary in which Hugo described himself complimenting his four-year-old granddaughter on her 'charming little *con*'.[35]

Barbey d'Aurevilly of all people should have seen that the petticoat-chasing adolescent was another of Hugo's personae, a mask beneath the mask, and that, demoralizing as it may seem for the biographically minded, certain aspects of Hugo's personality were principally pre-texts for varieties of poem, so that apparent contradictions in the whole moral picture are no more surprising than the fact that the same poet worked in different genres. The powerful effect of Hugo's *Chansons* on Verlaine, Rimbaud and the Symbolists suggests that influences passed more purely and freely between the generations of grandfather and grandchild. His amazing fluency was a machine driven by a set of image-producing devices which younger poets studied like engineers inspecting blueprints. Images like 'the fan of brightness', 'the shiver of the sky' or the 'diaphragm' of the sea showed a painter's ability to reproduce exactly what entered the eye, while the metaphors which now seem intolerably arch – 'A butterfly teaches a violet the facts of life / And flutters off' – proved that everyday preoccupations could be used, not for their thematic signifi-cance but as rhetorical paintbrushes. Morally, Hugo sounded like a relic of the eighteenth century; aesthetically, he was a giant of the avant-garde. Neither quality was likely to endear him to his own generation.

The composition of the *Chansons* proved once again that Hugo was able to be both types of poet at the same time: the consciously creative and the naturally inspired. If he suffered from writer's block, only one type of writing was blocked at a time. Exactly two-thirds of the poems had been written in the glorious summer of 1859. They germinated – at the same time and place as *Les Travailleurs de la Mer* – on the tiny island of Sark during a two-week holiday there with Charles and Juliette.[36] The remaining third was produced in the ten-week period preceding delivery of the manuscript (August–October 1865). Typically, the poems came at a rate of one a day for three or four days, followed by a break of about a week – somewhat analogous to a digestive system, with about ten days in the brain corresponding to one day in the rest of the body.

The sexual aspect of the *Chansons* tells us little that we did not already know, except perhaps that Hugo wrote poetry to rid himself of an obsession or to indulge an obsession as a holiday from other parts of himself. Of all the fields of human experience which the nineteenth century optimistically submitted to 'scientific' analysis, only love has remained relatively untouched: only since the 1970s has any systematic attempt been made to exploit the mass of insights preserved in romantic fiction and popular songs. In Hugo's case, the idea of drug-addiction seems particularly appropriate. The evidence of the *Chansons* is that he had organized his addiction to the psycho-physiological effects of enamoration so that it could be satisfied in small, regular doses. 'I cancel out one affair by having another.'[37] The fleeting affairs with maids and country girls were just that: diminutive love affairs, allowing the heart to run through its full repertoire of effects, but without the inconveniences of long-term exposure.

*

FOR THE NEXT two-and-a-half years, Hugo's life followed the pattern already described. The house continued to grow around him like the secretion of his brain, but the human furnishings were slowly stripped away. Mme Hugo spent more and more time on the Continent. Her sight was failing rapidly. Stretched out painfully on a chaise longue, she received visits from friends and journalists, serving as Victor Hugo's ambassador to Brussels.

Letters sometimes arrived from Adèle's landlady in Halifax. Hugo tried to decipher the foreign script and sent the letters on to François-Victor for decoding. According to Mrs Saunders, 'Miss Lewly' always wore black and sometimes went out dressed in men's clothing. In 1866, word came that Adèle had followed Pinson's regiment to Barbados. Then, from 1868 until her sad return in 1872, there was almost total silence. Army records show that the regiment left the West Indies in 1869. Adèle stayed on, an unidentified madwoman who watched the soldiers on parade and collected money orders every month from the post office. Children threw stones at her in the street. A freed slave called Mme Baa took pity on her and gave her a room. Hugo offered to pay her fare home. If she returned to Guernsey, he would 'make her a gift' of the money.

The more Hugo thought of his daughter, the more visits he received from ghosts, some of whom spoke in her voice. Unexplained lights appeared under the doors of empty rooms. Inquests in the morning often produced corroborations from the servants. Under a full moon, his bed swayed about like a boat on water.* He dreamt of funeral processions which stopped in front of Hauteville House. One night, a loud noise came from the library. An unopened package had fallen on to the floor. Hugo picked it up. It was a book titled *Maladies de Poitrine* ('Chest Complaints').

When darkness filled the house and the only sound was the whispering sea, one world dissolved into the other. References in the sexual account books to 'incubi' and 'succubi' may not mean that Hugo was a practising necrophiliac, but the thought was there. A servant who had known him sexually 'returned' several times after her death and gave rise to a short but pregnant entry in the diary: '+! prayer'[38].

These intimate moments with the dead coincided with some untypically reckless activity which probably reflects his increasing reluctance to sleep alone. In early February 1867, François-Victor wrote from Brussels with news of one of the servants: 'It seems that poor Philomena ... is five months pregnant and does not know by whom.' Hugo pasted this sentence into his diary. Then he answered the letter: 'I feel sorry for poor Philomena, but how the devil does a woman manage not to know?'

---

* The phenomenon of lunar influence on the mind is now sufficiently well established to require no appeal to personal belief. Leonard Ravitz discovered in the 1950s that mental patients had a greater electric potential between head and chest than 'normal' people, and that this increased at full moon. Several anecdotes suggest that Hugo's magnetic field was unusually active. Once, in the salon of Bertin the Elder, he attached a small weight to the end of a thread, held the other end to his forehead and made the weight describe circles inside the crown of a hat.[39] Pending proper research, Hugo's 'poetic year' (see p. 243) might tentatively be associated with seasonal fluctuations in the magnetic fields of vegetation.

If he turned back the pages of his diary he might have remembered the night of 5 August 1866: 'A las tres [at 3 a.m.]. Philomena toda.' Or 27 August: 5 francs to Philomena 'for having darned my sleeves'.

The child, if it was born, has left no trace. For Hugo, these incidents were little more than droplets in the cloud that enveloped him and which, ghosts notwithstanding, was about to produce one of the great storms of literature.

On 12 March 1866, two weeks after Hugo's sixty-fourth birthday, a novel quite unlike either *Notre-Dame de Paris* or *Les Misérables* appeared under the title *Les Travailleurs de la Mer*. Hugo's great story of the sea is only now being recognized as an important moment in the history of the novel.[40] It was once a summertime bestseller in the Channel Islands and two films were made of it.[41] Since then, it has fallen into obscurity, which is all the more annoying for English readers since the only available translations are prudishly incomplete: gone are the pebbles under water resembling the heads of green-haired babies; gone, too, the Dionysian evocation of Nature in the spring as the wet dream of the universe.

The bones of the story are this: a reclusive Guernsey fisherman called Gilliatt falls in love with the daughter of a local shipowner. The shipowner, Mess (Monsieur) Lethierry, has two passions: his daughter, Déruchette, and his steam-ship, *La Durande*. The latter is deliberately run aground by its trusted captain, Clubin. The captain's plan is to fake his own death and steal the 75,000 francs he was carrying back to Lethierry. The passengers and crew abandon ship, admiring Clubin's selflessness ... Only then does it dawn on the hypocrite that he has struck the wrong reef and is marooned, not on Les Hanois, a mere mile off the coast, but on the lugubrious Douvres, a full 5 leagues from Guernsey. But before the sea can claim him, a mysterious, rag-like thing moving swiftly underwater grabs him by the leg and pulls him to his death.

Back on Guernsey, the shipowner's daughter offers her hand to anyone who can save the ship. Gilliatt sets off and spends the larger part of the novel dislodging the steamer from the two stone pillars of Les Douvres, between which the storm has wedged it like the bar of a giant **H** : 'it appeared on the horizon in a kind of crepuscular majesty'.[42] This 60,000-word epic of amateur engineering, followed by Gilliatt's hand-to-tentacle struggle with the octopus-cum-squid called '*la pieuvre*'* is one of the great scenes in literature. A single human pitted against 'the dark coalition of forces', 'the silent inclemency of phenomena going their own way'.

In order to depict this battle with elemental forces, Hugo had first to break down the walls of the nineteenth-century novel and frighten off its chattering characters. A recent guide to French literature speculatively describes *Les Travailleurs de la Mer* as a 'novel about fishermen';[43] but the fishermen suggested by the title never appear, as *Fraser's Magazine* complained: there was 'a great deal in it about fishes, rocks, and boats, but very little about men and women'.[44]

This, however, is the point – and perhaps Hugo should have stuck to his original title, *L'Abîme*: 'The Abyss' or 'The Deep'. As in *Moby Dick* (a striking example of uninfluenced similarity), the real 'digressions' are the everyday deeds and thoughts of human beings. Even the jaded reviewer of *Fraser's Magazine* was affected by Hugo's hurricane of technical vocabulary, whipped up from a handful of half-read books and manuals: 'All that the author has ever thought about wind is heaped up here to burthen the narrative – troubling us, offending us, buffeting us in the face; we come out of this chapter in a dishevelled unseemly condition.'[45] It seems a pity that Hugo decided to omit the other nine chapters he had written on the subject of wind.

Les Travailleurs de la Mer can be read in several ways and tamed to a gentle allegory. Hugo claimed that it showed the final victory of Prayer over 'that most formidable of despots: the Infinite'.[46] Since the first English editions, illustrated by Gustave Doré,[47] the title has always been rendered as *Toilers of the Sea*. '*Workers* of the Sea', though less elegant, would preserve the political connotation and show the novel to be a metaphor for the nineteenth century – technical progress, creative genius and hard work overcoming the immanent evil of the material world: Gilliatt's mission, like that of any engineer, is to conquer gravity and thus, in Hugo's view, the dumb weight of original sin. It was a novel for the people and a summary of what separates Hugo from his literary roots: a collective title, an illiterate

---

* *Pieuvre*, now in common use, is Hugo's form of the old Norman/Channel Islands word for 'octopus' (*puerve*); it also meant 'prostitute' – a meaning it recovered almost immediately in modern French.

central character, and a preference for manual labour over idle musing.

It can also be read as the only great memorial in Hugo's work to his second daughter: a huge, obsessive monolith looming over the tidier, poetic mythology arranged around Léopoldine. At the end, Gilliatt returns in triumph to find that Lethierry's daughter is enamoured with an Anglican vicar. He relinquishes his prize, removes the last obstacle to the marriage, and, sitting in his rock armchair, watches the newly-weds sail over the horizon as the tide washes over him: 'That which escapes the sea does not escape woman.' This passive suicide, brilliantly conveyed with the impeccable sense of timing that enabled Hugo to coordinate huge blocks of text as if they were parts of a gigantic building, was almost universally condemned as implausible; a sign of the author's 'childishness' – in which case one can only advise readers of Hugo's novels not to grow up.

Yet another reading might show the novel to be an allegory of Hugo and the Second Empire: the racketeering Clubin/Louis Bonaparte deliberately wrecks the ship of State which is then salvaged by Gilliatt / Hugo.[48]

But the lasting impression is of the scenes which expand in the mind so much like childhood memories that it is a common experience to find, on re-reading Hugo's novels, that, far from being too long, they are not nearly as long as they should have been: the storm, which has the same effect on the brain as a sudden drop in barometric pressure; the 'haunted' watch-house on the cliff-top at Pleinmont Point where the smugglers meet;* and, of course, the *pieuvre*. According to Robert Sherard, locals boys were disgusted with Hugo for making the monster up, but paid a nice compliment to his imagination by curtailing their swimming expeditions.[49]

What is the *pieuvre*? 'It is a sucker.' 'It has no bones, no blood, no flesh. It is flaccid. There is nothing inside.' 'It resembles a closed umbrella without a handle.' 'Compared to the *pieuvre*, the hydras of old bring a smile to the lips.' 'A lump of slime that has an instinct.' 'Beyond the horrific – being eaten alive – there is the unspeakable:

---

* The house was demolished by the Nazis in 1940. The 'haunted house' which now stands near the same spot is an impostor, but a worthy substitute.

being drunk alive.'[50] Hugo claimed to have seen his son Charles pursued by a *pieuvre* when swimming off Sark,[51] and recent deep-sea expeditions have filmed monsters which are every bit as alarming as Hugo's, although some of the details dredged up from the deepest trench of the unconscious have not been confirmed: 'It has a single orifice. . . . Is it the anus? Is it the mouth? It is both.'[52]

Reviewers of *Les Travailleurs de la Mer* had an easy job: they simply translated it into a 'normal' register for humorous effect. A parody attributed to 'Victor Gogo' accused him of filling up pages with synonyms in order to increase the fee – as if he was in danger of running out of things to say. (In fact, Hugo refused an offer of half a million francs from *Le Siècle* because he knew the novel would not lend itself to serialization.)[53] In the Victor Gogo parody, the characters stand around waiting for the plot to begin when suddenly they notice 'a shadow, a shape, a thing, which must have been a sail, a mast, a boat, a sloop, a craft, a vessel, which slipped away, fled, disappeared, veered off', etc.

> 'Where the devil can that boat be going?' they said.
> Where is it going, dear readers? That is the great mystery: it is going to look for the toilers of the sea.[54]

There was just the merest suspicion of an insight here into Hugo's revolutionary use of words as cubical objects, expanding into their three dimensions – sound, sight and sense. The only critic of Hugo's generation who might have given the novel the review it deserved was the eternally silent Sainte-Beuve. It was left to Alexandre Dumas to express public support for Hugo. He issued invitations to a *pieuvre*-tasting party, which was harder for the Government to ban than a Shakespeare banquet. The question was: *pieuvre frite* or *pieuvre au gratin*?[55]

The other main criticism, interestingly, stung Hugo to the quick and is even now one of his chief claims to infamy in the English-speaking world. Misled by his source, Hugo had devoted a chapter to Gilliatt's 'bug-pipe'. 'A *u* for an *a*!' he commented later. 'Albion threw up its hands in horror. . . . A good many newspapers devoted editorials to the scandal.'[56]

To Hugo, this seemed particularly discourteous. He had dedicated his novel to the island of Guernsey. He even allowed England to have the first word: '*La Christmas de 182 ...*' 'Bug-pipe' however was only one of several Hugoisms. Captain Clubin was greeted after an absence with a hearty 'Good bye, Captain'. A 'cliff' in Scotland was identified as '*la Première des Quatre*' (the Firth of Forth). There was also something the English call 'a dick' (dyke). Twenty-seven years later, *The Saturday Review* was still making a meal of the 'bug-pipe' passage:

> Then Hugo proceeds to dress a Highlander ... The wandering Celt who sold the national instrument of torture to Gilliat [*sic*] must have been a travestied duniewassel, for he sported a bonnet decorated with a thistle instead of an eagle's feather. He wore likewise a 'scilt or philaberg', adorned with the 'purse-sporran' and the 'smushing mull.*'[57]

Hugo had also equipped the man with a 'swond', a claymore, a 'dirck', a skene dhu – four blades in all – and two '*ceintures*', 'la sashwise et le belts'.[58]

Robert Louis Stevenson was the only critic to suggest that these blunders were part of Hugo's lunatic charm.[59] Similarly ludicrous errors are still made by Englishmen talking about Scotland, and anyone who would prefer an accurate catalogue of Highland apparel to Hugo's orgy of spelling mistakes will probably not read the novel anyway. Hugo's resistance to the English language allowed him to preserve the sense of strangeness which language teaching usually eradicates. He grafted his own bizarre etymologies on to the foreign words: white 'ghouls' circled in the air above Gilliatt as he worked on his rock (sea-gulls); a poisonous fungus was called the '*tabouret de crapaud*' ('toad's stool');[60] and Queen Victoria was unaware that her title defined her as a 'prostitute' or 'homosexual'.†[61]

The other peculiarity that sets Hugo apart from common blunderers is his Oedipal relationship with the dictionary. When Vacquerie and Hugo's stationer pointed out the bug-pipe error, Hugo insisted he was right: 'BUG *pipe* is the true spelling. From *bugle*.'[62] If this

* Hugo (or his source) mistook the 'or' for part of the word. A 'philabeg' or 'filibeg' is a kilt. A 'mull' is a snuff-box.
† '*Gouine*', 'Quean' ('harlot') and 'Queen' are etymologically related.

seems strange, it should be remembered that the creator of Bug-Jargal was tenaciously attached to the hieroglyphs of his name as if, like a child, he felt that a significant part of his personality was invested in it. Mere usage was trying to rob him of his UG.[63]

*

THE MONTHS FOLLOWING *Les Travailleurs de la Mer* were taken up with the writing of another novel, *L'Homme Qui Rit* and the framing of some abortive projects: a *Victor Hugo de l'Exil*, designed to compete with counterfeit editions of *Châtiments* and *Napoléon-le-Petit*, and a massive people's encyclopedia, *Tout pour Tous. Répertoire de l'Esprit Humain au XIXe Siècle*, in which all human knowledge would be bathed in the light of Hugo's ideology.

There was a sense of repressed panic in these huge undertakings. Hugo told Adèle that he often had nosebleeds – 'I bleed from the nose like an ox' – and stoutly concluded: 'It clears my head.' But he noticed a curious phenomenon: as his mind grew younger and more vigorous, his life blood was draining away. 'It would be depressing to leave this earth, taking with me the secret of so many half-written, half-lit creations which already exist in my brain. Hence my furious work.'

Somewhat in contradiction of this, he gave up several weeks to supervise, at a distance, the revival of *Hernani* in Paris. The ambiguous nature of his final apotheosis was already emerging: the tentative relaxation of restrictions which signalled the decline of the Empire indirectly dealt a serious blow to Hugo's original work. From June to December 1867, *Hernani* was performed seventy-two times at the Comédie Française and was so successful that the French Government eventually had it taken off the stage. Mini-biographies and lithographs of Victor Hugo were sold in the streets. There were cries of '*Vive Victor Hugo!*' and even '*Vive le proscrit!*'[64] For the few ageing bohemians who had cheered at the first night of *Hernani* in 1830, it was a trip down amnesia lane, a reminder of the great days – far greater in the remembering; for the younger generation, it was a glimpse of the heroic, revolutionary origins of their introverted art and a rare opportunity to feel subversive. *Hernani* was so embedded in people's memories that the changes Hugo had made to the text were corrected out loud by the audience. Hugo alone saw the second victory of *Hernani* in the light of the future. It was a glimpse of the acclaim that awaited him in Paris, proof that he was more popular in the capital than Napoleon III.

But if the shadows were falling over the Empire, clouds were also massing over Hauteville House. Hugo had adopted the bankrupt Kesler as a kind of human pet – he paid his debts, gave him a room in the house and battered him into ideological submission. He looked forward to spending the summer in Brussels, where he would be able to keep an eye on the bills his sons were running up with the wine merchant. His installation there seemed so permanent that Baudelaire had assumed in 1865 that Hugo was settling in for good:

> It seems that he and the Ocean have fallen out. Either *he* was not strong enough to bear the Ocean, or the Ocean itself grew tired of him. – What a waste of time it was setting up a palace on a rock![65]

The great consolation which came in March 1867 – the birth of Charles's first son, Georges – was snatched away the following April when the baby died of meningitis. Worst of all, Adèle was showing signs of leaving him for ever.

Her exceptional life had been curiously typical in one respect. She had seen her biography of Victor Hugo appear in 1863. It was translated immediately as *Victor Hugo: A Life Related by one who has Witnessed it* and partially retranslated dozens of times without acknowledgement by hasty biographers. But Adèle had also seen it primped and teased into the flowery, Second Empire style – a style appropriate to a female hand – by two men: Charles Hugo and Auguste Vacquerie.

Despite what the hagiographical amendments suggest, Hugo read his biography only after publication. He found it 'exquisite' and pointed to 'some small inaccuracies I could easily have corrected had I read the proofs'. The original drafts show a late blossoming of Adèle's intellect, a sturdy, ironic wit, and a style which sometimes wanders off into contemplation of a past that was now illuminated by experience – a style which projects a clear image of the woman who loved to comb her hair for hours and who dipped her biscuit in her tea and forgot it was there.[66] A keen eye might find traces in the text of Sainte-Beuve's role in the family history, but Juliette (to whom Adèle gave a copy of the book) is entirely absent.

Her last letter to Victor might have been written by the daughter of Pierre Foucher half a century before – the girl who had been chosen to be the wife of Mme Hugo's son:

> As soon as I have you, I shall cling to you without asking your permission. I shall be so sweet and gentle that you will not have the courage to desert me. My dream is to die in your arms.

Victor and Adèle were reunited that summer in Brussels. On 24 August 1868, they went out in a carriage together like old lovers. The following afternoon, Adèle suffered a heart attack. She was paralysed on her right side and had difficulty breathing. Doctors came and went. On 27 August, at 6.30 a.m., Hugo closed her eyes.

> Alas! God will receive that great and gentle soul. I am returning her to Him. May she be blessed! According to her wish, we shall transport her coffin to Villequier, to be next to our sweet dead daughter. I shall go with her as far as the border.

There was no mention of the fact that Adèle had died without seeing her second daughter return.

When the body had been prepared for burial, Hugo arranged white daisies around her face and kissed her on the forehead.

> At five o'clock, the lead coffin was sealed and the oak coffin was screwed shut. Before the lid was closed, I took a small key that I had in my pocket and scratched into the lead above her head, 'V. H.'

The tombstone was to be engraved with the words, 'ADÈLE, FEMME DE VICTOR HUGO'.

The wife of Victor Hugo had been photographed on her death-bed. When the enlargement arrived, Hugo reminded himself of death's absolving power and cast a dark light over the last four decades by writing on the photograph: '*Chère morte pardonnée*'.

To forgive is not to forget.

CHAPTER NINETEEN

Stations of the Cross

(1868–1870)

H UGO STOOD BY a railway line at the Belgian border. The guard's van which contained his wife's coffin was disappearing in the direction of Paris. Seventeen years before, he had arrived at the same station in darkness, skulking under a worker's cap. Now, as the world's most popular dissident, he was about to emerge from the night of exile to shine on a new horizon.

The coffin left too late for Hugo to catch the return train. He slept at the home of an admirer in Quiévrain, signed a copy of *Les Misérables* which he found in his bedroom, and took the morning train to Brussels, where his diary shows him seeking the natural consolation: 'Louise, Marais 27, 5 francs'.

Adèle could hardly have died in more cheerful circumstances. Her death was one of several events which marked the hectic end to Hugo's exile like railway signals clattering into the up position. Eleven days before, Alice Hugo gave birth to Georges II, Hugo's treasured grandson, who was to survive long enough to spend a large part of his huge inheritance. Four days earlier, Hugo wrote the last words of his novel, *L'Homme Qui Rit* – the conclusion of fifteen months' hard labour. Then, a few weeks after the burial, work began on the next great nail to be driven into the Empire's coffin. Vacquerie, Meurice and Hugo's sons took advantage of a new law which allowed newspapers to be published without ministerial consent: a sign of Imperial unease dressed up as a generous concession. Weakened by strikes, scandals, an economic recession and the threat of Bismarck's Germany, the Government was hoping to stem the tide of republicanism by cracking open the floodgates. In practice, this 'liberal reform' caused a sudden increase in single-issue newspapers and in the number of journalists who were fined, imprisoned and deported. Censorship had simply passed from the civil service to the judiciary.

Hugo was asked to choose a name for the new paper. His first idea was *La Répu-gnance*, with a hyphen: when the Empire fell, the suffix could be changed from '-*gnance*' to '-*blique*'. Meurice preferred Hugo's later suggestion, *Le Rappel*, because it had 'all sorts of meanings, all of them excellent': 'the call to rally round the republican flag, a reminder of the past ... the recall of M. Bonaparte to a sense of decency, and so on'. In a letter to the editors, which was given pride of place in the first issue (3 May 1869), Hugo identified sixteen different meanings, all summed up in the cry, '*Fiat jus*!': 'Let there be justice!'

Naturally, Hugo himself would be 'a mere reader': he was bound by his oath not to make his political return, in print or in person, until 'freedom' had returned. This did not prevent *Le Rappel* from publishing all his speeches and messages, nor from supplying its 50,000 readers with regular reports from the island home of its guiding spirit. Meanwhile, Hugo would work quietly at his desk, sitting on the horizon like a gigantic innuendo, performing the function he had prophetically defined for himself in the 1840s:

> Knowing how to wait for the right day and time is the secret of the true genius. His patient serenity reassures and at the same time intimidates pygmies and predisposes them to surrender and obey. Many battles are won in advance ... by the spectacle of a mighty force at rest and dreaming.[1]

In other words, there were now two Victor Hugos running on parallel tracks: the writer who was racing against death to excavate and record the remaining contents of his brain, and the republican who was biding his time as if all eternity lay before him.

*

THE GROUP WHICH constituted Hugo's campaign headquarters was an odd assortment of revolutionaries for baby Georges to gaze at from his cradle – the closest thing to a royal family for anti-monarchists.

There was the long nose and black, plastered-down hair of Auguste

Vacquerie, sustained for the last seventeen years by his loathing of English people and Napoleon III. Vacquerie had managed to become an original playwright, but since his entire oeuvre positioned itself in orbit around Hugo's, it is difficult now to see it as anything other than a small, airless satellite.

There was the soft, grey old lady who half succeeded Mme Hugo, although there was never any question of remarriage. Since the Mme Biard fiasco, Hugo had been describing marriage as a form of legalized prostitution, a prophylactic against love.[2] This was largely academic now anyway since his diary shows that he and 'Juju' made love only twice between 1860 and 1870. Juliette herself suppressed any desire to enter the sanctum at whose door she had been sitting 'like an old dog' for the last thirty-five years. It was the century's longest-running Romantic drama. To change roles now would be to upset the order of the universe: 'It seems to me that I love you both with the great soul of your dear departed and with my own. I beg her permission to love you as long as I live in this world and in the next. . . . May all the haloes of heaven and earth be her starry crown for all eternity.'[3]

François-Victor was still mourning his fiancée, still seeking 'decorations' from his father by writing earnest, inflammatory editorials, but still refusing to marry. Nevertheless, Hugo had devised a future for him so unexpectedly majestic that it has entirely escaped attention. If successful, it would have turned the Hugos into the leading political dynasty of the United States of Europe and built a bridge between worlds which seemed destined to remain for ever apart: aristocracy and republic, nobility and bourgeoisie, England and France.

The plan was to marry François-Victor to the 'ravishing' Lady Diana Beauclerk, a frequent visitor to Hauteville House. This, in Hugo's mind, was the purple blood that would blot out the stain of Adèle's 'worthless little English trooper'. Lady Diana's brother was the tenth Duke of St Albans – 'very liberal, almost republican', Hugo assured his son,[4] failing to mention the fact that William Amelius Aubrey de Vere Beauclerk was a member of the Jockey Club, a friend of the Prince of Wales and the owner of a coal-mine in Nottingham-shire.[5] Since Lady Diana showed signs of mild insanity and seemed more interested in Hugo than in his son (she told him that she remembered 'having served him as a cat in a previous existence'),[6]

François-Victor probably made a wise choice. His father was even then recounting the adventures of the son of a republican English peer in *L'Homme Qui Rit* and was effectively offering François-Victor a role in the fantasy.[7]

Hugo's disappointment is understandable. With a Lady Diana in the family, he would have been even more highly connected in England than he was in France. He would have been intimate with that 'ruddy-faced bourgeoise', Queen Victoria,[8] and had a son-in-law in the British Parliament. Casting all this in the proper light would have been an interesting test of his diplomacy.

In contrast to François-Victor, Charles still behaved like the baby and was prone to do silly things like staying in an expensive hotel in Spa and losing 5000 francs at roulette (especially silly for a prominent republican journalist). Sometimes, he repaired his losses by roping Hugo into card games and arranging for him to lose. He intercepted gifts and sold them to his father.[9] He also encouraged him to draw on his letters because an illustrated Victor Hugo manuscript always fetched a good price.[10]

Hugo played along and pretended not to notice. Charles was that happy combination: a spoilt child with an engaging personality. It was a pleasure to forgive him. A description by Gautier's daughter Judith makes him sound like the human equivalent of his darling greyhound: sleek and handsome, with a tendency to bark at policemen.[11]

Not everyone saw the Hugo household in such a pleasant light. Baudelaire had been a regular visitor in Brussels while Mme Hugo was still alive. He was rumoured to be a '*mouchard*' ('spy'), which was Hugolian slang for someone who wrote in officially approved newspapers and did not review Hugo's books, which accounts for almost every living French writer. He was also known to believe that the human race was stuck in the quagmire of original sin, not seated happily on the conveyor-belt of progress. Baudelaire would have to be converted. Over dinner, he was tackled on the subject of what Hugo called 'the great washing of humanity by illumination':[12]

> Mme Hugo explained to me her majestic plan for *international education* . . . I had no end of a job explaining that there were great men BEFORE *international education*, and that since children have nothing

better to do than eat sweets, drink liqueurs in secret and go off to visit prostitutes, there will not be any more great men AFTER it.[13]

The remarkable thing about Baudelaire's doomed relationship with Hugo is not so much the witty insults, which were really a form of self-deprecation, as Hugo's astonishing persistence. 'To Charles Baudelaire, *jungamus dextras*', he wrote in a copy of *Les Chansons des Rues et des Bois*. Baudelaire translated for Manet: 'I don't think it means simply "Let's shake hands". I know the innuendoes of V. Hugo's Latin. It also means "*Let's join hands* TO SAVE THE HUMAN RACE". But I don't give a damn about the human race, and he never noticed.'[14] But it was precisely because Hugo *had* noticed that he was trying to set Baudelaire straight. It was impossible for him to believe that someone who attracted his interest could genuinely hold views so opposed to his own.

Paul Verlaine, whose generation was too young to have been exasperated by Hugo's cultural 'dictatorship' (Baudelaire's word), was more receptive. He found Hugo's Brussels home in a quiet, residential *quartier* of trees and stuccoed walls:

I was in a state. A terrible state. Of course I was! Like the rest of my generation, I was Hugolatrous twice over: 1830 and 2 December. I was haunted by those two dates. . . .

He quoted some of my poetry to me – that sublime, sweet crafty devil! He flattered my childish pride by paternally allowing me to sustain an argument. . . .

As for *Impassibility*, which we Parnassians had adopted as our slogan, he said, 'You'll get over it.'[15]

The best view of the Hugos' Belgian outpost comes from the man Hugo called his 'third son'. After a spell as a government clerk, Henri Rochefort had become one of the most successful journalists in French history, a mixture of anarchist and music-hall impresario. His pocket-sized newspaper, *La Lanterne* (May 1868–November 1869) dealt a significant left-hook to the Emperor's image. It had half a million readers and was one of the first serious attempts to reveal the lunatic bureaucracy that underpinned the Second Empire.

One of the key themes of *La Lanterne* was the notion that Victor Hugo was a future President. As an avid reader of comic papers,

Hugo was delighted to follow the weekly adventures of his image.[16] The issue for 13 June 1868 reported the Government's decision to authorize a lecture series on French theatre, 'on condition that the name of Victor Hugo not be uttered'.[17] Rochefort imagined a bureaucrat briefing the Minister of Education:

> 'Excellency, bad news. It has come to my attention that the name of Victor Hugo has been uttered 4852 times this week. I believe it advisable to reinforce the Paris garrison.'
>
> 'A worrying sign indeed,' the Minister must say. 'Last month, that baneful name was uttered only 2700 times.'

In August 1868, Rochefort fled from a flurry of fines and prison sentences totalling 16,250 francs, two years and five months and moved his *Lanterne* to Brussels. When he arrived at the Place des Barricades, Hugo's Christ-like greeting was, 'Sit here at my side, for you are also one of my sons.' He offered him free board and lodging – certainly a sign of personal affection since Hugo was keen to remain (or to be seen to remain) politically unaligned.

Rochefort later published a detailed description of life under Hugo in 1868–9.[18] The value of his account lies in the fact that he refused to tackle the Gordian knot of 'sincerity'. He knew that he was seeing the real Victor Hugo and that he was also seeing a performance. Hugo's study–bedroom, for instance – off-limits to the rest of the family – was set up as a kind of photo opportunity. At the appointed time, Rochefort would open the door to find the genius standing in a sea of wet manuscripts, his pen looping across large sheets of vellum, impervious to the weather: 'It was a tiny attic, so lightly roofed that the sky could be seen through the tiles, and, as Victor Hugo somewhat proudly declared, the rain occasionally found its way into the room.' Hugo had re-created the conditions in which his writing brain had first sprung to life. At his age and in his position, a leaking roof was a luxury.

In *Le Rappel*, he posed for his sons' readers as 'an old man who is anxious and at peace. At peace because I am at the bottom of the precipice; anxious because my country might fall into it.' Massive demonstrations at the tomb of Baudin – the *député* whose bullet-ridden body Hugo had seen being carried from the barricade in 1851

– brought a fresh spate of cheerfully abusive poems like 'They've been feasting now for nigh on seventeen years!'[19] But there was still no sign that he was preparing for his finest political hour. It seemed to be pure coincidence that his family now included two of Napoleon III's most powerful opponents: Rochefort and Alice's godfather, Jules Simon. His jottings on the subject of a possible return show how difficult it was at his age to make plans for the future – not because death might prevent their realization, but because time kept spinning itself into circles or disappearing altogether:

> To become a Minister, President, etc.?
> What's the point?
> Minister of what? President of whom?
> I am a Spirit on this earth.
> That is what I wish to remain.
> I have no need to become a functionary of men; I am a functionary of God.[20]

*

FOR THE TIME BEING, Hugo's divine duty consisted of publishing what he claimed was a study of 'Aristocracy': a novel called *L'Homme Qui Rit*.

The two volumes appeared in Paris, Brussels, Leipzig and Leghorn in April and May 1869. Critically and commercially, it was almost a failure, perhaps because minds were taken up with the elections which gave the Empire its first and last parliamentary government, or because it asked readers who now expected novels to reflect the trivia of their own lives to take an interest in seventeenth-century England, or rather, in the region of Hugo's mind which he had decided to locate on that fog-beshrouded island off the French coast.

The opening words might have sent many readers back to the title-page to make sure they had not accidentally bought a parody:

> Ursus and Homo were bound by close friendship. Ursus was a man, Homo was a wolf.... This association of man and wolf was a boon to fairs, parish fêtes and street-corners where crowds assemble.... The wolf, being docile and graciously subordinate, was pleasing to the crowd. Taming is always a pleasant sight. Nothing makes us happier

than to see all varieties of domestication pass before our eyes. That is why so many people line the routes of royal processions.

L'Homme Qui Rit was supposed to be 'a true picture of England painted by means of invented characters' and thus, according to Hugo, not a historical novel in the traditional sense.[21] It reached its 'truth' by what seemed a convoluted route: the story of a boy called Gwynplaine who was abducted in infancy by the 'Comprachicos' ('child-buyers') – a multinational tribe of nomads who practised the art of cosmetic mutilation and sold the fruits of their gruesome industry to circuses. The mutilation performed on Gwynplaine is a hideous, fixed laugh: 'whatever emotion he felt only served to increase and aggravate that strange face of joy'.

Abandoned on the English coast at a spot which Hugo would have seen from the Weymouth steamer, Gwynplaine is adopted by the fairground philosopher and kind-hearted misanthrope, Ursus, along with the blind orphan girl, Dea. Gwynplaine and Dea fall in love: the blind girl 'sees' the soul instead of the mask of twisted flesh. The three humans and their wolf travel through southern England in a painted caravan called 'The Green-Box', performing mystery plays with Gwynplaine's face as the star attraction.

While the Green-Box plays to ever-larger audiences, the obscure royal official known as the 'Uncorker of the Ocean's Bottles' has discovered that Gwynplaine is the long-lost son of an exiled republican peer: Lord Linnaeus Clancharlie. In London, Gwynplaine is snatched away by the equally mysterious official called 'the Wapentake'[22] and, after a blood-curdling insight into the workings of English 'justice', takes his seat in the House of Lords, where he proposes to regale the high and mighty with a faithful depiction of life among the *misérables*. The revolutionary message is drowned in waves of laughter.

Gwynplaine leaves Westminster in disgust and arrives at the coast to find Ursus setting sail in the belief that Gwynplaine is dead. The grief-stricken Dea dies in his arms. In the thickening shadows, Gwynplaine acquires her visionary sight and follows her soul over the edge of the ship into the starless sea.

L'Homme Qui Rit was instantly recognized as a novel about Victor

19. François-Victor, Adèle,
Mme Hugo, Charles and VH.

20. 'Victor Hugo listening to God',
by his sons, 1856.

21. Hauteville House.

22. Hauteville House: the Oak Gallery.

23. Hauteville House: the 'look-out'.

24. Adèle, daughter of VH.

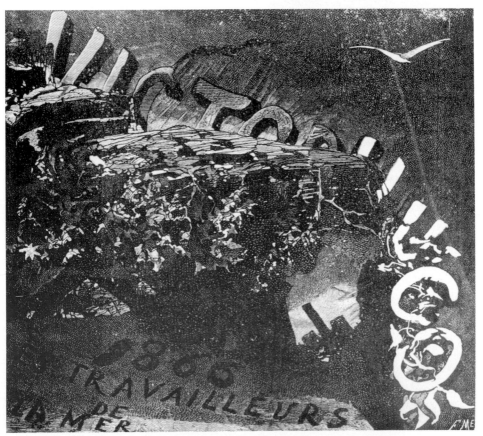

25. Frontispiece for *Les Travailleurs de la Mer*.

26. Manuscript of *L'Homme Qui Rit*, fo285

27. 'The Imperial Eagle blasted by *Les Châtiments*', by H. Daumier.

28. Funeral of Charles Hugo, Paris, 1871.

29. Blanche Lanvin.

30. VH in 1879, Leon Bonnat.

31. VH and his grandchildren,
Jeanne and Georges.

32. Juliette Drouet in 1883,
by Bastien-Lepage.

33. VH with Paul Meurice
and Auguste Vacquerie
at Veules-les-Roses,
c. 1883–4.

34. VH on his deathbed, by Nadar.

35. VH's funeral procession arrives at the Panthéon.

Hugo: the mutilated child, winning a perverse acceptance from the people he entertains with his deformity; the republican lord, ridiculed by his fellow peers for exposing social sores. Other similarities were assumed to be accidental: the half-tamed, hairy thing called Homo, the fairground quack called Ursus. The more subtle self-revelations went unnoticed. Years passed before a less gossipy approach to literature made it easier to see that Hugo's novels were not personal boasts but studies of possible extremes, the imaginary pursuit of one path to its disastrous conclusion while the rest of Hugo remained safely at the crossroads. Gwynplaine was an experimental Hugo who bottles up his visionary message and sails off to suicide and inner truth.

On the way, he survives the ultimate test of the hero: the unfathomable female body, incarnated by Duchess Josiane, a depraved idealist, fascinated by the thought of having sex with the ugliest man alive: 'She lived in some mysterious expectation of a supreme, lascivious ideal.' 'A peculiar thing about her – less rare than is generally believed – is that one of her eyes was blue and the other black. . . . Day and night mingled in her gaze.'

Hugo never commented on his characters' origins, only on their destinations, and so none of these analogies can be labelled conscious or unconscious. In any case, the distinction is not as useful as it sounds. Josiane represents the all-pervasive fear that Nature herself was trying to stop him obeying the dictates of his conscience and that, beyond rational good, lay a force that could only be described as Evil: 'A disquieting ecstasy, ending with the brutal triumph of instinct over duty'. 'Vices have an invisible path already prepared in our organism.'[23] The fact that Gwynplaine escapes the alluring *pieuvre* suggests the hope in Hugo of a final victory, an escape from the daily antithesis of good and evil, discipline and relapse.

France was in no mood for laughter. The few who read the novel from cover to cover saw it as one of the last bonfires of a decadent mind, an appalling reflection of the nation he had helped to corrupt.[24] In Britain, Hugo's claim that *L'Homme Qui Rit* was historically accurate brought guffaws of protest.[25]

This time, it was said, Hugo had gone completely off the rails. His England was infested with impossible creatures: the legendary *neitse*, which had the feet of a pig and the bleat of a calf; the fulmar which spewed lamp-oil from its beak; the mischievous chough which dropped burning twigs on to thatched roofs. The human population was similarly plagued with exoticism: Tom-Jim-Jack the boxer, Lord Desertum of Kilcarry, Lord Cantilupe, Queen Cuthbarghe and Dr Gumdraith of All Soules College. They lived in legendary cities like Winbuenminster, Umfraville and Srehwsbury. Hugo had practised the art of the spelling mistake with his usual immunity to correction. Nothing in this fantastic book, wrote Frank Marzials, 'bears any resemblance to anything that ever was or ever will be'.[26]

This is rather like complaining that Sir John Mandeville is useless as a guide to the Holy Land. Swinburne, who admired the 'Blakishness' of Hugo's religious poems,[27] was the only reviewer to suggest that the novel should not be read 'by the lamplight of realism'.[28] In fact, there is a remarkable Britishness about the novel, reminiscent of Swift, Lewis Carroll, Tolkien or Mervyn Peake. Hugo had after all been living on English soil for a period equivalent to the careers of many writers. His proper nouns may sound like cheap imported whiskies – Clancharlie, MacCallummore – they may have been found in old satires and assumed to be the names of real people,[29] but they show a wonderful sense of the riches of the English language, and perhaps the biggest surprise of all is that so many of them are real – even the oil-spitting fulmar and the pig-footed *neitse*.*

Hugo had teased out of what appeared to be something worse than ignorance a brilliant depiction of the solidified revolution that underlies British culture. The wraiths of older tongues – Saxon, Latin, Gaelic and one is tempted to say Prehistoric – return to claim their place in the dictionary. It was as if all of Britain's populations since the formation of the English Channel had been living at the same time in the Home Counties, as if the Celtic exodus had never taken place. Hugo had regallicized England and brought the extremities to the centre.

If enough people had read the novel to make the connection, instead of assuming that 'The Laughing Man' was another jibe at Napoleon the Little,[30] they might have been alarmed to see the

---

* *Neitser-soak*: Greenlandic for the hooded or bladder-nosed seal.

manner in which Hugo had tackled the subject of aristocracy. The sneering aristocrats of Westminster are too picturesque and anti-quated to suggest a present threat, and there is something comforting about Hugo's House of Lords, compared to the volcano-Parliament of his next novel, *Quatrevingt-treize*. 'The French like a complete revolution; the English prefer a well-behaved earthquake.'[31]

The lasting impression, ironically, is of a deep, visceral disgust and fascination with the seething plebs, and the comedian's desire to 'instruct' his public by rubbishing everything that passes for knowl-edge. *L'Homme Qui Rit*, like the recently Disneyfied, disinfected *Notre-Dame de Paris*, has a sentimental moral that can be used to render it harmless; but it can also be read as the manifesto of a massacre, a reminder that a poet who aspires to 'save' his country can just as easily dream of its annihilation.[32] *L'Homme Qui Rit* is the most representative novel of its age, written for a society that was on the verge of self-destruction. The great gilded speeches Hugo was to unfurl on his return to France are just as hilarious as Gwynplaine's grimace or the mock-philosophical tirades of Ursus. But Hugo's savage treatment of his clowns suggests that all the time he was laughing at the laughing reader:

> 'I am coming, Dea,' he said. 'Here I am.'
> He walked on. There was no parapet. The void lay before him. He put his foot in it.

*

THE UNEXPECTED IMAGE of Hugo as a laughing anarchist is reinforced by the corpus of eleven playlets and dramatic poems, most of which date from the last years of exile. They were eventually published in the posthumous volume, *Le Théâtre en Liberté* (1886), and remained a funny little island in French theatrical history until the plays of Brecht, Ionesco and Beckett showed them to be part of a new continent. Their settings range from a cloister on the Isle of Man to a railway track, and the characters include a talking stone and a 100-year-old woman in a sack. Only one was performed in Hugo's lifetime and they are still being rediscovered, along with their odd, ironic figures who poke fun at the author's little foibles – speech-tampering, pedantry, snobbishness and the sexual exploitation of women. It may be that this explains their neglect: they so spectacularly fail to confirm the received idea of a Victor Hugo blinded by his ego.

The largest and most remarkable of the unperformed plays (1869) is devoted to Torquemada, mastermind of the Spanish Inquisition, 'the healer with bloody hands' who wants to rescue the human race from the eternal fires of Hell by burning it at the stake: 'Save those lost souls with pitchforks, / And drive them into Eden!' It was published in 1882 as a protest against the pogrom in Russia.

Torquemada is not just another sanctimonious disquisition on the wickedness of fanaticism. It examines the results of imposing any system of beliefs on human life; the paradox of the social Messiah whose abstract love of humanity can express itself in cruelty as well as charity; the idea – that was still to make Hugo the bogeyman of conservatives and republicans alike – that the active contemplation of God's mysteries is preferable to a fossilized conviction and that, even in the aftermath of a holocaust, the desirable alternative to one disastrous ideology is not another ideology. The tragic hero of *Torquemada* is not a frazzled martyr but Torquemada himself and, by extension, Victor Hugo: the fearless 'functionary of God', following the dictates of his conscience . . .

As the Empire teetered on the brink of collapse, Hugo was pulling out the files on his past selves with a new urgency and openness, reconsidering the dilemmas of power. He now owed his influence to the fact that he was a victim. His power lay in impotence. What would happen if he became the next Napoleon?

One of the first casualties of war would be these more eccentric aspects of his writing. Large, unfinished texts litter his complete works like houses left in a hurry: the attempt to rediscover a primal language; speculations on extraterrestrial life, on the apparently chaotic proliferation of effects from tiny causes, on the need to devise a 'housekeeping' method for the planet.[33]

If *Torquemada* looks forward to the rise of fascism and the new, political 'religions', Hugo's abandoned projects are a farewell to the age of Romanticism and its dreams of the future. The complete story of his exile is not the story of a sacrifice eventually redeemed with interest, but the story of one sacrifice leading to another. The French poet banished from France, and the English visionary forced by events to leave his island tomb.

*

IN PARIS, 'that great blind mole, the Past' was about to stick its snout into the present. Something like the French Revolution was struggling to be reborn. The elections of May 1869 saw *Le Rappel* exercising its new legal right to support republican candidates: Henri Rochefort and a young lawyer called Léon Gambetta. As a result, its offices were ransacked and the editors threatened with imprisonment. Joke ballot papers circulated, inviting Parisians to vote for Louis Blanc, Félix Pyat or Victor Hugo, none of whom was eligible.[34] Rumours that Hugo was to be smuggled into the city brought huge crowds to demonstrations which were officially described as small gatherings of trouble-makers watched by large groups of sightseers.

In May, Rochefort and Gambetta were both elected. Official candidates suffered a crushing defeat in all the big cities, though the bulk of the population remained loyal to the Emperor. On the evening of 10 June 1869, 20,000 Parisians protested against the attempted closure of *Le Rappel*. Street kiosks were smashed, and for the first time since 1851 a barricade went up in the streets of Paris.

Hugo watched and waited, refusing to align himself with any republican faction, dissociating himself from his sons' newspaper, urging peaceful protest, and devising futures for himself like a novelist looking for a denouement. First, the epic conclusion: 'On the day they erect a barricade which is to my liking, I shall, if possible, go and die on it. It will be a sweet end.' Next, the understated ending:

> Boasting in advance of dying on a barricade which may never be built is pointless. I shall simply say that I shall try to make a good end.
>
> I am old, introspective, disinterested and useless. Apparently, I don't even have any literary talent any more.

Finally, a *modus moriendi*:

> Anyone can have the good fortune to be killed. I do not claim to be more favoured in that respect than anyone else, but I do not wish to be less favoured. One should not die on purpose, but one should not try to stay alive on purpose either.[35]

It might be expected that Hugo's self-centred view of developments in the Empire would make him a poor political analyst, and this is so often assumed to be inevitably the case that his analyses are usually dismissed as unprofessional ramblings. In fact, it had the opposite effect. Someone who habitually examines international affairs in the light of their own personality and ambitions has a much broader frame of reference and more reasons to go on thinking about the subject than most people. That September, Hugo agreed to chair the Lausanne Peace Conference. His opening speech was the usual panoply of stirring generalizations, which was fortunate, since he had mistaken the Conference for the more revolutionary Workers' Congress which was being held in Basel. But behind the rhetoric, the speech contained an unusually sensible diagnosis of the continental débâcle that began in 1870 and ended, temporarily, in 1918. Hugo's idea was that a final war might be necessary, but it would be a war to end all wars:

> Wars have all sorts of pretexts, but they only ever have one cause: armies. Remove the Army and you remove War. . . .
> Kings agree on one thing: perpetuating war. People think their kings are quarrelling. Not at all. They are helping each other out. The soldier must have his *raison d'être*. To perpetuate war is to perpetuate tyranny. The logic is impeccable. It is also ferocious.[36]

Hugo returned to Guernsey in November. It was a wet and miserable winter. He began to suffer from sciatic rheumatism and sent gloomy poems to *Le Rappel*, among them a Zolaesque slice-of-life from the coal-mines of Aubin where twenty-four strikers had been shot dead by Government troops: 'The miner is a negro,' says the sixteen-year-old prostitute narrator. 'It rains, though there is no sky.' 'Each gallery is a hole whose worm is a man.' Increasingly, the philosophical ray of hope came not from the content but from the form. These poems are to Hugo's speeches what prayers are to a sermon. God expressed himself through the mysterious coincidences of words. The names of the two communities where miners had been massacred – *Ricamarie, Aubin* – were also a gigantic rhyme-image of Babylonian Paris, where decadent despots amused themselves with whores: *ris qu'a Marie au bain* ('Marie's laughter in the bath').[37]

The sun was setting over the Empire but also over Hugo's island kingdom. The prospect of a Republic was forcing him to face the fact that exiles can never truly return. *Les Misérables* had celebrated the smelly, anarchic Paris of Hugo's childhood. But as Baudelaire had reminded him in the magnificent elegy, 'Le Cygne', which he dedicated to Hugo, 'the form of a city changes faster than a human heart'. Hugo knew that he would not be returning to ancient Rome or Athens, but to the European New York:

> How fine it is! From Pantin you can see all the way to Grenelle!
> Old Paris is nothing now but an everlasting
> Street, which stretches out, elegant and lovely as an *I*,
> Saying, 'Rivoli! Rivoli! Rivoli!'
>
> The Empire's a draughtboard locked away in its box.
> Everything there except conscience runs straight and true.[38]

*

IN ONE SENSE, Hugo had never left France. Several examples of himself were already fully implicated in French political life and it was with these other Victor Hugos that he would form a coalition on his return.

As far as the ruling class is concerned, the depressing conclusion to be drawn is that while censorship had only served to disseminate his work, real damage had been done by self-censorship. Almost everything written about the exiled Hugo is quite adequately represented by the entry in Flaubert's *Dictionnaire des Idées Reçues*, quoted here in its entirety:

> HUGO (VICTOR). – It was really quite wrong of him to go into politics.[39]

The desertion of Hugo by most of his contemporaries was noted by the younger generations. Banville's 'Ballade de Victor Hugo' became a famous anthem in the last months of the Empire with its refrain, 'Mais le père est là-bas, dans l'île.' 'The old man over on his island' was a schoolboy legend, the only living Romantic who had real adventures; proof that it was possible to grow up and still be subversive. Since 1856, all his new works had been available in France, but there were exciting signs of official disapproval: busts of Hugo sold under the counter,[40] spiv-like individuals hawking pornographic picture books and smutty copies of *Napoléon-le-Petit*. A history of France for schools intriguingly identified the opponents of the 1851 *coup d'état* as 'escaped convicts and members of secret societies'.[41]

Hugo's image in the proletariat is harder to reconstruct. Pictures of Hugo were a common sight on the walls of workers' homes where they took the place once occupied by that other saviour-in-exile, Napoleon Bonaparte.[42] Newspapers sold secretly in the *faubourgs* presented a muddier image. Hugo's works were revered; the man himself was tainted by his past. A fine example of this dual identity can be found in a paper which, in its attempts to dodge the censor, began life as *Jocko*, ended as *La Mère Michel* and, for six issues, went by the name *Le Misérable*. '*Misérable*' now had a plainly revolutionary connotation, as did '*Quasimodo*', who wrote to the paper in February 1870 to complain about living conditions in the suburban slums. But for a newspaper which encouraged its readers to go out and shoot policemen, Hugo was not necessarily to be trusted. The issue calling itself *RR_RR^RAN!* invited readers to visit the poor exiles' cemetery on Jersey and to conclude that Victor Hugo had saved his own bacon and abandoned his brothers in exile.

The aggressively purist, anarchist view of Hugo was almost identical to the extreme conservative view. A foul-mouthed proletarian rag called *La Mère Duchêne* (a.k.a. *La Guillotine*) devoted the front page of its first three issues to Victor Hugo.[43] The style is a foretaste of the Paris Commune and an example of the dangerous, pantomime approach to politics which Hugo's *Châtiments* had done so much to foster: 'This personage, the poet-chameleon, is the biggest braggart who has ever existed in the history of humanity since the fallen angel.' 'The son of a soldier of the first Empire, he was brought up with imperialist ideas.' With each new regime, the chameleon changed its colour. He cadged a pension from Louis XVIII, licked the boots of Charles X, deserted to the freemasons in 1830, served the evil government of Louis-Philippe, begged to be made a *pair de France*, and then bedded the wife of his best friend, Biard, and got off scot-free. All this time, he had been 'fabricating obscene, impious dramas' and 'consorting publicly with the courtesan Juliette'. Why had he

spent the last eighteen years in exile? Because Louis Bonaparte refused
to give him a ministry. The series ended with a long poem in which
Hugo was said to have the voice of a peacock, the head of a
hydrocephalic, poisonous bad breath and a cancerous growth in his
armpit which supplied him with his ink.

The significance of this mud-slinging is that it was obviously
intended for a proletarian audience which thought of Hugo as its
Bonnie Prince Charlie. In February 1870, *La Mère Duchêne* printed a
selection of readers' letters protesting about its treatment of 'a man
like Hugo'. One unsung hero called Durou offered to meet the writer
of the articles in the street outside his home at 10 Rue Cadet between
8.30 and 9 p.m. There were no further issues of *La Mère Duchêne*.

This radical disagreement about Hugo was inevitable in a period
in which political debate had been reduced to the endless reiteration
of passionately held views. On the other hand, how could anyone
identify the real Hugo with any confidence? Was he, for instance, the
contemplative soul who presented himself to readers of *Le Rappel* as a
kind of geological remnant, 'cut off by the escarpments which have
agglomerated around my conscience'?[44] Or the man who was furious
with Rochefort for not turning an anti-Government demonstration
into a full-scale riot when 100,000 Parisians protested at the murder
of a journalist by Napoleon's gun-toting cousin? Hugo was yearning
for a sudden solution, desperate to see the slow trickle of events
funnelled into one symbolic cataract. Perhaps *La Mère Duchêne* was
right to insist on his 'imperial' upbringing. Both sides of his family
had created blood-baths in the past.

For the next four months, Hugo went about the business of the
professional exile: the Poor Children's Christmas Dinner at which he
held out the prospect of a 'radiant' twentieth century to children who
would be of fighting age in 1914; a letter to the 'Seamen of the
Channel' who had thanked him in a collective letter for writing *Les
Travailleurs de la Mer* ('I am one of you,' he wrote, 'a combatant of
the abyss'; 'I am wet, I shiver, but I smile and sometimes, like you, I
sing'). In the same vein of incongruity, he sent a letter of support to
the British Ladies' National Association for the Repeal of the
Contagious [i.e. Venereal] Diseases Act. In April, he spoke at the
grave of his old sparring-partner, the atheist and communist, Hennett

de Kesler. As the coffin was lowered into the grave, Hugo won their last argument by observing, first, that Kesler was now in the next world, talking to great republicans of the past, and, second, that he had died owning property (his plot in the cemetery).

Compared to his other public pronouncements, the funeral oration was light relief.

*

1870 IS SUCH a momentous year in French history that it is natural to want to start packing Hugo's bags for him and to assume that he knew what was about to happen. But after the excitement of 1868 and 1869, there was every sign that the Empire would muddle through.

Napoleon III was tormented by his unpopularity and bullied by his wife, who was becoming increasingly keen on running the country. In 1870, he proved that he was still as slippery as ever. The nation was invited to approve the recent 'liberal reforms'. A 'Yes' would be a vote for the Empire as it was, and a 'No' would be a vote for the Empire as it would have been if all its citizens had understood the pre-eminent importance of economics.

Hugo's response appeared in *Le Rappel* and in several other papers. The plebiscite was 'the *coup d'état* in the form of a piece of paper'. 'Can arsenic be rendered edible? That is the question.' He proposed a question of his own: 'Should I leave the Tuileries for the Conciergerie and place myself at the disposal of the courts?' Signed 'Napoleon'. Answer: 'Yes.'

As a result, a warrant was issued for Hugo's arrest, his sons were sentenced to prison, again, and Napoleon III saw his reforms approved by 7,358,000 votes to 1,572,000, with 1,894,000 abstentions. The future looked imperial. Hugo found himself back at the starting-point. He continued to write poems for a collection he was thinking of calling *Nouveaux Châtiments* or *Tonnerres à l'Horizon* ('Thunder on the Horizon').[45] Some of the poems dated back to the 1850s and had originally been earmarked for a volume to be called *Boîte aux Lettres* ('Letter-Box').[46] They were eventually published posthumously as *Les Années Funestes*.

If Hugo truly believed, as some have claimed, that the Empire was about to fall, why did he spend so much time preparing a book that would be out-of-date as soon as it appeared? Though he later boasted of having predicted the Prussian invasion,[47] the poems in which he depicted the Empire as a *danse macabre* show its nemesis taking a divine, not a Prussian form. The last of the *Années Funestes* to be written before the war, 'Épizootie dans les Hommes de Décembre' is the work not of a man who is mentally priming his pistols but of a jovial old revolutionary who likes to start the day by reading the obituaries: 'Grave-digger, help them down. / Throw ashes on Morny / And mud on Troplong.'*

He also made a momentous discovery that summer which confirmed his cosmic view of human affairs. Charles and Alice arrived at Hauteville House with little Georges and their second child, Jeanne, born on 29 September 1869. Hugo had the pond and terrace cordoned off and addressed a poem to the garden birds, inviting them to come and feed on little Georges's window-sill. The cradles and nursemaid were installed in Adèle II's empty bedroom.

Suddenly, Hugo was reminded that human beings shared the planet with a separate human race. Every contact was recorded: '6 July 1870: *Jeanne a fait pipi sur moi. C'est la seconde fois.*' These 'divinely clumsy' creatures[48] were not imperfect forms of an adult imago but beings in their own right, with their own language and customs. 'Their obscure conversation opens up horizons for me. / They understand and explain things to each other. / Imagine how it scatters my thoughts.'

Babies and young children seem to have had the same dissolving effect on Hugo's mind as the Ocean. They gave the same sense of the roundness of time and the interpenetration of body and universe:

> An exile is a benevolent soul. . . . Through his reverie, he sees little three-year-old girls running on the strand, their bare feet in the sea, their skirts pulled up with both hands, showing their innocent belly to the immense fecundity.[49]

While Hugo listened to baby-talk like an anthropologist studying the language of a lost tribe, the leaders of the adult world were behaving like little boys. A Hohenzollern Prince was a candidate for

---

* Morny: President of the Legislative Assembly. Troplong: President of the Court of Appeal.

the Spanish throne. Since the head of the Hohenzollern family was Wilhelm I of Prussia, and since Prussia had been frustrating French ambitions in Europe for the last ten years, France objected. Apparently, it was time to make a stand. The Minister for Foreign Affairs let it be known that a Hohenzollern King of Spain would be a *casus belli*. Hohenzollern withdrew, and that should have been that.

Empress Eugénie, however, was bent on winning a diplomatic victory for her husband's discredited Empire. She insisted that King Wilhelm personally guarantee the withdrawal. Bismarck issued a curt statement in the form of a telegram. It was read in Paris on Bastille Day. No such assurance would be given. France considered itself insulted and declared war on Prussia on 19 July 1870. 'It has pleased certain men to condemn a part of the human race to death,' wrote Hugo. 'Masterpieces are announced. One rifle will kill twelve men, one cannon will kill a thousand.'[50] A great surge of mindless patriotism brought cheering crowds into the streets. There was a rush on maps of Germany: everyone wanted to chart the progress of the victorious French Army. *Paris Journal*, a family newspaper, suggested flinging the dead bodies of pacifists into the sewer.[51]

One of the few pleasant sights in the bloody twilight of the Second Empire is its greatest sentimental patriot betraying the patriotic cause. Hugo published an open letter 'To the Women of Guernsey' which appeared in most of the mainland newspapers. He appealed for bandages, to be distributed equally among French and German casualties: 'Since these blind men have forgotten they are brothers, be their sisters!'

Like everyone else, Hugo expected French soldiers to be celebrating in Berlin in a few days' time. France was winning the arms race and the confidence of its Army was reputed to be based on something concrete. Hugo's dream of a French Rhineland would come true. The two equal pillars of the United States of Europe would be established and the language of progress would be imposed on the federation: 'The United States of Europe speaking German would set us back five hundred years.' 'But none of this should be achieved through Bonaparte! Not by this atrocious war!'[52]

Despite his gloomy prognostication of victory, the man who had studied the inscrutable chaos of Waterloo half-suspected the final outcome: 'I believe that Prussia will be crushed; but complications may arise and pass through a series of collisions which will end in revolution.'[53]

Given the mood of absolute certainty in France, it is surprising to see that a bureaucrat in Paris had had the same idea. On 26 July, a week after war was declared, Hugo discovered that he had been accused by two Frenchmen – one of whom sent his children to the Poor Children's Dinners – of plotting with the exiled d'Orléans family to assassinate the Emperor.[54] Ex-convicts were apparently to be recruited in Rouen and armed with pistols. If need be, the 'plot' could be used to discredit republicans and monarchists at the same time. It would also 'prove' that Victor Hugo had been a closet royalist all along.

Hugo's first response to rumours of war had been a characteristically symbolic act. While Bismarck's telegram was being read in Paris, he was conducting a little ceremony in the garden of Hauteville House: the planting of the acorn (actually one of several acorns) that would grow into 'The Oak of the United States of Europe'. 'A hundred years from now, there will be no more war, no more Pope, and the oak will be tall.' He was right about the oak.

Three weeks later, on 9 August 1870, it was time for direct action:

> The papers have come. The war is turning into a catastrophe. Devastating news. Three battles lost one after the other, including a big one, by MacMahon. 8000 Frenchmen taken prisoner. 30 cannon, 6 machine-guns, 2 flags captured.
>
> I shall put all my manuscripts in the three trunks and prepare to place myself at the disposal of duty and events.
>
> Charles and all my guests are leaving today for Jersey. Jersey has the telegraph and Charles will hear all the latest news. If necessary, he will write to me every hour.[55]

Less than a month into the war, France had lost Alsace and Lorraine. The Army had been trained in the wilds of Algeria and was inexperienced in the use of heavy artillery and railways. Supplies were stranded a long way from the front line. Maps had to be requisitioned from local schools. It was becoming apparent that the excellence of French soldiers had been greatly exaggerated. Louis Bonaparte sat on his horse in agony, crippled with indecision and gallstones. The end of the Empire was at hand, which was not an absolute tragedy; but would there still be a nation called France?

On 13 August, Hugo took 12,000 francs from the Old Bank and had 11,000 sewn into his waistcoat. That night, he had a dream. He met Louis Bonaparte in the back shop of Mme Levert, Auguste Blanqui's friend in Brussels. 'He was going out. I was coming back in.' The imaginary companion of his exile, the rival brother and evil alter ego, ousted from a small, dark room belonging to a married woman ... The motherland was about to welcome home its vindicated son.

On 15 August, Hugo left Guernsey with Charles and Alice, Jeanne and Georges, three maids, Juliette and her nephew, Louis Koch. Hugo handed out an Italian remedy for seasickness. After an unusually nauseating crossing, they reached Southampton early the next morning. A customs officer who had written a poem in honour of Hugo the year before let them pass without opening the trunks. They boarded the train for Waterloo, caught a second train at Charing Cross, sailed from Dover, and reached Brussels at 9.30 p.m. on 17 August.

Meanwhile, a telegram had left the French embassy in London. It contained disturbing news for the Minister of the Interior: 'Hugo is said to be leaving Guernsey today for the little island of Sarks [sic]. In reality, he is headed for Bayeux.' Victor Hugo, said the telegram, had been holding secret talks with a Prussian agent. Forty thousand traitors were waiting in Bayeux for Oberleutnant Hugo to lead them to Paris.[56] It is interesting that this was considered believable. Hugo's works were still seen in some quarters as a deliberate attempt to undermine French civilization. Even as late as 1883, he was described, by the author of *Victor Hugo le Petit*, as a cultural German spy.[57] The hunt for scapegoats that would culminate in the Dreyfus Affair was already under way.

Hugo was to wait in Brussels for another three weeks, discussing the future with other exiles, leaving instructions for his executors, enjoying family life, and trying to save a medieval tower that was due to be demolished. The children were having nightmares. Hugo had decided to end his exile if the French were defeated; but he would be

defending Paris, not the Empire. He would return as a normal citizen
and take his place in the civilian Garde Nationale: 'To share the death
of Paris would be my glory . . . and if the people do not rise, I shall
return to exile.'

Hugo knew perfectly well that he would not be 'just another
guardsman'. Like the Empire, he was making contingency plans,
sketching out speeches and possible futures. Whatever happened, he
would be ready:

> Dictatorship. I shall bear the burden of it. If I fail, I shall punish
> myself by going into exile for ever.
>
> If I succeed, dictatorship is a crime. A crime is not absolved by
> success. I shall have committed this crime. I shall pass sentence on
> myself, and even if I save the Republic, I declare that I shall leave
> France never to return.[58]

This was Hugo holding a policy meeting with his super-ego. If he
was fortunate enough to save the motherland (when the fatherland
was in danger, it tended to change its gender), one Victor Hugo
would punish the other Victor Hugo for this act of hubris – union
with the mother – thus rendering it retrospectively acceptable. Having
discovered the absolving power of that 'atrocious, holy thing', exile,[59]
he would use it to the full. Napoleon III and Victor Hugo, the
banisher and the banished, would be merged in one super-Hugo. It
was the best ending he had written for himself so far.

On 31 August 1870, finding the eye of his own storm, he wrote a
poem entitled 'Au Moment de Rentrer en France'. It was written in a
rare stanzaic form which exactly reproduces the breathing of someone
who is mulling over drastic possibilities, arrested by a recurrent
thought, measuring the drop:

> Qui peut en ce moment où Dieu peut-être échoue,
> > Deviner
> Si c'est du côté sombre ou joyeux que la roue
> > Va tourner? . . .

('Now that God perhaps is helpless, who can tell which way the wheel
will turn – toward joy or gloom? . . .')

Four days later, newspaper vendors were passing in the street, shouting, 'Napoleon III a prisoner!' The French Army had surrendered at Sedan, eighteen years and three months after the *coup d'état*.

Paris fell silent. Nothing now stood between the Prussian horde and the capital. At the Rue d'Enfer station, crates marked 'Fragile' were being loaded up for Brest: paintings from the Louvre. The National Guard was doubled. Hugo wrote in his diary: 'To save France now would be to save Europe.'[60]

On 4 September, the Republic was proclaimed and a moderate Government appointed, with General Trochu in charge as a sop to conservatives. France was beginning to look distinctly Hugolian. Almost every member of the emergency cabinet had close ties with the exile: Arago (Hugo had been friendly with the Arago brothers since the 1820s), Adolphe Crémieux (lawyer and friend), Favre and Gambetta (defence lawyers at the trial of *Le Rappel*), Pelletan (a friend since 1840), Rochefort (Hugo's 'third son'), Jules Simon (Alice's godfather).

At three o'clock a telegram arrived from Paul Meurice in Paris: 'Bring the children immediately.' It was the agreed signal. Next morning, Hugo stood at the ticket office in Brussels station and asked for a ticket to Paris. A young republican journalist called Jules Claretie was with him and noticed he was trembling. 'I have been waiting for this moment for nineteen years,' Hugo explained. Then he looked at his wrist-watch as if to record the exact time;[61] but his diary mentions only the cost of eight first-class tickets to Paris: 272 francs.

> At noon, as I was about to leave, a young man, a Frenchman, came up to me on the Place de la Monnaie and said,
> 'Monsieur, I am told you are Victor Hugo?'
> 'I am.'
> 'Be so kind as to enlighten me. I wish to know whether it is safe to go to Paris at the moment.'
> I replied,
> 'Monsieur, it is very unsafe, but it is one's duty to go.'

At four o'clock that afternoon, Hugo's train crossed the border into France.

Part Four

CHAPTER TWENTY

L'Année Terrible

(1870–1871)

HISTORICALLY, THE HUMILIATION of France at Sedan seems almost reassuringly logical, the inevitable demise of a regime which had channelled its energy into image rather than substance and which, as a secret report on the mediocre crop of official candidates in the 1868 elections revealed, had stifled 'individual initiative' and been a charitable institution for sycophants and 'dandies'.[1] Psychologically, it was an unfathomable disaster and a complete surprise. Defeat without honour. The decorations suddenly stripped away.

*

WHEN HUGO CROSSED the border, he was only 70 miles from Sedan. The train passed columns of demoralized soldiers, pale and caked with mud. Hugo leaned out of the carriage window, shouting '*Vive la France!*' and 'It isn't your fault!'[2]

At the same moment, 100 miles to the west, a woman pretending to be a lunatic from a Paris asylum on a visit to relatives was heading for the coast in a tiny, uncomfortable carriage. It was Empress Eugénie in a foul mood, furious with General Trochu for siding with the new Republic. She was expecting to return quite soon.

Hugo's train pulled into the Gare du Nord at 9.35 p.m. He was planning to slip away through the darkened streets and find somewhere to spend the night. A masterpiece of false modesty – the exiled son snuggling into the old city like an animal returning to its lair.

He left the station with a leather satchel slung over his shoulder, and was engulfed by a madly cheering crowd. Gautier's daughter Judith took his arm.[3] They pushed their way across the square to a café. A window opened on the first floor and a robust old man appeared on the balcony. He launched a speech at the sea of heads which more or less resembled the version printed in *Actes et Paroles*: 'Citizens ... here I am.' 'I have come to do my duty. What is my duty? It is your duty and everyone's duty: to defend Paris.' 'Paris is the holy city. Whoever attacks Paris attacks the entire human race.' References in Hugo's speech to 'the people' and 'popular instinct' show that the crowd at the Gare du Nord was mainly working-class – hence his appeal for 'unity': when the Hun was on the horizon, it ill behoved the holy city to engage in civil war. Despite appearances, Hugo was making it up as he went along. The American ambassador, Elihu Washburne, was in the crowd and caught a fragment which does not appear in *Actes et Paroles*:

> Seeing our flag, he called attention to it, and said, 'That banner of stars speaks to-day to Paris and to France, proclaiming miracles of power which are easy to a great people, contending for a great principle; the liberty of every race and the fraternity of all.'[4]

In the storm of patriotic fervour, no one noticed the shocking implication of Hugo's speech. When he used the word 'fraternity', he intended it to include the Prussians . . .

An open carriage was brought and Hugo was paraded through the streets like a saviour or a circus act.[5] The boulevards were thick with promenaders and café-goers, dazzling in gaslight – nothing like a change of regime and an approaching enemy to create a carnival atmosphere. He spoke another three times, standing up in the carriage. In between speeches, two or three thousand people sang 'La Marseillaise' and shouted snatches of *Châtiments* and even, thanks to some mysterious process of dissemination, the little poem written for the birds on Georges's window-sill at Hauteville House. '*Vive le Petit Georges!*' cried the crowd. Some people tried to unhitch the horses: they wanted to carry Hugo to the Hôtel de Ville and give him his own *coup d'état* as a welcome-home present. 'I cried, "No, Citizens! I come not to upset the Republic's provisional government but to support it."'

Two hours and 'ten thousand handshakes' later, Hugo reached the home of Paul Meurice in the Rue de Laval (now 5 Avenue Frochot), one mile from the station. He was embraced by the local mayor, a young man called Georges Clemenceau who was intending to stand at the next election.[6] Then he flung a final oratorical bouquet at the crowd: 'In a single hour, you have repaid me for nineteen years of exile.' At two in the morning, he climbed into bed and fell asleep.

A few hours later, he was woken up by a tremendous thunderstorm. The welcome home was complete.

*

NEXT DAY, the hat-stand in the hall was a symbolic tableau of French society. Hugo was deluged with visits from writers, politicians, workers, and a flower-bearing deputation of market women from Les Halles. There was a rumour that Hugo was going to challenge the King of Prussia to single armed combat outside the city walls.[7] Hector Hugo defending Troy. In the circumstances, anything was plausible. Charles and François-Victor expected their father to be made emergency dictator at any minute.

To the relief of the provisional government, Hugo decided to remain symbolic: 'I have made a rule for myself: to efface my personality, the better to fulfil the great and humble duties of the citizen.'[8] For the time being, he confined his humble duties to the publication of two vibrant appeals which stamped his personality on the crisis – one 'Aux Allemands' (9 September) which Engels and Carlyle both described as 'nonsense':[9] why did Germany want to rape a woman (Paris) who opened her arms to all nations? The response of one German paper was gratifying – 'Hang the poet from the highest yardarm'[10] – although the general trend was less heroic: 'You are a great thinker, Herr Victor Hugo, but as a historian and a thinker you are, to put it simply, an ass!'[11] The other appeal, 'Aux Français' (17 September 1870), was a rallying cry for the city that was about to suffer indecent advances:

> Paris has fortresses, ramparts, ditches, cannon, blockhouses, barricades and sewers which can be mined. There is powder, petrol and nitro-glycerine. . . . The scarlet furnace of the Republic is swelling in its crater.

> Defend France heroically, desperately and tenderly. Patriots, be fear-some! Pause only when you pass before a cottage to kiss a sleeping infant on the brow.
>
> That child is the future, and the future is the Republic.

These rousing texts, which are often quoted as prime examples of Hugo's silliness, were read again, without a smile, in 1914. In 1870, they provided foreign correspondents with some light relief for their war reports. 'Paris is indeed formidable,' agreed the *Boston Morning Journal*. 'Her hair will rise like the forest monarchs of Argonnes. Her tooth-pick will leap from its scabbard like a sword; and this city, which yesterday was Paris, to-morrow may be Pekin or Porkopolis.'[12]

Two days later, Paris was completely surrounded – an island in a hostile sea.

*

IT TAKES A LONG TIME to return home after nineteen years abroad. The 132-day siege of Paris gave Hugo a chance to take his bearings in the new city. Every evening, he walked from one side of Paris to the other, inspecting Haussmann's 'improvements' – the dusty squares, the tall apartment blocks, the manicured Bois de Boulogne – happy to see them all in mourning, preparing for their come-uppance.[13] At night, he watched the balloons go up from the besieged city and saw the red glow on the horizon where satellite towns had fallen to the Prussians. Since 1851, the population had grown by a third, but large areas of the city seemed depopulated. Two days after Hugo's return, Zola fled with his wife, mother and dog to Provence. Jules Janin was in a chateau in Normandy. This exodus of the bourgeoisie and the influx of poor from the suburbs were to have serious consequences in the next elections.

Others had gone for ever. From the early days of the Cénacle, only Émile Deschamps remained: he was on his death-bed at Versailles. Lamartine and Sainte-Beuve, as if in anticipation of Hugo's return, had both died in 1869. The young *Hernanistes* of 1830 had been decimated by death, respectability and madness. Philothée O'Neddy was a clerk at the Ministry of Finance. Théophile Gautier had a son who ran the press section at the Ministry of the Interior: a dismal legacy for a Romantic poet – Gautier *fils* had been instrumental in silencing *Le Rappel*. The master had returned to count the talents and found some guilty faces. Over a month passed before Gautier came to pay his respects.

The generation which had been too young to attend the first night of *Hernani* had also begun to vanish, and most of the family Hugo had known before the *coup d'état* was gone. In a poem written nine months after his return, he pictured himself as a tall, dark cypress drawing its nutrients from the tombs of an ever-expanding graveyard, looming over a flower (Jeanne) and a shrub (Georges).[14] An exception to the divine rule, Hugo was starting out afresh. Edmond Goncourt thought he looked like one of Michelangelo's prophets, with 'beautiful rebellious streaks of white in his hair', 'on his face a strange, almost ecstatic placidity', and, at times, 'in the dark glint of his eye, a vague expression of evil cunning'.[15]

This was the wild look people often noticed in Hugo on the eve of battle. He seemed to believe that popular resistance and sheer sense of history could repel an army which, by way of epic encouragement to his compatriots, he overestimated at 'eight hundred thousand men'.[16] Positioning himself between the Government, which he suspected of wanting to capitulate, and the agitated revolutionaries who wanted to blow it up, he turned himself into the patron saint of Paris. He wore an old red sweater, bought a kepi (the cap worn by the Garde Nationale), and asked General Trochu for permission to go and endanger his life by doing sentry-duty with his sons on the ramparts. (There is no sign that he did.) 'An old man is nothing, but the example counts for something.'

He also kept a siege diary which fortunately was never tidied up into a coherent narrative. The following excerpts show how well Hugo's sense of time suited him for life under siege: the immediate present and the eternal future, between which the imminent occupation or starvation of Paris were of small concern.

The unexplained names in the diary fall into two categories. Poems from the new edition of *Châtiments* were recited in theatres to raise money for cannon. As a result, a stream of young actresses came to perform in front of Hugo, to receive a lesson in declamation or to experience a moment of intimacy with the god. Other names reflect his delight at rediscovering the consumer's paradise. As famine set in and inflation soared, two commodities remained cheap and readily available: mustard and sex.

29 September: As of now, I shall give up the two raw eggs I had every morning. There are no more eggs in Paris. No milk either. . . .

Little Jeanne is one year old today.

30 September: This morning I wrote my *Lettre aux Parisiens.* It will be dated 2 October and will appear on Sunday.

The house is still full of visitors.

Eugène [i.e. Eugénie], 6b, Rue Neuve-des-Martyrs; *n. sec.** 3 frs.

2 October: . . . We toured Paris on the perimeter railway. . . . Fascinating. Paris demolishing itself in order to defend itself – a magnificent sight. Turning its ruins into a barricade.

Toul and Strasbourg have fallen.

4 October: The popular photograph of myself is being sold in the streets. I bought one (25 centimes).

8 October: There is only enough sugar in Paris for ten days. Meat rationing began today. . . .

. . . The Prussian guns rumble continually, recommending unity.

9 October: Five delegates of the 9th *arrondissement* came 'to forbid me from getting myself killed, seeing as how anyone can get himself killed but only Victor Hugo can do what he does.'

10 October: Visit from M. Ernest Picard, Minister of Finance. I requested an immediate decree to liberate all pawn-shop deposits below 15 francs, since the present decree absurdly excludes certain items like linen. I told him that the poor could not wait. He promised the decree for tomorrow.

13 October: The decree I requested for the indigent is in this morning's *Journal Officiel.* M. Pallain . . . told me the decree would cost 800,000 francs. I replied, '800,000 francs? So be it! Taken from the rich. Given to the poor.'

* Code words used in the following entries:

n.: nue (naked)

sec.: secours (alms; i.e. payment)

poöle (stove) sounds the same as (*à*) *poil* (nude)

osc.: osculum or *oscula* (kiss or kisses)

N.B. Hugo often turns the women into men as a precaution: e.g. Émile instead of Émilie.

16 October: No more butter, no more cheese . . .

It has been confirmed that the Boulevard Haussmann is to be named after me. I did not go to see.

17 October: Tomorrow on the Place de la Concorde a mail balloon called the *Victor Hugo* is to be launched. I shall use it to send a letter to London.

Sec. to C. Montauban, *sick:* 10 frs.

18 October: J.J. came to fetch me. We went to see the Feuillantines. The house and garden of my childhood have disappeared. A road has been built over them.

20 October: The papers report that the *Victor Hugo* balloon has landed in Belgium. It is the first mail balloon to cross the border. [Thus beating The *George Sand* and sixty-six others. The *Victor Hugo* disappeared without trace.]

22 October: We are eating horse in every form. . . .

28 October: Sec. to Justin[e] Jullian, 60, Rue Saint-Laurent, 3rd floor, last door; has a twenty-year-old son, missing. *Poële;* 10 frs.

31 October: Skirmish at the Hôtel de Ville. Blanqui, Flourens and Delescluze want to overturn the provisional Trochu–Favre Government. I refuse to join them. Military parade. Immense crowd. My name is included in Government lists.[17] I persist in my refusal. . . .

10 November: It is snowing.

Osc. A. Desormeaux. R. Rousseil.

According to the version dragged out of Hugo by Juliette, Amélie Désormeaux hid behind his door one night and pounced on him when he returned home, asking him to call her 'Cosette' and to give her a baby.[18]

Details supplied by Mme Meurice enabled Edmond Goncourt to assemble a broader picture:

> Every night, at about ten o'clock, he would leave the Hôtel Rohan [172 Rue de Rivoli] where he had quartered Juliette . . . He would then return to the Meurice home where one, two or three women would be waiting for him, frightening the other tenants who bumped into them

on the stairs – all sorts of women, from the most distinguished to the dirtiest of drabs. This appears to have been Hugo's main preoccupation during the siege.[19]

12 November: After the rehearsal [for a *Châtiments* recital], the wounded at the Porte-Saint-Martin ambulance asked Mme Laurent to get me to pay them a visit. I said, 'With pleasure!' and went.

They are laid out in several rooms. The main room is the old theatre foyer with the large round mirrors where I read *Marion de Lorme* to the actors in 1831. . . .

On entering, I said to the wounded, 'You see before you an envious man. My only wish is to have one of your wounds. I salute you, children of France, favoured sons of the Republic, you who have been chosen to suffer for the fatherland.'

They seemed quite moved. I shook hands with them all. One of them held out his mutilated wrist. Another had lost his nose. . . . The nurses in white aprons (the Porte-Saint-Martin actresses) were in tears.

As I left, I gave 100 francs for the ambulance.[20]

15 November: Malvina de Ch., 5, Rue Frochot, 6th floor; *osc.* I shall recommend her to the Minister of Finance.

A widow, old. I shall recommend her to the mayor of the 8th *arrondissement*, M. Carnot.

23 November: It has been raining. The cannon are getting bogged down in the muddy plains. . . . Paris has been on a diet of salt meat for two days. A rat costs 8 sous.

27 November: People are making rat pâté. It is said to be quite good. . . .

People have stopped asking my permission to recite my works in the theatres. They are recited everywhere without my permission. This is as it should be. My writing is not my own. I am in the public domain.

29 November: The sortie has been halted. [Trochu's ill-fated attempt to break out of Paris and join up with Gambetta's army on the Loire.]

The mania for inventing miracle solutions was now at its height. Hugo's idea, which he explained some time after the siege to Sir Sidney Colvin, showed a keen sense of things to come:

What should have been done, he declared, was to send up a vast number of captive balloons from the beleaguered city to the greatest height possible above the Prussian lines, a height beyond the reach of their artillery: platforms should have been swung in the air from between pairs or groups of such balloons; and from those platforms the best scientific chemists of the city should have poured down deadly corrosive compounds upon the enemy's lines which should have caused his hosts to burn up and shrivel and be no more.[21]

1 December: ... On the Boulevard Victor-Hugo a *Victor Hugo* orphanage is being founded. . . .

3 December: ... I told Schoelcher that I wanted to go with my sons if their National Guard batteries made a sortie . . . We shall be together in battle. I am going to have a zouave hood* made for myself. I am worried about the night air.

  Yesterday we ate stag; the day before yesterday, bear; and the two days before that, antelope. Gifts from the Jardin des Plantes. . . .

4 December: A notice has just been pasted to my door indicating precautions to be taken *in case of bombardment.* . . .

14 December: Mlle Marguerite Héricourt (Doña Sol). *Osc.* . . .

  This evening we looked at Goya's *Disasters of War*, brought by Burty. Beautiful and hideous.

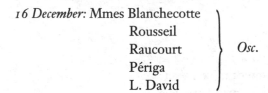

16 December: Mmes Blanchecotte
                    Rousseil
                    Raucourt   *Osc.*
                    Périga
                    L. David

29 December: Cannon all night long. . . .

  Th. Gautier has a horse. The horse has been arrested. It is to be eaten. Gautier has written asking me to obtain its pardon. I have appealed to the Minister. . . .

  I am being entreated ever more urgently to join the Government. . . .

---

* Zouaves: French infantry regiment formed in Algeria.

30 December: ... The bombs have begun to demolish Rosny fort. The first shell fell on Paris. The Prussians launched 6000 bombs at us today....

I am told that the King of Prussia has declared that if I am captured I will be taken to die in Spandau fortress.

Box of lead soldiers for Little Georges, 2 frs. 50....

We are not even eating horse now. It *may be* dog, or *perhaps* rat. I am beginning to have stomach pains. We are eating the Unknown....

January 1871: [Hugo writes a poem entitled 'Au Canon le V.H.' (one of the guns purchased with the proceeds of *Châtiments* recitals).]

> You who will scatter blind death in the air,
> Be blessed! ... Yesterday,
> You left the forge, redoubtable and proud.
> Women followed you, saying, 'How handsome he is!'
> ... Between the ruined slums you'll wend your way
> And take your lofty place in those great embrasures
> Where indignant Paris stands, sabre in fist!

2 January 1871: ... The elephant of the Jardin des Plantes has been killed. He cried. We are going to eat him.

8 January: Yesterday's news was brought by two pigeons....

Furious bombardment today. A shell damaged the Chapel of the Virgin at Saint-Sulpice where my mother was buried and where I was married....

10 January: [Hugo writes a letter in verse to Julie Chenay and sends it by balloon]:[22]

> ... Our stomachs are Noah's Ark.
> Decent or disreputable, every beast gains entrance
> To our bodies – cat, dog, mammoth,* chimpanzee,
> They all come in, and the mouse runs into the elephant.
> The trees have gone – cut, sawn and chopped;
> Paris has the Champs-Élysées on its hearth.
> ...
> Paris is a hero, Paris is a woman,

---

* In the original: *'mammon'* – a rare alternative for *'mammouth'*.[23] If Parisians were Trojans or Athenians, elephants could be mammoths.

Valiant and lovely. Smiling, pensive eyes
Gaze into the big, deep sky, following
The pigeon that returns, the balloon that flies away.
A beautiful sight: the formidable has come forth out of the frivolous.

18 January: . . . There is a cock in my little garden. Yesterday Louis Blanc was lunching with us. The cock crew. Louis Blanc stopped and said, 'Listen.' 'What is it?' 'The cock is singing.' 'So?' 'Can you hear what he's saying?' 'No.' 'He's saying, "Victor Hugo!"' We listened and laughed. Louis Blanc was right. . . .

20 January: . . . A child of fourteen was crushed in a crowd outside a bakery.

26 January: People came again to ask me to lead a demonstration against the Hôtel de Ville. I refused. All sorts of rumours are flying about. I am urging everyone to remain calm and united.

29 January: The armistice was signed yesterday. Published this morning. National Assembly. To be elected from 5 to 18 February. Will sit at Bordeaux. . . .

30 January: Little Jeanne is still sick and is not playing.
  Mlle Louise Périga. *Osc.*
  Louise David. *Osc.*
  Mlle Périga brought me a fresh egg for Jeanne.

*

COMPARED TO MOST PEOPLE, Hugo had had a good siege. While 'The Victor Hugo' cannon was pounding away on the ramparts, its human counterpart was doing something similar in the city. The cheering crowd at the Gare du Nord was gratifying in its way, but this carnal homage was the sort of welcome home an old hero should expect. A year from his seventieth birthday, Hugo was averaging almost one sexual encounter a day – a total of forty different partners in five months. If Paris was a woman, Victor Hugo was a man. The whole city had paid tribute, from the actress who called herself 'Cosette' to the schoolteacher who called herself 'Enjolras' (one of the young revolutionaries in *Les Misérables*). 'Enjolras' was Louise Michel, soon to be adored and detested as one of the fiercest anarchists of the Commune, the so-called 'Red Virgin'. The thought of this martyr of socialism baring herself in front of her childhood hero has caused some discomfort to her admirers. A broad-minded socialist regime might have made it the subject of a commemorative postage-stamp.

The women of Paris having voted with their bodies, the rest of the population expressed its support in the usual manner. On 8 February 1871, voting began for a National Assembly. Its task would be to negotiate the terms of surrender with Bismarck. By now, the psychological defence mechanism which was to play an important role in the Nazi Occupation had begun to take effect. Instead of being angry with the undefeatable Prussians, the French were starting to hate the 'Reds' who had threatened to seize control from General Trochu. But while the rest of the country returned a huge monarchist majority, Paris voted socialist, which meant that it was opposed to surrender. Hugo was elected with 214,169 votes, a close second behind Louis Blanc, ahead of Garibaldi, Quinet, Gambetta, Rochefort, Pyat, Clemenceau and thirty-five others. It was his greatest election victory. The dream of February 1848 had come back to life in the nightmare of 1871.

Shortly after noon on 13 February 1871, even before the final election results were in, Hugo left Paris with Juliette, Alice, his sons and grandchildren, the maids and Louis Blanc. The Assembly was to sit in the safety of Bordeaux. Hugo knew that he and his allies would be hopelessly outnumbered, sitting opposite men who had served the Emperor and who felt they had more in common with those disciplined Prussians than with the plebs of Paris. He half-expected the political disaster that was looming, but not the personal catastrophe that came with it.

At four o'clock, the Hugos' train was waiting to leave Étampes, where it had stopped for lunch. A crowd gathered round the carriage window, shouting '*Vive Victor Hugo!*' Hugo waved his kepi and was shouting back '*Vive la France!*' when 'the Prussian commander of the town came towards me with a menacing air and said something in German which was obviously meant to be fearsome'.

Staring in turn at the Prussian and at the crowd, I raised my voice and said again, '*Vive la France!*', at which the people cried enthusiastically, '*Vive la France!*' That put the old crabstick in his place. The Prussian soldiers did nothing.

A hard journey, slow and uncomfortable. The saloon-car is poorly lit and unheated. One senses the ruin of France in this dilapidation of the railways. At Vierzon, we bought a pheasant and a chicken and two bottles of wine for supper. Then we wrapped ourselves in some blankets and coats and slept on the seats.[24]

*

SOMETHING WAS WRONG from the very beginning. They left Paris on 13 February (luckily not a Friday), there were thirteen people in the carriage, and after a long search in Bordeaux, an apartment was found for Charles and Alice at 13 Rue Saint-Maur. (Hugo took lodgings at 37 Rue de la Course.) 'Alice observed that we are being pursued by the number 13.' In the morning, they ate breakfast at the Restaurant de Bayonne. The bill came to 13 francs 15.

At two o'clock, Hugo left for the Assembly, which had taken over Bordeaux's Grand Théâtre. The upper circle was the public gallery. Behind the President, the stage stood empty.

At the end of the session, Hugo donned his kepi and came out on to the square to find a huge crowd.[25] 'While the people cried in their enthusiasm, "*Vive la République!*", the members of the Assembly were emerging, stony-faced, almost furious, hats on their heads, they passed through the bare heads of the crowd and the kepis that were being waved in the air around me.'

Inside the Assembly, debates pursued their course with a sad inevitability. Adolphe Thiers had negotiated a humiliating treaty with Bismarck. It meant the loss of Alsace and part of Lorraine and the biggest national debt ever: five billion francs' reparation, payable by September 1875. On 1 March 1871, having failed to unite the left-wing representatives who chose him as their leader, Hugo spoke in his own right. It was his first parliamentary speech in two decades, but it looks forward with a long, dark stare to a more distant horizon, familiar to us from the other side. The title given to the speech in *Actes et Paroles* is 'For War in the Present and Peace in the Future'. Hugo still had some big surprises in store:

If this inexorable peace is signed, Europe will never sleep again. The world's immense insomnia will begin. (*Sensation.*) Henceforth there will be two European nations to fear: one because it is victorious, the other because it is vanquished.

One of the men who applauded this speech was the young mayor who had embraced Hugo on his return to Paris. In 1919, Georges Clemenceau presided over a different Peace Conference and, with the intransigence of the 'vanquished' of 1870, helped prepare the way for Adolf Hitler.

Thus far, Hugo's speech was controversial but an acceptable contribution to the debate. He now went on to offer his own solution to the crisis with a mixture of imperialism, internationalism and sheer cheek that might almost be called Churchillian: 'France will reconquer Lorraine and Alsace. (*Hear, hear!*) Is that all? No! ... Trier, Mainz, Cologne, Koblenz, the whole left bank of the Rhine.' The spirit of Napoleon I seemed to be making a comeback. It turned out that Hugo was indulging his dangerous penchant for giving his speeches the rhetorical form of jokes. The punch-line was that France would then restore these conquered cities to Germany on condition that the frontier be abolished and the 'continental federation' established.

This astonishing speech, which seems to have been instantly erased from the minds of all who have read it, raises several disturbing questions. First, the suggestion in *Actes et Paroles* is that the left-wing members failed to unite behind Hugo because of their own internal divisions; but to propose all-out war on an enemy which had just won a swift, crushing, total victory was not necessarily to wave the flag of compromise and reconciliation.

Second, Hugo's vision might appear from the vantage-point of the late twentieth century as a happily accelerated version of modern history – a single, Rhineland war followed immediately by the European Community; but it might also be seen as an example of the sort of politics that draws its confidence from long-term plans and personal utopias: the visionary eye fastened on its distant object and the blind boot underneath. If, as many people later claimed, Victor Hugo predicted both World Wars, he was also quite capable of starting one himself. Since 1869, the man who was thought to be blissfully devoid of practical solutions had come up with a surprising number of them: a spontaneous, mass riot on the streets of a heavily militarized city; the destruction of the city by underground explosives; the chemical dissolution of 800,000 fellow-Europeans; and now a 'holy' war at the end of which France would say to Germany, 'You delivered me from my Emperor; I am delivering you from yours' – if, that is, anyone was left alive to say it.

The best that can be said for Hugo's genocidal solution is that the spirit of the age was still finding its echo in his voice. This tendency of the dream to mutate into a ghastly re-creation of the past is in some ways even more characteristic of post-Sedan France than of Hugo himself. Experiencing the worst defeat since Waterloo had sent him back to the battlefields of his childhood. He was now proposing that 'science be summoned to the aid of war' and that 'those little ones who will grow into men and women be raised and nourished with sacred wrath'. A secular jihad. This was the language of Torquemada.

Pacifism in Hugo had always been a violent state, a contrast to the quiescence of the soldier. But now the self-contradiction was blatant and, as such, a splendid opportunity to map out his mental itinerary since the return to France.

As the siege diary makes clear, his ego had become dangerously over-inflated. The continual reminders of his own importance forced him to face the megalomaniac's dilemma: not the relatively straight-forward problem of acquiring absolute power but the far more delicate task of controlling the absolute power he already possesses. Hugo's answer, whether consciously devised or not, was to turn himself into a Gwynplaine, to make it impossible for his own policies to be taken seriously.

This is after all the great mystery of his political career: why, when Les Misérables is such a magnificently persuasive novel, are Hugo's speeches so humorously unpersuasive? Considering the mad solution he proposed at Bordeaux, it might be said that his greatest contribution to the future European Community was the deliberate sabotaging of his own political career, his refusal to become one of the first dictator-buffoons of modern times. It only remained for him now to send himself back into exile – the only position in which his own special form of madness could be turned to profit.

As far as the outside world was concerned, Hugo was forced to resign by sheer indignation. The penultimate straw was the vote to move the Assembly, not to Paris but to Versailles: news from the capital had dried up completely. It was feared that some revolutionary act had occurred. Hugo urged the Assembly not to turn its back on 'the dazzling and mysterious motor of universal progress', Paris: 'The Prussians have dismembered France; let us not decapitate her.'

Then, on 8 March, the Assembly voted to annul the election of Garibaldi, who had placed his Red Shirts at the disposal of the French and held out against the Germans in the South. Hugo stood up and passed the point of no return: 'I wish to offend no one in this Assembly,' he lied, 'but I am bound to say that Garibaldi is the only general who fought for France, the only general who was not defeated.'

Since Garibaldi was not a Frenchman and since Hugo was right, the Assembly erupted. In the hullabaloo, Hugo scribbled his resignation on a piece of paper, handed it to the President, declared that he would never return and left the Grand Théâtre.

Five days later, while the Assembly was packing its bags, Hugo was dining at a restaurant. He was expecting to leave the next day. The *garçon* asked him to step into the foyer where a messenger was waiting. A cab had been taking Charles Hugo to the Café de Bordeaux. When it arrived, the driver opened the door and found a man whose face appeared to have exploded: a heart attack followed by a massive haemorrhage caused by obesity, over-indulgence and the long winter nights spent manning the guns on the ramparts of Paris. Charles Hugo was dead at the age of forty-four. It was 13 March.

15 March: Crêpe for my hat, 4 frs. For the two workers who watched over Charles, 20 frs.

16 March: Undertakers, 428 frs.

17 March: Transport to Paris by express, 559 frs.
A saloon-car hired for ourselves (10 seats), 665 frs.

The funeral party travelled overnight and arrived at the Gare d'Orléans in Paris at 10.30 a.m. on Saturday, 18 March. Newspapers were brought: Victor Hugo was expected in the capital at midday. The stationmaster offered the use of his office and they waited there until the crowd had assembled. Edmond Goncourt, who had recently lost his brother, came to offer his condolences. 'It's not normal,' Hugo told him, 'two bombshells in one life.' He was thinking of Léopoldine.[26]

At midday, they set off across the city towards the Père Lachaise cemetery.

Even to the man who was following his son's coffin, it was obvious that something unusual was happening. That morning, Government troops had tried to seize the cannon positioned on the heights of Montmartre and Belleville, but a mass of local women protested and the soldiers disobeyed the order to shoot. The people of Paris had not survived the siege to be disarmed by M. Thiers. The National Guard had rebelled and the regular army was about to evacuate the city. Two generals had been executed by the mob in the Rue des Rosiers.

Barricades forced the coffin to take a long and devious route. As it passed through the eastern *faubourgs*, the cafés emptied and the procession grew into a cortège of writers, guardsmen and inebriated workers. At the Place de la Bastille, where Hugo had once attempted to proclaim the Regency, a red flag was flying. Seeing the hoary head of Victor Hugo, a battalion of the National Guard rolled its drums and presented arms. The crowd fell silent. As they left the square, the cry went up: '*Vive la République!*'

Hugo had detached himself from events only to see his private life stick itself to them more closely than ever. The funeral of Charles Hugo was the first public ceremony of the new city state. The revolution which Hugo had helped to crush in June 1848 had finally triumphed, and while another old man, General Thomas, was being shot forty times as 'one of the assassins of '48',[27] Hugo found himself the immaculate, half-reluctant hero of the revolution.

By the time they reached Père Lachaise, the crowd was several hundred strong, filling up the spaces between the tombs like a river in flood. Hugo knelt down and kissed the coffin.

Then something happened which, in almost every account, sounds as though it should have been a devastating experience. The entrance to the vault was too narrow for the coffin to pass. For half an hour, gravediggers hacked at the sides of the vault. 'Vacquerie', wrote Goncourt, 'took the opportunity to deliver a long speech in which he informed us that young Hugo was a martyr and that he died in harness, helping to found the Republic. Meanwhile, Busquet is telling me in a whisper that the cause of death was conjugal luxuriousness and material diarrhoea [profligacy].' Hugo's own account suggests a different mood:[28]

> While the stone was being filed down, I looked at the tomb of my father and the coffin of my son. At last, the coffin could be lowered. Charles will be with my father, my mother and my brother [Eugène]. People threw flowers on the tomb. The crowd surrounded me. They held my hands. How the people love me, and how I love the people!

Next day, the papers were dominated by two stories: the funeral of Charles Hugo and the announcement by the ruling Central Committee of the National Guard that elections were to be held in Paris.[29]

The siege appeared to be over, the cowards who had surrendered to the Prussians had run off to Versailles, and spring had arrived. History seemed to have ended in a carnival, and Victor Hugo was in danger of becoming the sacred cow of the new republic. The day after the funeral, four members of the Central Committee came to consult the sage of Guernsey. Hugo told them their cause was just but their means were criminal, which was a risky thing to say. He was remembering the massacre of June 1848 and its result: nineteen years of Napoleon III. If Hugo was elected to the Committee, he would be in an impossible position, forced to enact his own policies. It would probably end in his execution – by one side or the other – and the final defeat of French republicanism. As usual, the revolution had started too soon. It was time to leave Paris. A few days later, a note appeared in *Le Rappel*:

> Victor Hugo left for Brussels on Wednesday [22 March 1871]. His presence there is required by the formalities which are to be completed in the interests of the two little children left by our late lamented colleague. . . .

As soon as the legal prescriptions have been fulfilled and the children's future settled, Victor Hugo will return immediately to Paris.[30]

It was certainly true that the estate had to be wound up, but the superfluous repetition – 'as soon as', 'immediately' – suggests a slight colouring of the cheeks.

*

'AN ADMIRABLE THING, stupidly compromised by five or six deplorable ringleaders': Hugo's verdict on the Commune.[31] Admirable, because for almost two months, Paris was an autonomous state wrested from social collapse and political ignominy by a revolutionary committee, democratically elected. Deplorable, because it was infected by the spirit of revenge. In Hugo's view, the Commune was a giant leap backwards, the past pretending to be the future. The revolutionary calendar which had been in force at the time of his birth was reinstated. It was now the year '79. A newspaper called *Paris Libre* published the names and addresses of people who had asked to be employed as informers under the Second Empire.[32] Auguste Renoir was caught sketching by the Seine and arrested as a spy.[33] The column in the Place Vendôme was pulled down and eventually a large part of central Paris was destroyed by fire.

It is easy to revel in the ideological excesses of the Commune, in the same way that political correctness canards today are a comforting distraction from real injustice. The fact is that the Paris Commune of 1871 was elected with an 80 per cent majority. The worst acts of ideological cleansing were performed, not by the anarchists who ran Paris quite efficiently for two months and became an inspiration to Lenin, Mao and the students of May 1968, but by the monarchist parliament which rained incendiary bombs down on its own capital city from Versailles.

Hugo spent these two months in Brussels, horrified to find that Charles had been living in anticipation of his inheritance: he had run up debts of over 40,000 francs. Hugo consoled himself with his grandchildren and prostitutes. By the time the estate was settled, it was too late to return to Paris. The second siege had begun. In any case, addressing the masses in an amplified voice was best done at a distance. Hugo had pitched his tent between President Thiers and the Communards, the human synthesis of a dialectic. His poems in *Le Rappel* called for an equal condemnation of both sides. 'Les Deux Trophées' was an attempt to save the Arc de Triomphe from the artillery of the Versailles Government and the Vendôme Column from the Communards – an appeal to a common national heritage which did nothing to stop the bombing of the Étoile district but which delayed the demolition of the column for a few days.[34]

On 21 May, Government troops broke into the city and the week of street fighting known as the '*Semaine Sanglante*' began. On 25 May, Hugo wrote in his diary: 'Something monstrous. The Communards have set fire to Paris. Firemen are being called from as far away as Belgium.' By 27 May, the Commune had been extinguished. The Tuileries, the Louvre library, the Hôtel de Ville, the Préfecture de Police, two theatres, swathes of the Rue de Rivoli and countless other buildings lay in ruins. Neuilly and Saint-Cloud had been flattened. Photographs of Paris in June 1871 have the look of our own century about them. Hundreds of Communards were lined up against a wall in the Père Lachaise cemetery and shot. Trenches dug eight months before for the German siege were packed with corpses, many of them painstakingly mutilated: 'An impure blood', said *La Liberté*, sarcastically quoting 'La Marseillaise', 'will feed our furrows.'[35] As usual at times like this, the word 'our' had a sinister ring to it. 'Our soldiers', said *Le Figaro*, 'have simplified the work of the courts-martial of Versailles by shooting on the spot; but it must not be overlooked that a great many culprits have escaped chastisement.'[36]

History was speedily rewritten and illustrated with myths which lived on for many years: the *pétroleuses* (female incendiaries), beautifully faked photographs of priests being butchered on the boulevards,[37] torture chambers in the Paris sewers. The Communards who survived the massacre – and anyone else who happened to be arrested – were sentenced to death, deportation 'to a fortified enclosure' or hard labour for life, and ordered to pay costs (including those sentenced to death). Lists of the condemned and their professions paint an interesting picture of these slavering revolutionaries who were so far beyond the pale of decent society: accountant, mechanic, medical student, vet, silversmith, painter, ex-naval officer, man of letters, cashier, cobbler, head of primary school, etc.[38]

Not having been directly implicated in the Commune, Hugo himself was out of danger. He was free to pursue his new vocation as a grandfather, to go on publishing those grand, old-fashioned poems about progress and fraternity, to return to his next novel. Instead, he decided to jeopardize his life and his popularity. Now that 'order' had been restored and the episode was over, Hugo would supply the moral.

The Belgian Parliament had assured M. Thiers that any political refugees would be treated as criminals and extradited to France. It was the moment Hugo had been waiting for. He sent a letter to the leading Belgian newspaper, *L'Indépendance Belge*. He had never approved of the Commune, but 'asylum is an ancient right'. 'Even if he is my personal enemy – especially if he is my personal enemy – any Communard may knock at my door and I shall open it. In my house he will be safe.... I shall do Belgium this honour.' Even his socialist colleagues, Schoelcher and Louis Blanc, deemed the letter 'inopportune and excessive'.

Hugo was about to gain first-hand experience of that unpleasant phenomenon known to conscientious objectors and opponents of the death penalty: the fury induced by any attempt to take away the 'right' to kill and exact retribution. For Hugo, it was a chance to improve on his reaction to June 1848, to re-edit his *actes et paroles*. This time, his conscience would be satisfied, and the Church, which had already been taught its own lessons by Bishop Myriel in *Les Misérables*, would be shown up once again as a servile arm of the State.

That night (27–28 May 1871), a well-dressed mob gathered outside his home in the Place des Barricades, shouting 'Death to Victor Hugo! Death to Jean Valjean! . . . String him up!' The windows were smashed. A large stone narrowly missed Jeanne. The door downstairs shuddered under the blows of what Hugo assumed to be a battering-ram. Little Georges, struggling to keep up with events, was saying, 'It's the Prussians!'

No help came. Hugo was expecting to be taken out and crucified at any minute. 'It seems the police were otherwise engaged.' 'It was a reactionary, Bonapartist ambush which the clerical Belgian administration was inclined to tolerate' – perhaps because one of the stone-throwers was the son of the Belgian Minister of the Interior.

Two hours later, the mob dispersed and the police arrived; but no report was filed. François-Victor's florid account of the incident appeared in some newspapers and was understandably interpreted as a gross exaggeration. A simple statement of the facts would have been more effective.

The following night, the family slept at the Hôtel de la Poste while another mob assembled in the Place des Barricades. In the morning, Hugo and his son were bizarrely accused of stealing paintings from the Louvre, and 'Victor Hugo, man of letters, aged sixty-nine years, born in Besançon, residing in Brussels', was officially expelled from Belgium for 'breach of the peace'. The vote in Parliament was eighty-one votes in favour of expulsion to five against, but many people wrote or came in person to express support. A week later, a letter from Hugo appeared in *L'Indépendance Belge*: 'I persist in not confusing the Belgian people with the Belgian Government.... I forgive the Government and I thank the people.'

His 'fourth exile' had begun, nine months after his return to France.

*

To RETURN TO PARIS now would be to walk into an open grave. Swinburne heard that Hugo was sailing to England and started to prepare a welcome party.[39] Instead, Hugo and the family set off for Vianden in Luxembourg on 1 June 1871.[40] Luxembourg was a symbolic haven sandwiched between the two warring powers, and Vianden was a pretty little town with a ruined castle and a largely sympathetic population.

Overall, the reception was mixed. The Workers' Philharmonic Society serenaded Hugo twice during his stay and people walked miles to see him, but the local priest warned his flock that Satan had a new religion: Lutheranism, Calvinism, Jansenism and now Hugoism. The French press was treating him as a dangerous crackpot. The novelist Edmond About suggested that he go to America and apply for a job with Barnum's Circus[41] – Hugo as a forerunner of W. C. Fields. The Boulevard Victor Hugo reverted to its old name,

Boulevard Haussmann – the Prefect who had demolished more of the city than the Germans, the Versaillais and the Communards combined. There were also moves to silence him for ever, ranging from expulsion from the Société des Gens de Lettres to a bullet in the head.

Meanwhile, Satan's emissary enjoyed a surge of creativity comparable to the one he had experienced on arriving at St Helier in 1852 with a sense of duty done. He set to work on the next volume of his speeches, wrote more poems for the volume to be entitled *L'Année Terrible*, sketched ruins, played boule with François-Victor, allowed his ego to be resorbed by Nature, and kept up his vocabulary list of baby-talk. An eighteen-year-old called Marie Mercier arrived from Paris.[42] Her common-law husband had been director of Mazas prison under the Commune and had since been shot as a traitor. Hugo insisted that Alice take her on as a servant, which she did, for a few weeks, during which Hugo showed how to give asylum to a young, attractive woman. They went walking in the hills and Hugo watched her bathing naked in the River Our. Thirty years later, Marie Mercier remembered her happy holiday with the People's Friend. 'He praised everything my husband and I had loved: freedom, justice, the Republic.' 'He had his own special way of pleasing one.' She also supplied him with details of the atrocities in Paris, which explains why the poems of *L'Année Terrible* relating to the Commune have the smell of first-hand experience.

Hugo's Luxembourg idyll does however lead one to reflect on the nature and implications of the psychological state he had made the mainstay of his life: a cleansed conscience. Even as he wrote poems like 'La Question Sociale', in which it is claimed that Jesus Christ himself would have been expelled from Belgium, reports of the reprisals in Paris were flooding in. It was a good chance to get rid of unwanted neighbours: the Government received almost 400,000 denunciations, most of them anonymous. Blackened hands were assumed to have been stained by gunpowder. Several firemen and at least one chimney sweep were shot. Half the shoe-makers of Paris disappeared. A self-trained torturer called the Marquis de Galliffet, a future Minister of War and friend of Edward VII, shot 111 men for having white hair because they were old enough to have fought in the

1848 Revolution. Prisoners were tied to horses' tails or taken in carts to Versailles to be stoned by the respectable crowd and stabbed with parasols.[43]

Far more people were butchered in Paris in the last week of May 1871 than were killed in France under the Terror. French socialism had been exterminated and would not recover in Hugo's lifetime.

'You are right to congratulate me,' Hugo wrote to Janin. 'I have done my duty. I am banished and content.'[44] Excited by his latest adventures, he organized the poems of *L'Année Terrible*: '[The book] will end, after the fall of the Empire and the epic of the two sieges, with the present catastrophe, whence I shall extract a prophecy of light.'[45] 'And what do you think about the incredible story of the paintings stolen from the Louvre? ... The *farce* of 27 May [the attack on his home] almost attained the status of tragedy; this Louvre business is better than a comedy.'[46] 'Epic', 'farce', 'tragedy', 'comedy': the whole *année terrible* had been a writer's dream.

Hugo and the family left Vianden at the end of August and spent a month travelling through Luxembourg. They visited Thionville, where Hugo's father was still revered as the town saviour, and Mondorf, where a peasant's horse stopped in front of him and bowed. By now, Hugo had decided to return to Paris. Despite his refusal to stand, 57,854 people had voted for him in the July elections – not quite enough to be elected but amazing all the same, especially since there were now 40,000 fewer voters in Paris, and the bourgeois who had fled from Bismarck and then the Commune had all come home. It was his 'pressing and imperative duty' to plead for the Communards who were being shot or deported, although it seems the duty only became irresistible on 22 September when he learned that Henri Rochefort was to be sent to Cayenne.

On 24 September, they crossed the frontier, saw the battlefield at Sedan – 'covered with little humps' – and spent the night at Rheims. Hugo remembered his trip there as official poet at the coronation of Charles X. 'Today, in 1871, I return as an old man to this city which saw me in my youth, and in place of the coronation coach of the King of France, I see the black and white sentry-box of a Prussian soldier.' The aesthetic apprehension of things was a powerful consolation for the national disgrace.

The chief officer at the border post telegraphed to Paris to announce the imminent arrival of Victor Hugo.

Five months before his seventieth birthday, Hugo was sitting in a first-class compartment, heading for a city that was divided into those who loved him, those who hated him, and those who thought of him as an incorrigible clown.

It was raining. The summer was almost over. Paris was half destroyed and only one of Hugo's four children was still at his side. But as the train trundled over the battlefields of northern France, his eyes were brimming with sunny visions of the future:

> Left Rheims at half-past twelve. . . . It rained during the journey. Saw a beautiful ruin and a pretty woman at Crépy-en-Valois. I must go back there one day.

CHAPTER TWENTY-ONE

'Because'

(1871–1873)

I was the old savage prowler of the sea,
A sort of spectre on the edge of the salty abyss;
In the cruel Winter, in the gales and the ice,
In the storm, the spume and the night, I wrote a book;
. . .
I came, I saw the formidable city;
The city was hungry, I placed my book in her mouth . . .
And to Paris I said, like the klepht to the eagle,
'Eat my heart, your wing will grow by a span.'

L'Année Terrible, 'Octobre', i

THE HEART HUGO fed to Paris now was not a spume-spattered book of verse but the hours of an ever-shorter day. This time, there was no delirious crowd to welcome him back. He put up at the Hôtel Byron while an apartment was prepared at 66 Rue de La Rochefoucauld. Juliette was to stay across the road at 55 Rue Pigalle.

Photographs and tours of the ruins were being sold to foreign visitors. Hugo and Juliette bought the photographs and went to gaze at the burnt-out shells of the Tuileries Palace and the Hôtel de Ville. The ruined building is one of the key images of Hugo's work, the intersection of time and matter. Now, he confined his description to one word: 'Sinister'. Troops were patrolling the streets. There were rumours of conspiracies and almost daily news of executions. Worried wives and lawyers came to ask for Hugo's help. One of his guests had overheard two Corsicans talking in a café in dialect: 'Victor Hugo goes out every evening unaccompanied.' A monarchist *coup d'état* seemed likely. Officially, the Republic had been born, but it was 'April without birds, nests, sunbeams, flowers or bees'. 'Springtime with the institutions of Winter'.[1]

It was in this volatile atmosphere of recriminations that Hugo pleaded for the convicted Communards. He took the train to Versailles to meet the President. Adolphe Thiers found Hugo meddlesome and affected but appeared to lend a sympathetic ear and promised that Henri Rochefort would not be deported. Both men were manipulators who depended on appearing powerless, which made for a futile but pleasant conversation. They agreed on only one thing: the best way to survive the daily flood of insults was not to read the papers. Hugo supplied the conclusive image: 'To read diatribes is to sniff the latrines of one's fame.'[2]

Beyond the silk-lined salons of Versailles, reality pursued its backward path to the future, as if in total ignorance of Victor Hugo. 'Law has triumphed over Justice.' The guillotine had been replaced by the death camps of New Caledonia. Martial law remained in force until 1876. Forgiveness was considered unpolitic. Property owners were reassured, the economy recovered, and the war debt to Prussia was paid off by September 1873, two years ahead of schedule.

A society in which Victor Hugo was the voice of reason had obviously reached an unhealthy state of extremes. 'The rage that surrounds us is a state of madness,' he wrote in *Le Rappel*.

> Let us be suspicious of certain phrases like 'ordinary offence' or 'common criminal' – supple expressions which can easily be made to fit excessive sentences. . . . The elasticity of words corresponds to the cowardice of men. They are too obedient.

This was the word-wary poet whose least literate characters had always come closest to the truth, and who defined his poetic technique, not as a classical bending of language to the poet's will but as the incitement of words to revolt.

Hugo's jottings on post-Commune Paris describe a modern police state, more intent on justifying its neurotic accusations than on seeing justice done, unconsciously humiliating itself, perpetuating the massacre in private. His relationship with the motherland was identical to his relations with the human family: everything he loved destroyed itself. In one of his letters of complaint, he called the process 'self-denigration'.[3] And since Hugo was a Frenchman, disrespect for Victor Hugo was part of the national shame. He may have been a comedian, but it was History that supplied the jokes: 'I know I made myself ridiculous last week when I called ... for unity among Frenchmen, and I know I shall make a fool of myself again this week when I ask for the lives of convicted prisoners to be spared. I am resigned to it.'[4]

This refusal to stop protesting is perhaps more admirable in its way than his reckless behaviour at Bordeaux and Brussels: it called, not for courage, which came with its own reward, but for the suspension of disinclination. 'Duty' invaded every corner of his life. The hermit now found himself surrounded by po-faced priests, smug ministers of the political 'religion' he had helped to found. Goncourt's sketch of an evening chez Hugo shows that his reluctance to seize power was not simply a matter of ideology. It also had to do with the quality of life.

> The other day, when Thiers was the subject of discussion, Hugo said to that doctrinal Communard, Meurice, for whom he harbours a secret antipathy, 'Scribe* is just as guilty in his own way!' And when Meurice went on, like an idiot, 'But Thiers banned *Le Rappel*,' Hugo, indignant to see shop-talk intruding on higher things, burst out, 'What do I care about your *Rappel*?'[5]

Guests permitting, Hugo escaped to the home of Judith Gautier where a dog called Grimace had been trained to stand up whenever it heard the words 'Victor Hugo'.[6] Together, they fantasized about conspiring to bring Napoleon III back to France: 'We'd be able to go away, back to Jersey ... We could work together.'

The joke was more serious than it sounds. Hugo was in the ironic position of a revolutionary who sees some but not all of his dreams come true. Napoleon III was languishing in Chislehurst, where he died in 1873. Hugo would be forced to direct his adversarial energy against men who were supposed to be his allies, to fight ignorance

---

* Eugène Scribe (1791–1861), hugely prolific and successful author of unRomantic dramas.

instead of malevolence: 'Better to have an intelligent hell than a stupid paradise.'[7] He was homesick for exile.

In keeping with the irony of the situation, release took the form of two setbacks.

In January 1872, he failed to be re-elected to the National Assembly, which was bad news for the imprisoned Communards but a relief for Hugo. The result – 122,435 votes for Thiers's candidate, 95,900 for Hugo – is still described as a humiliating defeat. But since the official candidate enjoyed the uncensored support of the news-papers, and since Hugo was standing for unconditional amnesty and abolition of the death penalty, it was a surprising moral victory: it shows that he was not the irrelevant old misery most of his later biographers thought he must have been by now. Otherwise, the amazing transformation of Hugo's image in his last years would be inexplicable. The alarming Hugo vote was enough to persuade the National Assembly to remain for the time being at the safe distance of Versailles. Paris might become Hugopolis at any minute.

The second setback, something far more devastating than an election defeat, came a month later.

Two women left an American ocean-liner at Liverpool and boarded a ship which docked at Saint-Nazaire on 11 February 1872. Next day, they were at the home of Hugo's doctor in the Rue de Rivoli. François-Victor went to embrace his sister and found an emotionless, dark-haired woman of forty-one, chaperoned by a cheerful Barbadian. Adèle Hugo failed to recognize her brother.

Whether out of anxiety or a sense of chronological propriety, Hugo waited until the 13th. 'She recognized me. I kissed her. I said all the loving, hopeful things one can say. She is very calm and sometimes appears to sleep.' The entries for the following days were short, verging on silence: 'There are some emotions of which I wish to leave no trace.' 'I saw Adèle. My heart is broken.' 'Another door closed, darker than that of the tomb.' The doctor advised him to visit as seldom as possible.

Half a century before, Eugène had fallen into the same bottomless pit, though the illness (if it was the same illness) appears to have taken a more gentle form in Adèle. She spent the day squabbling with the voice in her head, dabbling at the piano, scribbling page after page, but refusing to show them to anyone. The daughter of Victor Hugo had returned from her great adventure with no story to tell.

From a physiological point of view, insanity had done her a world of good. She exercised and ate heartily. Sinister rumours that there was really nothing wrong with her at all have continued almost to the present – based on a belief that genuine lunatics behave like demented fiends twenty-four hours a day. It has even been claimed, in 1976, that Adèle's last known letter from the asylum (28 June 1878) is 'entirely lucid', 'controlled' and 'normal', which is a worrying statement in its own right. The letter is obsessive, emotionally disconnected and linguistically skewed:

My dear father,
    I already sent you a letter to ask for various things, among others, that you send me *some gold*.* I would have been happy to have the prompt results of it. But I didn't get any.
    Don't forget to come and fetch me, as well as Mme Léontine and another person [fellow inmates?], and to come today as soon as possible or tomorrow. Take us with you insistently. Come today or tomorrow.
    Be *insistent* about it. Send us *some gold*.
                            Your respectful loving daughter, Adèle.

    I shall expect you as soon as possible. Be *insistent* on taking us with you and coming to fetch us.[8]

This confused agitation is all that remained of the woman who, the year before her 'escape' in 1863, had written two paragraphs in her diary which would have made a splendid opening for a novel:

    It would be an incredible thing if a young woman, who is so enslaved that she cannot even go out to buy paper, went to sea and sailed from the Old World to the New to be with her lover. This thing I shall do.
    It would be an incredible thing if a young woman, whose only sustenance is the crust of bread her father deigns to give her, had in her possession, four years from now, money [literally, 'gold'] earned by honest toil, money of her own. This thing I shall do.[9]

* *'De l'or'*, i.e. cash, considered as a personal treasure. But this is an oddly specific use of the word.

Adèle was sent to an expensive nursing home at Saint-Mandé just outside Paris. It was chosen for its comfort and because it was run by a reputable psychiatrist, but perhaps, too, because Hugo already had in mind the poignant, antithetical notes which appear in his diary almost until his death. Juliette's daughter Claire had been buried in the graveyard there in 1846: 'We went together to Saint-Mandé. She goes to see her daughter in the cemetery, alas!, and I go to see mine.'

*

GRIEF RARELY EXISTS in complete isolation. Hugo's daughter was at least safe and free from scandal. He had no parliamentary duties, the latest volume of his speeches was ready for publication, and so was *L'Année Terrible*. It was an important moment in his life, an opportunity to make the final choice: either to sink into lethargy, pick through memories like the beads of a rosary, humour his visitors for the sake of company, and gloat over the intellectual and moral puniness of the generation in power; alternatively, forge new adventures, question old assumptions, cash in on the respect due to the old, and be a thorn in the flesh of people he despised.

Hugo did all these things, except become lethargic. Apart from creaky joints and an attack of nephritis, he was free from most of the reminders of creeping putrefaction: his 'loins' still had a good seven years' life in them, his sense of humour was intact, and his friendship with Judith Gautier had matured and blossomed into casual sex. He even – for the first time in his life – wrote some love sonnets, a form thought to be too constrictive for the broad hand of Victor Hugo, but which he had probably shunned because it was Sainte-Beuve, now dead, who had reintroduced the form to France. His idea of life after death was as comfortably settled as a well-written will. There was a God who was unknowable but whose judgements could be read on the internal meter called the conscience:

I have tried to introduce moral and human questions into what is known as politics. . . . I have spoken out for the oppressed of all lands and of all parties. I believe I have done well. My conscience tells me I am right. And if the future proves me wrong, I feel sorry for the future.[10]

Or, as a poem from *L'Année Terrible* put it, with an image dear to his heart, Hugo was the 'tranquil creditor of the abyss', Nature was the promissory note, and God was 'not insolvent'.[11]

For the first time in two decades, he was in complete control of his own works. He even seems to have worked out a special deal with Alice's godfather, the Minister of Education. Despite the lifting of the ban on political works imported from Belgium, crates containing *Napoléon-le-Petit* and *Châtiments* were still being impounded. Why? Because Hugo received no royalties on those editions. To publishers who had risked their freedom smuggling the works of Victor Hugo into France, this seemed a little ungrateful.[12] This time, Hugo would reap the rewards of a recovering economy: the French reading public was no more insolvent than God.

He also tightened his grip at home. Charles's young widow found that both her children and her body were the object of Grandfather's attentions. Georges and Jeanne were growing up in a highly irregular environment; pawns in a power-struggle. The pettiest dramas are always the best documented, but a single note in Hugo's diary sums up the relationship quite nicely: 'I am in favour of weaning little Jeanne. The nurse looks very tired to me. Alice does not appear to notice. The doctor agrees with me. Jeanne will be weaned immediately.'[13]

Even the dismal return of Adèle brought a ray of sun in the shape of Mme Baa, the woman who had accompanied her back to Europe. 'The first Negress in my life,' says the entry in Hugo's log, in Spanish, on 23 February, followed, six days later, by a new hieroglyphic – not one of his most ingenious: a thick capital 'O' resembling a dark hole.

Despite these consolations, Hugo was pining for the Ocean and the 'eyrie' in which he hoped to hatch his final prose masterpiece. The last labour he imposed on himself in Paris was a reminder of why he wanted to leave: the publication of the ninety-eight poems entitled *L'Année Terrible* – a great, clattering announcement that he had no intention of shuffling off into elegant retirement.

The book began with Sedan and ended with the current reprisals. It was repetitious, hyperbolic and deliberately irritating. The entire first print-run of 1600 sold out before noon on the day of publication (20 April 1872). The reddest rags to the reactionary bulls were Hugo's little lines of dots, voluntarily censored passages intended to show 'the future' that free expression still did not exist in the second year of the Third Republic.

Reviewing *L'Année Terrible*, a tetchy Robert Buchanan pointed to Hugo's interminability as a fine example of 'French waste generally' – 'power recklessly drivelled away'.[14] Since the 1830s, the trend had been to short, asthmatic poems, like the dainty ornaments of Second Empire salons, saving their perfumes from the materialist world that produced them. Hugo was poetry's response to miniaturization. His deliberate verbal incontinence gave a sense of the mad swirl of events which History, that 'concierge who thinks of herself as a great lady',[15] rarely manages to convey. Words were used for their weight, as books might be used as chairs and door-stops. Vast columns of alexandrines catapult tiny, super-significant phrases into the reader's brain: a long diatribe, for instance, against an imaginary anarchist who destroyed the Louvre library ends with the half-line response, 'I can't read'.

The best review was published by the humorous weekly, *Le Grelot*. It concocted a special phrase-book for bamboozled readers of *L'Année Terrible*, thereby serving the useful purpose of removing the scaffolding of Hugo's syntax to reveal the rude strangeness of his imagery. The question behind the tittering was this: was he using poetry for political ends, or was he using events as the raw material of verse? A question better asked than answered.

ABC of the Ideal: Library
Avatar incubated by an apocalypse: Something very uncommon
Curtain of destiny: Very thick when lined with enigma
Dark stain on the horizon: Poet
Dawn ray – to turn a dawn ray into a thunderclap: To use the 'Victor Hugo' cannon
Enormous eye: Paris
Minds on whom the eagle rests: Perch-minds of superior quality
Sublime prolongation: The tomb
Tearing of spider's webs: Destiny
Vomit which must be drunk: Remorse

*

ON 7 AUGUST 1872, Hugo left France to its vomit and sailed for the Channel Islands with Juliette, Alice, the children and a sickly François-Victor. He planned to stay there for the best part of a year. The great white page was waiting.

It was some time before he began, not the writing of his last novel, but its 'final incubation' – and not just its incubation: whole generations of embryos preceded the first, imperfect draft. Even now, there were signs of procrastination, but he had so many projects in so many stages of incompletion that only he himself was aware of the vice. To create the necessary state of emergency, he convinced himself that death was about to pounce: 'The lion lies down in his cavern to die. / Friends, like Shakespeare and like Aeschylus, I am entering / That period of oblivion that comes before death.' 'I am very old: I have time left only / For being a sage.'[16]

Despite Mme Chenay's caretaking, Hauteville House had suffered from the master's absence. A threat to burn it down at the time of the Brussels mob had fizzled out,[17] but the house was now 'a hovel', he wrote with a miser's humility: 'Everything is in tatters, the hangings are drooping, the gilt is falling off, the room I inhabit is a garret.'[18] Fortunately, as he told his correspondents, a 'Family Hotel' had opened across the road to catch the steady flow of Hugo tourists.

The ocean air had the usual effect. He swam in the sea, visited the haunted house on the cliff-top described in *Les Travailleurs de la Mer*, saw a storm cloud 'imitating' a page from the novel, and made up dozens of fairy-tales for the children – so many, over a period of ten years, that they would have formed a large volume had they been written down: a hermit who gorges himself in secret; a revamped 'Little Red Riding-Hood' which ends with the wolf being eaten by a lion; and a tale known only by its title: 'The Bad King and the Good Flea'.[19]

When François-Victor, Alice and the children left with the first leaves of autumn, Hugo settled down to the two great projects of the next nine months: the writing of *Quatrevingt-treize*[20] – which he did standing up, until a thorn punctured his foot – and the uncharacteristically earnest pursuit of Juliette's new maid, a timid twenty-three-year-old called Blanche.

The more challenging of the two projects – *Quatrevingt-treize* –

was Hugo's showdown with his last great subject: the French Revolution at its most horrific. 1793 was the year of the Terror and the decapitation of Louis XVI, the year of royalist rebellion in Brittany, the year of Danton, Robespierre and Marat, the climax of the period he had been brought up by his mother to loathe religiously. It was a glaring gap in the huge, dishevelled encyclopedia of his complete works. Even *Les Misérables* had sidestepped the entire Revolution and effectively blotted out the period immediately preceding Hugo's birth.[21] It was only now, after the nightmare of the Commune, when any attenuation of the Terror was likely to be seen as an act of treason, that Hugo set about filling the gap. The temptation to be tactless was irresistible.

One reason for the delay was that, in Hugo's mind, the French Revolution was the old dilemma of the individual conscience and the greater good, applied to history. How could such barbarism and cruelty have been the golden dawn of the modern age? How was it possible to be optimistic in the wake of a massacre? The challenge was to pull the Revolution from its bloody womb and to show its shining face, to 'cast on that terrifying figure, *93*, a ray of appeasement', 'to stop people being frightened of progress'.[22]

The story can be artificially boiled down to three characters. First, the Marquis de Lantenac, the white-haired aristocrat who is smuggled back to France to lead the peasant revolt. Though Lantenac was supposed to represent the past, many assumed that he was the true hero of the novel.[23] Second, Cimourdain, the ex-priest and 'sinister virgin' who espouses the cause of 'humanity' with an inhuman, theoretical rectitude. His manic ideological purity made a deep impression on a young Georgian seminarist called Dzhugashvili who was confined to his cell for reading *Quatrevingt-treize* and later changed his name to Stalin.[24] Finally, Gauvain, grand-nephew of the Marquis and beloved pupil of Cimourdain, the character who straddles the chasm between clemency and *raison d'état*. After a bloody guerrilla campaign, Gauvain allows his aristocrat enemy, Lantenac, to escape by a secret tunnel and, as revolutionary virtue demands, is executed by his mentor, Cimourdain. The novel ends with the simultaneous guillotining of Gauvain and the suicide of Cimourdain.

Ironically, the spirit of the Revolution is best represented by the three tiny children, trapped in the forest tower, who rip to shreds a priceless, ancient copy of St Bartholomew's Gospel (another St Bartholomew's Day Massacre): 'pink, laughing and ferocious, the three angels of prey fell on the defenceless evangelist'.[25] A lesson on the subject of mindless conservation: Nature the benign exterminator.

With such a theme, it is not surprising to find so many autobiographical threads. The novel is set in the Breton melting-pot where Hugo's parents' marriage had been forged, and the implicit message is that the bloody origins of the future United States of Europe were also the origins of Victor Hugo. In a rare first-person appearance, he mentions his father's role in repressing the Breton revolt;[26] yet he says nothing at all about his mother, despite the fact that he liked to boast about her heroic escapades, saving priests and staving off the Revolution.*[27] It is especially odd that the very parts of the novel that might have been placed under the sign of his mother are handed over to Juliette Drouet: the descriptions of Brittany are based on Juliette's memories of childhood and her trip there with Hugo in 1836. The central character, Gauvain, even bears her original surname.

Hugo had finally tackled the subject of the French Revolution, but there was still no attempt to investigate the chasm in his own life. Even if he didn't know that his great-aunt Louise had been the mistress of Carrier[28] – cited in the novel and elsewhere as one of the blackest examples of revolutionary 'malevolence'[29] – it is hard to believe that with his phenomenal memories of his mother's salon and first-hand experience of five regimes, he had not built up a more accurate picture of his past. His whole work suddenly appears to have been the longest psychological procrastination in the history of literature. The description of the spongy, spy-infested Breton forests where his parents had supposedly met and where the Revolution 'gave birth' to Civilization, owes its existence to memories of a different kind – a gloriously mad image of a mind enthralled by its dark regions:

* Hugo (and, it seems, everyone else) was unaware that his father's cousin Charles had a son, Joseph Hugo (1747–1827), who was a member of the Convention. Joseph Hugo was absent through illness when the death sentence was passed on Louis XVI.

It would be difficult nowadays to imagine what the Breton forests were. They were cities. Nothing could be more mute, uncommunicative and savage than those inextricable entanglements of thorns and branches. Those vast thickets were lairs of stillness and soundlessness. No solitude could be more deathlike or sepulchral. If, in a flash, one could have razed the trees, one would have seen all of a sudden in that blackness a swarming mass of people.[30]

The underlying lesson is that while Hugo's motherless male characters can only cling to their principles and destroy themselves, the author himself survives – but not simply by interpreting history 'in the spirit of protesting humanism':[31] however laudable or prophetic, this is part of the storyteller's charm. When the magic has worn off, it dawns on one that Hugo's optimism is based on the very flimsiest of pretexts. Its only theoretical justifications take the form of zany axioms – 'If God had wanted man to regress, he would have given him an eye in the back of his head'[32] – while the only firm proposal for the establishment of the future utopia (apart from abolishing priests and soldiers and making every citizen a property-owner) is the efficient use of human faeces: 'You fling your fertilizer down the drain,' says Gauvain shortly before his execution, 'you should cast it upon your furrow.'[33] To see *Quatrevingt-treize* as a protest against 'the growing barbarism of capitalism'[34] is to ignore Hugo's aversion to systems of every kind and his great baby-like taste for destruction – all part of what he was soon to call 'The Art of Being a Grandfather'.

If God had wanted Hugo to be a serious political thinker, he would not have given him the gift of profiting from self-deception. Hugo's survival had depended on the deliberate embracing of absurdity, the dogged phenomenological approach which fed his work with images. Hugo had turned himself into the water-wheel of History's river, and the source of the river was not to be investigated:

> Revolution is a form of the immanent phenomenon which besets us on every side and which we call Necessity.
>
> In the face of this mysterious entanglement of boons and afflictions rises up the *Why?* of History.
>
> *Because*. This is the answer of the man who knows nothing. It is also the answer of the man who knows everything. . . .

Above revolutions, truth and justice remain like the starry sky above the storm.[35]

*

GIVEN THIS ALMIGHTY EXCUSE – *'Because'* – the miracle at this late stage of Hugo's life is not that he had survived his origins but that he managed to remain in a sufficient state of crisis to nourish his writing.

The problem of necessity and morality was also being acted out in the bedrooms of Hauteville House. Juliette, who lived on a cycle of ignorance and rude reawakening, was coming to the end of a phase of blind worship. Copying out *Quatrevingt-treize* with an arthritic hand brought her to her knees with admiration: 'In the coming age, the calendar will be dated from Victor Hugo as it is from Jesus.'[36] But it was impossible to forget that the Messiah was corrupt: perfumed letters and unexplained absences, a sly attempt by Hugo to move her clock forward half an hour. She tried hard to believe – writing with that mixture of the earthy and the orotund that she shared with Hugo – that he was a sucker for 'trouser-hunters' and 'unsatisfied bitches'.

The new maid, Blanche, had been 'educated above her station', according to the wife of Hugo's last secretary, who seems to have been educated well below hers.[37] The official story was that, as a young girl, Blanche had lost both her parents and been taken in by Juliette's friends, the Lanvins. In fact, she was probably the Lanvins' illegitimate granddaughter.[38] It was M. Lanvin whose passport had enabled Hugo to escape from France in 1851. Having borrowed Lanvin's identity, Hugo was going to borrow his adopted child. The 'approach work' (Hugo's expression) began on Christmas Day, 1872. Blanche had been warned about M. Hugo's friendly ways, but since she knew several of his poems by heart, she had been as it were pre-seduced like most of the women he met.

The Blanche campaign differs from the others in two important respects. First, Hugo had nearly always shown a marked preference for what he euphemistically termed 'the first woman to come along'.[39] Sex by chance selection was convenient, physically and sociologically interesting, and the anonymity made it easy to grasp the essence in the individual: 'Woman is in those women.' Blanche, by contrast, was the object of a steady, single-minded passion, the first specific passion Hugo had experienced since Léonie Biard.

Second, he was clearly alarmed by the destructive potential of his craving. His diary reveals an unusually acute concern for his principal mistress. 'Accidental affliction,' he wrote on 5 January 1873. 'Take care not to wound that tender heart and great soul.' The urgent question now was not, 'Will Providence triumph over Evil?', but 'Will lust and obsession destroy domestic peace?'

The delicate balance was sustained all the way to consummation. It was on 1 April 1873 that Hugo watched himself precipitating a mystical transformation in the little maid:[40]

> Flames were quivering on my emboldened lips;
> She welcomed love and all its fires,
> Dreamt of saying '*tu*', took chances,
> Did not refuse, yet did not yield.
> Her sweet compliance was lofty and serene;
> She knew how to be a slave and yet remain a queen.
> . . .
> When love the conqueror entered her body,
> Heaven seemed to leap out of her heart;
> She caressed with light.
> . . .
> From her white shoulders, as I kissed her,
> Two wings slowly seemed to grow;
> Her eyes had the blueness of the skies;
> And that strange woman had such a noble soul
> That as she ceased to be a virgin she turned into an angel.[41]

For most poets of Hugo's generation, sex spells the end of romantic love. For Hugo, it was the opposite: an orgasm was one of Nature's beautiful sights, like the explosion of the sun in the morning sky, the birth of an Aphrodite, the completion of a poem. One of his finest sexual images never found its way out of the coded diary into verse: it was too precise for contemporary taste, but it defines the process nicely. When Blanche touched his penis, he told her, 'It's a lyre.' 'And only poets know how to play them.'[42]

Two months later, while Hugo was touring the island with his angel, Juliette was rummaging in his files and became the first person to attempt a decipherment of his log. The result was that Blanche left Guernsey for Paris on 1 July. Hugo and Juliette were reconciled, and the only sign of regret in Hugo's diary is a short note in approximate Spanish: '*A las 11, se ha disparacido el vapor.*'[43] He had stood watching from his look-out, like Gilliatt at the end of *Les Travailleurs de la Mer*, as the steamship carried Blanche over the horizon.

Ten days later, the steamship docked at St Peter Port and a young woman set off for rented lodgings in town. Blanche was back. The poem later included in the last series of *La Légende des Siècles*, 'En Grèce', is dated 12 July (it was published one month after Juliette's death in 1883): 'Listen, if you like, since we are in love, / We shall flee together over hill and dale / And head for Grecian skies, where the Muses live.' The curtain-call lasted nine days. A Guernsey native seems to have spotted 'Monsieur Hiougo' with his girlfriend.[44] It was hard to be a secret lover and the local tourist attraction at the same time. On 21 July, Blanche left again for Paris, under orders not to write 'until further notice'.

Hugo now had several reasons to return to Paris: Blanche was waiting for him in an apartment close to the Invalides; *Quatrevingt-treize* was almost ready for the printers; François-Victor was seriously ill with renal tuberculosis; and President Thiers, who had promised that Rochefort would not be deported, had been forced out of office. He was replaced by a soldier, Marshal MacMahon, whose most recent qualification was his crushing of the Paris Commune. Just the man to restore what he called 'moral order'. Work began on the giant wedding cake that now squats on Montmartre: the Sacré-Coeur de Jésus – a hypocritical act of national atonement which might more fittingly have been dedicated to Pontius Pilate. 'Moral order' also demanded that Rochefort be sent to expiate his crimes under the tropical sun.

On 31 July 1873, Hugo was back in Paris, this time in the plush suburb of Auteuil. He took rooms in the Villa Montmorency, where his son was wasting away. Three days after moving in, he sent a letter to his fellow Academician, the monarchist minister, the Duc de Broglie, begging him to countermand the deportation order:

[Rochefort's] very delicate constitution will not survive this deportation. He will either be broken by the long and atrocious voyage, devoured by the climate or will die of nostalgia. . . . You can and must intervene. By taking this generous initiative, you will bring honour on yourself.

The Duc de Broglie decided that he was already honourable enough and responded like a man who believes authority to be inherently correct: 'M. Rochefort will have been the object of a medical inspection performed with very particular attention'; 'the intellectual faculties M. Rochefort enjoys merely increase his responsibility', etc. On 12 August 1873, Hugo recorded the failure of his mission. Another *misérable* in the making: 'Rochefort has gone. He is no longer called Rochefort. His name is Number 116.'

Hugo's determination to keep poking his finger at France's 'shame' was not just the result of his patriotism and ethics. He was acting out his own moral drama on the national stage. The focusing of his political action onto one object – amnesty – corresponds to a similar concentration of his physical energy. Instead of the respectable miseries of decrepitude, he suffered the humiliation of a pert and lusty metabolism. Adèle had been swallowed by her mind; her father was being taken over by his body.

Every day after lunch, it put him on the Batignolles–Jardin des Plantes omnibus and made him get off at the stop closest to Blanche's apartment. This turned out to have a beneficial side-effect. He told his guests that he found the top deck of the bus conducive to the writing of poems, which was obviously an excuse but also true. The noise of the wheels and the horses' hooves, the irregular rhythms and the breeze in his hair set the syllables tripping out, in the same way that the twirling housemaid dusting his room had an inspiring, kinetic effect on his pen.[45] The process induced such fluency that on one occasion, some lines he had written on the bus proved to have a six-syllable gap. Hugo traced it back to the moment when the conductor had asked for his ticket: '*Votre place, Monsieur!*'[46]

It is a shame that no picture exists of the white-haired Hugo perched on his 'tuppenny Pegasus', surrounded by a cross-section of Parisians – a familiar sight to people on the route and a splendid image of the neo-Romantic poet, the man on the Batignolles omnibus in full flight.

Travelling by bus also had one serious disadvantage: it made him very easy to follow. Juliette hired a private detective ... The storm broke on 19 September: 'Catastrophe. Letter from Juliette. Terrible anxiety. A horrible night.' Juliette had disappeared, and for the first time in ages there was a glimpse of the fragile, half-existent creature that remained when 'Juju"'s flattering smile was no longer there to reflect its image:

> Three days of anguish ... And the bitter necessity of keeping it all secret: I must remain silent and appear normal.... Meanwhile, people are dying. There is cholera in Paris.... I seek her everywhere. I wish I were dead too ... Three nights without sleep, three days, almost without drinking or eating. Fever.

Telegrams were sent to Julie Chenay and Juliette's nephew, Louis Koch, in Belgium. He visited some clairvoyants, but the messages were 'vague and obscure'. He also visited a prostitute, but the anguish continued. Friends were told that Mme Drouet was on holiday in Brittany. Finally, news came from Brussels. Juliette was refusing to return. Hugo wrote and she returned on the evening train on 26 September: 'Happiness equal to despair. I gave her dinner at the corner restaurant. Then we took a cab and went to bed at midnight.'

The 'terrible week' was over. He swore 'on the life of his dying son' that he would never see Blanche again. The resolution held good for almost two days.

Like most addictions, in the short term, Hugo's craving for women's bodies was harmful only when it was frustrated. Considering his writing rhythms, it comes as no surprise to learn that the mood-enhancing and energizing effects of romantic love are produced by an amphetamine-related compound.[47] Before and after the crisis, he was writing superb poems for the next series of *La Légende des Siècles*. They were admired for their breadth and technical mastery by purists like Mallarmé and, later, Valéry – lines which seemed to have fallen from the tree like ripe fruit,[48] daring themselves to become ridiculous and carrying off the trick, expressing the infinite by the interminable:

> Elle monte, elle monte, et monte, et monte encore,
> Encore, et l'on dirait que le ciel la dévore.[49]

In his early seventies, Hugo was more thoroughly and paradoxically Romantic than ever before, thriving on the sources of his shame.

Another gaudy antithesis was forming itself in his diary as he charted the apparent recovery of François-Victor – pathetic notes of 'improvements' and doctors' lies which betray the inflated optimism of despair. François-Victor was dying under the blank stare of his father: 'The white marble bust crowned with laurel which David d'Angers made of me has been placed in my son's drawing-room. . . . He had the bust set on a large plinth draped with red velvet.'[50]

Edmond Goncourt was invited to dinner shortly after Hugo's return from Guernsey and mused on the reversal of generations:

> In the humid garden of the little house, François Hugo lies in a chaise longue, with waxen features, faraway, staring eyes, his arms clutched tightly around him against the cold. He is sad in the way that anaemic people are. Close to his chair, standing up, his father has the rigid frame of an old Huguenot in a play.[51]

During dinner, Hugo happily ate nothing but melon, having suffered a bout of cholerine (a mild form of cholera). He expatiated on his pet topics which, at that moment, included an Institut that would perform the function of an intellectual House of Lords, a government of Gwynplaines, its members elected by popular vote: 'On this theme, which seems to be one of his party pieces, he is very eloquent, full of insights, great phrases and flashes of brilliance.'[52]

> The evening air turns chilly. François Hugo's pallor takes on a livid hue. The great man is bare-headed and wears a little alpaca overcoat but does not feel the cold. He is full of life and *joie de vivre*, overflowing with vitality. Next to his son's agony, the obliviousness of his powerful and rugged good health is painful to behold. . . .
>
> As we leave the house, Bocher says to me, 'That man's a tiger! It's only because I urged him to that he came back. The last thing he's thinking about is his son! At the moment, he's busy fucking his tenant! It's the same with that tall young woman who caresses him . . .'*

The end of *Quatrevingt-treize*, which Hugo was then revising, was a sombre hymn to the distressing ironies of Nature: 'Nature is pitiless.

---

* Emmanuel Bocher, son of the *député*, Édouard Bocher. The 'tenant' is Blanche. The tall young woman could be one of several guests.

She refuses to withdraw her flowers, her music, her scents and her sunlight in the face of human abomination.' While François-Victor turned slowly green, Hugo was furiously fornicating and the little grandchildren – the shrubs under the cypress – were thriving merrily: 'I played in the garden with the little ones, who are adorable. Jeanne said to me, "I left my knickers at Gaston's place." Gaston is her boyfriend, five years old.'[53]

The Christmas of 1872 had seen the birth of the Angel Blanche. The Christmas of 1873 saw the death of Hugo's last sane child.

> I drew aside the curtains. Victor appeared to be sleeping. I lifted his hand and kissed it. It was warm and supple. He had just passed away, and though the breath had left his lips, his soul was on his face. . . . I shall see you all again, you whom I love and who love me.

A singer called Anatole Lionnet was asked by Hugo to produce a drawing of François-Victor on his death-bed. For two hours, while Lionnet sketched the emaciated face, Hugo sat in the death chamber, sharpening his pencils for him.[54]

The funeral took place on 28 December 1873 at Père Lachaise. Naturally, there was no church service. Louis Blanc was asked to speak and to 'declare the soul immortal and God eternal', which he did to Hugo's satisfaction. Flaubert attended the funeral. There was a large crowd but no unseemly political display, which, Flaubert observed, would disappoint the Catholic Church: 'Poor old Hugo (I couldn't help embracing him) was devastated but stoical.' The *Figaro* rebuked him for attending his son's funeral 'in a soft hat'.[55]

That night, Hugo lay awake in bed, half-dissolved in the spirit world: 'Very close, above my head, I heard something like the rustling sound of a bird's wings. It was pitch-black. I prayed, as I always do, and then I fell asleep.'

CHAPTER TWENTY-TWO

'A Man Who Thinks of Something Else'[1]

(1874–1878)

SHORTLY AFTER FRANÇOIS-VICTOR 'became invisible', Hugo made one of the most important decisions of his life: he decided to go on living. The first words written in 1874 – at two in the morning on New Year's Day – took the form of a final-sounding alexandrine:

What am I good for now? For dying.

But he was far too busy not to make his death last as long as possible. He had to supervise the publication of *Quatrevingt-treize* and the revival of his plays, marshal his manuscripts, patch up the quarrel between Blanche and the Lanvins, who were horrified to see their ward setting up as a poet's mistress. He also had to help bring up the grandchildren and the Third Republic, and look after Juliette – a task which he performed with the light heart of someone who loves an old story: 'I take care of my poor invalid by rubbing cottonseed oil on both her hips. I saw her almost naked, which had not happened for a long time. She still has a superb body.'[2]

The first poems he wrote after the loss of François-Victor were 'Le Lapidé' (5 January), in which God tells the poet that prophets are stoned to death in order to serve as a warning to the people who stoned them to death (another allusion to the Brussels mob), and 'Je Travaille' (12 January), in which hard work is said to be the divine remedy for suffering.

The gritting of the teeth suggested by these stoical poems was a grin of satisfaction, the philosophical smile of a man who saw everything that happened to him as an allegory of something else. Hugo's normal mental condition was the mood of illusion associated with leaving a cinema or finishing a novel (or, in Van Gogh's case, with 'finishing a book by Victor Hugo'):[3] contingency and tedium ceased to exist, 'all Nature seemed to speak', and there was a pleasant feeling of being shielded from life's insults. In 'Pensées de Nuit' (16 January 1874), Hugo imagined himself facing 'fortune' and 'jealous fate' like a '*belluaire*' (a gladiator or lion-tamer). He was not surprised therefore to learn from a hairy man who sat next to him on the bus one day – a lion-tamer called Pezon – that taming lions was simple: 'All you 'ave to do is jump on 'em. Easy-peasy.'[4]

This happy state, which looks like sheer good luck – merely a question of having the right temperament – was the result of a conscious decision, taken some time in February 1874. It beautifully illustrates the weaknesses and strengths of Hugo's thinking habits:

> As a mind, I belong to God; as a force, I belong to humanity. But an excess of generalization leads to abstraction in poetry and to denationalization in politics. The result is that one detaches oneself from life and dissociates oneself from the fatherland – a double pitfall which I try to avoid. I seek the ideal, but I make sure that one toe always remains in contact with reality. I wish neither to lose touch with the ground as a poet nor with France as a politician.[5]

Usually, these suspiciously neat formulations in which two equal copies of Hugo sit at either end of a rhetorical see-saw, going up and down for as long as it takes to exhaust the thought, are considered philosophically unsound: mere syntax whisks away the doubts that a reputable thinker would pause to consider. But this is to assume that an unobstructed passage ran directly from Hugo's mind on to the page. These rhetorical structures are the outward sign of a delicate mental discipline, expressed in all its beautiful power in the tiny autobiographical text, *Mes Fils* (May 1874), where Hugo manages to present the death of his sons as the opening of a door, almost as an intriguing distraction from present miseries. He was preparing to carry off one of his greatest victories over human nature: combining a sensible 'desire for death' with the desire to influence reality; to neutralize the usual effects of philosophical wisdom – relativism and a sense of indifference to the result – and yet remain wise.

*

HUGO'S ATTEMPT to remain fully 'nationalized' required a proper base of operations. That April, what was left of the family moved into two refurbished apartments at 21 Rue de Clichy.[6] It was decided that Hugo would live with Alice and the grandchildren. Juliette would have the floor with the reception rooms, ostensibly because she was to act as Hugo's stewardess.

The Rue de Clichy seemed an odd choice for a millionaire. It was a busy road of secondhand furniture shops and dingy cafés which joined the luxurious quarters around the Opéra to the working-class sprawl of Montmartre. Hugo's fourth-floor apartment looked out on to the new Paris Skating Rink. In fact, it was an excellent investment, without being conspicuously expensive, and although Hugo never mentions the fact, it was also the completion of a circle: the scene of his earliest conscious memories. His first Paris home, since demolished, had been at 24 Rue de Clichy. At number 19, Mme Hugo's lover had hidden from the imperial police in 1804.

Seventy years on, Hugo was a fugitive from his own fame. Number 21 is the birthplace of a phenomenon that would have astounded Mme Hugo: the mixture of religious and political fervour known to historians as Hugolatry.

For the next five years, Hugo's apartment was the most publicized dwelling in Europe, an enchanted oasis of flowery anecdotes which seemed to writers a century ago to be the main point of a Hugo biography. One biographer listed 142 people who regularly came 'to breathe the purer air' of Hugo's salon.[7] Most came to satisfy the sort of curiosity that spends more time feeding on titbits than discovering matters about which it might be more richly curious. One enterprising tour organizer succeeded in introducing a whole party of American sightseers into Hugo's salon. (They were politely ushered out.)

For those who were not invited to dinner but asked by a white-aproned maid to wait in a crimson-papered antechamber, the public performance took place in a vast, overheated salon lit by gas and chandelier and divided in two by a large bronze and gold elephant.

Hugo received his guests on a small green sofa. Juliette sat across from him, policing the conversation, correcting any remarks of an unHugolian nature with an apposite quotation from the master's works. Still celebrating the dawn of their love, she wore silk dresses in the early Romantic style, daringly décolletée – especially daring for a woman of sixty-eight – with lacy frills and huge 'pagoda' sleeves. Hugo's tastes in women's clothing were well known and there were more exposed bosoms at the Rue de Clichy than anywhere else in Paris. Ladies who were suitably unclothed were kissed from fingertip to elbow. Those who tactlessly wore gloves felt a digit inserted under the hem and a hairy kiss planted on their wrist. A token undressing.

Guests who came prepared to memorize poetic gems or ludicrous aphorisms were usually disappointed, though Hugo could always be persuaded to offer an opinion. His peculiar brand of literary criticism is best represented by a story from Turgenev:

> Once, when I was at his home, we were chatting about German poetry. Victor Hugo, who does not like people talking in his presence, cut me short and began to give a portrait of Goethe.
>
> 'His best work', he said in an Olympian tone, 'is *Wallenstein*.'
>
> 'Forgive me, dear master. *Wallenstein* is not by Goethe. It is by Schiller.'
>
> 'It matters not. I have read neither Goethe nor Schiller, but I know them better than those who have learnt their works by heart.'[8]

Whenever something out of the ordinary happened, it was reported by newspapers all over the world, especially if it matched what Hugo was now thought to represent. Once, when thirteen people were counted at the dinner-table (certainly not through any fault of Juliette), a cab-driver was invited up to fill the empty place. Changes in society have given this little story an ambiguous nuance; at the time, it was supposed to produce a warm glow in the reader – the great man stooping to fill the stomach of the humble tradesman – though the end of the story was usually omitted: the cab-driver, a man called Moore, overstepped his symbolic role and threw up on the carpet.[9] Often, the cab-driver story was told with the complementary tale of courtesies exchanged with Pedro II, Emperor of Brazil, who came to Paris in 1877 and did not want to leave without seeing

Victor Hugo and his grandchildren. Don Pedro had been a Hugophile since the age of six. Hugo recorded the interview in his diary:

> When I introduced him to Georges, I said, 'Sire, allow me to introduce my grandson to Your Majesty.' He said to Georges, 'My boy, there is only one Majesty here, and that is Victor Hugo.'[10]

Meatier stories came from those who were privy to Hugo's table activities. He drank cheap, heavily sugared wine, mashed up mounds of eggs, vegetables and sauces into a fearsome, pork-based *olla podrida*, munched his way through lobsters (including their shells, which he claimed were an aid to digestion – the gastronomic equivalent of Gilliatt's battle with the *pieuvre*), nibbled lumps of coal, and pushed whole oranges into his mouth, daring Georges and Jeanne to do the same.

Georges and Jeanne were an appreciative audience. Their grand-father doodled on the tablecloth, balanced plates and cutlery on top of wine bottles, and left little drawings under the children's napkins. If they had behaved themselves, they found an angel or a bird; if not, a devil, an ass or, in exceptionally bad cases, a chamber-pot.[11] For Hugo, the Rue de Clichy was more than just a geographical return to childhood.

The problem with many of the anecdotes associated with the Rue de Clichy is their source. Three well-thumbed Hugo memorialists – Gustave Rivet, Alfred Barbou and Maurice Coste – owed their jobs and good reputations to Hugo's influence. Richard Lesclide was his secretary, Georges Hugo his grandson and Édouard Lockroy his son-in-law. Though their accounts are not necessarily fictitious, they do represent a tactful selection.

Extreme cases of niceness to Hugo could be quoted quite literally ad nauseam. The fulsomest flatterers used a special convoluted syntax – plenty of subordinate clauses – and an antiquated vocabulary as if to stress that this was no ordinary reality: 'How should I forget that first visit to the flat in the Rue de Clichy – the modest apartment, so disproportionate to the glory of its inhabitant, which, in the estimate of his contemporaries, no palace could contain!' (Mme Daudet).[12] 'The course of time seems reluctant to touch his venerable head' (Barbou).[13] 'One cannot treat his utterances as those of lesser men'

(Anon.).[14] Some of this self-flagellating adulation verged on the insane. A poet called Adolphe Pelleport, who suffered from an intermittent delusion that he was Victor Hugo, appears to have died from a wasting illness caused by the agony of accidentally breaking one of Hugo's Chinese vases.[15] Swinburne, by contrast, retained the wit to enjoy his obsession. He had been reading Hugo since Eton and became so studiously besotted with 'the greatest writer of his century' that he produced a complete rhymed bibliography of Hugo's works. 'I wish I could polish Victor Hugo's boots every morning,' he wrote, after a visit to Hugo's home, 'so as to obtain from him daily a glance imbued with that adorable kindness he condescended to show me.'[16] Hugo responded by pleading his ignorance of English and eventually resorted to deafness.

Swinburne was indulging a characteristic, late-nineteenth-century perversion that might be called gerontophilia – something akin to the passion that was satisfied in Britain by Queen Victoria. Hugo was the hero of a nation which had seen its elders disgraced and which increasingly was being asked to take responsibility for its own fate. The manly virtues of chauvinism and anticlericalism went hand in hand with a cult of personal impotence and religious awe.

It comes almost as a relief to find that Hugo's salon was also infested with sniggering iconoclasts. This is where the distinction first appears between what Maurice Agulhon calls '*hugolâtrie populaire*' and '*hugolâtrie officielle*'.[17] To most politicians, Hugo was still the irresponsible demagogue, a vast and vacuous ego casting doubt on the seriousness of their profession. Even in republican circles, it was unfashionable to pay homage: Hugo was tainted with bizarre spiritual beliefs. Writing in 1927, Maurice Coste described the men who rode the Hugo bandwagon:

> This covert hostility of most of the leaders of the Third Republic toward the man whom they publicly lauded as one of their official glories, is one of the strongest memories I have of the republican milieux of that period. It was so much the done thing to ridicule him behind his back, in the very parties which employed him as their banner, that, in the end, many people who sincerely loved and admired his genius were afraid to show it and joined in with the sneering.[18]

However much of an embarrassment to the party, Hugo was too valuable to waste. The most famous man on Earth was a French republican. In the new world of international trade, Victor Hugo was worth at least a coal-field or a famous public monument. The monarchists were hoping to install the Comte de Chambord on the throne – the grandson of Charles X who had been hailed by Victor Hugo in 1820 as a national Baby Jesus but who was turning out to be an oblivious anachronism. Hugo was the republican answer to royalty, a personality as large as an election poster, the first of those adored figures, from General Boulanger to General de Gaulle, who eased the mental transition from monarchy to democracy – or perhaps it was the reverse. Hugo was ending his career almost as he had begun it: a court poet for post-monarchist France.

*

AS THE UNGUENTS poured over Hugo begin to solidify, it seems as though his attempt to remain in touch with reality by being patriotic had backfired. He was turning into the figment of a mass fantasy. Bulgaria made him an honorary citizen for no apparent reason. He was invited to the centenary celebration of American independence, promised a royal reception if he ever went to Egypt, and learned that the new Sultan of Turkey, Murad V, was having *Les Orientales* translated into Turkish – 'translated so well that he has just had [his predecessor] Abd-ul-Aziz strangled to death'.[19]

This heaping of honours on Hugo is a disaster for the truth. Medals parody the acts they commemorate. Hugo's contribution to the political life of his century is converted into an enormous pile of loose change: honorary presidencies and citizenships, the sponsoring of anti-vivisectionists, workers' cooperatives, freemasons, insurance companies and illegitimate children. If diatribes were 'the latrines of one's fame', honours were its disinfectant.

His real influence is more diffuse and intimate. His ploy of making the glory of the nation hinge on the question of amnesty showed that it was possible to be a patriot and a humanist at the same time. For many people – the 80,000, for example, who bought the illustrated edition of *L'Année Terrible* in April 1874 – Victor Hugo was an altar at which liberal ideas could be worshipped. Though the tricolour-waving Hugo now attracts more attention than the others, like a lighthouse where there is no longer a sea, his determination to apply personal morality to national and international behaviour was an important tempering influence on belligerent capitalism, not only in France. Perhaps most important of all, he had the comforting knack of finding a phrase for every event – the sort of philosophical confidence that is eventually missed even by the people it most irritated. This, for example, on the Turkish atrocities in Bosnia and Herzegovina (29 August 1876):

> Kill six men and you are Troppmann.* Kill six hundred thousand and you are Caesar. . . .
> Murdering a man is a crime. Murdering a people is a 'question'.[20]

The fact that this sort of subversive sentiment was enshrined in the works of the nation's greatest writer certainly helped to dignify what had once been seen as the dangerous fantasies of a disgruntled proletariat.

Hugolatry has the extra disadvantage of making Hugo look like the smoothly flowing fount of a few endlessly recycled opinions. The reality is far more complex. In the tiny fragments Hugo called his 'wood shavings',[21] there is evidence of almost every view that words are capable of forming – even of normal misgivings. This is a note for an abandoned poem written in 1877 or 1878:

> When I think of all the enemies I have,
> It seems to me I must after all be wrong about something,
> But I know not how . . . [end of fragment][22]

It may be that Hugo simply felt that self-doubt was a poor subject for a poem and a poor example to the reader. 'I leave the door of my mind open', he had written, 'but my work remains personal.'

What now appears as the monumental façade of Hugo's oeuvre is largely the result of work carried out in this period. He divided his manuscripts into administrative regions with all-absorbing titles, which later editors would use to mop up the miscellanea: *Les Quatre Vents de l'Esprit, Toute la Lyre, Tas de Pierres, Océan.* In 1875 and 1876,

* J.-B. Troppmann butchered five children and their mother and became a focus for national paranoia at the end of the Second Empire.

his last thirty-four years of public utterances were presented, largely unchanged, in three volumes of 'words and deeds': *Actes et Paroles* – a title which almost asks to be misheard as *Actes des Apôtres* (Acts of the Apostles). The whole edifice was laid out like a pyramid around the years of exile – *Avant l'Exil, Pendant l'Exil, Après l'Exil* – and bolted together by three gigantic prefaces, beginning with an evocation of the Feuillantines garden, haunted by the misremembered ghosts of his father and Lahorie.

This final organization of Hugo's complete works into what are effectively 1000-page epitaphs is highly misleading. He himself admitted, at least to himself, that he did not have the faintest idea what the final significance of his work would be, and the fact that he wanted even his 'wood shavings' to be published suggests a desire to undermine his own pharaonic constructions. Discovering Hugo's work should ideally be a process of watching these huge agglomerations crumble back into their constituent parts. If publishing practice allowed, some of the tomes that stand to attention in the library could usefully be replaced with cardboard boxes filled with wandering scraps of paper and deprived of an index.

Behind the façade of his complete works and the decorative front of the Rue de Clichy, the happy evidence is that Hugo was enjoying himself, an ageing Gavroche, using his published work as a magic play-pen in which any kind of bad behaviour was turned into an acceptable public display.

The best examples of his mischief-making come under the respectable heading of 'anticlericalism' – perhaps better described as priest-bashing. The Church had been wrestling with republicans over the vital question of primary education. Infant brains had become the great battleground of French politics. It was now that Hugo's Voltairean tendencies reached their peak. He condemned the moral confidence trick known as original sin, slandered his first teacher, Larivière, by talking of the bigoted education he had received at the hands of a 'priest' – the root of all his later 'errors' – and described his ideal paradise as a 'wide-gated garden' with 'a sweet, mysterious WC' for the edicts of the Catholic Church.[23]

This was the Hugo whose slow, slightly muted voice – 'a finely pitched guttural'[24] – could suddenly sound rowdy and overexcited, who wedged puppets into his back trouser pockets to entertain the children while he talked to important guests,[25] the man who could still wake up at half-past four in the morning to write an insulting poem on that 'little poet', Musset, who had been dead for seventeen years.[26]

The last masterpiece of the priest-bashing Hugo was a long poem in two 'scenes', published in 1878: *Le Pape*. Pope Pius IX undergoes a shattering conversion which effectively turns him into Victor Hugo, the humble righter of wrongs. Scene 1 – Hugo's programme for turning the Roman Catholic Church into a Christian organization – takes up over 1000 lines. Scene 2 is much shorter:

The Vatican. The Pope's bedchamber. Morning.

THE POPE, *waking up*: What a terrible dream I've just had!

*

BY THE TIME *Le Pape* appeared, one of the nightmares of the clerical party had come true. The 1875 Constitution had divided the legislature into a Senate and a Chamber of Deputies. The President was to be elected by both Chambers, not by the people, who had shown a regrettable tendency to vote for tyrants. Proposed by Clemenceau, Hugo was narrowly elected as a senator for Paris on 30 January 1876. On the day of the vote, a huge crowd gathered in the street and showed that Hugomania was more prevalent than it had been since his return in 1870.

The Senate itself was frosty: Republican senators were still in a minority and the motion to call the Third Republic a republic had been carried by only one vote. Hugo's maiden speech (22 May 1876) was another passionately sarcastic plea for amnesty which ensured that his influence in the Senate would be negligible. He compared the perpetrators of the 1851 *coup d'état*, who had had city streets named after them, to the Communards, who were still being deported. The speech was greeted with absolute quiet, which Hugo took as a silent roar of approval from the Senate's conscience. Only ten senators voted with him.

This final phase of Hugo's political career has often been described as a failure, which it certainly was in purely parliamentary terms. He seems to have used the Senate primarily as a source of free headed notepaper and played the part of the fruitlessly stubborn old man to perfection. But without an artificial division between the literary and the political Hugo, it looks more like a skilful campaign to deposit the huge weight of popular feeling in the political scales.

The first of the three works which marked Hugo's debut as a senator was the 'new series' of *La Légende des Siècles* (26 February 1877). It brought together the 'little epics' written over the last twenty years, and since all but one of the poems were undated, confirmed the impression of his inexhaustible fertility. Beginning with a terrifying vision of 'the wall of ages' – a vast, vertical charnel-house of history – it applied the philosophy of love and progress to everything that had occurred since creation. An election campaign launched by God. The subjects ranged from prehistory to the present, including the pontifications of 'The Seven Wonders of the World' (the last word goes to a gleeful 'worm of the sepulchre'), and the famously lachrymose 'Petit Paul': a sad little orphan who leaves his horrid stepmother and falls asleep for ever on the tomb of his kindly old grandfather. Not entirely unconnected, one imagines, with the imminent marriage of Édouard Lockroy and Alice, whom Hugo persisted in calling 'Mme Charles', even after the wedding.

Immediately after sending *La Légende des Siècles* to the printers, Hugo began his next piece of indirect politicking. It came out three months later under the title, *L'Art d'Être Grand-Père* ('How to be a Grandfather'): a sixty-eight-poem hymn to his favourite form of human being. An English critic said that to read it was to be sick of children,[27] but this was probably in exasperation at the popularity of Hugo's nice-old-man image in Victorian Britain. The poems detailing the adorable *actes et paroles* of Georges and Jeanne may have been spawned by a great soppiness at the heart of Hugo, but, taken as a whole, they were his most cunning collection. Improbable as it may seem, his dual self-portrait as a frisky, breast-grabbing old greybeard and as a role model for God was not the result of some embarrassing, senile miscalculation. The doting over grandchildren was almost as much a front as kissing babies is for politicians. Whatever the apparent subject of the poem, Hugo was always ploughing more than one furrow. The best-known and most frequently misrepresented poem is 'Les Enfants Gâtés':

When they see that the children don't fear me,
When they see me so dreamy with the jubilant tots,
Serious men knit their dreary brows.
An addlepated granddad who can't behave,
That's me. . . . A ruler who doesn't know his job.
I don't want my people to tremble.
My people, that's Jeanne and Georges. I'm the old gaffer,
The unbridled patriarch with a nasty habit of being nice.
I get them to break the law. I even dare incite
Their pink republic to revolt.
Unhealthy popularity I can't resist.
I ask you, should a grandfather be so anarchic
That he points out as a source of dark adventures
The august cupboard which contains the pots of jam?
The bane of housekeepers, I confess to having on occasion
Consummated the violation of those sacred urns.
I'm a disgrace. To make them happy, I climb on chairs!
If I spy a plate of strawberries in a corner,
Set aside for us adults' dessert, I say to them,
'Darling little greedy birds of paradise,
Take it, it's yours! See, down there in the street,
Those little paupers – one has scarce been born –
They are hungry. Invite them up and share.' . . .

The spoilt children of the title turn out to be children in long trousers – the unforgiving Mr Murdstones of bourgeois society who 'want to debar children from happiness and love from alabaster breasts': an interesting equation of the children's illicit treats with Grandfather's girlfriends. That plate of strawberries is particularly suspicious. In context, it conjures up the expression, *aller aux fraises* (to go a-frolicking in the woods), perhaps, too, *sucrer les fraises* (to go soft in the head).

Half a century after *Les Feuilles d'Automne*, the Romantic theme of childhood innocence had been demolished and reconstructed twice over: complicated by Hugo's insights into infantile sexuality, it was now being used as political propaganda. The drooling old softy was the public face of a socialist Machiavelli, revelling in his orgy of tolerance, the lonely child who would have started a civil war if he thought it would make the people like him, who had spent the best part of his career pointing out pots of jam to the *misérables*, scoffing at convention, delighting the little ones with tales of excrement and insubordination.

The effect of *L'Art d'Être Grand-Père* is impossible to gauge, except by two obvious results: first, Georges and Jeanne were doted over like royal babies, which was another propaganda blow to the monarchist cause; second, they experienced severe emotional and financial set-backs later in life which Georges attributed to a lack of emphasis on self-restraint.

The last of Hugo's 'senatorial' publications was overtly political and demonstrably effective: the two-volume *Histoire d'un Crime. Déposition d'un Témoin* (October 1877 and March 1878). Shelved in 1852, either because of its size or inaccuracies, Hugo's full-scale account of the *coup d'état* could now be unleashed, complete with damning anecdotes about men who had subsequently become enemies or died: 'There was Sainte-Beuve, a distinguished inferior man who had the sort of envious nature that is forgivable in the ugly. . . . There was Abbatucci: a conscience that allowed everything to pass. Today, Abbatucci is a street.'*[28]

Parts of *Histoire d'un Crime* may be more story than history, more slapstick than tragedy, but it was still the best-documented account of the *coup d'état*, and it served its modern purpose brilliantly. In May 1877, President MacMahon dismissed the republican cabinet of Jules Simon: 'a semi-*coup d'état*', Hugo called it. The monarchist Duc de Broglie, who did not represent a majority, was appointed in his place and an 'election campaign' was launched – actually a Church-backed programme of censorship, propaganda and intimidation. Volume I of Hugo's rip-roaring tale of presidential misdeeds shot off the presses, just in time, as a giant, retaliatory custard-pie: 'This book is more than topical. It is urgent. I publish it.'

As the elections drew near, there were rumours that the book was to be banned and its author assassinated. Hugo slept soundly: 'The matter concerns my assassins.' MacMahon and Broglie decided not to take the risk. The election-rigging tactics used by Napoleon III had lost their bite. The Monarchists remained in a minority, and it is

* J.-P.-C. Abbatucci (1792–1857), Minister of Justice.

generally agreed that Hugo's *Histoire d'un Crime* was a major factor in what proved to be a decisive victory for democracy and the Republic.

The following May, speaking at the celebration of Voltaire's centenary – a writer he had once described as 'an ape of genius sent by Satan'[29] – Hugo pronounced what sounded like his own funeral oration. Everything seemed to be coming to a happy conclusion – his own life and the nineteenth century:

> A hundred years ago today, a man was dying. He was dying immortal, laden with years and works and the most illustrious and redoubtable of responsibilities – responsibility for the conscience of the human race, alerted and rectified. As he departed, he was cursed and blessed: cursed by the past, blessed by the future. . . . He was more than a man, he was a century. He had exercised a function and fulfilled a mission.[30]

Reading these speeches, it is possible to believe that Hugo himself thought that life was simple, that everything had gone according to plan, and that he had always known what the plan was.

*

COMPLICATIONS – and even that vague, primal force called Evil – had been consigned to certain places and hours of the day. Since the discovery of his secret diary by Juliette, Hugo had been forced to take greater precautions, which is to say, to make improvements to his code. 'Olocin 83' was 38 Rue Nicolo backwards, *'lenta vinea'* ('pliant vine') was Lanvin, and 'Aristote', with some mark of disappointment, referred to menstruation:* precautions of a more serious kind were obviously left up to the woman. Some phrases in Spanish remain suggestively obscure, even in translation: *'A los dos lugares y yo también'* ('In both places, and me too').[31]

Hugo was toying with words in the same way that he played with his food: a mish-mash of tongues, sense spilling over from one word to the next or setting off in the wrong direction altogether. A verbal equivalent of sex.

On 18 April 1878, in her daily letter to Hugo, Juliette produced a

---

* Probably from 'the rules (*règles*) of Aristotle'. '*Règles*' also means menstruation.

piece of wisdom which, for once, was not a quotation from the works of Victor Hugo: 'Men are always in a permanent state of infidelity, whether retrospectively, in the present, in thought, or in word and deed.'[32] Along with the pain of betrayal and the effort of ignoring it, there was now the worry that Hugo's sense of invulnerability would be the death of him. The benefits of regular exercise were being outweighed by the health hazard. In June 1875, his memory had blanked out for two hours and the diary showed a sudden attack of chastity lasting several days. But he was still gadding about Paris on the omnibus and using the revival of his plays to familiarize himself with the new generation of actresses – especially the most desirable actress in Europe: Sarah Bernhardt, who was persuaded to stop acting the fool at rehearsals by Hugo's gentle manner and his trick of scolding the actresses in rhyming verse.

'He wasn't exactly what you'd call a paragon of elegance,' she remembered, 'but there was such moderation in his gestures and something of the old *pair de France* in his soft way of speaking.' In 1875, she told her doctor that 'the *real reason*' her trip to England had been postponed was 'one's fear of having *problems* à propos of Victor Hugo'. The note in Hugo's diary, after a visit from Sarah Bernhardt, is more explicit: '*No será el chico hecho*' (supposed to mean, 'There will be no child').[33]

Sex was now everywhere in Hugo's life and work. Forests were 'orgies', Nature was an 'alcove', and the moon was the 'bruised bottom' of the goddess Venus.[34] This was the fertile imagination of a normal, healthy adolescent. But sex was not necessarily an attempt to hang on to life; increasingly, it was associated with the opposite: the final consummation.

'The darker the night, the brighter the star' – Hugo's cheering comment on the advantages of having an *idée fixe*.[35] Suicide by sexual intercourse must logically have occurred to him. It would be the final scattering of seed before the death of the plant. The next best thing to dying with one's boots on.

An extraordinary spate of activity suddenly began on 21 June 1878. That day, Hugo wrote another poem in which the dying man is seized by life as if by an inverted Grim Reaper. The same day, at a literary congress, he asserted the writer's moral obligation to give posterity full access to the untidy kitchens that produced his work, and the duty of the heirs not to suppress a single line. It was a long speech which, according to Hugo's arithmetic, was equivalent to making love three times.

The days that followed were an unprecedented feast of sex with Blanche: 22, 23, 25, 26 and 27 June. On the 25th, he delivered another long speech. On the 26th, he wrote another poem – one of the finest in the posthumous collection, *Toute la Lyre*:

> Spring! Sacred woods! Deep blue sky!
> One senses a breath of living air penetrating one's body
> And the distant opening of a white window.[36]

On the evening of 27 June, after a hefty meal and a furious discussion of the relative merits of Rousseau (who abandoned his illegitimate children) and Voltaire (who 'pleaded the cause of the human race'), he suddenly became confused. His speech was slurred. Three doctors were called. Hugo had suffered a mild stroke, more serious than first appeared. The poem-writing part of his brain seems to have taken a direct hit.

It might have been a splendid, energetic end to Victor Hugo as he knew himself. But the half-natural, half-man-made thing he called his destiny had something much better up its sleeve.

CHAPTER TWENTY-THREE

'To Love Is To Act'

(1878–1885)

T HE TRUTH WAS HIDDEN from him, but his body gave it away. He felt as though he had been struck by lightning; gutted like an old tree. There was a terrifying sense of emptiness. The story that Hugo cheered himself up with Blanche on the morning after the attack is plainly untrue.[1] His 'lyre' lay inactive. The poet Banville met Hugo towards the end of 1878 and heard a sorry tale of irreparable damage:

> He had wanted to make a sacrifice to Venus and found himself incapable of it. This flaccidity, which the man of granite had never before experienced, cast him into profound sadness. He saw in his penis the signs of imminent death.[2]

Hugo had recently estimated that a reasonable length for human life was 200 years[3] – just enough time to put everything down on paper. Now, there was barely time to write instructions for executors. Incredible treasures would be lost. His complete works would be a mere fragment, the capitals of a buried temple.

The disciples, the doctors and Juliette were determined to make him leave for Guernsey. Juliette had the trunks brought down from the attic, and a touching plea was elicited from little Jeanne. Hugo found himself on the train for Granville, grumbling and uncomfortable. He was delivered to Hauteville House like an old trunk on 5 July 1878.

'Paradise' was hell. In the interests of his 'health and glory', Juliette tried to convince him 'of the necessity of breaking with an odious and terrible past'. He had the familiar old-age experience of being deprived of an addiction just when its comforts were most needed. He was tetchy and morose. He tottered to the carriage that took him on his daily ride around the island. Every few minutes, the driver was ordered to stop, not, as before, so that Hugo could record a thought, but to allow him to urinate in the bushes. The only metaphorical fertilizing of furrows was a tiny scrap of poem with unusually weak rhymes: 'Let a voice be heard / Murmuring in the seas, murmuring in the woods: / Be my beloved for ever!'[4]

A palace coup had taken place and rival factions formed. Juliette seemed to have gained the upper hand and was determined to consolidate her position. She compared her love to a battered fortress: standing on the battlements, she scoured the horizon for those evil creatures 'who claim the honour (what an honour!) of exciting your senses at the peril of your health', defending the old king against Cupid's 'catapults'. The great literary romance had long since entered the age of realism. On 17 July 1878, she wrote to her nephew in Paris:

> You must try to track down the creature [Blanche] who has destroyed my happiness, which is of no account, but who is also perhaps, alas!, destroying the world's greatest genius! . . .
>
> You could either resort to Mme Noël [housekeeper at the Rue de Clichy], who is, I think, absolutely discreet and devoted, or you could ask a policeman. There are some at the Préfecture de Police who offer such services, for a fat fee, of course. . . .
>
> . . . I shall send you my list of phrases in Spanish, written every day for two years in notebooks with every date and detail carefully recorded. Please have them translated word by word by someone who knows Spanish well enough to understand the abbreviations and any grammatical mistakes they may contain.
>
> I have just noticed that I forgot to give you a description of the creature: between 26 and 28, short, very dark complexion, very frizzy hair, impossible to comb; divergent eyes – the result of an old eye complaint; intelligent, half-educated, very cunning and very depraved; looks like a second-class *grisette*. This would enable a good agent to discover her whereabouts and her current habits. without compromising the man I continue to admire and, alas!, to love.[5]

This splendid letter clearly establishes Juliette Drouet as one of Hugo's first investigative biographers, the benevolent Inspector Javert to Hugo's Jean Valjean. A reminder to Hugophiles who try to cover up his foibles that love and a desire to know the truth are not incompatible.

Back in Paris, Meurice and Vacquerie were scheming to save the master's guilty secrets. Reputation before life. The men who were to act as Hugo's go-betweens with posterity seem to have performed a similar function with respect to his women. On 16 August 1878, Meurice wrote to Richard Lesclide (who volunteered his secretarial services every Sunday), suggesting that the locked drawer in Hugo's desk be forced and any compromising papers be placed beyond the reach of 'a certain person', by which he meant Juliette Drouet.[6]

This was the new order to which Hugo returned on 10 November, shattered but stable. The scene had changed. He found himself, not in the Rue de Clichy, but in a modest two-storey house with mansard rooms at 130 Avenue d'Eylau – one of the avenues which fan out from the Arc de Triomphe. It was the latest extension of the city, a plush but rustic *quartier*, popular with retired people and religious communities. A stone staircase led from the drawing-room into a garden of shady trees. Hugo's first-floor window opened on to the branches: a convenient arrangement for his last known cat, Gavroche. Juliette's bedroom was on the same floor: the closest she had ever come to sharing a room with her lover.

For the outside world, the illusion of vitality was preserved by Vacquerie and Meurice. The effects of their editorial ventriloquism can be seen in the misleading list of Hugo's final publications: three long poems – *La Pitié Suprême* (1879), *Religions et Religion* and *L'Âne* (1880); an anthology, *Les Quatre Vents de l'Esprit* (1881); a play, *Torquemada* (1882), and the 'final series' of *La Légende des Siècles* (1883). All these works had been written many years before. But since Hugo had often described his writings as messages from the dead to the living, it was appropriate that his 'posthumous' works should begin to appear while he was still alive.

The crucial fact about Hugo's new home was that it was attached to number 132, where Alice lived with the children and her husband. Édouard Lockroy had fought with Garibaldi, collaborated with Rochefort, served a gaol sentence after the Commune and been elected to Parliament as one of the leading lights of Hugolatrous republicanism. He now faced his greatest challenge: sharing a house with Victor Hugo.

The problem was that the blasted tree was already putting out new shoots. At first, this seemed impossible. Hugo was sleeping until noon, which was a disaster for his work since he could only write in the morning, before lunch diverted his energy from brain to stomach. Blanche had been frightened off with a warning from Juliette that she might suddenly find herself embracing a corpse. She was married off to a desk clerk. A small victoria was purchased so that Hugo would never again have to take the bus . . .

His last full-length poem however (17 November 1879) shows signs of a remarkable recovery. It describes the thinker who hopes to penetrate the mystery of creation by using the image of a man excited by his lover's resistance: 'Trying to snatch a "yes" from voices which say "no".'[7] There is a vagueness about the verse, an interesting clumsiness in the phrasing which suggests that a loss of agility in the mind of an old poet can be as aesthetically profitable as failing sight in a painter.

Hugo, it seemed, was still slipping out the back door on amorous excursions. Lockroy was appalled. His stepchildren had been pressed into service as icons of Hugolatry, his wife had told him tales of senile bottom-pinching, and whenever Hugo was deprived of sex the house filled up at night with supernatural knockings – sounds of mirrors smashing and huge sails crashing to the floor. The old man was found to be actively involved with three women, including a former mistress of the indispensable Paul Meurice. And then there were the blackmailing letters: Blanche's husband had discovered a cache of obscene messages among his wife's papers. Lockroy, whose political reputation was bound up with Hugo's, called in the Sûreté. There was to be no repetition of the Mme Biard incident. Rumours were rife, but this time they had a different effect on his reputation. Hugo's energy was admired as if it somehow reflected the vitality of the nation:

> It was said that at that time every detective and every police officer carried in his pocket the photographs of two remarkable old men, of whom Victor Hugo was one, so that in case their tastes for exploring

the *bas-fonds* of Paris might lead them into perilous adventures, the public scandal of an arrest might be avoided.[8]

The details of Lockroy's life with Hugo – the unconscious rivalries, the irritating habits – naturally escape us. His reaction to living with a sexual generator is preserved only in the crude form of Léon Daudet's memoirs. 'Where are you off to, you disgusting old man?' he is reported as saying to Hugo, who was creeping downstairs in his slippers and vest. 'Leave the cook alone!'[9]

Léon Daudet was a boyhood friend of Georges Hugo and later married Jeanne. His memoirs are heavily dosed with fiction and invented conversations but they probably quite faithfully reflect the point of view of orphan Georges. Hugo had taken on all the congenial duties of fatherhood, leaving the less popular aspects, such as discipline, to Lockroy. The psychological accuracy of Daudet's fantasy is confirmed by a letter written by Georges Hugo to his stepfather in 1894:

> I observed your treatment of Victor Hugo, whose memory you now jealously defend. I witnessed scenes between that great old man and yourself when you had the temerity to defy him, saying things which horrified me.[10]

Whether or not Lockroy actively frustrated Hugo's sexual expeditions, the new domestic regime was clearly more oppressive than the Second Empire. His poetry had dried up, his tyrannical charm had lost its power, and his principal means of self-expression was treated as a disgusting vice.

*

5 JULY 1879, 1000 feet in the air: Juliette was clinging on to Hugo.[11] Far below, her lover's city was spread out like a relief map of his life: domes, spires and turrets that bore the names of some of his best-known works. Surrounding him in the basket was a group of middle-aged men – his hagiographers past and future: Richard Lesclide, Paul de Saint-Victor, Maurice Talmeyr and Paul Meurice.

They had all gone up in the captive balloon of the Tuileries Gardens. Hugo may have remembered his first aerial view of Paris, from the dome of the Sorbonne, when the Allies were approaching

Paris in 1815. Since then, the city had been rewriting itself in his image, and it was possible to believe, especially from 1000 feet in the air, that his optimism was justified.

The first law granting amnesty to the Communards had been promulgated that April. A general amnesty was proclaimed the following year. Secular primary education was made compulsory in 1882, with rote learning of Victor Hugo poems as an important consequence. Beyond the hills of Paris, the torch of progress was being carried through the Dark Continent by inspired explorers, as Hugo observed in May at a banquet celebrating the abolition of slavery by the Government of 1848: 'Lakes have been sighted ... Gigantic hydraulic apparatuses have been prepared by Nature and are awaiting Man.'[12] The balloon itself was a joyful symbol, like the phonograph at the Ministre des Postes ('most curious') and the new high-speed tram which scared the wits out of Juliette. 'In the twentieth century', he informed the first Socialist Workers' Congress a month later, 'war will be dead; the scaffold, hate, royalty, frontiers and dogmas will all be dead. Man will live.'[13]

Hugo was devoting himself to his symbolic function so efficiently that it is easy to forget that his poetry had all but withered away. This was the man who sat for hours like a snow-covered mountain having his portrait painted for the salon by Léon Bonnat. Only his mouth moved – to hail the providential greatness of Lesseps, engineer of the Suez Canal, who called in during the sitting, and to urge an exhausted Bonnat to finish the portrait.[14] Flaubert claimed that the portrait was 'true to life, down to the very form of the fingernails'.[15] True to life as Hugo lived it: a Napoleonic hand nestles in the waistcoat (stains disguised by deep shade) while a heavy elbow leans on a prostrate Homer. The left eye is cavernous – dull with age or filled with invisible visions.

The great image-maker had fallen prey to other image-makers. The common view of Hugo in the 1880s is largely a product of the posthumous volume of *Actes et Paroles* (1889), decorated by its editors with mawkish verbal vignettes. Hugo's last long utterance – at a party for the children of Veules (Meurice's home on the Channel coast) – is made to end with a truly awful picture, almost a case of assassination by syrup: 'Victor Hugo sits down, the only "big person" in the midst of his seventy-four young guests, served by the three daughters of Paul Meurice.' A tombola had been held:

> Fate was intelligent. First prize went to a poor woman with four children, a widow who had never remarried. Shedding tears of joy, she came to receive the prize for the little girl who was asleep in her arms.[16]

The Meurice–Vacquerie editions of Hugo's work, perpetuated in their purifying spirit by later editors, show a stupidly defensive discretion which reflects the sort of intransigent, party-political convictions that have dogged him ever since. The quality he felt was missing from Voltaire's work – 'monstrosity' – was carefully removed from his own like a cancerous growth.

There was no escaping his apotheosis. After the final decree of amnesty in 1880, Hugo could no longer claim to be a one-man opposition. Though he continued to do embarrassing things like pleading for the lives of Russian nihilists and Kabyle rebels in Algeria, his declarations were sufficiently imprecise to be dissolved in republican dogma. Hugo had given the Third Republic its mythology: its evil Ancien Régime was the Second Empire, its savage but necessary Revolution was the Paris Commune. The view of Marx's son-in-law, Paul Lafargue – that Hugo had been upholding bourgeois values and interests all along – now seems quite accurate. In the dark night of the Second Empire, he had kept alight the torch of free enterprise and philanthropic capitalism, defending bourgeois ideology when it had become unacceptable to the bourgeoisie itself.[17] *Châtiments* and *Napoléon-le-Petit* had after all been two of the great commercial successes of the age. Bankers had paid small fortunes for the first editions.

In February 1881, Hugo's transcendental significance was recognized in the greatest public tribute ever paid to a living writer. 26 February was his seventy-ninth birthday, but it was described, with a proper sense of urgency, as Victor Hugo 'entering his eightieth year'. The choice of date was clearly political. In the past, the celebration would have fallen on the saint's day, the Saint-Victor; but this was the modern, secular Republic, celebrating a strictly pagan apotheosis.[18]

Festivities began on the 25th: Hugo was presented with a Sèvres vase – a traditional gift for visiting sovereigns – and all schoolchildren who had punishments outstanding were absolved of their crimes. Next day, *Lucrèce Borgia* was performed at the Gaîté Theatre, a triumphal arch was erected at the entrance to the Avenue d'Eylau, and Hugo's house was cordoned off with a tricolour ribbon. In the front garden, a large plane tree that threatened to spoil the view was cut down.

On the morning of the 27th, a Sunday, the longest procession seen in Paris since the days of Napoleon Bonaparte stretched from the Avenue d'Eylau, down the Champs-Élysées, along the *quais*, all the way to the centre of Paris. Cheap trains brought reinforcements from the provinces and emptied the Parisian basin. Official guides were distinguishable by a rose and a cornflower (an allusion to Cosette's song in *Les Misérables*). The whole event was beautifully organized by the same people who had stage-managed the pageants of Napoleon III.

Braving the bitter cold and the snow flurries that were blowing down Haussmann's wide avenues, the procession set off at noon. Six hours later, over half a million people had passed in front of Hugo. He sat at the window with Georges and Jeanne, urging them to engrave the sight in their memories. Occasionally, he stood on the balcony. It was generally agreed that he had tears in his eyes.

First came the Senators and the *députés*, then a band of children carrying a festive banner marked 'L'Art d'Être Grand-Père'. Five thousand musicians performed 'La Marseillaise'. There were deputations from cities and countries Hugo had never seen, the Democratic Union of Anticlerical Propaganda, the 'Friends of Divorce', every school in Paris, the members of twenty gymnastics clubs in leotards, and a group of typesetters carrying an old hand press said to have been used to print Hugo's first poems. A huge cake went past, representing the works of Victor Hugo.

By the time the lamps were lit, Hugo's home was awash in a sea of flags and fresh flowers (in February). When a group labelled 'Municipal Council of Paris' hove into view, Hugo rose from his seat and said a few words: 'I salute Paris. I salute the immense city. I salute her, not in my own name, for I am nothing, but in the name of all on

Earth that lives, reasons, thinks, loves and hopes.' He could write this kind of speech in his sleep and, in fact, sometimes did.[19] Its most significant phrase came near the end, though it seems to have escaped comment, even by the Catholic press: 'He who speaks to Paris speaks to the entire world. *Urbi et orbi*.' Hugo was nodding at his rival in the Vatican.

Celebrations were also held in other French cities, including his native Besançon, which had finally worked out in which house Victor Hugo must have been born. Two thousand telegrams arrived from places which had to be looked for in an atlas. The French delegate of the Internationale presented Hugo with two enormous volumes containing 10,000 signatures. Irish Republican leaders, grateful for Hugo's continuing support, were well represented.[20] Partly for that reason, there was no official message from Her Majesty's Government, though everyone knew that the Poet Laureate, Lord Tennyson, had sent his son over in 1877 with a dreadful sonnet proclaiming Hugo 'Victor in Poesy, Victor in Romance':

> Weird Titan by thy winter weight of years
> As yet unbroken, Stormy voice of France!
> Who dost not love our England – so they say . . .[21]

Since the end of the Second Empire, Hugo had been comparing himself to Voltaire, not just because of his humanism but also because of his triumphal return to Paris in 1778. Statistically, Hugo had now out-triumphed Voltaire. No writer had ever seen so much of his audience face to face. Ten weeks later, his section of the Avenue d'Eylau was renamed Avenue Victor Hugo and a nearby crossroads was called Place Victor Hugo. Letters posted anywhere in the world could now be addressed 'To Victor Hugo, in his Avenue'.

His diary shows only one reaction to his apotheosis: 'In certain cases, though one has done nothing to deserve it, allowing oneself to be rewarded is a duty. I bow before the honour bestowed on me by the Republic as a humble citizen.' A different response was couched in a symbolic arrangement. On 31 August 1881, he redrafted his will. This time, he left 40,000 francs to 'the poor', reiterated his desire to be borne to the grave in a pauper's hearse, and, without consulting them, appointed Jules Grévy, Léon Say and Léon Gambetta as his executors – a choice which seems inexplicable until one realizes that these men were respectively President of the Republic, President of the Senate and President of the Chamber of Deputies.[22] The three last servants of the nation's adoptive father, Pope, arch-President and leading humble citizen.

*

'DEATH IS UNCLEAN.' 'It is humiliating to expire. The final floating visions are abject.'[23] The state of Hugo's mind after the stroke of 1878 and the potentially more damaging spectacle of organized mass adulation is difficult to determine and is usually passed over out of respect for the moribund in a kind of moral euthanasia. Hugo's declarations had always been several nuances short of apparent sanity, and there is no reason to mistake his sense of humour for senility. A thirteenth-century tower was found to be standing in the way of a new block designed by an architect who was a distant relative of Hugo: 'Demolish the tower?' wrote Hugo. 'No. Demolish the architect? Yes.'[24]

Whether or not Hugo's conviction that he was the direct successor to Jesus Christ and Voltaire indicates a loss of perspective is open to interpretation. Turgenev remembered a young man in Hugo's salon protesting that the Avenue d'Eylau was too trifling a thoroughfare to be named after Victor Hugo. The whole city should be renamed. 'That will come, that will come,' Hugo is reported as saying.[25] The story is not entirely incredible, though an octogenarian with an increasing tendency to somnolence and deafness is easily misunderstood.

There are signs, however, that Hugo was falling prey to his ego or that his skill in masking certain facets of his personality was being lost. When a request for more money came from Adèle's asylum on 8 August 1881, he denied that he had ever known Mme Baa, Adèle's companion ('the first Negress in my life'), though the diary records a pleasing visit to the asylum five days before: 'Mme Baa brought me a very beautiful bouquet of coloured birds' feathers.'

Blanche appears to have been forgotten altogether. Even more remarkable, so were the poor of Paris. Hugo eventually increased the size of his bequest to 50,000 francs. This, of course, was in addition to several irregular donations which, in one generous estimate, totalled approximately 200,000 francs since his return from exile.[26]

The 1952 volume of Hugo's *Correspondance* invites the reader to marvel at this 'example to the rich'.[27] And yet the final bequest falls a long way short of 1 per cent of Hugo's fortune – an example 'the rich' would have been only too glad to follow. Hugo had consistently failed to take opportunities to lend money to former acquaintances in distress, though an interesting exception, until her death in 1879, was Léonie Biard.

It may be that he was simply too disorganized to calculate or to keep track of reasonable donations. When clearing out the study at the Rue de Clichy, Lesclide had come across several old royalty cheques that had never been cashed, including one for 17,000 francs.[28] More probably, Hugo had never mentally recovered from his precarious childhood and the habits of economy inculcated by Mme Hugo. Apron strings and purse strings are closely entwined, and he is certainly not alone in scrimping out of context. Earned by honest toil, his fortune, in his view, was inherently virtuous.

He was conscious in any case of having donated his life to the poor. The most instructive text in this respect is one of the longest personal notes of his last three years. It appears to concern the attempt by Blanche's husband to blackmail him:

> A long life of integrity. Eighty years. Devotion; good deeds with women, for women, through women; on my knees before woman – that charming creature who makes the Earth acceptable to man. Ending in calumny, low, base, abject; ending in filth. The man of integrity has nothing left to do ... [Here, Hugo notices his thought turning into a poem]
>
> He has but to turn with a smile towards God,

or:

> The decent man has nothing to do, nothing to say;
> He has but to turn towards God his gentle smile.[29]

The rhyming couplet, which had once been the mainspring of a sacred discipline, was now a pair of crutches, holding up the ego.

*

THE SADDEST SIGHT at the dinner-table now was not the old, deaf poet, already half absent like someone about to leave on a long journey, but Juliette Drouet. She sat behind her plate in constant pain, concentrating on not throwing up, while Hugo urged her to eat and stay healthy.[30] Since the first stabs of pain, in the spring of 1879, laudanum had proved useless. She had stomach cancer. Her only medicine was her 'domestic duties'. She survived a horribly long time on sheer devotion. Every morning, she took Hugo his two eggs, opened his letters ('shelling peas', she called it), read out the order of the day from the Senate, reminded him to wear his new overcoat, worried about his cough, and, when Hugo attended the Senate, waited outside in the victoria.

Hugo instructed his female acquaintances to address their letters to Paul Meurice, but even the official correspondence was stained with his doings: frivolous notes from women whom Juliette was forced to invite to dinner – having first made sure that their husbands or lovers had not been invited to the same soirée.

> I spend my time gluing the pieces of my idol back together again as best I can, but without managing to hide the cracks. Perhaps in heaven there is a divine cement that will wipe them all away.[31]

Hugo's insistence that she eat her food was a polite pretence in front of guests. His letters looked forward to the final return from exile, to a paradise that was already showing its age – a mystico-socialist Eden which he was able to describe with an impression of being reasonably correct by putting himself in God's position: they would live together with their children and their 'angels', 'in love, in usefulness and in light'. 'It is only right. I feel that that is what I would do. How could He not do the same?'[32]

Juliette died, still trying to convince her lover that she felt no pain, on 11 May 1883, aged seventy-seven. A huge crowd followed her to Saint-Mandé, where she was buried with her daughter. The names in the book of condolences included those of Georges Clemenceau, Stéphane Mallarmé, Alfred Nobel, Ernest Renan and Auguste Rodin.[33] Hugo stayed at home. He was flattened by her death. The doctors had ordered him not to move.

Two years before, Juliette had chosen a marble slab for her

grave and discussed the epitaph with Hugo. They settled on one of the many unpublished poems she kept in her private Victor Hugo archive:

> When I am nothing but cold ashes,
> When my weary eyes are closed to the light,
> Say to yourself, if my memory is engraved in your heart,
> > The world has his thoughts
> > But I had his love![34]

Strangely, the slab remained blank. It was not engraved until long after Hugo's death – not until all the people who had known Juliette were dead.[35]

Most of the obituaries recognized how much of the monument called Victor Hugo had been built by Juliette Drouet. But at the cemetery, the only speech was Auguste Vacquerie's: Mme Drouet, he declared, had 'a right to her share of glory, having shared in the struggle'.

There was of course no priest to point it out, but Vacquerie's mealy-mouthed rhetoric of 'rights' and 'shares' was a sufficient reminder of her married status. The death of Mme Hugo had been tearfully recorded in its proper place in Volume III of *Actes et Paroles*. The pompous Vacquerie–Meurice volume passes from a speech in honour of a train-driver who saved a train, to Hugo's oration at the funeral of Louis Blanc, a birthday banquet and the nauseating tombola at Veules with its weeping widow 'who remained a widow'. Somewhere in the middle of these piffling events, Juliette Drouet had died.

When 1001 of her letters to Hugo were published in 1951 – with a strong editorial emphasis on slavish devotion – she was hailed as one of the great *épistolières* of French literature. A generous but well-earned exaggeration. If Paul Meurice had edited the works that were entrusted to him with the same love and care with which Juliette had copied out Hugo's manuscripts and maintained his body, mind and reputation for fifty years, he might almost have deserved the image of selfless devotion that sweetened the rest of his life.

That year, Hugo made only one entry in his diary, on 20 June: '*Je vais bientôt te rejoindre, ma bien-aimée*' ('I shall soon be with you, my beloved'). A single, imperfect alexandrine. Its main verb straddles the caesura like a soul yearning to cross the great divide.

*

ON THE BANKS OF Lake Leman near Villeneuve, a French tricolour fluttered outside the Hôtel Byron. Victor Hugo was in residence, nursing his grief, waving at crowds from the terrace. He received a few visitors, among them a pastor from Nîmes: 'Yes,' said Hugo, 'I believe in God.' 'There is nothing useless in the universe.'[36] He had begun to speak in 'last words'. It was a literary genre in which he proved to be as prolific as in all the others; perhaps it was the genre he had been practising all along.

After the summer in Switzerland, Hugo returned to his Avenue and the weekly receptions. Vacquerie brought along his latest acquaintance, Oscar Wilde, who sparkled as usual but failed to keep Hugo awake.[37] The words of dissenters also reached his ears – the first of those oxymoronic judgements that tried to capture his hugeness between two opposites: 'sublime cretin' (Dumas *fils*), 'as stupid as the Himalayas' (Leconte de Lisle). 'I do not find the remark unpleasant,' wrote Hugo, 'and I forgive Leconte de Lisle, who seems to me to be just plain stupid.'[38] Whatever the audience, Hugo tried to make himself available like a coffee-table book. 'Leaf through me,' he told his guests;[39] but some of them came only to admire the binding:

> A loud-voiced and brass-faced American girl stood up before him and, to his obvious anguish, recited one of his beautiful poems. Her mother went and sat by his side upon the sofa and smothered his dainty hand within her fat fist and told him he was by all odds the greatest of living men.[40]

That June, the 'final series' of *La Légende des Siècles* appeared.[41] The opening poem, dated 2 June 1883, had been written ten years before. The themes were old favourites: the punishment of the wicked, the stubborn serenity of prophets and heroes. Dante is woken up so that he can update his *Inferno* and include that wolf-eyed hypocrite, Napoleon III, among the damned. In 'Ténèbres', it is said that if the sinister paw of the sphinx could be raised, the answer to the riddle of creation would be found underneath: 'Love'. There were also some old poems inspired by the woman who had apparently ceased to exist even as a memory: Blanche. 'We shall head for Grecian skies, where the Muses live.' ''Tis the noble land of chasms and peaks, / My beauty, where the heart of man grows forgetful / Of all that is not the dawn and lofty places.'

Hugo remained socially active well into 1884. He went to the Senate and sat through a performance of Saint-Saëns's 'Hymne à Victor Hugo'. He was often seen without a stick, an umbrella or a raincoat. An American visitor records an amazing display of abbreviated erudition as late as 1884: Hugo appears to have had an opinion on almost every living American writer (a contrast to his occasional failure to recognize members of his own family).[42] Is it possible that he had started reading books again? The last, wizened remnants of verse also show a return to old habits: turning Horace into French verse. He chose the ode on the granitic tenacity of the just: 'Crumbling, the universe / Would crush my bones without shaking my soul'[43] (28 April 1884).

The last lines of all (9 May 1884) were a faint, domestic echo of the sphinx, a final act of lion-taming: 'I bid the cat good morning; / I offer my paw, he gives me his claw; / We are good friends.'[44]

Hugo watched his last summer fade into autumn at Paul Meurice's home on the Channel coast between Dieppe and Fécamp. On the day of departure, when the bags were packed and the carriage was waiting, there was no sign of Hugo. The house and garden were searched. Both were deserted. Eventually, he was found on the terrace of the summer house, sitting in a chair, staring out to sea.[45]

More last words ... To Georges and Léon Daudet, who were playing in the garden: 'The earth is calling me.'[46] To his secretary, Lesclide, repeatedly, like an incantation: 'Sad, deaf and old, / Thrice silent, / Close your eyes on earth, / Open them in heaven.'[47] And, on his last important public appearance, in Bartholdi's workshop, after climbing up inside the Statue of Liberty – one monument to another: 'The sea, that great restless being, observes the union of the two great lands at peace.'[48]

Having taken his leave of the Ocean, Hugo said farewell, several times, to that other 'abyss' – woman. Symbols indicating a sexual act appear eight times in his diary in the spring of 1885.[49] The last one of all comes on 5 April, thirty-eight days after his eighty-third birthday. The last words he ever wrote (19 May) thus acquire an appropriately ambiguous nuance:

> To love is to act.

*

ON 14 MAY 1885, after a dinner with Ferdinand de Lesseps, Hugo began his final performance, carving out his own Canal to the world beyond.

In bed that night, he suddenly felt queasy. The doctors diagnosed lesion of the heart and congestion of the lungs. He had pneumonia. He should have worn his hat, said *Le Figaro*, whose reporter had seen him bare-headed the day before at the Academy. By the following Tuesday, the pavement outside the house was permanently occupied by a crowd.

Inside, Hugo lay in his four-poster bed, facing the mantelpiece with its old bronze clock, wondering how long it would take him to die. He was already finding it difficult to breathe. Now and then, the illness picked him up and shook him like a rag. 'Friend,' he said to Lockroy, 'this is a dead man who speaks to you.' Georges and Jeanne stood where their grandfather could see them when he opened his eyes, but Georges kept bursting into tears and had to be hidden away. Downstairs, a book was filling up with signatures. The minute, global coverage of Hugo's agony proved that he was right to identify Voltaire and Goethe as his closest modern rivals. No other writer had exported his reputation so widely. Hugo's decline was front-page news from St Petersburg to Sacramento.[50]

The night of 19–20 May was horrific. Hugo was spewing out phrases in French, instantly translating them into Latin and then into Spanish, as if for the international audience. At two in the morning, he suddenly leaped out of bed and had to be forced back in. Then he flung himself to the other side and stood on the floor for a few seconds, shouting, '*C'est ici le combat du jour et de la nuit*': 'This is the struggle of day and night' (or 'light and dark'). A perfect alexandrine. The extraterrestrial audience was also in attendance – the family 'angels' and his fellow magi: Homer, Jesus Christ, Dante, Shakespeare. 'You know that I believe', he had written on the occasion of his funeral ode to Gautier, 'that *up there* they read poetry (when the poetry is very beautiful). My poem will have delighted our poor friend. It is good that everything should return to heaven, but sad that nothing comes back down again.'[51]

The alexandrine was certainly beautiful enough in its deceptive clarity: a typical Victor Hugo antithesis which, contrary to the popular prejudice, dissolves the opposites it appears to posit so conclusively. On which side of life was the night and on which the day? Another phrase snatched from his lips in the final moments – 'I see dark light' – was more clearly equivocal: a resolution of opposites, or confirmation of the horrifying vision of 'Ce que Dit la Bouche d'Ombre': 'A dreadful black sun radiating darkness'?

At dawn, he collapsed from the exertion of the night. Reporters rushed to their offices. Meanwhile, Hugo was making a recovery. 'How hard it is to die,' he said. 'I was all ready.' A constant stream of last words was transmitted to the crowd outside. 'Here is the end, my heart is dead.' 'I am well. It is death.' The Catholic newspaper, *L'Univers*, found Hugo's last words 'heartbreaking by the absence of any religious thought' and showed its Christian piety by predicting an eternity of suffering, 'which will seem a lot longer to him than an agony of a few hours or days'. Hugo reported 'slight pain' – still the master of the modest understatement. The doctors administered morphine, cinchona, nux vomica and oxygen. The crowd outside was admiring the lovely spectacle of Sarah Bernhardt descending from a carriage. She had come to pay her respects.

At five o'clock that afternoon, an unexpected development: Hugo felt better than he had done for ages. The illness seemed to have purged him. Georges told Jeanne that Grandfather was going to live. The doctors wondered how to write the next press release. Hugo was sitting up in a chair, asking after Alice, who was ill from lack of sleep. For his curtain-call, he drank three bowls of bouillon, followed by a glass of white wine. Newspaper editors had prepared special editions and cursed their luck. The Archbishop of Paris, though apparently 'convalescing from an illness very similar to his own', offered to administer the last rights. A cartoon showed him squatting on Hugo's roof with a butterfly net, waiting to catch the errant soul.[52] Lockroy reminded the Archbishop of Hugo's last wishes. His will was common knowledge: 'I shall close my terrestrial eye, but the spiritual eye will remain open, wider than ever. I reject the prayers of all churches. I ask for a prayer from every soul.' A death-bed conversion of Victor Hugo would have been one of the greatest coups ever for the Catholic Church. Devout journalists were writing some unusually vicious obituaries. Others had already decided to improve on the truth by pretending that Victor Hugo had called for a priest at the last moment.

That night, a thunderstorm broke over Paris. In the morning, a crowd of umbrellas that Hugo might have compared to a Roman testudo besieging a fortress heard that he had bid '*Adieu!*' to Jeanne. A terrible struggle began at 7 a.m. The word '*Séparation*' was heard. Policemen kept the crowd at bay. Hugo raised his head, appeared to take a bow, and fell back on to the pillow. This time, he was gone for good. The clock was stopped at 1.27 on the afternoon of Friday, 22 May 1885. The unofficial end of the nineteenth century. It was a death he had every right to be proud of.

The Transatlantic Cable, which Hugo had once used as an image for communion with God,[53] hummed with headlines: 'Hugo Called Hence.' 'Victor Hugo Crosses the River of Death and Enters the Dark Valley.' '*FINIS*. The Life of Victor Hugo is Brought to a Fitting Close.'[54]

In Paris, news of the death spread with the speed of gossip. The hotels were already filling up, and in the *faubourgs*, the dregs of society, who could always be depended on to ruin any orderly display, were getting ready for the biggest birthday party of all.

CHAPTER TWENTY-FOUR

God

(1885)

A T FIVE-THIRTY in the morning of Saturday, 30 May, a small group of people had gathered on the Place du Panthéon and were staring up at the temple which until recently had been the Church of Saint Geneviève, patron saint of Paris. High above the Latin Quarter, a workman was hacking the arms off the Cross.[1]

A decree had been rushed through Parliament, restoring the Panthéon to the cult of 'great men'. God had been served with an eviction order; Victor Hugo was moving in. Atheists and clergymen were hurling insults at each other in the papers. Extra prayers were ordered for the day of Hugo's funeral.

It was the fourth time the Panthéon had been deconsecrated. It had once contained the bones of Voltaire and Rousseau, reportedly tipped down the nearest sewer during the Restoration. More recently, it had served as a munitions store, then as a headquarters for the Commune. A peace-making *député* was shot on its steps by Government troops. The blood was washed away, the tomb-like interior purged of the Communards' breadcrumbs and tobacco, and the Panthéon reverted to the Catholic Church. A fitting monument to the last 100 years of French history.

Today, tourists standing in the gale that blows around its blank walls can be heard wondering what purpose it serves. The Panthéon was one of Hugo's least favourite buildings, a poor man's Saint Peter's, entirely devoid of 'sacred horror'. It reminded him of a giant sponge cake.[2]

The Panthéon was to be his final resting place. For the Third

Republic, one vote-winning god was worth another, and Victor Hugo had the inestimable advantage of being exclusively French.

The only problem was that, by the time the law had completed its journey through the Chambers, Hugo would have turned into that disreputable object he described as 'a nameless somebody' – a rotting corpse. On Saturday evening, thirty hours after death, the body was embalmed and a solution of zinc chloride injected into the carotid artery. His features, which had sunk, regained a recognizable expression that could reasonably be described as 'serene'.[3]

But ten days separated his death from the funeral. The plan to expose his face to the doting crowd had to be abandoned. The Catholic papers were delighted. As usual on such occasions, they gloated over the unusually 'rapid decomposition of the body': Victor Hugo was falling to bits – clearly several days less eternal than the average Christian.

> Victor Hugo was the greatest poet of our century.
> He had been mad for more than thirty years [since his 'conversion' to socialism].
> May his madness serve him as an excuse before God.
> We should pity those who are about to grant him an apotheosis. Let us pray for him.[4]

The Catholic Léon Bloy, perhaps remembering Hugo's poem, 'Mazeppa', suggested that his corpse should have been dragged through the streets on a three-kilometre-long cable and spattered all over the city, shared out equally among his admirers.[5]

The family also came under attack from the other side for refusing to release the brain.[6] A valuable scientific opportunity had been lost. The pre-emptive verdict was congenital insanity. Physiologists had to be content with the death mask, which turned out to be amazingly revealing: 'Distance between the two eyes: 31 mm.' 'Length of nose: 38 mm.' 'All measurements of width are above average.' The nose was 'thick' and the lips 'quite strong'. The famous 'brow of genius' was an effect of 'premature baldness'. Sadly, in view of Hugo's penchant for antithesis, he was 'asymmetrical': 'The left ear is slightly higher than the right.' In summary, 'an almost average brain, in which the organic and appetitive representations are preponderant, served by an extremely vigorous temperament.'[7] So much for the mystery of creative genius.

*

ONE OF THE HUNDREDS of obituaries in the British press assured its readers that 'To understand Victor Hugo's life is to understand the nineteenth century'.[8] A similar claim could be made for the ten days immediately following his death. While his body waited to be enclosed in a triple coffin with photographs of his children and grand-children, roses from Villequier and a bronze medallion stamped with the face of Vacquerie, unusual events were occurring all over the city.

On 24 May, in the Père Lachaise cemetery, between fifty and eighty people were wounded and several killed in 'scuffles' with police: the first official murders in Paris since 1871. The victims had been marking the anniversary of the massacre of Communards. Increased activity was reported in the anarchist societies. It was feared that Hugo's funeral – like other funerals in the past – would be the signal for an uprising. A special funeral budget of 20,000 francs had been approved by Parliament. Some of it would have to be spent on safeguarding the Republic. The world was watching. The three regiments that accompanied Hugo to his final resting place were not there just for show.

All went well until the night before the funeral. Hugo's coffins were placed under the Arc de Triomphe in a towering catafalque fitted with a huge monogram:

M

'*Veau Humain*' ('human calf'), said *La Croix*, alluding to the Mardi Gras. The Arch itself was draped in black, guarded by torch-bearing horsemen and bathed in electric light.

When Napoleon's ashes were returned in 1840, Hugo had admired the 'beautiful effect' of Napoleon's catafalque framed by the Arc de Triomphe. He would have been pleased to see himself in the same position, blotting out the setting sun. It was generally agreed to be an impressive spectacle, especially if seen from a distance: everything had been done in such a hurry. Close up, it had the flimsiness of a stage-set.

As darkness fell, the area around the Arc de Triomphe began to look like a fairground. Thousands came to enjoy the free spectacle of Victor Hugo lying in state; but one could only stare at a catafalque and electric lighting for so long. The Hippodrome circus nearby was doing a roaring trade. Hugo souvenirs were being sold by an army of pedlars: photographs and song-sheets, bouquets of artificial flowers with Hugo's face peering from the centre like a giant corolla, 'ghostcards' which imprinted a negative image of 'the illustrious poet' on the retina. A man claiming to have been Hugo's body-servant sold 400 pairs of trousers that had once 'encased the legs of the greatest lyric poet of all time'.[9]

Soon, drunken bodies littered the Champs-Élysées. Wine-shops stayed open, and as the night of the wake wore on, the singing became merrier and politically suspect. Edmond Goncourt heard from a police source that the brothels had closed and that the whores of Paris had draped their pudenda in black crêpe as a mark of respect. Perhaps the whole apparatus shimmering up at the Arc de Triomphe was a huge, unconscious representation of something obscene. Other prostitutes were hard at work in the grassy avenues surrounding Hugo's sarcophagus. It was the last spontaneous outbreak of the carnival spirit. The people's day of rebellion; the Cour des Miracles of *Notre-Dame de Paris*. The Catholic papers used the word 'Babylonian'. Behind the bushes in the Avenue Victor Hugo, 'abominable outrages' were taking place 'which the police are impotent to repress'.[10] The mood of national mourning was being conjured away by fresh conceptions.

This extraordinary display of erotic energy and commercial verve – not the absurd procession the following day – was Hugo's true apotheosis. Something between a mythical regeneration and a moral disgrace. A great clanking platitude brought spectacularly to life. It would have made a splendid concluding poem for *La Légende des Siècles*.

*

NEXT DAY, just before noon, for the first time in fourteen years, the hills around Paris resounded to the rumble of heavy artillery – a twenty-one-gun salute, signalling the start of the funeral. The procession set off down the Champs-Élysées towards a city which seemed to have been infested by a giant swarm of ants: over two million people, outnumbering the usual population of Paris.

Almost everything that could constitute a delegation had done so: war veterans, civil servants, artists and writers, animal-lovers and schoolchildren, clubs that no one had heard of before, including the Béni-Bouffe-Toujours – a society whose single purpose was to ensure that one of its members was always smoking a pipe – and a mysterious, presumably underground organization called the Potato Club, which attracted reprobation by refusing to remove its hats.

In the week leading up to the funeral, there had been some violent public bickering over the order of the procession. Everyone had been able to find a quotation in Hugo's works supporting their claim to pre-eminence. The militant feminist journal, *La Citoyenne*, complained that the suffragettes had been placed a long way behind the gymnasts and the department stores: 'They were forced to remain in the full sun on their little feet for ten hours.'[11] One journalist retorted that 'a single, very pretty woman' would have been a more fitting tribute.[12] He might have noticed the vast wreath, topped with an artificial dove, inscribed 'To God's Ambassador, She Who Hopes. Amélie Désormeaux'[13] – the woman who had pounced on Hugo during the Siege of Paris, calling herself 'Cosette' and asking for a baby.

The route itself had been criticized by subversive groups which used to call themselves 'republican' before the Third Republic changed the meaning of the word: Champs-Élysées, Place and Pont de la Concorde, Boulevard Saint-Germain, Boulevard Saint-Michel, Rue Soufflot – 5 kilometres of Haussmann's Paris without the slightest deviation through the poorer quarters. Hugo's hearse had been hijacked by the State. But the anarchists failed to organize. Socialist clubs had their banners confiscated by armed policemen, cheered on by the crowd with cries of '*Vive la République!*' Everything was going back to normal. The reporter from *La République Française* cast his mind back fourteen years and felt a distinct sense of progress: 'On the pavement of the Rue Soufflot, I find myself slipping, as once before, in a little red puddle. But this time, it's a puddle of wine!'[14]

As Napoleon III had discovered, a rousing parade worked wonders for morale and was also very good for business. All along the route, windows and balconies had been rented out at the price of a year's lodging. Florists had taken on extra staff. Seen from above, gigantic flower arrangements appeared to move under their own steam, while tiny children tottered along underneath. Queen Victoria had asked her ambassador for a report: 'The general impression', he lied diplomatically, 'was one of weariness and unconcern.' 'There was nothing mournful or solemn in the demeanour of the people.'[15] The second statement was quite true. Like Hugo's own orations, the funeral was also a gala performance, 'an orgy of bad taste and self-admiration', according to Nietzsche.[16] 'One of the most remarkable funerals in the world's history,' said *The Chicago Tribune*. 'Many of [the wreaths] are colossal and superb works of art and of untold value at the present price of flowers.'[17]

Hugo's own contribution – the pauper's hearse – turned out to be a stroke of genius. It was so blatantly symbolic and immodest that most of the intelligentsia expected it to cast a pall over the proceedings. Ford Madox Ford saw the eleven carriages of flowers approaching and the full magnificence of a State in mourning, 'and then . . . something like a scream!':

> The *corbillard des pauvres*, like a blacked packing case drawn by two spavined horses, produced a shocking effect, really an inconceivably shocking effect of grinning hypocrisy.[18]

Verlaine had a firmer grasp of the matter and imagined the hearse, 'that vainglorious vehicle', speaking on behalf of its client:

> Ha! ha! You bunch of idiots, you gawping masses, you made fun of my antitheses while I was still alive. Well, here's my last one – and it's the best one of all![19]

Hugo knew his audience better than any other writer or politician. He knew exactly how incongruous it was possible to be, how to produce an effect that would never be forgotten. A shabby old truck surrounded by imperial splendour perfectly matched the mood of melodrama. This was a jolly Day of Judgement. All of Hugo's acts, past, present and posthumous, were bathed in virtue. His measly bequest to the poor would have bought a Victor Hugo postcard for about one person in ten who attended the funeral, or a chair, ladder or mirror on a stick for about one in 200. Yet there were already rumours that Hugo had left millions to the *misérables*, founding hospitals and charitable institutions.

As the procession seethed into the Place de la Concorde, the whole of Paris came into view like a theatre packed to the rafters. Every statue, fountain, advertising column and chimney-stack had been occupied since early morning. Trees had been privatized: 10 centimes for a leg-up, 2 francs later on for a leg down. Boys and small men perched on top of lampstands, using the lamps as lunch-boxes. In what would now seem a superfluous measure, 150 pigeons were released at the Pont de la Concorde because Hugo, the lover of 'wingèd things', was said to have banned pigeon from his dinner-table.

As the hearse crossed the Seine, which several journalists compared to the River Styx, a woman fell off the parapet and was drowned along with the man who tried to save her. Further on, an overpopulated tree branch snapped, fell on to a step-ladder and injured five people. When the cortège wheeled into the Boulevard Saint-Michel, an argument broke out at the Café de Cluny. Ladders fell like toy soldiers and a woman was trampled underfoot. Her screams caused a slight delay. An arrest was made and then 'the procession pursued its course, painfully impressed by this incident'.[20] On the Boulevard Saint-Germain, a woman gave birth.

It was exactly the kind of 'regal and popular' funeral that Hugo felt should have been given to Napoleon in 1840: 'In this affair, all that comes from the people is great; all that comes from the State is small.'[21]

Two hours after leaving the Arc de Triomphe, the river of humanity turned into a dark, malodorous sea washing up on the steps of the Panthéon. A stand had been erected for important delegates. The last of nineteen tediously uncontroversial speeches was delivered. All around the square, well-dressed people could be seen on the balconies – the most expensive on the route. One eagle-eyed journalist spotted an elegant young woman, high up on the roof of the Hôtel des Grands Hommes, breast-feeding her baby.[22]

Hugo's coffin was carried out of the sun and into the torch-lit interior of the Panthéon, where it lay until the entire procession had filed past it. The suffragettes finally reached it at six o'clock that evening. Several days later, it was removed to the crypt, facing the tomb of Jean-Jacques Rousseau, where an official guide would invite shivering tourists to admire the echo. Hugo now shares cell number XXIV with Émile Zola in the wing dedicated to 'Martyrs of the Revolution'. Through the grille in the locked door, a mould- and grime-covered window can be seen high up at the far end. Shades of *Les Misérables* . . .

> The transition was astounding. In the very heart of the city, Jean Valjean had left the city. In the blink of an eye, in the time it takes to lift a lid and let it fall, he had passed from the light of day to total darkness, from noon to midnight, noise to silence, from the thunderous commotion to the stagnation of the tomb. . . . For a few moments, he seemed to be dazed; listening, stupefied. The trap-door of salvation had suddenly opened beneath him. Divine benevolence had as it were caught him by treachery. The adorable ambushes of Providence![23]

Despite the unseemly squabbling, the injuries and deaths, and the official insult to the Catholic Church, there was a general feeling of satisfaction. Twenty thousand francs well spent. For years afterwards, the funeral was one of the commonest shared memories of people all over France. Victor Hugo had supplied a worthy conclusion to the epic adventure begun by Napoleon – even if it had turned into farce along the way.

Hugo After Hugo

I T WAS NOT immediately clear which Victor Hugo had just been
enshrined – the poet, playwright and novelist; the socialist, exile,
campaigner and philanthropist; the grandfather who upheld family
values or the patriarch who made a mockery of them; the *pair de
France*, the *député*, the Senator, or simply the very famous Frenchman.
Was it the Hugo of 1830, 1851, 1870 or 1885? The only apparent
agreement – though not quite general – was that Victor Hugo had
been an atheist . . .

> He democratized the French language. . . . Despite the revolution-
> ary pretensions of his youth . . . Victor Hugo became a Classic in his
> own lifetime.
>
> (René Goblet, Minister of Education)[1]

> That idiotic lama whose pitiful intellectual senility, sordid avarice,
> monstrous egotism and complete hypocrisy as *grandfather* and as citizen
> are known to everyone.
>
> (Léon Bloy)[2]

> Comet whose flux will perhaps illumine
> Other stars that cradle on the Ocean of Being
> Another human race!
> (Marquis de Saint-Yves d'Alveydre)[3]

> The bourgeoisie showed that it identified with 'the great man' it
> was burying in the Panthéon. While it invited all nations to the funeral,
> it kept the Stock Exchange open . . . the First of June being the day on
> which bills of exchange and public dividends matured.
>
> (Paul Lafargue)[4]

Born a citizen of France, died a citizen of humanity.... Champion of the workers, apostle of world civilization and liberty.... Column of light.... Great educator.... All peasants mourn him, even those that are illiterate.

(*Le Rappel*)

His passport to immortality is stamped with the visas of all anti-revolutionary powers.... The new '93 that Hugo feared will cast him, not into the Panthéon, but into the sewer!

(*Le Cri du Peuple*)[5]

Funerals and executions are closely related.

Two days after the death, Edmond Goncourt saw Émile Zola almost rubbing his hands with glee.[6] Right up to the end, it had looked as though Hugo would go on for ever. The reverential reviews of his last works appeared to Zola as a plot to smother his own brainchild, Naturalism: 'Victor Hugo has become a religion in French letters, by which I mean a sort of police force for maintaining order.'[7] It did not help that Hugo was reported to have 'mistaken' Zola for an Italian novelist who had been 'badly let down by his Swiss translator'.[8]

It soon became apparent that Hugo's work would be largely unaffected by the end of his life. 'Death' had given him some excellent advice in the drawing-room of Marine Terrace: 'Jesus Christ rose from the dead only once. You can fill your tomb with resurrections.' Meurice and Vacquerie set to work on the huge deposit of unpublished manuscripts and kept up a steady flow of 'new' masterpieces right into the twentieth century. The personal absence of Hugo was almost a return to normality.

These posthumous publications were not just leftovers. They were long, important works which retrospectively changed the landscape of nineteenth-century French literature and increased the size of Hugo's *Oeuvres Complètes* by about a third: the unfinished epics, *La Fin de Satan* (1886) and *Dieu* (1891); the unperformed plays of the *Théâtre en Liberté* (1886); Hugo's eyewitness accounts of historical events – *Choses Vues* (1887 and 1900) – and the final volume of *Actes et Paroles* (1889); oceans of unused poems – *Les Années Funestes*, abandoned when the Empire fell (1898), *Toute la Lyre* (1888 and 1893) and *Dernière Gerbe* (1902); travel accounts – *Alpes et Pyrénées*

(1890) and *France et Belgique* (1892); a general introduction to his works dating back to the 1860s – *Post-Scriptum de ma Vie* (1901). Two volumes of carefully selected letters appeared in 1896 and 1898, followed by the *Lettres à la Fiancée* (Adèle) in 1901.

Unknown fragments have been emerging ever since. It will be a long time before any edition of his correspondence can be described as 'complete'.

*

HUGO'S HUMAN LEGACY was racked with all the usual ironies of family connections. Four weeks after the funeral, in the glory of Hugo's setting sun, Édouard Lockroy was elected to Parliament with a massive majority and began a distinguished career as an opportunist Minister: Commerce, Education, Navy (twice) and War.

Georges Hugo was seventeen years old at the death of his grandfather and settled into a long adolescence. Despite Lockroy's attempts to stem the flow, a large part of Hugo's fortune continued to be spent on women. Famous before he could speak, little Georges's desire to fritter away what the old man had so laboriously amassed is understandable. But he also inherited his grandfather's artistic genius. It came to full fruition in the following generation: Georges's first son was the painter, Jean Hugo, who died in 1984.

Six years after the funeral, Jeanne married her brother's friend, Léon Daudet – co-founder of the extreme monarchist, Catholic and anti-semitic *Action Française* group, which later found redeeming features in the Nazi Occupation. When the marriage collapsed, the heroine of *L'Art d'Être Grand-Père* married the son of Freud's teacher, Charcot – the polar explorer who went down with the *Pourquoi Pas?* Thanks to Charcot, a lonely island off the west coast of the Antarctic Peninsula now bears the name of Victor Hugo.

Hugo's houses had mixed fortunes. 3 Marine Terrace was painted yellow and turned into the 'Hôtel Maison Victor Hugo – Private Boarding House'. Neither it nor the address has survived. The house in the Avenue Victor Hugo was torn down in 1907. The building which stands on the site (124 Avenue Victor Hugo, with a bas-relief Hugo looking down on the entrance) was for a time the home of a religious order, the Filles de la Sagesse.

Hauteville House and its contents were donated to the Ville de Paris in 1927 by Jeanne and the children of Georges, Paris being 'the worthy custodian of all that might serve the poet's glory'. The Maison de Victor Hugo museum in the Place des Vosges (formerly Place Royale) was inaugurated during the week-long celebration of Hugo's centenary in 1902. On that occasion, a statue was erected in the Place Victor Hugo – still one of the least Hugolian parts of Paris. During the Occupation, the statue was seized by the Nazis and probably ended up in a munitions factory. After the War, a decision was taken not to replace it because it would have impeded the flow of traffic. The site was marked for a time by a car advertisement.[9]

The ill-fated statue, by Ernest Barrias, had been commissioned by the State. Not to be outdone, the Ville de Paris commissioned its own statue: Georges Bareau's 'La Vision du Poète'.[10] It spent eighty years in the municipal warehouse and was exhumed on the centenary of Hugo's death in 1985 to be dumped at the northern corner of the Jardin du Ranelagh. It shows a naked, creamy-white Victor Hugo demurely inspecting a frozen cascade of figures representing 'the wall of centuries' from *La Légende des Siècles*. A few yards up the road, at the end of the Avenue Victor Hugo, Auguste Rodin's more potent Victor Hugo listens to an angry Muse, one hand outstretched to silence the traffic.

The object that had first placed Hugo in continuous communication with the Beyond – the pedestal table from Marine Terrace – was given to Jeanne, who passed it on to her husband's grandmother, who left it to her maid. It was useless as a piece of furniture. It kept jumping about. Eventually it was thrown on the fire, its final messages unrecorded.[11]

The last witness of the great adventure died in 1915 in a luxurious nursing home at Suresnes on the edge of the Bois de Boulogne – an old lady in a long-ribboned bonnet. A quiet funeral took place in the Chapel of the Virgin at Saint-Sulpice, where Victor Hugo had married Adèle Foucher ninety-three years before, to the everlasting distress of brother Eugène. A few brief obituaries appeared in Brussels, Geneva and Tunis, but only two in Paris.[12] The papers were filled with more important news. A few miles to the East, French soldiers were rotting in trenches, scorched by poison gas, defending an image of France that had been inspired in large part by the anti-Prussian poems of Victor Hugo – the same Victor Hugo who was an inspiration to the international peace movement.[13] Among the reports of civilization's latest leap backwards, an old, half-guessed story was dug up: the illegitimate daughter of Sainte-Beuve who ran away with an English soldier and went mad with grief.

Adèle II had spent the three decades since her father's death in the company of the world's greatest composers, playing incomprehensibly beautiful songs on the piano, tapping every night on her bedroom wall according to some superstitious ritual, acknowledging visitors from the world of the living with a few hostile words uttered in 'a metallic voice'. While Hugo's writings continued to grow into one of the most majestic monuments in literature, the last survivor of his life was sitting in her room, shredding books and sheets of paper, stuffing the pieces carefully into her bag.

*

FOR HUGO'S WORK, the period of discernible influences was already long past. His clearest effect had been on writers whose entire careers were swallowed up by his own: Gautier, Baudelaire, Flaubert, Dostoevsky, Rimbaud. Whole generations had copied or parodied his poems: long before he was ensconced in the school curriculum, Hugo had been a one-man education system through which every writer had to pass before achieving originality or sinking into the obscurity of helpless imitation. The story of Hugo's influence after death is the story of a river after it reaches the sea. It was so pervasive that he was sometimes thought not to have had an influence at all. Joseph Conrad, whose father translated *Les Travailleurs de la Mer*, was once said to be Hugo's only foreign 'disciple'.[14] Yet anyone who reads Hugo's works for the first time will be aware of a nagging familiarity, far more eloquent than any deliberate allusion.

In the first decades of the new age, his effect on French literature appeared to be wholly negative. A reaction against the patriotic, school-desk sort of poetry that Hugo was thought to represent produced some of the great modernist experiments, like Mallarmé's bizarre typographical shipwreck, *Un Coup de Dés* (1897), in which a Hugo-like 'Master' sinks beneath the waves, surrounded by the wreckage of his alexandrines. In *Crise de Vers*, Mallarmé precisely divided all French literature into two epochs – before and after Hugo: the man who was 'verse personified', who 'practically confiscated the right to self-expression from all who think, discourse or narrate.'[15]

Après lui, le déluge.

Hugo had condemned the following generations to a chronic adolescence. Whatever the biological reality, writers who wrote in his wake seem to have lived and died young. It was not until after the First World War, when André Breton included him among the prophets of Surrealism ('Hugo is Surrealist when he isn't stupid')[16] that Hugo was seen to have contributed in a positive way to the literary revolution. Even then, his vast shadow had to be conjured away with trite aphorisms and convenient half-truths: André Gide's 'Hugo – hélas!' (when asked to name his favourite poet),[17] or Cocteau's 'Victor Hugo was a madman who thought he was Victor Hugo.'[18] It would be true to the spirit of Hugo to observe that these are now the best-known quotations from the works of Gide and Cocteau.

The irony was too enormous to be credible: for all his egotism, Hugo's single greatest contribution to modern literature was a kind of transcendant modesty: the revelation that words were creatures with a life of their own, that to write a poem or a novel was not to go shopping for the best verbal approximation to a known reality, but to engage in a mysterious collaboration, to invent a new reality.

The phenomenon of post-Hugolian *tristesse* was also the result of a French peculiarity of which Hugo is the most spectacular example: like Voltaire, Chateaubriand or Sartre, he was also a politician and a cultural symbol. His audience extended far beyond the minority that actually read his works. By the time the centenary of his birth was celebrated in 1902, Hugo had entered the fabric of French life with the force of a multinational corporation. The bearded sage looked down on pupils who memorized his odes and learned a history of Romanticism boiled down to *Hernani* and the *Préface de Cromwell*. His face was seen on plates, table-mats, bottles, pens, paperweights, pipe-racks, tobacco-tins, cuff-links, braces, tie-pins, fans and walking-sticks. It stared out of hearths, sphinx-like, on the end of fire-dogs, loomed over lampstands, proliferated on curtains and wallpaper. It appeared on stamps, laundry books, blotting-pads and bars of soap, and on decorative receptacles designed to contain all those little knick-knacks that mysteriously accumulate: Victor Hugo as his own litter-bin. Later, it lent its authority to the lowest denomination of bank-note. Most cities in France named something after Hugo – usually a boulevard or a main square. Victor Hugo was to France what Queen Victoria was to England, a perch for pigeons and an indicator of air quality. The damage to his literary reputation is incalculable.[19]

This proliferation of Hugo-emblazoned garbage was as influential in its own way as his poems and plays and helped to fuel a reaction which smoulders on to this day. The purification of his works by successive editors had a similarly inflammatory effect: Ionesco's first full-length work, *Viata Grotescă şi Tragică a lui Victor Hugo* (1935–6), was inspired by the pious lies of Hugo's admirers: 'The only chance of survival for Victor Hugo's work is the impossibility of reading it even once.'[20] Everyone knew that Victor Hugo had been a genius, but it was sometimes difficult to say exactly how this genius had manifested itself.

The savage, nit-picking biographies of Edmond Biré, the Satan of Hugo-worshippers, actually did a huge service to Hugo's reputation by stressing the fickleness of his opinions, the craftiness that lay behind his grand illusions, and other sins that later became modernist virtues. Gradually, the lower layers of Hugo's trunks were explored and strange creatures like his sex diaries and the transcriptions of the Jersey séances came to light. When the big batteries of his unpublished epics fell silent and the flotsam of *Océan* and *Tas de Pierres* were collected in editorial buckets, Hugo began to look like the poet of ruin and fragmentation – almost as if he had planned the dissemination of his unknown works in advance to match the artistic developments of the twentieth century.

*

FORTY-ONE YEARS after his death, Hugo officially became a saint. A small group of Vietnamese civil servants with revolutionary aspirations had been meeting secretly after work in Saigon, contacting spirits by means of a tapping table. A form of Buddhism known as

Cao Dai had been pieced together from the spirits' revelations.[21] The French authorities kept a close eye on the new religion, afraid that it might become a focus for nationalist revolt.

The most important of these spirits was called Nguyet-Tam-Chon-Nhon, though he sometimes gave his name as 'Symbole'. He communicated in alexandrines and described a strange East–West blend of karma, Christian morality, metempsychosis and vegetarianism. The alexandrines were shaky and imperfectly rhymed but had an unmistakable tone – chatty and apocalyptic:

> The universe is a school for spirits
> Who attend it to increase their erudition.
> Those who often play truant
> Must take the year again.[22]

Hugo had returned, along with several members of his family, via the French education system – an ambiguous, Janus-like figure who could easily be construed as the epitome of official, Third Republic culture, but who might also have been the warrior-prophet, come back to fight a final battle with the man who had initiated the conquest of Indo-China: Napoleon III. Hugo and his sons have since been reincarnated several times as Cao Dai priests. The first temple at Phnom Penh was dedicated in 1937 on the occasion of General Hugo's 164th birthday. During the long years of conflict, the military wing of Cao Dai changed sides so often that its political history is as complicated as Hugo's. There are now 1000 temples in Vietnam and perhaps three million followers, many of them in Paris.

This is surely a better place to leave Hugo than in the basement of the Panthéon – enshrined in the heaven of a collective mind, transmitting divine axioms to a nation wasted by war.

Hugo's latest incarnation in the West is in some ways remarkably similar. The 'oriental', meditative qualities of his poetry and novels, in which the surface meanings are continually eroded by the oceanic flow of words and rhythms, have fostered the image of a prophet of modernism. This induction of Hugo into a renovated pantheon has produced some fine critical studies, but it also signals the severance of his work from its original mass audience.

The ideological pleading of textual critics and the unwieldy ouija board of biography share a refusal to allow the past to die, a fear of universal decay. When Hugo dreamed of posterity, he thought of the nets that were strung across the Seine at Saint-Cloud to catch the drowned as they washed downstream from Paris. But even a corpus as large as Hugo's eventually disintegrates and heads for the open sea. With time, the most majestic work falls into disrepair and becomes indecipherable. Quasimodo and Esmeralda end up as dust, Jean Valjean's tombstone is wiped clean by the wind and the rain, Gwynplaine and Gilliatt are swallowed by the waves. Hugo's best-known tales have already suffered the fate of Homer's epics. *Les Misérables* is 'the world's most popular musical'. *The Hunchback of Notre Dame* is a Disney cartoon, visually inspired by Hugo's drawings, in which a dorsally challenged teenager called Quasi overcomes the appalling handicap of shyness.

It is all the more unfortunate that Hugo's last novels, which stand like weird towers on the frontier of Romanticism and Modernism, are practically unobtainable in English.[23] The two finest prose works of English literature in French – *Les Travailleurs de la Mer* and *L'Homme Qui Rit* – have effectively disappeared beneath the English Channel like the ancient pathways that once connected Britain to the mainland. At least one Victor Hugo is now an obscure, eccentric writer on the fringes of late Romanticism, relegated to unrefreshed libraries and secondhand bookshops.

These products of the most lucid case of madness in literature should be liberated and read while there is still time – preferably in an armchair of granite, with a view of a coastline, and the tide coming in.

Appendices

APPENDICES

Family Trees

Principal sources:
Bertault, *CF*, Tribout de Morembert,
Venzac, Origines Religieuses,
Ville de Châteaubriant

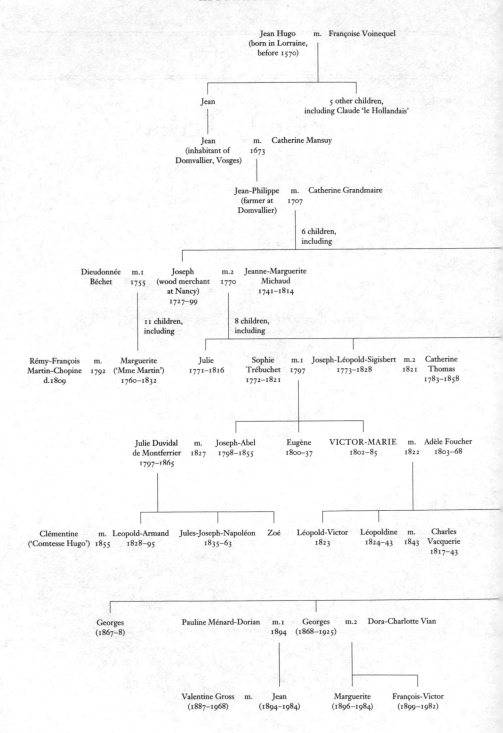

Jean Hugo   m.   Françoise Voinequel
(born in Lorraine,
before 1570)

Jean   5 other children,
                        including Claude 'le Hollandais'

Jean   m.   Catherine Mansuy
(inhabitant of 1673
Domvallier, Vosges)

Jean-Philippe   m.   Catherine Grandmaire
(farmer at   1707
Domvallier)

6 children,
including

Dieudonnée   m.1   Joseph   m.2   Jeanne-Marguerite
Béchet   1755   (wood merchant 1770   Michaud
                    at Nancy)   1741–1814
                    1727–99

11 children,   8 children,
including   including

Rémy-François   m.   Marguerite   Julie   Sophie   m.1   Joseph-Léopold-Sigisbert   m.2   Catherine
Martin-Chopine 1792 ('Mme Martin') 1771–1816   Trébuchet   1797   1773–1828   1821   Thomas
d.1809   1760–1832   1772–1821   1783–1858

Julie Duvidal   m.   Joseph-Abel   Eugène   VICTOR-MARIE   m.   Adèle Foucher
de Montferrier 1827   1798–1855   1800–37   1802–85   1822   1803–68
1797–1865

Clémentine   m.   Leopold-Armand   Jules-Joseph-Napoléon   Zoé   Léopold-Victor   Léopoldine   m.   Charles
('Comtesse Hugo') 1855   1828–95   1835–63   1823   1824–43   1843   Vacquerie
                                                                                                          1817–43

Georges   Pauline Ménard-Dorian   m.1   Georges   m.2   Dora-Charlotte Vian
(1867–8)   1894   (1868–1925)

Valentine Gross   m.   Jean   Marguerite   François-Victor
(1887–1968)   (1894–1984)   (1896–1984)   (1899–1982)

The Hugos

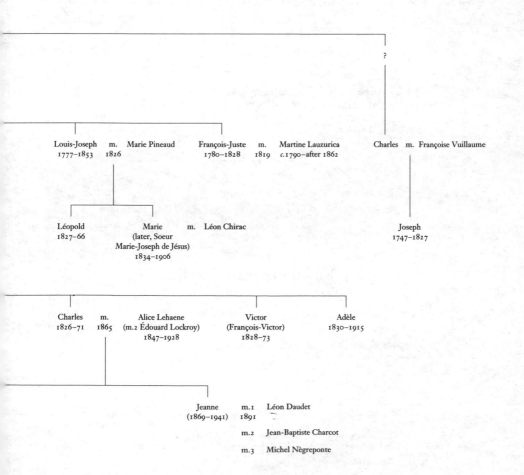

The Le Normands and Trébuchets

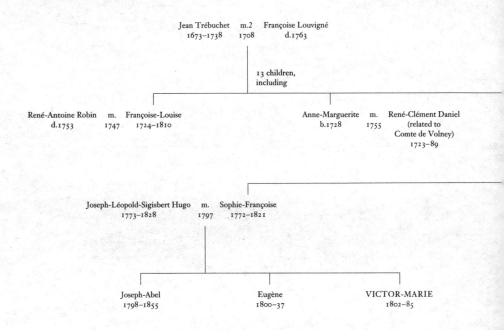

Jean Trébuchet   m.2   Françoise Louvigné
1673–1738   1708   d.1763

13 children,
including

René-Antoine Robin   m.   Françoise-Louise
d.1753   1747   1724–1810

Anne-Marguerite   m.   René-Clément Daniel
b.1728   1755   (related to
Comte de Volney)
1723–89

Joseph-Léopold-Sigisbert Hugo   m.   Sophie-Françoise
1773–1828   1797   1772–1821

Joseph-Abel   Eugène   VICTOR-MARIE
1798–1855   1800–37   1802–85

The Fouchers and Asselines

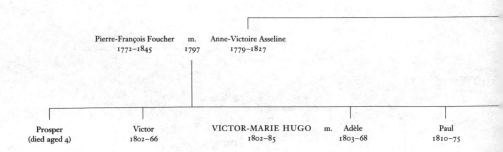

Pierre-François Foucher   m.   Anne-Victoire Asseline
1772–1845   1797   1779–1827

Prosper   Victor   VICTOR-MARIE HUGO   m.   Adèle   Paul
(died aged 4)   1802–66   1802–85   1803–68   1810–75

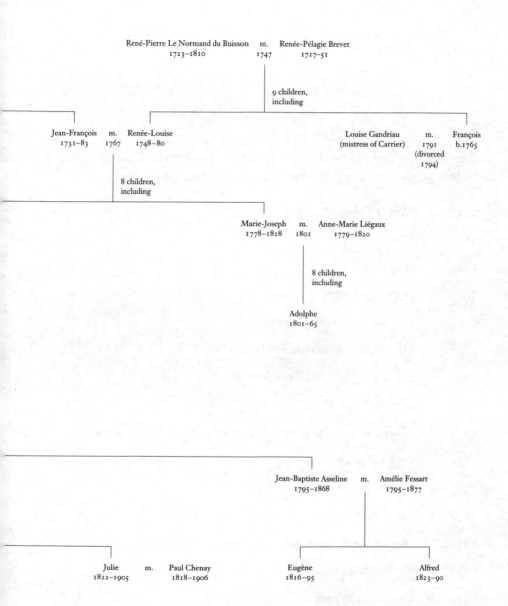

René-Pierre Le Normand du Buisson   m.   Renée-Pélagie Brevet
1723–1810   1747   1727–51

9 children,
including

Jean-François   m.   Renée-Louise
1731–83   1767   1748–80

Louise Gandriau   m.   François
(mistress of Carrier)   1791   b.1765
(divorced
1794)

8 children,
including

Marie-Joseph   m.   Anne-Marie Liégaux
1778–1828   1801   1779–1820

8 children,
including

Adolphe
1801–65

Jean-Baptiste Asseline   m.   Amélie Fessart
1795–1868   1795–1877

Julie   m.   Paul Chenay   Eugène   Alfred
1822–1905   1818–1906   1816–95   1823–90

APPENDIX II

Principal Published Works

The dates are those of the first publication in book form. This list does not include poems, speeches and letters published separately.

1822   *Odes et Poésies Diverses*

1823   *Odes; Han d'Islande*

1824   *Nouvelles Odes*

1826   *Bug-Jargal; Odes et Ballades*

1827   *Cromwell*, including *Préface*

1828   *Odes et Ballades* (augmented)

1829   *Les Orientales; Le Dernier Jour d'un Condamné*

1830   *Hernani*

1831   *Notre-Dame de Paris; Marion de Lorme; Les Feuilles d'Automne*

1832   *Le Roi S'Amuse*

1833   *Lucrèce Borgia; Marie Tudor*

1834   *Littérature et Philosophie Mêlées; Claude Gueux*

1835   *Angelo, Tyran de Padoue; Les Chants du Crépuscule*

1836   *La Esmeralda* (libretto)

1837   *Les Voix Intérieures*

1838   *Ruy Blas*

1840   *Les Rayons et les Ombres*

1842   *Le Rhin*

1843   *Les Burgraves*

1851   *Douze Discours; Treize Discours; Quatorze Discours*

1852   *Napoléon-le-Petit*

1853   *Châtiments; Oeuvres Oratoires*

1855   *Discours de l'Exil, 1851–1854* (= first ten speeches of *Actes et Paroles II*)

1856   *Les Contemplations*

1859   *La Légende des Siècles, Première Série*

1862   *Les Misérables*

1864   *William Shakespeare*

1865   *Les Chansons des Rues et des Bois*

1866   *Les Travailleurs de la Mer*

1867   *La Voix de Guernesey* (*Mentana*)

1869   *L'Homme Qui Rit*

1870   *Les Châtiments*

1872   *Actes et Paroles, 1870–1871–1872; L'Année Terrible*

1874   *Quatrevingt-treize; Mes Fils* (incorporated into Charles Hugo's *Les Hommes de l'Exil*)

1875   *Actes et Paroles I. Avant l'Exil, 1841–1851; Actes et Paroles II. Pendant l'Exil, 1852–1870*

1876   *Paris et Rome; Actes et Paroles III. Depuis l'Exil, 1870–1876*

1877   *La Légende des Siècles, Nouvelle Série; L'Art d'Être Grand-Père; Histoire d'un Crime*, I

1878   *Histoire d'un Crime*, II; *Le Pape*

1879   *La Pitié Suprême*

1880   *Religions et Religion; L'Âne*

1881   *Les Quatre Vents de l'Esprit*

1882   *Torquemada*

1883   *L'Archipel de la Manche; La Légende des Siècles, Dernière Série*

1886   *La Fin de Satan; Théâtre en Liberté*

1887   *Choses Vues*

1888   *Toute la Lyre*

1889   *Amy Robsart; Les Jumeaux; Actes et Paroles IV. Depuis l'Exil, 1876–1885*

1890   *Alpes et Pyrénées*

1891   *Dieu*

1892   *France et Belgique*

1893   *Toute la Lyre, Dernière Série*

1898   *Les Années Funestes*

1900   *Choses Vues, Nouvelle Série*

1901   *Post-Scriptum de ma Vie*

1902   *Dernière Gerbe*

1934   *Mille Francs de Récompense*

1942   *Océan, Tas de Pierres*

1951   *L'Intervention*

'Gastibelza, le Fou de Tolède'*

Music by Hippolyte Monpou

Gas - ti - bel - za l'homme à la ca - ra -
bi - ne chan - tait ain - si:
quel - qu'un a - t - il con - nu Do - ña Sa -
bi - ne, quel - qu'un d'i - ci?
Dan - sez, chan - tez, Vil - la - geois, la nuit
ga - gne le mont Fa - lou, Le vent qui

* See pages 236–240.

vient ____ à tra - vers la mon - ta - gne ____ me ren - dra

fou, oui ____ me ren - dra fou ____

Notes

Single-name references are to works listed in the bibliography. Hugo divided his longer works into sub-sections small enough to provide adequate references, applicable to any edition. For convenience, most other references are to the latest edition of Hugo's *Oeuvres Complètes* (Laffont, 1985–90).

The following abbreviations are used (for full details, see the Bibliography).

AP   *Actes et Paroles.*

CF   *Correspondance Familiale*, ed. J. and S. Gaudon and B. Leuilliot, 2 vols.

Corr   *Correspondance*, ed. C. Daubray, 4 vols.

Massin   *Oeuvres Complètes. Édition Chronologique*, ed. J. Massin, 18 vols.

MVH   Maison de Victor Hugo.

OC   *Oeuvres Complètes*, gen. eds J. Seebacher and G. Rosa, 15 vols. – identified by volume title instead of by number. In the following notes, numbers have been assigned to the 15 volumes: I–III (Roman), IV–VII (Poésie), VIII–IX (Théâtre), X (Politique), XI (Histoire), XII (Critique), XIII (Voyages), XIV (Océan), XV (Chantiers). (NB the promised volume of 'lists, tables and general index' was never published.)

OP   *Oeuvres Poétiques*, ed. P. Albouy, 3 vols.

PRO   Public Record Office, Kew

VHR   *Victor Hugo Raconté par Adèle Hugo*, ed. E. Blewer *et al.*

INTRODUCTION

1. Magnin, 733–4
2. Quoted by G. Rosa and A. Ubersfeld in *Dictionnaire des littératures de langue française* (1984).
3. Cocteau, 28.
4. *OED*, quoting E. Saltus and J. Lodwick.
5. Saintsbury, II, 122.
6. *Les Misérables*, IV, 7, 4.
7. Palmerston to General Love, 21 October 1855: PRO HO 45.
8. '[La Civilisation]', *OC*, XII, 608.

PART ONE

1. A Sabre in the Night (1802–1803)

1. General Hugo to Victor, 10 November 1821 (*CF*, I, 215 and note 2); Claretie (1904), 106; Cordier, 30; Paul Foucher (1873), 367. Also R. Escholier, letter to Hans Haug in Braun, and J. Y. Mariotte, Director of the Strasbourg Municipal Archives, letter to the author.
2. Hugo also claimed to have been conceived on the Montenvers: Stapfer (1905), 190; Baldensperger (1925); Cordier, 270–73.
3. This detail appears only in the official version: Mme Hugo (1863). See Family Tree.
4. *France et Belgique*, *OC*, XIII, 570 and 573.
5. *Quatrevingt-treize*, III, I, 1–7.
6. On Hugo's father: *VHR*; Barthou (1926); Guimbaud (1930): fantasies corrected by Bertault (1984). Victor Hugo's paternal grandfather is normally described as a carpenter. However, General Hugo's birth certificate identifies him as a *'maître menuisier'* (master carpenter) simply because he belonged to the carpenters' guild: Bertault, 122.
7. A. Duruy, 404; Guimbaud (1930), 68.
8. *Littérature et Philosophie Mêlées*, *OC*, XII, 117–18; *Les Feuilles d'Automne*,

Préface; 'Le Droit et la Loi', *AP*, *OC*, X, 75; *VHR*, chs 1–3; Adèle Hugo, II, 45. Also, by implication, *Les Misérables*, III, 3, 3. Allusions in verse: *Châtiments* (Suite), *OC*, XV, 156 and in *Moi Vers*, *OC*, XIV, 315; *Les Contemplations*, V, 3, part 2; *Les Quatre Vents de l'Esprit*, I, 29. Earliest echo of the legend in Sainte-Beuve (1831). See also Rabbe and Vapereau.

9. *CF*, I, 399–400.
10. Bertault.
11. *Les Misérables*, II, 5, 1.
12. Ibid., V, 2, 3.
13. On Lahorie: Le Barbier.
14. Guimbaud (1930), 159.
15. Barthou (1926), 26.
16. R. Lesclide, 310. The song does not appear in 'Napoléon et sa Légende', *Histoire de France par les Chansons*, V (Barbier and Vernillat).
17. See *CF*, I, 30–36 and 42–4.
18. 'Ce siècle avait deux ans . . .', *Les Feuilles d'Automne*.
19. *CF*, I, 463, 479 and 484; Massin, II, 1371.
20. *VHR*, 97.
21. Ibid., 97 and 684 n. 10.
22. A possible reference to Émile Deschanel's determinist *Physiologie des Écrivains et des Artistes* (on *Comtois*: p. 46). Hugo claimed to owe his 'triple stubbornness' to Brittany, Lorrain and the Franche-Comté (*OC*, XV, 297).
23. *AP*, *OC*, X, 633.
24. 27 December 1880: *AP*, 1022.
25. See Metzidakis, 82 n. 9; Feller, 150–67. Cf. *Corr*, III, 268: 'I was the first to use the term *The United States of Europe*.' See *AP*, *OC*, X, 275. In fact, he first used it at the Paris Peace Conference on 21 August 1849.
26. 'Le Droit et la Loi', *AP*, 74; *Carnets*, *OC*, XIII, 1098.
27. Dumas (1966), 137.
28. Claretie (1902), 7.
29. *VHR*, 98.
30. 'Tristesse d'Olympio', *Les Rayons et les Ombres*.
31. 16 November 1804 and Barthou (1926), 48.
32. 30 August 1800: Barthou (1926), 26; dated 10 December 1802 in *Victor Hugo, 1885–1985*, no. 2.

33. Barthou (1926), 36.
34. Foresi (14), from his uncle's friend. The Hugos' house has not been identified.
35. Barbou (1886), 23.
36. 16 November 1804: Barthou (1926), 48.
37. February 1815: *CF*, I, 30–36.
38. *Les Misérables*, III, 3, 6; *Littérature et Philosophie Mêlées*, *OC*, XII, 117.
39. 'Mon Enfance', part 1, *Odes et Ballades*. See also *Toute la Lyre*, VI, 50 and *Océan Vers*, *OC*, VII, 965.

2. SECRETS (1804–1810)

1. On biting female flesh: Stendhal, *Vie de Henry Brulard*, ch. 3; Balzac, *Le Lys dans la Vallée*: Balzac (1976–81), IX, 984; André Gide, *Si le Grain ne Meurt* (1926), paragraph 12. Hugo's oldest images are a good example of screen memories: Freud (1914), ch. 4; Baudouin, 66–7, and on the resonance of wells in Hugo's work: 83–6.
2. *VHR*, 123, and cf. Freud on the infant Leonardo's encounter with a bird of prey: Freud (1963), ch. 2. ('Freud' is used here to refer to the author of his books, not as the label of a doctrine. Remarks in *Psychopathology of Everyday Life* concern common fantasies rather than memories of actual events.)
3. Judith, 115–16. In 1829, Hugo claimed to be planning a book entitled *Les Souvenirs d'un Enfant de Neuf Ans* ('Memoirs of a Nine-Year-Old'): Denis, 41.
4. Stapfer (1905), 125.
5. Freud (1914), ch. 10; also *Jokes and their Relation to the Unconscious* (1905).
6. *VHR*, 103.
7. Hillairet, I, 338.
8. Sainte-Beuve (1831), 103; Le Barbier.
9. *Les Misérables*, III, 4, 6.
10. The word 'guerrilla' entered French and English during the Peninsular War a few months later.
11. *VHR*, 106; also 205.
12. *Hernani*, II, 3.
13. 13 February and 11 March 1806: Barthou (1926), 61 and 63.
14. Dumas (1966), 142–3.

15. *Promontorium Somnii*, *OC*, XII, 660; *Religions et Religion*, *OC*, VI, 996.
16. 'À Charles Hugo', *AP*, *OC*, X, 633.
17. *VHR*; Pierre Foucher, 118.
18. Stendhal (1936), IV, 130–47.
19. 9 June 1806: Barthou (1926), 68.
20. *Odes et Ballades*, V, 9.
21. See below, p. 57.
22. Dumas (1966), 143.
23. *L'Art d'Être Grand-Père*, I, 6.
24. Barthou (1926), 78.
25. In the original: 'à nous en inspirer le respect', etc.: *CF*, I, 221.
26. *VHR*, 134; Hillairet, I, 522–3. A plaque in the Rue des Feuillantines (5th *arrondissement*) marks the approximate site of the garden.
27. 6 *arpents*, according to *VHR* (127). The *arpent* was a variable measure; in Paris, approximately one third of a hectare.
28. Balzac (1976–81), VIII, 89.
29. References to the Feuillantines: 'Mes Adieux à l'Enfance', *Cahiers* (*OP*, I); 'Novembre', *Les Orientales*; 'A Eugène Vte H.', *Les Voix Intérieures*; 'Ce qui se Passait aux Feuillantines vers 1813' and 'Sagesse', *Les Rayons et les Ombres*; 'À André Chénier' and 'Aux Feuillantines', *Les Contemplations*, I and V; 'Une Bombe aux Feuillantines', *L'Année Terrible*, Janvier; 'À une Religieuse', *Toute la Lyre*, V; *Le Dernier Jour d'un Condamné*, chs 33 and 36; 'Le Droit et la Loi', *AP*, I; *Les Misérables*, IV, 3, 3.
30. 'Ce qui se Passait aux Feuillantines vers 1813', *Les Rayons et les Ombres*.
31. Pierre Foucher, 113; *VHR*, 100–101.
32. *VHR*, 125.
33. *Les Misérables*, III, I, 2. '*Sourd*' is also the Breton name for the salamander (Galand, quoting Littré).
34. For a partial catalogue: Duchet and Seebacher (1962).
35. *Les Misérables*, I, IV, 2.
36. See Uncle Louis's account of his miraculous survival of the Battle of Eylau (February 1807) in *La Légende des Siècles*, II.
37. 'Souvenir d'Enfance', *Les Feuilles d'Automne* and 'À la Colonne', *Les Chants du Crépuscule*.
38. *AP*, *OC*, X, 73.
39. Venzac was unable to confirm Hugo's claim that Larivière was a member of the Oratory: *Premiers Maîtres*, 42–8. On Larivière: *VHR*, 136–7 and 699 n. 32; *AP*, 69; *Moi Vers*, *OC*, XIV, 318; R. Lesclide, 53; 'Sagesse', part 3, *Les Rayons et les Ombres*.

40. Venzac, *Premiers Maîtres*, 32–3.
41. *Notre-Dame de Paris*, II, 5.
42. *AP, OC*, X, 650, 991 and 999.
43. *AP*, 69–70.
44. *Histoire d'un Crime*, II, 3.
45. *CF*, I, 700.
46. *VHR*, 146.
47. *CF*, I, 43 and Pierre Foucher, 142–3.
48. Suspicions of Pierre Foucher: 142–3.
49. *AP, OC*, X, 73.
50. *AP*, 71.
51. *CF*, I, 42.
52. Ibid., 31.
53. Guimbaud (1930), 195.
54. Caron, 84. In 1814, a student with 3000 francs a year was considered '*un vrai milord*' (ibid., 85).

3. The Disasters of War (1811–1815)

1. J. Lesclide, 11.
2. *AP, OC*, X, 634–5.
3. *Corr*, II, 404.
4. *Alpes et Pyrénées, OC*, X, 765–6.
5. Ibid., 786–7.
6. Rivet (1878); *CF*, I, 551.
7. *Océan Prose, OC*, XIV, 12; *VHR*, 199. Southey gives a detailed account of the destruction of Burgos (III, 622–3; also 548): 'Some of the French officers at the commencement of this treacherous invasion used to visit the church and spout passages from Corneille's tragedy over [the] tomb' of El Cid.
8. Hugo's letters in Spanish appear to owe more to letter-writing manuals than to first-hand knowledge. Elementary mistakes appear as early as 1827: Hugo–Nodier, 88 and 96, and the epigraph of 'Dédain' in *Les Feuilles d'Automne*. The smugglers' language in *Les Travailleurs de la Mer* is dialect or 'mountain Spanish' mainly because of Hugo's mistakes (I, II, 3).
9. Hugo himself calls it 'Hernani', without comment, in 1843: *OC*, XIII, 788. He may have been responding to a more recent desecration –

Verdi's amputation of the 'H' in his unauthorized *Ernani* (1844). On thieving operatic composers, see *Corr*, II, 185 and IV, 266; also Adèle Hugo, II, 431, and III, 489 on suing Donizetti over *Lucrèce Borgia*.

10. *VHR*, 213–15; Dumas (1966), 163; but cf. Abel Hugo (1833), 302–3; Hugo to Fontaney, 9 February 1831: Massin, IV, 1122–6.

11. *VHR*, 216; Gassier.

12. Abel Hugo (1833), 306.

13. *Odes et Ballades*, V, 9.

14. 'Novembre', *Les Orientales*.

15. Venzac, *Premiers Maîtres*, 426 n. 4.

16. The name of another bully, Belverana, is the nickname of Gubetta in *Lucrèce Borgia*.

17. *Les Misérables*, V, 7, 1.

18. Adèle Hugo, III, 516–17.

19. *VHR*, 186–7, 200 and 242–3.

20. *Les Misérables*, I, 4, 1.

21. *AP*, *OC*, X, 75.

22. 24 September 1813: Barthou (1926), 87–8.

23. *CF*, I, 34.

24. Ibid., I, 26.

25. *L'Âne*, *OC*, VI, 1061–2.

26. Simond, I, 325–6. The paper reverted to its earlier title, *Journal de l'Empire*, on 20 March 1815.

27. *Les Misérables*, II, I, 13 and 17.

28. Ibid., 2; and Dossier: *OC*, XV, 887–8.

29. *Carnets*, *OC*, XIII, 1178–9.

30. Chateaubriand, II, 669 (XXIV, 5).

31. *AP*, *OC*, X, 75–6; also *Les Misérables*, V, 5, 6: 'Anyone who has had a mysterious childhood is always prepared to resign himself to ignorance.'

32. 'Ce que Dit la Bouche d'Ombre', *Les Contemplations*, VI, 26, l. 186; also 'Les Fénians', *AP*, *OC*, X, II, 584. Edmond Grégoire's *L'Astronomie de Victor Hugo* (Droz, 1933) was written before astronomy had caught up with Hugo's intuitions.

4. METROMANIA (1815–1818)

1. *L'Homme Qui Rit*, II, I, 1, 4. The following details from *William Shakespeare* (Reliquat), *OC*, XV, 1004; *Les Misérables*, I, 3, 1 and II, 1, 18; *Littérature et Philosophie Mêlées*, *OC*, XII, 66; *AP*, *OC*, X, I, 120.

2. Palmerston, 39.

3. *Journal de ce que J'Apprends Chaque Jour*, 5 December 1847: *Choses Vues*, *OC*, XI, 656.

4. J. Seebacher, review of *Boîte aux Lettres*, ed. R. Journet and G. Robert, *Revue d'Histoire Littéraire de la France*, October–December 1967, p. 854.

5. On the Pension Cordier: *Choses Vues*, *OC*, XI, 1178.

6. *CF*, I, 45.

7. Ibid., I, 60.

8. Ibid., I, 56–7.

9. Ibid., I, 50.

10. Adèle Hugo, II, 20.

11. *VHR*, 281 and 285–6.

12. Barbou (1886), 50; R. Lesclide, 52.

13. *Les Contemplations*, I, 13; *Les Misérables*, IV, 12, 3 ('My father always hated me because I couldn't understand Mathematics').

14. Venzac, *Premiers Maîtres*, 276–87.

15. Sainte-Beuve (1831), 34; also Adèle Hugo, III, 214 and Stapfer (1905), 29.

16. Barbou (1886), 477.

17. 'Le calcul, c'est l'abîme...': *Toute la Lyre*, III, 67. See also *Moi, l'Amour, la Femme*, *OC*, XIV, 274. This was the new mathematics of Monge, Legendre *et al.*, filtering down from the École Polytechnique.

18. Adèle Hugo, III, 214; *Faits et Croyances*, *OC*, XIV, 134.

19. Barbou (1886), 51; Adèle Hugo, II, 430.

20. Olivier, 23 June 1830.

21. See *Préface de Cromwell*, *OC*, XII, 28; *Faits et Croyances*, *OC*, XIV, 186.

22. J. Lesclide, 278.

23. Robb (1993), 9.

24. Fontanes, 18 December 1812: Venzac, *Premiers Maîtres*, 143–4 n. 2.

25. Quicherat.

26. *Le Conservateur Littéraire*, 25 December 1819. It appeared as an

unpublished poem in a pirated edition of *Les Feuilles d'Automne, suivies de Plusieurs Pièces Nouvelles* (Brussels: Méline, 1835).

27. 'Sur une Corniche Brisée' appears to describe football rather than *choule*, which allowed the use of any part of the body.

28. 'Les Places', *OP*, I, 148–9; also *Littérature et Philosophie Mêlées*, *OC*, XII, 78.

29. *Étude sur Mirabeau* in *Littérature et Philosophie Mêlées*, 227. Sainte-Beuve points out that this image describes Hugo's own style (fragment dated February 1834, in *Les Grands Écrivains Français*, ed. M. Allem (Garnier, 1926), p. 99).

30. *A.Q.C.H.E.B.* [= *A Quelque Chose Hasard Est Bon*] (1817): *OP*, I, 91.

31. *Quatrevingt-treize*, III, 2, 12.

32. Venzac, *Premiers Maîtres*, 152.

33. Barthou (1926).

34. Venzac, *Premiers Maîtres*, 172.

35. Barthou (1926) and *OP*, I, 124–5 (Hugo translated Achaemenides' description of the Cyclops' cave).

36. *William Shakespeare*, II, III, 5.

37. *Toute la Lyre*, VI, 18; also in *Dernière Gerbe*, 75, and *Moi, l'Amour, la Femme*, *OC*, XIV, 358.

38. Clearly a favourite topic since Hugo's son wrote a poem on the same theme for the same competition a quarter of a century later: Guille, 32 n. 42.

39. *OP*, I, 39 and 1150.

40. *Les Misérables*, III, 6, 4; Adèle Hugo, II, 246–8 (August 1853). Another account by Paul Lacroix: Biré (1883), 108–11, and Legay, 39.

5. *PASSION* (1818–1820)

1. *CF*, I, 261.

2. On Mme Hugo's 'salon': Barbou (1886), 16; Venzac, *Origines Religieuses*, 644–9; echoed in *Les Misérables*, III, 3, 3. Venzac (648–9) confirms the family connection with the Comte de Volney (see Family Tree).

3. Now the courtyard of the École des Beaux-Arts.

4. Abel Hugo (1825). See also *VHR*, 314–15; *Carnets*, *OC*, XIII, 1100–1101.

5. Birkbeck, 95 (1 October 1814).

6. 'À l'Arc de Triomphe', part 3, *Les Voix Intérieures*. See J. Gaudon (1969), 94–5.

7. *VHR*, 338; Barbou (1886), 44.

8. *Les Misérables*, III, 6, 1.

9. Ibid., III, 5, 2.

10. Ibid., III, 6, 1.

11. Ibid., III, 4, 1.

12. Ibid., III, 4, 1.

13. *Le Rhin*, letter 4.

14. Stapfer (1905), 193.

15. *Tas de Pierres*, *OC*, XIV, 492.

16. Robb (1993), 50 and 397 n. 22; Baudelaire: II, 129–30.

17. Séché (1908), ch. 1; Ségu (1935–6). For a list of the Hugos' entries and awards: Ségu (1935–6), II, 272. There were eighty-seven submissions in 1818, eighty-six in 1819, and sixty-two in 1820.

18. See the epigraph of 'La Pente de la Rêverie', perhaps invented by Hugo (*Les Feuilles d'Automne*, 29): '*Obscuritate rerum verba saepe obscurantur*' ('Often it is the obscurity of things that makes the words obscure').

19. Dufay (1924). For a balanced account of Eugène's illness: Gourevitch.

20. Balzac considered lunacy a family trait: 'Hugo has the skull of a madman, and his brother the great unknown poet died insane' (Balzac (1990), II, 8).

21. *Les Jumeaux*, II, 1. On *Les Jumeaux*: Ubersfeld, 39 and 351–86. Dumas's *L'Homme au Masque de Fer* appeared in 1840.

22. *Notre-Dame de Paris*, VII, 4.

23. 'À Madame la Comtesse A. H.' (19–20 December 27): *Odes et Ballades*, V, 23.

24. *OC*, XV, 1009: supposedly, Nodier found a copy of the 'unknown' *Romancero* in a junk shop in Soissons and Hugo translated it on the spot – four years after Abel's edition; Abel Hugo (1821 and 1822). Lockhart's English translation appeared in 1820.

25. Blewer (1985); Abel Hugo (1835).

26. A! A! A!, 10, 32, 33–4, 13 and 79.

27. e.g. A! A! A!, 48.

28. *Le Conservateur Littéraire*, ed. Marsan. On Hugo's alterations: A. R. W. James's edition of *Littérature et Philosophie Mêlées*.

29. 'Réponse à un Acte d'Accusation' (24 October 1854), *Les Contemplations*, I, 7.

30. Adèle Hugo, II, 31 (January 1853).
31. 'But de cette Publication', *Littérature et Philosophie Mêlées*, OC, XII, 47.
32. Léopold Hugo (1818); attributed to General Hugo in Rabbe. The idea was to populate the French colonies with orphans.
33. *CF*, I, 290; cf. *Les Misérables*, III, 6, 5.
34. *CF*, I, 82.
35. Described by Balzac in *Le Bal de Sceaux* (1829).
36. 23 May 1829: Vigny (1948), 892.
37. *CF*, I, 259.
38. Ibid., I, 200 and 198.
39. Ibid., I, 196.
40. Ibid., I, 82. On the horrors of waltzing: Larousse.
41. Ibid., I, 411.
42. Ibid., I, 289.
43. Ibid., I, 323. 'French women shew their legs ... sooner than get draggle-tailed': Hazlitt, 130–1.
44. *Les Misérables*, III, 6, 8.
45. *VHR*, 333–7; *Choses Vues*, OC, XI, 697–8.
46. *CF*, I, 140.
47. In fact, the albatross sleeps on water.
48. *VHR*, 354–5.
49. Soumet to Guiraud, 5 July 1820, in Séché (1908), 41–2. *Mouchoir* made its first public appearance in French literature in Vigny's verse translation of *Othello*, *Le More de Venise* (1829), III, 15: Vigny (1926), 109. The French word has the disadvantage of drawing attention to the act itself (*se moucher*).
50. Hundreds of pages have been devoted to the question of whether or not Chateaubriand dubbed Hugo *'l'enfant sublime'*. The story was widely known and believed in the 1820s. Chateaubriand later denied having said it, but in the salon of Mme Récamier and at a time (1841) when Hugo was considered a renegade. Sainte-Beuve points out that Chateaubriand was quite capable of forgetting something he wished he had never said. He may also have forgotten, for instance, that Hugo's ode on Quiberon made him cry (*Corr*, I, 322, with a different text but the same editor in Daubray (1947), 26–7). See Barbou, 60; Biré (1883), 223–7; Dumas (1966), 172; Giraud (1926); Legay, 61–3; R. Lesclide, 178; Loménie, 148; Sainte-Beuve (1831), 40; Séché (1912), 51–5; Venzac, *Origines Religieuses*, 650–3; Trollope, I, 152; *VHR*, 333.

51. Letter to an unknown correspondent, August (?) 1821: Lamennais, II, 190.
52. *CF*, I, 98, 195–6, 211 and 233.

6. The Demon Dwarf (1821–1824)

1. *CF*, I, 212.
2. Ibid., I, 148.
3. Ibid., I, 220.
4. Ibid., I, 751: 'récip' = '*réciproquement*'; 'd.l.b.' = '*donnant le bras*'.
5. Ibid., I, 475.
6. Ibid., I, 757, 749 and 751.
7. *New Monthly Magazine*, April 1823: Hooker, 18.
8. *CF*, I, 308; see also 452.
9. *Han d'Islande*, ch. 5: translations (corrected), from Hugo, *Hans of Iceland* (1825 and 1897).
10. Legoyt, 345; Pouchain and Sabourin, 342.
11. Heine, 54–5. Hetzel's account in Parménie, 271–4.
12. On the pre-eminence of Hugo's 'G': Bellet.
13. *CF*, I, 321. The notebooks may have contained the first chapters of *Han d'Islande*.
14. *VHR*, 360–1, and Pierre Foucher, 201–2. On the house: Miquel, 155–61.
15. *CF*, I, 230–1. Hugo had been reading Joseph de Maistre. See Savey-Casard, 21–6.
16. *CF*, I, 278; 473; 452.
17. See Juliette's letter, below, p. 210. Nine appears to be the conventional indeterminate number. Cf. the puny lover of Baudelaire's '*Sed non Satiata*': 'No Styx am I to embrace you nine times.'
18. *Les Misérables*, III, 1, 5 and III, 8, 10.
19. *Choses Vues*, *OC*, XI, 708 and 917. Also *AP*, *OC*, X, 464; *Le Dernier Jour d'un Condamné*, preface; *Bug-Jargal*, ch. 12.
20. *Faits et Croyances*, *OC*, XIV, 128; *AP*, *OC*, X, 544. Branding was reintroduced under Napoleon and not abolished until 28 April 1832. Thieves were marked with a 'V' for '*Voleur*'.
21. *VHR*, 441–2; R. Lesclide, 279–80.
22. *Han d'Islande*, ch. 48.
23. Letter to Vigny, 20 July 1821: *Corr*, I, 327.

24. 20 July 1821: *CF*, I, 162–3.
25. 'La Chauve-souris', *Odes et Ballades*.
26. *CF*, I, 366.
27. Ibid., I, 470.
28. Ibid., I, 430.
29. 'Le Cauchemar', *Odes et Ballades*, perhaps inspired by Fuseli.
30. *CF*, I, 169.
31. Ibid., I, 348.
32. Ibid., I, 167.
33. Ibid., I, 438.
34. Ibid., I, 193.
35. R. Lesclide, 58.
36. *Les Misérables*, III, 5, 2.
37. *CF*, I, 249.
38. Blagdon, 171.
39. Leroux (1979), 554–5; Evans, 10.
40. *CF*, I, 256; also *VHR*, 375–7 and Sainte-Beuve (1831), 42–3.
41. Carbonari: The Italian resistance, formed in 1814 to fight Napoleon, became a focus for Bonapartist opposition in France. Its Paris membership was estimated at 20,000.
42. *CF*, I, 479 and 483, and Jean Massin's summary in Massin, II, 1371.
43. *CF*, I, 483–4.
44. Ibid., I, 486.
45. 'À Madame Victor Hugo, Souvenir de Ses Noces' (5 June 1856): Lamartine (1963), 1471–2, reflecting Lamartine's personal experience of the marriage, though he was almost certainly in England at the time of the wedding.
46. *CF*, I, 223–5 and 241.
47. Ibid., I, 374.
48. Ibid., I, 373.
49. Ibid., I, 519–20.
50. Ibid., I, 524.
51. *Promontorium Somnii*, *OC*, XII, 652.
52. *CF*, I, 494.
53. Ibid., I, 573–4.
54. Not until 1827: Sainte-Beuve (1827), 4.
55. Preface to *Marion de Lorme*.
56. *VHR*, 365.
57. For instance, Maturin's *Fredolfo* (1819) has an intrepid dwarf called

Berthold ('What dares not he whom nature's self hath cursed?') (II, 1; Fierobe, 394–6); Grenville Fletcher's *Rosalviva, or The Demon Dwarf. A Romance* was published in 1824. See also *OG*, a parody of *Han d'Islande* by Victor Vignon. The eponymous Og is 'a cannibalistic giant' identified with Og, King of Bashan (Deuteronomy 3).

58. All but six published in the USA.

59. *Iislaenderen i Norge. Med nogle Forandringer oversat efter Victor Hugos franske Original: Han d'Islande*. 3 vols. Christiania (Oslo): J. W. Cappelens Forlag, 1831. Copies of the novel exist in Iceland but not in Icelandic.

60. Hugo, *Hans of Iceland* (1825); Lady Pollock in 1885: Hooker, 18. Hugo's opinion of the engravings: 'The effect is unpleasant, but they are terrific' (*CF*, I, 667). The anonymous translator also made some picturesque additions, notably in the form of epigraphs (25): 'He had long claws, and in his jaws / Four-and-forty teeth of iron; / With a hide as tough as any buff, / Which did him round environ.' George Saintsbury (II, 97) knew several people who read *Han d'Islande* as schoolboys.

61. *Literary Gazette*: 15 February 1823: Hooker, 18.

62. *La Quotidienne*, 12 March 1823; reprinted in Hugo–Nodier, 130–5.

63. Anonymous, but taken from Abel's translation of the Spanish Ballads.

64. *CF*, I, 559.

65. Ibid., I, 585. The same superstition is the basis of 'Le Revenant': *Les Contemplations*, III.

66. Sainte-Beuve, article on J.-B. Rousseau in *Revue de Paris*, 7 June 1829: *OP*, I, 1249.

PART TWO

7. TRAITORS (1824–1827)

1. *Corr*, I, 338.
2. *Littérature et Philosophie Mêlées, OC*, XII, 155.
3. Ibid., 157.

4. *CF*, I, 632 and 704; II, 173.
5. Séché (1908), 305. The figure has desiccated breasts and a headful of snakes and is not, therefore, Lucifer. Cf. Séché (1908), 67.
6. Peoples, 2.
7. *Le Réveil*, 11 December 1822: *CF*, I, 499 n. 3.
8. *Philosophie Prose*, *OC*, XIV, 75.
9. In the fifth edition (1798), *romantique* is said to be applicable 'to sites and landscapes which bring to mind descriptions in poems and novels'. The sixth edition (1835) shows the tendentious addition: 'Of certain writers who affect to free themselves from the rules of composition and style established by the example of classical authors; also applied to the works of these writers.'
10. Auger.
11. *CF*, I, 588 and 587.
12. *Corr*, I, 399, 402, 403.
13. *CF*, I, 646.
14. Ibid., I, 633; *VHR*, 372.
15. Guimbaud (1928), 10.
16. *CF*, I, 580.
17. *AP*, *OC*, X, 691.
18. R. Grant.
19. *Corr*, I, 402.
20. *Odes et Ballades* (1826); removed to *Les Orientales* and retitled, 'La Ville Prise'.
21. 'Suite', *Les Contemplations*, I.
22. See General Hugo (1825), 37, on the 'wise law which now calls all young French citizens to serve the King and thus the fatherland'.
23. *CF*, I, 621. The editors of *CF* correct Barthou's reading: '*eau de navets*' (turnip water) instead of '*eau de pavots*'.
24. See Hayter. The effects of culture and chemicals are inseparable. Many visions reflect expectations in the opium-eater. M. H. Abrams draws an important distinction between the effects of an isolated dose and the more spectacular withdrawal symptoms.
25. *Les Misérables*, IV, 14, 1; *Dieu* (Fragments), *OC*, XV, 490; *Mangeront-Ils?*, I, 6; *Dernière Gerbe*, 39.
26. Rossetti, 53 (1 April 1871); this 'imprudent' act is mentioned in *Notre-Dame de Paris*, VIII, 4.
27. 'Du Génie', *OC*, XII, 563.

28. For a biography of Nodier in English: A. R. Oliver.

29. Nodier (1808). Words which Nodier considers onomatopoetic: *asthme, canard, fanfare, horreur, loup* ('wolf'), *violon, whist,* etc.

30. Ancelot, 124–5; 'Cécile L.' (identified as Adèle by Sainte-Beuve) in *L'Événement,* 9 January 1849: in *VHR,* 641–6, and Hugo–Nodier, 177–84.

31. Baldensperger, 165.

32. *Corr,* I, 399.

33. Baldensperger, 168–9 (19 April 1825).

34. *CF,* I, 639.

35. *VHR,* 379–83; letters in *CF,* I.

36. *CF,* I, 677.

37. *William Shakespeare* (Reliquat), *OC,* XV, 1006.

38. *CF,* I, 768.

39. *Carnets, OC,* XIII, 1190.

40. *CF,* I, 659.

41. Ibid., I, 701; Baldensperger, 175–6.

42. S. P. Oliver, 721. Hugo's other sources include Stendhal, Mme de Staël, and the Abbot-Kemble troupe.

43. e.g. Nodier's 'Impromptu Classique' in *L'Oriflamme,* 2 February 1824 (Vivier, 304) and cf. the three *Chants* in Hugo's *Nouvelles Odes.*

44. Hugo's 1823 ode on the *'bande noire'* – a consortium of businessmen who demolished abbeys and chateaux and sold off their treasures – has an epigraph from Nodier.

45. *La Quotidienne,* 12 March 1823 and 10 February 1827; Hugo–Nodier, 130–5.

46. *CF,* I, 708.

47. One of his chief creditors was Balzac, whose printing business had collapsed.

48. Smith, 32: from *The Edinburgh Review,* also quoted in *The Hunchback of Notre-Dame* (1833), xi; Morgan, I, 184–5.

49. *Le Globe,* 2 March 1826: Blémont. See also Aragon (1952), 19.

50. *Les Misérables,* III, 7, 4.

51. *Bug-Jargal,* ch. 9.

52. Havelock Ellis, quoting Papillault's study of Dalou's cast (Ellis, 258–9; Papillault).

53. Reported to Heine by Hugo's publisher, Renduel: Heine, 54–5.

54. *Mes Fils,* i.

55. *Les Misérables*, V, 7, 2 – a crucial passage – reduced without warning in the Penguin translation of *Les Misérables* to 'an imaginative haziness that pervaded his whole being'. On the influence of the Ocean: *Océan Vers*, *OC*, VII, 1014; *Moi, l'Amour, la Femme*, *OC*, XIV, 273; *Corr*, II, 238.

56. Gautier's poem on the Vendôme column, 'Le Godemichet de la Gloire' is a sarcastic echo of Hugo's ode: recited to Adèle's cousin, Alfred Asseline: Gautier (1968), 100; Asseline (1853).

57. e.g. letter to Dubois, 5 November 1826; *Les Affiches d'Angers*, 31 December 1826.

58. Picat-Guinoiseau, 210.

59. 'Byron et Moore', *La Quotidienne*, 1 November 1829: Hugo–Nodier, 98.

60. 2 November 1829: *Corr*, I, 460 and Hugo–Nodier, 99–100.

61. November 1829: Hugo–Nodier, 104; John 1:27.

62. Summary of reviews in Bauer, 155–82.

63. *VHR*, 414; Guimbaud (1928), 11–12.

64. Séché (1912), 68–70.

65. *Amy Robsart*, V, 2. Reviews: Biré (1883), 450–3. Generally: *VHR*, 425–9; Paul Foucher (1873), 245–6 and 369–71.

66. Jullien, 58–9; Larousse; Verlaine, 537.

67. *Corr*, I, 459; see also I, 446.

68. Gourevitch, 770.

69. Not in the Gospels but in Revelation 3:17: 'poor, and blind, and naked'.

70. *Corr*, I, 446.

71. 'La Conscience': *La Légende des Siècles*, I.

8. ▆ (1828–1830)

1. *Faits et Croyances*, *OC*, XIV, 212 (5 May 1839). Same image applied to a Madrid cemetery in a letter to Fontaney, 9 February 1831: Massin, IV, 1125.

2. *CF*, I, 734. Also autobiographical notes dated 26 May 1828, claiming the title of baron after his father's death: Biré (1891), II, 235–6. Émile Deschamps addressed a letter to 'Baron Hugo' on 20 September 1828. The General's full, assumed title is given in Abel Hugo's *Romancero* (1821).

3. Baudelaire (1975–6), II, 28.
4. *CF*, I, 620 and 630.
5. Ibid., I, 735–6.
6. *Les Misérables*, III, 3, 6.
7. *Corr*, I, 456.
8. Louis Hugo, a sixteenth-century scholar. *Corr*, III, 18.
9. Biré (1869), 155–6, quoting Cayon, 353 (see also Cayon, 433); Biré (1883), ch. 1; Hozier; Méry; Rabbe. Origins of Jesus: *Dieu* (Fragments), *OC*, XV, 542; *Carnets*, *OC*, XIII, 1103; 'Bourgeois Parlant de Jésus-Christ', *Toute la Lyre*, I.
10. *Tas de Pierres*, *OC*, XIV, 497.
11. Vigny (1948), 893 (23 May 1829).
12. Ibid., 892.
13. *Volupté*, ch. 3: Sainte-Beuve (1969), 68.
14. Gautier (1872), 17–18.
15. Musset, 839.
16. Cocteau, 28.
17. Reynolds, II, 12. Generally: Brombert, 25–48.
18. Dostoevsky, 227. See also Chardin.
19. Fontaney (1832), 378 n. 1.
20. Sometimes attributed to Harold Bloom (cf. Bloom, 102–3).
21. *Le Dernier Jour d'un Condamné*, ch. 3; *Han d'Islande*, ch. 48.
22. *Le Dernier Jour d'un Condamné*, ch. 13.
23. *VHR*, 498–9; Adèle Hugo, III, 200.
24. See especially Chételat.
25. Used by Baudelaire, in 'Harmonie du Soir'. For a history of the form: Robb (1993), 223–4.
26. Géraud, 250–1.
27. See Riffaterre, 257–8.
28. Nerval, 'Histoire Véridique du Canard', *Le Diable à Paris* (1844): Nerval, I, 859.
29. *Littérature et Philosophie Mêlées*, *OC*, XII, 167–72.
30. Then known as the Théâtre Français.
31. Blagdon, 195–8.
32. Hazlitt, 50–1.
33. *Henri III et Sa Cour* and adaptation of *Othello*.
34. Morgan, I, 169 and II, 96.
35. Morgan, I, 181.
36. *Revue de Paris*, October 1829; Ségu (1931), 349–52.

37. *Corr*, I, 458.
38. The story that Hugo earned his credentials as a censored playwright as early as 1822 is suspect. One of his first attempts at melodrama, *Iñez de Castro*, was accepted by a tiny avant-garde theatre, the Panorama Dramatique (1821–3), only to be banned, supposedly, because the subject was the marriage of a prince and a commoner. The origin of this rumour is a note in the 1912 edition of *Odes et Ballades* by Gustave Simon, who was exposed to Hugo's oral autobiographies. Since Hugo's chronicles of battles with the censor contain no reference to *Iñez de Castro*, since the Archives Nationales have no record of it, and since the Panorama Dramatique was allowed to have only two actors on the stage at a time, the story is probably apocryphal. See Brazier, I, 175–87; Krakovitch (1982 and 1985); Langlois, letter dated 5 December 1822 (Massin, I, 429–32, i). The only critic who casts doubt on the story is also the only critic who cites a source for it: Benoit-Lévy, 181.
39. On this incident: *VHR* and *Corr*.
40. Dumas (1986), 483.
41. *VHR*.
42. Schneider, 17.
43. Legay, 119.
44. Ibid., 111.
45. *Le Rouge et le Noir*, II, 10; also Marnay, 89, and Jay (with a useful list of rhetorical devices used by Romantics). Hence Gautier's 'Daniel Jovard, ou la Conversion d'un Classique' in *Les Jeunes France* (1833).
46. Legay, 155.
47. *Littérature et Philosophie Mêlées*, *OC*, XII, 205.
48. *CF*, II, 669, 679 and 681.
49. Allusion to the war cry used as the epigraph of the sixth *Orientale*, '*Hierro, despierta te!*'
50. Gautier (1872), 51–2; Pichois–Brix, 73–80.
51. No connection with the modern Moulin Rouge.
52. First recorded use of 'cigarette' in French: 1831. In English, *re* 'French ladies': 1842.
53. Karr (1880), II, 176.
54. Hugo's accusation that his play was leaked by the censor (letter to Minister of Interior, 5 January 1830) ignores the fact that he had given readings, left the manuscript with a disgruntled troupe of actors – one of whom supplied the author of *Harnali* with a secret copy – and effectively wandered through Paris allowing pieces of *Hernani* to fall

out of his pocket. He later suggested to the author of *Harnali* that they collaborate on a parody of *Marie Tudor* (by Victor Hugo) ... Hugo deliberately exposed his unperformed play to approximately 10 per cent of the literary population of Paris – enough to ensure near-total dissemination. See Francisque Sarcey in Duvert, VI, xii–xiv; Schneider, 16. Legoyt's statistics, based on death certificates, show 1,257 'men of letters' in Paris in 1831.

55. *VHR*, 463; Adèle Hugo, III, 87.
56. Chasles, II, 13–15; Pichois (1965), II, 322–3.
57. *VHR*, 463.
58. *Dernière Gerbe*, 83.
59. Pendell, 36.
60. Act III, scene 7. Molière uses '*as de pique*' in the sense of 'scandal-monger'.
61. Alexandre Duval, in Legay, 180.
62. Confirmed by Anon. (1830), 6. Other accounts of *Hernani*: Cuvillier-Fleury, 168–9; Olivier, 26 May; Pontmartin.
63. Gautier (1874), 8.
64. Porel and Monval, I, 241.
65. On the political nature of *Hernani*: J. Gaudon (1985), 26–38 and 165–78.
66. Schneider, 122–4. Leveson-Gower's was the third English translation. In 1857, an adaptation of *Hernani* by F. M. Piave was 'rendered into English from the Italian' by J. W. Mould. Liberal tendencies were also ascribed to Hugo by Hazlitt the Younger in the preface to his 1833 translation of *Notre-Dame de Paris*.
67. Du Camp (1895), 28.
68. J. Gaudon (1985), 179–85.
69. Joanny in Descotes, 67; last performance of *Hernani* on 11 August 1830.
70. *Corr*, I, 467–8.
71. Pichois (1965), I, 323 and II, 252–3.
72. R. Lesclide, 72–3; see also Read, 89.
73. Schneider, 36.
74. Sainte-Beuve to Hugo, February 1830: Sainte-Beuve (1935–83), I, 179.
75. *Corr*, I, 472.
76. Olivier, 21 July.
77. Schneider, 16.

78. Fontaney (1925), 10.
79. Bertin.
80. Letter to Papion du Château, early April 1832: Nerval, I, 1284.
81. Fontaney (1925), 124.
82. Ibid., 81.
83. *VHR*, 482–3.
84. Sainte-Beuve (1880), 39.
85. See however Nerval's ode, 'À Victor Hugo. Les Doctrinaires' (16 October 1830), asking for a less equivocal statement: Nerval, I, 307–9.

9. What the Concierge Saw (1831–1833)

1. Goethe: Eckermann, 655–6.
2. *Madame Bovary*, I, 7.
3. On 'vertical perspective' in *Notre-Dame de Paris*: Brombert, 77–82.
4. See Stevenson, 12 and 23.
5. *Les Misérables*, II, 7, 3.
6. *Littérature et Philosophie Mêlées*, OC, XII, 122.
7. There is a splendid description of the novel's effect on the 'unprofessional' majority in the diary of the actress Fanny Kemble: Kemble (1878), III, 175–7. See also, below, p. 577 n. 45, her *Records of Later Life* (1882), III, 302, and a translation in Llewellyn Williams.
8. *Corr*, III, 158 (12 January 1869).
9. Hugo (1833) and Fitz-Ball.
10. Stevenson, 11–12.
11. R. Lesclide, 166–7.
12. *Notre-Dame de Paris*, XI, 1.
13. Morgan, I, 196–7.
14. Manuscript note in the *Livre d'Amour*: Sainte-Beuve (1843), 77.
15. Billy, I, 148–9, quoting Octave Lacroix and Jules Troubat.
16. Sainte-Beuve (1843), no. 24.
17. Ibid., no. 15.
18. Sainte-Beuve (1935–83), I, 392.
19. Mérimée, IV, 202 (16 October 1844) and V, 542 (12 November 1849).
20. *Tas de Pierres*, OC, XIV, 521.
21. *Corr*, I, 485.
22. *CF*, II, 381.

23. Montalembert, II, 32 (19 June 1830) and 150 (23 February 1831).

24. Sainte-Beuve to U. Guttinguer, 18 May 1838: Sainte-Beuve (1935–83), II, 365.

25. e.g. 'Oh! pourquoi te cacher...', *Les Feuilles d'Automne*, with 'Sainte-Beuve' as phonetic motif; 'À mes Amis S.-B. et L.B.', *Les Feuilles d'Automne*: Sainte-Beuve 'pursuing a dark eye beneath the shutter' (*jalousie*) – recalling Sainte-Beuve's notorious synecdoche in 'Voeu' (*Joseph Delorme*): 'Oh! that I could have for just three years / Pure milk on my table, a dark eye in my bed / And leisure all day long!': Sainte-Beuve (1829), 77 and 189.

26. *Corr*, I, 519. Snakes: *Dernière Gerbe*, 127; 'La haine, tantôt fière...', in *OP*, I, 1132 and comment by Juliette Drouet, p. 1591. The snake image is applied to a would-be seducer in *Amy Robsart*, III, 5.

27. *Châtiments* (Suite), *OC*, XV, 244–5. The poem denies rumours that Sainte-Beuve was funded by the Government of Napoleon III ('Are frogs paid to be horrid?'), and refers to his famous change of mind about Balzac in 1850: 'He tears Balzac apart, then admires him in the tomb.'

28. *Océan Vers*, *OC*, VII, 934; *L'Homme Qui Rit*, II, I, 9; *Châtiments* (Suite), *OC*, XV, 92; Goncourt, III, 1296 (11 June 1896): Léon Daudet reporting Édouard Lockroy. See also Goncourt, II, 548, and L. Daudet, 238 (from Georges Hugo). Oscar Wilde borrowed the cuckolds aphorism: Latourette, in Ellmann, 206.

29. *Le Rhin*, ch. 15.

30. *CF*, II, 123.

31. Ibid., 135.

32. *Corr*, II, 290.

33. *VHR*, 506.

34. Birth certificate: *CF*, II, 35. The myth appeared to be confirmed by a letter dated 'morning of the 28th', announcing the birth of 'a big, healthy, chubby-cheeked girl'. In fact, this was Léopoldine. The correct date (28 August 1824) is given by J.-R. Dahan in Hugo–Nodier, 30 n. 1.

35. *Notre-Dame de Paris*, X, 5.

36. *Les Misérables*, IV, 10, 4.

37. *Choses Vues*, 6–7 June 1830.

38. *Les Misérables*, IV, 1, 2.

39. 'O Dieu! si vous avez la France sous vos ailes...', *Les Chants du*

Crépuscule, dated August 1832 in the book, 30 August 1835 on the manuscript.

40. *CF*, II, 723.

41. Ibid., II, 81.

42. Letter to Countess of Blessington, 27 January 1847: Dickens (1981), 15.

43. Challamel, 153.

44. *AP*, 706; R. Lesclide, 92–3.

45. Hugo may have noticed a review by Gustave Planche of Fanny Kemble's tragedy, *Francis the First* (with an important role for Triboulet): Kemble (1832). It appeared in the issue of the *Revue des Deux Mondes* which contained Fontaney's review of Hugo's novels. A month later, Hugo began work on his play.

46. Paul Foucher (1867), 322.

47. Pendell, 62.

48. 9 December 1832.

49. Letter to *Le Constitutionnel*, 26 November 1832: *Corr*, I, 516.

50. *Les Misérables*, IV, 1, 2.

51. 'À Ol', *Les Voix Intérieures* (26 May 1837 – perhaps the anniversary date). Juliette had acted in Dumas's *Térésa* and *Jeanne Vaubernier*. *Pace* Jean Savant, 'À Ol', with its orchestra and costumes, is not a description of a play-reading. The idea that Hugo first saw Juliette at a *'bal d'artistes'* comes, without evidence, from Louis Guimbaud.

52. *Les Misérables*, IV, 5, 4.

53. *Corr*, III, 47.

54. Sainte-Beuve (1973), 363.

55. Pradier, II, 108 n. 9 and Juliette to Hugo, 5 September 1870: Souchon (1943), 27; Poisson, 114–16.

56. e.g. MVH (1953), nos 496–500.

57. Pradier, I, 165 (10 November 1828).

58. Barthou (1919), 129–30.

59. *Faits et Croyances*, *OC*, XIV, 197.

60. *Une Heure Trop Tard* (1833). See correspondence of Karr and Juliette in Barthou (1919), 170–7, and Savant, IV.

61. Pradier, I, 291 and n. 1. (8 January 1833 and undated).

62. Bulwer, 290–303.

63. Du Camp, 440.

64. *La Revue Théâtrale, Journal Littéraire, non Romantique*, 5 May and 26 May 1833.

65. *CF*, II, 103.
66. *Le Figaro*, 29 October 1837: Gautier (1874), 379–81; also Massin, IV, 1159–60.
67. Drouet (1951), 13 and (1985), 3.
68. Hugo (1964), 113–14 (20 February 1849).
69. Ibid., 167 (26 February 1874).

10. OLYMPIO (1833–1839)

1. Balzac (1990), I, 35 (end March 1833) and 42 (1 June 1833).
2. Letter to Trébutien, 23 August 1833: Barbey d'Aurevilly, I, 27.
3. Bonnerot, I, 538.
4. e.g. Béranger to Sainte-Beuve: Daubray, 307 (23 September 1835) and 308 (7 December 1835).
5. Hugo, *Lettres à Juliette Drouet*, 1.
6. Pradier, I, 267 (11 July 1832).
7. Drouet (1985), 4.
8. 'Le Soleil', *Les Fleurs du Mal* (1857).
9. Drouet (1951), 26.
10. 13 August 1833: Drouet (1951), 19.
11. Pouchain and Sabourin, 128 and 437; also Charlier, 59–74.
12. Hugo, *Lettres à Juliette Drouet*, 14.
13. Boulay-Paty, in Séché (1912), 206–8; Barbier, 357–8.
14. Hugo, *Lettres à Juliette Drouet*, 3.
15. *Moi, l'Amour, la Femme*, *OC*, XIV, 339.
16. *Toute la Lyre*, III, 21 (1838–42?).
17. Sainte-Beuve (1973), 363.
18. Guimbaud, *Victor Hugo et Juliette Drouet*, 344–5 (December 1837).
19. Dubois and Boussel, 97.
20. Drouet (1951), 56.
21. Karr (1880), I, 77.
22. *CF*, II, 127.
23. Ibid., II, 537–8.
24. Simon, 236 (July 1840).
25. *Le Figaro*, 12 January 1897: Pouchain and Sabourin, 116–17.
26. *Moi, l'Amour, la Femme*, *OC*, XIV, 292.
27. *Corr*, II, 84–5.
28. Letter to Hugo, 31 May 1839: Massin, VI, 1257.

29. In *William Shakespeare* (II, 6, 2), Hugo claims to have used the expression when discussing Voltaire's tragedies 'thirty-five years ago' (i.e. in 1829).

30. Cf., in 1837, 'High drama is like the ocean wave: 'some people are exhilarated, others are sick': ms. of 'Écrit sur la Vitre d'une Fenêtre Flamande', *Les Rayons et les Ombres*: *OP*, I, 1553.

31. Letter to Hugo, 10 June 1841: Drouet (1951), 214.

32. Drouet (1951), 109 and 141.

33. 'Sagesse', part 5, *Les Rayons et les Ombres*.

34. *OP*, I, 1516–17 (fragment bound with ms. of *Les Voix Intérieures*). See 'À Ol', *Les Voix Intérieures*; 'Tristesse d'Olympio', *Les Rayons et les Ombres*; also 'À Olympio', *Les Voix Intérieures*; 'À Ol' (2 poems), *Toute la Lyre*, III and V. A nice example of Olympio's universality in Custine's reading of 'À Olympio' as a gay love poem (letter to Hugo, 27 August 1837): Luppé, 191.

35. Planche (1837), 177.

36. *OP*, I, 1516–17.

37. *Le Rhin*, Preface.

38. Letter to Paul Demeny, 15 May 1871: Rimbaud, 250.

39. T. Meredith, 316.

40. Another victim of anti-Hugo activity: *La Esmeralda* (1836), Louise Bertin's fourth opera, based on *Notre-Dame de Paris*, libretto by Hugo, directed by Berlioz. Hugo blamed its failure on the fact that his own suggestions were rejected – he wanted to show Quasimodo climbing Notre-Dame by having the scenery lowered – and on fate: the soprano later lost her voice, the tenor committed suicide, a ship called the *Esmeralda* sank, and the Duc d'Orléans had a mare of the same name which smashed its brains out in a steeplechase. See Berlioz, II, 318–19; Macdonald; *VHR*, 568–70; also 'La Bertinhugolâtre', *Le Charivari*, 30 November 1836: Pirot (1958), 255; and Arnaud Laster in *The New Grove Dictionary*. Fifty-six operas and three ballets based on Hugo's works were written in the nineteenth century. Three others were planned, including a *Han d'Islande* opera by Musorgsky.

41. 'Jeune homme, ce méchant fait une lâche guerre...', *Les Voix Intérieures*.

42. Hugo obtained expert information on sunspots from the astronomer, François Arago: Arago to Hugo, 17 April 1841 (Massin, VI, 1206–7).

43. Pendell, 82.

44. Hugo, *Lettres à Juliette Drouet*, 4.

45. Drouet (1951), 71.
46. Ibid., 75.
47. Letter to Hugo, 13 April 1843: '*Some kicks in the stomach* are more passionate and tender than certain kisses on the forehead': Drouet (1951), 261; her emphasis. The Juliette Drouet file at the Comédie Française contains a gossipy report suggesting that 'an indisposition which is fairly common in the theatre kept her off the stage for nine months' ... : Archives Nationales F21. 1085: Pouchain and Sabourin, 173.
48. The Bertins' home has been restored and is now known as the 'Maison Littéraire de Victor Hugo'.
49. Drouet (1951), 105.
50. Chenay, 162–4 (quoting Paul Chenavard).
51. *CF*, II, 178.
52. Ibid., II, 213.
53. *Les Misérables*, II, 3, 2 and 9.
54. *CF*, II, 515.
55. Trollope, I, 156 (London edition) 110 (Paris edition).
56. *CF*, II, 318.
57. Ibid., II, 302.
58. Ibid., II, 460.
59. Ibid., II, 307–9; also Adèle Hugo, III, 224–5.
60. R. Lesclide, 142–4.
61. Ibid., II, 279.
62. Ibid., II, 462.
63. Ibid., II, 225.
64. Ibid., II, 454.
65. 'La Statue' (19 March 1837), *Les Rayons et les Ombres*.
66. *CF*, II, 413; 414 and 421–3. On the literary effects of speed: Pichois (1973), 21.
67. *CF*, II, 421–3.
68. Nisard, III, 266.
69. Bremond, 228 (15 September 1837); Sainte-Beuve (1935–83), II, 262.
70. *CF*, II, 220.
71. Letter to Gautier, 17 April 1852: *Corr*, II, 91.
72. *CF*, II, 341.
73. Georgel (1967), 113.
74. Death certificate in Gourevitch, 772.
75. Nichol, 129. Cf. Léon-Paul Fargue, quoted by Escholier (1951), vi–vii:

Hugo 'authorized, as it were ... the Eiffel Tower, Dada and Surrealism'.

76. Drouet (1951), 91 (1836).
77. Drouet (1985), 41.
78. Ibid., 45 (12 December 1839).

11. 'Dark Doors Stand Open in the Invisible' (1839–1843)

1. *L'Homme Qui Rit*, I, 1, 5.
2. 'Saturne', *Les Contemplations*, III.
3. An idea developed in the *Revue des Mondes* in 1850: Thomas, 925–6.
4. R. Lesclide, 240; also *Choses Vues*, OC, XI, 684.
5. Also to celebrate the opening of the Musée Historique.
6. Hemmings, 40.
7. Vitu, 158.
8. *Ruy Blas*, II, 2; Ubersfeld (1971–2), 16 n. 29.
9. Drouet (1951), 244 (20 August 1842).
10. Drouet (1985), 50 and 54.
11. Letter to Hugo, 17 December 1841: Savant, I, 55.
12. Claudel, 514.
13. *VHR*, 655.
14. Liszt, II, 155 (13 June 1841).
15. Balzac (1990), I, 516 (3 July 1840).
16. *VHR*, 475; Challamel, 25.
17. *VHR*, 475; Smith, 63.
18. Petrus Borel, in *Les Français Peints par eux-mêmes*, II (1840); Champfleury (1845).
19. Tuffet, 418–19.
20. *France et Belgique*, OC, XIII, 555.
21. Heine, 54.
22. Unknown letter dated 15 February 1864 (no. 5, p. 33).
23. Du Camp, 144–5; see also Asseline (1885), 94.
24. See Nisard, III, 256–62.
25. Flaubert, I, 195 (3 December 1843).
26. *CF*, II, 312.
27. Adèle Hugo, II, 79–80.
28. Balzac (1976–81), I, 510 (*Modeste Mignon*); Gautier (1833), 104 (*Daniel Jovard*).

29. Karr (1880), I, 201.
30. Bertin. Also in *La Gazette des Femmes*, 14 August 1841, a syrupy story of Adèle and Victor's young love, and E. Woestyn, 'Contes pour les Grands Enfants et les Petits Hommes, Dédiés aux Enfants de Victor Hugo', *L'Âge d'Or. Journal de l'Enfance*, April and May 1842.
31. Goncourt, I, 934–5 (14 February 1863); R. Lesclide, 147–8; Pontmartin (1885), 133–4; Sainte-Beuve (1831).
32. *CF*, II, 354, 390, 488, 314, 363; Matthew 8:8.
33. Vacquerie (1872), 12.
34. *CF*, II, 345.
35. Ibid., II, 333.
36. Letter to Trébutien, 28 June 1855: Barbey d'Aurevilly, IV, 234.
37. Du Camp, 153.
38. Farcinet, 2 (unknown letter, 18 June 1851).
39. Houssaye, 143–5. On Hugo's archetypal vision: Péguy, III, 253–4.
40. Other visits: Andersen, 108–9 (1833), 185–6 (1843). Baudelaire: Prarond, 19; Robb (1993), 50–1. Dickens: Forster, 451–2. Flaubert, I, 195 (3 December 1843). Oehlenschläger, IV, 190–4 (1845).
41. Guérin, 228 (30 July 1838).
42. Jouin, 120 (letter to Victor Pavie, 3 February 1837).
43. *Tas de Pierres*, *OC*, XIV, 511.
44. *Moi, l'Amour, la Femme*, *OC*, XIV, 329.
45. Drouet (1951), 188 (27 March 1840).
46. Gautier (1985-), II, 154 and 185.
47. Drouet (1951), 249 (17 January 1843).
48. Letter to Gautier, 16 May 1845: 'For Mme Bouclier, you are a charming poet; for you, she will be a charming woman': *Corr*, I, 620–1; also *Océan Vers*, *OC*, VII, 961; Guillemin (1954), 29.
49. Massin, VI, 1105.
50. Drouet (1951), 211 (3 June 1841).
51. Magnin, 733–4. Magnin called this an exaggeration. Hugo was guilty only of using inelegant metaphors, odd word-combinations, inappropriate plurals, inaccurate images, repetitions, ambiguities and peculiar expressions.
52. Sainte-Beuve (1935–83), IV, 118 (17 July 1841).
53. *AP*, *OC*, X, 92.
54. Ibid., 104.
55. Henri Hignard, quoted by J. Bonnerot in Sainte-Beuve (1935–83), IV, 104 n. 1.

56. Magnin; also in *Réception de M. Victor Hugo*, 67.

57. *Le Rhin*, letter 28. Quotations below are from the definitive, augmented edition (Renouard, 1845).

58. Ibid., letter 36.

59. Ibid., letter 20.

60. e.g. the poem, '?' (*Les Contemplations*, III), in which the Earth is seen from space.

61. *Le Rhin*, 'Conclusion', 15; also preface to François-Victor's translation of Shakespeare, v; '[La Civilisation]', *OC*, XII, 608. Similar remark on French combining the 'hardness' of German and 'softness' of Italian, made to Robert Waldmüller in 1867 (Feller, 283–4): '"For who, apart from the English, can speak that senseless language?"'

62. *Le Rhin*, 'Conclusion', 15.

63. *Choses Vues*, *OC*, XI, 951 and 830. See also 1460–1, Hugo's letter to the Minister of War, 16 April 1847.

64. *Choses Vues* – almost certainly not Hugo's title – first appeared as the title of a posthumous selection of fragments (1887); it has since been applied to several different compendia covering the years 1845–50. See Rosa.

65. *Faits et Croyances*, *OC*, XIV, 143.

66. *Choses Vues*, *OC*, XI, 827–9.

67. Massin, VI, 1315.

68. Barrère (1952), 108. *Les Burgraves* was not translated into English until 1862, and then only as an adaptation: *The Robber Lords of the Rhine*, by Edwin F. Roberts (London: Lea's Sixpenny Library, 1862). The Taylor Institution has an unknown (probably pirated) English edition: *Les Burgraves. Trilogie* (London: *Courrier de l'Europe*'s Office, 1843).

69. *Les Burgraves*, I, 6.

70. Claretie (1904), 84.

71. Sartre, I, 841 (Hugo was 'God's favourite interviewer').

72. 'Pierre Dupont' (1861): Baudelaire (1975–6), II, 169: 'The Just' refers to Aristides; the idol to La Fontaine's fable, 'Les Grenouilles qui Demandent un Roi'.

73. *Faits et Croyances*, *OC*, XIV, 151. See also Woestyn, quoting Hugo: 'The Odéon no longer exists. It is a provincial theatre in the centre of Paris.'

74. Léopoldine Hugo, 297 (to Julie Foucher, April–May 1842?).

75. The section beginning 'Sois pure sous les cieux!' was published as 'À une Jeune Fille' in the *Journal du Dimanche*, 3 January 1847, p. 26.

76. *Les Misérables*, V, 1, 10.
77. Simone-André Maurois, 'Les Malheurs de Julie', *Revue de Paris*, September–October 1957 (not mentioned in her husband's biography of Hugo). On Julie Chenay: Mercié.
78. *Corr*, I, 595 (16 March 1843).
79. Léopoldine Hugo, 403 (27 April 1843).
80. *OC*, XIII, 752.
81. Ibid., XIII, 779–80. See Burroughs, 43 (writing in 1814): 'The people entertain an idea that the noise made by the wheels of the car, stimulates the oxen to exertion, for which reason, they never grease them.'
82. Monpou's version differs from the original. It was the subject of an opera by Louis Maillart (Paris Opera, November 1847). *Gastibelza* is best known today in the version by Georges Brassens.
83. '*Estrangero*' for '*extranjero*'.
84. *OC*, XIII, 775. Pasajes: the house where Hugo stayed is now a Victor Hugo Museum and Basque cultural centre.
85. Ibid., XIII, 855; also *Corr*, I, 610: letter 'to Toto', 25 August 1843.
86. *OC*, XIII, 856–7.
87. Carrington, 22, quoting Abbé Cochet.
88. *OC*, XIII, 864–6; also Leroux (1979) 454, and Leroux's journal, *L'Espérance, Revue Philosophique, Politique, Littéraire* (Jersey), April 1859.
89. *OC*, XIII, 986; Delteil.
90. *OC*, XIII, 872.

12. CRIMINAL CONVERSATION (1843–1848)

1. 18 December 1843: Balzac (1990), I, 755.
2. Levaillant, 51.
3. '*Umbra*', *Toute la Lyre*, III.
4. Letter to Paul Foucher, 16 September 1843: *Corr*, I, 613. Also: Roger de Beauvoir, 'À Victor Hugo', *La Chronique. Revue Universelle*, 1843, p. 200; Henri Couturier, *Satires et Poésies* (G.-A. Dentu, 1846); Pierre Dupont, 'Sur le Terrible Événement du Havre' (MVH (1953), no. 486).
5. David d'Angers, II, 172–3; Jouin, 224–5.
6. *Corr*, I, 614–15.

7. 'L'enfant, voyant l'aïeule...' and 'Le poète s'en va dans les champs...', *Les Contemplations*, III and I.

8. The pattern is reproduced in the fictitious dates of *Les Contemplations*, except that September, the anniversary of the drowning, is promoted to second place.

9. Drouet (1951), 270 and 273.

10. 3 October 1843: *Corr*, I, 615.

11. *OC*, XIII, 889.

12. *Corr*, I, 601 and 615.

13. 9 April 1843: Balzac (1990), I, 666. See also Janin, I, 394.

14. Letter to Countess of Blessington, 27 January 1847: Dickens (1981), 15.

15. Adèle Hugo, III, 36 and 60–2.

16. Vacquerie (1872), V, 7. Earliest allusion in a letter from Jules Janin to his wife, 28 July 1848: Janin, I, 394.

17. On Mme Biard: Guimbaud, *Victor Hugo et Madame Biard*; Hugo (1990); Mercer; Savant, II and III; Souchon (1941). W. Mercer has also edited Léonie Biard's *Voyage d'une Femme au Spitzberg* and her play, *Jane Osborn*. A drawing given to Léonie (MVH (1985), no. 928) shows a 'V' at the feet of an 'L', with an 'H' under an 'A-'shaped easel supporting a landscape. The unsolved rebus can be construed thus: 'L I A V *couché*' ('V' lying down): '*Elle y avait couché*' ('This is where she slept').

18. Baudelaire (1975–6), II, 479.

19. Savant, II, 17.

20. Flaubert to Louise Colet: Flaubert, II, 330 (21 May 1853).

21. Hugo (1990), no. 76 (date unknown). On transcriptions: Guillemin (1954), 55–56 and 60.

22. Drouet (1951), 310.

23. Ibid., 115.

24. Massin, VII, 781.

25. *Les Misérables*, IV, 8, 1.

26. 17 December 1841 and 30 July 1842: Savant, I, 54–5.

27. Savant, I, 62.

28. 26 July 1842: Savant, I, 60.

29. Reconstituted by Jean Gaudon: Gaudon (1969), 460–2.

30. Verlaine, 107.

31. *Toute la Lyre*, VI, 19.

32. Hugo (1990), no. 100.

33. Mabilleau, 104–5.
34. *Faits et Croyances*, *OC*, XIV, 158.
35. 'Le Poëte', *Les Contemplations*, III. See also 'Fonction du Poète', part 2, *Les Rayons et les Ombres*; 'Les Mages', part 5, *Les Contemplations*, VI.
36. 'Lueur au Couchant', *Les Contemplations*, V.
37. Mérimée, IV, 254.
38. Sainte-Beuve, in *Les Grands Écrivains Français*, ed. M. Allem, 289.
39. Saint-Marc Girardin (advising his students never to become writers), 164–80.
40. Allusions to the past in Hugo's speech: 'In order to reach the suffering, your thoughts wear a veil . . . In order to be one of them, you wrap yourself in their cloak. Hence a penetrating yet timid form of poetry.' Sainte-Beuve had described his affair in a *roman à clé* published in the *Revue des Deux Mondes*: Sainte-Beuve (1837).
41. *Les Misérables*, IV, 1, 3.
42. *Choses Vues*, 896.
43. Karr (1853), II, 138–40.
44. See Robb (1985).
45. Anon., 20 July 1845; also 13 July 1845, and *Le Corsaire-Satan*, 5 July 1845 (commented on by Weill (1890), 23). Echoes in Chopin, 14 (20 July 1845); Gautier (1985–), II, 261 (8 July 1845); Lamartine (1873–5), VI, 170 (9 July 1845). On Hugo's confession: Chenay, 129–30; Mérimée, IV, 321–2 (1 August 1845). Alfred Asseline consulted the police file on his Uncle Victor in February 1848: Asseline (1885), 126–9.
46. Balzac's *La Cousine Bette* (1846) shows how much was known. Baron Hector Hulot, husband of Adeline Fischer (cf. Adèle Foucher), is arrested in bed with a courtesan in a street adjoining the Passage Saint-Roch. Balzac's Hulot ends his life chasing cooks and chambermaids: Balzac (1976–81), VII, 303–10; Lorant, I, 120–8. Mallarmé believed that he was born in the house where Hugo was arrested (12 Rue Laferrière was a later address of Léonie Biard): Mallarmé (1959–85), VI, 273 n. 2.
47. Gayot, 260–1 (18 July 1846).
48. Hugo had announced a sequel to *Notre-Dame de Paris*: *Le Fils de la Bossue* or *La Quiquengrogne*. The title had since been borrowed, with Hugo's permission, by Émile Chevalet (unknown letter, 4 March 1845: Chevalet).
49. *OC*, XIII, 948.

50. *Moi, l'Amour, la Femme, OC*, XIV, 286 (1868).
51. Anon. (27 July 1845). Bernay's name is associated with two anti-Hugo titles, *Le Roi S'Ennuie* (a play) and *Égoïste et Myope* (poetry; both unpublished): Larousse.
52. There were rumours that Hugo was planning a new volume of verse: *Revue Suisse*, September 1846, p. 703: based on notes sent by Sainte-Beuve. J. Gaudon (1995) points out that large parts of the future *Misérables* also belong to this lyrical 'explosion'.
53. *Les Contemplations*, IV, 14 and 15, redated 3 and 4 September 1847.
54. e.g. Hugo (1964), 104 (10 December 1846).
55. To be absolutely precise: nineteen syllables a day. This excludes a few poems stolen from the Place Royale in 1848 and some versified Bible passages dating from 1846.
56. *Les Misérables*, I, 1, 5; *Moi Vers, OC*, VII, 1000.
57. Adèle Hugo, II, 191.
58. Texier, ch. 12, 'Le Poète de Salon': in the album of a certain Guillot, full of Guillot's own verse: 'Il aurait volontiers écrit sur son *chapum* : / C'est moi qui suis Guillot, berger de cet album. / Victor Hugum.' Cf. Karr (1880), III, 67–8.
59. *Le Courrier de Paris*, 1 October 1844, p. 166: 'Mon illusion se dissipe, / Car je vois que vous me trompiez; / Vous devriez être tulipe, / Ayant des oignons à vos pieds.' Hence the allusion in *Océan Vers, OC*, VII, 967 (and 1166 n. 44); also *Choses Vues, OC*, XI, 617 and 621–2.
60. R. Lesclide, 245–6; seen on the Boulevard des Italiens by the painter Hector Giacomelli (b. 1822): Blémont, 66–7.
61. *Corr*, I, 625.
62. Drouet (1985), 78–9; *Choses Vues, OC*, XI, 933–4.
63. Drouet (1951), 343.
64. Hugo, *Journal*, 66 and 98 (20 May and 21 December 1847), and notes by R. Journet and G. Robert, 220, 226–7 and 242.
65. Hugo, *Journal*, 73, 143 and 218.
66. Ibid., 104, 107 and 163.
67. Ibid. 68 and 142.
68. *Choses Vues, OC*, XI, 1456 n. 7.
69. *Moi, l'Amour, la Femme, OC*, XIV, 352–4; *Choses Vues*, 1187–90; Drouet (1951), 347 (20 September 1847); Judith, 123–6, and Bassanville, IV, 276. Generally: Massin, VII, 785–9 and Hugo, *Journal*, 149–53.
70. See also *Esca*, II, 2: *Les Quatre Vents de l'Esprit*, II (*OC*, VI, 1266).
71. Escholier (1953), 293.

72. *Tas de Pierres*, OC, XIV, 492.

73. *Choses Vues*, OC, XI, 928.

74. Reported by Philippe Burty: Goncourt, II, 505 (26 March 1872).

75. *L'Homme Qui Rit*, II, VIII, 7.

76. Ibid., II, VIII, 7.

77. In *AP*, Hugo truthfully (but misleadingly) calls 'Question Polonaise' his 'first political speech'. 'Propriété des Oeuvres d'Art' (his first intervention) is relegated to the 'Notes' and dated simply '1846'.

78. *Choses Vues*, OC, XI, 970.

79. Hugo on February 1848: *Choses Vues*, 1006–15; *Toute la Lyre*, III, 26.

80. *Choses Vues*, OC, XI, 1010.

81. Ibid., 1015.

82. 'Réplique à M. de Montalembert', *AP*, OC, X, 253; Auguste Barbier, quoting the painter Paul Huet: Barbier, 160–1.

83. La Morvonnais, 74, 95–6, 98 and 100. See also Delaage (1850), 121, Richard, 229–31, and Nadaud, in which a trowel-wielding Hugo builds poems like a bricklayer. On Hugo as an involuntary socialist: Viatte.

84. *Choses Vues*, OC, XI, 1031 (6 April 1848).

85. On the writers' meeting at the Assemblée Nationale: Anon. (1848) and Blewer (1996). Hugo so eloquently refused to stand that many people voted for him.

86. *Choses Vues*, OC, XI, 1048.

87. Ibid., 1049.

88. Ibid., 1048.

89. On June Days: *Corr*, I, 638–41; *Les Misérables*, V, 1, 1; *Histoire d'un Crime*, I, 17; *Choses Vues*, 1052–9; 1290; *AP*, OC, X, 352–6; and texts quoted by Leuilliot (1985) – the best summary, with E. Grant's.

90. Confirmed by Paul de Molènes: Molènes, 193.

91. *Choses Vues*, 1055.

92. Ibid., 1053.

93. Ibid., 1056.

94. Ibid., 1059.

95. Ibid., 1058.

PART THREE

13. MOUNT SINAI AND A PILE OF RUBBISH (1848–1851)

1. Seure.
2. *Les Misérables*, V, 1, 1.
3. Antoine Galy-Cazalat, *Gazette des Tribunaux*, 29 July 1848: Leuilliot (1985), 128–9. Also François-Victor Hugo (1867), 1336: Hugo 'ordered the cannon to fire at the white flag hoisted on a barricade in the Rue Boucherat'. Drawings by Mérimée show Hugo and François-Victor attacking a barricade: 'The citizen representative fires the cannon, which makes a great impression on Toto' (MVH (1953), no. 1105).
4. Cahagne de Cey: Massin, VII, 750. See also *L'Émancipation*, 2 July 1848 and *Le Moniteur Universel*, 11 July 1848: E. Grant, 11.
5. Adèle Hugo, 27 June 1855: Leuilliot (1985), 130.
6. *Les Misérables*, V, 1, 18.
7. *Histoire d'un Crime*, I, 17; also III, 13.
8. *Gazette des Tribunaux*, 19 September 1848: Leuilliot (1985), 132.
9. See letter from E. Daubterre: MVH (1956), no. 240.
10. *AP, OC*, X, 703–6; Hugo to Karr, 3 July 1848: Karr (1853), IV, 409; François-Victor Hugo (1867), 1336.
11. *Corr*, II, 1.
12. Exodus 33:23.
13. *Corr*, IV, 207; *Choses Vues, OC*, XI, 1098–9.
14. MVH (1985), no. 804. Description in Charles Hugo (1859), 30–2. On Hugo's drawings see pp. 390–4.
15. 'Vénus rit toute nue . . .', *Toute la Lyre*, V: quoted from Hetzel edition (V, 8).
16. See an unknown letter to Eugénie Foa, 11 August 1851 in *Les Muses de la Mode, Journal en Vers et en Prose*, 1 September 1851, p. 7: 'C'est moi qui suis l'aveugle et c'est vous qui êtes la voyante. / Je me trompe, je ne suis pas aveugle, car je vois clairement les ténèbres où l'on voudrait replonger notre radieux pays. Je lutte contre ces ténèbres.' Other letters in the same vein, also unknown: to Bénédict Gallet, 8 January 1849 (*Le*

Voleur Littéraire et Artistique, 25 January 1849, p. 79); to Charles Farcinet, 18 June 1851 (Farcinet, 2); to Nicolas Martin, 1847 (Martin, viii).

17. The word was not adopted until 1969.
18. Hugo, *Lettres à Juliette Drouet*, 111 (22 September 1848).
19. *Choses Vues*, *OC*, XI, 1091 (September 1848).
20. *Philosophie Prose*, *OC*, XIV, 105.
21. See below, p. 320.
22. *Corr*, II, 15 and 19; IV, 210–11.
23. *Choses Vues*, *OC*, XI, 1222; *Châtiments*, III, 1.
24. *Napoléon-le-Petit*, I, 6.
25. Philipps, 31.
26. *Napoléon-le-Petit*, II, 8.
27. Editor of *The Brooklyn Advertiser* in Schoelcher, 136–7.
28. *Histoire d'un Crime*, I, 1; also *Choses Vues*, *OC*, XI, 1171.
29. *AP*, *OC*, X, 388.
30. Ibid., 155.
31. *Corr*, IV, 212.
32. Wallon, 103.
33. Guénot, 16 November 1850.
34. Inscribed, '*Hommage de Haute Estime et de profonde Considération*': Adèle Hugo, II, 377.
35. Maurois, 355.
36. *OC*, XI, 1480 n. 32 (note by C. Trévisan).
37. *AP*, *OC*, X, 204.
38. Ibid., 196, 189 and 200.
39. 'La Misère', 9 July 1849: *AP*, 204–5.
40. e.g. Delaage (1851), 83. (*Bibliographie de la France*: 16 November 1850.)
41. See E. Grant, 37.
42. *AP*, *OC*, X, 77.
43. Ibid., 209.
44. Verlaine, 728.
45. Granier de Cassagnac, 76–7.
46. *William Shakespeare*, II, 1, 4.
47. *Moi, l'Amour, la Femme*, *OC*, XIV, 286.
48. *Choses Vues*, *OC*, XI, 1210–11.
49. Karr (1853), I, 384–5; (1880), I, 97–8.
50. Champfleury (1855), 83–4; *Choses Vues*, *OC*, XI, 616 and 622–3.

51. Guénot, 21 July 1850. On Hugo's salon in 1850: Berlioz, III, 704 (3 April 1850).
52. *Choses Vues*, OC, XI, 1237.
53. *Corr*, II, 20.
54. *Moi, l'Amour, la Femme*, OC, XIV, 311; *Corr*, II, 5.
55. Letter to Armand Fraisse, 18 February 1860: Baudelaire (1973), I, 675.
56. Adèle Hugo, II, 56.
57. Castille, 9 and 19–21.
58. *Choses Vues*, OC, XI, 1225; Apponyi, 162–3 and 202.
59. Letter from Mulot, '*ex-garde républicain*', Préfecture de Police, 28 May 1850: MVH (1956), no. 319.
60. Marx contrasts Hugo's 'bitter and witty invective' in *Napoléon-le-Petit* with his own analysis: '[Hugo] sees in [the *coup d'état*] only the violent act of a single individual. He does not notice that he makes this individual great instead of little by ascribing to him a personal power of initiative such as would be without parallel in world history' (Marx and Engels, 295).
61. The word '*Mouvement*' ('stir'), inserted here in *Actes et Paroles*, does not appear in the official transcript.
62. 'Écrit le 17 Juillet, en Descendant de la Tribune', *Châtiments*, IV and Note I.
63. Viel-Castel, I, 80–1 (18 July 1851).
64. 'Révision de la Constitution', 17 July 51: *AP*, OC, X, 270–98.
65. Planned preface for a collection of *Quinze Discours*. Other pre-*coup d'état* speeches were published as *Douze Discours*, *Treize Discours* and *Quatorze Discours* (Librairie Nouvelle, 1851).
66. *AP*, OC, X, 275.
67. Ibid., 290.
68. 'Après la Bataille', *La Légende des Siècles*, I, XIII.
69. Janin, II, 58 (13 June 1851); also Ménière, 9 (13 June 1851).
70. Proudhon, IV, 294 (1 August 1851).
71. Ibid., 343–4 (5 September 1851). See also Léon Faucher to the Garde des Sceaux, Rouher, 3 October 1851: MVH (1956), no. 343. The 'actresses' were probably Alice Ozy and Esther Guimont. For Proudhon's annotated copy of Hugo's plays: Pirot (1959), 188–9.
72. Auguste Nefftzer, quoted by Goncourt, II, 336 (9 November 1870).
73. St John, II, 301.
74. Drouet (1951), 391–409.

75. Ibid., 433 (18 July 1852).
76. St John, II, 305.
77. *Histoire d'un Crime*, I, 3.

14. POETIC INJUSTICE (1851–1852)

1. Account from *Histoire d'un Crime*; *Napoléon-le-Petit*; Angrand, 65–6.
2. Mayer, 122.
3. *Histoire d'un Crime*, II, 2.
4. Magen, 74–5.
5. 'Burgraves' was later applied to Brezhnev and Tito by Antoine Vitez (production of *Les Burgraves*, Paris, 1977): Baron.
6. St John, II, 308.
7. *Histoire d'un Crime*, II, 2. It is hard to tell which 'apologia' Hugo had in mind. Most of the early accounts published in Britain were opposed to the *coup d'état*. There is only one minor reference to Hugo in *Letters Published in the 'Sun', by C. W. S., Justifying the Coup d'État of the Second of December* 'by one who is really "an Englishman"' (London: Pelham Richardson, 1853). Pascoe Grenfell Hill's *Life of Napoleon III* (London: Edward Moxon, 1869) makes a similar comment about 'members of the late Assembly' inciting 'the lowest class of the populace' to insurrection on 4 December (92–3). Some reviewers of *Napoléon-le-Petit* suggested that Hugo and his cronies caused the *coup d'état* by waving the red flag (Hooker, 103), but the comment so closely resembles remarks made by the Police Chief, Maupas, that the likely source is French propaganda.
8. Baudin is also mentioned in a letter (not in *Corr*) dated 18 September 1853: Strugnell, 803–4.
9. Granier de Cassagnac, 77–8 and 253.
10. Adèle Hugo, I, 189 and III, 297; *Histoire d'un Crime*, 'Cahier Complémentaire', II (letters from Adèle).
11. Capt. William Jesse, *The Times*, 13 December 1851; Schoelcher (1854), 104.
12. Magen, 97–8; Schoelcher (1854), 104; also Senior, 226, 279 and 284.
13. St John, II, 325–6.
14. *Histoire d'un Crime*, IV, 2.
15. Wauwermans, 11.
16. Maupas (1884–5) and (1884), I, 488–97.

17. 27 September 1878: Granier de Cassagnac, 261.
18. *VHR*, 580–1; *Choses Vues*, *OC*, XI, 840. See also 794: Hugo nearly lynched for carrying the works of Saint-Simon (the memorialist, mistaken for the social reformer).
19. Escamps (2 editions), 75: the Empire 'is the will of the people and of God'. See *Corr*, II, 32–3, 69, 251–2. On 16 January 1850, d'Escamps, originally republican, congratulated Hugo on his education speech (MVH (1956), no. 305). H was made Inspecteur des Beaux-Arts in 1862.
20. Drouet (1851), 1134.
21. Passport dated 8 December 1851: MVH (1956), no. 362.
22. Drouet (1851), 1133.
23. *Mes Fils*, i.
24. 300,000 francs in 1845 (approximately £900,000 today): *Corr*, I, 625; Massin, VII, 734. For a song on Hugo's stinginess: Alexandre Pothey, 'La Golgothe': Lemercier de Neuville, 148–9.
25. *Choses Vues*, *OC*, XI, 1253.
26. Wauwermans, 9–10.
27. Charles Hugo (1875), 104–16; Wauwermans, 122–3.
28. *La Fin de Satan*, *OC*, VII, 129.
29. *Histoire d'un Crime*, IV, 5. Cf. J. Bruhat's defensive note in Massin, VIII, 7. But the fact that Hugo had political reasons for publishing *Histoire d'un Crime* in 1877 (see p. 503) does not explain why he shelved it in 1852. Publishers' conditions may also have played a role.
30. Browning, II, 90: to John Kenyon, Paris, November 1852. Her letter reflects opinion in France.
31. Victoria, II, 391.
32. See for example the otherwise excellent study by K. W. Hooker: *The Fortunes of Victor Hugo in England* [*sic* for Britain] (1938): Hooker is suspicious of any anti-government activity, whatever the government. The result is an impressive mass of material with tendentious omissions and misleading juxtapositions. It should be complemented by Victor Bowley's thesis, which has more generous quotations but a narrower sweep.
33. *Corr*, II, 55 and n.
34. Ibid., II, 56.
35. Ibid., II, 67.
36. Charles Hugo (1859), 26.
37. Nerval, II, 1302.

38. *Mes Fils*, iii.
39. *Corr*, II, 70.
40. Charles Hugo (1859), 23.
41. Simon, 288 and 294–5; Clément-Janin, 45–53; Gautier, *La Presse*, 7 June 1852: Massin, VIII, 1142–4.
42. J. Vizetelly to Hugo, 11 September 1852: Hugo (1979), 150. James was the brother of Henry Vizetelly, who first exposed the British to the novels of Zola.
43. *Corr*, II, 118.
44. Ibid., II, 119.
45. Hugo's draft, dated 31 July 1852, in Massin, VIII, 1024. The letter was obviously published or otherwise broadcast, since Bassano quotes a passage from it in his report to Drouyn de Lhuys on 2 August 1852 (Angrand, 31).
46. Angrand, 31.

15. STRANGE HORIZON (1852–1855)

1. PRO: HO 3 66 (2 August 1852).
2. Quoted by Barrère (1965), 88–90.
3. Pelletan, 228; also *Corr*, II, 122 and *Moi, l'Amour, la Femme*, *OC*, XIV, 273.
4. On Hugo and London: Barrère (1965), 88–90; S. Gaudon, 'Anglophobie?', in James (1986). Also *William Shakespeare*, I, I, 3, 3; '[Les Traducteurs]', *OC*, XII, 636–7; Adèle Hugo, I, 240–1; *Les Travailleurs de la Mer*, II, 2, 4; *VHR*, 114.
5. 1864 Carnet, quoted by S. Gaudon in James (1986), 55.
6. *Châtiments* (Suite), *OC*, XV, 204–5.
7. Adèle Hugo, I, 241–2.
8. Vacquerie (1863), 448.
9. Angrand, 42 and n.
10. Émile Laurent to Drouyn de Lhuys, 10 August 1852: Angrand, 50.
11. *AP*, *OC*, X, 424.
12. *William Shakespeare*, I, 1, 1; Adèle Hugo, I, 262–3; *Moi, l'Amour, la Femme*, *OC*, XIV, 306.
13. Angrand, 129–31.
14. *Corr*, II, 127.

15. Advertisement in Mercié, 173 n. 17. Perry, 114–15. Messrs Perry had an agent on Jersey: Chadwick Le Lièvre.
16. Smuggling details: Angrand, 55, 63, 70, 86, 94–5, 102–3, 108–10, 153; Barbou (1886), 269; Griffiths, 573 (19 December 1853); Adèle Hugo, I, 314, 328; II, 450; Charles Hugo (1875), ch. 14; Karr (1880), III, 161; Martin-Dupont, 39–40; *Corr*, II, 129 and 180.
17. Hugo–Hetzel, 38–9, 92–3, 190 and 519.
18. Adèle Hugo, II, 104 and 491.
19. Hugo–Hetzel, 150.
20. Massin, VIII, 1118.
21. According to Biré, the published texts are not the speeches that were actually delivered but bastardized versions designed to mislead. This slur has been widely accepted, even by Hugophiles. However:

    a) Hugo's main criterion was aesthetic rather than ideological. Many insulting interruptions are omitted, but the idea was to preserve the rhythm and integrity of the speech, to prevent the yahoos from robbing posterity of his oratorical gems.

    b) It was common practice for orators to improve their speeches before publication. Biré does not mention the fact that one of his mentors, Hugo's enemy, Bishop (and *député*) Dupanloup, was notorious in typesetting circles for returning the proofs of his speeches with as many corrections as a Balzac manuscript (Bosq, 87–8).

    c) Some passages apparently added by Hugo may have been taken from his own record of proceedings. Not everything was preserved in *Le Moniteur* (e.g. the passage quoted on p. 287). There is some support for this view in the fact that many of the passages apparently added by Hugo are of no obvious advantage to himself.

    Examples of alterations, accelerating Hugo's drift to the Left or creating dramatic effect:

    Omitted: 'Terrorism' (applied to the June insurgents).

    Added: 'As a socialist myself'.

    'The delusions of socialism' changed to 'The delusions of a certain form of socialism'.

    Added: 'An expectant tremor in the Assembly'.

    The President asks for silence because 'M. Victor Hugo is hoarse': changed to 'Total silence falls over the Assembly.'

    (Quotations from *Compte Rendu des Séances de l'Assemblée Nationale Législative*. For a stylistic analysis: Fizaine.)

22. James, ed. (1985).

23. Angrand, 63.

24. Hugo–Hetzel, 496 (contract).

25. Flaubert to Louise Colet, 1 June 1853: Flaubert, II, 336–7.

26. Chernov, 140.

27. Anon. (1854), 6; O'Brien, 4–5.

28. O'Brien, 4.

29. PRO: HO 45 4302 (19 January 1852).

30. *Paris*, V.

31. Massin, X, 1523.

32. Barbou (1886), 260.

33. *Les Misérables*, I, 3, 1.

34. *L'Homme Qui Rit*, II, III, 1. On English as 'brute jargon': François-Victor Hugo, *Les Sonnets de Shakespeare*, 22.

35. Stapfer (1905), 190–1.

36. Adèle to Léonie, 23 September 1852.

37. *Moi, l'Amour, la Femme*, OC, XIV, 304.

38. Hugo–Hetzel (18 November 1852), 173.

39. Ibid., (6 February 1853), 232.

40. *Choses Vues*, OC, XI, 1259.

41. *Châtiments* (Brussels: Henri Samuel, 1853), 16mo (expurgated); *Châtiments* (Geneva and New York: Imprimerie Universelle, St Helier, 1853), 32mo (unexpurgated). The definite article appeared with the 1870 edition: *Les Châtiments, seule édition complète, revue par l'auteur, augmentée de plusieurs pièces nouvelles* (Hetzel, s.d.).

42. Hugo–Hetzel, 214 and 220.

43. St John, I, 6. *Re* the ban on flower-pots, cf. Baudelaire's 'Le Mauvais Vitrier'.

44. Cf. Charles Péguy's suggestion for an all-purpose footnote: 'Whenever one finds an unfamiliar name in *Les Châtiments* (and sometimes in all his other works), it is the name of a murderer' (Péguy, III, 1106).

45. Zola (1966–70), part i.

46. Flaubert, II, 382–3; 386, and Jean Bruneau's note.

47. *Châtiments* might be counted as the first major work of Anglo-French poetry since Robert Wace. (Hugo considered himself a successor of 'the first French poet', born on Jersey in the early twelfth century: François-Victor Hugo, *La Normandie Inconnue*, 92.) For the combination of pantomime and Gallic chauvinism, see a 'translation' of *The Poetic Works of Louis Napoleon*, published in London the year before,

and, for the similarly metaphysical bent of British socialism, the identification of Napoleon III as the Beast of the Apocalypse in Anon. (1863); also Macrae, 96. Hugo claimed that British papers quoted the poems in French because they were obscene (*Corr*, II, 176). Cf. *The Beacon*: 'We will not spoil the following ['Le Chant de ceux qui s'en vont sur Mer', *Châtiments*, V, 9] by any attempt at translation': Anon. (1853).

48. Adèle Hugo, III, 509.
49. Drouet (1951), 446 (12 May 1853).
50. *L'Archipel de la Manche*, i; and preface by French *attaché culturel* in Hugo, *L'Archipel de la Manche. The Channel Islands*. The last people to cross from France on foot did so *c.* 6500 BC.
51. *L'Archipel de la Manche*, i; and Vacquerie (1856), 292–3.
52. Adèle Hugo, III, 439.
53. *Corr*, II, 238: written as a preface for Franz Stevens's *Poésies Nationales* (1856).
54. *Moi, l'Amour, la Femme*, OC, XIV, 273.
55. The fullest edition of the séance texts is J. and S. Gaudon's in Massin, IX, 1167–489. See also Simon (1923) and J. Gaudon (1963).
56. Text dated 29 September 1854; approximately 66,000 taps in 195 minutes. A similar calculation in De Mutigny, 86.
57. On Charles's fear of becoming 'the Dumas *fils* of Victor Hugo': letter to Hetzel, 30 October 1855 (Parménie, 251).
58. See Benjamin, 64.
59. e.g. Adèle Hugo, II, 279 and 283.
60. Ibid., III, 109.
61. Ibid., II, 283.
62. Quoted in this context by J. and S. Gaudon in Massin, IX.
63. Cf. Adèle's diary: 'I wish', says Hugo, 'that you would abandon the piano and take up the organ, which is a serious instrument' (Adèle Hugo, III, 425–6).
64. J. Gaudon (1969), 559 n. 25 (on 'Pleurs dans la Nuit').
65. Paraphrenia: De Mutigny, 83.
66. *The Times Literary Supplement*, 22 April 1965, p. 308.
67. Adèle Hugo, II, 268.
68. 'Christianity,' says Jesus, 'like all human things, is both an advance and an ill, a door of light with a lock of darkness.' 'God is not at home.'
69. Adèle Hugo, III, 108.
70. Hugo to Delphine de Girardin, 4 January 1855: *Corr*, II, 205.

71. *Les Misérables*, I, IV, 2.
72. Martin-Dupont, 75.
73. Adèle Hugo, III, 417.
74. Vacquerie (1863), 412.
75. Adèle Hugo, III, 155–6; Massin, IX, 1337–9.

16. '*HU!* GO!' (1855–1861)

1. *Moi, l'Amour, la Femme, OC*, XIV, 269–70.
2. PRO: HO 45 5194/A (misdated February 1852). Love sent Palmerston copies of all Hugo's pronouncements: HO 45 5180 (e.g. 4 October 1854).
3. Letter to Governor General Love, 2 November 1855: PRO: HO 45 / 6188.
4. PRO: HO 45 / 6188 [1855].
5. *AP, OC*, X, 461.
6. Hansard's, CXXXVI, 128 (12 December 1854) – usually quoted from Hooker (p. 593 n.32, above), who omits part of the speech so as to suggest that Hugo was a mere afterthought. Peel devoted equal amounts of invective to Hugo and Kossuth.
7. Adèle Hugo, III, 520–1 (14 December 1854).
8. Day, 158.
9. PRO: HO 45 / 6188.
10. *Moi, l'Amour, la Femme, OC*, XIV, 272 (11 June 1855).
11. *Corr*, II, 210 (25 June 1855).
12. Carneiro Leão, 70–4 and illustration facing p. 81.
13. Unpublished letter in PRO: HO 45 / 6188 (14 August 1855). Hugo met Palmerston at a dinner in 1846 and talked about the famine in Ireland: *Choses Vues, OC*, XI, 883.
14. PRO: HO 45 / 6188.
15. Unpublished letter to Sir George Grey, the new Home Secretary: PRO: HO 45 / 6188 (23 October 1855).
16. This was also the view of George Julian Harney, convincingly argued in his reply to W. E. Henley's obituary in *The Athenaeum*, 30 May 1885, pp. 695–8: Harney.
17. PRO: HO 45 / 6188.
18. Angrand, 163 n. 1.

19. PRO: HO 45 / 6188 (30 October 1855).

20. Hooker, 119–23.

21. PRO: HO 45 / 6188 (3 November 1855).

22. Pelleport, 46. Governor Love sent a protest pamphlet to Home Secretary Grey – *Vérité ou Mensonge. Loi ou Violence* (Jersey, December 1855) – by George Vickery, 'a young lawyer, a great friend of Victor Hugo': PRO: HO 45 6333. See also François-Victor Hugo, *La Normandie Inconnue*, 3–19.

23. *Moi, l'Amour, la Femme*, *OC*, XIV, 311.

24. See *La Gazette de Guernesey* on 'the folly of our Jersey brothers': Hooker, 134.

25. *Corr*, II, 225.

26. Martin Tupper, who published faster than he could think, claims that Hugo 'greatly offended my cousin (the chief of our clan) by stealing for his hired abode [*sic*] the title of our ancestral mansion, Haute Ville House [*sic*]' – a remark perhaps related to Hugo's refusal to see Tupper when he called. In his *History of Guernsey*, the cousin has nothing but praise for Hugo. Hugo also enjoyed excellent relations with the consular official, Henry Tupper: M. Tupper, 186; F. Tupper, 481; Delalande, 57 n. 1.

27. Vacquerie (1856), 309.

28. *Dieu* (Fragments), *OC*, XV, 486.

29. *Corr*, II, 540 (2 April 1866).

30. Ibid., II, 319.

31. Bergerat, II, 74.

32. *Corr*, II, 404; cf. *William Shakespeare*, II, VI, 3 (on Fingal); and 'La Chaise Gild-Holm-'Ur' in *Les Travailleurs de la Mer*, I, I, 8.

33. *Toute la Lyre*, V, 23.

34. *Corr*, II, 206–7.

35. Translation slightly adapted from Hugo, *L'Archipel de la Manche. The Channel Islands*.

36. *Corr*, II, 235 and 236; *Faits et Croyances*, *OC*, XIV, 153. Also 162: '*abyme*' instead of '*abîme*' (abyss).

37. *Corr*, II, 240. Vacquerie's book was *Profils et Grimaces*.

38. Adèle Hugo, III, 560 (13 August 1854).

39. e.g. a review in Edmond Duranty's *Réalisme*, of '*Les Contemplations, ou le Gouffre Géant des Sombres Abîmes Romantiques*' (15 January 1857).

40. Cf. 'Écrit en Exil', written two years after the return from exile.

41. Browning: II, 261–2 (April? 1857). The letter may not have been sent. See also letter to Mrs Jameson, 9 April 1857: Browning, II, 260.

42. Baudelaire (1975–6), II, 134.

43. Rimbaud referred to his mother as '*La Bouche d'Ombre*'.

44. *Corr*, II, 227.

45. *Gazette de France*, 14 June 1856: Hugo (1922), I, 131.

46. See for example J. Gaudon (1969) and Nash.

47. 'Le Goût', *OC*, XII, 575–6. The Star of the Dragon is Thuban (Alpha Draconis), the pole star at the time the Pyramids were built.

48. Patty.

49. On the reliability of Hugo's manuscript dates: Barrère (1965), 241–3.

50. *Dieu* (Fragments), *OC*, XV, 634.

51. *Corr*, II, 350.

52. *Les Contemplations*, III, 2.

53. Generally: Benjamin, 144, and Bhaktin, quoted *re Notre-Dame de Paris* in Brombert, 71–2; Zeldin, 802–3.

54. Lockroy, 290.

55. Vacquerie (1856), 298.

56. Adèle Hugo, III, 36.

57. Ibid., III, 18–20.

58. Dr Terrier: Guillemin (1985), 41 n. 2.

59. Massin, X, 1282.

60. Parménie, 232.

61. Massin, X, 1462.

62. 9 February 1857.

63. Massin, X, 1267.

64. From 'Choses Écrites à Créteil' (27 September 1859) in *Les Chansons des Rues et des Bois*, I, 4: 'A girl who in the Marne / Was washing her *torchons radieux*.'

65. e.g. R. Waldmüller (visitor in 1867): Feller, 283; etc.

66. *Corr*, III, 120; Sherard (1905), 2–3.

67. Stapfer (1905), 153–4.

68. Thomas Gore, letter dated 10 April 1903: Wack, 41.

69. Massin, XIII, 925 (22 June 1865).

70. Stapfer (1905), 155.

71. Baudouin, 281–2.

72. Hugo to Hetzel, 12 September 1859: *Corr*, II, 305.

73. Berret, 106–16.

74. NB: many of Hugo's fragments begin with an unrhymed, 'orphan' line.
75. *La Fin de Satan*, I (*Le Glaive*), IV, 1–2.
76. Reviews of *LS* I: Hooker, 139–41.
77. Mérimée (10 December 1862) said that *Salammbô* was 'like a bad pastiche of Vr Hugo'.
78. Flaubert, III, 41–2 (end September, 30 September and 1 October 1859).
79. J. Lesclide, 82–3.
80. *William Shakespeare*, II, III.
81. Proust, 619.
82. Hudson, 142 n.
83. Goncourt, I, 742.
84. *Les Misérables*, I, 3, 7.
85. Wack, 43.
86. The editors of the Massin edition wonder why Mazzini asked Hugo for a letter (X, 704). A British spy told the Home Office on 14 August 1852 that there was correspondence between Mazzini and 'the Son of Victor Hugo'. Two days later, Mazzini was reported to have 'somewhere in London deposited 2000 pieces of fire-arms, to be sent when occasion requires to Italy': PRO: HO 45 4302.
87. On John Brown: *AP*, *OC*, X, 512–14 and 525–6; Hoffman. US reaction in Lebreton-Savigny, part 4.
88. Delalande, 75. Scraps of the original silks remain above the fireplace in the Salon Rouge.
89. Black, 125–7; Harney; Hambrick. Hugo's relations with Ernest Jones: S. Gaudon, 'Anglophobie?', in James, ed. (1986). See also unpublished note (Taylor Institution, MS F/HUGO V.3) dated 29 November 1863: 'Souscrivons tous pour le million de fusils que Garibaldi demande et qui délivrera Rome et Venise. Victor Hugo.' (Perhaps originally enclosed with Hugo's letter to Meurice of the same date.)
90. S. P. Oliver, 715.
91. *Corr*, II, 338.
92. 9 September 1860: Massin, XII, 1342.
93. Angrand, 200–3.
94. Now in the Orsini file at the Archives Nationales: Angrand, 189.
95. Hugo to Hetzel, 4 July 1861: Parménie, 368.
96. *Corr*, II, 348.
97. Guillemin (1954), 89.
98. Rossetti, 23 (2 October 1870).

99. Hugo to François-Victor, 20 May 1861: *Corr*, II, 351.
100. *Les Misérables*, II, 1, 1; also *OC*, XV, 885–91.

17. '*MERDE*!' (1862)

1. Summary by J. Seebacher: 'Victor Hugo et ses Éditeurs avant l'Exil', in Massin, VI, i–xv; also Seebacher (1993), 43–56.
2. Parménie, 374.
3. Goncourt, I, 808.
4. See Mollier, 157–8.
5. Biré (1891), 14, 39–40; Derôme, 24–9; Jullien, 98–100 (but Jullien was a close friend of the Renduel family); Stapfer (1905), 83. Contemporary (adverse) comments in the *Bibliographie de la France*, 1833, nos 78, 1128, 6468 and 6842.
6. On the publication of *Les Misérables*: Leuilliot (1970); Despy-Meyer and Sartorius.
7. Hugo to Lacroix, 8 May 1862: *Corr*, II, 388.
8. Leuilliot (1970), 250.
9. Goncourt, I, 809.
10. Strachey, 223.
11. Leuilliot (1970), 258 n. 2.
12. *Les Misérables* appropriately has two entries in *The Guinness Book of Records*. It contains the longest sentence in Western literature before Proust (823 words, 93 commas, 51 semi-colons and 4 dashes), and it gave rise to the shortest recorded correspondence. Hugo reportedly asked the publishers of the English translation how the novel was selling: '?' To which the reply was '!'
13. Lamartine suggested '*L'Homme contre la Société*', '*Les Coupables*' or '*Les Scélérats*': *Corr*, II, 401. See also II, 273 n. 1: Lamartine is thought to have lied when he told Hugo that no insulting allusion was intended to *Châtiments* in one of his *Entretiens*. In fact, since he mentions a stay in Italy and, twice, '*œuvres de colère*', the allusion is clearly to Amédée Pommier's *Colères* (Dolin, 1844). On relations with Lamartine: unknown letter to Charles Fillieu, 21 June [1850?]: Taylor Institution, MS.F/HUGO V.5.
14. Letter to Georges Izambard, 4 May 1870: facsimile in Matarasso–Petitfils, p. 37. Cf. Izambard, 58–60.
15. Angrand, 218–20; Pirot (1958), 263–4.

16. Hugo (1862), I, iii–iv. See G. Meredith, I, 333: 'a part of his grotesque greatness. It costs me nothing to overlook it – especially in this age of satin.'

17. *Moi, l'Amour, la Femme*, OC, XIV, 278.

18. Maillard, 19. Maillard's *Les Derniers Bohèmes* (Sartorius, 1874) contains an unknown quatrain by Hugo (probably 1860–61): 'Poète, je donne des ailes / Aux faibles de l'Humanité; / Je n'aime que la liberté / Et ses trois couleurs immortelles.' (170)

19. Angrand, 214–16. Generally: chap. 11, and *Revue d'Histoire Littéraire de la France*, July–September 1960, pp. 334–44.

20. Stevenson, 12.

21. Dostoevsky, 227.

22. '[Les Traducteurs]', OC, XII, 625.

23. *William Shakespeare*, I, IV, 1.

24. Ibid., II, I, 4.

25. 'Geometry deceives; only the hurricane is accurate': *Les Misérables*, II, 1, 5. Also 'Les Fleurs', OC, XII, 557 ('Cloud forms are rigorous'), and below, p. 608 and note 33.

26. Sewage recycling was treated by Sue in *La Marquise d'Alfi* (Sue, xix–xx) and by Hugo's Jersey neighbour, Leroux, in a pamphlet 'on a means of quintupling, to say the least, the agricultural production of the region' (1853).

27. *Les Misérables*, III, 1, 13.

28. *Corr*, II, 395.

29. Claretie (1883?), 496.

30. Rochefort (1896), I, 193–4; cf. *Corr*, IV, 370: 400.000 or 500,000 francs a year.

31. A commemorative book was published: Frédérix; also Despy-Meyer and Sartorius.

32. *Les Quatre Vents de l'Esprit*, I, 39.

33. *William Shakespeare*, II, II, 5.

34. On Hauteville House: Delalande; 'Documents Iconographiques', Massin, XV.

35. Hugo to sons, 20 October 1867: *Corr*, III, 78. The visitors book has disappeared.

36. P. Georgel, paper delivered at Colloque de Cérisy, July 1985: not among the talks 'whose texts arrived on time' collected in *Hugo le Fabuleux*, ed. J. Seebacher and A. Ubersfeld (Seghers, 1985).

37. Delalande, 91–2; Lecanu (i.e. Charles Hugo), 59.

38. Hugo's library: Barrère (1965); Delalande.

39. *Corr*, III, 229.

40. Ibid., II, 367. Not to be confused with an earlier room on the floor below, also called the 'look-out'.

41. S. P. Oliver, 724–5.

42. Wack, 41–2; Delalande, 26 n. 2. Tom Gore would have been trained in the traditions brought to Guernsey by Thomas Chippendale, whose 'designs of houshold [*sic*] furniture' recommend a combination of Chinese, Gothic and 'modern' (i.e. rococo): Chippendale; Delalande, 159 n. 3.

43. The publication of an album had been announced prematurely in 1848: Robin, 73–4.

44. Hugo to Paul Chenay, 13 November 1862: *Corr*, II, 424.

45. Hugo to Philippe Burty, 18–19 April 1864: *Corr*, II, 468–9.

46. Hugo to Baudelaire, 29 April 1860: *Corr*, II, 334–5; Barbou (1886), 435; Georges Hugo, 38–9 (and Goncourt, III, 120); Lecanu, 33; R. Lesclide, 220; and texts quoted by Delalande, 32 n. 1.

47. R. Journet and G. Robert, in Hugo, *Trois Albums*, 6–7; Sergent, 24.

48. *Faits et Croyances*, *OC*, XIV, 189. See also Journet and Robert's introduction to *Trois Albums*, 5–12.

49. *Tas de Pierres*, *OC*, VII, 913.

50. Van Gogh, I, 493 (end November 1882).

51. Van Gogh, II, 19 (1883).

52. Barbou (1886), 403.

53. Baudelaire (1975–76), II, 430; see also II, 366.

54. Ibid., 668; Hugo's reply: 29 April 1860: *Corr*, II, 334–54.

55. Georges Hugo, 18.

56. 'Colère de la Bête', II: *L'Âne*, *OC*, VI, 1044.

18. Salvage (1863–1868)

1. Hugo to wife and Charles, 10 October 1863: *in toto* in Guillemin (1985), 105–6.

2. See Guille, including rumours later recorded in Halifax – notably the tales of Mr Gossip, the bookseller.

3. Guillemin (1985), 118–19.

4. *Les Misérables*, II, 8, 8.

5. There were also signs of odd obsessions in Abel's son, Hugo's nephew

(see Bibliography: Léopold-Armand Hugo). Clémentine Hugo, author of *Comedy and Comedians in Politics* (London: Ward & Downey, 1892) was Léopold's wife. On Clémentine: J. Lesclide, 256–8.

6. *Corr*, II, 475.

7. Angrand, 252.

8. 'Le Bout de l'Oreille', *Les Quatre Vents de l'Esprit*, I; and see p. 1490 nn. 21–2.

9. *AP, OC*, X, 678.

10. The original *Voix de Guernesey*, printed on Guernsey, has escaped editions of Hugo's *Oeuvres Complètes*. The Taylor Institution owns a copy, inscribed by Hugo 'Au lieutenant Butler, son ami'. The text is the same as the Brussels edition reproduced in Laffont. Butler is the addressee of Hugo's 'L'Expédition de Chine': *AP, OC*, X, 527. *La Voix de Guernesey* was republished (with variants) with the apocryphal *Le Christ au Vatican* in 1868 (London and Geneva: Chez les Principaux Libraires): Bodleian Library.

11. *Corr*, II, 549.

12. *Paris*, I.

13. Stapfer (1869), xi–xii; (1905), 19–22.

14. Stapfer (1905), 62 and 181.

15. S. P. Oliver, 720–1. '*Sanglante*' was still used as a synonym of '*saignante*'.

16. Wack, 49.

17. Ibid., 48.

18. Bergerat, I, 10–12.

19. Stapfer (1905), 76–77.

20. Goncourt, I, 802 (8 April 1862).

21. 23 August 1860: Massin, XII, 1340.

22. Stapfer (1905), 131.

23. Judith, ch. 11.

24. Rochefort (1896), I, 187–8.

25. Drouet (1851), 589–91 (30 October and 21 November 1863).

26. *Corr*, II, 404.

27. Drouet (1851), 639–40 (20 February 1868).

28. *Corr*, III, 144.

29. *Les Chansons des Rues et des Bois*, I, II, 4. See J. Gaudon's edition, especially 8–10 and 14–15.

30. *Les Chansons des Rues et des Bois*, I, I, 1.

31. Claretie (1902), 114.

32. *Le Nain Jaune*, 15 November 1865; also Baudelaire (1973), II, 541 (3 November 1865).

33. *Châtiments* (Suite), *OC*, XV, 221.

34. Davidson, 261–2.

35. 27 January 1874: Savant, V, 28.

36. Hugo's stay on Sark: Barrère (1965), 103–57. The grotto which Hugo named after Charles is now called Victor Hugo's Cave.

37. 'La belle s'appelait mademoiselle Amable . . .', *Toute la Lyre*, VI.

38. Delécluze, quoted in Séché (1912), 61; also Stapfer (1905), 148–9.

39. 16 June 1865. (Mary Green died on 13 June 1865.)

40. See for example Brombert, 165.

41. Mass, 129.

42. *Les Travailleurs de la Mer*, II, I, 1.

43. K. Ross, in *A New History of French Literature*, gen. ed. D. Hollier (Harvard University Press, 1989), p. 753.

44. *Fraser's Magazine*: Anon. (1866), 740. See also Henry James's review in *The Nation*, 12 April 1866: James (1921), 199.

45. Anon. (1866), 741.

46. *Corr*, II, 537.

47. First translation by William Moy Thomas (reprinted by Everyman in 1961): eight editions from 1866 to 1872; the Doré illustrations first appeared in 1867.

48. D. Bancel gave a similar interpretation in a letter to the 'pilot of the abyss' (Hugo): Massin, XIII, 784–5 (16 April 1866).

49. Sherard (1905), 5.

50. *Les Travailleurs de la Mer*, II, IV, 2.

51. Stapfer (1905), 41.

52. Hugo's anatomical knowledge discussed by H. Crosse in *Un Mollusque Bien Maltraité, ou Comment M. Victor Hugo Comprend l'Organisation du Poulpe* (Savy, 1866).

53. *Corr*, II, 530.

54. *Les Travailleurs dans la Mer* (1866): Bersaucourt, 197–206.

55. North Peat, 186 (23 May 1866).

56. *L'Archipel de la Manche*, xii; also letter in *The Gentleman's Magazine*, December 1869 – May 1870, p. 710. On mistakes, see also Bowley, 404–9.

57. Anon. (18 March 1893).

58. *Les Travailleurs de la Mer*, I, IV, 1.

59. Stevenson, 19.
60. *L'Archipel de la Manche*, xii.
61. *Faits et Croyances*, *OC*, XIV, 165.
62. Hugo to Vacquerie, 22 February 1866: *Corr*, IV, 360. Also to his stationer, T. B. Banks: Wack, 44.
63. J.-L. Mercié: Massin, XII, 501. Mercié's 'corrections' are equally fantastic.
64. North Peat, 253–4 (21 June 1867); also Weill (1867) on the emasculated 'nation of Hernanis'.
65. 12 February 1865: Baudelaire (1973), II, 460.
66. J. Gautier, 307.

19. STATIONS OF THE CROSS (1868–1870)

1. *Philosophie Prose*, *OC*, XIV, 61.
2. *Océan Prose*, *Faits et Croyances* and *Moi, l'Amour, la Femme*, *OC*, XIV, 28, 119, 122 and 277; *Dernière Gerbe*, 55.
3. Drouet (1951), 652 (10 October 1868).
4. Hugo to François-Victor, 17 February 1870: Guille, 248.
5. Adamson and Beauclerk Dewar, 154–5. The Hugo connection is not mentioned. For Hugo's public views on coal-mining: 'Les Génies Appartenant au Peuple' and '[Le Tyran]', *OC*, XII, 594 and 618; 'Aubin', *Les Années Funestes*.
6. *Océan Vers*, *OC*, VII, 1018–19.
7. One of the Duke's ancestors, Charles Beauclerk, is mentioned in *L'Homme Qui Rit*, I, I ('Chapitre Préliminaire'), 3, and II, VIII, 7.
8. Hugo to François-Victor, 15 August 1859: *Corr*, II, 301.
9. Rochefort (1896), I, 196–7. The painting mentioned by Rochefort is probably the dubious Salvator Rosa seascape pointed out to visitors in Hauteville House: S. P. Oliver, 717. Another trace of filial deception in *Corr*, III, 164.
10. Goncourt, II, 664 (11 November 1875).
11. J. Gautier, 308.
12. 'Les Fleurs', *OC*, XII, 559.
13. 24 May 1865: Baudelaire (1973), II, 501. See also II, 495.
14. 28 October 1865: Baudelaire (1973), II, 539; also Baudelaire (1975–6), II, 884.

15. Verlaine, 560–4.
16. Rochefort (1868–9), no. 3 (13 June 1868); also nos 11, 14, 19, 21, 22, 32, 36, 41 and 48.
17. Lectures to be given by Charles Boissière.
18. Rochefort (1896), I, 172–84. On *'Le Christ au Vatican'* – an imitation which appears in some catalogues as the work of Victor Hugo – and Hugo's occasional apparent indifference to his published works: I, 190–1. Hugo vowed to correct a mistake discovered by Rochefort in 'Fantômes' (*Les Orientales*): 'Des fleurs, à *paver* [not *'payer'*] un palais!' The correction was never made: all editions still show *'payer'*.
19. 'Et voilà dix-sept ans bientôt qu'il sont à table! . . .', *Les Années Funestes*, 55.
20. *Moi, l'Amour, la Femme, OC*, XIV, 286–7.
21. *Corr*, III, 153.
22. A wapentake is 'a subdivision of certain English shires' and 'the judicial court of such a subdivision' (*OED*).
23. *L'Homme Qui Rit*, II, VII, 3.
24. e.g. Champfleury to Jules Troubat, 24 July 1869: Troubat, 251.
25. e.g. a review in *St Paul's Magazine* inspired (perhaps written) by Anthony Trollope, whose latest tale was set aside to make room for the English translation of Hugo's novel. The English title was taken from the title of Part II, 'Par Ordre du Roi': *By Order of the King. A Romance of English History*.
26. Marzials, 186.
27. Swinburne to W. Rossetti, 23 November 1891: Swinburne (1959–62), VI, 23. See also Bowley, 39.
28. Swinburne (1875), 2.
29. See C. Thompson in *'L'Homme Qui Rit' ou la Parole-Monstre de Victor Hugo*. On humour in *L'Homme Qui Rit*: articles in the same volume by B. Leuilliot and A. Zielonka.
30. e.g. *Le Père Duchêne*, no. 7 (9 December 1869). Perhaps by confusion with the poem of *Châtiments*, 'L'Homme a Ri'.
31. *L'Homme Qui Rit, OC*, III, 1081 (fragment).
32. On Hugo as Nero: Swinburne (1959–62), II, 123 (28 August 1870).
33. Expressive vowels: *Faits et Croyances, OC*, XIV, 210–11; see also figurative letters in *Alpes et Pyrénées, OC*, XIII, 684: translated by Paul Standard for Hermann Zapf's *Manuale Typographicum* (1954), reprinted in Hugo (1991); figurative numbers – 'The number 22 is sailing on the pond in the shape of a pair of ducks' (Barrère (1965), 121); housekeep-

ing of globe: 'Les Fleurs', *OC*, XII, 555 (also 687, '[La Mer et le Vent]', on 'our cosmic dependency'); extraterrestrials: 'Philosophie. Commencement d'un Livre', *OC*, XII, 488 and 509. Part III of 'Saturne', was quoted by Camille Flammarion in his *La Pluralité des Mondes Habités*, 276. Hauteville House has a signed copy. Butterfly effect: 'No thinker would dare to say that the scent of hawthorn is of no use to constellations' (*Les Misérables*, IV, 3, 3); 'There are no absolute logical links in the human heart any more than there are perfect geometrical figures in celestial mechanics' (*Les Misérables*, IV, 8, 2). See also, above, p. 603 n. 25.

34. Poulet-Malassis, 372 (note by F. Giraudeau dated 30 March 1868); Rochefort (1868–9), 27 February 1869: *La Lanterne*, no. 40.
35. *Moi, l'Amour, la Femme*, *OC*, XIV, 289 and 293.
36. *AP*, *OC*, X, 624.
37. *Châtiments* (Suite), *OC*, XV, 273.
38. 'Quant à Paris . . .', *Les Années Funestes*.
39. Cf. Hugo's 'Bourgeois Parlant de Jésus-Christ', *Toute la Lyre*, I: 'How unfortunate that he meddled in politics!'
40. North Peat, 20–21 (29 August 1864) (bust by Leboeuf).
41. V. Duruy, 264. Hugo's image in the younger generation: Badesco, I, 116–18 and 258; II, 1309–16.
42. See Zola (1966–70).
43. *La Mère Duchêne*, nos 1–3 (December 1869 – January 1870).
44. *AP*, *OC*, X, 635.
45. Other titles: *Le Septième Coup de Clairon, L'Épopée Noire, Rugissements*.
46. See Hugo, *Boîte aux Lettres*, 5.
47. Stapfer (1905), 224.
48. *L'Art d'Être Grand-Père*, I, 6.
49. *AP*, *OC*, X, 405.
50. Ibid., 661.
51. Quoted by Christiansen, 138.
52. Hugo to d'Alton-Shée, 2 August 1870: *Corr*, III, 263.
53. Hugo to Meurice, 17 July 1870: Ibid., 262.
54. Hugo, *Carnets Intimes*, 26; Angrand, 284.
55. *Carnets Intimes*, 29.
56. Angrand, 285.
57. Leffondrey, 20–7.
58. *Carnets Intimes*, 205.
59. 'En Quittant Bruxelles', *L'Année Terrible*, Juin.

60. *Carnets Intimes*, 39.
61. Claretie (1882), 6.

PART FOUR

20. *L'Année Terrible* (1870–1871)

1. Poulet-Malassis, 195–9 (report dated 6 August 1868).
2. Claretie (1882), 10; also Antonin Proust, *Le Figaro*, 1 June 1895: Feller, 277–81.
3. Escholier (1953), 453.
4. Washburne, I, 137–8.
5. E. Vizetelly, 89.
6. According to Clemenceau himself: Escholier (1970), 277.
7. François Coppée, in Wack, 11.
8. To voters of the 15th *arrondissement*, 5 November 1870: *Corr*, III, 271.
9. Engels to Marx, 13 September 1870: Marx and Engels, 296. Also 297: 'Notes on the War', *Pall Mall Gazette*, 13 October 1870. Hooker, 190.
10. *AP*, *OC*, X, 729 – possibly apocryphal: see Feller, 195 (based on a reading of twenty-five German newspapers). However, *Le Rappel* had a German correspondent, and similar sentiments were expressed. See Feller, 198. In a similar spirit, Wagner – who set four Hugo poems to music in 1839 – composed *Eine Kapitulation* (1870), in which a pompous Hugo emerges from the sewer to save France. Hugo called Wagner 'a talent containing an imbecile' (*OC*, XIV, 176). Hugo's apocryphal 'Letter to Bismarck', published in Germany in 1941 by Hans Bethge ('I love you, for I am greater than you', etc.) is interesting only because it was believed to be genuine. See Feller, 232–7.
11. Feller, 197.
12. Lebreton-Savigny, 127. Cf. *AP*, *OC*, X, 727.
13. Goncourt, II, 332 (7 November 1870).
14. *L'Année Terrible*, Juillet, 10.
15. Goncourt, II, 332 (7 November 1870).
16. 'Aux Français', *AP*, *OC*, X, 730.

17. See also Bondois, 170.
18. Hugo (1992), 7–8.
19. Goncourt, II, 438 (17 May 1871).
20. See also *Toute la Lyre*, V, 30.
21. Colvin, 271.
22. *L'Année Terrible*, Janvier, 2.
23. *OP*, III, 983 n. 2.
24. *Carnets, OC*, XIII, 1106–7.
25. Bosq, 11.
26. Goncourt, II, 395 (18 March 1871).
27. André Gill and Edmond Lepelletier quoted by Edwards, 141.
28. Goncourt, II, 396 (18 March 1871).
29. e.g. *Le Rappel*, 20 March 1871; *Le Journal des Débats*, 19 March 1871; *L'Ouvrier de l'Avenir*, 19 March 1871.
30. Hugo, *Carnets Intimes*, 264 n. 3. See also *AP, OC*, X, 794 (open letter to Meurice and Vacquerie supposedly written during the Commune but, for an unexplained though apparently 'well known' reason, not published until 6 March 1872).
31. *Corr*, III, 281 (18 April 1871).
32. *Paris Libre. Journal du Soir*, 12 April 1871 – 24 May 1871. The lists were republished in an illustrated brochure, *Pilori des Mouchards*.
33. Edwards, 212.
34. Hugo, *Carnets Intimes*, 134. Hugo's opinion shared by *Le Corsaire*, no. 3 (10 May 1871).
35. Lissagaray, 392.
36. Ibid., 403.
37. Christiansen, illustration.
38. *Documents sur les Événements de 1870–71*, IX, 12–15. The painter in this list is Gustave Courbet.
39. Rossetti, 65 (2 June 1871); also Marmier, II, 260 and *Choses Vues*, 1 June 1871. Larousse, 'Hugo' (1873) also reports a spell in England (434, col. iv).
40. On Hugo in Luxembourg: Bourg, 273–88, 306–21 and 469–511. Hugo's Vianden residence is now a Victor Hugo Museum (Bourg, 274 and 483).
41. Hugo, *Carnets Intimes*, 271 n. 1; also Marmier, II, 260; *Le Grelot*, no. 9 (11 June 1871): a playlet set in Hugo's home at the Place des Barricades.
42. G. Stiegler, *Le Figaro*, 5 May 1893: Maurois, 511; Escholier (1951), 313–14.

43. Edwards, 343–6.
44. *Corr*, III, 283.
45. Ibid.
46. Ibid., 285.

21. 'BECAUSE' (1871–1873)

1. *Choses Vues, OC*, XI, 1331.
2. *Carnets, OC*, XIII, 1194.
3. *AP, OC*, X, 827; *Le Rappel*, 1 November 1871.
4. *AP*, 833; *Le Rappel*, 8 November 1871; *Qui Vive!*, 10–11 November 1871. Also in *Qui Vive!*, 22 November 1871: two poems from *L'Année Terrible*.
5. Goncourt, II, 504–5 (24 March 1872).
6. *Choses Vues*, 30 July 1872.
7. *Quatrevingt-treize*, III, VII, 5.
8. Guillemin (1985), 155.
9. Ibid., 83.
10. *Corr*, IV, 2.
11. *L'Année Terrible*, Juillet, 12. Cf. *L'Art d'Être Grand-Père*, X, 3, line 19.
12. Poulet-Malassis: Pichois (1996), 213.
13. 3 April 1871.
14. Buchanan, 146–51.
15. *L'Homme Qui Rit* (Reliquat), *OC*, III, 1083.
16. *Moi, l'Amour, la Femme, OC*, XIV, 319.
17. *Carnets, OC*, XIII, 1200.
18. *Corr*, III, 369.
19. R. Lesclide, 29; *Choses Vues*, 8 March 1878.
20. The usual spelling is '*quatre-vingt-treize*'.
21. The central, Bastille section of *La Fin de Satan* was never written (see p. 365). Hugo's longest attempt to cram the Revolution into verse was *Le Verso de la Page* (1857–8), dismembered in 1870 to feed other poems.
22. *Corr*, IV, 6.
23. Hooker, 192. For Saintsbury (II, 129), Lantenac 'annihilates Dickens's caricature [of the *ancienne noblesse*] in *A Tale of Two Cities*.' Readers often disagreed with Hugo's judgement of his own characters: e.g.

Hennett de Kesler, quoted in Blémont, criticized him for preferring Cosette to Éponine in *Les Misérables*. The daughter of the Paris executioner, Sanson, considered Phoebus 'far more guilty' than Frollo: Marquand, 43–4.

24. R. Tucker, in Brombert, 267 n. 4. Also Deutscher, 553: in the Soviet Union before World War II, Hugo and Maupassant were published more often than any other foreign writers.

25. *Quatrevingt-treize*, III, III, 1, 6.

26. Ibid., III, I, 4.

27. See p. 556, note 8 – a myth preserved notably by Vapereau (1865). On Joseph Hugo, see Family Tree; Kuscinski; Robert *et al.*; Tribout de Morembert. Cf. the erroneous reference in *VHR* to a Louis-Antoine Hugo: Mme Hugo (1863), I, 1–2.

28. See p. 7.

29. *Autographes Anciens et Modernes*, no. 269.

30. *Quatrevingt-treize*, III, I, 2.

31. Lukács, 256.

32. *Quatrevingt-treize*, III, VII, 5.

33. Ibid., III, VII, 5.

34. Lukács, 280.

35. *Quatrevingt-treize*, II, III, 1, 11.

36. Drouet (1951), 697 (17 February 1873).

37. J. Lesclide, 199.

38. Savant, VI, 33.

39. *Tas de Pierres*, OC, XIV, 492.

40. Notebook belonging to Louis Barthou (now lost): Guillemin (1954), 110.

41. *Toute la Lyre*, VI, 7.

42. *Choses Vues*, 15 August 1873.

43. For '*A las 11, ha desaparecido el vapor.*'

44. Interpreted thus by Juin, III, 161. Savant (VI, 46–7) thinks the woman who left the island on 21 July was either Marie Mercier or Judith Gautier (who was then in Normandy). 'En Grèce' is addressed to a working woman, a 'wild and naive' beauty. It contains several allusions to her name, Blanche, and her code-name in Hugo's diaries, 'Alba' ('*blanche*', '*candeur*', '*albâtre*', etc.).

45. Arico (manuscript memoirs of Juliette Adam), 438.

46. Judith, 119; see also Amicis, 196.

47. Phenylethylamine: Sternberg and Barnes, 199.

48. Zola (1966–70).

49. 'Idolâtries et Philosophies', *Les Quatre Vents de l'Esprit* (*c.* 1872); cf. *OC*, XV, 457: 'On monte, on monte, on monte, on monte, on monte encore'. Also, on God: 'Il est! il est! il est! il est! éperdument!' Cf. 'Est-il? est-il? est-il? est-il? Moi-même suis-je?' (*Religions et Religion*, V; *Dieu*, *OC*, VII, 638). Other examples: *OC*, XV, 685; *OC*, VI, 224, 783, 855, 884, 908, 1000; VII, 274 (cf. Mallarmé's, 'L'Azur') and 703.

50. *Choses Vues*, 21 November 1873.

51. Goncourt, II, 546–8 (5 August 1873).

52. Goncourt, ibid.; also R. Lesclide, 242–3.

53. *Choses Vues*, 31 July 1873.

54. Lionnet, 237–9.

55. Flaubert to George Sand, 30 December 1873.

22. 'A MAN WHO THINKS OF SOMETHING ELSE' (1874–1878)

1. Hugo, *Post-Scriptum de Ma Vie*, 117 (1863).

2. *Choses Vues*, 30 January 1874.

3. Van Gogh, I, 493 (end November 1882).

4. *Choses Vues*, 5 April 1876. Also *AP*, *OC*, X, 856: the Revolution is the 'lion-tamer' of Emperors (*Le Rappel*, 23 September 1872; manuscript copy in the Taylor Institution: MS.F/HUGO V.6).

5. *Choses Vues*, February 1874.

6. Barbou, Calmettes, Colvin, Duclaux, Lesclide, Lockroy, Talmeyr, Yates.

7. Rivet, 17–19.

8. Isaac Pavlovsky, in Biré (1891), II, 12–13.

9. L. Daudet, 236.

10. *Choses Vues*, 22 May 1877; Carneiro Leão, 61–3.

11. Georges Hugo, 21–2.

12. Mme Daudet, in Duclaux, 246.

13. Barbou (1882), 396–7. See also a variation on the Lord's Prayer by Catulle Mendès: 'Victor Hugo' (22 January 1869): Mendès, 36.

14. Article published in *The London Daily News*, *The New York Times* and *Appleton's Journal*: Lebreton-Savigny, 273.

15. Martin-Dupont, 106–15 and 126–8; R. Lesclide, 255–6; Pelleport, v.

16. Swinburne to Tola Dorian, *c.* 26 November 1882: Swinburne (1959–62), IV, 318.

17. Agulhon, 27.

18. Talmeyr, 71.
19. *Choses Vues*, 21 November 1876; 4 and 5 June 1876.
20. *AP, OC*, X, 950–1.
21. Claretie (1882), 17.
22. *Moi, l'Amour, la Femme, OC*, XIV, 293.
23. *L'Art d'Être Grand-Père*, VI, 10.
24. Claretie, quoted in Hugo, *Victor Hugo's Intellectual Autobiography*, lviii; also Colvin, 268; Goncourt, II, 549, 693 and 727.
25. R. Lesclide, 15.
26. 'Quand ce charmant petit poète . . .', *Toute la Lyre*, IV.
27. Hooker, 265. Cf. Swinburne (1886), 81: 'the most adorable book ever written'.
28. *Histoire d'un Crime*, III, 4. The Rue de la Pépinière was known as the Rue Abbatucci from 1868 to 1879. It now forms part of the Rue La Boétie.
29. 'Regard Jeté dans une Mansarde', *Les Rayons et les Ombres*.
30. *AP, OC*, X, 984.
31. *Choses Vues*, 29 October 1875. Literally '*to* both places', but probably confused with the French, '*aux deux endroits*'.
32. Drouet (1951), 772.
33. Maurois, 517; *Choses Vues*, 2 November 1875; Escholier (1953), 514. Phrase should be '*No se hará el chico.*'
34. Unfinished section of 'Après l'Hiver', *Toute la Lyre, OC*, VII, 1143 n. 127; *Toute la Lyre*, VII, 23, 16 and 14.
35. 'Le Dîner d'*Hernani*', *AP, OC*, X, 979.
36. 'Après l'Hiver', *Toute la Lyre*, V.

23. 'To Love Is To Act' (1878–1885)

1. J. Lesclide, 5.
2. Goncourt, II, 809 (21 December 1878).
3. R. Lesclide, 187–8.
4. *Moi, l'Amour, la Femme, OC*, XIV, 364.
5. 17 July 1878: Pouchain and Sabourin, 384–5.
6. 16 August 1878: Guillemin (1954), 129–30; Massin, XVI, 603 n. 31.
7. *Toute la Lyre*, III, 5.
8. Sherard (1905), 6. The other remarkable old man has not been identified.

9. L. Daudet, 233.

10. Juin, III, 258; echo in Goncourt, III, 1066.

11. *Choses Vues*, 5 July 1879; *Le Rappel*, 8 July 1879; R. Lesclide, 152–5.

12. *AP, OC*, X, 1011.

13. Ibid., 1059.

14. Claretie (1883), 289–90.

15. Flaubert, 12 June 1879.

16. *AP*, 1034.

17. Lafargue; Lacroux, 133–8; also P. Albouy, 'La Vie Posthume de Victor Hugo': Massin, XVI, ii.

18. Agulhon, 24.

19. See *Choses Vues*, 25 February 1884 (speech for the Senate).

20. Letter from Parnell in Lebreton-Savigny, 128. See also Maxse, 15: a plea for Hugo to maintain 'a generous silence' on the Irish question.

21. 'To Victor Hugo', *The Nineteenth Century*, June 1877; in a slightly different form in *Ballads and Other Poems* (1880): see S. Gaudon, 'Anglophobie?', in James, ed. (1986), quoting Hugo's reply: 'How could I not love England when she produces men like yourself!' (4 June 1877). Tennyson's private opinion, according to his son, was that 'Victor Hugo is an unequal genius ... he reminds one that there is only one step between the sublime and the ridiculous.'

22. Agulhon, 24.

23. *Les Misérables*, V, 3, 5.

24. The Tour du Vertbois, on the Rue Saint-Martin: *AP, OC*, X, 1042–3; Hillairet, II, 469.

25. I. Pavlovsky, in Biré (1891), II, 237–8.

26. Bellosta.

27. *Corr*, IV, 79 n. 6.

28. R. Lesclide, 169–70; Lockroy, 285.

29. *Choses Vues*, 1882.

30. Mme Daudet, 46.

31. Drouet (1951), 809 (8 August 1880).

32. Hugo, *Lettres à Juliette Drouet*, 179–80 (21 May 1880).

33. *Le Rappel*, 14 May 1883: Pouchain and Sabourin, 422.

34. 'Quand je ne serai plus ...', *Dernière Gerbe*.

35. Guimbaud, *Victor Hugo et Juliette Drouet*, 255; Drouet (1951), 823.

36. Fabre, 10. On a visit from Count von Moltke: Lockroy, 291–2.

37. Sherard (1902), 18 and (1905), 9.

38. 8 August 1872; Calmettes, 320–1.

39. Claretie (1902), 3 and 113.
40. *The Detroit Free Press*, 24 May 1885: Lebreton-Savigny, 281.
41. A clumsy, composite edition of *La Légende des Siècles* also appeared in 1883 in the Hetzel–Quantin '*ne varietur*' edition of Hugo's complete works.
42. 'Mont.', 'A Chat with Victor Hugo', *The Baltimore Sun*, c. 1884: Bandy, 482–3.
43. *Océan Vers*, OC, VII, 1075; Horace, *Odes*, III, 3.
44. *Océan Vers*, 1075.
45. According to Mme Clemenceau-Meurice, daughter of Paul Meurice: Levaillant, 273.
46. L. Daudet, 246.
47. R. Lesclide, 314; *Moi, l'Amour, la Femme*, OC, XIV, 326.
48. *AP*, OC, X, 1035.
49. Guillemin (1954), 134.
50. Articles in Lacroux; Lebreton-Savigny.
51. Hugo to Hetzel, September 1873: Parménie, 586.
52. Alfred Le Petit, in *Le Grelot*, 31 May 1885: Lacroux, 57.
53. *Dieu* (Fragments), OC, XV, 611.
54. *The Daily Inter Ocean* (Chicago); *Courier Journal* (Louisville, KY); *The Minneapolis Daily Tribune*: Lebreton-Savigny, 138.

24. GOD (1885)

1. Biré (1894), 364–5; Lebreton-Savigny, 142. On protests: Abbé Vidieu (historian of Saint Geneviève and the Paris Commune).
2. *Notre-Dame de Paris*, III, 2; R. Lesclide, 292–3.
3. *Le Temps*, 25 May 1885; *Le Soleil*, 28 May 1885: Lacroux, 35. See also Le Faure and Abeniacar.
4. *La Croix*, 23 May 1885: Lacroux, 34.
5. Bloy, 123.
6. *Le Cri du Peuple*, 3 June 1885; *La Croix*, 11 June 1885: Lacroux, 104.
7. Papillault, 3–5, 7.
8. Heath, 809.
9. Giese, 15.
10. *La Croix*, 2 June 1885: Lacroux, 75. Generally: Bingham, II, 297; Goncourt, II, 1162 (2 June 1885) – volume published in 1894; Maurice Barrès, *Les Déracinés* (1897), ch. 18: 'La Vertu Sociale d'un Cadavre';

Biré (1894), 368; J.-K. Huysmans, letter to J. Destrée, 3 June 1885 (Lacroux, 152). Cf. account in *Le Rappel*: Massin, XVI, 953–60.

11. *La Citoyenne*, June 1885: Lacroux, 88.
12. *Le Figaro*, 3 June 1885: Lacroux, 99.
13. *La Citoyenne*, June 1885: Lacroux, 87.
14. *La République Française*, 3 June 1885: Lacroux, 101.
15. Lord Lyons to Queen Victoria, 4 June 1885: Newton, II, 355.
16. Nietzsche, *Jenseits von Gut und Böse* (1886), no. 254.
17. *The Chicago Tribune*, 1 June 1885: Lebreton-Savigny, 143.
18. Ford, 671.
19. *Mémoires d'un Veuf*: Verlaine, 89.
20. *Gil Blas*, *Le Pays* and *Le Temps*, 3 June 1885: Lacroux, 91–2.
21. *Choses Vues*, OC, XI, 813–14 (quoting the Prince de Joinville).
22. *La République Française*, 3 June 1885: Lacroux, 101.
23. *Les Misérables*, V, 3, 1.

EPILOGUE

1. Funeral oration: Lacroux, 115.
2. 'Causeries sur Quelques Charognes', *Le Pal*, 4 March 1885: Legay, 562; Pirot (1958), 268.
3. Viatte, 266–7.
4. Lacroux, 138; Lafargue.
5. Jules Guesde, *Le Cri du Peuple*, 6 June 1885: Lacroux, 145.
6. Goncourt, II, 1160 (24 May 1885).
7. Zola, review of *Les Quatre Vents de l'Esprit*, *Le Figaro*, 13 June 1881.
8. Bergerat, I, 17.
9. Paul Claudel, 'Le Double Abîme de Victor Hugo' (15 May 1952): Claudel, 478.
10. On statues of Hugo: Poisson, 114–16.
11. L. Daudet, 41 n.
12. Adèle Hugo, I, 114–16; Guillemin (1985), 156–7.
13. e.g. Hugo, *The United States of Europe* (1914): translation of Hugo's presidential address at the Paris Peace Conference (21 August 1849).
14. James Payn, review of *An Outcast of the Islands*, *Illustrated London News*, 4 April 1896: Conrad, I, 271 n. 2. Conrad's father also translated parts of *La Légende des Siècles*. His translation of *Les Travailleurs de la Mer* was never published. See also Gosse, 361.

15. Mallarmé (1993), 240.
16. Breton, 329.
17. Replying to a survey in *L'Ermitage*, February 1902, p. 109: 'Quel est votre poète?' 'Hugo – hélas!'; see also Gide, 32–5.
18. Cocteau, 28.
19. Hugo paraphernalia in Beuve and Daragon.
20. Ionesco, 23.
21. On Cao Dai: Gobron. See also Graham Greene, *The Quiet American* (1955).
22. Gobron, 65.
23. Well over two million copies of Hugo's novels in English were in circulation in Britain before World War I – in order of popularity: *Les Misérables, Notre-Dame de Paris, Les Travailleurs de la Mer, L'Homme Qui Rit, Quatrevingt-treize*. All his major works could be found in translation. Today, the list is shorter, though the quality has improved. There are excellent translations of *Notre-Dame de Paris* by John Sturrock (Penguin Classics, 1978) and Alban Krailsheimer (Oxford World's Classics, 1993), and, in the same collection, *The Last Day of a Condemned Man and Other Prison Writings* (*Claude Gueux* and two passages from *Choses Vues*) by Geoff Woollen (1992). An unannotated selection of *Choses Vues* was published by David Kimber as *Things Seen* (Oxford University Press, 1964). *The Distance, the Shadows* is a solid rendition by Harry Guest of sixty-six major poems spanning Hugo's career (London: Anvil Press, 1981). The Penguin translation of *Les Misérables* (1976; 1982) has been described on page 382. Tony Harrison's *The Prince's Play* (1996) is a modernized but curiously faithful version of *Le Roi S'Amuse*, with Triboulet as a Glaswegian comic called Scotty Scott.

    Beyond these works, the Anglophone reader is adrift. Print-runs of many of the nineteenth-century translations – especially *The History of a Crime* – were large enough to ensure their survival in secondhand bookshops. In the case of the novels, this is not necessarily a good thing. *The Laughing Man* and *'Ninety-Three* last appeared in English in the 1920s, pruned and disinfected. *The Toilers of the Sea* was republished as a paperback in 1990 (Stroud: Alan Sutton; Vale, Guernsey: The Guernsey Press Co.) with no indication of its origin: like the 1961 Everyman edition, it is based on the original 1866 translation by William Moy Thomas, which, even after being 'completed', is a miserable travesty (see p. 413). Approximately half of Hugo's oeuvre has never been translated into English.

Select Bibliography

(Unless otherwise indicated, the place of publication is Paris.)

A ! A ! A ! [Abel Hugo, Jean-Joseph Ader and Armand Malitourne]. *Traité du Mélodrame*. Delaunay; Pélicier; Plancher; et chez les Marchands de Nouveautés, 1817.

Abrams, Meyer Howard. *The Milk of Paradise*. New York: Harper & Row, 1970.

Adamson, Donald and Peter Beauclerk Dewar. *The House of Nell Gwyn. The Fortunes of the Beauclerk Family 1670–1974*. London: Kimber, 1974.

Agoult, Marie de Flavigny, Comtesse d', *see* Liszt.

Agulhon, Maurice. *La République de Jules Ferry à François Mitterand. 1880 à Nos Jours*. Hachette, 1990.

Albouy, Pierre. *La Création Mythologique chez Victor Hugo*. Corti, 1963.

Amicis, Edmondo de. *Ricordi di Parigi*. Milan: Treves, 1879.

Ancelot, Virginie. *Les Salons de Paris. Foyers Éteints*. Tardieu, 1858.

Andersen, Hans Christian. *Le Conte de Ma Vie*. Trans. C. Lund and J. Bernard. Stock; Delamain et Boutelleau, 1930.

Angrand, Pierre. *Victor Hugo Raconté par les Papiers d'État*. Gallimard, NRF, 1961.

Anon. *Réflexions d'un Infirmier de l'Hospice de la Pitié sur le Drame d'Hernani, de M. Victor Hugo*. Roy-Terry, 1830.

Anon. *The Strangers' Guide to the Island of Jersey*. Guernsey: J. E. Collins, States' Arcade Library, 1833.

Anon. 'Véritable Légende du Beau Pécopin' and 'Olympio Ier'. *La Silhouette*, 20 and 27 July 1845.

Anon. 'Le Candidat de la Société des Gens de Lettres'. *L'Égalité, Journal des Intérêts de Tous*, 20 April 1848.

Anon. *The Poetic Works of Louis Napoleon Now First Done Into Plain English*. London: David Bogue, and may be had of all French booksellers who have a weakness for Cayenne, 1852.

Anon. 'The Decembrists in the Pillory'. *The Beacon* (London), 28 December 1853, 155.

Anon. *A Week on the Norman Coast, by a Commonwealth Man. With a Few Remarks on Jersey and the Other Channel Islands. With the Addendum of the Declaration of Independence of the United States*. London: Tweedie, 1854.

Anon. *Is Louis Napoleon, the Present Emperor of France, the Personal Anti-Christ of the Last Days, the Beast (or Eighth Head) Described in Rev. xiii.4; Rev. xvii.8–11?* London, Newcastle-Upon-Tyne, Sunderland, Morpeth and Edinburgh, 1863.

Anon. Review of *Les Travailleurs de la Mer*. *Fraser's Magazine*, June 1866, 735–45.

Anon. *Guide du lecteur de 'L'Année Terrible'. Petit Vocabulaire Hugo-Français, Indispensable pour l'Intelligence du Texte*. Le Grelot, 1872.

Anon. 'Hugonica'. *The Saturday Review*, 18 March 1893, 292–3; 8 April 1893, 374–5.

Apponyi, Rodolphe. *De la Révolution au Coup d'État, 1848–1851*. Ed. C. Samaran. Geneva: La Palatine, 1948.

Aragon, Louis. *Hugo, Poète Réaliste*. Éditions Sociales, 1952.

Arico, Santo. 'Mme Juliette Adam and Victor Hugo'. *Studi Francesi*, September–December 1990, 437–41.

Asseline, Alfred. *Le Cœur et l'Estomac*. Michel Lévy, 1853.

Asseline, A. *Victor Hugo Intime*. Marpon et Flammarion, 1885.

[Assemblée Nationale]. *Compte Rendu des Séances de l'Assemblée Nationale Législative*. 17 vols. Panckoucke.

Auger, Louis-Simon. [Manifeste contre le Romantisme]. Institut Royal de France, 24 April 1824. In Stendhal. *Racine et Shakespeare*. Ed. R. Fayolle. Garnier-Flammarion, 1970.

Autographes Anciens et Modernes. No. 50. Pierre Berès, [1962].

Badesco, Luc. *La Génération Poétique de 1860*. 2 vols. Nizet, 1971.

Baldensperger, Fernand. 'Documents Officiels sur Victor Hugo "Chantre du Sacre" de Charles X'. *Revue de Littérature Comparée*, January–March 1927, 164–77.

Balzac, Honoré de. *Oeuvres Complètes*. 40 vols. Ed. M. Bouteron and H. Longnon. Conard, 1912–40.

Balzac, H. de. *La Comédie Humaine*. 12 vols. Gen. ed. P.-G. Castex. Gallimard, Pléiade, 1976–81.

Balzac, H. de. *Lettres à Madame Hanska*. 2 vols. Ed. R. Pierrot. Laffont, 1990.

Bandy, W. T. 'Hugo's View of Poe'. *Revue de Littérature Comparée*, July–September 1975, 480–3.

Banville, Théodore de. *Mes Souvenirs*. Charpentier, 1883.

Barbey d'Aurevilly, Jules. *Correspondance Générale*. 9 vols. Ed. J. Petit *et al.* Les Belles Lettres, 1980–89.

Barbier, Auguste. *Souvenirs Personnels et Silhouettes Contemporaines*. Dentu, 1883.

Barbier, Pierre and France Vernillat, ed. *Histoire de France par les Chansons*. Gallimard, NRF, 1958.

Barbou, Alfred. *Victor Hugo et son Temps*. Charpentier, 1881.

Barbou, A. *Victor Hugo and his Time*. Trans. E. Frewer. London: Sampson Low, Marston, Searle & Rivington, 1882.

Barbou, A. *La Vie de Victor Hugo (Victor Hugo et son Temps)*. Charpentier; Marpon et Flammarion, 1886.

Baron, Philippe. 'Les Représentations des *Burgraves* à Paris'. *Francofonia*, Spring 1988, 109–18.

Barrère, Jean-Bertrand. *La Fantaisie de Victor Hugo*. 3 vols. Corti, 1949–50.

Barrère, J.-B. *Hugo, l'Homme et l'Oeuvre*. Boivin, 1952.

Barrère, J.-B. *Victor Hugo à l'Oeuvre*. Klincksieck, 1965.

Barthou, Louis. *Les Amours d'un Poète*. Conard, 1919.

Barthou, L. *Le Général Hugo, 1773–1828*. Hachette, 1926.

Bassanville, Comtesse Anaïs de. *Les Salons d'Autrefois*. 4 vols. Brunet, 1864–70.

Baudelaire, Charles. *Correspondance*. 2 vols. Ed. C. Pichois and J. Ziegler. Gallimard, Pléiade, 1973.

Baudelaire, C. *Oeuvres Complètes*. 2 vols. Ed. C. Pichois. Gallimard, Pléiade, 1975–6.

Baudouin, Charles. *Psychanalyse de Victor Hugo*. 1943. Ed. P. Albouy. Armand Colin, 1972.

Bauer, Henri François. *Les 'Ballades' de Victor Hugo. Leurs Origines Françaises et Étrangères*. Champion, 1936.

Bellet, Roger. 'Le G Majuscule dans l'Onomastique Hugolienne'. In *G comme Hugo*. Ed. A. Court and R. Bellet. Université de Saint-Étienne, 1987.

Bellosta, Marie-Christine. 'Dons de Caractère Public Faits par Hugo après son Exil'. *Revue d'Histoire Littéraire de la France*, November–December 1986, 1114–16.

Benjamin, Walter. *Charles Baudelaire. A Lyric Poet in the Era of High Capitalism*. Trans. H. Zohn. Verso, 1983.

Benoit-Lévy, Edmond. *La Jeunesse de Victor Hugo. Ouvrage Documentaire*. Albin Michel, 1928.

Bergerat, Émile. *Souvenirs d'un Enfant de Paris*. 4 vols. Charpentier, 1911–13.

Berlioz, Hector. *Correspondance Générale*. 5 vols. Ed. P. Citron. Flammarion, 1972–89.

Berret, Paul. *La Philosophie de Victor Hugo en 1854–1859 et Deux Mythes de la Légende des Siècles*. Paulin, 1910.

Bersaucourt, Albert de. *Les Pamphlets Contre Victor Hugo*. Mercure de France, 1912.

Bertault, Marialys. *Sophie et Brutus. Le Sang Lorrain et Breton de Victor Hugo*. France-Empire, 1984.

Bertin, Louise. 'Les Joujoux des Enfants de Victor Hugo'. *La Gazette des Femmes*, 25 December 1841, 1.

Beuve, Paul and Henri Daragon. *Victor Hugo par le Bibelot. Le Populaire, l'Annonce, la Chanson*. Daragon, 1902.

Billy, André. *Sainte-Beuve, sa Vie et son Temps*. 2 vols. Flammarion, 1952.

Bingham, Capt. the Hon. D. *Recollections of Paris*. 2 vols. London: Chapman and Hall, 1896.

Biré, Edmond. *Victor Hugo et la Restauration. Étude Historique et Littéraire*. Lecoffre; Nantes: Forest et Grimaud, 1869.

Biré, E. *Victor Hugo avant 1830*. Gervais; Nantes: Grimaud, 1883.

Biré, E. *Victor Hugo après 1830*. 2 vols. Didier; Perrin, 1891.

Biré, E. *Victor Hugo après 1852. L'Exil, les Dernières Années et la Mort du Poète*. Didier; Perrin, 1894.

Birkbeck, Morris. *Notes on a Journey Through France [. . .] in July, August and September, 1814, Describing the Habits of the People, and the Agriculture of the Country*. 3rd ed. London: William Phillips, 1815.

Black, Frank Gees and Renee Métivier. *The Harney Papers*. Assen: Van Gorcum, 1969.

Blagdon, Francis William. *The French Interpreter, Consisting of Copious and Familiar Conversations on Every Topic which can be Useful or Interesting to Families, Travellers, Merchants, or Men of Business, Together with a*

Complete Vocabulary [. . .], the Whole Exhibiting, in a Very Distinct Manner, the Exact Mode of Pronunciation, with the True Parisian Accent. London: Samuel Leigh, 1816.

Blémont, Émile [Léon-Émile Petitdidier], ed. *Le Livre d'Or de Victor Hugo, par l'Élite des Artistes et des Écrivains Contemporains*. Librairie Artistique; Launette, 1883.

Blewer, Evelyn. 'Abel et Victor, les Frères Amis'. *Europe*, March 1985, 104–15.

Blewer, E. 'Victor Hugo, Élu des Lettres et des Arts'. In *Pratiques d'Écriture. Mélanges Jean Gaudon*. Ed. P. Laforgue. Klincksieck, 1996.

Bloom, Harold. *Poetics of Influence*. Ed. J. Hollander. New York: Schwab, 1988.

Bloy, Léon. *Le Désespéré*. 1886; Mercure de France, 1933.

Boisjolin, *see* Rabbe.

Bondois, Paul. *Histoire de la Révolution de 1870–71 et des Origines de la Troisième République*. Picard et Kaan, 1888.

Bonnerot, Jean. 'Les Lettres de Madame Adèle Victor-Hugo à Sainte-Beuve. Rapport de Henry Havard sur leur Destruction en Novembre 1885'. *Revue des Sciences Humaines*, October–December 1957, 353–92.

Bosq, Paul. *Souvenirs de l'Assemblée Nationale, 1871–1875*. Plon, Nourrit, 1908.

Bourg, Tony. *Recherches et Conférences Littéraires*. Ed. J.-C. Frisch, C. Meder, J.-C. Muller and F. Wilhelm. Luxembourg: Publications Nationales, 1994.

Bourquelot, Félix and Alfred Maury. *La Littérature Française Contemporaine, 1827–1849*. IV. Delaroque aîné, 1852.

Bowley, Victor. 'Victor Hugo in the Light of English Criticism and Opinion During the Nineteenth Century'. PhD Thesis. London University, 1944.

Braun, Jean, 'A Propos d'une Pierre Gravée au Donon'. *Les Vosges. Revue du Club Vosgien*, no. 4 (1983), 1–2.

Brazier, Nicolas. *Chroniques des Petits Théâtres de Paris*. Ed. G. d'Heylli. Rouveyre et Blond, 1883.

Bremond, Henri. *Le Roman et l'Histoire d'une Conversion. Ulric Guttinguer et Sainte-Beuve d'après des Correspondances Inédites*. Plon, Nourrit, 1925.

Breton, André. *Manifeste du Surréalisme* (1924). In *Oeuvres Complètes*. Vol. I. Ed. M. Bonnet *et al*. Gallimard, Pléiade, 1988.

Brombert, Victor. *Victor Hugo and the Visionary Novel*. Cambridge, Mass. and London: Harvard University Press, 1984.

Browning, Elizabeth Barrett. *Letters*. 2 vols. Ed. F. G. Kenyon. London: Smith, Elder, & Co., 1897.

Buchanan, Robert. *Master-Spirits*. London: Henry S. King, 1873.

Bulwer, Henry Lytton. *France, Social, Literary, Political*. Galignani, 1834.

Burroughs, George Frederick. *A Narrative of the Retreat of the British Army from Burgos*. Bristol: Joseph Routh, 1814.

Calmettes, Fernand. *Leconte de Lisle et Ses Amis*. Librairies-Imprimeries Réunies, [1902].

Carneiro Leão, A. *Victor Hugo no Brasil*. Rio de Janeiro: José Olympio, 1960.

Caron, Jean-Claude. *Générations Romantiques. Les Étudiants de Paris et le Quartier Latin (1814–1851)*. Armand Colin, 1991.

Carrington, Henry, Dean of Bocking. *Translations from the Poems of Victor Hugo*. 'Prefatory Notice' by E. Martinengo-Cesaresco. London: Walter Scott; Newcastle-on-Tyne, 'The Canterbury Poets', 1885.

Castille, Hippolyte. *Portraits Politiques au Dix-Neuvième Siècle. Victor Hugo*. Sartorius, 1857.

Cayon, Jean. *Histoire Physique, Civile, Morale et Politique de Nancy*. Nancy: Cayon-Liébault, 1846.

Challamel, Augustin. *Souvenirs d'un Hugolâtre. La Génération de 1830*. Jules Lévy, 1885.

Champfleury. *Les Excentriques* (1852). 2nd edn. Michel Lévy, 1855.

Champfleury. 'Les Grands Hommes du Ruisseau: Bug-Jargal'. *Le Corsaire*, 29 December 1845. In *Les Excentriques*, and *Chien-Caillou*. Ed. B. Leuilliot. Éditions des Cendres, 1988.

Chardin, Philippe. 'Dostoïevski Lecteur de V. Hugo'. In *Le Rayonnement International de Victor Hugo*. Ed. F. Claudon. New York: Peter Lang, 1989.

Charlier, Gustave. *Passages*. Brussels: La Renaissance du Livre, 1947.

Chasles, Philarète. *Mémoires*. 2 vols. Charpentier, 1876–7.

Chateaubriand, François-René, Vicomte de. *Mémoires d'Outre-Tombe*. 2 vols. Ed. J.-C. Berchet. Garnier, 1989, 1992.

Chenay, Paul. *Victor Hugo à Guernesey*. Juven, [1902].

Chernov, I. *Le Parti Républicain au Coup d'État et sous le Second Empire*. Pedone, 1906.

Chételat, E. J. *Les Occidentales, ou Lettres Critiques sur Les Orientales de M. Victor Hugo*. Hautecoeur-Martinet et chez tous les Marchands de Nouveautés, 1829. Geneva: Slatkine, 1970.

Chevalet, Émile. *La Quiquengrogne*. 2 vols. Gabriel Roux et Cassanet; chez Bazouge-Pigoreau, 1846.

Chippendale, Thomas. *The Gentleman and Cabinet-Maker's Director. Being a Large Collection of the Most Elegant and Useful Designs of Houshold* [sic] *Furniture in the Gothic, Chinese and Modern Taste: Including a Great Variety of Book-Cases for Libraries or Private Rooms* [etc.]. 2nd edn. London: Haberkorn, 1755.

Chopin, Frédéric. *Souvenirs Inédits*. Ed. M. Karlowicz. Trans. L. Disière. Paris and Leipzig: Welter, 1904.

Christiansen, Rupert. *Tales of the New Babylon. Paris 1869–1875*. London: Sinclair-Stevenson, 1994.

Claretie, Jules. *Célébrités Contemporaines. Victor Hugo*. Quantin, 1882.

Claretie, J. *La Vie à Paris, 1882*. Havard, [1883?].

Claretie, J. *Victor Hugo, Souvenirs Intimes*. Librairie Molière, [1902].

Claretie, J. *La Vie à Paris, 1901–1903*. Charpentier et Fasquelle, 1904.

Claudel, Paul. *Oeuvres en Prose*. Ed. J. Petit and C. Galpérine. Gallimard, Pléiade, 1965.

Clément-Janin, Noël. *Victor Hugo en Exil, d'après sa Correspondance avec Jules Janin*. 5th edn. Éditions du Monde Nouveau, 1922.

Cocteau, Jean. 'Le Mystère Laïc', part I of *Essai de Critique Indirecte*. Grasset, 1932.

Colvin, Sidney. *Memories & Notes of Persons and Places, 1852–1912*. London: Arnold, 1921.

Conrad, Joseph. *The Collected Letters*. 5 vols. Ed. F. Karl and L. Davies. Cambridge University Press, 1983–.

Le Conservateur Littéraire. 4 vols. Ed. J. Marsan. Hachette, 1922–6; Droz, 1935–8.

Cordier, Marcel. *Victor Hugo, Homme de l'Est*. Sarreguemines: Pierron, 1985.

Coste, Maurice, *see* Talmeyr.

Cuvillier-Fleury, Alfred-Auguste. *Journal Intime*. Ed. E. Bertin. Vol. I: 1828–1831. Plon, Nourrit, 1900.

Daubray, Cécile. *Victor Hugo et ses Correspondants*. Avant-Propos de Paul Valéry. Albin Michel, 1947.

Daudet, Mme Alphonse (Julia Allard). *Souvenirs Autour d'un Groupe Littéraire*. Charpentier et Fasquelle, 1910.

Daudet, Léon. *La Tragique Existence de Victor Hugo*. Albin Michel, 1937.

David, Sylvain-Christian. *Philoxène Boyer. Un Sale Ami de Baudelaire*. Ramsay, 1987.

David d'Angers [Pierre-Jean David]. *Les Carnets de David d'Angers*. 2 vols. Ed. A. Bruel. Plon, 1958.

Davidson, A. F. *Victor Hugo. His Life and Work*. London: Eveleigh Nash, 1912.

Day, Samuel Phillips. *The True Story of Louis Napoleon's Life*. London: *Reynold's Newspaper*, [1871].

Delaage, Henri. *Perfectionnement Physique de la Race Humaine ou Moyens d'Acquérir la Beauté d'après les Procédés Occultes des Mages de Chaldée, des Philosophes Hermétiques, d'Albert-le-Grand, de Paracelse, et des Principaux Thaumaturges des Siècles Écoulés*. Lesigne, 1850.

Delaage, H. *Le Monde Occulte, ou Mystères du Magnétisme Dévoilés par le Somnambulisme, Précédé d'une Introduction sur le Magnétisme par le Père Lacordaire*. Lesigne, 1851.

Delalande, Jean. *Victor Hugo à Hauteville House*. Albin Michel, 1947.

Delécluze, Étienne-Jean. *Souvenirs de Soixante Années*. Michel Lévy, 1862.

Delteil, Yvan. *La Fin Tragique du Voyage de Victor Hugo en 1843 d'après le Journal de Voyage Autographe de Juliette Drouet*. Nizet, 1970.

De Mutigny, Jean. *Victor Hugo et le Spiritisme*. Nathan, 1981.

Denis, Ferdinand. *Journal (1829–1848)*. Ed. P. Moreau. Fribourg: Librairie de l'Université; Paris: Plon, 1932.

Derôme, Léopold. *Les Éditions Originales des Romantiques*. 2 vols. Rouveyre, 1887.

Deschanel, Émile. *Physiologie des Écrivains et des Artistes, ou Essai de Critique Naturelle*. Hachette, 1864.

Descotes, Maurice. *L'Acteur Joanny et son Journal Inédit*. P.U.F., n.d.

Despy-Meyer, A. and Francis Sartorius, eds. *Les Éditeurs Belges de Victor Hugo et le Banquet des 'Misérables'*. Brussels: Crédit Communal, 1986.

Deutscher, Isaac. *Stalin. A Political Biography*. 1949; Penguin, 1990.

Dickens, Charles. *The Letters of Charles Dickens*. Vol. V. Ed. G. Storey and K. J. Fielding. Oxford: Clarendon Press, 1981.

Dictionnaire de l'Académie Française. 5th edn., 1798; 6th edn., 1835.

Documents sur les Événements de 1870–71. 10 vols. Librairie des Bibliophiles, 1871–2.

Dostoevsky, Anna. *Dostoevsky. Reminiscences*. Trans. B. Stillman. London: Wildwood House, 1975.

Drouet, Juliette. *Mille et Une Lettres d'Amour à Victor Hugo*. Ed. P. Souchon. Gallimard, NRF, 1951.

Drouet, J. *Lettres de Juliette Drouet à Victor Hugo*. Ed. E. Blewer. Preface by J. Gaudon. Pauvert et Silène-Har/Po, 1985.

Drouet, J. 'Fin du Voyage de 1843'. Ed. C. Chuat. In *OC*, XIII, 965–94.

Drouet, J. 'Relation sur les Événements du 2 au 11 Décembre 1851'. In Massin, VIII, 1123–36.

Dubois, Madeleine and Patrice Boussel. *De Quoi Vivait Victor Hugo?* Les Deux Rives, 1952.

Dubois, Abbé Pierre. *Bio-Bibliographie de Victor Hugo de 1802 à 1825* [*sic* for 1824]. Champion, 1913.

Du Camp, Maxime. *Souvenirs Littéraires.* (1882). Ed. D. Oster. Aubier, 'Critiques', 1994.

Du Camp, M. *Théophile Gautier.* 2nd edn. Hachette, 1895.

Duchet, Claude. 'Un Libraire Libéral sous l'Empire et la Restauration: du Nouveau sur Royol'. *Revue d'Histoire Littéraire de la France*, July–September 1965, 485–93.

Duclaux, Mme [Agnes Mary]. *Victor Hugo.* London: Constable, 'Makers of the Nineteenth Century', 1921.

Dufay, Pierre. *Celui Dont on ne Parle pas. Eugène Hugo, sa Vie, sa Folie, son Oeuvre.* Fort, 1924.

Dumas, Alexandre. *Mes Mémoires.* Ed. P. Josserand. Vol. III. Gallimard, NRF, 1966.

Dumas, A. *Mes Mémoires.* Ed. I. Chanteur and C. Schopp. Plon, 1986.

Duruy, Albert. 'Le Brigadier Muscar. Histoire du Temps des Guerres de la Révolution'. *Revue des Deux Mondes*, 15 November 1885, 380–404.

Duruy, Victor. *Petite Histoire de France, Depuis les Temps les Plus Reculés Jusqu'à Nos Jours.* Hachette, 1868.

Duvert, Félix-Auguste. *Théâtre Choisi.* Charpentier, 1877–8.

Eckermann, Johann Peter. *Gespräche mit Goethe in den letzten Jahren seines Lebens.* Munich: Beck, 1984.

Edwards, Stewart. *The Paris Commune. 1871.* 1971; New York: Quadrangle, 1977.

Ellis, Havelock. *From Rousseau to Proust.* London: Constable, 1936.

Ellmann, Richard. *Oscar Wilde.* London: Hamish Hamilton, 1987.

Enciclopedia Universal Ilustrada Europeo-Americana. Vol. XXVIII. Bilbao, Madrid, Barcelona: Espasa-Calpe, [1925].

Engels, Friedrich, *see* Karl Marx.

Escamps, Henry d'. *Du Rétablissement de l'Empire.* Garnier; Plon, 1852.

Escholier, Raymond. *Un Amant de Génie: Victor Hugo.* Fayard, 1953.

Escholier, R. *Victor Hugo, cet Inconnu.* Plon, 1951.

Escholier, R. *Hugo, Roi de son Siècle.* Arthaud, 1970.

Evans, David Owen. *Le Socialisme Romantique. Pierre Leroux et ses Contemporains*. Rivière, 1948.

Fabre, Gustave. *Une Visite à Victor Hugo en 1883*. Nîmes: Clavel et Chastanier, 1889.

Farcinet, Charles. *Trois Lettres Inédites de Victor Hugo, Alfred de Vigny et Béranger*. Vannes: Lafolye; Fontenay-le-Comte: Bureaux de la *Revue du Bas-Poitou*, 1894.

Feller, Martin. *Der Dichter in der Politik: Victor Hugo und der Deutsch-Französische Krieg von 1870/71*. Doctoral Dissertation. Marburg an der Lahn, 1988.

Fierobe, Claude. *Charles Robert Maturin (1780–1824), l'Homme et l'Oeuvre*. Université de Lille, 1974.

Fitz-Ball, Edward. *Esmeralda, or The Deformed of Notre Dame. A Drama, in Three Acts, Founded on Victor Hugo's Popular Novel of 'Notre Dame'*. (Surrey Theatre, 14 April 1834.) London: John Miller, 1834.

Fizaine, Michèle. '*Provisam Rem*: Les Manuscrits des Discours de 1848 à 1851'. In *Hugo de l'Écrit au Livre*. Ed. B. Didier and J. Neefs. Presses Universitaires de Vincennes, 1987.

Flammarion, Camille. *La Pluralité des Mondes Habités*. 2nd edn. Didier; Gauthier Villars, 1864.

Flaubert, Gustave. *Correspondance*. Ed. J. Bruneau. 4 vols. Gallimard, Pléiade, 1973–.

Fontaney, Antoine. 'Romans de Victor Hugo, nouvelle édition'. *Revue des Deux Mondes*, 1 May 1832, 375–9.

Fontaney, A. *Journal Intime*. Ed. R. Jasinski. Les Presses Françaises, 1925.

Ford, Ford Madox. *The March of Literature. From Confucius to Modern Times*. 1938; London: Allen & Unwin; Readers Union, 1947.

Foresi, Mario. *Vittore Hugo all'Isola d'Elba*. Florence: Salvadore Landi, 1889.

Forster, John. *The Life of Charles Dickens*. London: Cecil Palmer, 1928.

Foucher, Paul. *Les Coulisses du Passé*. Dentu, 1873.

Foucher, Paul. *Entre Cour et Jardin. Études et Souvenirs du Théâtre*. Amyot, 1867.

Foucher, Pierre. *Souvenirs de Pierre Foucher*. Ed. L. Guimbaud. Plon, 1929.

François de Neufchâteau, *see* Le Sage.

Frédérix, Gustave. *Souvenir du Banquet Offert à Victor Hugo par MM. A. Lacroix, Verboeckhoven et Cie*. Brussels: [Lacroix, Verboeckhoven et Cie], 1862.

Freud, Sigmund. *Psychopathology of Everyday Life*. Trans. A. A. Brill. London and Leipzig: Fisher Unwin, 1914.

Freud, S. *Leonardo da Vinci and a Memory of His Childhood*. 1910. Trans. A. Tyson. Penguin, Pelican, 1963.

Galand, René. 'Le Monstre des Feuillantines: Une Énigme Hugolienne'. *Revue d'Histoire Littéraire de la France*, September–October 1994, 805–8.

Gassier, Pierre. 'Goya and the Hugo Family in Madrid, 1811–12'. *Apollo. The Magazine of the Arts*, October 1981, 248–51.

Gaudon, Jean, ed. *Ce que Disent les Tables Parlantes*. Pauvert, 1963.

Gaudon, J. *Le Temps de la Contemplation, L'Oeuvre Poétique de Victor Hugo des Misères au Seuil du Gouffre (1845–1856)*. Flammarion, 1969.

Gaudon, J. *Victor Hugo et le Théâtre. Stratégie et Dramaturgie*. Suger, 1985.

Gaudon, J. '"Je ne sais quel jour de soupirail . . ."'. In Guy Rosa, ed. *Victor Hugo. Les Misérables*. Klincksieck, 1995.

Gaudon, Sheila. 'Prophétisme et Utopie: le Problème du Destinataire dans *Les Châtiments*'. *Saggi e Ricerche di Letteratura Francese*, XVI (1977), 403–26.

Gautier, Judith. *Le Collier des Jours. Le Second Rang du Collier*. Juven, n.d.

Gautier, Théophile. *Les Jeunes France, Romans Goguenards*. 1833; Ed. R. Jasinski. Flammarion, 1974.

Gautier, T. *Correspondance Générale*. 8 vols. Ed. P. Laubriet, C. Lacoste-Veysseyre *et al*. Geneva: Droz, 1985–.

Gautier, T. *Histoire du Romantisme* (unfinished article written for *Le Bien Public* in 1872). In *Souvenirs Romantiques*. Ed. A. Boschot. Garnier, 1929.

Gautier, T. *Lettres à la Présidente et Poésies Libertines*. Ed. P. Pia. Bibliothèque Privée, 1968.

Gautier, T. *Portraits Contemporains*. 3rd edn. Charpentier, 1874.

Gayot, André. *Une Ancienne Muscadine, Fortunée Hamelin. Lettres Inédites, 1839–1851*. Émile-Paul, n.d.

Georgel, Pierre. *Léopoldine Hugo, une Jeune Fille Romantique*. Villequier: Musée Victor Hugo, 1967.

Georgel, P. *Drawings by Victor Hugo*. Exhibition Catalogue, Victoria and Albert Museum. London: HMSO; The Curwen Press, 1974.

Géraud, Edmond. *Un Homme de Lettres sous l'Empire et la Restauration. Fragments de Journal Intime*. Ed. M. Albert. Flammarion, n.d.

Gide, André, ed. *Anthologie de la Poésie Française*. Gallimard, Pléiade, 1959.

Giese, William F. *Victor Hugo, the Man and the Poet*. London: Melrose, [1927].

Giraud, Victor. 'Chateaubriand et Victor Hugo: la Légende de "l'Enfant Sublime"'. *Revue d'Histoire Littéraire de la France*, July–September 1926, 419.

Gobron, Gabriel. *Histoire et Philosophie du Caodaïsme. Bouddhisme Rénové, Spiritisme Vietnamien, Religion Nouvelle en Eurasie*. Dervy, 1949.

Goncourt, Edmond and Jules. *Journal. Mémoires de la Vie Littéraire*. 3 vols. Ed. R. Ricatte. Laffont, 1989.

Gosse, Edmund. *French Profiles*. London: Heinemann, 1905.

Gourevitch, Michel and Danielle. 'La Folie d'Eugène Hugo'. In *CF*, II, 755–83.

Goya y Lucientes, Francisco José de. *Los Desastres de la Guerra: Coleccion de Ochenta Láminas Inventadas y Grabadas al Agua Fuerte. – The Disasters of War*. Ed. P. Hofer. New York: Dover, 1967.

Granier de Cassagnac, Adolphe. *Souvenirs du Second Empire*. I. *La Présidence et le Coup d'État*. Dentu, 1879.

Grant, Elliott. *Victor Hugo During the Second Republic. Smith College Studies in Modern Languages*, XVII, 1 (October 1935).

Grant, Richard. 'Victor Hugo's "Les Deux Archers": Patterns of Disguise and Revelation'. *Romance Notes*, Spring 1992, 215–20.

Griffiths, David. 'Victor Hugo et Victor Schoelcher au Ban de l'Empire'. *Revue d'Histoire Littéraire de la France*, October–December 1963, 545–80.

Guénot, Georges. 'Courrier de Paris'. *Le Courrier de Paris*, 21 July and 16 November 1850.

Guérin, Eugénie de. *Journal et Fragments, publiés avec l'assentiment de sa famille*. Ed. G. S. Trébutien. 60th ed. [*sic*]. Lecoffre; Gabalda, 1931.

Guille, Frances Vernor. *François-Victor Hugo et son Oeuvre*. Nizet, 1950.

Guillemin, Henri. *Hugo et la Sexualité*. Gallimard, NRF, 1954.

Guillemin, H. *L'Engloutie: Adèle, Fille de Victor Hugo, 1830–1915*. Seuil, 1985.

Guimbaud, Louis. *Victor Hugo et Juliette Drouet*. Blaizot, 1927.

Guimbaud, L. *Victor Hugo et Madame Biard*. Blaizot, 1927.

Guimbaud, L. *Les Orientales de Victor Hugo*. Amiens: Malfère, 1928.

Guimbaud, L. *La Mère de Victor Hugo, 1772–1821*. Plon, 1930.

Guttinguer, Ulric. *Arthur*. Ed. H. Bremond. Les Presses Françaises, n.d.

Hambrick, Margaret. *A Chartist's Library*. London and New York: Mansell, 1986.

Hansard's Parliamentary Debates. 3rd series. London: Cornelius Buck.

Harney, George Julian. 'Victor Hugo in Jersey'. *The Athenaeum*, 20 June 1885, 791.

Hayter, Alethea. *Opium and the Romantic Imagination. Addiction and Creativity in De Quincey, Coleridge, Baudelaire and Others*. Revised edn. Wellingborough: Crucible, 1988.

Hazlitt, William. *Notes of a Journey Through France and Italy*. London: Hunt and Clarke, 1826.

Hazlitt, William, the Younger, *see* Victor Hugo, *Notre Dame*.

Heath, Richard. 'Victor Hugo'. *The Leisure Hour*, XXXIV (1885), 809–16.

Heine, Heinrich. *Lutèce. Lettres sur la Vie Politique, Artistique et Sociale de la France*. Michel Lévy, 1855.

Hemmings, F. W. J. *The Theatre Industry in Nineteenth-Century France*. Cambridge University Press, 1993.

Hetzel, Pierre-Jules, *see* Victor Hugo (1979).

Hillairet, Jacques. *Dictionnaire Historique des Rues de Paris*. 6th edn. 2 vols. Éditions de Minuit, 1976.

Hoffman, Léon-François. 'Victor Hugo, John Brown et les Haïtiens'. *Nineteenth-Century French Studies*, Fall–Winter 1987–8, 47–58.

Hooker, Kenneth Ward. *The Fortunes of Victor Hugo in England*. New York: Columbia University Press, 1938.

Houssaye, Arsène. *Souvenirs de Jeunesse, 1830–1850*. Flammarion, [1896].

Hozier, Louis-Pierre d' and D'Hozier de Sérigny. *Armorial Général, ou Registres de la Noblesse de France*. IV. Didot, 1867.

Huas, Jeanine. *Juliette Drouet, le Bel Amour de Victor Hugo*. Lachurié, 1985.

Hudson, William Henry. *Victor Hugo and His Poetry*. London: Harrap, 1918.

Hugo, Abel, ed. *Romancero e Historia del Rey de España Don Rodrigo, Postrero de los Godos. En Lenguage [sic] Antiguo*. Pélicier; Rodriguez; Baudry, 1821.

Hugo, Abel, trans. *Romances Historiques, Traduites de l'Espagnol*. Pélicier, 1822.

[Hugo, Abel]. J. A. ***. *Les Tombeaux de Saint-Denis* [and] *Récit de la Violation des Tombeaux en 1793*. Maurice, 1825.

Hugo, Abel. 'Souvenirs et Mémoires sur Joseph Napoléon: sa Cour, l'Armée Française et l'Espagne en 1811, 1812 et 1813'. *Revue des Deux Mondes*, 1 February 1833, 300–24, and 15 April 1833, 113–42.

Hugo, Abel. *La France Pittoresque, ou Description Pittoresque, Topographique et*

Statistique des Départements et Colonies de la France. 3 vols. Delloye, 1835.

Hugo, Abel, *see* A ! A ! A !

[Hugo, Adèle (Mme Hugo)]. *Victor Hugo Raconté par un Témoin de sa Vie, avec des Oeuvres Inédites, entre autres un Drame en Trois Actes: Iñez de Castro.* 2 vols. Brussels and Leipzig: Lacroix, Verboeckhoven, 1863. (On authorship, see p. 17.)

[Hugo, Adèle (Mme Hugo)]. *Victor Hugo Raconté par Adèle Hugo.* Ed. E. Blewer, J. and S. Gaudon, G. Malandain, J.-C. Nabet, G. Rosa, C. Trévisan and A. Ubersfeld. Plon, 1985.

Hugo, Adèle (Mlle Hugo). *Le Journal d'Adèle Hugo.* Ed. F. V. Guille. 3 vols. Minard, Lettres Modernes, 1968–84.

Hugo, Charles. 'A Ma Mère'. In *La Bohême Dorée.* Vol. I. Michel Lévy, 1859.

Hugo, Charles. *Les Hommes de l'Exil, Précédés de Mes Fils, par Victor Hugo.* 2nd edn. Lemerre, 1875. [Title page: 1874.]

Hugo, Charles, *see* Lecanu.

Hugo, François-Victor. *La Normandie Inconnue.* Pagnerre, 1857.

Hugo, François-Victor. *Les Sonnets de Shakespeare Traduits pour la Première Fois en entier.* Michel Lévy, 1857.

Hugo, François-Victor. 'La Place Royale'. In *Paris Guide, par les Principaux Écrivains et Artistes de la France.* 2 vols. Librairie Internationale; Brussels, Leipzig and Leghorn: Lacroix, Verboeckhoven, 1867.

Hugo, Georges. *Mon Grand-Père.* Calmann-Lévy, 1902. Reprinted in Massin, XVI, 927–39.

[Hugo, Joseph-Léopold-Sigisbert]. S. Sigisbert. *L'Aventurière Tyrolienne.* Delaforest, 1825.

[Hugo, J.-L.-S.]. Genty. *Mémoire sur les Moyens de Suppléer à la Traite des Nègres par des Individus Libres, et d'une Manière qui Garantisse pour l'Avenir la Sûreté des Colons et la Dépendance des Colonies.* Blois: Verdier, January 1818.

Hugo, Léopold-Armand. *La Théorie Hugodécimale ou la Base Scientifique et Définitive de l'Arithmologistique Universelle.* Chez tous les Libraires, 1877.

Hugo, Léopoldine. *Correspondance.* Ed. P. Georgel. Klincksieck, 1976.

Hugo, Victor. *L'Archipel de la Manche. The Channel Islands.* Trans. J. W. Watson. Jersey: La Haule, 1985.

Hugo, V. *Boîte aux Lettres.* Ed. R. Journet and G. Robert. Flammarion, 1965.

Hugo, V. *Carnets Intimes, 1870–1871.* Ed. H. Guillemin. Gallimard, NRF, 1953.

Hugo, V. *Les Chansons des Rues et des Bois*. Ed. J. Gaudon. Gallimard, 'Poésie', 1982.

Hugo, V. *Choses Vues. Souvenirs, Journaux, Cahiers, 1870–1885*. Ed. H. Juin. Gallimard, 'Folio', 1972.

Hugo, V. *Les Contemplations*. 3 vols. Ed. J. Vianey. Hachette, 1922.

Hugo, V. *Correspondance*. 4 vols. Ed. C. Daubray. Imprimerie Nationale; Ollendorff, 1947–52. [Part of *Oeuvres Complètes*, 1904–52.]

Hugo, V. *Correspondance Familiale et Écrits Intimes*. 2 vols. Gen. eds. J. and S. Gaudon and B. Leuilliot. Laffont, 1988, 1991.

Hugo, V. *Correspondance entre Victor Hugo et Paul Meurice*. Preface by Jules Claretie. Charpentier et Fasquelle, 1909.

Hugo, V. *Correspondance entre Victor Hugo et Pierre-Jules Hetzel*. Vol. I. Ed. S. Gaudon. Klincksieck, 1979.

Hugo, V. *Les Enfants (Le Livre des Mères)*. Preface by P.-J. Stahl [Hetzel]. Hachette, 1858.

Hugo, V. *Excursions Along the Banks of the Rhine*. (Translation.) London: Henry Colburn, 1843.

Hugo, V. *Hans of Iceland*. With four etchings by George Cruikshank. London: J. Robins, 1825.

Hugo, V. *Hans of Iceland*. Trans. A. Langdon Alger. London: Routledge, 1897.

Hugo, V. *The Hunchback of Notre-Dame. Translated Expressly for this Edition, with a Sketch of the Life and Writings of the Author*. Trans. F. Shoberl. Galignani; London: Richard Bentley; Edinburgh: Bell and Bradfute; Dublin: Cumming, 1833.

Hugo, V. *Journal de ce que J'Apprends Chaque Jour (Juillet 1846–Février 1848)*. Ed. R. Journet and G. Robert. Flammarion, 1965.

Hugo, V. *Lettres à Juliette Drouet, 1833–1883. Le Livre de l'Anniversaire*. Ed. J. Gaudon. Pauvert, 1964.

Hugo, V. *Lettres de Victor Hugo à Léonie Biard*. Ed. J. Gaudon. Blaizot, 1990.

Hugo, V. *Lettres Inédites à Juliette Drouet (1873)*. Ed. T. Bodin. Pref. J. Gaudon. Beugné l'Abbé, privately printed, 1992.

Hugo, V. *Littérature et Philosophie Mêlées*. 2 vols. Ed. A. R. W. James. Klincksieck, 1976.

Hugo, V. *Man and his World in the Alphabet*. Trans. P. Standard. 1954; Moreton-in-Marsh: Kit-Cat Press, 1991.

Hugo, V. *Les Misérables*. 3 vols. Trans. Lascelles Wraxall. London: Hurst and Blackett, 1862.

Hugo, V. *Les Misérables*. 2 vols. Trans. C. E. Wilbour. London: Routledge, 1887.

Hugo, V. *Napoléon-le-Petit*. London: Jeffs; Brussels: Mertens, 1852.

Hugo, V. *Napoleon the Little*. London: Vizetelly, 1852.

Hugo, V. *Notre Dame. A Tale of the Ancient Regime. From the French of M. Victor Hugo, with a Prefatory Notice, Literary and Political of His Romances.* Trans. William Hazlitt the Younger. Effingham Wilson, 1833.

Hugo, V. *Oeuvres Complètes*. ['Édition de l'Imprimerie Nationale'.] 45 vols. Ed. P. Meurice; G. Simon; C. Daubray. Ollendorff; Albin Michel, 1904–52.

Hugo, V. *Oeuvres Complètes. Édition Chronologique*. Gen. ed. Jean Massin. 18 vols. Club Français du Livre, 1967–71. Ed. P. Albouy, J.-B. Barrère, M. Billington, H. Bonnier, J.-P. Brisson, J. Bruhat, M. Butor, L. Cellier, C. Duchet, J. Gaudon, S. Gaudon, C. Gély, P. Georgel, Y. Gohin, B. Grynberg, H. Guillemin, P. Halbwachs, A. R. W. James, R. Journet, A. Laster, B. Leuilliot, A. Martin, C. Mauron, J.-L. Mercié, H. Meschonnic, R. Molho, P. Moreau, G. Mounin, G. Picon, G. Piroué, R. Ricatte, G. Robert, G. Rosa, S. S. de Sacy, F. Schneeberg, J. Seebacher, J. Téphany, A. Ubersfeld, É. Vasseur, J.-P. Wytteman, P. Zumthor.

Hugo, V. *Oeuvres Complètes*. Gen. eds Jacques Seebacher and Guy Rosa. 15 vols. Laffont, 'Bouquins', 1985–90. Ed. J. Acher, M.-C. Bellosta, E. Blewer, H. Cellier, C. Chuat, B. de Cornulier, J. Delabroy, J.-C. Fizaine, M. Fizaine, D. Gasiglia-Laster, J. Gaudon, S. Gaudon, C. Gély, Y. Gohin, A. R. W. James, R. Journet, P. Laforgue, A. Laster, B. Leuilliot, G. Malandain, A. Maurel, C. Millet, J.-C. Nabet, Y. Parent, C. Raineri, J.-P. Reynaud, A. Rosa, N. Savy, C. Trévisan, A. Ubersfeld.

Hugo, V. *Oeuvres Poétiques*. 3 vols. Ed. P. Albouy. Gallimard, Pléiade, 1964–74.

Hugo, V. *Post-Scriptum de Ma Vie*. Ed. H. Guillemin. Neuchâtel: Ides et Calendes, n.d.

Hugo, V. *The Rhine. To Which is Added A Guide for Tourists on the Rhine, from Notes by the Translator*. Trans. D. M. Aird. London: Ingram, Cooke and Co., 1843; 1853.

Hugo, V. *Trois Albums (Choix de Lavis et Inventaire)*. Ed. R. Journet and G. Robert. Les Belles Lettres, 1963.

Hugo, V. *The United States of Europe*. Boston: World Peace Foundation, October 1914.

Hugo, V. *Victor Hugo's Intellectual Autobiography (Postscriptum de Ma Vie)*,

Being the Last of the Unpublished Works and Embodying the Author's Ideas on Literature, Philosophy and Religion. Translated with a Study of the Last Phase of His Genius by Lorenzo O'Rourke. New York and London: Funk & Wagnall, 1907.

Hugo, V. *La Voix de Guernesey*. Guernsey: T.-M. Bichard, November 1867.

Hugo, V. and Charles Nodier. *Correspondance Croisée*. Ed. J.-R. Dahan. Bassac: Plein Chant, 1986.

Ionesco, Eugène. *Hugoliade*. Trans. D. Costineanu. Gallimard, NRF, 1982. (Translation of *Viata Grotescă şi Tragică a lui Victor Hugo*, 1935–6.)

Izambard, Georges. *Rimbaud tel que je l'ai Connu*. Ed. H. de Bouillane de Lacoste and P. Izambard. Mercure de France, 1946.

James, Anthony R. W., ed. *Victor Hugo: A Story of Resistance. A Centenary Exhibition*. John Rylands University Library of Manchester, 15 April–14 June 1985.

James, A. R. W., ed. *Victor Hugo et la Grande-Bretagne. Actes du Deuxième Colloque Vinaver, Manchester 1985*. Liverpool: Cairns, 1986.

James, Henry. *Notes and Reviews*. Ed. P. de Chaignon la Rose. Cambridge, Mass.: Dunster House, 1921.

James, H. *Literary Reviews and Essays*. Ed. A. Mordell. New York: Grove, 1957.

Janin, Jules. *735 Lettres à sa Femme*. 3 vols. Ed. Mergier-Bourdeix. Klinck-sieck, 1973–9.

Jay, Antoine. *La Conversion d'un Romantique, Manuscrit de Joseph Delorme*. Moutardier, 1830.

Jouin, Henry. *David d'Angers et ses Relations Littéraires. Correspondance du Maître*. Plon, Nourrit, 1890.

Judith, Mme [Julie Bernard]. *La Vie d'une Grande Comédienne. Mémoires de Madame Judith de la Comédie Française et Souvenirs sur ses Contemporains*. Ghost-written by Paul Gsell. Tallandier, 1911.

Juin, Hubert. *Victor Hugo*. 3 vols. Flammarion, 1980–86.

Jullien, Adolphe. *Le Romantisme et l'Éditeur Renduel*. Charpentier et Fasquelle, 1897.

Karr, Alphonse. *Les Guêpes*. 2nd edn. 4 vols. Lecou; Blanchard, 1853.

Karr, A. *Le Livre de Bord*. 3 vols. Calmann Lévy; Librairie Nouvelle, 1880.

Kemble, Frances Ann. *Francis the First. A Tragedy in Five Acts. As Performed at the Theatre Royal, Covent Garden*. London: John Murray, 1832.

Kemble, F. A. *Record of a Girlhood.* 3 vols. London: Richard Bentley, 1878.

Kemble, F. A. *Records of Later Life.* 3 vols. London: Richard Bentley, 1882.

Krakovitch, Odile. *Hugo Censuré. La Liberté au Théâtre au XIXe Siècle.* Calmann-Lévy, 1985.

Krakovitch, O. *Les Pièces de Théâtre Soumises à la Censure (1800–1830). Inventaire.* Archives Nationales, 1982.

Kuscinski, A. *Dictionnaire des Conventionnels.* Société de l'Histoire de la Révolution Française, 1916.

Lacroux, Jean-Pierre, ed. *La Fin du Siècle. Tombeau de Victor Hugo. Le 22 Mai 1885.* Quintette, 1985.

Lafargue, Paul. *La Légende de Victor Hugo.* Le Dilettante, 1985.

Lamartine, Alphonse de. *Correspondance.* 6 vols. Ed. Valentine de Lamartine. Hachette; Furne, Jouvet, 1873–5.

Lamartine, A. de. *Oeuvres Poétiques.* Ed. M.-F. Guyard. Gallimard, Pléiade, 1963.

Lamennais, Félicité-Robert de. *Correspondance Générale.* 9 vols. Ed. L. Le Guillou. Armand Colin, 1971–1981.

La Morvonnais, Hippolyte Michel de. *L'Ordre Nouveau ou Gouvernement du Monde par les Mieux Inspirés, les Plus Instruits, et les Plus Capables. Évangélisation du Globe et des Ames.* Saint-Malo: Hamel, 1848.

Larousse, Pierre. *Grand Dictionnaire Universel du XIXe Siècle.* 1866–79.

Le Barbier, Louis. *Le Général De la Horie, 1766–1812.* Dujarric, 1904.

Lebreton-Savigny, Monique. *Victor Hugo et les Américains (1825–1885).* Klincksieck, 1971.

[Lecanu, Alphonse]. *Chez Victor Hugo, par un Passant, avec 12 Eaux-Fortes par M. Maxime Lalanne.* Cadart et Luquet, 1864. (Text by Charles Hugo.)

Le Faure, G. and H. Abeniacar. *Victor Hugo devant l'Opinion. Presse Française. Presse Étrangère.* Office de la Presse, 1885.

Leffondrey, Jules. *Victor Hugo le Petit.* Vanier, 1883.

Legay, Tristan. *Victor Hugo Jugé Par Son Siècle.* 3rd edn. Éditions de *La Plume,* 1902.

Legoyt, A. 'Statistique de la Ville de Paris'. In *Le Diable à Paris. Paris et les Parisiens.* II. Hetzel, 1846.

Lemercier de Neuville, Louis. *Souvenirs d'un Montreur de Marionnettes.* Bauche, 1911.

Leroux, Pierre. *Aux États de Jersey, sur un Moyen de Quintupler, pour ne pas dire plus, la Production Agricole du Pays.* London: Universal Library; Jersey: Nétré, 1853.

Leroux, Pierre. *La Grève de Samarez, Poème Philosophique.* Ed. J.-P. Lacassagne. Klincksieck, 1979.

Le Sage, Alain-René. *Histoire de Gil Blas de Santillane.* Vol. I. Ed. François de Neufchâteau. Didot, 'Collection des Meilleurs Ouvrages de la Langue Française, Dédiée aux Amateurs de l'Art Typographique, ou d'Éditions Soignées et Correctes', 1819.

Lesclide, Juana. *Victor Hugo Intime.* Juven, [1903].

Lesclide, Richard. *Propos de Table de Victor Hugo.* Dentu, 1885.

Leuilliot, Bernard. *Victor Hugo Publie Les Misérables. Correspondance avec Albert Lacroix, Août 1861 – Juillet 1862.* Klincksieck, 1970.

Leuilliot, B. 'Les Barricades Mystérieuses'. *Europe,* March 1985, 127–36.

Levaillant, Maurice. *La Crise Mystique de Victor Hugo.* Corti, 1954.

Lionnet, Anatole and Hippolyte. *Souvenirs et Anecdotes.* Ollendorff, 1888.

Lissagaray, Prosper. *History of the Commune of 1871.* 1876; Trans. Eleanor Marx Aveling. London: Reeves and Turner, 1886.

Liszt, Franz. *Correspondance de Liszt et de la Comtesse d'Agoult.* 2 vols. Ed. D. Ollivier. Grasset, 1933–4.

Littré, Émile. *Dictionnaire de la Langue Française.* Hachette, 1873–5.

Llewellyn Williams, Henry, ed. *Selections Chiefly Lyrical from the Poetical Works of Victor Hugo. Translated into English by Various Authors.* London: George Bell, 1885.

Lockroy, Édouard. *Au Hasard de la Vie. Notes et Souvenirs.* Grasset, 1913.

[Loménie, Louis de]. *Galerie des Contemporains Illustres, par un Homme de Rien.* Brussels: Hen, 1841.

Lorant, André. *Les Parents Pauvres d'Honoré de Balzac.* Droz, 1967.

Lukács, Georg. *The Historical Novel.* Trans. H. and S. Mitchell. London: Merlin Press, 1962.

Luppé, Alfred, Marquis de. *Astolphe de Custine.* Monaco: Éditions du Rocher, n.d.

Mabilleau, Léopold. *Victor Hugo.* Hachette, 1893.

Macdonald, Hugh. 'Louise Bertin'. In *The New Grove Dictionary of Music and Musicians.* Ed. S. Sadie. London: Macmillan, 1980.

Macrae, David. *Life of Napoleon III.* Glasgow: Marr; Edinburgh: Menzies; London: Simpkin, Marshall, 1870.

Magen, Hippolyte. *Histoire du Second Empire.* 3rd edn. Dreyfous, 1878.

Magnin, Charles. '*Les Rayons et les Ombres*, par M. Victor Hugo'. *Revue des Deux Mondes*, 1 June 1840, 729–37.

Maillard, Firmin. *La Cité des Intellectuels. Scènes Cruelles et Plaisantes de la Vie Littéraire des Gens de Lettres au XIXe Siècle*. Daragon, n.d.

Maison de Victor Hugo. *Dessins de Victor Hugo*. Musées de la Ville de Paris, 1985.

Maison de Victor Hugo. *Maturité de Victor Hugo (1828–1848)*. Ed. J. Sergent. Ville de Paris, Maison de Victor Hugo, May–July 1953.

Maison de Victor Hugo. *Victor Hugo, Homme Politique*. Introduction by J. Sergent. Catalogue by Mme Dane. Ville de Paris, Maison de Victor Hugo, June–October 1956.

Mallarmé, Stéphane. *Correspondance*. 11 vols. Ed. H. Mondor and L. J. Austin. Gallimard, NRF, 1959–85.

Mallarmé, S. *Igitur. Divagations. Un Coup de Dés*. Preface by Y. Bonnefoy. Gallimard, NRF, 1993.

Marmier, Xavier. *Journal (1848–1890)*. 2 vols. Ed. E. Kaye. Geneva: Droz, 1968.

Marquand, Henri-E. *Ma Visite à Henri Sanson, Bourreau de Paris*. London: Rolandi, 1875.

Martin, Nicolas. *Poésies*. Renouard, 1847.

Martin-Dupont, N. *Victor Hugo Anecdotique*. Storck, 1904.

Marx, Karl and Friedrich Engels. *On Literature and Art*. Moscow: Progress Publishers, 1976.

Marzials, Frank T. *Life of Victor Hugo*. London: Walter Scott, 1888.

Mass, Edgar. 'Fortune de Victor Hugo au Cinéma'. In *Lectures de Victor Hugo. Colloque Franco-Allemand de Heidelberg*. Ed. M. Calle-Gruber and A. Rothe. Nizet, 1986.

Matarasso, Henri and Pierre Petitfils. *Album Rimbaud*. Gallimard, Pléiade, 1967.

Maupas, Charlemagne-Émile de. *Mémoires sur le Second Empire*. 2 vols. Dentu, 1884–5.

Maupas, C.-É. de. *The Story of the Coup d'État*. 2 vols. Trans. A. Vandam. London: Virtue, 1884.

Maurois, André. *Olympio ou la Vie de Victor Hugo*. Hachette, 1954.

Maury, Alfred, *see* Bourquelot.

Maxse, Admiral Frederick Augustus. *The Irish Question and Victor Hugo*. London: Ridgway, 1881.

Mayer, Paul. *Histoire du Deux Décembre*. 3rd edn. Ledoyen, 1852.

Menche de Loisne, Charles. *Influence de la Littérature Française de 1830 à 1850 sur l'Esprit Public et les Moeurs*. Garnier, 1852.

Mendès, Catulle. *Figurines de Poètes*. In *Portraits Littéraires*. Ed. M. Pakenham. University of Exeter, 1979.

Ménière, Prosper. *Mémoires Anecdotiques sur les Salons du Second Empire*. Ed. É. Ménière. Plon, Nourrit, 1903.

Mercer, Wendy. 'Léonie d'Aunet (1820–1879) in the Shade of Victor Hugo: Talent Hidden by Sex'. *Studi Francesi*, January–April 1993, 31–46.

Mercié, Jean-Luc. *Victor Hugo et Julie Chenay. Documents Inédits*. Minard, Lettres Modernes, 1967.

Meredith, George. *The Letters of George Meredith*. 3 vols. Ed. C. L. Cline. Oxford: Clarendon Press, 1970.

Meredith, Thérèse. 'Victor Hugo aux États-Unis'. *Revue de la Société d'Histoire du Théâtre*, 1987, 311–25.

Mérimée, Prosper. *Correspondance Générale*. 17 vols. Ed. M. Parturier *et al.* Le Divan; Toulouse: Privat, 1941–64.

Méry, Joseph. 'Victor Hugo'. *Galerie de la Presse, de la Littérature et des Beaux-Arts*. Vol. I. Ed. L. Huart, M. Raoul and C. Philippon. Aubert, 1839.

Metzidakis, Angelo. 'Victor Hugo and the Idea of the United States of Europe'. *Nineteenth-Century French Studies*, Fall–Winter 1994–5, 72–84.

Miquel, Pierre. *Hugo Touriste, 1819–1824. Les Vacances d'un Jeune Romantique*. Paris and Geneva: La Palatine, 1958.

Molènes, Paul Gaschon de. 'La Garde Mobile. Souvenirs des Premiers Temps de la Révolution de Février'. *Caractères et Récits du Temps*, 2nd edn. Michel Lévy, 1853.

Mollier, Jean-Yves. *L'Argent et les Lettres, Histoire du Capitalisme d'Édition, 1880–1920*. Fayard, 1988.

Montalembert, Charles de. *Journal Intime Inédit*. 2 vols. Ed. L. Le Guillou and N. Roger-Taillade. CNRS, 1990.

Morgan, Lady Sydney. *France in 1829–30*. 2 vols. London: Saunders and Otley, 1830.

Musset, Alfred de. 'Lettres de Dupuis et Cotonet'. *Revue des Deux Mondes*, 15 September 1836–15 April 1837. In *Oeuvres Complètes en Prose*. Ed. M. Allem. Gallimard, Pléiade, 1951.

Nadaud, Gustave. *Le Carnaval à l'Assemblée Nationale*. Boisseau, [1850].

Nash, Suzanne. *Les Contemplations of Victor Hugo: An Allegory of the Creative Process*. Princeton University Press, 1976.

Nerval, Gérard de. *Oeuvres Complètes*. 3 vols. Ed. J. Guillaume, C. Pichois *et al*. Gallimard, Pléiade, 1984–93.

Newton, Lord (Thomas Wodehouse Legh). *Lord Lyons. A Record of British Diplomacy*. 2 vols. London: Arnold, 1913.

Nichol, John Pringle. *Victor Hugo, a Sketch of his Life and Work*. London: Swan Sonnenschein & Co.; New York: Macmillan, 'Dilettante Library', no. 11, 1893.

Nisard, Désiré. *Études de Moeurs et de Critique sur les Poètes Latins de la Décadence*. 3 vols. Brussels: Hauman, 1834.

Nodier, Charles. *Dictionnaire Raisonné des Onomatopées Françaises*. Demonville, 1808. Ed. H. Meschonnic. Mauvezin: Trans-Europ-Repress, 1984.

Nodier, C., *see* Victor Hugo and Charles Nodier.

North Peat, Anthony B. *Gossip from Paris During the Second Empire. Correspondence (1864–1869)*. Ed. A. R. Waller. London: Kegan Paul, Trench, Trübner, 1903.

O'Brien, P. *Notes of Interviews with the Ministers and Principal Statesmen of France, in Reference to the Domestic and Foreign Policy of Louis Napoleon*. London: Colburn, 1852.

Oehlenschläger, Adam. *Meine Lebens-Erinnerungen. Ein Nachlaß*. 4 vols. Leipzig: Lorck, 1850.

Oliver, A. Richard. *Charles Nodier, Pilot of Romanticism*. Syracuse University Press, 1964.

Oliver, Samuel Pasfield. 'Victor Hugo At Home'. *The Gentleman's Magazine*, December 1869–May 1870, 713–25.

Olivier, Juste. *Paris en 1830. Journal*. Ed. A. Delattre and M. Denkinger. Mercure de France, 1951.

Palmerston, Henry John Temple, 3rd Viscount. *Selections from Private Journals of Tours in France in 1815 and 1818*. Richard Bentley, 1871.

Papillault, Georges. *Essai d'Étude Anthropologique sur V. Hugo. Extrait de la Revue de Psychiatrie*. Clermont (Oise): Daix, 1898.

Parménie, A. and C. Bonnier de la Chapelle. *Histoire d'un Éditeur et de ses Auteurs. P.-J. Hetzel (Stahl)*. Albin Michel, 1953.

Patty, James S. 'Hugo's Miniature Pyramid ("Lettre", *Les Contemplations*, II, 6)'. *Romance Notes*, Fall 1985, 27–30.

Péguy, Charles. *Oeuvres en Prose Complètes*. 3 vols. Ed. R. Burac. Gallimard, Pléiade, 1987–92.

Pelleport, Adolphe. *Tous les Amours, avec une Lettre de Victor Hugo, une Préface d'Auguste Vacquerie et l'Adieu de Louis Blanc.* Charpentier, 1882.

Pelletan, Camille. *Victor Hugo Homme Politique.* 3rd edn. Société d'Éditions Littéraires et Artistiques; Ollendorff, 1907.

Pendell, William D. *Victor Hugo's Acted Dramas and the Contemporary Press.* Les Belles Lettres; Baltimore: Johns Hopkins Press; London: Humphrey Milford, Oxford University Press, 1947.

Peoples, Margaret H. *La Société des Bonnes Lettres (1821–1830). Smith College Studies in Modern Languages*, V, 1 (October 1923).

Perry, R. and L. & Co. *The Silent Friend. A Medical Work Treating on the Anatomy and Physiology of the Organs of Generation, and their Diseases, with Observations on Onanism and its Baneful Results* [etc.]. London: Published by the Authors, 1847.

Phillips, Charles. *Napoleon the Third, by a Man of the World.* 3rd edn. London: Richard Bentley, 1854.

Picat-Guinoiseau, Ginette. *Nodier et le Théâtre.* Champion, 1990.

Pichois, Claude. 'Les Vrais "Mémoires" de Philarète Chasles'. *Revue des Sciences Humaines*, January–March 1956, 71–97.

Pichois, C. *Philarète Chasles et la Vie Littéraire au Temps du Romantisme.* 2 vols. Corti, 1965.

Pichois, C. *Littérature et Progrès. Vitesse et Vision du Monde.* Neuchâtel: La Baconnière, 1973.

Pichois, C. 'Victor Hugo'. In *Littérature Française.* Ed. C. Pichois. Vol. XIII. Arthaud, 1979.

Pichois, C. *Auguste Poulet-Malassis. L'Éditeur de Baudelaire.* Fayard, 1996.

Pichois, Claude and Michel Brix. *Gérard de Nerval.* Fayard, 1995.

Pirot, Henri. 'Études Bibliographiques sur les Parodies, Pamphlets et Charges Contre Victor Hugo'. *Bulletin du Bibliophile*, 1958, 177–271; 1959, 187–250.

Planche, Gustave. 'Les Voix Intérieures de M. Victor Hugo', *Revue des Deux Mondes*, 15 July 1837, 161–84.

Poisson, Georges. *Guide des Statues de Paris.* Hazan, 1990.

Pontmartin, Armand de. *Mes Mémoires. Enfance et Jeunesse.* Vol. I. Calmann Lévy, 1885.

Porel, Paul [Paul Parfouru] and Georges Monval. *L'Odéon. Histoire Administrative, Anecdotique et Littéraire du Second Théâtre Français.* 2 vols. Lemerre, 1876, 1882.

Pouchain, Gérard and Robert Sabourin. *Juliette Drouet ou la Dépaysée.* Fayard, 1992.

Poulet-Malassis, Auguste, ed. *Papiers Secrets et Correspondance du Second Empire*. 11th edn. Ghio, 1878.

Pradier, James. *Correspondance*. 2 vols. Ed. D. Siler. Geneva: Droz, 1984.

Prarond, Ernest. Letter to Eugène Crépet. In Claude Pichois. *Baudelaire. Études et Témoignages*. Neuchâtel: La Baconnière, 1976.

Proudhon, Pierre-Joseph. *Carnets*. 4 vols. Ed. P. Haubtmann. Rivière, 1960–74.

Proust, Marcel. *Contre Sainte-Beuve*. Ed. P. Clarac and Y. Sandre. Gallimard, Pléiade, 1971.

Pyat, Félix, *et al*. ('Le Comité de la Commune Révolutionnaire'). *Lettre à la Reine d'Angleterre*. London, 22 September 1855.

Quicherat, Louis-Marie. *Traité de Versification Française*. Hachette, 1838.

Rabbe, Alphonse, Vieilh de Boisjolin and Sainte-Preuve. *Biographie Universelle et Portative des Contemporains, ou Dictionnaire Historique des Hommes Vivants, et des Hommes Morts Depuis 1788 Jusqu'à Nos Jours*. Vol. II. Levrault, 1834.

[Read, Charles]. A.-J. de Marnay. *D'une Chute à l'Autre, 1830–1848. Charles X. Royauté de Juillet. Louis-Philippe*. Fischbacher, 1880.

Réception de M. Victor Hugo à l'Académie Française. Séance du 3 Juin. Palermo: Polygraphie Empedocle, 1842.

Reid, Sir Thomas Wemyss. *The Life, Letters, and Friendships of Richard Monckton Milnes, First Lord Houghton*. 2 vols. 2nd edn. London, Paris and Melbourne: Cassell, 1890.

Reynolds, George W. M. *The Modern Literature of France*. 2 vols. London: Henderson, 1839.

Richard, Charles. *Les Lois de Dieu et l'Esprit Moderne. Issue aux Contradictions Humaines*. Pagnerre, 1858.

Riffaterre, Michael. 'En Relisant *Les Orientales*'. In *Essais de Stylistique Structurale*. Flammarion, 1971.

Rimbaud, Arthur. *Oeuvres Complètes*. Ed. A. Adam. Gallimard, Pléiade, 1972.

Rivet, Gustave. *Victor Hugo Chez Lui*. Dreyfous, [1878].

Robb, Graham. *La Poésie de Baudelaire et la Poésie Française, 1838–1852*. Aubier, 'Critiques', 1993.

Robb, G. *Balzac. A Biography*. London: Picador; New York: Norton, 1994.

Robert, Adolphe *et al*. *Dictionnaire Historique et Biographique de la Révolution et de l'Empire, 1789–1815*. 2 vols. Librairie Historique de la Révolution et de l'Empire, n.d.

Robin, Charles. *Galerie des Gens de Lettres au XIXe Siècle*. Lecou; Martinon, 1848.

Rochefort, Henri. *La Lanterne*. Nos 1–77. Brussels: Rozez, 1868–9.

Rochefort, H. *The Adventures of My Life*. 2 vols. Ed. E. W. Smith. London and New York: Arnold, 1896.

Rosa, Guy. 'Génétique et Obstétrique: l'Édition de *Choses Vues*'. In *Hugo de l'Écrit au Livre*. Ed. B. Didier and J. Neefs. Presses Universitaires de Vincennes, 1987.

Rossetti, William Michael. *The Diary of W. M. Rossetti, 1870–1873*. Ed. O. Bornand. Oxford: Clarendon Press, 1977.

Sainte-Beuve, Charles-Augustin. '*Odes et Ballades*'. *Le Globe*, 2 and 9 January 1827. In *Oeuvres*. Vol. I. Ed. M. Leroy. Gallimard, Pléiade, 1956.

[Sainte-Beuve, C.-A.]. *Vie, Poesies et Pensées de Joseph Delorme* (1829). Ed. G. Antoine. Nouvelles Éditions Latines, 1956.

[Sainte-Beuve, C.-A.]. 'De l'Audience Accordée à M. Victor Hugo par S.M. Charles X'. *Revue de Paris*, August 1829. In *Oeuvres*.

Sainte-Beuve, C.-A. 'Victor Hugo en 1831'. *Revue des Deux Mondes*, 1 August 1831. In *Les Grands Écrivains Français. XIXe Siècle. Les Poètes*. II. Ed. M. Allem. Garnier, 1926. 24–51.

Sainte-Beuve, C.-A. 'Les Feuilles d'Automne'. *Revue des Deux Mondes*, 15 December 1831. Ibid., 52–64.

Sainte-Beuve, C.-A. 'Madame de Pontivy'. *Revue des Deux Mondes*, 15 March 1837, 728–47.

Sainte-Beuve, C.-A. *Livre d'Amour* (1843). Ed. J. Troubat. Durel, 1904.

Sainte-Beuve, C.-A. 'Ma Biographie'. In *Souvenirs et Indiscrétions*. Ed. C. Monselet. Calmann Lévy; Librairie Nouvelle, 1880.

Sainte-Beuve, C.-A. *Correspondance Générale*. 19 vols. Ed. J. Bonnerot; continued by A. Bonnerot. Stock, 1935–83.

Sainte-Beuve, C.-A. *Volupté*. Ed. R. Molho. Garnier–Flammarion, 1969.

Sainte-Beuve, C.-A. *Cahiers. I. Le Cahier Vert (1834–1847)*. Ed. R. Molho. Gallimard, NRF, 1973.

Saint-Marc Girardin [Marc Girardin]. *Essais de Littérature et de Morale*. Vol. II. Charpentier, 1845.

Saintsbury, George. *A History of the French Novel (To the Close of the 19th Century)*. 2 vols. Macmillan, 1917, 1919.

Saint-Victor, Paul de. *Victor Hugo*. Calmann Lévy, 1892.

Sartre, Jean-Paul. *L'Idiot de la Famille. Gustave Flaubert de 1821 à 1857*. 3 vols. Gallimard, NRF, 1971–72.

Savant, Jean. *La Vie Sentimentale de Victor Hugo*. 6. Chez l'Auteur, 1982–5.

Savey-Casard, P. *Le Crime et la Peine dans l'Oeuvre de Victor Hugo*. P.U.F., 1956.

Schneider, Erwin. *Victor Hugos 'Hernani' in der Kritik eines Jahrhunderts*. Erlangen: Junge, 1933.

Schoelcher, Victor. *Dangers to England of the Alliance with the Men of the Coup d'État. To Which are Added, the Personal Confessions of the December Conspirators, and Some Biographical Notices of the Most Notorious of Them*. London: Trübner, 1854.

Séché, Léon. *Le Cénacle de La Muse Française, 1823–1827*. Mercure de France, 1908.

Séché, L. *Le Cénacle de Joseph Delorme (1827–1830). I. Victor Hugo et les Poètes, de Cromwell à Hernani*. Mercure de France, 1912.

Seebacher, Jacques. 'Le Bonhomme Royol et son Cabinet de Lecture'. *Revue d'Histoire Littéraire de la France*, October–December 1962, 575–89.

Seebacher, J. *Victor Hugo ou le Calcul des Profondeurs*. P.U.F., 1993.

Ségu, Frédéric. *Un Romantique Républicain. H. de Latouche, 1785–1851*. Les Belles Lettres, 1931.

Ségu, F. *L'Académie des Jeux-Floraux et le Romantisme, de 1818 à 1824*. 2 vols. Les Belles Lettres, 1935–6.

Senior, Nassau William. *Journals Kept in France amd Italy from 1848 to 1852, with a Sketch of the Revolution of 1848*. 2 vols. Ed. M. C. M. Simpson. London: Henry S. King, 1871.

Sergent, Jean. *Dessins de Victor Hugo*. Paris and Geneva: La Palatine, 1955.

Seure, Onézime. *Le Divorce*. Chaumerot, 1848.

Sherard, Robert Harborough. *Oscar Wilde. The Story of an Unhappy Friendship*. London: Hermes Press, 1902.

Sherard, R. H. *Twenty Years in Paris, Being Some Recollections of a Literary Life*. London: Hutchinson, 1905.

Simon, Gustave. *La Vie d'une Femme*. Paul Ollendorff, Société d'Éditions Littéraires et Artistiques, 1914.

Simon, G., ed. *Les Tables Tournantes de Jersey*. Conard, 1923.

Simond, Charles. *Paris de 1800 à 1900, d'après les Estampes et les Mémoires du Temps*. Vol. I. Plon, Nourrit, 1900.

Smith, George Barnett. *Victor Hugo, His Life and Work*. London: Ward and Downey, 1885.

Soubiranne, F. *Le Chaos: Réponse au Plus Grand des Hugolins*. Chez tous les Libraires, [1853].

Souchon, Paul. *La Plus Aimante, ou Victor Hugo entre Juliette et Mme Biard*. Albin Michel, 1941.

Souchon, P. *La Servitude Amoureuse de Juliette Drouet à Victor Hugo*. Albin Michel, 1943.

Southey, Robert. *History of the Peninsular War*. 3 vols. John Murray, 1823, 1827, 1832.

Staël, Mme de. *De l'Allemagne*. 5 vols. Ed. Comtesse J. de Pange and S. Balayé. Hachette, 1958–60.

Stapfer, Paul. *Causeries Guernesiaises*. Guernsey: Le Lièvre; Paris, Saint-Jorre, 1869.

Stapfer, P. *Victor Hugo à Guernesey. Souvenirs Personnels*. Société Française d'Imprimerie et de Librairie, 1905.

Stendhal. *Journal*. Ed. H. Debraye and L. Royer. Gallimard, NRF, 1936.

Sternberg, Robert J. and Michael L. Barnes, eds. *The Psychology of Love*. New Haven and London: Yale University Press, 1988.

Stevenson, Robert Louis. *Familiar Studies of Men and Books*. London: Chatto & Windus, 1917.

St. John, Bayle. *Purple Tints of Paris. Character and Manners in the New Empire*. 2 vols. London: Chapman and Hall, 1854.

Strachey, Lytton. *Landmarks in French Literature*. 1912; Oxford University Press, 1943.

Strugnell, Anthony. 'Contribution à l'Étude du Républicanisme de Victor Hugo'. *Revue d'Histoire Littéraire de la France*, September–October 1978, 796–809.

Sue, Eugène. *La Marquise d'Alfi*. Vol. I. Cadot, 1853.

Swinburne, Algernon Charles. *Essays and Studies*. London: Chatto & Windus, 1875.

Swinburne, A. C. *A Study of Victor Hugo*. London: Chatto & Windus, 1886.

Swinburne, A. C. *The Swinburne Letters*. 6 vols. Ed. Cecil Y. Lang. New Haven: Yale University Press, 1959–62.

Talmeyr, Maurice [Maurice Coste]. *Souvenirs d'avant le Déluge, 1870–1914*. Perrin, 1927.

[Texier, Edmond]. *Physiologie du Poëte, par Sylvius. Illustrations de Daumier*. Laisné; Aubert; Lavigne, 1842.

Thomas, Alexandre. 'La Carmagnole d'Olympio'. *Revue des Deux Mondes*, 1 June 1850, 913–34.

Thomas, John Heywood. *L'Angleterre dans l'Oeuvre de Victor Hugo*. Pedone, 1934.

Thompson, C. W. 'À Propos des Lecteurs Anglais de *L'Homme Qui Rit*'. In *'L'Homme Qui Rit' ou la Parole-Monstre de Victor Hugo*. C.D.U. and SEDES, 1985.

Tribout de Morembert, H. 'Hugo (Familles)'. In *Dictionnaire de Biographie Française*. Letouzey et Ané, 1929 – .

Trollope, Frances. *Paris and the Parisians in 1835*. 2 vols. Baudry's European Library; London: Richard Bentley, 1836.

Troubat, Jules. *Un Coin de Littérature sous le Second Empire. Sainte-Beuve et Champfleury. Lettres de Champfleury à sa Mère, à son Frère et à Divers*. Mercure de France, 1908.

[Tuffet, Salvador-Jean-Baptiste]. *Les Mystères des Théâtres de Paris. Observations! Indiscrétions!! Révélations!!! par un Vieux Comparse*. Marchant, 1844.

Tupper, Ferdinand Brock. *The History of Guernsey and its Bailiwick*. 2nd edn. Guernsey: Le Lièvre; London: Simpkin, Marshall, 1876.

Tupper, Martin Farquhar. *My Life as an Author*. London: Sampson Low, Marston, Searle & Rivington, 1886.

Ubersfeld, Anne, ed. *Victor Hugo. Ruy Blas*. 2 vols. Les Belles Lettres, 1971–2.

Ubersfeld, A. *Le Roi et le Bouffon. Étude sur le Théâtre de Hugo de 1830 à 1839*. Corti, 1974.

Ulbach, Louis. *Almanach de Victor Hugo, avec un Beau Portrait de Victor Hugo et des Fac-Simile d'Autographes*. Calmann Lévy, 1885.

Vacquerie, Auguste. *Profils et Grimaces*. Michel Lévy, 1856.

Vacquerie, A. *Les Miettes de l'Histoire*. Pagnerre, 1863.

Vacquerie, A. *Mes Premières Années de Paris*. Michel Lévy; Librairie Nouvelle, 1872.

Van Gogh, Vincent. *The Complete Letters of Vincent Van Gogh*. 3 vols. London: Thames and Hudson, 1958.

Vapereau, Gustave. *Dictionnaire Universel des Contemporains*. 3rd edn. Hachette, 1865.

Venzac, Géraud. *Les Origines Religieuses de Victor Hugo*. Bloud et Gay, 'Travaux de l'Institut Catholique de Paris', 1955.

Venzac, G. *Les Premiers Maîtres de Victor Hugo*. Bloud et Gay, 'Travaux de l'Institut Catholique de Paris', 1955.

Verlaine, Paul. *Oeuvres en Prose Complètes*. Ed. J. Borel. Gallimard, Pléiade, 1972.

Viatte, Auguste. *Victor Hugo et les Illuminés de son Temps*. Ottawa: Éditions de l'Arbre, 1942.

Victor Hugo, 1885–1985. Les Autographes. T. Bodin, expert. No. 25 (1985).

Le Victor Huguenot, exclusivement littéraire. Ed. R. Delorme. Nos 1–9 (15 December 1863–15 April 1864).

Victoria, Queen. *The Letters of Queen Victoria*. Ed. A. C. Benson and Viscount Esher. 3 vols. London: John Murray, 1908.

Vidieu, Abbé Auguste. *Victor Hugo et le Panthéon*. Dentu, [1885].

Viel-Castel, Comte Horace de. *Mémoires sur le Règne de Napoléon III, 1851–1864*. 2 vols. Ed. P. Josserand. Le Prat, 1942.

Viennet, Jean-Pons-Guillaume. 'Extraits des Mémoires de Viennet'. Ed. P. Jourda. *Revue des Deux Mondes*, 1 July 1929, 123–53.

[Vignon-Restif de la Bretonne, Victor]. *OG*. Hubert, et tous les Libraires du Palais-Royal; Locard et Davi; et au *Salon Littéraire*, 1824.

Vigny, Alfred de. *Journal d'un Poète*. In *Oeuvres Complètes*. Ed. F. Baldensperger. Vol. II. Gallimard, Pléiade, 1948.

Vigny, A. de. *Oeuvres Complètes. Théâtre. I*. Ed. F. Baldensperger. Conard, 1926.

Ville de Châteaubriant. *Des Trébuchet à Victor Hugo*. Châteaubriant: Bibliothèque Municipale, 1985.

Villemessant, H. de and B. Jouvin. 'Histoire de l'Ancien *Figaro*'. *Figaro*, 2 and 9 April 1854.

Vitu, Auguste. *Les Mille et Une Nuits du Théâtre. 1re série*. Ollendorff, 1884.

Vivier, Michel. 'Victor Hugo et Charles Nodier, Collaborateurs de *L'Oriflamme* (1823–1824)'. *Revue d'Histoire Littéraire de la France*, July–September 1958, 297–323.

[Vizetelly, Ernest Alfred]. Le Petit Homme Rouge. *My Days of Adventure. The Fall of France, 1870–71*. London: Chatto & Windus, 1914.

Vizetelly, Henry. *Glances Back Through Seventy Years: Autobiographical and Other Reminiscences*. 2 vols. London: Kegan Paul, Trench, Trübner, 1893.

Wack, Henry Wellington. *The Romance of Victor Hugo and Juliette Drouet*. Introduction by F. Coppée. New York and London: Putnam, Knickerbocker Press, 1905.

Wagner, Richard. *Eine Kapitulation. Lustspiel in antiker Manier* (1870). In *Sämtliche Schriften und Dichtungen*. Vol. IX. Leipzig: Breitkopf & Härtel, n.d.

Wallon, Jean. *La Presse de 1848, ou Revue Critique des Journaux Publiés à Paris depuis la Révolution de Février Jusqu'à la Fin de Décembre*. Pillet fils aîné, 1849.

Washburne, E. B. *Recollections of a Minister to France, 1869–1877*. 2 vols. London: Sampson Low, Marston, Searle & Rivington, 1887.

Wauwermans, P. *Les Proscrits du Coup d'État en Belgique*. Brussels: Société Belge de Librairie, 1892.

Weill, Alexandre. *La Méprise d'Hernani, ou un Peuple d'Histrions*. Dentu, [1867].

Weill, A. *Introduction à Mes Mémoires*. Sauvaître, 1890.

Woestyn, Eugène. 'Une Soirée chez Victor Hugo'. *Journal du Dimanche*, 4 October 1846.

Yates, Edmund. *Celebrities at Home*. 2nd series. London: Office of *The World*, 1878.

Zeldin, Theodore. *France, 1848–1945*. Vol. II. Oxford: Clarendon Press, 1977.

Zola, Émile. 'Victor Hugo et sa *Légende des Siècles*'. In *Oeuvres Complètes*. 15 vols. Ed. H. Mitterand. Cercle du Livre Précieux, 1966–70.

Zola, É. *Correspondance*. 10 vols. Ed. B. H. Bakker. Presses de l'Université de Montréal / CNRS, 1978–95.

General Index

Abbatucci, Jacques-Pierre-Charles (1792–1857), 503 and n.
Abd-ul-Aziz, Sultan of Turkey (1830–76), 497
About, Edmond (1828–85), 468
Abraham, 387
Académie des Jeux Floraux, 71–2, 94, 117
Académie Française, 108, 242, 306; VH wins prize, 61–3; and Romanticism, 84–5, 110; VH attempts to join, 210–11, 212, 214; VH's membership of, 225–6, 250–1; Prix Montyon, 262
L'Action Française, 535
Adèle H. (film), 398
The Aeneid (Virgil), 60, 63
Aeschylus (c.525–c.456 BC), 231, 382n., 386, 399, 480
Agoult, Marie de Flavigny, Comtesse d' (1805–76), 217–18
Agulhon, Maurice, 496
'A la Petite Ad . . .' (Sainte-Beuve), 164
Alaux, Jean (1786–1864), 108
'Albert the worker' (Alexandre Martin) (1815–95), 266
Albouy, Pierre, xvi
Alderney, 388
Algeria, 229, 441, 513
Allix, Jules (1818–97), 341
Alps, 121–2

Alsace, 441, 459, 460
Amaury-Duval (Eugène-Emmanuel Amaury Pineau-Duval), nephew of Alexandre Duval (1808–85), 150
American Civil War, 371, 381
Amiens, 306
Androcles' Lion (spirit), 334, 337
Animal Farm (Orwell), 309
Antarctic Peninsula, 535
L'Anti-Romantique, 184
Antwerp, 314, 315
'Apollo, M.', 253
Aquila (ship), 374
The Arabian Nights, 32
Arago, Emmanuel (1812–96), 444
Arc de Triomphe, Paris, 209, 210, 527–8
Aristotle, 504
Army, 403; Léopold Hugo's military career, 5–6, 9, 12, 20, 23, 45, 482; 1848 Revolution, 279–80; Napoleon III's coup, 301; 'Commissions Mixtes', 309; Franco-Prussian War, 440, 441, 443–4
Arnold, Sir Edwin (1832–1904), 403
Artaud, Antonin (1896–1948), 231
Assemblée Nationale *see* National Assembly
'Atala' (Chateaubriand), 49
Ateliers Nationaux, 268

Index of Works by Hugo

Index of Characters

'The ABC Society', 69–70
Auverney, Léopold d', 123

Borgia, Lucrezia, 179
Bug-Jargal, 123, 124, 218, 418

Cantilupe, Lord, 430
Carlos, Don *see* Charles V
Charles V, Holy Roman Emperor,
   145–6, 150
Cimourdain, 481
Clancharlie, Lord Linnaeus, 428
Clubin ('Sieur Clubin'), 413, 415, 417
Cosette, 65, 82, 379, 384, 399, 514
Cuthbarghe, Queen, 430

Dea, 428
Déruchette, niece of Lethierry, 413
Desertum of Kilcarry, Lord, 430
Didier, 175–6, 192
Dirry-Moir, Lord David *alias* Tom-Jim-
   Jack, illegitimate son of Lord
   Linnaeus Clancharlie, 430
Djali (goat), 158
Don Carlos *see* Charles V
Doña Sol *see* Sol de Silva

Elespuru, 39
Enjolras, 457–8

Esmeralda, 158, 159, 174, 541
Ethel *see* Schumacher, Ethel

Fabiani, 198
Fantine, 379
Flibbertigibbet, 127
François I, King, 176
Friend (polar bear), 89
Frollo, Claude, 74, 158

Gauvain, 481, 482, 483
Gavroche, 379
Gennaro, 179
Gilbert, 198
Gilliatt, 413–14, 415, 416, 417, 485–6,
   495, 541
Gormon, 90
Gringoire, 158, 161
Gueux, Claude, 192
Guldon, 90
Gumdraith, Dr, 430
Guth, 90
Gwynplaine, 262, 428, 429, 431, 461,
   489, 541

Habibrah, 123
Han d'Islande, 89–90, 101 n., 147
Hernani, 21, 145, 149–50, 151
Homo, 427, 429